"To borrow from guitarist Robert Fripp, we progressive rockers 'didn't know what we couldn't do'. Mike Barnes's masterly evocation of what it meant to be an actor in this untidy, sprawling music genre examines every nook and cranny, leaves no stone unturned, and interrogates anyone who knew anyone connected to it. The result rings true, providing as complete a picture as you're likely to find anywhere."

Bill Bruford, (King Crimson, Yes, U.K.)

"An epic portrayal of the cultural revolution and evolution of popular music from the end of 1967 to 1977. This masterpiece evokes fertile times of cross-pollination and reinvention, experimental extemporisation, blending folk, jazz, rock, technology and psychedelics. It is the experience of a new generation, created for future readers as vividly as being there."

Sonja Kristina, (Curved Air)

"If you like progressive rock, read this."   Viv Albertine, (The Slits)

"Prog rock's essential guidebook."

Sir Ian Rankin, (author of Knots & Crosses, The Rise)

"A New Day Yesterday is an extremely impressive and comprehensive study of progressive rock! From its roots in jazz and psychedelia, to its initial vague acceptance as an art form, to its influential effect on the beauty and lyrical power of an iconic British musical form . . . In fact, I'm sure Mike Barnes knows more about Yes than I do!"

Steve Howe, (Yes, Asia, Tomorrow)

"A heroic account of the story of prog: affectionate, funny and packed with weird and impressive detail."

Dame Joanne Harris, (author of Chocolat)

"Celebrates the era when prog was the coolest sound on the planet. Lucid and deeply researched. . . this exhaustive tome may well be the last word on the subject."   MOJO, 4★

"A grand survey of the most ambitious and pretentious British rock of the age."   Uncut

"There's plenty here for hardcore aficionados and the prog-curious alike."
Shindig!

"Epic overview of revolutionary times. Spot on in so many ways, Barnes beautifully captures that time when music was flying by the seat of its pants to explode into a multi-tentacled hydra of exploration and mini-revolutions, charged with resonating wonder and often necessary humour."
Record Collector

"A time of glorious eccentricity and bold creative adventure remembered in fond and fascinating detail."
Mark Ellen

"Astute handling of such a wide-ranging genre."
Long Live Vinyl

"Head and shoulders above the crowd. A remarkable book."
Prog Magazine

"If the mark of a great rock book is how much it makes you want to go out and buy the music it covers, then this book is a classic. 9/10."
Classic Rock

A New Day Yesterday

Mike Barnes

A New Day Yesterday

UK PROGRESSIVE ROCK & THE 70s

Contents

FOREWORD

In the sweltering summer of 1969, I was 19 years old and thrillingly engaged in banging nails into the sticky black tarmac of a London road. So far, I'd refused offers of going on the dole from my bass playing friend at the local labour exchange; I was just treading water until I could make it as a professional musician. This felt like a distant dream while stuck in a rut of dead-end jobs, when my labours were interrupted by a young pal, Mike Docker.

"Come to the Marquee on Sunday to see a band named King Crimson," he said, "I promise you won't be disappointed . . ."

I did as I was told – he wasn't wrong. Crimson had invested in intelligence and precision over instinct, auguring a new era from the 'let it all hang out' 1960s.

In later years, as I came to know the group's guitarist, Robert Fripp, he said he felt that many of our peers had favoured 'form over spirit'. I took it to mean that improvisation was essential to a band's progress, taking a leaf out of the jazz bible. I was just about to talk Genesis into doing 'The Waiting Room' on *The Lamb Lies Down on Broadway*, where the band briefly embraced dissonance and sidelined melodic certainty.

Not long afterwards, when the lead singer of Genesis Peter Gabriel began working with Robert, the lines between certain groups were starting to blur. Cutting-edge musos began to function like atoms, revolving around a nucleus of radical ideas.

Mike Barnes's reflective book is a beautifully-crafted, insightful look at that era of music which, for all its indulgences, was to change mankind for the better. Today, in a fast-fracturing, decoupling world we may well be jealous of a time that saw the sweeping away of much social prejudice under the twin banners of civil rights and pacifism.

If you could make an oppressive political machine unhip, armed with a few songs and an enthusiastic following from listeners that refused to buy into nationalism at all costs, you had a real chance to evoke change. In a few years the Vietnam war would be over, arguably heralded by Jimi Hendrix's reworking of 'The Star-Spangled Banner' at Woodstock and John Lennon's dictum of "War is over if you want it."

Where the 1960s embraced musical multiculturalism, the 1970s took that 'world' music a stage further; an invitation to the dance didn't always require audience participation, but rather audience appreciation. As music became more inclusive, listeners themselves became ever more discerning and selective. Within progressive music, all forms were welcome. Blues met baroque as raga met rock. Telepathy was possible during the best moments among players when spontaneous creativity took over. Hooray for those little glimpses of heaven when click tracks were temporarily consigned to the coffin and the conductor's baton given a decent burial.

If folk music was the ancestor of jazz, and blues ceded a child that became rock, what happened to all the other styles? Inclusivity seems the fastest route to Valhalla, involving the element of surprise, whereas a pan-genre approach fuels endless thrills, sometimes forcing us to be historians but also pointing the way to a brave new world. What did the original bone orchestras really sound like? Or the ancient Greek cithara, the forerunner of the modern guitar? We have to look back in spirit to move forward and complete the circle.

Mike Barnes's exhaustively researched book surely took a lifetime to write while assimilating all the data, including the musings of the actual entertainers. The thing that ultimately links J. S. Bach, George Formby and John Lennon is that they, like us all, made a noise for a living. Whether you prefer Gracie Fields or 'Strawberry Fields', all music starts as a doodle in the dark.

Some audiences are way ahead of what they are fed. In praise of progressive music, challenges were part of the package. That's what Mike's book is all about; the motivation towards taking risks and chances that thrill. Radical ideas don't have to be thrown away with the beads, flowers and flares. Give music a chance, as well as peace.

Bless you, Mike, for throwing light on an area of music so often criticised for overcomplexity, but which really involves pushing creative boundaries to give birth to new, hybrid forms and at its best expresses a deep feeling about the future of mankind.

Steve Hackett
February 2024

More Songs About Wizards and Hobbits

"Progressive rock – isn't that about wizards?" asked a considerably younger friend via email when I told her that I was thinking of writing this book. "Well, yes and no," I replied, and then changed the subject, amused but also rather embarrassed by her perception of my literary intention.

Afterwards I had a bit of a think: there was a band called Silly Wizard, but they were more folk rock; The Wizard Of The Keys was a minor character in Gong's *Radio Gnome* trilogy; Uriah Heep released an album *Demons And Wizards* in 1972, but although they had some aspects in common with the progressive rockers, they also had another stack-heeled boot in the hard rock camp; Rick Wakeman was known in Seventies parlance as a keyboard wizard, and had posed for promotional photographs for his 1975 concept album *The Myths And Legends Of King Arthur And The Knights Of The Round Table* wearing a conical wizard's hat... but best stop there.

The heyday of progressive rock is long enough ago now for received wisdom to suggest that it was all about wizards, elves and hobbits, and so it should be retrofitted thus and consigned en masse to the dustbin of history. But in fact almost none of it had anything to do with this fantastical roll call. So, what are we actually talking about here? What is, or was, progressive rock?

Labelling music into genres may be a journalistic construct, but there is usually a rough consensus. Free jazz, jazz rock, Britpop, soul, blues, funk, grunge, hardcore, rave, folk and ambient all conjure up an aural image of their typical sounds. If we are talking about Merseybeat, then we know we are dealing with beat music that was initially played in the Liverpool area in the early to mid-Sixties.

But progressive rock defies easy categorisation. It's a term that, according to the majority of the musicians I have spoken to, was rarely used to describe the music as it was made in the Seventies, but has since become a way of labelling a wide-ranging genre, while its modern shorthand, prog, can be used pejoratively. Imagine saying it while pulling a face.

But one has to start somewhere, and for the purposes of this book, progressive rock was essentially ushered in by the burst of creativity in the psychedelic era, from 1966–68 – although "era" seems a bit of a grand title for a shift in creative thinking whose first phase lasted only a couple of years. But such are the ways that we attempt to make sense of changes within an artistic continuum.

The first major wave of progressive rock swelled up in 1969, reached its peak in the mid-Seventies and then began to dissipate into different tributaries towards the end of the decade. But the Seventies was a particularly open, fertile and mutable time musically, with so many different influences and styles feeding into what was played, that borders and definitions remain contestable.

After psychedelia had thrown open the doors of perception, the challenge was to impose order on its lengthy, expressive freakouts – and the chaos that these could potentially lead to – and to experiment with form, structure and dynamics: the imperative was to make new musical shapes. With progressive rock anything was creatively possible and, stylistically, everything was up for grabs, and so the groups mixed up elements of rock'n'roll, R&B, psychedelia, classical, the avant-garde, folk, jazz, free improvisation, non-Western influences and more soul than is generally acknowledged – even attempts at multi-media – into brand-new musical hybrids. Lyrics encompassed social satire, invented worlds, sci-fi, ideas from literature, stream of consciousness word paintings, a hippieish striving for enlightenment, a few love songs and even a smattering of politics.

As always with these musical shifts, there was no clear beginning. The earliest example this writer has seen of "progressive" in print, as an adjective to describe rock music, was with reference to the psychedelic group, Tomorrow, in early 1968, while in that year the Small Faces were referred to by Keith Altham in the *New Musical Express* as "progressive pop". Jimi Hendrix was also labelled "progressive" in some quarters, an accolade he certainly deserved. The "p" word was used to describe Caravan in the sleeve notes of their self-titled debut album in October 1968. But it was in use even before then.

Melody Maker journalist Chris Welch claims he was the first writer to coin the phrase "progressive rock" when writing about Cream in 1967, in a nod back to "progressive jazz", the way pianist Stan Kenton described his music of the late Forties. Writing in *International Times* in 1970, Mark Williams described Caravan, Soft Machine, Mighty Baby and Family as "British ethnic rock music" – an interesting idea, but the label never stuck.

In the late Sixties, rock'n'roll music was still alive and well, with many of its pioneers still playing, but it was beginning to show its age. In this new, post-psychedelic artistic climate, rock'n'roll was suddenly expanded by a mass of new ideas, creating a different kind of rock music. Calling it "progressive" was as good a nomenclature as any. Music is constantly progressing anyway, but in the early Seventies, developments in rock music happened at an unusual speed, with musicians eager to stride into the new creative space that was opening before them.

Suddenly, basic 4/4 twelve-bar rock'n'roll seemed anachronistic, like something from the distant past, as rock was now open-ended and could potentially go anywhere and everywhere. Ian Anderson of Jethro Tull has this to say on progressive rock's questing spirit: "When I was asked to define what makes a progressive rock musician, I said, well it's a person who just gets bored easily. People who think, 'Well, I can do that, but what's next?'"

What was initially envisaged as a sustainable, imaginative alternative to mainstream pop, with one foot still in the counterculture, could, on paper, have been a minority interest, but eventually became – in the case of some groups – commercially huge in the heyday of the album. Major labels caught on and invested substantial amounts of money in this new thing, and there was enough of a market to allow a number of independent labels to spring up. And with a record-buying public looking for new kicks, it also infiltrated the charts, with hit singles in the early Seventies by Jethro Tull and Family in particular, who made appearances on the BBC TV singles charts showcase, *Top Of The Pops*.

Other reactions from friends to the news of this book project ranged from raised eyebrows of interest to lip-curling sneers of disdain. Such divided reactions are nothing new. Progressive rock was both revered and reviled in its heyday from 1969-74. And there's the rub. One musician I talked to, a practising punk of a certain age, admitted that although he'd like to read the book, he couldn't stand the music and that "obviously Yes were shit". I was concerned, although not entirely surprised, that to some, this music was simply synonymous with "naff" – or less polite descriptors.

Although this easy way of dismissing nearly a decade's worth of music bothered me, I could see why it had arisen. At its height, progressive rock was powerful and potent enough to attract millions of fervent true believers, but when it began to lose its way in the mid to late Seventies – a view shared by many of the musicians I have spoken to – it did what no other form of 20th-century popular music had managed to do. It provoked a backlash of epic proportions: the emergence of UK punk rock in 1976.

Punk signalled a huge shift in attitudes as to what rock music was for, particularly in the relationship between the musicians and their audience. It was fundamentally opposed, not just to progressive rock, but to all big, established rock acts who had lost touch with their audience.

Whereas the sheer scale of the most commercially successful specimens had once been impressive in itself, progressive rock groups of all shapes and sizes became classified as dinosaurs, while the punks were portrayed in some sections of the music press as avenging angels who had emerged sui generis to preside over a Year Zero cull, standing on the shores, brandishing their weapons as these giant musical sauropods, who had once ruled the world unopposed, now slid sadly off into the swamps to their extinction.

Except it wasn't quite like that.

Like many Seventies teenagers, I embraced punk and the enormous amount of new music that followed in its wake, but I also had an abiding affection for progressive rock, having grown up with the big boys like Emerson, Lake & Palmer, Jethro Tull, Pink Floyd, Yes, Genesis and Mike Oldfield, as well as the more esoteric strains of King Crimson, Gong and Hatfield And The North.

From the early Nineties, I went on a trip around the musical world, becoming a published music journalist, perennially drawn to the new, and largely writing about music to the left of the mainstream. And progressive rock groups seemed more a thing of the past than of the present.

So why did I decide to write this book? Well, put simply, I was approached. I immediately turned down the offer, but the more I churned the idea over in my mind, the more I was drawn back to the music of that era. I was also beginning to notice more Seventies progressive rock groups being mentioned positively in the music press, these views now coming from a different generation to the ones who had called for the cull back in the day. They were able to hear the music as it was, without all of its historical and critical baggage.

Although I was brought up with progressive rock, I had been away from it for long enough to not be a partisan apologist. But as the connections were still there, I was curious enough to be able to retrace my steps back to it, to attempt to make sense of it and look at it with some kind of objectivity. Importantly, I wanted to try to get rid of the barrier of received wisdom and to show there an alternative viewpoint to that of Yes obviously being shit.

One of the highlights of the 2009 BBC Four documentary *Prog Rock Britannia* was keyboard player Rick Wakeman's tongue-in-cheek portrayal of a punter going into a record store to buy some prog albums long after its heyday. He acted out the protagonist's furtiveness as like that of a man buying a top-shelf mag in a newsagent's full of female customers, keen to have the vendor slip his purchase into an inconspicuous brown paper bag as quickly as possible to allow a hasty exit. It was exaggerated for comic effect, but exemplified contemporary prog fans as lonely male misfits harbouring a love that dared not speak its name – at least not in public.

I grimaced at some of my taste lapses as an impressionable youth, and also recognised things that had completely escaped me in my younger days. But although this involved me undergoing some self-administered regression therapy sessions – including one memorable night spent with numerous bottles of strong cider, a jar of home grown weed and a pile of Emerson, Lake & Palmer vinyl LPs in an attempt to establish what had fired me up about their music in the first place – my intention was not just to go on some kind of "rock heritage" nostalgia trip. There was a story that needed to be told in a particular way.

To get this story, my aim was to speak to as many musicians as was reasonably practical, as well as radio DJs, record company people and journalists. And also the fans, the longhaired kids who bought the music – for progressive rock was made for and consumed by young people. I intended to investigate the era, to get as close as I could to the feeling of being back in the Seventies. Crucially, the narrative has been largely shaped by hundreds of hours of interviews with those who were there, and many of their observations have been both fascinating and unexpected.

In the early Seventies, progressive rock was hallmarked by musicians who let their imaginations off the leash, producing music that moved away from previous givens, in synch with an audience who wanted – demanded – to be presented with something new. The decade was a time of cultural and countercultural change in terms of politics, the media, idealism, literature, philosophy and personal aspirations. These were woven, to greater and lesser extents, into the music, together with the developments in technology that made it all possible.

I also explore the fads and fashions, the sights, sounds and even smells of the era – the whiff of dope smoke, joss sticks and patchouli oil clinging to scoop-neck shirts, and the reek of the poorly cured leather of cheap afghan coats and desert boots all waft through the story.

The remit of the book is deliberately restricted. I felt that as progressive rock started in the UK, then that would be the geographical focus of my investigations, which also wouldn't stray temporally beyond the Seventies and would concentrate on the first half of that decade. Music scenes in other countries will be briefly mentioned, but I will leave an in-depth exploration of these to others.

My survey is detailed, but doesn't pretend to be exhaustive. It soon proved too repetitious to chart every group's history in detail, so my narrative concentrates on particular areas and elements, and is interspersed with more detailed surveys of key albums.

To write all this in chronological order would have resulted in an unholy pile-up of information, so after sending out markers to the late Seventies early on, I have hopped back and forth filling in the gaps. I'm sure that those readers who like their music with twists and turns, time changes, abrupt halts and recapitulation of themes will find no problem with this approach.

The inclusion of certain groups will run counter to some notions of what was progressive rock, but they are included because so much invention was taking place within the same milieu. And as always, stylistic labels came later. In the early Seventies, as the bass player and guitarist in Kevin Ayers' group The Whole World, Mike Oldfield had played on some stylistically diverse bills.

"In the days that prog rock started, there were no differences between any kind of music," he recalls. "You'd get to mix with everyone from Pink Floyd to Free to Hawkwind – there was no difference. None of these categories existed. Prog didn't even exist. Nobody said, 'I'm in a progressive band'. We were all in there together."

Some musicians wished to distance themselves from their Seventies peers and also the very notion of progressive rock. "Progressive rock? Don't know anything about it," snapped one particularly cantankerous lead vocalist, who accused me of trying to make money out of him before the interview ground to a halt.

The inclusion of Hawkwind raised eyebrows among friends, some of whom thought they were part of a different scene altogether, but the group's saxophonist Nik Turner was happy to be included and that was good enough for me. Similarly, jazz pianist Keith Tippett, who was the creative force behind Centipede – one of the more groundbreaking projects of the Seventies, a large ensemble drawing on players from classical, rock, jazz and free improvisation – claimed, with some justification, that they were "the most progressive group of the era", so I was hardly going to shut him out.

Robert Wyatt, who had played with Soft Machine and Matching Mole – and Centipede – was, as always, an entertaining and gracious interviewee, but was particularly keen to distance himself from progressive rock for reasons that will become clear later on. However, Wyatt also delivered two startlingly new-sounding solo albums in the mid-Seventies. So sorry, Robert, but you were progressive something-or-other and it wouldn't be the same without you, so you are in. Other groups missed out completely, so apologies to the excellent Jade Warrior, to Manfred Mann's Earth Band, Gnidrolog and more.

The heyday of progressive rock was a heady time of artistic freedom and accelerated creativity unique in rock music's history. At best it found groups fearlessly breaking into new areas and initiating new musical forms. At worst it saw them exhibiting delusions of grandeur, over-reaching themselves and getting lost in the maze of possibilities in which they had been allowed to roam free.

When musing on the birth of King Crimson back in 1969, the group's guitarist Robert Fripp had this to say about lyricist Pete Sinfield's flamboyant modus operandi: "He did not know what he could not do". By implication, this applied to Fripp, the rest of the group and many other musicians besides.

And so this book is dedicated to all those musicians who did not know what they could not do, and this is their story.

Mike Barnes, 2019

CHAPTER 1

It's All Too Beautiful: Psychedelia and the British Psyche

The date is April 22, the first spring day of 2016 that actually feels like spring. There is sun and birdsong, and the warming air seems animated, alive, slowly dispelling the last vestiges of winter gloom. It's the time when those who have been hibernating most deeply experience the slightly disturbing pleasure of being wrenched, blinking, back out into the daylight.

The walk south towards Ilford from Gants Hill tube station takes me along a wide and busy street lined with substantial mock Tudor semis. This indicates that I am in suburbia now, just beyond the edge of London's East End. As I walk in through the gates of Valentines Park, I come across a pond with scattered slices of white bread and a pile of cheese puffs left on the bankside for the wildfowl. Canada geese sail away, snootily disdaining this human being's idea of an avian smorgasbord, although the park's noisy crow population are taking an interest and one flies off with a cheesy snack in its beak.

Valentines Park, like many parks in London, was once the grounds and gardens of a substantial property. Valentines Mansion was built in 1696 and, paid for by National Lottery money, extensive renovation was carried out in 2007, including restoration of the walled gardens. The architectural features of particular interest in the grounds are the three 18th-century grottos bordering the Long Water, a narrow man-made lake about 100 metres long. Two of these grottos stand at each end of the lake at water level, one of which is occupied by a swan. A third grotto overlooks the water from terra firma, and is occupied by a man with a mobile phone and several cans of lager.

Mallards, swans, moorhens and tufted ducks paddle around. One broody moorhen has built a nest of twigs on the bank. The Fish Pond, an adjoining lake with a large island in the middle, would have been a safer site.

A little girl rolls away from her mother on unwieldy roller skates, joggers jog by in succession and groups of kids in school uniform cut through the park on their way home. But still the atmosphere is unexpectedly tranquil.

In case this all seems a little less than relevant to the subject matter of this book, all journeys start with a single step and mine finds me in Itchycoo Park, the subject of a 1967 single by the Small Faces. The "itchycoos" of the title were nettles, which could give a nasty sting to an unsuspecting Fifties schoolboy dressed in shorts.

This is also the book's first contentious point. The song was written by bass guitarist Ronnie Lane, and singer and guitarist Steve Marriott. Lane has said it was written about a park in Ilford. Some of Marriott's school friends remember the nettles being at Little Ilford Park about a mile to the south, but Marriott has specifically identified it as Valentines Park. Drummer Kenney Jones prefers to think it is referring to King Edward Memorial Park in Shadwell. But Valentines Park seems the best fit for the venue. In the bridge passages into the choruses of the song, Marriott sings of feeding the ducks (with a bun) and while Little Ilford Park contains no bodies of water, Valentines has three lakes and ducks aplenty.

It's unclear exactly which one park – if indeed it were just one – inspired the song, and references to Oxford's *"dreaming spires"* and Cambridge's Bridge Of Sighs are thrown in to make up a composite place. But that only adds to the mystery.

There are no dreaming spires in sight of Valentines Park, just a single, rather wary-looking tower block. And as I stand reflecting on all this, I realise that being in one of a number of its possible locations is rather like standing atop Glastonbury Tor, which some claim to be the Isle Of Avalon, collaring a passer-by and asking: "Excuse me, where is Camelot?" It's a question without an answer.

The reason I had gone looking for its location is that the song epitomises a peculiarly late-Sixties English way of looking through a metaphorical lens – be it drug induced or not – at the everyday and transforming it, via the imagination, into something transcendental, almost mystical, and as such it was one of the most potent songs of the psychedelic era, which, at most, lasted just a couple of years from 1966 to the beginning of 1968.

Mythical places are so entrenched in our race memory that the fact that one only has access to them through the imagination strengthens their allure. Millions of people will have an image in their minds of Itchycoo Park. And in the mind is where the action was taking place.

Most importantly, the song was inspired by memories of the group members' youths and, in common with many late-Sixties British musicians, the Small Faces were re-evaluating who they were musically by travelling back to their childhoods, a time when they could dream and play in a relatively untroubled way, and when days were always sunny and full of untested possibilities.

Musically, the times were changing fast. The Small Faces had started out in 1965 as fresh-faced, sharply dressed teenage mods purveying a mixture of soul, R&B and Brill Building pop. Into 1967 fellow mods The Who were purveying an updated image of aggressive dandyism, both in the expanded range of their music and their onstage equipment smashing. But the Small Faces were still seen as teen pin-ups and locked into something akin to Beatlemania.

With 'Itchycoo Park' the group began to veer into more personal territory, while still making a brilliant experimental pop single. They epitomised the way that many British musicians at this time were moving away from their influences and pursuing more individual ideas.

Ian McLagan weaves piano and organ phrases around Marriott's jaunty acoustic strum. Lane's dreamy, conspiratorial backing vocals agree with the singer in how cool it would be to miss out school, then with his voice swathed in flanging – a new technique of manually putting tape signals out of phase, making a disorientating whooshing sound, which is pretty much synonymous with phasing – Marriott sings about his intention to blow his mind before leaving a two-bar gap for Jones's flanged drums and cymbals to travel across the soundfield, leaving sonic vapour trails in their wake, and leading into a simple chorus in which the scene is described as *"all too beautiful"*.

Given the locale that spawned the song, these gushing sentiments might be taken as ironic, but Marriott sounds genuinely, unabashedly overwhelmed by the beauty of things, by these thoughts of a sunny afternoon stoned in the park, a precious oasis of green in the capital city.

By 1967 this exploration and re-establishment of self was probably practised more vigorously by musicians like the Small Faces than, say, trainee surveyors, but this pop song, with its memorable tune and alluring soundworld – and a Top 10 hit for the group – re-imagined humdrum Britain as somewhere that really could be perceived as being all too beautiful. The idea was immensely attractive.

But before we immerse ourselves more fully in psychedelia, we need to wind back to the first musical memories of the Small Faces and their peers, those musicians born around the end of World War Two and their audience, of similar age or born up to the end of the Fifties.

In the decade or so following World War Two, the principal remit of mainstream public broadcasting was to be educational and impartial along the lines drawn by Lord Reith at the foundation of the BBC in the

Twenties. In terms of music, the idea was to provide a sense of comfort and order, which in turn fostered a largely static and conservative mainstream culture. There was initially little aimed at youths specifically, but then what would the demand have been?

The Anglo-Italian band leader Mantovani was the most commercially successful recording artist in the UK up to the end of the Fifties. BBC orchestras would play approximations of his trademark lush string arrangements on the BBC Light Programme on morning shows like *Housewives' Choice*. As its name suggested the Light Programme also played Light music – the theme tune to *Music While You Work* was Eric Coates' ebullient wartime march, 'Calling All Workers' – as well as big band music and songs from musicals.

Elsewhere you might hear popular tunes sung by The Andrews Sisters, or proto-pop stars like Jimmy Young and a young Petula Clark singing songs arranged by Ron Goodwin; or The Cliff Adams Singers and their soothing medleys of "the old songs" on their early Sunday evening radio show *Sing Something Simple*, which ran from 1959. For younger listeners the programme not to miss was the Sunday evening singles chart rundown, *Pick Of The Pops*, which ran from 1955.

The December 1944 copy of the American *Life* magazine had carried the first high-profile recognition of the cultural phenomenon known as "the teenager", as those in the transitional phase between puberty and adulthood would become known. Within the affluent US, which was not as affected by the war as the UK, this group developed its own fashions, vernacular and modes of behaviour, but one can safely assume that happened largely within the more liberal white middle class groups. At the time the cultural significance of this new species had yet to be felt, and some of it would definitely not be welcomed.

In the mid-Fifties, the new phenomenon of rock'n'roll caused a huge stir in the USA because it saw a young generation symbolically shearing away from, and at times kicking against, the notion of an idealised, near utopian post-war American lifestyle. At least musically: typically the teenagers' lives were otherwise as conservative as those of their parents. But once they had hold of the notion of self-expression it wasn't going to go away.

In the mid-Fifties Brian Eno was a young boy growing up in the small Suffolk town of Woodbridge. Just a couple of miles outside of town lay the RAF facility of Bentwaters, which had been handed over to the Americans as a Cold War airbase. The number of American personnel living in Bentwaters and the former RAF Woodbridge, which had also been handed over to NATO, was around 17,000 – over four times the population of Woodbridge itself. A number of cafés and milk bars with jukeboxes sprang up in town to cope with the demand and they would play the latest American rock'n'roll and doowop, as well as Tommy Steele, who came onto the scene in 1957 as Britain's answer to Elvis Presley, and Cliff Richard who followed a couple of years later.

A record buyer from the age of nine, Eno was captivated by these sounds, but has since noted that you didn't necessarily need to have an airbase in your back yard to have been affected by this new music.

"The combination of the three-minute single and the radio station is in my opinion what gave birth to rock'n'roll," he says. "Suddenly it was possible to make a three-minute piece of music stand alone, and it could be heard globally in a very short space of time through radio stations and distributed globally as well, and this created a new way of thinking about music."

This applied just as much to the music from the Detroit label Tamla Motown. Formed in 1959, its singles – a peerless combination of soul, doowop, R&B and pop songwriting craft – were soon in the UK charts and on the radio.

While some of this music was played on BBC radio, its dedicated pop music station, Radio 1, only came on air in 1967. Before its inception you could catch the latest sounds on Radio Luxembourg and the UK pirate radio stations like Radio London and Radio Caroline that had broadcast from the early Sixties to over 10 million listeners. Many teenage music fans living with their parents were surreptitiously tuning in to the stations' inconsistent signals at night, their transistor radios pressed to their ears as they lay in bed.

From the early to mid-Sixties, the Liverpool-based Merseybeat groups purveyed pop-oriented appropriations of American soul and R&B in a way that carried a subtly distinctive English feel in their driving rhythms and vocal delivery. This was the scene that ushered in The Beatles, who were to dominate the Sixties on both sides of the Atlantic.

Into the Sixties, distinct tribal strands of youth culture were forming. Those who would become known as the modernists, or mods, were sharply dressed teens, initially dancing to jazz and then soul and R&B in London clubs. Their nemeses, the rockers, had morphed from the teddy boys of the Fifties and were steeped in rock'n'roll music with its accompanying signature style of pompadour haircuts and leathers, and although not much separated these rival factions age-wise, the mods were seen as upstarts against the old guard.

Prolonged fights in spring 1964 along the south and east coast from Brighton to Hastings, and in Clacton, prompted the UK's very own "moral panic", with the media also proclaiming the imminent disintegration of society.

Away from the testosterone-fuelled world of knuckle-dusters and bike chains by the sea, for those more keen on discovering traditional forms, there was a revival in the performance of folk music, which had been collected, researched and championed by the likes of Ewan MacColl and A. L. Lloyd in the Fifties and Sixties. This extended to the appreciation of American folk, and one young singer was of particular importance in speaking to the youth of America and the UK: Bob Dylan.

Others explored the recordings of American blues artists and as this music was relatively easy to learn, skiffle groups, playing an amalgam of folk and blues with a primitive jazzy swing, began to spring up in the UK from the Fifties, emulating homegrown artists like Lonnie Donegan. This huge groundswell of interest in blues music prompted a bunch of London-based students and their mates to form a group called The Rolling Stones in 1962.

They played R&B with an arrogant, sexually charged performance style and a lot of attitude. The Rolling Stones might have been serious about their blues, but they also had far more teen appeal than most blues outfits. Alan Barnes, a teenage music fan in the Sixties, remembers their impact.

"Going to parties aged 15 or 16, there used to be a kind of divide between the melodic, early Beatles-type things against the Stones, who were the slightly riskier option and that's when I decided that it was my kind of music, even though it wasn't quite as popular. It was edgier and you felt like you were more a rebel without a cause.

"A lot of the time, groups just used to stand there in suits playing their instruments and so having someone like Jagger commanding the stage was exciting."

Elvis Presley never came over to the UK and it was a rarity to be able to see other American rock'n'roll legends over here. But it was relatively easy to go to provincial theatres to see less remote stars like The Dave Clark Five and their stomping beat music or The Swinging Blue Jeans, or expat American P. J. Proby, infamously banned from all ABC theatres in 1965 for causing a ruckus after publicly splitting his tight trousers.

Or if you wanted to see something a bit nearer the source, soul groups like Herbie Goins & The Nightimers regularly played UK clubs in the Sixties as did Geno Washington. A US airman formerly stationed at the Air Force base at Bentwaters, once demobbed, Washington became a favourite on the UK club scene leading the Ram Jam Band, who scored two Top 10 album placings.

Barnes recalls the thrill of seeing Washington playing in the cellar of the Orford Arms in Norwich in the mid-to-late Sixties: "It was never more than a dive and it would probably never be opened now for health and safety reasons. I can remember all the people packed in there and looking at the walls and seeing the sweat trickling down. But the atmosphere was fantastic and the fact that you couldn't move was just part of it."

A wider British electric "blues boom" had begun in the early Sixties and expanded into the mid-Sixties, based on catalytic band leaders like Alexis Korner and John Mayall, and so it became worthwhile for some of the original American blues artists like Howlin' Wolf and Muddy Waters to come over as middle-aged men and play to enthusiastic audiences of young Brits. A young American promoter, Joe Boyd, brought over a package tour, the Blues And Gospel Caravan in 1964, featuring Muddy Waters, Brownie McGhee and Sonny Terry, the Reverend Gary Davis and Sister Rosetta Tharpe. The line-up toured the UK, playing to sold-out venues.

In this stylistically diverse time it was inevitable that hybrid forms would start to emerge. It would be these that took us through the brief flowering of psychedelia and onto progressive rock at the end of the decade.

One of the most remarkable and influential characters of the mid-Sixties was Graham Bond. His group The Graham Bond Organisation formed in 1964 and played a freshly minted, jazz-inflected take on R&B, including some classical influences. The group comprised Ginger Baker on drums, Jack Bruce on bass and vocals, and saxophonist Dick Heckstall-Smith, as well as Bond himself, who sang and played sax and Hammond organ. Their album *The Sound Of 65* was the first to feature the Mellotron, the keyboard instrument where depressing keys activated tape loops of strings, bass or woodwind. The instrument will crop up regularly throughout the rest of this book.

Underneath the surface, the group was less than stable. Bruce and Baker might have been a powerful rhythm section that vigorously swung, but there was a great animosity between them, while Bond was having problems with his drug consumption. Against all odds, Baker and Bruce left and eventually rejoined as the rhythm section of Cream in 1966.

At this time a young Keith Emerson was the keyboard player in The V.I.P.s. "He was totally in thrall to Graham," says poet, lyricist and singer Pete Brown. "He used to apparently stand by the side of the stage in the Marquee and check everything that he was doing. Obviously he became one of the leading lights in the progressive thing and what he did was a sort of extension of what Graham did. He couldn't do the jazz part – he wasn't in that actual mode – but he could certainly use the classical influences and because of the incredible chops that he had, he could use them more effectively than Graham."

"Graham Bond – oh gosh, yes," Emerson assents. "I saw him play with Ginger Baker and Jack Bruce and I don't think at that time I'd managed to purchase my first Hammond. But one of the first singles I bought was his version of 'Wade In The Water'. It started off with Bach's *Toccata And Fugue In D Minor*, which I thought was cool."

One of the tricks that Bond used live, which could be viewed as showmanship or simply practical – and has been used many times since – was wedging two keys down on the organ by putting a piece of folded card between them and pressing them down simultaneously to make drones and bigger spreads of sound. We will find out how Emerson expanded on this idea in a later chapter.

Drummer John Hiseman joined Bond in 1966, as Bruce and Baker left, and formed a trio with the organist and Heckstall-Smith. He recalls that the creative momentum of the group was more and more geared towards creating something new, not with any plan per se, but avoiding adhering to a handed-down blues or R&B stylistic template. Instead the musicians were let loose on the music.

"The thing about Graham was what he wanted you to do was to be you," Hiseman says. "And his was a very interesting concept, as you can't change people. You might be able to for one evening, but not over time. Graham chose the right people and let them get on with it."

Bond's individual music provided a bridge between mid–Sixties R&B and psychedelia, while signposting progressive rock. He would undoubtedly have been a major force himself, but was losing his personal battle with heroin addiction.

"The Organisation broke up around June or July '67," says Hiseman. "I had to get out. Graham was trying to go cold turkey, and it made him go a bit crazy. It was all too difficult to live with." Bond died in 1974 under a train at Finsbury Park Underground station.

Hiseman went off with Heckstall-Smith to form a group called Colosseum, who would take jazz and R&B into a new direction as we shall find out later.

And so back to the all too beautiful environs of 'Itchycoo Park' and into psychedelia and the subtle – and with some musicians the not so subtle – shift in consciousness in the way music was made. Psychedelic means "mind expanding" and is inextricably linked with psychedelic drugs, namely lysergic acid diethylamide or LSD-25, which was first formulated in 1938 and remained legal in the US until 1968, but was banned by the UN in 1971.

One of the drug's early advocates was American psychologist Timothy Leary. His most famous dictat, which he delivered to tens of thousands at the 'Human Be-In' in San Francisco in 1967, was that you should "turn on, tune in, drop out". This was radical – revolutionary, even – in that he was exhorting us to basically veer away from the strictures of "straight" society, to turn inward, to tap the potential of the mind. Clocking in for work every day seemed trivial when one had travelled through a kaleidoscopic inner space and glimpsed what appeared to be revelations of universal truths.

This prompted a questioning of the point of it all, an abstract question that the establishment couldn't answer, and prompted plans for a revolution fuelled by psychedelics – although quite who was going to empty the bins if the populace was all high on acid was never fully addressed. But these were ideas flying high, caught up like kites in spring. Now the youthful voicings of love, lust and discontent, the visceral needs of the everyday that came with rock'n'roll had ceded – in the views of some – into an exploration of one's interior landscape.

One way of looking at it was that the acid trip's negation of the ego, hopefully leading to enlightenment, was akin to many strands of religious and mystical thought, from Zen Buddhism to Hinduism, to the mystics and monastic orders of Christianity. Except that rather than achieving this state through a regime of meditation, contemplation and/or bodily deprivation, you achieved it through the ingestion of a drug, an instant hit. This left the ingester essentially a tourist in their own mind, on a "trip" whose effects could not be controlled. It could also be fearsomely strong.

Pete Brown's poetic imagery, with its pithy surrealist twists, was a peculiarly English take on the Beats. But although he might have seemed a prime candidate for such mental exploration, after accidentally setting fire to one of his poems typed on a roll of paper while speeding on amphetamines in 1967, he decided it best to just say no and has abstained ever since.

"I always thought that people with no imagination took acid and then imagined that they had an imagination, which was nice for them briefly," he says. "And the people who did have imagination, but took it anyway, it really sent them right over the fucking top to somewhere horrible. The results were not good."

In the UK the LSD option was generally only open to those who had connections in metropolitan areas. And more importantly, you didn't actually need to be high on acid to join in the fun or to visit the swinging, groovy West End fashion hub, Carnaby Street, or other London clothes emporia like Granny Takes A Trip or I Was Lord Kitchener's Valet, the latter an affectionate lampooning of the fading British Empire, with a range of military jackets for sale.

Those of the burgeoning hippie movement were characteristically less sartorially ostentatious, more dressed down, more in keeping with their aims, which were to try to establish a peaceful alternative to what had previously been learned by rote in a restrictive Christian capitalist society – or question it all at the very least. The idea was, broadly speaking, to gain enlightenment, to see beyond the everyday.

The hippies – or freaks – originated in mid-Sixties America and became most visible in 1967 in what was dubbed by the media, rather cutely, as "The Summer Of Love", which had been achieved through "Flower Power". This phrase had been coined by American Beat poet Allen Ginsberg back in 1965 as a positive and provocative moniker for peaceful anti-Vietnam protests: photographs and footage of demonstrators handing out flowers to tooled-up police and the military were so gently mocking – and potentially dangerous – that they became talismanic.

Oddly enough, "freaking out" has since become part of common parlance, although now it generally means extreme mental disturbance. But back in the Sixties freak-outs were collective gatherings of "freaks", who would "let it all hang out", expressing themselves through music, drama, art, stoned pranks and general exhibitionism. In California The Mothers Of Invention played such events in provocative, theatrical performances that were sometimes accompanied by dancers.

In the USA the hippies or freaks were, generally speaking, more politicised than their UK counterparts, what with the possibility that any of them might receive the dreaded letter in the post, enlisting them to go fight in the ongoing Vietnam War.

For example, Country Joe & The Fish's 1967 album *Electric Music For The Mind And Body* is overtly fuelled by psychedelics, with Joe McDonald half whispering the letters *"L... S... D..."* at the end of 'Bass Strings', a song about tripping in the Californian desert and by the ocean, feeling or realising that you are part of everything. But then on 'Super Bird', he criticises American president Lyndon B. Johnson and his involvement in Vietnam. On their next album, also from 1967, *I-Feel-Like-I'm-Fixin'-To-Die*, the title track is a scurrilous and scathing take on the senseless deaths in that conflict, set to a "good ole boy" country stomp.

English hippies shared many of these sentiments, but back in Blighty that sort of imminent threat was absent. They had memories of World War Two, which the Allies had won, and apart from prompting ideological indignation, Vietnam had little direct impact on British society. If anything, the prevailing view was exemplified by The West Coast Pop Art Experimental Band's 1967 song, 'Suppose They Gave A War And No One Comes', accompanied by a benign smile and the flash of a peace sign.

The whole peace, love and flowers business was a striking development in youth culture, and was latched onto by Scott McKenzie in his 1967 hit single 'San Francisco' with its evocation of a generation that had a "*new explanation*" – made attractive and romantic to both sexes when it conjured up images of wistful youths with flowers in their hair.

To espouse peace and love might have seemed a bit dopey to some, a bit pat, but then there was the ongoing Cold War, with Russia and China the potential adversaries. For the "straight" societies of both East and West to have spent a huge amount of money amassing an arsenal that could lay waste to the planet, but was balanced so that hopefully neither side would use theirs, was, looked at logically, completely insane.

The generation who were youths and young adults in 1967 had been told rather boldly back in 1957 that they had "never had it so good" by Prime Minister Harold Macmillan. They enjoyed greater leisure time and started to become more self-aware. For record producer and writer Joe Boyd, life in the Sixties was not as pressured. It was easier to get by.

"The atmosphere in which music flourished then had a lot to do with economics," he wrote in his memoir *White Bicycles: Making Music In The 1960s*. "It was a time of unprecedented prosperity. People are supposedly wealthier now, yet most feel they haven't enough money, and time is at an even greater premium.

"The economy of the Sixties cut us a lot of slack, leaving time to travel, take drugs, write songs and rethink the universe. There was a feeling that nothing was nailed down, that an assumption held was one worth challenging."

Attitudes to life were changing, with people beginning to challenge the givens regarding hitherto prim sexuality, Western religion and a job for life. But was it literally all too beautiful? Do we exaggerate it as if looking back through multi-coloured glasses at the so-called "beautiful people" frolicking in some giant, Eden-like psychedelic playpen?

In 1967 Peter Daltrey was the singer of Kaleidoscope, one of the premier British psychedelic groups. Their style ranged from wah-wah infused rock with swooning melodies to more baroque pop settings of his extravagant lyrics. The only reason they didn't make a bigger splash was down to bad luck and bad management. He remembers the time fondly, when they transcended their early beat group roots as The Sidekicks and began to write more personal material:

"Obviously we were being influenced by everything around us – this was '67. It was an absolutely amazing year to be 21 and making music living in London. It was a truly magical time. I don't expect to experience anything like it again. It's difficult to explain to people because there was so much going on. It wasn't just music, it was photography as well; in acting you had Terence Stamp and Julie Christie; in painting David Hockney; in fashion Mary Quant and Biba.

"As a band, we were lucky that our first recording period was that magical eighteen months when psychedelia was being formed and we were at the heart of it. But it was a very short period."

One could add to the above list TV shows like *The Avengers*, which had been going since the early Sixties, but whose plots were becoming progressively surreal. Even more bizarre was *The Prisoner*, first aired in 1967, which mixed up Cold War paranoia and brainwashing with the disorienting atmosphere of Franz Kafka's *The Castle* and Lewis Carroll's *Alice's Adventures In Wonderland*.

Daltrey also notes the magnitude of The Beatles' influence at the time, when the release of each of their singles was viewed as a significant cultural event.

"When you heard that a new Beatles single was coming out, all the conversation was, 'Have you heard it yet?' Songs like 'Paperback Writer' [1966] were breathtaking. You can't explain to people what it was like hearing that sort of music for the first time. But for me it was *Revolver* [1966] that changed the landscape. And you realised that you didn't have to write little love songs, you could write about anything."

In 1966, by all accounts, John Lennon had taken to LSD like a duck to water and had consequently become a semi-recluse in his pop star's mansion in Weybridge, negating his ego through daily ingestion of the hallucinogen. He later tried to achieve a similar end through the rather safer route of meditation, but this mind-altering course did help produce some startling creativity.

Lennon's simmering, acid-fuelled introspection boiled over most spectacularly on 'Strawberry Fields Forever', one of the first truly psychedelic English pop songs, written and recorded in late 1966 and released in early 1967 as a double A-side single with 'Penny Lane'. It stands as a signpost into a kind of parallel world where nothing is real, while referencing Strawberry Field, then a Salvation Army children's home in Liverpool, near where Lennon had played as a child. This experience was evoked in a confused, contradictory delivery as if Lennon was trying to make sense of memorial flashbacks buffeted and distorted by the effects of LSD.

The haunting tune is set to a low-key band performance with ringing guitar arpeggios and Ringo Starr rumbling along on snare and tom-toms at his idiosyncratic best. It was given a stately and sombre arrangement of cellos and trumpets – echoing the Salvation Army brass bands that the young Lennon heard there on open days – by producer George Martin, who famously spliced together two different takes.

Most people wouldn't have heard anything like it before and even now it sounds as strange and disturbing as a dark fairy tale. But it was an experiment that worked, as it also had an alluring quality, with Lennon offering to metaphorically take the listener by the hand and lead them down the rabbit hole. And it was by The Beatles, so people could hear it on the radio, and they listened. Paul McCartney's 'Penny Lane' is an equally remarkable but more focused revisiting of childhood in which another area of Liverpool is reviewed under halcyon blue skies, even if the memories it evokes are somewhat chemically amplified.

The Beatles' following album *Sgt Pepper's Lonely Hearts Club Band* might not have been quite as musically potent as *Revolver* in Peter Daltrey's estimation – a view echoed by many – but landing when it did, in May 1967, its effect was seismic. The album was packaged and sequenced as a single piece of art, but it wasn't, as many have stated, a "concept album". Instead it was a series of vignettes that featured teenage runaways, sexy traffic wardens, dance band nostalgia, Victorian fairgrounds, Eastern mysticism, and ideas borrowed from the musical avant-garde: a near-perfect distillation of young, hip Britishness, particularly Englishness, circa 1967.

Photographs of The Beatles as the titular band carry a whiff of Empire, of Lord Kitchener in a satin military suit, moustache bristling, freaking out on the electric guitar. The reprise of the main theme is a brilliant device in that it's so nearly the neat show-closer, but instead segues into the enigmatic, allusive 'A Day In The Life'. The song chronicles the demise of a young man who was seemingly one of the most blessed of mid-Sixties scenesters, the heir to the Guinness fortune Tara Browne – with whom McCartney had his first acid trip in 1965 – who lost control of his Lotus Elan sports car while driving at excessive speed and crashed into a parked van.

The way Lennon intones the news in neutral, slightly weary tones only adds to the poignancy of the situation. George Martin's orchestral arrangements add gravitas, but the two upward-swooping full orchestral glissandi, so dramatically inclined that the sensitive listener will experience g-forces, betrays the group's interest in the experimental end of modern composition. At the apex of the second of these the song ends on a multiple-piano chord. Now the four young Scousers who had come to prominence when rock'n'roll was basically still part of the variety circuit in the UK, led the way in British pop music and allied it to untrammelled self-expression and sonic innovation – and a certain self-importance – which is why the album is regarded by some as one of the first examples of progressive rock.

Although the UK singles charts in 1967 were by no means full of mind-expanding fare, some prime examples were Pink Floyd's 'See Emily Play', Traffic's 'Hole In My Shoe', 'Purple Haze' by Jimi Hendrix, Donovan's 'Sunshine Superman' and 'A Whiter Shade Of Pale' by Procol Harum. The Move gave a nod to the synaesthetic effects of LSD – when sensory inputs get cross-wired – with 'I Can Hear The Grass Grow'.

Another group who could and should have been big in 1967 and who were already sowing the seeds for progressive rock, were Tomorrow. The group developed out of a mid-Sixties mod band, The In Crowd, and guitarist Steve Howe recalls how this happened.

"There was a turning point when we were in a rehearsal, when [vocalist] Keith West said, 'I've got a number of my own songs and maybe we could collaborate?' Because we were kind of getting tired of playing soul, like Otis Redding, and we started to improvise. We wanted to get our own music to do that to – not other people's songs."

A new song 'My White Bicycle' ticked all the psychedelic boxes, with drummer Twink's whooshing hi-hats, backwards tapes trailing like the rider's slipstream, Howe's incisive guitar playing, including some Eastern-style licks on the chorus, and de rigueur whispered backing vocals. The song is a paean to two-wheeled transport akin to Sixties car songs, except it's way hipper, as the white bicycles in question were provided in Amsterdam by the Dutch countercultural movement, Provo, an ostensibly anarchistic movement which also organised protests and "happenings" in the city.

It was released as a single in 1967, but the delays in getting their debut album out meant the group missed out, commercially, on the Summer Of Love.

This was partly due to vocalist Keith West's involvement in producer Mark Wirtz's *Teenage Opera* project. A tantalisingly titled single, 'Excerpt From A Teenage Opera', was released under West's name, but the opera was never fully realised. However, despite being a side project, the single became a hit in 1967, which disrupted Tomorrow's schedule.

UK psychedelia's greatest delver into his own childhood was Pink Floyd's singer and guitarist Syd Barrett. On the group's 1967 debut, *The Piper At The Gates Of Dawn* – its title fittingly taken from Kenneth Grahame's children's novel *The Wind In The Willows* – Barrett sounds positively infantilised on 'The Gnome', a song about a little man named Grimble Gromble, as if leafing through one of the children's story books he had read as a seven-year-old.

'Matilda Mother' is a different matter. It feels more like an adult's reminiscences of a strange room in which a child is entranced by fairy stories, exploring a doll's house, chests of trinkets and fusty old clothes, idyllically held high by *"fairy stories"*. It's a prime example of a psychedelic view of the warm security of childhood as some kind of haven to revisit and from which to re-emerge, albeit slightly thrilled by those stories' attendant creepiness. By contrast, the group's vision was also directed outwards on 'Astronomy Domine' with Barrett, starry-eyed, looking up to the cosmos, regarding and naming some of the planets, stars and constellations.

In London there were a handful of clubs that were focal points of the psychedelic scene: Happening 44 in Gerard Street, The Electric Garden in King Street and the most famous, the UFO Club. UFO was started by Joe Boyd and John "Hoppy" Hopkins, an important figure in the underground scene. Hoppy had been the main instigator of the London Free School. This was ostensibly an adult education project founded in Notting Hill in March 1966, whose members and associates included Pink Floyd manager and London School Of Economics lecturer Peter Jenner; radical psychologist R. D. Laing; civil rights activist and black revolutionary Michael X; writer, performance artist, anarchist and happening organiser Jeff Nuttall; singer-songwriter Julie Felix; and Scottish novelist Alexander Trocchi. The School's activities were publicised via a magazine, *The Gate*. Basically the London Free School was a short-lived idea that didn't actually get off the ground, but its first "happening" was a benefit gig to help fund itself, billed as the Sound/Light Workshop and featuring Pink Floyd. It took place in All Saints Hall, Powis Gardens in West London, on September 30, 1966. For something that for its short life span only nominally existed, the School's influence was considerable, leading to Hopkins and Barry Miles of Indica

Books and Gallery co-founding the underground magazine *International Times* in 1966.

"I saw all the early concerts by Pink Floyd at the church hall and all their UFO club performances; they were the 'house band' of the scene," says Miles. "I paid them their £15 to play at the launch party for *International Times* and the posters for their UFO gigs were all Michael English and Nigel Waymouth designs. They were central to the small 1966–67 scene."

The UFO Club was situated in the basement of 31 Tottenham Court Road, under the Blarney Club, with a small stage and for the year or so it was in operation it hosted the cream of the psychedelic scene augmented by "theatrical happenings". It was also a place where information was disseminated and various causes publicised: there was talk that it would be the epicentre of the revolution.

Without an alcohol licence UFO just sold soft drinks, but it didn't take much initiative to find the guy selling blotters of LSD. To those who didn't partake, the place was disorientating enough with films projected on the walls and projections by visual artist Mark Boyle, who had premiered the infamous *Son Et Lumière For Bodily Fluids And Functions* at the Bluecoat Society Of Arts, Liverpool, in January 1967, which included projections of semen and vomit. In among the coloured slides and oil wheels, it was not always easy to tell what you were looking at, which for the squeamish was probably just as well.

Tomorrow were another of the main attractions, with Howe quickly gaining a reputation as a phenomenally gifted guitarist, who was occasionally left holding it all together solo when drummer Twink left his kit to engage in some mime. Jimi Hendrix came onstage to jam with them on one occasion at UFO.

Soft Machine were also a popular draw at the club. Looking back, the group's drummer Robert Wyatt had this to say about playing there: "We felt like suburban fakes dressed up on Saturday and visiting the city. I never dared take LSD. I was in awe of the audience at UFO... the [underground magazine] *Oz* crowd. We used to come in on the train and pretend we were like them. Just because we played long solos, people assumed we were stoned, which was great for our credibility.

"[Guitarist] Daevid Allen had connections with a whole generation of people there with advanced ideas. Daevid was the internationalist of the group, he got all of us into that. The rest of us were all provincial."

Wyatt remembers a particular Soft Machine gig there on May 5, 1967. "One of the biggest influences was the atmosphere at UFO. In keeping with the general ersatz orientalism of the social set-up you'd have an audience sitting down. I mean, everything was done sitting down in those days.

"If you've got a room of beer-swigging people standing up waiting for action, it's very hard starting with a drone. But if you've got a floor full of people, even the few that are listening, they're quite happy to wait for half an hour for the first tune to get off the ground. So that was a wonderful influence, or a terrible one according to your taste, but it was an influence on what the musicians played."

There were times when the more energetic and coordinated audience members would dance to the music.

"Stoned people are really sleepy and wave their arms around," Wyatt recalls. "They are rubbish dancers. Obviously they haven't being paying attention to The Temptations' nifty footwork. But people did dance to us in the early days, something I missed later on."

At a venue like UFO, time was an elastic concept. The venue was open until 6 a.m., so improvising at length was fine. No one was in a hurry. And to play at length was a defining aspect of psychedelic music in that it put you at a remove from pop music. This was about expression, not playing your hits to the kids. So if, say, Pink Floyd played their cosmic improvisation 'Interstellar Overdrive' for twenty minutes or more, that was definitely OK and became part of the blur of the evening.

Judy Dyble was the original vocalist in Fairport Convention, who would become associated with Joe Boyd as their producer and manager. She has these recollections of playing at UFO.

"You'd go down these very steep steps and you'd end up in this underground room with people sitting on the floor and leaning on walls in the dark. You'd have these blobby oil wheel lightshows and black-and-white films running at the same time out of focus, and a band playing in a corner. The room was absolutely crammed with people all smoking dope, being cool and dancing. For me it was a question of trying to pick my way carefully through this heap of people, carrying my incredibly heavy autoharp to get to the dressing room, which held about two people but was for about four or five bands. So where would you tune your harp or your guitar? You'd do your best and then you would go on and play and people would listen, while others were dancing and others just talking."

It seemed that apart from the pungent smoke, there was a tangible whiff of change and liberation in the air at the time. Was that the case?

"Most definitely," she says. "I was 18 in 1967 and some of us were the first teenagers to not be wearing the same clothes as our mothers. You think of the beautiful people lounging around on settees in their glorious clothes, but it wasn't quite like that; it was a lot messier than that. You could ignore the fact that it was filthy, but you didn't want to see it in daylight.

"The music and the atmosphere were great. [Fairport Convention] were all 17–18, and in London and alive in a wonderful time. We didn't realise how important this period was. I wish I'd taken photographs, but to take photographs then was expensive."

Dyble notes that the audiences in 1967 were particularly receptive, not just to psychedelic rock, but to any combination of performance styles that was presented to them.

"I think you can go back to the era of the Beats," she says. "That's when you first got someone reciting poetry over a bongo player – it was perfectly cool and proper to have poetry and jazz and that turned into the psychedelic scene where you've got a band playing, poets, a small jazz group, or [improvisers] Spontaneous Music Ensemble. You could do anything and it would be accepted."

Pink Floyd had gained a reputation as being in the psychedelic vanguard by 1967 and Syd Barrett represented the best and worst aspects of psychedelic mind expansion. He was a bright, sparky youth, but exacerbated by his relentless ingestion of LSD, his descent into mental instability – the time when the lights went out, as many have said – was alarmingly rapid.

In those days to be weird was good and there was a hip cachet attached to drugs, to being "out of it". It was against the constrictive rules of "straight" society. The label "acid casualty" was in its infancy, but behind the druggy bonhomie these were young people who basically didn't fully know what they or others were taking, or how to react to someone experiencing mental problems, or whether these problems were as a direct result of the drug or would have manifested themselves anyway.

Pete Brown frequented London psychedelic venues like the UFO Club in 1967. He was on speaking terms with Barrett and has this to say about the guitarist.

"Syd Barrett came from a background of blues and within his limitations was a very good improviser. Sometimes, of course, he was a sonic improviser, which was a different thing. It wasn't until Hendrix and Jeff Beck that you got people who could play absolutely incredibly and could do the sonic things well. But certainly Syd was extremely inventive both in terms of texture and in terms of actual content. When he was on, he was really interesting. And some of the progressive influences there were from free jazz, because he was liking people like [guitarist] Derek Bailey and AMM – he always claimed that."

In 1967 AMM were a free improvising quartet, and guitarist Keith Rowe explored the possibilities of his instrument beyond conventional playing. But as a testament to the broad tastes of the day, their supposedly difficult music occasionally found them on the same bill as Pink Floyd. Their own approach to musical freedom was considered, while late into his tenure in Pink Floyd, Barrett would sit on the stage playing his Fender Telecaster through a Binson Echorec echo unit with a cigarette lighter as a slide, quite independently and perhaps completely oblivious to what his bandmates were doing. Sadly, this freedom from constraints culminated in him playing nothing for entire sets. The Nice guitarist Davy O'List deputised for him at some shows when he had taken this freedom further still by not appearing at all.

Lest we forget, this psychedelic scene was largely a London phenomenon. Arthur Brown, who played at UFO, describes it as a "cultural melting pot". But its effects soon spread out. "I think a lot of bands in the provinces heard and they started to be psychedelic," Brown says. "It didn't all start at the same time in those days, and so you had jazz, classical, blues, rock and Indian influences creeping in."

Psychedelia spread out from metropolitan centres, but not before some of the psychedelic groups suffered at the hands of provincial fans who had no intention of sitting around listening to twenty-minute freak-outs, but as Robert Wyatt described, were swilling beer and wanted some action. And in some cases the action was the group themselves.

And if one night encapsulated the stark difference between London clubs and provincial ballrooms, it was the evening of July 29, 1967. Pink Floyd's Roger Waters recalled that the group played a "double header": firstly at the Wellington Club, East Dereham, to a 500-strong crowd, "hurling abuse and fighting", with beer glasses smashing against the drum kit. They then travelled the hundred miles south to play a late headlining slot at the International Love In Festival at Alexandra Palace, north London.

Joe Boyd has said that the hardcore UFO regulars, who had made the club a rallying point for countercultural activity – as well as simply getting high – were steadily being joined by the "weekend hippies", hipsters sporting psychedelic trappings, and dodgy geezers who were searching out the groovy late-night places to hang out. Out of London, this is exactly what was happening.

In 1967 Pete Brown was performing a mix of jazz and poetry in The First Real Poetry Band. He has this memory of one particular show: "We were doing a gig in Bristol when John McLaughlin was in that band and the support band came into the dressing room, all looking quite normal. There was one guy with a beard and curly hair and the rest of them all looking fairly straight, and a black singer, smartly dressed. And they all proceeded to don wigs and kaftans. It was quite a big band, there were eight of them, and they went on stage and proceeded to play 'In The Midnight Hour' and other soul classics in psychedelic clothing, which was the first manifestation of some kind of weird provincial fashion."

Whereas good old Blighty might have seemed like a benign kaleidoscope world given the right mindset, the establishment took a dim view towards the insurrectionist activity of the counterculture. The underground press were a prime target and the *International Times* office was raided under the strict laws on obscenity.

In response, Hoppy and Joe Boyd organised the mother of all benefit gigs on April 29, 1967. Named The 14 Hour Technicolor Dream, it was a financially risky enterprise and no simple fund raiser, but a defining moment of British counterculture. Held at the enormous Victorian edifice of Alexandra Palace in north London, the show involved dance troupes, poets, films, a helter skelter and forty-one groups, with two simultaneously playing on stages at each end of the huge main space. A considerable amount of drugs were consumed. Pink Floyd headlined as the sun was coming up, around 5 a.m.

Nik Turner, later the saxophonist in Hawkwind, was in attendance. "I saw John Lennon there, just hanging out, I saw Marc Bolan playing with John's Children, and saw another band called The Flies, who were hurling bags of flour around," he recalls.

"The 14 Hour Technicolor Dream was quite an event, really, because it had all these creative people that were of that era – Unicorn Press, and the Osiris Agency, who printed psychedelic posters for the UFO Club, and all psychedelic people who were agitating for something different, for social change. They were also having a good time and getting high together."

Somewhat dazed come the morning, Joe Boyd recalls the feeling with which he was left: "I lay outside on the grass surrounded by crowds streaming away in the bright sunshine. There was no stopping this juggernaut: the underground was becoming the mainstream," he wrote in his book *White Bicycles*.

Instead, by October 1967, the UFO Club, which had moved to the larger venue of the Roundhouse in Camden Town had closed. Hoppy had been busted for possession of cannabis – drug laws were far stricter then – and in June was sentenced to nine months in jail.

Covent Garden club Middle Earth (formerly the Electric Garden), which promoted gigs at the Roundhouse after UFO, was subjected to several police raids for breaching age restrictions and for drug possession among its clientele, and closed down in mid-1968. Maybe it wasn't all too beautiful after all.

CHAPTER 2

Notes from the Underground

As we have noted, the term "progressive rock" was coined by Chris Welch of *Melody Maker* in 1967. This snappy turn of journalese was certainly appropriate because, put simply, things were progressing and at some rate.

That might sound trite or obvious, but compare the Sixties to the contemporary music scene, where we exist in a simultaneity of different eras, with a massive library of music that can be accessed by anyone. The first decade of the 21st century might have seen a few sub-genres introduced, like grime and freak folk and, as always, each year throws up some new music of high quality. But however you look at it, the Sixties was a pioneering time, with new developments in technology and a desire for exploration that produced an exponential development of pop culture, the like of which had never been witnessed before, nor has it since.

The transition from 1967 to 1968 was so marked that if you had raised a wetted finger in the early spring of 1968 it would have been clear that the prevailing wind had changed.

For example, Tomorrow's self-titled debut album was eventually released by EMI in February 1968, complete with money-saving black-and-white cover, and stereo mix hastily derived from producer Mark Wirtz's original mono. The group lost out doubly, as not only did they turn up to the party just as everyone was leaving, but they were now seen rather as last year's thing. Make that triply, for they split up just before the album was released.

In guitarist Steve Howe's assessment it could and should have been better. "There was some new kind of stuff that was innocently naïve. I don't know what the hell it was doing there, but somehow we twisted ourselves into that," he says, amused at the memory. "I wouldn't say that the Tomorrow album is a thoroughbred album and in a way that was its weakness; it had too many quirky songs. 'Three Jolly Little Dwarfs' was appropriately quirky, but 'Auntie Mary's Dress Shop' and 'Shy Boy' weren't really rock songs of the psychedelic era.

"Besides 'My White Bicycle', which was a project that we did by itself as a single, the rest of the album didn't really reflect the power and excitement that the group had. With a few more tracks [to record on] and a producer in a studio you start messing around, and in a way you can very easily lose the plot. We went into 'record' mode and songs like 'Real Life Permanent Dream' got the overproduction job with sitars, but the way we played it live was much more involving and exciting. We were using experimentation like everybody was, but the way we rocked out onstage was very different from the studio."

With hindsight, *Tomorrow* is a fine piece of work and while it contains some whimsical songs, there were as many aspects of the music that pointed to the future. Not for nothing had they been referred to as a "progressive group" in *New Musical Express*, as they were adept at improvisation and their songs often incorporated unusual structural quirks and unison passages. For example, on 'The Incredible Journey Of Timothy Chase', Keith West's vocal melody rides smoothly over a particularly odd series of time changes.

Tomorrow was favourably viewed in the music papers, but this review in *Melody Maker* was also particularly telling.

"Somehow 'My White Bicycle', the opening track, sums up the long dead days of the hippie summer of '67. It brings back a whiff of burning incense, the jingling of bells, and sights and sounds of the UFO, the Saville Theatre, Primrose Hill, Chalk Farm and various scenes around Marylebone, Earl's Court and Paddington. The madness may have faded but the music lingers on and these Keith West compositions have a charm of their own. Songs like 'Shy Boy' should have been hits. Well produced and performed, above average material."

But hang on, what's all this "long dead" business? The "madness" was all at its height only a few months previously, but this kind of comment feels like the remembrance of things long since past. And as the year of the Summer Of Love had been such an experience and ushered in so much exciting, innovative music that still stands the test of time, why were there not subsequent summers of love?

It seems that with the ringing in of the New Year, something had subtly changed. Kaleidoscope was one group who metamorphosed stylistically and, in 1969, changed their name to Fairfield Parlour. Vocalist Peter Daltrey offers these views.

"Psychedelia was this amazing firework that burst into the sky, multicoloured and multifaceted, when fashion and music came together in such an intrinsic way. But when that firework died, you couldn't then carry on doing that or you would have been out of style, and so-called 'progressive' music was coming in.

"Into '68 it started to change – you could almost put it down to a season," he continues. "We couldn't stay being psychedelic or we'd have been old hat and looked very silly indeed. We were lucky that our songwriting leant itself to maturing and you can tell [that] from [Kaleidoscope's 1967 debut] *Tangerine Dream* to [second album released in 1969] *Faintly Blowing* to *From Home To Home* [1970, as Fairfield Parlour]. Even on *Faintly Blowing* you can see a lot more mature songs like 'Black Fjord', 'If You So Wish', 'Bless The Executioner'. Fortunately it suited this new progressive period. When music changed we were right there making this progressive-psych-folk music, which has a place in people's hearts now."

One way of looking at it is that psychedelic music was full of sonic detail to evoke a feeling of transcendence: guitars and organs played through wah-wah pedals, fuzz boxes and echo units; backwards, phased or flanged guitar, vocals and other instruments; tape manipulation and collages; more "avant" orchestrations; the use of faux-Eastern scales; sitars; and swooning backing vocals singing words like *"sky"* or just *"aaah"*.

This love of the manipulation of sound reflects the difference that Pete Brown highlights between sonic improvisers and more conventional soloists on guitar. And a lot of the seemingly peripheral aspects of psychedelia – the drones, the exotica, the decoration-in-sound – were its most important legacy. You were allowing the music to carry you along, happily losing yourself in the jams or improvisations. As with classical symphonies and jazz excursions, the length of the piece, the journey, became as important as the destination. It was like the difference between hopping on the bus down into town and going on a mystery tour.

The Beatles, who to many people defined psychedelia with *Sgt Pepper's*, were already set to leave it behind. But the *Magical Mystery Tour* double EP, released right at the end of 1967, contained one song, 'I Am The Walrus', that was a pinnacle of English psychedelia, only this time it was part Lewis Carroll fantasy, part bad acid trip. Music journalist Ian MacDonald has referred to it as "the most idiosyncratic protest song ever written". He describes it as a "Damn-you-England tirade that blasts education, art, culture, law, order, class, religion and even sense itself".

Lennon again regressed back to schooldays, but recast playground chants as sinister mantras, while sneering at contemporary mores and morals. He had been fascinated by – and wary of – Bob Dylan's stream of consciousness lyrics, and on 'I Am The Walrus' his verse delivery is somewhat reminiscent of Dylan's 'Subterranean Homesick Blues', in that both involved a pile-up of images delivered on a melody seesawing largely between a couple of notes. But whereas Dylan's was a sage word to the kids on the street, Lennon's was so disturbing precisely because it was surrealism delivered as invective. Even the brief interlude that finds him sitting in an English garden patiently waiting for the comforting appearance of the sun is ushered in by disquieting string glissandi.

George Martin's arrangement has a touch of genius about it, with rich, resiny cellos and a woozy brass band melody giving an air of distressed formality, heightened by the normally sedate Mike Sammes Singers yelping and grunting with vigour.

The song ends in chaos with a refrain of the rather quaint children's insult, "Stick it up your jumper", juxtaposed with an ironic interjection of high art, an extract of a radio broadcast of Shakespeare's *King Lear*.

In terms of freedom of expression and shocking originality this was the most outré Beatles song, but it was the last one to embark on such an exploration. Into 1968, like many groups, they pulled back from the brink and took stock. Their first single of that year was 'Lady Madonna', which although a superior pop song, was grounded in R&B.

March 1968 brought a swift killing of a sacred cow with The Mothers Of Invention's *We're Only In It For The Money*. The cover is a delicious parody of the *Sgt Pepper's* sleeve and the inference, which singer, guitarist and main writer Frank Zappa later confirmed, was that The Beatles were no gods, but just after your hard-earned cash like everyone else.

But if, as Zappa claimed, they were only in it for the money, they wouldn't have released *Sgt Pepper's*, because although The Beatles were given unlimited time at Abbey Road studios, both EMI and manager Brian Epstein were concerned about the commercial viability of the album to the extent that there were payback clauses if it sold less than 100,000 copies. To have quickly knocked out an album of more standard pop songs would have been the easy option.

The psychedelic glad rags were being metaphorically folded and packed away, and the communal vibe of the 1967 underground was beginning to dissolve. The massed ranks of hippies never went away, but in the cold grey light of early 1968, their psychedelically inspired State Of Grace involved too much of a suspension of disbelief to be sustainable. It was lampooned by others who were wary of their "all too beautiful" passivity.

Arthur Brown, then the leader of The Crazy World Of Arthur Brown, pursued an alternative, countercultural lifestyle, but wrote a song, released as the B-side of the 1967 single 'The Devil's Grip' called 'Give

Him A Flower'. The title partly referred to American anti-war demonstrators putting flowers down gun barrels. He explains the meaning of the song.

"It was a lot of fun [to think] that you could put a flower down the barrel of a gun and that would be the answer to everything," Brown says. "If a teddy boy is coming after you with a bike chain and you give him a flower, it doesn't always work is the point. It can work and then it's a huge symbol. It was about a lot the things of the day, and the idea that now we've got a slogan, 'Give him a flower'. It was obvious that there was going to be a need to look much deeper than that.

"There were guys with beads who were actually hard-headed mods. And as soon as there was any trouble, it was, ''Ere, you fucking on at my mate? I'll have you!'"

On March 17, 1968, demonstrations took place outside the American Embassy in London's Grosvenor Square prompted by the escalation in the Vietnam War, with demonstrators clashing with police. Mick Jagger was photographed participating – in one shot standing close to a young and ambulant Stephen Hawking – and another high-profile demonstrator eagerly snapped was the actress Vanessa Redgrave in the company of leftwing radical, Tariq Ali.

Over in France, unrest culminating in the May 1968 Paris riots came close to bringing down the government. Quite to what extent this influenced the course of rock music in the UK in 1968 is debatable. Now those calls for revolution by paisley-clad musicians seemed a little effete when compared with students and workers scrapping it out with police on the streets in Paris. The two songs that were most overtly influenced by this unrest were The Beatles' 'Revolution' and The Rolling Stones' 'Street Fighting Man'.

John Lennon's 'Revolution' first emerged as the B-side of 'Hey Jude' in August 1968, although it had been written earlier in the year. It showed Lennon taking an observational stance, equivocal about whether or not he was to be counted either "out" or "in" of what might lead to violent clashes. He also enraged the far left by criticising Chairman Mao. That seems incredible now, but pro-Mao factions would have been largely unaware of the pitiless brutality that was a by-product of the Chinese Cultural Revolution achieving its "egalitarian" aims.

Lennon simply shrugged his shoulders and assured us that it was all going to be alright, without offering any explanation as to *how* it was going to be alright. But then his confusion, summarised as "I want to change things but I don't really know how to go about it", reflected the thoughts of many.

Mick Jagger's 'Street Fighting Man', released on The Rolling Stones' *Beggars Banquet* and written shortly after the Grosvenor Square demos, was similarly delivered without a manifesto. Although Jagger's sentiments were set to acoustic guitars and tamboura drones, there was nothing remotely hippieish about them. But the denouement of each line again resulted in a rather bathetic, metaphorical shoulder shrug that undermines its apparent braggadocio. Yes, there was fighting in the street *"everywhere"*, but in London what could you do to make any difference but play in a rock'n'roll band?

The turbulence of 1968 prompted a surprise move into the arena of protest by another "progressive" group, The Nice. American composer and conductor Leonard Bernstein had showcased some of the more adventurous new music on his US TV show, *Inside Pop: The Rock Revolution* in 1967, giving tacit endorsement and kudos to, for example, Brian Wilson playing a strange, strikingly beautiful new composition on piano entitled 'Surf's Up'.

But he was less than enamoured by The Nice's radical 1968 reworking of 'America' from his musical *West Side Story*. It's cleverly cut with a theme from the fourth movement of Antonin Dvorak's *Symphony No. 9: From The New World*, together with some aggressive instrumental extemporising. Emerson has described it as the first instrumental protest song – against the US involvement in Vietnam – and his burning of the American Flag onstage at the Royal Albert Hall in 1969 earned him a lifetime ban from the venue.

As many groups retrenched a bit and reined in their ambitions, phrases like "back to basics" or "back to the roots" were bandied about in the music press, as if groups had been getting ideas above their station – but what exactly were these roots? This habitually resulted in more common-denominator rock riffs and motifs. A band like Blossom Toes couldn't really have carried on in the imaginative, but occasionally daft, psychedelic vein of *We Are Ever So Clean* (1967), but by the time they had got to *If Only For A Moment* in 1969, they had become a harder-rocking, less appealing and less original group. And in common with many groups who stretched out into this kind of territory, the songwriting, the shape of the tunes, rather suffered as a result.

Many groups went down this route, with the British blues boom morphing into the harder, riff-based music by the likes of Uriah Heep and Led Zeppelin, both of whom had progressive tendencies, but created their own genre, which lies outside the remit of this book.

So why did so many groups pull back rather than go further out? It was like they had put a tentative toe in the water, decided that it would feel warmer when they were in, dived in off the middle board, but then came straight out again.

Pink Floyd's 'Interstellar Overdrive' had been conceived as a structurally indeterminate improvisation, which could go on for something like half an hour. Soft Machine played Kevin Ayers' two-chord mantra, 'We Did It Again' – which had been conceived as a study in repetition – for twenty minutes or more, partly because they could. And people danced. But then how much further did you want to "freak out" before you either became unbearably tedious or completely lost your bearings?

As was borne out from 1968 onwards, exploring extended forms was something that appealed hugely to the more questing rock musicians but, crucially, rather than going headfirst into the flames and doing, say, forty-minute slices of abstract mayhem, they started to experiment with structure.

The groin-level communiqués of "rock'n'roll" morphed into "rock", to separate it further from pop music. But if this losing of the "'n'roll" implied a certain neutering of the music to make it less primal and more cerebral, that was a by-product of the way things were heading.

One of the key factors in the transition from psychedelia to progressive rock was the significant number of groups who took this path. "Self-indulgence" was a term that was prevalent in the music press, although it was almost always used pejoratively by the back-to-basics brigade. But if one looks at it all from a different angle, it can just as easily be synonymous with risk-taking, experimentation, boundary-pushing and unfettered self-expression – doing exactly what one wants. Most of The Beatles' best work from 1966–68 was gloriously and unapologetically self-indulgent, and self-indulgence was, by this twist of definition, what spurred musicians on to make the original new music that hallmarked progressive rock rather than falling back on tried and trusted forms. And into the Seventies, the musicians generally had the blessings of record companies to do just that, to be part of the development of this new thing. Artistically speaking, it was knowing your limitations and knowing when to stop that became the difficult factor.

Rewinding back to 1966, The Who had recorded a multipart nine-minute suite, 'A Quick One While He's Away' on their second album *A Quick One*. In 1968, rather than going back to mod basics, the Small Faces sailed further away from the environs of 'Itchycoo Park' with the album *Ogdens' Nutgone Flake* and its sidelong story-in-song, 'Happiness Stan', made up of a number of discrete parts.

One of the most significant releases of that year was *S.F. Sorrow* by The Pretty Things. The group had come into prominence in 1963 as a feisty R&B combo. Guitarist Dick Taylor had played with Mick Jagger and Keith Richards in the group Little Boy Blue & The Blue Boys, which morphed into The Rolling Stones, for whom Taylor briefly played bass. In early 1967 The Pretty Things had flirted with psychedelia on *Emotions*, but had totally embraced it as the year drew to a close on their single 'Defecting Grey' – a mind-boggling song collage and one of the high water marks of that brief era.

They began recording *S.F. Sorrow* in late 1967 at Abbey Road studios, with Pink Floyd producer Norman Smith. The LP was one of the first true concept albums in that it had a narrative, with its subject the panoramic sweep of the protagonist's life. It was based on an idea by vocalist Phil May, who linked the song lyrics with annotations on the album's sleeve notes.

The record was released at the end of 1968 and was performed at the Middle Earth club in London, with the band miming to backing tracks and new drummer Twink, who had joined from Tomorrow, continuing his penchant for mime in performing the part of Sebastian F. Sorrow. Thereafter the group ditched this idea of staging the album and integrated some of its songs into their live set.

There have been arguments since that *S.F. Sorrow* was the first "rock opera", predating *Tommy*, the 1969 double album by The Who – which the group actually played at the Metropolitan Opera House in New York City in that year. The idea of calling it a rock opera came from The Who's manager Kit Lambert, and it now seems symptomatic of those not directly involved in the music, be they management or journalists, coming up with grandiose ideas whereby a series of thematically linked rock songs would be seen on a par with Puccini or Wagner.

It may seem pedantic, but if one wants to put these extended rock compositions into a pseudo-classical classification, a song cycle seems more appropriate, as an opera is essentially a dramatic work and, initially, these weren't. That said, Lambert's point was strengthened by later, semi-staged performances of *Tommy* at the Rainbow Theatre in London in 1972 with the London Symphony Orchestra and a stellar cast of guest vocalists. And it was a fun term to throw around.

Going back to The Nice, they had come along the route of so many groups at the time, when they first coalesced as the backing band of

American soul singer Patricia "P. P." Arnold who was operating in England and was signed to Andrew Loog Oldham's Immediate Records.

The group signed to the label and comprised Keith Emerson on keyboards, Lee Jackson on bass guitar and vocals, drummer Brian Davison, and Davy O'List on guitar. They released their debut album, *The Thoughts Of Emerlist Davjack*, in 1967 and the results were ostensibly psychedelic, but included the track 'Rondo', which was derived from jazz pianist, composer and band leader Dave Brubeck's 'Blue Rondo A La Turk', with a brief snatch of J. S. Bach's *Toccata And Fugue In D Minor* – as had been integrated into 'Wade In The Water' by one of Emerson's influences, Graham Bond.

Into late 1968, their second album *Ars Longa Vita Brevis* includes themes by Bach and Sibelius and the title track on the second side is one composition, split into four movements and a coda. This has been mentioned as being a groundbreaking album and is certainly one of the candidates for the first progressive rock album. Their third album, from 1969, *Nice (Everything As Nice As Mother Makes It)*, showed another side of the group with lengthy fantasias on songs by Tim Hardin and Bob Dylan.

Keith Emerson's theatrics while playing the organ began in The Nice. While rock guitarists could pose with the guitar, throw it around, even use it to repel stage-crashers, playing the bulky Hammond was like standing behind a large chest of drawers. Emerson, though, rocked it around, pivoted it on one of its corners, played it from behind, jumped on it as if he were humping it, lay under it as if it were humping him, and stuck knives between the keys, which appeared to expand rather dramatically on Graham Bond's pieces of cardboard.

"I didn't know that," Emerson says. "It might have been subconsciously, I may have seen him do that. But it was Lemmy from Motörhead. He used to be The Nice's roadie and when I started to stick knives in the organ, Lemmy came up to me with two Hitler Youth daggers and said in his gruff voice, 'If you're gonna use a knife, use a real one'. My very good mate Brian Auger apparently played one gig where he tried to copy me with plastic knives and forks."

There is no doubt that classical music was a significant influence in helping to shape the longer compositions associated with progressive rock. Over the years received wisdom has often equated it with simply rocking up the classics, however that was only a part of what was going on at the end of the Sixties.

Nick Kent wrote for *New Musical Express* during the Seventies, and became established as one of the most acclaimed and at times controversial music journalists of that decade. He also played guitar in an early version of the Sex Pistols around 1975. Although his tastes lay almost exclusively outside the music produced by progressive rock groups, he saw The Nice play live in their earliest incarnation.

"I count myself as one of the first people outside of London who saw prog rock kind of created before our very eyes [at the Sophia Gardens, Cardiff]," he recalls. "When I was 15 in November of 1967 there was a package tour with the Jimi Hendrix Experience, Pink Floyd with Syd Barrett – some of his last gigs with the group – The Move and at the bottom of the bill, The Nice. And those gigs with The Nice are where psychedelic rock ends and prog rock begins, because The Nice almost stole the show from all the other acts – but not quite, because you can't really steal the show from Jimi Hendrix when he's on good form.

"But they left a huge impression. They only had a six-minute slot on the tour – six minutes! They did one song, 'Rondo', and they rocked it up. Keith Emerson threw daggers into his organ and did all sorts of crazy stuff, and everyone in the room was completely gobsmacked by it. Because this wasn't psychedelic rock. This was music where they took a classical music piece and kind of rocked it up with a lot of virtuosity, and a lot of good old-fashioned shock-rock tactics.

"The Nice were the first prog rock group as far as I'm concerned. They were the ones that said, 'OK, the next step is away from just howling guitars – what we put in here is virtuosity'. And, you know, everyone is talking about how rock has suddenly become an art form – 'We'll play the old classics, but we'll do it our way, to show the academic world that rock really has grown up'".

Kent was witnessing a pivotal moment in rock music's development and his account seems to prove a point. But it doesn't quite tell the whole story and, in fact, confuses it further, as 'Rondo' was based on Dave Brubeck's 'Blue Rondo A La Turk', not *Rondo Alla Turca* by Mozart, so this ur-progressive rock composition was, in fact, jazz based. And despite its title, Brubeck had been influenced less by Mozart and more by Turkish musicians, composing the song in 9/8 and 4/4, although The Nice's version was played just in 4/4.

At the time of writing Toby Manning, a journalist and teacher, runs a course on progressive rock, *Sgt Pepper's Children*, at City Lit, a further education college in London. The age range is mostly between 40–60 years, but with a couple of students about 30. He says: "There's often quite a strong push in the classes to 'explain' prog as rock classical, whether that's how prog numbers mirror the symphonic form, or how exactly specific prog numbers were influenced by specific classical melody lines. Even after I thought I had explained myself thoroughly about classical being one of a number of things prog drew on (along with jazz, avant-garde, and particularly folk), there was in several different classes a sense of minority discontent, culminating in complaints that these comparisons hadn't been sufficiently delivered."

This is a prime example of time flattening out perspective and received wisdom taking over. There are many examples in progressive rock where classical influences have helped shape this emergent music, but there are far more examples where classical influences were either less overt or were completely absent. To put in a classical quotation or filch a melody wasn't in itself progressive – pop songwriters had been helping themselves to tunes from the classical repertoire for years – and in the late Sixties, German band leader James Last was taking classical themes and churning them out in his trademark bland easy listening medleys.

The Move were a group that flitted along the outskirts of psychedelia, with superior, somewhat eccentric, pop songs in the late Sixties. They used a cheeky quote from Tchaikovsky's *1812 Overture* in the guitar line of their 1967 single, 'Night Of Fear' and on 'Cherry Blossom Clinic Revisited' on their 1970 album *Shazam*, they ran through a number of classical quotations in the lengthy piece, but as the song was about a mental institution, it felt like some kind of tongue-in-cheek recital for the patients.

And winding forward slightly along this tack, in 1970 the Argentine arranger Waldo De Los Rios scored a hit with 'Mozart 40', a cheesy, rocked-up version of the opening movement of Mozart's *Symphony No. 40*, one of the tracks from his *Symphonies For The Seventies* album. His desire, as suggested by its title, was to make these compositions more "relevant" to the time.

If simply appropriating classic music and adding a few rock instruments to an orchestra was synonymous with progressive rock, then this was its acme. But of course it wasn't.

In fact, one slightly annoyed *Melody Maker* reader, Colin Fenn of Cuffley, Hertfordshire, saw the influence of classical music on rock as being more regressive than progressive. He wrote in to the paper in 1970. Unfortunately, the reasons for his alternative genre title are left unexplained.

"When will people refrain from using the term 'progressive music'? When applied to group like The Nice or King Crimson, who frequently feature classical pieces of music in their stage acts, the phrase becomes laughable. Let's have some suggestions for a new name. For example, how about 'intrinsic pop'?"

Given the expanding remit of 20th-century music, this merger of classical and rock music forms was inevitable. And as Judy Dyble noted in the previous chapter, the essence of a psychedelic event was that different combinations of artistic pursuit were combined. And so progressive rock became an all-gates-open way of expanding rock music by incorporating elements from classical, jazz, R&B, free improvisation, folk, blues, soul, electronics and Eastern music. And although few groups pursued the mixed or multi-media angle, further into the Seventies some favoured an increasing theatricality of presentation, and those who could afford it really went to town.

Looking at the above list, soul and R&B might seem anomalous as they are rarely mentioned inputs into what was a music played almost entirely by white musicians. But then most of the musicians had grown up playing soul or R&B. Into the Seventies Van Der Graaf Generator became one of the most extreme progressive rock groups, but their music is absolutely full of soul music references, many hiding in plain sight. Pye Hastings of Caravan, that most quintessentially English group and figureheads of the so-called Canterbury Scene – although he himself is Scottish – admits he has always thought of himself as a soul rhythm guitarist. Hastings also makes the semantic distinction between "progressive" – which he claims he never used – and "underground".

This is more than pedantry, as before the massive success of some progressive rock groups, "underground" was a much-used description of this increasingly popular but off-mainstream music. A trip to your local record store in 1970 would have revealed racks of records labelled "UNDERGROUND".

Just as this new kind of music was rarely ever about wizards and hobbits, so it was not all pseudo-classical, but among its players were a proliferation of classically trained keyboard players, and drummers who had learned their chops playing jazz, but who wanted to play rock, and who had a greater facility with unusual rhythms and timing than many self-taught rock players.

They were keen to progress and forge their own signature styles. Ditto with guitarists who knew their way around a few jazz chords. And with greater power of amplification and a greater range of timbres available to keyboard players with their instrument fed through effects, and the advent of the synthesizer and the string, brass or choral tape loops of the Mellotron, progressive rock groups might not have been playing music of symphonic intricacy but the sounds they were making was also a long way from 'Green Onions', and they now had the means to approximate the heft of a big classical string section that went some way, at least, to evoking the grandeur, the effect, of an orchestra.

Nick Kent offers these views: "What prog rock did was open up the door to a whole class of young musicians, the middle class, basically, whose parents had been well-off enough to force them to have piano lessons, and to read music and to learn classical pieces, [as I did] when I was 11 years old. By the time we were in our late teens, a little bit of Debussy wasn't beyond us, but we couldn't play rock'n'roll piano like Jerry Lee Lewis and Nicky Hopkins, and that's where prog rock began.

"Having worked very briefly with the Sex Pistols, I understand very well the difference between the working-class English or British musician and the middle-class musician. And prog rock was an invention purely of the middle class, because it wanted to be clever.

"I mean, you've got a working-class guy, and you can give him a really basic, primitive, AC/DC-type guitar riff, and he can play that riff over and over again with incredible conviction. Now, a middle-class guitarist, like Johnny Greenwood from Radiohead, he can play those heavy, grinding Neanderthal riffs as well. But after half a minute he's going to get bored, and he's going to throw in some really clever jazz chord, just to break it up.

"The middle-class brain is like, 'I want to make music that challenges me. I don't want to make music like I'm working on a lathe, where I'm just banging out the same thing over and over and over again, like the Pistols and the Ramones."

Tony Banks, who played keyboards and guitar with Genesis has a different take: "[As this] branch of music got more sophisticated it lent itself more to keyboard players. When you sit down with a guitar and play E, A and B, it sounds great and you often don't want to look any further than that. And it's much more difficult to play complicated chord sequences on guitar.

"I love simple music, but I also love more complex music and the way that harmony can change, and I really wanted to do that. It came naturally to me to do this within a rock setting, to use more elaborate harmony and also play around with structure, and playing keyboards lent itself more to that. With keyboards, rather than play a straight C chord you arpeggiate it, and it's quite easy to play fairly fast."

Noting that progressive rock was largely a white, middle-class male enterprise, some commentators have criticised it as being inherently exclusive. Demographically speaking that's an accurate description, but in my view that's not in itself either a good or a bad thing: it's just the way it was.

There were surprisingly few women instrumentalists or vocalists in Seventies progressive rock, but unless there is proper research done into what creative avenues women actually wanted to pursue – maybe not many wished to be in progressive rock groups – and what obstacles women musicians experienced, we shouldn't jump to conclusions. In the Seventies, many institutions were undeniably sexist, including the music business, but from what I have gleaned, and have detailed in subsequent pages, that sort of overt prejudice was not echoed by the musicians, and so the burden of proof should fall on those who maintain that progressive rock musicians were actively exclusive.

It's rather like criticising any form of music that grew out of a particular combination of cultural and demographic factors for not having grown out of a different combination. Similar questions can be asked of any genre. For example, why were there so few women instrumentalists in Seventies Jamaican reggae? Why so few Sino-Caribbeans?

As regards racial inclusion – or implied exclusion, with its shadow criticism of racism – it's easy to forget that in the early Seventies people from all ethnic minorities resident in the UK made up just over two per cent of the population, a number that would have been far lower outside the metropolitan areas.

Progressive rock was essentially played by young white male musicians – mainly middle class and often friends – who coalesced into groups. I have found no evidence to suggest any plan or scheme to exclude anyone from participating in the music that they produced.

This new, eclectic approach to music that had been fermenting away over the past year or so was starting to take off. So what was the first progressive rock album? Or perhaps the question should be how long is a piece of string? Or maybe a philosophical debate on how we can prove that the piece of string exists? Or does any of the above matter?

But to mix a metaphor, the nettle is there to be grasped and so here is a personal choice of some important albums to be considered, all with a claim on the title.

The Moody Blues – *Days Of Future Passed* (Deram)
November 1967

This was certainly an early example of a concept album by a rock group, but it's more a collection of songs with separate orchestrated links – by arranger Peter Knight – than some grand fusion of orchestral and pop music.

Family – *Music In A Doll's House* (Reprise) July 1968

Produced by Traffic's Dave Mason, it carried on a number of the hallmarks of psychedelia, like its use of flanging, but it included a number of esoteric influences and is clearly on the brink of something new.

The Nice – *Ars Longa Vita Brevis* (Immediate) September 1968

The group's second album is a very strong contender with its questing mix of classical, blues and rock elements, mixed together with the remnants of psychedelia.

Procol Harum – *Shine On Brightly* (Regal Zonophone) September 1968

The cryptic, episodic, sidelong 'In Held 'Twas In I' puts in a claim by itself in this mysterious melding of image-rich lyrics, stately bluesy songs and musical ideas explored at length.

Family – *Family Entertainment* (Reprise) March 1969

A particularly eclectic shift in style for the group, including blues, rock, folk, jazz and Eastern influences.

The Moody Blues – *In Search Of The Lost Chord* (Deram) July 1968

A collection poised on the cusp of psychedelia and progressive rock containing some structurally adventurous material, it finds the group integrating Indian instruments, mellotron, oboe and cello into their sound.

Procol Harum – *A Salty Dog* (Regal Zonophone) June 1969

The anthemic orchestrated title track is an evocative, haunting creation, but a lot of the music only partially flexes itself away from the group's blues and rock roots.

Jethro Tull – *Stand Up* (Island) July 1969

After their bluesy 1968 debut *This Was*, Jethro Tull achieved an individual synthesis of blues, folk, rock, jazz and string-swathed ballads on *Stand Up*, which remains one of the group's finest achievements.

Yes – *Yes* (Atlantic) July 1969

An adventurous mix of original material and some dazzling cover versions, all played with brio. It finds a group bursting with ideas, which would soon become more fully realised in spectacular fashion.

Van Der Graaf Generator – *The Aerosol Grey Machine* (Mercury) September 1969

There were many hallmarks here of Peter Hammill's solo work, with some questing ensemble playing in parts, hinting at a group identity that would be more convincingly established on later albums.

The Soft Machine – *Volume Two* (Probe) September 1969

The group's Robert Wyatt would have none of the "progressive" labelling, but their second album had them juggling post-psychedelic pop songs and jazz-tinged instrumental passages with aplomb.

King Crimson – *In The Court Of The Crimson King* (Island) October 1969

On their debut, King Crimson constructed an entirely new world in microcosm with their lyrics and cover design, and a musical menu of pseudo-orchestral ballads, and a previously unheard combination of jazz, rock and free improvisation.

Pink Floyd – *Ummagumma* (Harvest) October 1969

The live half of this double album set showed that psychedelic invention was not dead, but was reaching even further out, into the realm of space rock. The studio album is uneven but contains some of rock music's first dalliances with the avant-garde.

Renaissance – *Renaissance* (Island) Autumn 1969

A surprising departure from Keith Relf, formerly of The Yardbirds, who helped deliver a freshly minted amalgam of classical, rock and folk influences with vocals by his younger sister Jane.

Opening the sealed envelope, the winner is... [*unnecessarily long, dramatic pause*]... King Crimson!

No other album of that time was so new sounding, so musically adventurous, caused such a stir and raised the bar so high in terms of ambition. Feel free to argue amongst yourselves, but in the meantime, over to them.

CHAPTER 3

Hyde Park Incident: King Crimson Part One

"We were just exploring and finding out what could be done that was different from what everybody else was doing. King Crimson was probably the first of progressive rock music. Was it? Well, you tell me. I don't care, actually, if we were the first, second or third. But I think it did make a pretty major statement coming from nowhere." – Michael Giles, interview with the author, 2013

"Today as a young man thinking, 'What is needed in this world? Where is the juice at the moment?' ... Well, back then it was in music. If you wanted to change the world, go into rock music. That's really how we saw it.

"...It entirely worked. It did change the world for a generation. I am apolitical, but to actually be a hairy playing rock music in 1969 was in itself a political statement." – Robert Fripp, interview with the author, 2013

Open your mind, relax awhile and float downstream. Picture yourself in London's Hyde Park on a sunny summer afternoon – Saturday, July 5, 1969, to be precise – sitting on the grass and soaking up the rays as part of a crowd who are there to see The Rolling Stones. It was the group's first concert in a couple of years and an emotional occasion, taking place only two days after the death of former guitarist and founder member Brian Jones, who had been replaced by Mick Taylor. The night before there had been a candlelit vigil for Jones in the park and by show time, between 250,000 and 500,000 fans had gathered in anticipation.

The Stones were rather ragged, with tuning problems, but something epochal had happened earlier on in proceedings. It was a typically eclectic late-Sixties bill, featuring the acoustic, oboe-led urban ragas of the Third Ear Band, the blues of Alexis Korner's New Church, Family, The Battered Ornaments, and Screw, who quickly disappeared into obscurity – but at least they played to a gathering that few other groups could even dream about. But the group that the cognoscenti were particularly looking forward to seeing and who, for many, stole the show, was King Crimson.

They had only been in existence since January, but had already caused a stir on the London gig circuit. Concurrently they had invited journalists and record company representatives over for salons in their rehearsal studio in the basement of the Fulham Palace Café in west London. In March an impressed Simon Stable of *International Times* likened them to a cross between Family, The Moody Blues and The Pretty Things.

King Crimson's first concert had taken place at the Speakeasy in London on April 9 and guitarist Robert Fripp, an assiduous diarist, mentions in his entry of that day: "Massive Success, the word starts to creep about in the business". The Moody Blues had come to see them rehearsing in March, but a mooted tour support slot was abandoned. Fripp had it on very good authority – from one of the group members via manager David Enthoven – that The Moody Blues had considered King Crimson "too strong" for a support. They almost certainly would have been.

At Hyde Park, Mick Jagger opened a box full of butterflies in memory of Brian Jones. King Crimson let loose something else entirely. Rather than delivering some soothing sounds to waft across the long-haired crowd, or some groovy blues-rock to get heads nodding, King Crimson's set roared off into the concentrated aggression of '21st Century Schizoid Man', all acute, jagged lines, with a fiercely swinging, almost bebop instrumental section and a breathtaking, high-velocity unison passage, the like of which no one would have heard before.

The set crackled with energy and intensity. Dramatic Mellotron-led ballads, not so far removed from some of The Moody Blues' songs, were played alongside a cover of Donovan's 'Get Thy Bearings'. The song's hippieish exhortation for us all to *"get stoned"* prompted the flashing of a few peace signs, but Crimson's version was cut with episodes of free improvisation remarkable for a rock group, particularly Ian McDonald's torrential sax solo, which stretched the song to breaking point. No "new band" had played like this before to such a big audience. In terms of exposure and impact, a showcase at such a high-profile event was a godsend.

New Musical Express journalist and Stones fan Nick Kent has these recollections of their set: "They blew The Rolling Stones off the stage. King Crimson came on and they were just fucking amazing. They were seriously good at what they did."

If fate had not dealt such a generous hand to King Crimson, who were still to release a record, they might have been playing that Saturday in some small, smoky, sticky-floored provincial dive in the back of beyond to thirty people and the proverbial dog. But how did it feel playing to, depending on estimates, around half a million people?

Drummer Michael Giles remembers it this way: "When you are onstage you can't hear much as the open air sucks the sound away. You don't get any reflections like you do in indoor venues. It's a lot easier to play to a huge number of people, as it's just a sea of faces and very impersonal: it enables you to just get on and do it. But if you are in a small club and someone is a few feet away looking at you it can be quite intimidating."

Back in the mid-Sixties, Fripp was following in his estate agent father's footsteps taking his A-levels at Bournemouth College and his musical activities were geared towards helping him fund a degree course at the London College Of Estate Management. Principally these engagements found him playing in the house band at the Majestic Hotel in Bournemouth. "My particular responsibility was providing the band with what they called the Twists," he says. "Being a young guitarist, I was supposed to have my finger on the currents of pop."

Sundays were cabaret nights, when the band would back comedians like Bob Monkhouse and Dave Allen, and singers like Julie Rogers and Lita Roza, who was best known for her version of the novelty song, 'How Much Is That Doggie In The Window?' Luckily she disliked the song so much that Fripp was spared from playing it live.

"My heart was not engaged in the music, but it was part of my education as a player," he says. "The life of a professional musician was the best liberal education for a young man I could have conceived – far more useful than economics."

Together with Bournemouth musicians Michael Giles and his bass-playing brother Peter, Fripp formed Giles, Giles & Fripp, a group whose name sounds, rather fittingly, like a company of provincial estate agents. Their debut album, *The Cheerful Insanity Of Giles, Giles & Fripp*, was released on Decca's "progressive" subsidiary, Deram, in autumn 1968.

It includes the surreal image-parades of 'Elephant Song'; some clunky word plays on 'Digging My Lawn'; and a particularly English sensibility that hones in on the potential for wonder in the humdrum midweek on 'Thursday Morning'. Fripp acts as the narrator in the spoken word interludes of the side-long suite, 'The Saga Of Rodney Toady', a rather daft story of a solitary misfit with a penchant for girlie magazines.

On the album sleeve the group grin in exaggerated fashion, as if the "insanity" is of the "You don't have to be mad to work here, but it helps" variety. Promo photos show Fripp sporting a bald wig and dressed like a gardener who you might grudgingly allow to come round to cut back your wisteria. In another shot he is besuited, sporting a set of joke plastic teeth. Michael Giles is pictured in his pyjamas carrying a briefcase. This was a world away from the soon to be very serious King Crimson. What was the inspiration?

"We didn't want to do those posey pop photos," Giles recalls. "It was meant to be incongruous and absurd. But that's the way we were expressing ourselves at that time. It was from Edward Lear, and there was such a strong satirical, subversive look at life coming from Peter Cook and Dudley Moore, and Spike Milligan. All the material's there; you don't have to invent."

With little sales or airplay and, as Fripp says, "Nothing for the musicians to really play", the trio had a major rethink.

Ian McDonald had previously auditioned for a band that included Pete Sinfield on vocals and rudimentary guitar. "He said, 'Your band's crap but would you like to write some songs?'" Sinfield recalls. "I just thought he was extraordinary – he played several instruments and I didn't know anybody who actually played more than one. We got on very well and wrote some things."

Vocalist Judy Dyble had just left Fairport Convention and was going out with McDonald. Together they were working on some songs written by McDonald and Sinfield. In 1968 she put an ad in *Melody Maker* "to see who turned up, because that's what you did then", and got a collective response from Giles, Giles & Fripp. "We got these three very strange people," she says. "Over cups of tea, while they interrogated us, we tried to fathom them out.

"I don't know if it was because it was my name on there and they thought that sounded interesting, but when they spoke to Ian they found out that he had fantastic ideas and was probably more what they needed," she says. "I think the best way I can describe them is that they were English eccentrics but very stylised. It felt like they could have stepped out of the pages of *Country Life*. Robert had a beard and was quite plump. He was extremely focused on what he was doing.

"They were all contradictions of themselves, like masks within masks, although I don't think they would have thought they were like that. I didn't know them long enough to get through all the masks. So I went and bought the album from the record shop in Bounds Green tube station. I took it home and listened to it. Very strange."

The five piece made some demos in Giles, Giles & Fripp's flat in Brondesbury, north London, of material pooled from all of the musicians, including 'I Talk To The Wind', showcasing Dyble's sweet, clear vocals.

"I could see that these were four very gifted musicians," Dyble says. "I didn't see where I could fit in because Giles, Giles & Fripp were cool. There was a sense of being weighed up and found slightly wanting, so I left. I'm glad they developed into what they did. I don't think I could have been part of [King Crimson] as it is such a male band. If I had stayed with them, it would have gone in a different direction altogether."

Fripp, McDonald and the Giles brothers formed King Crimson with Sinfield, who had happily abandoned his own group and came on board as the lyricist and lighting man. He also gave the group its name. Greg Lake, a vocalist and guitarist from Poole, Dorset, who had played in local groups The Shame and The Gods, and who had taken lessons from the same guitar teacher as Fripp, was asked to join as lead singer. Peter Giles soon quit for a career in computer programming, and so Lake changed instruments and became the group's bassist and vocalist.

Given something more challenging to play, Michael Giles soon blossomed into one of the most original British drummers of his generation, with exquisite timing, a jazz-derived ability to keep playing around the "one", swinging the rhythm until it ended up inside-out, and with an at times perverse, cliff-hanging approach to drum fills. Lake possessed a commanding vocal style and was a dextrous and fluid bass player.

Fripp admits the influences of Scotty Moore, Jimi Hendrix and 20th-century composer Béla Bartók, and one could also hear in his early style the sweet chordings of jazz guitarists like Wes Montgomery. But he was already staking out a unique stylistic territory with his angular rhythms and buzzing lead lines with their lengthy sustain, in scales far removed from the blues idioms that dominated much of the lead guitar playing of the era.

Once rehearsals had commenced in the basement of the Fulham Palace Café, Fripp recalls vividly that King Crimson immediately seemed to draw on something outside of themselves: "There are times when music comes alive, you know it's real and you know it has nothing to do with you. In the Crimson of 1969, the muse descended and music leant over and took us into its confidence. And the power of that is so remarkable that if you are touched by it sufficiently, you go hunting for an elevator to the roof, to get beyond the ceilings, get to the roof and fly."

Looking back, Fripp turns the idea of consciously forging out a musical career on its head and into something far more metaphysical: that King Crimson came into being because there was a need for King Crimson music to be played.

"When you move into creative time, everything changes. In sequential time, today leads to tomorrow. In the creative world, today doesn't move to tomorrow; tomorrow reaches back and pulls today towards it," he explains. "So, something like the young players in 1969 didn't come together and form a band in order to make In The Court Of The Crimson

King; In The Court Of The Crimson King reached back and pulled those young players towards it in order that it could be made.

"I remember telepathic situations, precognition. Something remarkable was going on in the effect that the band had on people and the effect it had on us. And clearly this wasn't coming from the young players – something else was going on."

Within months of their inception, and leading up to Hyde Park, King Crimson's shows on the London gig circuit were characterised by a thrilling, of-the-moment risk-taking. Rock groups were adept at jamming – and at increasing length as the Sixties reached its close – but this was, more accurately, improvising.

Greg Lake recalls that you had to be on your mettle to play in the group: "With most bands, once you get going you just play, but with King Crimson you had to listen, because the chemistry of the personalities in the band was so peculiar, anything could happen at any time. You could be singing and the whole band would stop playing and you'd be left alone. Or they would start playing in a different time signature. It could go from lounge music to something ferocious, and it was that sense of it being a nightly adventure that kept it exciting and dynamic."

McDonald recognised the difference between King Crimson and a lot of their contemporaries. "One of the great things about it was there was this very aggressive, unified sound," he says. "And that kind of jazz capability set it apart from a lot of bands of the time, the heavy, ploddy rock stuff."

Live, the group were so original and powerful that it really did seem that there had been a hitherto unfulfilled need for the music of King Crimson to be played. Writing in *International Times*, Mark Williams pleaded: "Please, please see them. Cynicism will be forgotten, appetites whetted. Rock music can discover its identity in King Crimson. So can you."

Alongside the hippie homilies of cover versions like 'Get Thy Bearings', there was an aspect of the group's music that was, crucially, far removed from the benevolent, dreamy themes of English psychedelia that had been prevalent a year or two before. There was something about it that was hard-edged and forbidding. And at times quite frightening.

"Now, King Crimson, is it benign? Yes," says Fripp now. "What is scary about King Crimson is that there is something real about and when we come up against something real, a real intelligence a real presence, it can be overwhelming."

But some contemporary accounts of the group's live shows found little that felt benign, with the correspondents, in the parlance of the day, being somewhat "bummed out" by King Crimson's music. *Melody Maker*'s Alan Lewis wrote: "They created an almost overpowering atmosphere of power and evil."

This was mainly in reference to the set closer, a version of Gustav Holst's 'Mars, The Bringer Of War' from his orchestral suite, *The Planets* (1916). The crowd at Hyde Park heard just a couple of minutes of this, but in concert, it would typically stretch out to ten minutes or more. King Crimson's version of this piece was one of the first and best classical adaptions of the whole progressive rock era.

King Crimson took the main "riff", the ominous backbone of the piece in 5/4, decelerated it slightly and repeated it in the most single-mindedly brutal way, with McDonald's Mellotron playing the upwelling melody line and gradually cutting loose into discordant chaos. One can imagine that any audience members who had decided to illegally expand their minds before or during the show would have been sweating, hanging on, hoping it would end soon.

Not everyone was so taken by this radical new music. The year 1969 was a transitional period in which pop and rock culture was moving from psychedelia and into what was then generally referred to as underground. But to some of the late-Sixties freak scene, the underground was essentially something of the street rather than this new, rarefied art music. At a Speakeasy concert in 1969, members of Tyrannosaurus Rex (presumably Steve Took) and The Deviants crashed the stage in an attempt to stop King Crimson from playing. Deviants drummer Russell Hunter abstained from this demonstration and later apologised to Fripp for the group's behaviour.

Later, Mick Farren, singer with The Deviants, told Richard Williams in *Melody Maker*: "I think we've been going against what's been happening in the so-called underground pop scene. We're not interested in dexterity, in this big technical thing represented by King Crimson. That's so sterile."

IN THE COURT OF THE CRIMSON KING
Original label: Island
Producer: King Crimson
Recorded: June–August 1969
Release date: October 1969
Chart position: 5 (UK), 28 (US)

In amongst all these positive and negative reactions, King Crimson first went into the studio with Moody Blues producer Tony Clarke, but the sessions were abandoned. "It was one of those situations where artists and producers just don't fit," says Giles.

The financing of the group's debut, *In The Court Of The Crimson King*, was unusual for the time. The group didn't have a record deal when they went into Wessex Studios to record the album and so, nothing if not ambitious, they produced it themselves and the recordings were partly financed by manager David Enthoven re-mortgaging his house.

"It wasn't standard practice, exactly, but we'd already heard of people in the mid-Sixties doing a lease tape deal, whereby you are your own production company and the record company leases the tape from you for a certain period of time so you get a higher royalty rate," says Giles. "You control the music, the artwork, as much as you can, so there is much more creative and artistic freedom."

The album opens with the song that had shocked the masses at Hyde Park, '21st Century Schizoid Man'. It is basically progressive rock's firstborn and a testament to the group's ideology: that they went out of their way to avoid doing anything that had been done before. Even now it sounds completely original. And even McDonald found himself disorientated by the group's new creation during the rehearsal process: "There was one particular moment when I took the tape of 'Schizoid Man' home and I thought 'What *is* this?' It was new to me too."

The song begins with a menacing two-bar riff led by McDonald's saxes into a verse underpinned by staccato guitar chords from Fripp. Lake's vocals are distorted and barked out, a warning of mental collapse for the titular post-millennial everyman amidst images of turmoil and violence, like *"death seed"*, *"blood rack"* and *"iron claw"*. "On 'Schizoid Man', there are a few bits in there I'd change, only to make them more violent if I could," Sinfield has since commented.

The most striking aspect of the song was what the group called the "tutti" section, which came after Fripp's guitar solo and McDonald's garish double-tracked sax break played over a rolling 6/8 rhythm. This was originally conceived as a fast, convoluted melody, written out on manuscript paper by Fripp, to run over the top of the rhythm section, but instead the musicians decided to play it in unison, to the silent, but significant, reaction of jaws dropping en masse. The song culminates in a cacophonous ending.

'I Talk To The Wind' is a McDonald tune with a Sinfield lyric, that had initially been demoed with Dyble. Sinfield had worked as a computer programmer before joining the group and his employers even offered to keep his job open for him while he pursued his songwriting, but these lyrics show that his mind was already elsewhere. It's a conversation between *"the straight man"* and *"the late man"*, but rather than being metaphorical characters, they represent Sinfield's "straight" – or "square" – boss, while he is the tardy worker arriving late, whose daydreaming mind is already drifting onto more abstract subjects than the daily grind.

"The lyrics on 'I Talk To The Wind' I'm very fond of, I think it still stands up as a sort of folk tune about a person that doesn't enjoy going to a nine-to-five job very much – it's still valid," Sinfield says.

The song features exquisite flute playing by McDonald, a lovely lyrical solo by Fripp, and Giles's dextrous drumming patterns are a delight. But what had happened to the singing? Lake harmonises with McDonald, but taking the lower line, his pitching lets him down. He sounds lacklustre and a little flat in the verse.

McDonald had wanted real strings for their two big ballad-like numbers, 'Epitaph' and 'In The Court Of The Crimson King', and admits that the Mellotron was a "needs must" move. But as a result of its peculiar construction, the instrument was almost impossible to get completely in tune and produced an astringent, wheezing sound – more reminiscent of wind whistling across a barren landscape than the smooth sweep of a string section – which gave these songs a chilly grandeur. McDonald's arrangements are original and inspired, particularly the wind and flute lines.

King Crimson's collective desire to be as different as possible to other groups was reinforced by the fact that the album was subtitled *An Observation By King Crimson*. Each track has its subtitles, so the full title of '21st Century Schizoid Man' has 'including Mirrors' – presumably the aforementioned "tutti" section – while the track once simply known as 'Epitaph' was now subtitled, 'including March For No Reason and Tomorrow And Tomorrow'.

McDonald's view was that "Some people used to say it was pretentious, but I think we were able to back it up with the musicianship and the power of the live show. There were certain grandiose moments, but I think it was within the bounds of good taste."

Sinfield was credited on the sleeve with "Words and Illuminations". To the many who didn't realise that he worked the onstage light show, this helped to reinforce his burgeoning reputation as something of a seer.

Says Sinfield: "When I did the first album I was very naïve and the words just came out and I had some organisational ability. And I thought I was terribly clever."

Lyrically the songs appeared like the oral tradition of some strange future – or ancient – world and on the title track they chart the goings-on in the mythical court, but 'Epitaph' is like an update on the verses of Wilfred Owen's *Anthem For Doomed Youth* for the post-psychedelic generation, a portal into a not-so-distant future full of foreboding, with the human race in the *"hands of fools"*. It does smack rather of a young person's fetishisation of death and horror, but like all Sinfield's lyrics on the album, this song is one of the first examples of a new style of rock music moving away lyrically from sex, love and drug references, or slice-of-life observations of the day-to-day, and creating newly formed lyrical fantasies. Fantasy has formed an integral part of creative endeavour since time immemorial, so why not claim its place in rock music lyrics? And if Sinfield's lyrics may have prompted hundreds of teens to pen purple prose in their bedrooms, it served as much of a purpose as endlessly rehashing imagery from blues and rock'n'roll.

All this pontificating about some self-constructed mythos was many worlds away from The Deviants' anthem of insurrection, 'Let's Loot The Supermarket'. But to many kids who were averse to shoplifting, this fantastical music ticked all the boxes.

The prospective buyer had to look on the spine to see who the album was by, but the artwork was striking. By this time, Sinfield was officially a fifth member of the group and commissioned the cover, a striking painting by a young artist friend, Barry Godber, of a face, eyeballs looking hard to the right, nostrils flaring, contorted with anguish, like a contemporary version of the distressed character in Edvard Munch's nightmarish painting, *The Scream*.

What is rarely ever mentioned about *In The Court Of The Crimson King* is that a quarter of its running time is given over to free improvisation. The group were already known for their live improvisations and these were often full-throttle affairs, but at times the volume went down to almost nothing.

The case in point, 'Moonchild', is a lovely if eerie, two-verse and chorus song, which then drifts for ten minutes into a subdued, impressionistic landscape sketched out by Fripp's guitar, McDonald's vibraphone and Giles's drum kit dampened with dusters. The group had other original music that could have been included: 'Travel Weary Capricorn', the meditative guitar-led piece 'Mantra', and 'Drop In', which dated back to Giles, Giles & Fripp and 'Drop In'. The latter was a freewheeling highlight of their live set. It would have been more in keeping with the album's overall mood, but Giles thinks it might have sounded too derivative. Perhaps more so than the rest of the group he was interested in European free improvisation, particularly John Stevens' Spontaneous Music Ensemble.

The term free jazz came into common parlance in 1961 with Ornette Coleman's album *Free Jazz: A Collective Improvisation*, a forty-minute improvisation by two quartets. It was an extension of modal jazz, where players refer to modes, or scales, rather than the chord structure of the melodic "head" that had underpinned solos in earlier forms like bebop.

This cutting loose into freedom had occurred on parts of Miles Davis's *Kind Of Blue*, just a couple of years prior, but the players on *Free Jazz* went further out into a mix of the visceral and the cerebral, which included dissonance, and so much rhythmic and melodic detail it was difficult for the mind to follow. Subsequent free jazz albums include John Coltrane's album *Ascension* and Archie Shepp's *Fire Music*, both recorded in 1965, and albums by Cecil Taylor, Albert Ayler and Sun Ra.

Its European cousin – free improvisation – was significantly different. It was made by jazz players, but had little to do with jazz as such. *Karyobin*, the 1968 album by the Spontaneous Music Ensemble, is a case in point. As evidence of the index of possibilities at the time it was released on Island Records, an independent label originally home to Jamaican artistes and soon to become the home of many progressive rock groups. Although it contained some dramatic flare-ups, it also carried influences from European avant-garde classical music, like the pithy, spartan musical language that Anton Webern employed in his later works, and sometimes its conversation of fragmentary lines nodded towards the abstract landscapes of improvisers AMM.

Giles explains why the group chose this radical approach: "['Moonchild'] was an opportunity. We had recorded the material that we wanted to be on the album, so we thought, why not record something that is not improvisation in a jazz way, but is free of structure? You are just dealing with time and space. Music, of all the art forms, is just abstract; you can't pick it up or hold it, or put it on the wall. We started off with the little ditty and then we just took off into outer space, into nothingness, to see what happened. If it had been rubbish we wouldn't have left it on there. I keep looking at the other side of things. What about if we *hadn't* done it? What about if it *wasn't* there?"

Giles observes that there was a clear empathy, even telepathy, between the three players on the instrumental section.

"There are some bits on there which I think are just outstanding. Ian would do a trill on the vibraphone at exactly the same time that I would do a trill on the cymbal. It's a gift, it's been given to you and only because you put yourself in that area: you surrendered; you allowed these things to happen. And also it's all very low key, it's all quiet and drifting, and there was such a lot of listening – you open up your awareness."

'Moonchild' rarely got more than a passing mention in contemporary reviews and is still barely mentioned in more recent commentaries. One gets the feeling that it was a track that some listeners would skip – in the way that Beatles fans might have passed on 'Revolution 9' – but in its own contemplative way, 'Moonchild' was both beautifully played and the most adventurous track by a British rock group to date.

In November 1969 readers of *Disc* would have probably only semi-comprehended the section in which Fripp, referring to the praise, criticism and the stress caused by King Crimson's meteoric rise, said: "If there's one thing we have not learned to do properly yet, that's how to balance our life correctly and work hard yet remain healthy... Three of us have been ill in the past month." Just another quote in a music paper, perhaps, and nothing spectacular, but it portended the end of phase one of the group.

King Crimson embarked on their first American tour in November. Notices had been mixed, with some critics rather sniffy about this new phenomenon, but recordings of their US tour showed that they put in some spectacular performances, the set bolstered by a new song, a companion piece to '21ˢᵗ Century Schizoid Man', rather grandiloquently titled 'A Man, A City'.

But the group were soon rocked by news that both McDonald, the main composer and multi-instrumentalist, and drummer extraordinare Giles, had decided to quit. Fripp has said that he had offered to leave the group instead if that would help, but their problems were a mix of musical and personal. McDonald described King Crimson's music to interviewers as both "paranoiac" and "evil", which, on the surface, sounds like a musician taken in by their own press. A spokesman for the group told *Melody Maker*, in the parlance of the day, that McDonald and Giles had found the American tour "a total experience of plasticity".

With twenty years' hindsight McDonald had this to say: "I do regret leaving. It was an impulsive decision based on a number of things that perhaps I should have given more thought to at the time. It affected a lot of people's lives and I felt sorry about that decision. Would I do it all over again? No, I would stay with the band.

"I was young and I hadn't had much experience in the world. My youth was spent in army bands. Everything was fresh and it was difficult to deal with. At the time it was frightening for me. I was just a kid."

Fans always want more and more, and even as years pass they still think, "What if?" Many musicians are unable to get off the treadmill of adulation, expectations and record company and management demands. But the young Giles soon alighted. Put simply, he found the demands of being in a group incompatible with the way he wanted to live his life.

"It wasn't something that needed much thinking about: I didn't like touring in a rock'n'roll circus," he says. "I'm not a traveller. I find it all turgid and tawdry and tiresome and tedious, and spending twelve, fourteen, sixteen hours a day getting to a place where you break loose like lions in the circus for a couple of hours. I wanted to be close to my children and lead a balanced life. I knew that if I was to continue I was to need drugs and I didn't want to get into drugs, or stress-alleviating substances. But it was a terrible wrench because I'd spent the previous ten years of my life working up to doing something and it had been as much my baby as anyone else's."

On the subject of the band supposedly being evil, Giles says: "Well, certainly there were times when I felt what they call evil and I didn't really want to be a part of it, but I didn't want to be part of the peace and love thing either."

Fripp, Sinfield and Lake were left from the group that returned to the UK, but when King Crimson played at Fillmore West, San Francisco, on December 16, 1969, The Nice were also on the bill and their keyboard player Keith Emerson talked to Lake about joining him in a new group. But it wouldn't happen just yet.

The group's second album *In The Wake Of Poseidon* arrived after a complex round of musical chairs. With McDonald gone, Fripp was determined to continue the group, so assumed the role of principal composer and musical director, while Giles stuck around to help out. McDonald's place on reeds and woodwind was taken by an equally gifted young player, Mel Collins, who had been playing in a group called Cirkus.

Lake has said that if McDonald and Giles had stayed, he would have continued in the group, but Fripp encouraged him to join Emerson as the vocalist and bass player in Emerson, Lake & Palmer. The minutiae of the situation are somewhat unclear, but Elton John was mooted as a replacement singer for the album, for a £250 session fee. Fripp, however, wasn't keen on his records, and declined. Lake continued as vocalist only and didn't quite finish the sessions so Gordon Haskell, an old school friend of Fripp's, sang vocals on one song, 'Cadence And Cascade'.

Peter Giles was drafted in on bass guitar as a temporary measure, but the surprise addition to the line-up was exploratory jazz pianist Keith

Tippett. As we will see later on, Tippett was a catalyst in breaking down boundaries between jazz and rock in the UK, and creating new stylistic hybrids in his own music, but for a short while he did this to great effect in King Crimson.

Sinfield put a positive spin on the group's instability, telling David Hughes of *Disc*: "King Crimson is a pyramid or cone with Bob Fripp and me sitting at the top. Underneath are various musicians and friends upon whom we can call, who form a very solid foundation." Fripp said that, "It's a way of getting people together to play music and a way of thinking about things."

Even with all this to-ing and fro-ing, the transition to the new album was surprisingly seamless. The first side of *In The Wake Of Poseidon* in particular was very similar in structure to its predecessor. 'A Man, A City', now retitled 'Pictures Of A City' and a live favourite on Crimson's US tour, had much in common with '21st Century Schizoid Man' in its similarly shaped verses and instrumental passages, including a complicated unison section, and a mass freak-out ending. It had its own identity, though, with Collins' baritone sax theme on the verse giving it a sleazy strip-show vibe and a slow, bluesy middle section that evokes empty streets in a dangerous neighbourhood. Although Giles had effectively left the band, his drumming here with its exploratory whole-kit scurryings across the beat, transcended his playing on their debut.

'Cadence And Cascade' is similar in mood to 'I Talk To The Wind', with lyrical flute and piano, while the title track is a widescreen mini-epic structurally similar to 'Epitaph'.

Much of side two is taken up with a multi-part reworking of *Mars* as 'The Devil's Triangle', with Mellotrons blasting out hideous fanfares as the piece gradually disintegrates. The album also yielded a single, 'Cat Food'. This song made a break with the mood of serious import, with a Beatlesy melody, urgently sung by Lake, over a loose, funky ensemble arrangement. He sings some delicious Sinfield lyrics on the not-so-delicious topic of the barely edible, additive-rich products available in your local supermarket.

King Crimson's peculiar music got some critics particularly excited. Writing in *Melody Maker*, Richard Williams enthused that "It has a scale and grandeur unparalleled in rock and its inner complexities rival those of the great classical composers. You get the feeling if Wagner were alive today he'd be working with Crimson".

When I reminded Williams of that quote during an interview for this book, he grimaced and mimed banging his head on the café table. Was it a case of him getting carried away at the time and in the moment?

"Yeah, absolutely," he replied. "That ridiculous phrase was an example of a desire to draw attention to something that I thought was worthwhile, in an over-dramatic way. So, it's not a phrase I would want on my tombstone. But nevertheless, perhaps it was true, who knows?" he added, laughing.

The rogue sonic element on 'Cat Food' – and elsewhere on the album – is Tippett. He plays an exciting, virtuosic piano style that breaks out quickly from lyricism into dissonance and back again, and his splintered lines run playfully roughshod all over the song. In circumstances that he could never have envisaged, it was released as a single and he was required to mime to these lines on BBC TV's chart show *Top Of The Pops*.

"We were there all day," Tippett recalls of the session. "I only lived around the corner then, in Earl's Court, and the record company sent a bloody Rolls-Royce to pick us up. I'd rather have had the money. We get there and you do your thing and then you wait. We were miming, which I thought was against the law even then.

"I was given this little upright piano. Well, I improvised all that, so I couldn't do that again. I remember annoying one of the senior television people because I'd do a little break [on the record] and I'd just put one finger down. I don't know if they showed that bit or if it was just in rehearsal, but he got annoyed because I wasn't playing the game. When I think about it now, I should have got more money."

Sartorially speaking, the group looked rather a hotch-potch. Fripp had gone the whole hog with a billowing scarf and satin flares and Lake looked like a more sharply dressed hippie. But while Tippett looked cool, albeit fairly anonymous, the Giles brothers were something else. Michael sported a leonine barnet, with a casual jacket and tie, while Peter looked like he had just got in from the office.

"I tried all the hippie stuff just for a couple of months – the kaftan and the flares – and it didn't feel right to me," says Giles. "So I reverted to my Englishness and thought that I would just be straightforward English and to hell with what everybody else is doing."

Tippett had liked *In The Court Of The Crimson King* and enjoyed the sessions for its successor, but when Fripp asked him to join the group full time he declined.

"I considered it, but I told him I couldn't do it as the only reason I'd be playing with the band was for money and I respected the band and

Robert, certainly, too much for that. They were working quite a lot in those days, so if I'd have joined I would have been going around the world and the only live music I would have heard would have been support bands probably and at this time, in '70–'71, in London there was a lot happening."

The two absconders, McDonald and Giles, proved Michael Giles's idea that you could make happy, positive music without it being trite, with a self-titled debut album released in 1971. 'Suite In C', in particular, is a brilliantly realised long-form composition, with rich melodies – even though the vocals are rather diffidently mixed back – with guest musician Steve Winwood from Traffic on organ laying down some astringent lines to McDonald's agitated flute, and Giles and brother Peter on bass playing with astonishing sibling empathy in between the more melodic sections. 'Birdman', with lyrics by Sinfield, had been mooted as a King Crimson piece and occupies all of side two, and is another joyous mix of particularly English post-psychedelic pop tunes, and inspired playing with orchestration at the climax.

Now something of a cult LP, *McDonald And Giles* is such a strong, original collection that the question, "What if?" raises its head again.

"It took a lot of studio time and money, and Ian and I still didn't have any desire to be touring," says Giles. "I wanted to stay close to home and do session work, and he wanted to go to New York, so there wasn't much chance of us putting a live band together anyway."

Back to King Crimson, Fripp has since claimed that he knew the years following *In The Court Of The Crimson King* would be full of mistakes, with the group – himself in particular – finding its way. As noted, *In The Wake Of Poseidon* was something of a retread of their debut album – even though many journalists thought it was better – but its successor *Lizard* is a bizarre, flawed, but at times brilliant departure. It remains King Crimson's strangest offering.

Housed in a spectacular sleeve, like a contemporary take on an illuminated manuscript, there's a strange anti-chemistry at work with the group's grand compositional constructions headed by Sinfield's most opulent, rococo lyrics, jammed up against a skronky jazz sensibility from Tippett and horn players from his group – Nick Evans on trombone and Mark Charig on cornet. Classical oboist Robin Miller features, and Mel Collins was retained on saxes and flute, while Gordon Haskell who had sung on 'Cadence And Cascade' was now full-time on vocals and bass, except on 'Prince Rupert Awakes', where Jon Anderson from Yes was drafted in as the song was in too high a key for Haskell to sing comfortably – which begs the question why it wasn't transposed down a key or two. The new drummer was Andy McCulloch, an accomplished player who went on to play in Greenslade, whose approach here is almost incessantly over-decorative.

Fripp was now the sole composer of the music and 'Cirkus' is one of his slightly "scary" compositions, with ugly Mellotron fanfares oscillating around minor thirds, and McCulloch producing towering snare rolls and flamboyant breaks for all he is worth. The song is nightmarish, with the narrator having the paybox clerk write on his tongue on entering the big top and once inside, the cirkus is described in all its teeming grotesquerie, a *"pandemonium seesaw"*, including elephants eating the floors of their cages and gloves racing around the ring, as some kind of metaphor... but for what, exactly?

Rewinding back to a roughly contemporary vox pop, a bright young kid at the author's school in Norwich, who had copied out the lyrics to 'Epitaph' as his own in an English exam, sagely nodded and answered the question with: "It's about society". In his estimation, David Bowie's 'Life On Mars' was also "about society". In fact, since Bob Dylan began penning songs like 'It's Alright Ma, I'm Only Bleeding', any song with a welter of strange, disjunctive images could conceivably be "about society", including 'Cirkus'.

Although Sinfield has since described himself in this phase as a "flash little harlequin git", some of his lyrics on *Lizard* are inspired, albeit by mixing a narrative of sorts with flights of barely comprehensible linguistic fantasy, as on 'Indoor Games' with its decadent cast of characters amusing themselves in the strangest of fashions.

Musically, the multi-part title track is all over the place. The section 'Bolero: The Peacock's Tale' sounds like a slightly tentative take on Gil Evans's arrangements for Miles Davis's 1960 album, *Sketches Of Spain*, with Tippett and the brass players stretching its Iberian moods to breaking point. Even after scores of listenings, *Lizard* remains one long conundrum. Richard Williams again felt that it showed that "rock could be built on a scale that could rival classical music".

The *Lizard* line-up never played live and again it was all change. Gordon Haskell was on the move and bass guitarist Rick Kemp, who had played with Michael Chapman, passed the audition, but left almost immediately to go onto a lengthy career with Steeleye Span. One of the singers who had auditioned impressively, but was ultimately deemed unsuitable, was Bryan Ferry, although Fripp recommended him to EG Management, who less than two years later were handling his group, Roxy Music. The incumbent rhythm section was drummer Ian Wallace and guitarist turned bass guitarist Boz Burrell. Tippett had stayed on as a session player with Charig.

This new line-up recorded the group's fourth album, *Islands*, in October 1971. Although generally more direct than *Lizard*, it has its expansive moments, such as 'Formentera Lady' on which flute and piano lines cascade around each other, the Balearic island recast as a sunbaked place of myth and mystery.

The album's directness came as a relief after the convoluted architecture of *Lizard* and the dramatic end theme of 'Formentera Lady' is handed over baton-like as the main guitar theme of 'A Sailor's Tale'. Here Collins and Fripp cut loose in turn over the main riff before a sparse, loping mid-section where the trebly "klang" of Fripp's guitar builds into a thrilling solo excursion of fast jagged chords, which culminates in what would become his trademark, a sudden upward swoop of high-velocity strumming.

Where the new group come into their own is on the cartoonishly sleazy 'Ladies Of The Road', which title-wise is a rather archaic and romanticised description of groupies. Lyrically it feels as if Sinfield had come down from his lofty perch in a state of advanced priapism, fondly remembering one hippie chick from 'Frisco who ate the ample portion of *"meat"* that he gave her. Collins' greasy, leering tenor break is a potent mating call in keeping with the song's lubricious sentiments. Even Wallace's whomping bass drum and insolently open-and-shut hi-hat work sounds in context quite luridly sexual.

'Prelude: Song Of The Gulls' is a surprise, a succinct, stately string piece in a regular tread with Miller's oboe carrying the top line. 'Islands' ends the album with Fripp on harmonium and Charig breaking free on cornet. Sinfield's final lyrics on the album find him musing on the interconnectedness of things, with all islands metaphorically joining hands beneath the sea.

Islands was, then, another oddity, encompassing sleazy R&B, pastoralia and pseudo-baroque. A subsequent US tour featuring harder-edged performances gained favourable notices and was captured on the rather ropey sounding *Earthbound*, including an interminable drum solo on 'Groon' with Wallace's kit fed through a VCS3 synthesizer operated by Sinfield – which must have sounded amazingly new in 1971, but now comes over as something very much of its time.

So what next from this powerful, confident new ensemble? They began to break up. Firstly, the cone structure that Sinfield had recently described crumbled and the lyricist, sound and lights man went his way, with Fripp claiming that he had lost faith in what his lyrics stood for.

King Crimson played again in the US and the disappointed group stayed on for a while as Fripp ultimately pulled the plug in April. Claiming that the group's differences were "philosophical" he travelled back to Dorset, rumour had it, with a "witch". Had he shot himself in the smartly booted foot once more? The music papers were certainly wondering if he could get a new group together. The whole thing looked a bit of a mess from the outside, but Fripp had some big ideas that were soon to be realised.

CHAPTER 4

The Drive to 1974: King Crimson Part Two

"Crimson was remarkable. For, I think, nearly everyone in the band, it was the only place where they could really become who they were. The demands to be true are very high demands. You might have to do things you don't like all the time."
– Robert Fripp, interview with the author, *MOJO* 231 February 2013

As another incarnation of King Crimson went the way of all things, the group that had caused such a stir in their inaugural year of 1969 had gone through four major line-up changes – not just the odd musician coming and going – in three years. And while many assumed that King Crimson had now puttered to a halt, in May 1972 the guitarist told Caroline Boucher of *Disc* that "Crimso is a very long way from being shelved. When it goes out again it's a magic band". Their identity had been in flux, but Fripp, now effectively the group leader, was en route to finding his true voice.

And maybe fulfil another role. In his metaphysical assessments, King Crimson comes together when there is a need for King Crimson music to be played. And if King Crimson really did have its own existence outside the players, whatever "it" was, it was now making high demands.

In the UK, developments in rock music were carrying on apace and all the doors were still open. In the progressive field, Yes had just finished recording *Close To The Edge*, an amalgam of melody and inspired playing in lengthy compositions brimful of invention. It was released in September and would cast a very long shadow.

The drummer of Yes, the young, prodigiously talented Bill Bruford was made an offer he couldn't refuse by Robert Fripp and shocked many by jumping ship to join King Crimson in the summer, just after the album was in the can.

Given the lifespan of the group's previous incarnations, The Raver – *Melody Maker*'s anonymous gossip column – opined: "All that work down the drain and for what? Gigs with King Crimson don't last, at least on present form. Good luck to all parties – it's a bit like Rolls quitting Royce."

Bruford was clearly looking for something new, something that he had not experienced before. He was already a fan of King Crimson, having walked miles home in the small hours back in April 1969 after seeing them support Tyrannosaurus Rex at the Lyceum, buzzing from what he had just witnessed.

Fripp had built a completely new group, which also included bass guitarist and vocalist John Wetton, who had been close to joining on a couple of occasions previously and who had recently been playing in Family; the relatively unknown violinist, violist and keyboard player David Cross; and percussionist Jamie Muir.

Muir was the odd one out, as he would have been in virtually any ensemble operating in any field of music, so for Fripp to employ him in what was ostensibly a rock group was a statement of intent to rattle a few cages. This is what Muir did almost literally, as he prowled around an enormous percussion set-up that was more like an art installation, which included a compact drum kit, bowed saw, metal containers filled with nut shells, toys, gongs, glass tubing, metal sheets, and a bike frame.

He reinforced the group's relationship with improvisation in a major way and carried on the slightly tenuous link between King Crimson and the Spontaneous Music Ensemble beloved of Michael Giles. Muir had played at SME drummer John Stevens' Little Theatre Club off St Martins Lane in the Music Improvisation Company with two other luminaries of the admittedly small-scale London improv scene, guitarist Derek Bailey and saxophonist Evan Parker.

Muir had initially been inspired by the music of American drummer Milford Graves and saxophonists Pharoah Sanders and Albert Ayler, but in the true spirit of improvisation he charted an idiosyncratic path which began to veer towards rock and included spells in the improvisational group Boris and a brief period playing in Assagai, a South African group based in the UK, which include saxophonist Dudu Pukwana, trumpeter Mongezi Feza and English keyboard player Alan Gowen. Muir then played with Gowen and guitarist Allan Holdsworth in Sunship before he got the phone call from Fripp, partly on the recommendation of *Melody Maker*'s assistant editor Richard Williams.

Looking back in the early Nineties, Muir noted that Fripp was unquestionably the band leader and that he led the band well, adding: "I think I was a wee bit too much for him, simply because I was so involved in improvisation. He was very much concerned with logic and function."

In the autumn of 1972, King Crimson toured the UK playing largely improvised sets. This was an unusual tactic for a rock group and gained them positive notices from the likes of Williams and *NME*'s Ian MacDonald. They both sensed that something important was happening and the group was earning comparisons to Tony Williams' Lifetime and John McLaughlin's Mahavishnu Orchestra. Muir was clearly enjoying himself, clad in a boiler suit with fur wings or with an animal skin around his torso like a circus strong man, and with a penchant for biting on a blood capsule during a particularly intense percussive barrage.

The tour opened at Hull Technical College on November 10. On the first night the dangers of having Muir in the group were shown to be more than just his musical disruption. Looking back on the inaugural performance of the new line-up, Fripp noted: "At one point I heard a whistling sound and leaned forward attentively as a heavy chain flew through the space that my head had just occupied. It had been spun around by Jamie and then released with vigour."

Muir reckoned that "Bill Bruford and I got on very well together musically it seemed to me. He was a solid, tight, thinking studio type and I was very much into doing imaginative odd things." But the hotshot former Yes drummer was finding things unexpectedly difficult. Although Muir wasn't averse, in the parlance of the time, to "looning around" onstage, the combination of his fierce originality, his formidable technical skill and his exacting standards made him an intimidating musician to work with.

"He influenced me as a person completely," Bruford says with hindsight. "He was older than I was and a much more experienced musician. I was a jumped-up little best kid in my small town, and he told me that was a load of rubbish in no uncertain terms and I began seeing the music from beyond the drum set.

"That's a problem for young musicians: you end up just listening to your own instrument and not only are you not listening to what anyone else is playing, you are not serving the music to the best of your abilities.

"These were grown-up ideas and I'd never heard them before. He was very powerful and he reduced me to tears on several occasions, tore me to shreds saying everything that I stood for was a joke. I calmed down a lot after that."

The only album this line-up recorded was *Larks' Tongues In Aspic,* which was released in March 1973. Part one of the title track opens with a lovely double-tracked solo played by Muir on the mbira or African thumb piano, which fades out into a drizzle of metallic percussion. Then David Cross enters playing staccato violin lines over John Wetton's ominous bass lines and Fripp's malevolently buzzing guitar. As it increases in intensity Bruford and Muir play a colossal drum roll and the group hit a brutal five-chord riff, a manifestation of the "monstrous power" that Muir claims they had been collectively seeking.

The episodic composition goes into a percussion-led groove with Fripp playing an astonishingly convoluted picking figure. A section of completely free improvisation follows, involving Wetton's wah-wah bass, Fripp's agitated chord work and Muir at full throttle in a high-velocity rampage across toms, metal sheets and bells, some of the clattering coming from a baking tray that was receiving the full force of his bass drum pedal. Respite comes with Cross's reflective intermezzo on violin, accompanied by exceptionally delicate percussion and the group finish with a variation on the staccato lines from the opening section, substituting the brutal riff with a warm, melodic finale.

Although 'Larks' Tongues In Aspic Part One' could be criticised as being structurally a little incoherent, it's teeming with fecund musical ideas and inspired playing.

It may be pure coincidence, but in his violin solo, Cross plays what sounds like a nod towards one of the more delicate moments of Béla Bartók's *String Quartet No.5*. Fripp is guarded about his influences, but has cited Bartók as one and he was beginning to develop a style in which it feels like some of the angularities of Bartók's chamber pieces were taken into a rock context and played in motifs of hard-edged metric regularity.

This was apparent in a new compositional style in which Fripp's musical fastidiousness generates power through repetition in a way quite different from any of his guitarist peers. 'Larks' Tongues In Aspic Part Two' begins with stark, gimlet-eyed riffing, initially based on two chords, reminiscent of the unison cello stabs a few minutes into Stravinsky's *The Rite Of Spring*. A second, equally obsessive theme is then introduced that slips up a notch each time it is repeated, building up a huge tension through its inexorable logic.

Muir has opined that his playing should have been "a lot wilder sheets of tin rattling and ripping, piles of crockery breaking, those sorts of sounds. One or two things that Robert would have found just too much." That said it did feature him making the ripping sound of rapidly unreeling a roll of Sellotape and manipulating a laughing box on 'Easy Money'.

On 'Larks' Tongues In Aspic Part Two' Muir's contribution is the polar opposite to the steely formality of the group's ensemble playing, with Bruford's crisp, elegant snare drum work a foil to his free role. In the final section, Muir makes such an intense racket it sounds like he is laying siege to the composition, trying to derail it through sheer force.

There was an aspect of familiarity to the album, in the graceful Mellotron ballad 'Exiles'. It begins with a tape-manipulated atmospheric backdrop, which finds Muir playing glass tubing and zither to the chords of 'Mantra', which had featured in Crimson's live sets back in 1969.

Three tracks on the album have lyrics courtesy of Wetton's friend Richard Palmer-James, who was an early member of Supertramp. His lyrics are a world away from Sinfield's with 'Exiles' a neatly phrased tale of the narrator's lonely escape to a far-flung seaside town to preserve his sanity, which is in keeping with the bittersweet musical mood.

Who knows what King Crimson might have achieved had Muir stayed, but dissatisfaction began around his extensive percussion set-up being insufficiently well miked onstage to compete with a rock group, and there were run-ins about this with the road crew. His discontent and dislike of touring, plus a strengthening desire to follow his Buddhist calling, resulted in a meeting with EG Management. He offered to work his notice, but they declined and, bizarrely, put out a claim of injury. Muir cleared out his house and, with a few pangs of guilt for blowing out the tour, disappeared in February, retreating to a Tibetan monastery in Scotland. But he had left his mark.

Photographs of the four-piece King Crimson taken after Muir's departure in 1973 show a group that looked little sharper than the t-shirt and jeans anti-image favoured by some of their peers. Fripp was dressed in black with white boots, and positively chandeliered with crosses, ankhs and amulets. His image had always been that of a serious, bookish type, but with all this talk of wicca and witches going around, Ian MacDonald's *NME* piece of September 1973 cast him in another light – as a "sex crazed" bedroom athlete, while Fripp expounded on his enthusiasm for "helpless rutting".

The group continued as a four piece, with Bruford playing a standard kit – quite small for the time – augmented by a rack of tuned percussion, gongs and a metal sheet. King Crimson's live performances became increasingly concentrated and powerful, and they kept both probing at the boundaries of the compositions and also playing completely improvised music.

The group's next album, *Starless And Bible Black* was mostly recorded live, half of it from a concert at the Concertgebouw in Amsterdam on November 23, 1973, although that was not made apparent on the record sleeve. That night the chemistry was particularly potent.

On 1972's *Earthbound*, 'Orlando' and 'Peoria' are basically jams on a couple of chords. But from the Concertgebouw concert, the piece that was edited down and later titled 'Starless And Bible Black' showed the difference between a jam and an improvisation: it gradually built up from an abstract beginning of electric piano chords and Bruford's percussion into a powerful, fluid, full band section with melodic flourishes and skilfully navigated time changes. It sounds coherently structured but was completely improvised.

"It was ridiculous how telepathic we could be and it worked," says Wetton. "It was an adventure every time onstage; it was something to look forward to and you knew it would be rewarding."

'The Mincer' was recorded live in Zurich on November 15, 1973, and then edited down. It announces itself on slow, lopsided drum footfalls, its sense of unease heightened by queasy Mellotron and Fripp's agitated, wasp-like guitar. Wetton's subsequently overdubbed vocal melody makes it seem like a particularly strange composition. This way of constructing a song was virtually unheard of at the time.

The most beguiling improvisation on the album, and also from the Amsterdam concert is 'Trio'. Wetton describes the occasion: "'Trio' sounds like it was written from start to finish, but it was completely improvised. People think it sounds like a guitar piece, but there's no guitar on it. It's bass played an octave up. It's a bit like [Procol Harum's] 'A Whiter Shade Of Pale', a descending Bach-like sequence. For some reason we just hit on the right combination – bass, Mellotron flute and violin. The chemistry of the band was very good at times."

Bruford sat listening with his sticks across his chest and was credited with "admirable restraint". Fripp has added, with regard to 'Trio': "The finest quality of improvisation is spontaneous composition where it lands fully formed."

By 1973–74, in a live context Fripp was coming into his own. On a version of the old warhorse, '21st Century Schizoid Man' recorded at the Palace Threatre, Providence, Rhode Island, on June 6, 1974, Fripp's playing is a heady mix of the visceral and the technical.

His solo starts off on the edge of feedback, with long bent notes, wide intervallic leaps and sudden plunges, and lavish high-velocity pull-offs. He re-emerges with a frantically strummed chord-swoop up the fretboard. As he gradually climbs higher, Bruford suddenly launches off, playing in four across the 6/8 rhythm, adding to the mounting tension. After holding this chord for a number of bars, Fripp, as any gifted lover would do, increases the tension still further and shifts up to the very top of the fretboard. With nowhere else to go, the ensemble hit suddenly the cue for the riff leading into main theme, leaving the receptive listener somewhat short of breath.

King Crimson were beginning to draw bigger audiences, especially in the US, appealing to progressive and experimental music fans and those who craved heavy rock kicks. On the improvisation 'Asbury Park' recorded at that town's Casino Arena on June 28, 1974, the rhythm section lock into a highly effective, taut sub-funk groove. Wetton's colossal bass sounds like something that you would complain about if it were digging up the pavement outside your bedroom window at 8 a.m., while Fripp utilises a sulphurous fuzz guitar sound, with long sustained notes and quicksilver flurries.

"You can hear me shout 'F!' at the start," says Fripp. But does he ever remember playing these improvisations? "I remember shouting 'F!'" he laughs. "All you can really say at the time as the player is if you enjoyed it or not. You might have had a sense that there was something going on here, but if you listen to the tape, what was going on might have been in the atmosphere rather than the notes. The audience, the musicians and the music can come together in a way that is very special, so key performances were not necessarily the best played, but there was something in the atmosphere that made them stunning."

Bruford has commented that King Crimson's English or European-ness was maybe one of the reasons that they were embraced by American audiences.

"We always, to the Americans, sounded so British because the improvisations didn't involve much of their heralded pentatonic blues scale. We didn't use that in King Crimson. It was more European classical scales, like altered scales, some jazz scales, and whole tone scales and half step/whole step scales.

"I don't mean Eric [Clapton] playing blues licks, wailing away on top and I don't mean The Allman Brothers chugging away on one chord either, so it had more to do with new music in Europe, the avant-garde. And gradually we found out more about timbre and the quality of sound – how you could improvise with timbre was as interesting as anything else. Now rock music is so mass marketed that King Crimson are marginalised, but in those days, King Crimson were pretty much mainstream. They were open times."

Wetton offers a slightly different perspective on what fuelled the rhythm section: "We were totally tuned in. We were listening to the same stuff, Herbie Hancock, we were just so immersed in music at that time. Although it might have been in 13/8 we had this good grounding in Motown and jazz and blues. That's what made it click. If you had a standard stodgy English rhythm section it wouldn't have worked at all· we were more into playing around with the beat."

Listening now to live performances showcasing four young men pushing at musical boundaries with great force, it's easy to get somewhat romantic about it all, but King Crimson were clearly on the edge of something very significant in the development of rock music. But not all was rosy in the Crimson camp.

Fripp's diary of the USA tour in 1974 reveals a wearying schedule, with much intra-band bickering, and his sage advice that it was always best to pack for the next day no matter how late the hour, as you will always feel worse tomorrow.

Wetton's bass was going through a cheap pedal he had bought in a Soho music store, the JEN Double Sound, a fuzz-wah set-up that created an enormous, gnashing bass sound and in tandem with Bruford was creating a rhythm section of considerable volume, and both Fripp and Cross, playing on the sides of the stage found difficulties hearing themselves through their monitors with this monster in their midst.

On July 1, 1974, this incarnation of King Crimson played what would be their last concert in Central Park, New York City.

"It might have been a bit ropey tuning-wise and there was a buzz going through the PA most of the time, but for energy it was unbelievable," recalls Wetton. "I bump into people in the street who were at that concert and they go, 'Excuse me, I was there, it was fucking incredible. Bye!'"

Says Fripp: "As the sunlight was going down and the lights on the stage were coming up and we were going into the slow wind-up, the coda of 'Starless', the electricity went up the back of my spine and it was the power I recognised from 1969, and that was the last show we did."

When the group got back to the UK, Cross was eventually told that he was no longer in the group. This was in itself a contentious issue among the remaining trio and as usual in band situations was not dealt with very well. But the talented, empathetic violinist, whose lines had worked so well with Fripp's guitar had already planned to leave.

King Crimson recorded *Red* at Olympic studios shortly after coming off the US tour. The sound is dark, dense and exceptionally heavy. Fripp's composition 'Red' was in the mould of the singleminded insistence of 'Larks' Tongues In Aspic Part Two'. After its melodic opening theme, then a work-in-progress called 'Blue', one could imagine the licks of Fripp's beloved Scotty Moore made terse and carbon-hard in this brutal re-imagining of rock.

Bruford has been criticised in Fripp's diaries in that he apparently didn't "get" the composition, but his flamboyant playing makes the track – a vital force pulling against its regular, forbidding structure.

'One More Red Nightmare', the main theme of which had been road tested in live improvisations, had regular two-bar spaces within the riff for Bruford's drum fills, which were deliciously audacious, including one which found him playing ever more quietly around the kit. "Diminuendo is always very effective on drums," he says of the break. "It's like speech: if you want someone to listen to you, you get quieter."

He also put to good use a battered Zilco cymbal that he had found in one of the studio bins, its metallic clatter somewhere between a Chinese cymbal and one of Muir's baking trays.

Eyebrows were raised at both the alto sax playing on this track and who was playing it. The prodigal Ian McDonald had returned to the group as a guest player.

'Fallen Angel' effectively uses two other old stalwarts: Robin Miller plays a lovely oboe line over the verses, while Mark Charig gets stuck into some blazing cornet soloing against Fripp's metallic grid pattern in the choruses, this jazz element sounding startling juxtaposed with King Crimson's new, heavier music.

'Providence' is an improvisation recorded at the Palace Theatre, Providence, Rhode Island, on June 30, 1974, and is one of the first recorded examples of avant rock, *avant la lettre*. The mercurial rhythmic relationship between Bruford's fidgety drum patters and Wetton's bass is such that they play across each other in a kind of implied momentum. It's powerful, but its apparent instability adds an extra frisson, while Fripp buzzes and squalls ominously over the top.

The twelve-minute 'Starless' features McDonald and Mel Collins on soprano and alto saxophone respectively. It was already a staple of their live set. A minor-key melody with brooding Mellotron, it looked back to the sombre ballads of 1969, with Wetton in especially fine voice. A slowly climbing section, led by Fripp playing a series of minimal repetitive figures, finds the musicians building up an enormous tension. At its apex, it suddenly shifted into double speed, with McDonald's sax solo and Fripp's nagging two-note line still maintaining the tension, which is resolved by a glorious restatement of the initial melody.

But King Crimson had split before it was released, prompting more "What if?"'s. Fripp had made up his mind not to carry on with this most singular of groups.

Bruford writes in his autobiography that during the sessions for *Red*, Fripp had become insular, refusing to contribute views to the ways that the music should progress. "I was in Olympic for fifteen days with John and Robert, but it could have been fifteen months. Robert had neglected to tell us that, a few days before the sessions, he had undergone a spiritual awakening comparable to the one that Jamie Muir had undergone two years earlier, and which it now transpired was the reason for Muir's sudden and unexplained departure from the group.

"Presumably it was in relationship to this that Our Fearless Leader decided to withhold his opinion on all proceedings in the studio so a minor chord was as good, or not, as a major chord and Take 4 was as good or as lousy as Take 5. All this spiritual awakening certainly wasn't making the music any easier to produce."

In this difficult atmosphere, the album was mixed by Wetton and George Chkiantz. Looking back, Fripp says: "How I would put that now is that I would offer 'radical neutrality'. We have yes and we have no and that we understand, but what makes that possible is the one in between, the reconciling factor." The guitarist has always loved coming up with rather clever aphorisms, but this one feels a little too cute and a tad contrived.

Bruford's words still seem to carry a certain bitterness and Wetton has said they were both "distraught". This is hardly surprising. They had just made *Red*, which has influenced a myriad of musicians, including Nirvana's Kurt Cobain, and of which both are proud. They must have felt like the possibilities were limitless. They were, but the possibilities were suddenly cut off.

"It was like the carpet had been pulled from under us at exactly the time that we were looking the best, selling more records and doing better business," Wetton says. "Those two years of real hard work, three albums and 250 shows looked like they were going to pay off and then it ended. We were a bit cheesed off to say the least.

"I drifted after that, went to Roxy Music and Uriah Heep and lost my way a bit. But what do you do once you've been in one of the most avant-garde bands in the world? You can't go and just find the right combination of people again. It was a magical combination and after that I had needed to get paid. I'm not saying that in a cynical way, but I needed to pay the bills. I'm a working musician and I don't like to sit around all day on my arse."

Wetton was unhappy about being made redundant, aged 25, and was also dismayed that the group fell apart when Ian McDonald was ostensibly back in the fold. Fripp has said that he had invited him back in so that the group could continue without his own involvement and with his blessing, but unsurprisingly EG Management would have none of it.

McDonald has said that he feels that being invited back into a group that, unbeknown to him, was about to be disbanded carried a certain amount of payback for his absconding in 1969.

The decision to split the band had been down to Fripp. By late 1974 he saw that the thing that was called progressive rock was going in a way that he couldn't follow.

Fripp: "King Crimson ceased to exist in 1974 before the mass eruption in '75/'76 with ELP and the large sillinesses of Yes and Rick Wakeman."

That was partly an assessment blessed with hindsight. It was also something of a generalisation, as ELP released nothing between 1973 and 1977, and Yes were no more silly in these years than before or after. But with Rick Wakeman gearing up to do the ice pageant of *King Arthur*, it's fair to say that Fripp's view was prescient. Not that King Crimson were obliged to be a part of all that, of course.

"I think some people are as wary of success as they are of failure," says Wetton. "There were two of us champing at the bit to make the band as successful as possible because we could see what was possible, what we could do. And one third of the band was going, 'Hang on a minute'. The more popular the band is, the less control there is. There you have a fairly big factor on the demise of the band."

Ironically, this lack of control that had driven McDonald and Giles to leave in 1969 – which had so shaken the guitarist at the time – seems to be what ultimately got to Fripp. Giles had said that once a musician gets stuck in that sort of machine, their life is not their own. Then there was the fact that as the group's popularity was increasing in America, so they would be required to play over there more often.

Robert Fripp has described his early time in King Crimson as a superb liberal education. But to what end had this education been leading?

"The point is a band comes together when it has music to play," Fripp says. "When it's played that music it moves on. It has to do with the nature of the creative current and creative work. As soon as you say, 'Look this really works, let's keep doing it', you have a successful professional undertaking, which is entirely honourable, but the creative necessity for the band may not be there."

Maybe Fripp had become metaphysically disconnected from King Crimson because the muse had decided to turn her back on him. Maybe there really was no need now for King Crimson's music to be played, no King Crimson-sized hole in the universe to be plugged. Maybe the force that reached back from the future pulling the musicians towards it had had enough. And maybe it's worth calling a halt to this musing.

CHAPTER 5

Orchestral Variations 1967–74

From 1967, rock music's horizons expanded at a greater rate than ever before, with an ever-widening range of instrumentation used in compositions of greater length and so inevitably, some groups decided to augment their line-up in a major way: with an orchestra. A pop song with orchestral backing was nothing new in itself, but now musicians were becoming excited at the possibilities of a new hybrid artform, which integrated rock with elements of classical music.

From one viewpoint the more serious and questing rock musicians were hoping to receive a blessing from the classical establishment, to have their music rubber-stamped and to be taken seriously. There was a thin dividing line between going metaphorically cap-in-hand to the classical establishment and seeking a pat on the head, and youthfully asserting that this is *our* music and should be taken just as seriously – although both approaches ultimately amount to seeking approval.

The most high-profile melding of rock and orchestral music of the late Sixties was *Concerto For Group And Orchestra* composed by keyboard player Jon Lord – who had been classically trained up to the age of 17 – and performed by his group Deep Purple and the Royal Philharmonic Orchestra on September 24, 1969, at the Royal Albert Hall. The concert was conducted by British composer, Sir Malcolm Arnold.

Deep Purple formed in 1968 and on their early recordings virtually modelled themselves on the American group, Vanilla Fudge, best known for their melodramatic, bombastic take on The Supremes' 'You Keep Me Hangin' On', which was a hit for the group in 1967. Deep Purple's approach gave rise to 'Exposition'/'We Can Work It Out' on their 1969 album *The Book Of Taliesyn*, which featured a fantasia of sorts on the second movement (Allegretto) of Beethoven's *Symphony No. 7*, before going into a cover of the Lennon/McCartney song.

This writer admits to an abiding interest in *Deep Purple In Concert*, the album of the *Concerto For Group And Orchestra*, as at 12 years of age it was my first ever rock album purchase. It seemed logical – I liked classical music and had a burgeoning interest in heavy rock, so why not buy an album that was a mix of both? Problem solved. If only life could have continued to be that straightforward.

Whatever one might think of the results, it scored an 'A' for both ambition and audacity, and Arnold should be praised for agreeing to be involved. Given developments in orchestral music in the second half of the 20th century, with avant-garde composers like Stockhausen and Penderecki using pre-recorded tape with orchestral instruments, there was a feeling that now any combination were possible. Arnold himself wrote a tongue-in-cheek piece, *A Grand, Grand Overture* (1956), which involved a small orchestra augmented by four vacuum cleaners, the players of which were "shot" by people wielding four rifles – a parody of sorts of the cannonades used in Tchaikovsky's *1812 Overture*. A concerto for a rock group and an orchestra was bound to happen somewhere down the line.

"What does it feel like playing with us squares?" Arnold asked Jon Lord, with a grin, following the final rehearsal in a documentary film made of the event. "That's not the word… it's been exciting," said Lord. "I hope the concert will be as exciting as the rehearsals." "It will be more exciting," said Arnold exuding avuncular assurance. The film was called *The Best Of Both Worlds*, the narrator of which described it as a unique event, "a combination of symphony and pop," albeit presented with a horrible cut in the footage of the first movement. "Jon Lord believes the musicianship in pop is getting so good that this collaboration can happen more and more often," said the narrator.

This diplomatically covered up what had actually taken place behind closed doors in rehearsals. After the group had learned their parts, there came the time when it all needed to be stitched together with the orchestra. Deep Purple's co-manager Tony Edwards had spurred Lord on to realise his oft-mentioned idea of the concerto by booking the Royal Albert Hall for September 24. Given the touring commitments of the group, Lord was forced into all-night composing sessions to complete the piece, and the budget only stretched to two full rehearsals.

But this didn't prepare Lord for the reception given to himself and his hairy group mates by the orchestra. When they arrived at the first of the two rehearsals, some of the players behaved in an astonishingly juvenile manner, blowing wolf whistles. There were also practical problems with the group being too loud, and timing problems between the two factions. It was such a mess to begin with that Lord was nearly in tears. To make matters worse, one of the female cellists flounced out in a fit of pique, complaining that she hadn't become a member of the Royal

Philharmonic to play with "a second-rate Beatles". Faced with this shambles Arnold was forced to assert his authority.

Interviewed in the Nineties, Deep Purple vocalist Ian Gillan vividly recalled the situation: "The first rehearsal with orchestra and band ended with emotions running high... There was another very lacklustre effort by the RPO, which prompted our conductor to stop all resentment in a no-nonsense manner that quite shocked us.

"Increasingly irritated by their attitude, halfway through the first movement, he rapped his baton furiously, raised his hands in the air and said words to the effect of, 'I don't know what you think you're doing. You're supposed to be the finest orchestra in Britain, and you're playing like a bunch of cunts. Quite frankly, with the way it's going, you're not fit to be on stage with these guys, so pick yourself up and let's hear some bollocks. We're going to make history tonight, so we might as well make music while we're doing it.'"

Arnold's angry blast of Anglo-Saxon did the trick and thereafter the run-throughs improved dramatically, and the performance was of high quality. The most exciting part of the concerto is in the first movement where the six minutes or so of dramatic orchestral introduction leads into a theme that sounds like it could have danced off the pages of Igor Stravinsky's *Petrushka*, and then the group join the orchestra and take up the principal theme.

At this point it seems like all possibilities have been thrown open, but then, rather disappointingly, Deep Purple meander off on a rock jam. Lord wrote in the sleeve notes of the album that in this first movement he wanted to present the group and orchestra as "antagonists" – which they had been in more ways than one – and the two forces tend to disrupt each other or play episodically rather than meshing together. This carries on throughout the piece. There are some magical moments, but Ian Paice's "drum cadenza", stuck like a wedge into the galloping themes of the third movement, although played with flair, feels completely superfluous.

All that said, on the night, the concerto received a tumultuous reception. Lord realised that he had set himself up for a critical panning, as classical critics and enthusiasts could – and can still – be terribly snobbish and reactionary, and rock critics were often dismissive about those who seem to be getting ideas above their station. So he pre-emptively noted that music critics were themselves essentially archaic and that the occasion had turned out to be fun.

During the documentary footage of Ritchie Blackmore's brief, but flash "guitar cadenza", two seasoned members of the (resting) string section situated behind the guitarist noticeably swap telling glances. Blackmore was dissatisfied with the experience on many levels. For him it had been far from the best of both worlds.

"I was not into classical music then. I was very, very moody and just wanted to play very, very loudly and jump around a lot," he said when interviewed in 1979. "In '69 we went into the classical stuff because it was Jon Lord's big thing to write a concerto for group and orchestra. He was very sincere. But I didn't like playing it or respect the fact that we were doing it. The orchestra was very condescending towards us and I didn't like playing with them, so it was one big calamity onstage. But Jon was happy with it and management was happy with it because we had a press angle, which I resented very much."

The abrupt end for the group's participation in such ventures was the epochal *Deep Purple In Rock*, released in 1970. Gone were the post-psychedelic extravaganzas, classical snippets, grandiose cover versions and orchestral works, to be replaced by one of the landmark albums of heavy rock. Having found their métier, the five-piece became one of the most successful rock groups on the planet.

Interviewed after this deliberate and dramatic change of Deep Purple's musical direction, Jon Lord was asked if the group would continue to combine these different influences.

"No, I feel we're moving away from it now because it was never intended to be part of the direction of the group; it was merely an experiment," he said. "As you know, we did experiment with classical themes in the beginning – and with classical chord structures in the music, but it all got a bit soulless... planned, you know?

"I love classical music; I love the way it's worked... all those chord sequences, so I often use that sort of effect in my solos. The actual group now is trying to develop into being good at what we're best at – which is what we call rock'n'roll."

But Lord wasn't done with this kind of fusion by any means. In fact, he was commissioned to write a follow-up to *Concerto For Group And Orchestra*, a piece that involved an orchestra and rock soloists, which was titled *The Gemini Suite*. Malcolm Arnold was again the conductor, this time with the London Symphony Orchestra, and it was performed at the Royal Festival Hall in 1971. Lord explored these musical avenues on future albums *Windows* (1974) and *Sarabande* (1976), but it's safe to say that this fusion between rock groups and orchestras didn't have quite the legs that some had predicted.

The Five Bridges Suite was composed by Keith Emerson and was played by his group The Nice, with lyrics by Lee Jackson, the group's bass player and vocalist. The orchestra was the Sinfonia Of London, made up of players from the London Symphony Orchestra. The piece had been commissioned by the Newcastle Arts Festival, and Emerson used the (then) five bridges that spanned the River Tyne as a symbolic musical metaphor. In the sleeve notes, Emerson says: "I worked on building a musical bridge combining early baroque forms to more contemporary ideas, allowing the progression to move rather neurotically through a fantasia form." At only eighteen minutes, it's a smart, concise piece of music.

As with the *Concerto For Group And Orchestra*, *The Five Bridges Suite* opens with a purely orchestral section, before Emerson's piano makes its entrance. The second movement is a driving pop/rock song with Lee Jackson singing about getting on with life while breathing the dirty air of the city. The third movement, 'Chorale', has Jackson in a rather strained, breathy voice describing the landmarks of his home town over orchestral strings with interludes that are reminiscent of the Jacques Loussier Trio who specialised in jazz versions of J. S. Bach. 'High Level Fugue' is by Emerson's admission closely related to maverick Austrian composer Friedrich Gulda's Sixties composition, *Prelude And Fugue*, which is also a baroque-style keyboard fugue given jazz phrasings.

While Emerson is far from original here, the group and orchestra work the material convincingly, with the pianist hurtling along like a cross between Glenn Gould and Pinetop Perkins. The suite concludes with a recapitulation of material from the first and second movement, including Lee Jackson's opening song, given extra bite by a horn section of top players, including Kenny Wheeler on trumpet, and Alan Skidmore and Joe Harriott on saxophones.

Emerson later revealed that inspiration for the piece had struck him in the unlikeliest of places – on an Aer Lingus flight in July 1969, coming back from a cancelled gig in Cork with Yes and The Bonzo Dog Band. He wrote one of the main themes on an airsick bag and then, in a gesture of confident pragmatism, went and bought Walter Piston's *Guide To Orchestration* to write the orchestral parts.

The piece was premiered in Newcastle on October 10, 1969, with another performance soon after at the Fairfield Halls, Croydon, both with American conductor Joseph Eger. Emerson felt dejected and upset before the concert, having found the jazz players sequestered in a dressing room visibly stoned from smoking weed and noticed that some of the orchestral players had conspicuously and rather childishly stuffed their ears with cotton wool. It's all too easy for cynics to look back on this as being some kind of pretentious indulgence on Emerson's part without considering the financial risk that he was taking on. This was still virtually unknown territory.

"We are trying to reawaken an interest in classical music by introducing a more modern element to those young people who might never go to a classical concert," said Emerson in 1970. "We are trying to build bridges to those musical shores which seem determined to remain apart from that which is a whole.

"Joseph Eger who conducted the orchestra for us was sincerely knocked out because instead of a bunch of pretentious pseudo-intellectuals clapping politely and shouting, 'Well done maestro', he got a crowd of young college students shaking his hand and saying, 'Thanks Joe – we really enjoyed it'. I don't think he had been called Joe in his entire career!"

If *The Five Bridges Suite* had been artistically successful enough to point towards more such collaborations, two of the other concert pieces released on the resultant album, *Five Bridges*, were far less so. Emerson's grand idea of making a holistic statement through the merging of group and orchestra on pieces from the classical repertoire was laudable, but at times the results felt much more like a reminder of their essential incompatibility.

He said that when he first met Eger they were going in different directions – and there, frankly, is the rub. The versions of the *Karelia Suite* by Sibelius and the martial third movement of Tchaikovsky's *Symphony No.6: Pathetique* were, again, exercises that probably had to be done sometime, but although Eger helped Emerson to arrange these pieces for performance, to hear a rock group footling about in 4/4 as the orchestra played these big themes might have seemed like a new dawn at the time, but now sounds quite unedifying, very limited in scope and ultimately rather pointless.

American composer Steve Reich, himself a former jazz drummer, recognised the rhythmic limitations of this kind of stylistic synthesis when he said: "You can play Bach with a drummer, but you ain't gonna play no Mahler with a drummer."

On a brief section of the *Karelia Suite*, with scant regard for the overall atmosphere of the piece, Emerson unleashes a solo through a fuzz box, which makes his Hammond organ sound more like his Norton motorbike doing donuts in a field. After this display of what feels like reckless and pointless musical vandalism, both musical parties start up where they had left off, finishing the performance in a way that can best be described as bathetic.

On its 1970 release, *Five Bridges* made number two in the UK album charts. For what it's worth, *Concerto For Group And Orchestra* only made number thirty.

These classically trained rock musicians had been gravitating towards integrating classical approaches, themes or even entire compositions into what was becoming progressive rock music, but there was far less interest from the classical establishment. One of the few exceptions was David Bedford, who was unique in being a classical composer moving over to work in rock music. Even more extraordinary was the fact that he was a card-carrying member of the modernist avant-garde.

Bedford had failed his studies at the Royal Academy Of Music having signed off with "an extremely discordant and weird" composition, but left in 1961 with a generous grant to study abroad. He went to Venice under the tutelage of Luigi Nono, attracted by the Italian composer's musical and political radicalism. But with an avowed desire to do something "slightly different" in music, as he has said with considerable understatement, he followed a singular path.

Critically acclaimed compositions like 1965's *Music For Albion Moonlight*, for soprano and small ensemble, suggested a potentially successful niche career in modern composition. But from the close of the 1960s, through a combination of pragmatism, economic necessity, natural restlessness and serendipity, his career took a quite different turn.

Bedford was born in 1937 into a musical household. His father's mother was Lisa Lehmann, a composer of popular songs, and his own mother was an opera singer. His father was a jazz enthusiast and Bedford's brother Steuart became a respected conductor. Bedford learned the piano and then the oboe, but he had no knowledge of pop music. "Elvis Presley could not even have existed as far as our family knew," he says.

But just as he was always drawn to new developments in classical music, he was also "knocked silly" on hearing The Beach Boys' 'I Get Around' in 1964. "It was the first time I thought, 'Hang on, all my snobby classical music friends say it's all rubbish, this pop music', but that, I thought, was absolutely stunning. And I got into The Beatles, then the Stones."

Bedford's publishers were Universal Edition Ltd, based in Vienna, and his first foray into the world of pop music came in 1969 when Universal asked him to arrange a selection of left-wing songs for a stage show, *Revolutionary Songs From Marie Antoinette To The Beatles*, by Bettina Jonic, who Bedford has described as "a sort of modern Edith Piaf". Stage-managing the show at The Roundhouse, London, that night was Ian

Knight, manager of The Soft Machine. Kevin Ayers was about to leave the group and was looking for an arranger for his debut solo album, *Joy Of A Toy*, and so Knight recommended Bedford.

Bedford was then commissioned by the London Sinfonietta in 1969 to write a piece for instrumental ensemble and rock group, and he came up with *The Garden Of Love*. If rock musicians were seeking credibility by association with classical music, this sparse, angular composition – which Bedford feels was integral in bringing together the worlds of atonality and tonality in his own compositional process – feels like the two opposing forces have been smashed together leaving only a few large, jagged shards remaining.

There is no rock music as such in this piece, but the ensemble of himself on keyboards, Robert Wyatt (drums), Kevin Ayers (guitar), Mike Oldfield (guitar) and Lol Coxhill (saxophone) – then Ayers's group, The Whole World – take on the role as punctuators, playing short motifs both scored and improvised in a series of calls and responses with the Sinfonietta. Ayers brings events to a more melodic conclusion by singing the titular poem by William Blake.

The Garden Of Love was typical of Bedford's work in that it was an odd mix of the experimental and the irreverent, and found him playing Swanee whistle and bird calls as part of his "plinky plonk" music. The piece is also partly conceptual in a tongue-in-cheek way, as the score requires six pretty girls to work as page turners. "It's very sexist... now," he qualifies.

The piece was performed at the Queen Elizabeth Hall, London, on September 26, 1970. Unsurprisingly it fell below the media spotlight that had captured the works by The Nice and Deep Purple, and the recording was only released in 1997.

But again, the question is, does it work as a mix of rock and orchestral music? And again the answer is "kind of", but for different reasons: here the uncompromisingly modernist structures of the orchestra and the far less nuanced contribution of the rock musicians seem to be engaged in two different planes of activity.

A member of The Whole World until it broke up in 1971, Bedford sort of crept into the side door of progressive rock and onto DJ John Peel's Dandelion label, releasing *Nurse's Song With Elephants* in 1972. The title track is written for 10 acoustic guitars, and involves extended techniques like the player rubbing their moistened thumb across the back of the soundbox. 'Some Bright Stars For Queen's College' utilises twenty-seven plastic pipe twirlers.

Mike Oldfield's debut solo album, *Tubular Bells* – which will be dealt with in Chapter 12 – came out in 1973 and after the album's unexpected and considerable commercial success, there was talk of its "symphonic" qualities and Virgin Records' boss Richard Branson asked Bedford if he would orchestrate Oldfield's composition. Bedford did so, but was aware of what was going on.

"I didn't agree that it was a sort of symphonic piece," Bedford says. "What it seemed to me was a set of separate three or four minute pieces. Branson asked me to do an orchestral version of it, which is interesting but flawed. He was milking it for all he was worth."

Virgin Records were, however, certainly adventurous in their commissioning, and out of all this emerged the most anomalous record in their catalogue, an album of Bedford's orchestral piece, *Star's End*, released in 1974. It was recorded with the Royal Philharmonic Orchestra, conducted by Vernon Handley, and with Mike Oldfield on guitar and bass, and Chris Cutler of Henry Cow on drums, it was presented as a kind of progressive rock/avant-garde classical hybrid. It was recorded with the Manor Mobile at Barking Town Hall.

Bedford had an interest in cosmology and astronomy, and the composition, inspired by the death of a star, was originally titled *Heat Death Of The Universe*. That was thought by Virgin to be too forbidding and he agreed to change it.

The idea, hatched by Virgin, was that if Universal could get funding for the piece from the Arts Council, Virgin would release the album and book a premiere at the Royal Festival Hall in London. Bedford: "One of my classical composer friends rang me and said, 'I suppose you're going to use cheaper manuscript paper to write it on'. It was supposed to sound like a joke, but with a hidden sting.

"It's very challenging, because it's not at all like *Concerto for Group And Orchestra* by Deep Purple: it's quite atonal at times and very loud. But it introduced that sort of music to listeners who wouldn't normally have been into that sort of music at all. And you make allowances when you know that the subject is the universe, all the stars and the galaxies. You realise the music has to be slightly more adventurous."

The concert at the Royal Festival Hall featured Steve Hillage on guitar, Darryl Runswick on bass and Chris Cutler on drums and the trio dovetailed well with the convulsive orchestral parts. But while Bedford's (unnamed) composer friend might have been coolly dismissive of the idea, it was all too much for some.

"There were some walk-outs and it ends very quietly, fading away to nothing and a voice said, 'Thank God that's over'."

Bedford has noted that *Star's End* sold exceptionally well for a classical album, but relatively poorly for a rock album. And that was the problem in a nutshell. Such concerts were expensive to stage and although some of the audience were lured in by the Mike Oldfield connection, what they were faced with was something quite different and for which, ultimately, there was only ever going to be a niche market.

Although there was none of the sort of tomfoolery of the orchestral players blowing wolf whistles or stuffing their ears with cotton wool, rehearsals for *Star's End* exposed a difference in timing between rock and orchestral playing, as Chris Cutler soon found out.

"When I played *Star's End* I had to learn in double quick time that when I was playing in unison with a percussionist, I had to play on the beat; when I had a unison part with the brass, I had to wait a bit and then play; with the strings it was somewhere in between.

"[With a brass instrument] it takes a finite amount of time for a column of air to shift through the tube; if you play a violin it takes slightly less time to get the note out; if you play a drum or piano you get the note immediately.

"Orchestras have to learn with every new conductor where to place the beat. When you know the music, when you've played the *Jupiter* fifty times, you know what's coming and you can anticipate and prepare and produce your notes correctly. But when an orchestra plays a new piece and hasn't had enough time to rehearse, it can't really co-ordinate. I know that with *Star's End* I was leaving different amounts of time before I came in with the different sections, and therefore they were definitely and categorically not in time with each other."

Bedford went on to make a number of solo albums for Virgin and along the way, proved himself to be an inspired orchestral and ensemble arranger for songs, especially on Roy Harper's Seventies albums, like *Stormcock* and *Valentine*. But although Virgin Records stuck their neck out by getting behind *Star's End*, such big ventures proved essentially unprofitable. And while he stayed on the label until 1977, his future albums were written, in classical parlance, for smaller forces.

The most commercially popular album conceived as progressive rock music with orchestra in the Seventies was undoubtedly Rick Wakeman's 1974 album, *Journey To The Centre Of The Earth*. Wakeman had studied at the Royal College Of Music from 1968, but he had left the following year, by mutual consent, to continue his extra-curricular activities: as a successful session musician. Wakeman played with the Strawbs from 1970–71, then as a session player with David Bowie on 1971's *Hunky Dory*, where he beautifully elaborated songs like 'Life On Mars'.

Then, on the same day, Wakeman was asked to stay with Bowie as a band member and invited to join Yes. He opted for the latter, first appearing on Yes's 1971 album, *Fragile*. But he pursued a parallel solo career and from 1971, over a period of thirteen months, he began putting together his debut solo album *The Six Wives Of Henry VIII*, which was released in 1973. His penchant for concept albums dated back to hearing Sergei Prokofiev's 1936 composition *Peter And The Wolf* as a child, when he was entranced by its enchanting succession of animal characters depicted by themes played on different orchestral instruments. This is what he wanted to do in his own music.

An avid reader, Wakeman researched the lives of the Tudor wives and decided to create their musical portraits, but in a personally interpretive rather than a literal manner. "Somebody said to me, 'What is it? Is this bit Catherine Howard when she was young and is this the bit where she got bumped off?' I said, 'No, think surrealistically. Think Dali, think Picasso, think cubism, think all of that.' Because basically what I did is what these guys do. It was never meant to be a depiction of their lives. But I can hand-on-heart say that every single bit of that album came from thoughts of one of the wives."

The resulting album is Wakeman's most attractive and beguiling solo effort. It sounds fresh and capricious, then sombre, then joyous. At times it's flash and modern, at other times hushed and hymnal. 'Jane Seymour' is mainly recorded on the organ of the church of St Giles-without-Cripplegate in London, the composition's toccata-like organ excursions ultimately augmented by exultant, upward-arcing synthesizer lines. But in those early days of the Seventies, there was no guarantee that an album like this would shift units; Wakeman was basically walking the tightrope and hoping not to fall off.

"A&M records at that time were very unhappy about it," says Wakeman. "The American branch said, 'We've got to sell twelve and a half thousand of this to break even. How the hell are we going to sell twelve and half thousand copies of a guy with electronic instruments who doesn't even sing?'

"It had a chequered reception initially. The press absolutely hated it. It was one of the first sort of instrumental keyboards albums and they didn't get it. I must admit I was very hurt, I was really, really upset.

"It was saved by two things," he continues. "By [BBC TV rock music programme] *The Old Grey Whistle Test* – we did three tracks, because [executive producer] Mike Appleton, Colin Strong, who was the producer, and [presenter] Bob Harris loved it – and by the general public who warmed to it. A&M didn't mind too much when they gave me a platinum disc."

Wakeman had another musical idea in mind, one that he had sketched out before *The Six Wives*... And now, with some royalties coming in from that album, he set about realising this new, more ambitious project, which was based on Jules Verne's story, *Journey To The Centre Of The Earth*. The album features the London Symphony Orchestra and the New Chamber Choir, conducted by David Measham, and a rock ensemble comprising Wakeman and some musicians that he had played with in his Buckinghamshire locale.

"I love storytelling, and *Journey*... was always something I wanted to do when I knew I had the money, because I [only] got £4,500 [from the record company as an advance] and that didn't cover the rehearsals with the orchestra. I hate to say it, but money can rule the roost."

Without knowing this background information, it might again all look like progressive rock excess with a lot of money being thrown at an overblown project. But most of that money – about £40,000 – was Wakeman's own. As well as investing the royalties from *The Six Wives...*, he remortgaged his house, sold off a number of his assets, including cars, and in this period of thrift, he even ended up getting a court writ for an unpaid milk bill.

The injection of his own capital was probably the only reason that A&M – who really didn't get this album at all – agreed to release it. And then only on the say-so of label founder Jerry Moss. The label also could not understand why Wakeman wouldn't put a band together featuring established hot-shot stars, but he was keen to play with the musicians he knew and let the music speak for itself. To save costs, the album was recorded at its Royal Festival Hall premiere on January 18, 1974, and released five months later.

Journey To The Centre Of The Earth is stylistically completely different from *The Six Wives Of Henry VIII* and tells a distinct story, with excerpts from the text narrated by actor David Hemmings, followed by musical evocations of the scenes.

With its big, dramatic, whistleable orchestral and choral themes, cut with Moog extravaganzas, *Journey*... feels like a musical equivalent of the Fifties adventure films the young Wakeman would have seen on TV. He even throws in a snatch of Grieg's *In The Hall Of The Mountain King* into Part Two, as if to indicate beyond doubt that it was a rollicking musical yarn, rather than some chin-scratching high art statement.

Wakeman also had problems getting the orchestral musicians onside, and timing differences were again an issue. "Back then the classical players couldn't actually play that stuff," says Wakeman. "I could write music and give it to classical players and to blues rock musicians and their feel for the music was completely different to each other's."

The narration of Verne's century-old text helps give the piece its structure, and sounds rather quaint and quite charmingly preposterous. But Wakeman got the balance just right and this stylistic oddity struck a chord across a wide cross section of record buyers. Amazingly, it went to number one in the UK album charts; even more amazingly it peaked at number three in the US *Billboard* 200 chart, in which it stayed for twenty-seven weeks.

Reviewing the album in *Melody Maker*, Chris Welch caught its mood perfectly: "From the opening shout of the orchestra, the rumble of tympani and the delicate ringing of the vibraphone, the mood is set for romance and adventure.

"In classical music terms, this composition might be described as 'lightweight' or of 'little consequence'. But as far as popular music is concerned, Rick's composition for choir, orchestra and group is entertaining, fresh and disarmingly unpretentious.

"There are no attempts to be arty, clever or super-technical. This could be a score for a Hollywood musical – tuneful, but with epic overtones."

Whereas Jon Lord had hoped that *Concerto For Group And Orchestra* would be fun, this really was fun. The piece was also played at the Crystal Palace Bowl in 1974, with the added bonus of inflatable dinosaurs rearing up out of the lake at the front of the stage. Then, at the tender age of 25, Wakeman had a heart attack and was put out of action – but not for long.

Attempts to integrate the orchestra and an amplified rock group had mixed results. Orchestral lines added to songs had worked well, from Procol Harum's *Live In Concert With The Edmonton Symphony Orchestra* in 1972, to Caravan who made a live album with the New Symphonia in 1974.

But to actually write a standalone piece that integrated group and orchestra to any degree of complexity was another matter. The Moody Blues' *Days Of Future Passed* (1967) has perennially been lauded as an early fusion of classical and rock music, but it was nothing of the sort. Indeed, the most noticeable aspect of the album is the almost complete lack of fusion of rock and classical music, except on brief sections of 'Nights In White Satin'. The group were never in the same room as the orchestra, and Peter Knight's orchestral interludes, composed and recorded separately, have the punch and gloss of TV and film soundtrack music at odds with the group's songs. And orchestration isn't easy. Keith

Emerson was classically trained but had to buy a DIY book on the subject for the *Five Bridges Suite* and was also helped in this regard by Joseph Eger. His friend Rick Wakeman's score for *Journey...* was arrived at in conjunction with arrangers Will Malone and Danny Beckerman. It was one thing being a keyboard virtuoso, but being an orchestrator involved wearing an even bigger hat.

To successfully integrate rock and classical elements, one needs to overcome the fact that texturally and timbrally, the elements can get in the way of each other. Mont Campbell, a classically trained French horn player who also played bass in Egg and National Health notes that: "The Western symphony orchestra evolved on its own with all the sonorities complementing each other and going together nicely, and there were certain things that would not work with a rock group.

"They aren't sonorities that combine happily. You have percussion sections within an orchestra, but a rock band would rob too much of the sonority from the string ensemble.

"It's OK if you have a top line like you do with the Tamla Motown hits or Burt Bacharach, with a single violin line that sits quite nicely on a pop track, but not all the different pitches from double basses to cellos, through violas. The lower register will get completely lost and will muddy the overall effect, and that's why the only way an orchestra can play with a rock band is by following the top line."

Graeme Downes, singer and guitarist with New Zealand group The Verlaines is also senior lecturer in music at Otago University. To him the essential structural point of difference between classical music and progressive rock is that the latter is usually episodic, basically bits stuck together.

"It's the surplus of ideas: one idea leading to another idea, leading to another idea as opposed to something being developed out of a small idea. It's oftentimes the Paganini thing, the virtuoso aspect of classical music that has been mined [by rock music] more than the organisational aspect."

Which brings us onto claims of some branches of progressive rock as "symphonic rock" or "symphonic prog", a term that has unfortunately gained ground in recent years.

Firstly, one needs to pin down what "symphonic" means. The symphony was a name given to the hurdy gurdy in medieval times and "symphony", from the Greek, essentially means "sounding together", hence Stravinsky's relatively brief wind ensemble piece, *Symphonies Of Wind Instruments*. So in this context it could be applied to the music of any ensemble. But the contemporary meaning here is more in trying to equate a long progressive rock piece with a large-scale classical orchestral work. This is, in most cases, an attempt to claim classical credibility-by-association on behalf of groups by their admirers, rather than by the musicians themselves.

Symphonic form began as a formal four-movement structure back in the 18th century but, although it has changed and developed since then, its inherent complexity has never been approached by rock music.

For example, 'Close To The Edge' (1972) by Yes, is a seventeen-minute piece that has been deemed "symphonic" by some, but the group's admittedly inspired, but intuitive and somewhat chaotic compositional process yielded a number of sections accreted together to form a suite of sorts. And the fact that an earlier section reappears at the end does not make it "symphonic".

The Yes Album (1970) has also been cited as being "symphonic" because it contains "classical elements". But it doesn't. These ears can't pick out any, apart from one bass line that is vaguely reminiscent of Bach and the fact that the group produced a big and at times grandiose sound. Tony Kaye's organ lines derive more from R&B than from Bach; the vocal harmonies are redolent of Crosby, Stills & Nash; Steve Howe's guitar lines encompass psychedelia and bluegrass; Bill Bruford's drumming is syncopated rock playing that nods towards jazz; and Chris Squire was making up his own unique style on bass. According to Wikipedia: "Their approach was similar to classical music; each instrument played its own melodic line to generate a grand musical theme."

That description is so tenuous that it could also apply to hundreds of different pop and rock groups. In the classical field, Bach is an exemplar of "one instrument, one line" in some of his smaller-scale pieces like his cantatas, instrumental suites and sonatas – which weren't necessarily "grand" and were anything but symphonic.

A Wikipedia entry on symphonic prog groups offers this definition: "Additionally, they may play with the accompaniment of a symphony orchestra or use a synthesizer or Mellotron to emulate orchestral instruments." Which exemplifies the inescapable fact that the term is a misnomer to begin with or is so vague as to be meaningless, and someone playing a few chords on a Mellotron doesn't even approach orchestral string writing. "Faux orchestral" or "faux symphonic" would be more accurate.

If loosely used as an adjective, "symphonic" has its uses, of course, but to use it as a description of a genre of rock feels jarringly wrong. It's better that the term and the baggage that comes with it be discarded, except for a description in the loosest terms, and for these exploratory compositions to be taken for what they are, rather than having them pulling, rather gauchely, at classical music's coat tails.

The Enid, who formed in 1973, are, to some, the epitome of the popular idea of symphonic rock and have even played and recorded with orchestras. Founder member Robert John Godfrey has this to say on the term: "It doesn't mean anything. I have been loath to allow myself to be described as [being in] a symphonic rock band. There are always going to be references, but The Enid are unique."

Amen to that.

CHAPTER 6

Suburban Spacemen: Pink Floyd

Pink Floyd's debut LP, *The Piper At The Gates Of Dawn*, was a landmark album of Sixties psychedelia. Fittingly, it was released in August 1967, capturing the last heat of the Summer Of Love just before it poignantly tipped over into autumn.

The group's musical metamorphosis from a rather primitive R&B combo into the paisley-clad darlings of the London-based UK underground was more remarkable still. Their career, at least up until 1973, was one of the oddest pursued by any rock group, while producing some of the most inventive music of the whole progressive rock era.

Prior to Syd Barrett's ascendancy as a songwriter, *Melody Maker*'s Nick Jones, a reviewer of one of their earliest concerts at underground hub, All Saints Church Hall in Powis Gardens, west London, in October 1966, wrote: "The slides were excellent – colourful, frightening, grotesque, beautiful – and the group's trip into outer space sounds promised very interesting things to come.

"The Floyd need to write more of their own material – 'psychedelic' versions of 'Louie Louie' won't come off – but if they can incorporate their electronic prowess with some melodic and lyrical songs – getting away from dated R&B things – they could well score in the near future."

And they did just that, expanding out of R&B at such speed that they had soon left all stylistic clichés behind them. In 1967 they made a mark with pop singles like 'Arnold Layne', which reached the Top 20, and 'See Emily Play', which charted at number six. And then there was the audacious ten-minute, mainly improvised 'Interstellar Overdrive'.

The Who's guitarist and songwriter Pete Townshend saw the group play at psychedelic clubs like the UFO and was impressed by their sheer sonic assault, delivered at considerable volume, but was less than impressed by some of the album's childlike moments like 'The Scarecrow' and 'Bike'.

Melody Maker journalist Chris Welch interviewed bass guitarist Roger Waters in August 1967, and if he had already heard the album, he doesn't mention it in the piece. He took the opposite view.

"Are the Pink Floyd being quite honest when they make coy and attractive records like 'See Emily Play' and then proceed to make the night hideous with a thunderous, incomprehensible, screaming, sonic torture that five American doctors agree could permanently damage the senses?"

Welch's standpoint at this early stage involved further questioning the "honesty" of the group in that they found it difficult to play a song like 'See Emily Play' live. Waters counters, asking how could The Beatles hope to play 'A Day In The Life' live and stating "a lot of stuff on our LP is completely impossible to do live. We've got the recording side together and not the playing side." There was an underlying notion that these studio effects and overdubs were somehow artificial constructs.

His view might seem a bit quaint now, but at the time these were the sort of questions being asked about this new music. Outside of London or the metropolitan areas where psychedelia was embraced by the burgeoning ranks of hipsters and hippies, similar questions were being asked by provincial audiences who might have heard the group's singles and gone to see the new psychedelic pop sensation.

But when faced by elongated abstract "beautiful" instrumentals – in Waters' words – and the group's inordinate volume drowning out the vocal performance of the increasingly unreliable Barrett, some decided to make their feelings known. At the California Ballroom, Dunstable, the locals threw coins and infamously poured beer over the group from the balcony. All this prompted Waters to tell Welch: "We want a brand-new environment, and we've hit on the idea of using a big top. We'll have a huge tent and go around like a travelling circus. We'll have a huge screen 120 feet wide and forty feet high inside and project films and slides." He admitted that they'd been faced with technical problems, but had got to the nub of the matter, saying: "We're trying to solve problems that haven't existed before." Waters sounded genuinely concerned, concluding that if they didn't solve the problems they would end up "on the dole".

Another factor that prompted this idea of a moveable venue is that like many groups of the era who had achieved chart success, Pink Floyd's bookings were coming in on an ad hoc basis, giving them this schedule on six consecutive days in July 1967: London to Stowmarket and back (distance 180 miles); London to Redcar (260 miles); Redcar to London (260 miles); London to Douglas, Isle Of Man (330 miles); Douglas to Gorleston (370 miles); Gorleston to Elgin (570 miles).

The big top concept didn't happen, but by this point Pink Floyd had already made the unusual step of trying to transplant some of the eclectic vibes of the underground clubs into London's Queen Elizabeth Hall for their Games For May concert on May 12, 1967, subtitled 'Space Age Relaxation For The Climax Of Spring – Electronic Composition, Colour And Image Projection, Girls, And The Pink Floyd'. They used an early version of a joystick mixer for their quadraphonic sound system, the Azimuth Co-ordinator, pre-recorded tapes, a bit of performance art and a bubble machine to enhance their music.

Pink Floyd attracted the attention of the BBC TV arts magazine programme *Look Of The Week* and performed 'Astronomy Domine' and an extract of 'Pow R. Toc H.' two days later. It marked their first meeting with the classical establishment in the shape of Hans Keller, musicologist and musician and an authority on 20th-century music. It also felt like the Square versus the Kids.

Keller asked Waters and Barrett, who were charm personified throughout: "Why has it all got to be so terribly loud? I just can't bear it. I grew up with a string quartet, which is much softer, so why has it all got to be so loud?" Waters said: "We haven't grown up with a string quartet, so it doesn't sound terribly loud to us." Barrett followed with: "We don't need it very loud to hear it. Personally I like quiet music just as much as loud music." Keller finished by saying: "Well, there it is. My verdict is that it is a little bit a regression to childhood, but after all, why not?" delivered as if he had simply lost interest in it all already.

Barrett's rapid mental decline – due to underlying problems exacerbated by an excessive ingestion of LSD – gave them another problem to solve that hadn't existed before. Pink Floyd have been circumspect to the point of pleading guilty about the way that they left Barrett by the wayside in December 1967, but he had become unwilling or incapable of playing onstage. And none of the group, in their early twenties, could have hoped to have understood what was going on – even now it's not clear. Radical psychiatrist R. D. Laing, after having heard a tape of Barrett talking, apparently claimed he was "incurable". Considering Laing's idiosyncratic views on sanity and madness, this seems rather unlikely. Waters actually booked Barrett in to see Laing, but he refused to attend the session.

Without Barrett in the group, Pink Floyd were dropped by their managers Peter Jenner and Andrew King, who decided to stick with their former singer and guitarist. He had been their main songwriter, so surely he would deliver the goods? He did, after a fashion, with the beautiful, if disturbingly fractured, *The Madcap Laughs* (1969) and *Barrett* (1970), which rather painfully captured the last flowering of his remarkable talent before it withered and died.

Some commentators latched onto Syd Barrett's comment that while he was an art student, the rest of the original group were ex-architecture students who had met at Regent Street Polytechnic, with all its implications of logic over inspiration and laborious creation over spontaneity.

But being of a technical bent, Pink Floyd were adept at organising sound and were learning on the hoof, incrementally building up a lightshow and an ever more elaborate PA system. But now they had to prove themselves if they really weren't going to end up on the dole and so drafted in Cambridge guitarist David Gilmour – for a short, uncomfortable time in the same line-up as Barrett.

With their main songwriter now gone, they were forced to step up their own efforts. Roger Waters came up with 'Let There Be More Light', with his memorable beginners' bass line hooks, and lyrics referencing Hereward The Wake and a UFO making a close encounter at the RAF base of Mildenhall in Suffolk, to Rick Wright's looming organ and David Gilmour's keening guitar lines. Similarly, the bass player's mantric 'Set The Controls For The Heart Of The Sun', with his cool, subdued vocals sitting just under Mason's tom-tom patterns, Wright's organ lines and vibes, and taped bird cries – the group's first use of pre-recorded tapes and sound effects – saw them heading out towards the stars.

Wright's 'See-Saw' is an underrated song, not least by Pink Floyd themselves, and evokes the idyllic, sunny, very English Sunday afternoons of childhood, but this nostalgia brushes up against the futuristic, with Mellotron chords announcing great downward glissandi of overdubbed sounds leading into the swooning vocal choruses. His dreamy 'Remember A Day' was a leftover from a 1967 recording session with Barrett and features the latter's unpredictable slide guitar.

The big step forward was the twelve-minute title track, a staking out of new territory. As 'Interstellar Overdrive' had seen their blues–rock jams turned into something that – initially rather creakily – ventured into free improvisation, and so relied more on texture and timbre, on 'A Saucerful Of Secrets' they looked more at structure.

Pink Floyd's love of outré sounds was helped in no small way by Rick Wright's admiration of the iconoclastic German composer Karlheinz Stockhausen and Waters had come up with the idea of organising the composition via a graphic score, a compositional device first used by avant-garde composers in the early to mid 20th century – and of course handy if you couldn't write music.

A meditative opening section, structured around Waters' slowly probing bass figures, with plucked piano strings, and hovering organ and Mellotron, suddenly dissolves into a middle section. This section is anchored by Mason's ominous two-bar rotating drum pattern, with outbursts of the "space age" sounds the group had developed live, like echoed slide guitar and organ, along with Waters' crashing cymbals and Wright's fractured piano lines. The closing section is a hymnal organ theme with choral vocals, and Gilmour's slide guitar spiralling skywards.

Waters' 'Corporal Clegg' exemplifies the long shadow that World War Two still cast and the younger generation's desire to escape from it. It's a rather silly satirical song, with Waters telling us that the titular serviceman won a *"wooden leg"* in 1944, although nuance was added by the fact that Waters' own father, Eric, died in service that year, a theme that would recur much more seriously in his work later on.

The album closes with a recording made in October 1967 of Syd Barrett's 'Jugband Blues', which had already been aired on a BBC Radio 1 session. Although it's a bit pat to assume that a song's lyrics are necessarily about the writer, in it Barrett proclaims his own absence and questions his own identity. After the mid-section, which finds a Salvation Army brass band playing a jaunty tune accompanied by kazoo and Barrett's syllabic ululations, it veers into a grotesque section of free-form brass playing and guitar feedback, and concludes with Barrett solo, strumming a lyrically unfathomable coda. Unbeknown to him when recording, it would be a fittingly enigmatic full stop to his time with the group.

In early July 1968, shortly after the album was released, DJ John Peel, a champion of Pink Floyd, played the group's first post-Barrett session on his Radio 1 show *Top Gear*, opining that: "It's ever so nice that the Pink Floyd have got things together again." He claimed that "that thing they did in the park" (the recent Hyde Park Free Concert) was still spinning around in his head. This was delivered with a rather studied vagueness, which put him once removed from the grinning forced jollity of his Radio 1 peers. On their version of 'A Saucerful Of Secrets', retitled for the session as 'The Massed Gadgets Of Hercules', he gently enthused: "Now that is the sort of music that there should be coming out of churches and things."

Pink Floyd were one of the few groups to develop the sonic potential of psychedelia and move it on into the Seventies. They released a few singles with a lingering Barrett influence: 'Let There Be More Light', Rick Wright's charmingly gauche 'It Would Be So Nice' and Waters' and Gilmour's 'Point Me At The Sky', but soon realised that their strengths lay elsewhere.

"By the time we'd done *Saucer* we realised that we couldn't write singles and our interest switched much more to long tracks and more elaborate pieces," Nick Mason told Tony Stewart of *New Musical Express*. "I think the most important thing was the move towards concert appearances, of taking the whole evening and creating some sort of awareness. It's much better to take a concert hall, get the audience comfortable and, hopefully, the sound system right, and do it all properly with nothing to break the mood."

Although *A Saucerful Of Secrets* had breached the Top 10, EMI were unconvinced that this more exploratory approach would have legs and were applying pressure for Pink Floyd to come up with something more conventional.

Unusually for such a young group, they had already made music for John Latham, an experimental British film director, in 1967, as well as appearing in *Tonite Let's All Make Love In London*, a film by Peter Whitehead about the psychedelic scene of Swinging London that was released in 1968. In that year they also provided soundtrack material for Peter Sykes' noir film *The Committee*.

In April 1969, Chris Welch was more impressed by the group's show at the Royal Festival Hall in his *Melody Maker* review. The concert was billed as 'The Massed Gadgets of Auximines – More Furious Madness From Pink Floyd'.

"Two pieces were performed, 'The Man' and 'The Journey'. Burbling bird calls twittered overhead depicting daybreak, a mood broken by the group hammering and sawing up amplified logs, symbolising the day's work, followed by sleep, nightmares and a return to daybreak.

"In the second piece, the Floyd took us on a journey through a pink jungle to the temples of light, beset by creatures of the deep. A creature made a guest appearance among the audience at one point, but failed to arouse any terror in the heart of the sophisticated Floydians.

"A stream of events held our attention. In parts the pace flagged and it seemed the machines were in danger of playing the group."

These two pieces were never recorded in their entirety and, with hindsight, they come across as if the group had felt some obligation to make a conceptual narrative.

On June 26 the group played 'The Man' and 'The Journey' at the Royal Albert Hall featuring the Ealing Central Amateur Choir conducted by the group's producer, Norman Smith, on the finale of 'A Saucerful Of Secrets', reworked as part of 'The Journey'.

Back in February, Pink Floyd had been commissioned by Franco-Swiss director Barbet Schroeder to provide some music for his film *More*, a story about an inexorable descent into hard drugs, with a smattering of sex, played out on the island of Ibiza.

The soundtrack was put together with some haste and was a mixture of band instrumentals like 'Main Theme' and the eerie, abstract atmospherics of 'Quicksilver', and a batch of Waters songs like 'Cymbaline', which had been part of the 'Nightmare' section of 'The Journey'.

One song in particular encapsulated the essence of Pink Floyd in these early years, 'Cirrus Minor'. Lyrically, the group hadn't reached Barrett's standard of writing, but were exploring their instrumental palette. The song is introduced by a recording of birdsong, then over an acoustic strum and tremulous keyboards we are transported into an idyllic, characteristically English scene, lazing in a riverside churchyard in the haze of a warm summer's day. A weeping willow is waving to a *"river daughter"*, a character out of *Lord Of The Rings*, and then lyrically it changes to a journey to Cirrus Minor, a conflagration of a cloud formation and a star in an unknown constellation. The song then ascends, via Wright's organ chords, into a radiant refrain, with echoed single notes twinkling in the firmament above the main song, yet still umbilically connected to that pastoral scene.

The idea of escaping to space via music had been most famously put forward by Herman Blount, aka Sun Ra. He was born in Birmingham, Alabama, in 1914 and was a respected pianist working in jazz groups from the Thirties, in an age when racial discrimination was rife. But after an early vision of astral travel and communication with alien beings on Saturn, he disowned his birthplace and decided that the ringed planet was his real home. He was an Afro Futurist, envisaging that black people could achieve a symbolic freedom from the strictures of a white-dominated society through the metaphor of space exploration.

Pink Floyd's early yearning for space was nowhere near as radical, but thrived on those glimpses of otherness in the suburban everyday when everything suddenly seems illuminated and completely real, and they linked this expansion of consciousness with space. As well as the overt space references, there was also structural space in the group's music, which in itself evoked a wider space beyond the physical bounds of each piece.

Pink Floyd were also being accepted as the group who could provide hip music for TV arts programmes hosted by men wearing neckerchiefs, and produced some improvised music to accompany BBC coverage of the Apollo 11 moon landing in July 1969.

More charted in the UK at number nine. And although the record company would have been perturbed if they had known what the group had planned to deliver next, clearly what they were doing was selling.

With musical horizons widening by the month, Floyd fans were hoping for some far out sounds to follow *More* and they certainly got that with *Ummagumma*. The group have always admitted that technically speaking, they weren't great musicians, but in a way that was to their advantage, as without the technique needed to show off – as was the wont of many of their peers – they instead concentrated on the sound in total.

On a personal note, if I had not gone round to a school friend's house in Norwich aged 13 and been subjected to *Ummagumma*, I might be sitting comfortably now as, say, a town planner or a landscape architect, both of which were considered career options, rather than writing this. I was brought up on classical music, and by that age enjoyed pop music like T. Rex and The Beach Boys. I had also bought an LP by Herb Alpert, much to the derision of my friends, so let's just say that my musical taste was in its formative stage.

Before even realising what 'hip' was, my senses were sent on a dizzying fast track when my friend and I explored the record collection of his older brother by six years. It had the effect of, in the vernacular, blowing my mind. While playing snooker on a miniature table with my friend Mike and others, he put on side three of *Ummagumma*. We had listened to *Electric Ladyland*, *In The Court Of The Crimson King*, *The Man Who Sold The World*, Doctor Strangely Strange's *Heavy Petting* and *McDonald And Giles*, but this was something else entirely.

The extraordinary cover, one of the most evocative by design group Hipgnosis, was enough to get any young mind racing. It showed the group members portrayed in a middle-class lounge with the French doors open, looking out onto a garden, with the picture on the lounge wall showing a similar photo but with a different configuration of group members and the picture on that wall a different one still – the Droste effect – which visually regresses three times to the cover artwork of *A Saucerful Of Secrets*.

I was deliciously disturbed by the looming Mellotron opening to Rick Wright's 'Sysyphus', with its subsequent rhapsodic piano that gradually fractures into avant racket and the weird, shadowy, proto-ambient interludes before the eruption of multi-tracked noise that ushers in a re-introduction of the Mellotron theme in Part Four, which by that point was something of a relief, a way of getting my bearings. I also loved Roger Waters' 'Grantchester Meadows', a haunting acoustic track – again with birdsong – and an evocation of the sublime in a Wordsworthian way, with the author evoking the distilled memory of that halcyon time, back in his *"city room"*. It concludes with a recording of a person walking down wooden steps and running across a wooden floor to swat a fly.

The studio album of *Ummagumma* was conceived as half a side per group member. With hindsight it feels like self-indulgence run amok, but such is the way that new ideas can be born. Nick Mason's 'The Grand Vizier's Garden Party', has a certain charm with a double tracked flute intro and outro played by his wife, Lindy. The main section, 'Entertainment', is a manipulated and edited sequence of pedal tympani, snare and cymbals; a deconstruction of a drum solo.

Dave Gilmour's 'The Narrow Way' takes the song that was part of 'The Journey' and adds a breezy acoustic opening – which the group had recorded for a *Top Gear* session as 'Baby Blue Shuffle In D Minor' – and a grumbling, riffy mid section, both of which are accompanied by a plethora of echoed, looped and otherwise effected guitar and vocals. On the final song section, Gilmour, who had been uncomfortable in having to compose his bit, decided to go the whole hog and played drums himself. He starts well enough, but ends up dragging along like Mason under heavy sedation.

The live album, loved even more by my schoolboy self, sounds just as good today and is the commercially released apogee of Pink Floyd's space rock journey. The sound quality might be just a little hazy, but that adds to the mystery and distance of the four tracks.

'Astronomy Domine' eclipses the original on *Piper...* in terms of dynamics and the highlight of the song is a section where Wright's reedy Farfisa organ is left beautifully alone, fed through an echo unit, transmitting mysteriously through space, before the group rejoin. 'Careful With That Axe, Eugene' had been 'The Murderotic Woman', another part of 'The Journey', and Waters' two-note bass riff ushers in a languid, spacey 4/4 rhythm, before his spectacular screams up the intensity.

Gongs and cymbals usher in 'Set The Controls For The Heart Of The Sun' and live, the song is transformed into a soundtrack for a cosmic hashish ritual. 'A Saucerful Of Secrets' is also far darker and stranger than the studio version. I managed to get a tape recording of the album on my old reel-to-reel and played it obsessively: in my bedroom, in the garage when mending my bike, even out in the garden if the weather was good. Each time it felt like I was visiting a world of the utmost strangeness and beauty.

Some journalists were excited to see that the group were moving at speed into unknown territory. *Ummagumma* was released in October 1969 and a review in the UK's *Record Mirror* claimed it to be "a truly great progressive album. They mix psychedelic and classical patterns, and explore sounds, music, and gimmicks to their fullest extent. The recordings are beautiful."

John Peel, also a music journalist, had penned a review of the Mothers concert as "sounding like dying galaxies lost in sheer corridors of time and space". All of which sounds quite reasonable to this writer, but won him the dubious honour of inclusion in the Pseuds' Corner section of satirical magazine *Private Eye*. The album reached number five in the UK charts.

Waters' composition, 'Several Species Of Small Furry Animals Gathered Together In A Cave And Grooving With A Pict' is a looped incantation accompanied by a cabal of vocals, which are varispeeded into nightmarish "chipmunk" cries and screams. Then, as Waters takes on the guise of the troglodyte pict, he launches into an outburst of impenetrable faux Scottish phonetics. At one point he sighs and pauses, and if any listeners have a record deck that plays at 16rpm, they can enjoy Waters laughing and saying "That was pretty avant-garde wasn't it?" This might not be the most revered song in the Pink Floyd canon, exactly, but it takes us onto his relationship with Ron Geesin.

Born in Ayrshire, Geesin is one of the few musicians who emerged from the Sixties milieu who can be described as unique. He first played in a Dixieland jazz group The Original Downtown Syncopators, which he describes as "an adolescent fling before settling down", except that, artistically speaking, he never did.

He had also once worked in an architect's office and as a solo artist established a precarious balance between the practical and cerebral, and the visceral.

In the mid-Sixties, Geesin experimented with a double reel-to-reel set up to record, loop and layer sounds, with customised arms to help guide the tape. This pre-dated Brian Eno's set-up on which he recorded *Discreet Music*, by a decade at least.

He would make precisely timed electronic music to accompany schools' TV programmes, and compose considered melodic guitar and keyboard pieces, then play his solo performances that he has referred to as "one person erupting", unleashing his inner Dadaist in a kind of one-man variety performance with poems, fierce tracts of gobbledegook and crazed piano and banjo solos that parodied the rather hysterical end of trad jazz.

Geesin was the antithesis of a druggy Sixties artist, disliking the effects of smoking cannabis. Instead his performances were driven by a deep restlessness, a constant questioning both of his own work and its effect on others. His singular shows had won him places on bills with Pink Floyd at venues like Middle Earth – he even played at the 14 Hour Technicolor Dream – and he befriended Nick Mason and Roger Waters in 1968.

Waters' pictish rants on 'Several Species...' are clearly indebted to Geesin, who had also shown Waters some of his tape manipulation techniques. He and Waters became golfing buddies and collaborated on a delightful obscurity of the time, *Music From The Body*, for which recording began in 1970.

Geesin had already made collaborative music for a number of avant-garde films by directors like Steve Dwoskin and so when he agreed to director Roy Battersby's proposal to make the soundtrack for a film on the human body he was further asked if he could write songs. He said: "No but I know a man who does." Waters contributes a number of songs, with Pink Floyd playing on 'Give Birth To A Smile', with a female gospel backing that would appear in a slightly different form in their music later in the story.

Although not actually used in the film, 'Our Song' opens the record in spectacular fashion, with a tape collage of Waters grinding his teeth and doing armpit squeaks; a gurgling baby (Ron's son, Joe); Geesin drumming on his knees, burping and otherwise vocalising; and sonorous farts that he recorded with microphones in the toilet bowl – "stereo panning" as he describes them. Geesin provided a number of more orthodox musical interludes including sombre chamber pieces with cellos and violins, and massed overdubbed voices on 'More Than Seven Dwarfs In Penis Land'. Waters helped with the segueing and the mixing.

"I know that when we were alone in those days, and a lot of that was on a golf course, he was always getting dissatisfied with the Floyd," says Geesin of Waters. "And I said that as an artist he should leave the group environment. He couldn't, but the unrest was there right at the beginning."

ATOM HEART MOTHER
Original label: Harvest
Producer: Pink Floyd/Norman Smith
Recorded: March–August 1970
Release date: October 1970
Chart position: 1 (UK), 55 (US)

In the winter of 1969, Pink Floyd had been offered another soundtrack commission, this time for the new film by Michelangelo Antonioni who had just directed *Blow Up*, the enigmatic mystery set in Swinging London. The new film was *Zabriskie Point*, for which Pink Floyd came up with an album's worth of music from breezy acoustic harmony numbers like 'Crumbling Land' to abstract pieces like 'Oenone'. But while they were enjoying themselves recording, and wining and dining in style in Rome, Antonioni was exceptionally fussy and found a reason for rejecting most of what they offered him, and so only two tracks by the group appear on the soundtrack. The group had also been working on a long piece called 'The Amazing Pudding', sections of which they had played live.

Pink Floyd recorded the piece in March 1970, with Norman Smith producing. Waters and Mason initially played the whole twenty-three-minute rhythm track in one take because EMI had just taken delivery of state-of-the-art eight-track Studer recorders and issued a directive that no edits were to be done on this equipment, as they were worried about the quality of any tape splicing. Mason has often talked about the fluctuations of tempo that this caused, but they lean on the tempo just slightly in places and in a way that most listeners would be hard pressed to even notice.

Pink Floyd realised that the piece, which was then also referred to as 'Epic', needed something extra. They were booked to go on tour to the US in April 1970 and at a concert at the Fillmore West, San Francisco, Waters introduced it *sans* title as being "one side of our new album".

Looking back in 2004, Mason wrote: "Ron seemed the ideal choice to create the arrangements on 'Atom Heart Mother'. He understood the technicalities of composing and arranging, and his ideas were radical enough to steer us away from the increasingly fashionable but extremely ponderous rock orchestral works of the era."

Geesin had also been busy in 1970, embarking on his first major foray into audio-visual work when he provided music for an installation in the British Pavilion at Expo 70 in Osaka and was ready to meet the challenge of working with an established rock group. He notes that the group all looked drained before departing on the tour and remembers having about an hour-long meeting discussing melodic ideas with Gilmour, and with Wright about the choir.

Waters and Mason had said that they wanted something big, but Floyd manager Steve O'Rourke reminded Geesin that he was on a budget so he decided to hire a cellist, a brass ensemble and the John Alldis choir, four each of bass, tenor, contralto and soprano – which rather belies its reputation as an "orchestral" piece. Geesin took a quarter-inch rough mix to the small soundproofed studio he built in the middle floor at his home at 208 Ladbroke Grove to work out the chords and then score the piece.

He is keen to emphasise that he not only arranged, but co-composed the piece and is credited as such – he is also keen to point out that this was done "with the absolute minimum of creative suggestions from them". Get anyone who knows the piece to hum a melody and they would almost certainly give you Geesin's main brass and choral themes; or the second theme, the cello line over keyboard and bass arpeggios, which acts as a kind of surrogate lead vocal.

Geesin recalls working on the album during the hot summer of 1970 "stripped to my underpants" in his home studio bringing out the melodies in the piece.

Whereas the tape that Geesin used had an intro with gong-like cymbals, and in the live versions Mason played a few bars of quavers on the tom-toms as a cue for the group to begin the main theme, Geesin then wrote an inspired brass prelude, with a snatch of the main theme followed by a spiky, Stravinsky-esque passage, and then a descending two-note swoop to cue in the group.

"I only used wherever possible the best classical brass players," says Geesin. "[In the intro] there's not a lot of notes but they have got to be played bang on. The timing is one of the problems. And so anyone who is less than shit hot could fluff it slightly. It's meant to give the impression of something breaking out and stuttering into life."

But EMI were keen to keep what they could in-house and so the EMI Pops Orchestra was drafted in. I've always wondered why the kids who did music at school were rarely the hip ones, but more likely to be the nerdy, uncool ones, with the worst haircuts. One imagines that the nerdiest of these brass players had trickled down to find their places in the brass section of the EMI Pops Orchestra.

The introduction to the piece caused more problems than Geesin had been expecting, and when he was conducting at the recording sessions at Abbey Road studios in August, he received some rather childish and sarcastic comments from the players, that they didn't understand what he was wanting from them. Geesin had to be physically restrained from hitting one of the musicians.

"That was uncomfortable and I was exhausted from doing the work," he admits. "I obviously cared a lot about it and I cracked up. I had to hand over to the choirmaster fellow [John Alldis], who just happened to have dropped in and who conducted the rest of the sessions. But because he was a classical man, he didn't know about pushing the beat, or hot rhythm, playing just ahead of the beat, and so it's a bit spongy. If I had more experience at the time and got the brass players to give it out, it would be a little edgier, tighter."

The John Alldis choir then came in to overdub their parts on two separate sessions. In Geesin's opinion some of the repeats in the score were rather superfluous, so he was keen that the choir and brass added different melody lines as the piece progressed. During the first choir section, which is based on two organ chords, the choristers sing wordless melodic lines. But the 'Funky Dung' section in which Gilmour solos expansively – and where the rhythm section is as stodgy and un-funky as you can get – develops into long looming horn lines and the choir singing Geesin's "international phonetics", like an absurdist Esperanto, which give the section a considerable lift.

In among the choir and main horn themes, which have a feel of a panoramic Western movie soundtrack, 'Mind Your Throats Please' oscillates between discordant chords on the Mellotron with a *musique concrète* assemblage of sounds. In a droll nod towards the classical idea of recapitulation, snatches of the preceding music are featured in a brief tape collage leading into the main theme and the final section, 'Remergence'.

The cover, again by Hipgnosis, features a photograph by Storm Thorgerson of a Hertfordshire cow and bears no title or group name. The record company was apparently horrified, but played along to the extent that publicity shots were arranged of a herd of cows on the Mall in London at dawn. The title came from a news story of a woman with a plutonium-powered pacemaker.

The cover – the black-and-white inside gatefold pictured the herd grazing – helped establish a thematic link to the rather patchy side two, again that of pastoralia and post-psychedelia. Waters explores insanity on 'If' with a kind of neo-folk song construction. Rick Wright's 'Summer '68' – originally titled 'One Night Stand' – is rarely given more than a half-hearted dismissal, but is one of the group's best early songs. On it Wright muses that he would rather be lying in the sun with his friends than touring and waking up with a different woman in his bed every night. It's hard to muster up a great deal of sympathy with Wright's plight, but it was obviously causing him some spiritual bother. The song's mix of summery acoustic guitar and lovely piano playing weaves an atmosphere of dislocation and nostalgia with sumptuous Brian Wilson-esque harmony vocal arrangements. There are also three dramatic instrumental choruses featuring the EMI Pops brass players.

Gilmour's 'Fat Old Sun' evokes the warm glow of a summer evening in the country, the smell of ripening grain, and church bells. Gilmour plays most of the instruments and as on 'The Narrow Way', he writes his vocal lines punishingly high and so the vocal performance sounds rather strained.

'Alan's Psychedelic Breakfast' derives from the 'Tea Time' idea from 'The Man' and this time it involves recordings of kitchen sounds, starting with a dripping tap and Pink Floyd roadie Alan Styles running through his preferred breakfast menu – edited together by Waters and Mason – before the group are cued, by striking matches, into three largely acoustic instrumental sections. It was clearly filler, but good quality filler. *Atom Heart Mother* reached number one in the UK album charts.

The album has stood the test of time, with side one an inspired collaboration and one of the group's most enduring achievements. Mason had his wish that it should sound like nothing else at the time, and it was more radical than ponderous.

In time Pink Floyd became critical or even disparaging about the album, which rather upset Geesin. Mason told him that the group decided that it didn't represent an artistic direction that they would pursue in future and so they "played it down". One can surmise there was also a certain amount of professional jealousy to do with Geesin's involvement.

Pink Floyd played a number of live appearances with the choir and the more sympathetic Philip Jones Brass Ensemble – although on the evidence of live recordings, the intro always caused problems.

They headlined the second night of the Bath Festival Of Blues & Progressive Music on June 27. Their late-night set included 'Atom Heart Mother', which is introduced to the audience under the title of 'The Amazing Pudding'. The group was augmented by The John Aldiss Choir and The Philip Jones Brass Ensemble. One of the brass players later recalled accidentally spilling a pint of beer into his tuba before the concert began, which necessitated a rather more comprehensive emptying out of the instrument than usual during a break in the performance.

On July 18, Geesin left the Hyde Park concert in tears, unhappy at the way the music had been performed. There were to be no further collaborations between the two parties. Geesin noted that Waters was beginning a process of shedding friends and in the end found him "impossible to deal with". Geesin did, however, record a bizarre valedictory piece, 'To Roger Waters Wherever You Are', on his 1973 album *As He Stands*, which features Geesin trying to light a fire in a high wind and declaiming in the "pict" voice to a barrage of electronics, all of which still stands as a rather defiant aural exclamation-cum-question mark.

Pink Floyd's next album, the self-produced *Meddle*, was recorded at Abbey Road throughout 1971 in between tours and is similar in structure to *Atom Heart Mother* in that it has some shorter songs on one side and another side-long epic, this time 'Echoes'.

The opening piece 'One Of These Days', is a prime example of Pink Floyd making their lack of virtuosity work for them. It features both Waters and Gilmour playing the juddering, relentless bass line – much of it on one note – but with the difference in timbre and inflection of the up and down plectrum strokes accentuated by the instruments going through a Binson Echorec echo unit, which makes it sound more complex than it actually is. The drums knock on the door before their full entry and then Gilmour plays long overdriven slide lines that remind us that he wasn't just the best musician in the band, but one of the best guitarists of his generation – although nowhere near as fast or fiddly as some of his peers, he could really make the instrument sing.

The rest of the first side is a mixed bag of songs; the whole of side two, however, is Pink Floyd in excelsis, the last gasp of their psychedelic phase. 'Echoes' was premiered as 'The Return Of The Son Of Nothing' at the Norwich Lads Club in April 1971, albeit with different lyrics. The title is no great existential statement but instead derives from the fact that it was assembled from instrumental sections, all of which were numbered parts of a work-in-progress called 'Nothing'. 'Echoes' begins with single electric piano notes fed through a Leslie speaker to give an asdic-like "ping", before morphing into a typical Floyd slow groove with harmony vocals and an instrumental hook, a figure that rises and then descends on five notes.

There's a two-note "funky" section – well, funkier than 'Funky Dung' on *Atom Heart Mother*, anyway. But its stiff, locked groove bass pattern, with Mason playing an unchanging basic rhythm is its strength, as it creates a mounting tension, which is alleviated in part by Wright's decorative R&B-style flourishes on Hammond organ and then blown open by Gilmour's searing guitar outbursts.

The abstract section finds the "bird noise", that Gilmour achieved from mis-connecting his wah-wah pedal and had already used on other numbers onstage, crying out across a drift of keyboards and Waters rubbing his bass strings with a slide while going through an echo unit, and taped sounds of wind and cawing corvids, just in case we hadn't got the message. The section that follows is one of the most beautiful Pink Floyd achieved, a kind of luminous organ drone around four chords slowly filled in with more detail with Waters playing the juggernaut 'One Of These Days' riff in a four-note pattern and Mason freestyling around the cymbals and toms. Gilmour joins in with a glorious picking section before the dramatic descent into the final verse and a long fade out with more of Wright's asdic pings and upward-arcing glissandi of electronics, mixed in with Wright and Gilmour's falsetto vocals. 'Echoes' just avoids the sagging effect of extended length, but the results are spectacular.

Tony Stewart of *New Musical Express* quizzed Mason as to whether the way 'Echoes' was put together led on from the similarly lengthy 'Atom Heart Mother'.

"You're obviously right about the construction," Mason replied. "There are various things that have a Pink Floyd flavour, but are also very dangerous Pink Floyd clichés. One is the possible tendency to get stuck into a sort of slow four tempo. And the other thing is to take a melody line or the chorus or something and flog it to death."

In the last line he refers to some of the repeats in *Atom Heart Mother*. But in terms of the tempo, seldom, if ever, has a musician so clearly identified warning signs in his own music and so manifestly failed to heed them.

Nowadays it's not unusual to go to a concert and, within hours, access a reasonably well shot and recorded video of proceedings on YouTube. But back in the day, punters would be searched and if you were foolish enough to be caught smuggling a recording device in to see Led Zeppelin, for example, you would almost certainly be dealt with on the spot in a way that circumvented legal process.

In the early Seventies Pink Floyd's best work was made in live performances, which appeared on bootleg LPs, illicit pressings that could notch up big sales from which the group received no royalties. They were prized items and if you wanted one, you had to be prepared to search, and fork out more than you would on an official LP.

Pink Floyd were one of the most bootlegged groups of the time because they habitually road tested new material to audiences. And live the group was almost always more improvisatory, more powerful, less foursquare and more adventurous than on record. Mason, especially, sounds less stilted when playing onstage.

'Embryo' was a live staple around this time and was unreleased except for a hushed, low-key demo version that crept out on the 1970 Harvest Records sampler, *Picnic – A Breath Of Fresh Air*. In concert it became a ten-minute tour de force with a middle section of backing tapes of crying babies. The group were not afraid to be rather literal with their choice of extra-musical sounds.

At one show in Cincinnati in 1971, the group played a twenty-nine-minute version of the song with some questing improvisation, and spectacular and rather relentless exploratory guitar from Gilmour. In concert Pink Floyd produced a huge, enveloping sound.

For armchair explorers of inner space the 1972 film *Pink Floyd: Live At Pompeii* is an audiovisual document of the group at their best and is, basically, a live set played to no audience in a ruined amphitheatre.

Pink Floyd had shown themselves as prolific and were now well beyond the point of worrying about having to queue up at the Labour Exchange on a Monday. From late 1971 they were working on an ambitious new project for which they had already written the majority of the material, called *Eclipse* or *The Dark Side Of The Moon* – the uncertainty resulting from Medicine Head's 1972 album *Dark Side Of The Moon*.

It was kept on the back burner as a work-in-progress as the group had been commissioned to produce yet another film soundtrack, this time for *La Vallée*, again directed by Barbet Schroder, in which some white travellers find a sort of modern-day Shangri La in a valley in Papua New Guinea, a place "obscured by clouds".

The music for the soundtrack album *Obscured By Clouds* was recorded between February and March 1972. It's often cited as a precursor to their change of style on *The Dark Side Of The Moon*, but it was actually written after an early version of that album had been performed live. But to fans at the time it saw Pink Floyd effectively honing down their songwriting and playing, with only 'Absolutely Curtains' approaching the impressionistic. One music paper headline proclaimed "Floyd Joy For All", which largely summed up the album's serene and sunny mood, although on the grimly jocular 'Free Four', Waters addresses the rigours of touring in America, the inevitability of aging and the death of his father in World War Two. The song was released in the US as a single but failed to chart, although the album reached number forty-six in the US, their highest chart placing thus far.

By 1972, via their own mazy route, Pink Floyd had become both commercially and artistically successful. It's so easy with hindsight to think that such success must have been somehow planned, but Mason had this to say on the matter: "We had absolutely no policy whatsoever and we don't really have one now… But in the early days we had very little idea of what we were doing, or really how to do it."

But with *The Dark Side Of The Moon*, Waters was keen to establish a framework that had specific meaning. In group meetings they ran through some ideas, all of which were far from joyous.

Mason: "The various pressures that we talked about when we wrote it were physical violence, travelling, money, religion. Those were the things which we thought sidetracked people from things we thought might be important. And religion for us is one of those things. I mean, not religion as much as Christianity as practised by a large section of the population of Britain."

This was another big project, twice as long as the 'Atom Heart Mother' suite or 'Echoes'. And while Pink Floyd's lyrics had – in common with the majority of rock lyrics – often been poetically effective without really meaning anything in particular, on *The Dark Side Of The Moon*, their meaning is unequivocal.

Speaking to Chris Charlesworth of *Melody Maker*, Rick Wright said: "We always like to write numbers, go on the road with them and record them later. We did this with *Dark Side Of The Moon* and we think it's easily the best way to go about it."

The downside of this tack was that bootleggers had a field day with *The Best Of Tour 72*, which was recorded at the Rainbow Theatre, London on February 20, 1972. Released thirteen months before the official release of *The Dark Side Of The Moon*, the recording of its live prototype sold 120,000 copies.

The set starts with 'Breathe', which compared to the later studio version has an extra instrumental verse. Then, instead of the high-velocity synthesizer-based rush-hour-in-sound of 'On The Run', there is a six-minute instrumental, 'The Travel Sequence', with choppy rhythm guitar from Gilmour and some animated drumming by Mason. 'Time' comes without the introductory explosion of chimes on the album, but utilises the metronomic tick-tock backing tape of the original. It gets a bit draggy until Gilmour's guitar solo, which sounds like it was delivered at massive volume, with the rhythm section playing in a more loose-limbed manner than on the record.

In the place of 'The Great Gig In The Sky' is 'The Mortality Sequence', a piece that starts and ends with ecclesiastical organ and a tape collage of voices, some incomprehensible and groaning, some loosely based on religious rituals, with a brief appearance of Malcolm Muggeridge, a religious thinker and TV broadcaster on programmes like *The Question Why*.

'Money' starts with Waters and Mason's cash till loop, before Waters' 7/4 bass line ushers in the group. Where Dick Parry plays a sax solo on the album version, Wright plays a rather average solo of keyboard noodling before Gilmour's elongated solo. More of the groaning voices follow as Wright's organ chords introduce 'Us And Them'. This is one of the pieces left over from the *Zabriskie Point* recording sessions known as 'The Violent Sequence'. Unfortunately there is a tape cut after the first verse into halfway through the last chorus. The perils of buying bootleg albums.

The instrumental composition, 'Any Colour You Like' has a similar structure to the studio recording, although the playing is looser and livelier. Rick Wright described the track as: "Just improvisations but various parts are very arranged... almost like a score." It cuts into a few bars of 'Breathe' before leading into 'Brain Damage' with tapes of the voices from 'The Mortality Sequence'. 'Eclipse' had yet to be written.

The backing tapes and some of the looser moments still connect with the group's past, but overall *The Dark Side Of The Moon* was going somewhere different. Most of the changes made to this initial version worked to the advantage of the piece, and the idea of asking the group's friends and associates to be interviewed on tape yielded some memorable results, which were deployed throughout the album in an inspired way. They were a kind of commentary on the songs, the most effective being an unidentified man who casually informs the listener that he is not frightened of dying on 'The Great Gig In The Sky', before Claire Torry's gospel-derived wordless vocal bloodletting over Rick Wright's stately piano lines.

The album was released in March 1973 and the first pressings included two posters and two stickers. Gilmour referred to it as a "good package". Thematically it feels like the personal concerns and introspective contemplation of the early Seventies wave of singer-songwriters taken and writ large. There is a great sadness in *The Dark Side Of The Moon* born out of fear: fear of being left behind, fear of insanity, fear of wasting time, fear of opportunities slipping away, fear of death. Waters sings, on 'Time', about how the English way is to hang on in *"quiet desperation"*, as if all the whimsical dreams of psychedelia and hippiedom had evaporated into the Seventies, with nothing substantial to take their place. A popular poster that adorned many a teenage Head's bedroom wall at the time proclaimed: *"Today is the first day of the rest of your life."* In Waters' view, as expressed on 'Time', each new day is simply taking us all one day closer to death. It really was a bummer.

Many critics – and Waters himself – have criticised the lyrics as being basically sixth form poetry, but that's doing them a disservice. They *are* clunky at times, particularly when he looks at poverty and class divisions on 'Us And Them', and links them to the slaughter of working class soldiers in the war.

But there's poignancy, too. Waters sings in the near hymnal closer, 'Eclipse', that everything we try to do is a necessary distraction from the fact that that our fate is ultimately out of our hands. And although everything may be apparently in tune under the sun, there is the ever-present chance of an eclipse by the moon, with its unseen, occult dark side holding a particular threat.

But 'Brain Damage' is the key song, with Waters stating to the listener, with a defiant shrug, that if this catastrophe does happen, there's no reason that he will be spared just because he is a rock star, and so he'll see us all on the other side, even if that happens to be on the dark side of the moon.

'Money' has also been derided by some, but its lyrics are very droll. It was released before Pink Floyd had hit the really big league and, as Waters was an avowed socialist, it was a critique of rock star excess, but the way it was pitched suggests that a part of him would have rather liked a piece of the action himself.

There was a certain coolness about *The Dark Side Of The Moon* and a typical slow 4/4 grandeur that Mason had been keen to avoid as a potential cliché, but from *Atom Heart Mother* onwards it was a feature of almost every track that he and Waters played on. Certainly by the end of side two, this kind of uni-pace begins to feel like a trudge.

Despite its prevailing mood of pessimistic gloom, the album somehow both tapped into the zeitgeist and stood the test of time as it remained in the *Billboard* Top 100 for a staggering 14 years, and has become one of the best-selling albums of all time. The group were not expecting anything of the sort and even now it's hard to understand the extent of its appeal.

It got to the point where it was so ubiquitous that one almost felt an obligation to buy the damn thing, and with the growth of listeners who had good-quality hi-fi systems came the stereotypical buyer who would get a copy "because it sounds good on my stereo". It most certainly did as it was beautifully produced by the group, with Chris Thomas helping with the mix, with both a heft and a spaciousness to the group's sound. But there were sniggers in the music press at the thought of Pink Floyd appealing to such a lowest common denominator audience, as if it was some kind of miserablist stereo demonstration record.

But as soon as the recording was finished and before anyone but the bootleg buyers had heard this new piece, Pink Floyd added working with dance to their CV in a collaboration with the Roland Petit's Ballets De Marseille. Although the group had just recorded a concept album, their ambition was trumped by Petit's idea of doing a choreographed production featuring all new music based on Marcel Proust's *À La Recherche Du Temps Perdu*. Each group member struggled with the book and instead they ended up using tracks from *Meddle*, *Obscured By Clouds* and 'Careful With That Axe, Eugene' for performances at Paris in

February. But it was the group's last commission to collaborate with artists in other media, something that had hallmarked their early years.

With *The Dark Side Of The Moon* selling in unprecedented quantities worldwide, reaching number two in the UK and number one in the US, the group felt trapped by the album's success and were unsure what to do next.

Mason had this to say back in 1972: "It's very difficult to find the right way of working anyway. We don't know whether to give ourselves lots and lots of free time or to put on a lot of pressure, specifically for new material."

Speaking to Chris Charlesworth in 1974, Rick Wright looked back on the period immediately after the album. "We have made a lot of new fans as a result because it was the first time we ever had an AM airplay in America. 'Money' was played on AM radio and for a lot of people it was the first time they'd heard us.

"I like to think this hasn't put a pressure on us in terms of what we write next, but for a whole year we never did anything. We all sat around and got heavily into our reasons for being and our group. We got into a bad period when we didn't do anything at all creatively."

This was the first time that one of the progressive rock groups had grown to the extent that they were effectively ground to a halt by their own success. Pink Floyd were struggling with the psychological burden of topping their big artistic statement and were under pressure now as a major cash cow to tour more, record more and make more money.

This prompted a twenty-day sojourn at Abbey Road Studios in October 1973 to work on the aborted *Household Objects* project for which, looking back to their earlier avant-garde ways for inspiration, they attempted to make music from everyday items like wine glasses and elastic bands.

"Group momentum was pretty well non-existent. The early days of total commitment were beginning to dissipate," Mason wrote in 2004, also admitting that the group had been on the verge of "calling it a day".

The group members all enjoyed themselves in various leisure activities outside of Pink Floyd, but for their autumn 1974 UK tour, Mason notes that Gilmour, a keen squash player and Waters, still a keen golfer, were booking in at hotels with close access to such facilities. Although not crimes in themselves, these apparent priorities indicated a lack of focus.

When they played at the Empire Pool, Wembley, gone were Waters' onstage announcements. Gone also were Mason's benevolent ideas of "making the audience comfortable" and "creating some kind of awareness", to be replaced by the appearance of an aloof, remote quartet, who played competently, but with a distinct lack of inspiration. They had come up with three new songs, 'Shine On You Crazy Diamond', 'Raving And Drooling' and 'Gotta Be Crazy' and played *The Dark Side Of The Moon* in its entirety, encoring with 'Echoes'. They were joined onstage by the female vocal trio, The Blackberries.

Back in 1970 American rock critic Lester Bangs, with typical perspicacity, wrote that even then there was a widening divide between the audience and rock stars who were showing signs of entitlement and arrogance. He made a list of these musicians who he felt warranted a comedy pie slapped full in the face to bring them back down to the level of their fans. Adding: "Most rock stars have their audience so cowed, it's nauseating." It would be unfair to say that Pink Floyd or their fans were in that category, but something had clearly got out of synch with their performance, which taking away the lights, the back-projected animations and the crashing model aircraft they had used at some venues, was lacklustre.

The particularly English musical experiments and explorations that had hallmarked their earlier days had seen them regarded as paragons of integrity, the good old Floyd, a kind of post-psychedelic royalty. But that was all now in jeopardy.

New Musical Express journalist Nick Kent wrote an infamously scathing review of the Empire Pool concert, bemoaning the group's lack of inspiration and deeming them "incredibly limited as musicians". He went on to say: "As a rhythm section, Mason and Waters are perhaps the dullest I've ever witnessed filling a large auditorium, the former going through his tedious tricks most of the time, and falling apart at those unscripted junctures when the band are forced to involve themselves at attempts at spontaneity.

"Wright is merely an adequate keyboard player, and always seems uncomfortable when forced to take action. Finally there's Gilmour – who, although an adequate guitarist, projects little personality in his playing.

"The above constituted what could easily be the most boring concert I've ever been forced to sit through for review purposes."

Kent also wrote that Dave Gilmour's hair "looked filthy there on stage, seemingly anchored down by a surfeit of scalp grease". "Waters and Gilmour were very pissed off," says Kent. "I've apologised to Gilmour. Rick Wright came up to me at a party a year after that review came out and thanked me for writing the stuff that I did. He said, 'Listen, I don't agree with you, but that review forced us to sit down and actually talk about our problems as a group in a way that we wouldn't have done if we'd just got more, like, 'how-wonderful-you-are' reviews."

These included a rather florid rave review of the concert by *The Times* critic Derek Jewell. But journalists get carried away at both ends of the critical spectrum and surely it was up to the group to give performances that could merit that sort of praise, rather than resenting it if they had not played well.

All the punters were given free concert programmes, which included the lyrics to the new songs and Kent took exception to the sentiments expressed in 'Gotta Be Crazy': that Waters had to keep the audience *"buying this shit"*.

The huge number of fans who had purchased Pink Floyd's albums and concert tickets ultimately helped vindicate the group's existence. The darlings of the 1967 underground had become big commercial stars and the yobbos who had thrown glasses and poured beer over them had been replaced by crowds of true believers, who, like irritating dogs, loved their masters unconditionally.

This might seem to be a lot to pin on a line in a programme of a particular song lyric that was excised from its ultimate recorded form – 'Dogs' on their 1977 album *Animals* – but this kind of sour, po-faced comment by Waters about his current position felt like a kind of self-loathing that was also aimed at those who actually did keep on buying this shit. Contractual obligations aside, if that was what it had all come to, then the question was surely, why did Waters keep on producing this shit?

To put Waters' griping into perspective, it would have been sweet if a fan had clambered onstage and slapped a pie in his face at the precise moment that he was singing those lyrics.

In a stinging denouement to his review Kent wrote: "The Floyd in fact seem so incredibly tired and seemingly bereft of true creative ideas one wonders if they really care about their music anymore. I mean, one can easily envisage a Floyd concert in the future consisting of the band simply wandering on stage, setting all their tapes into action, putting their instruments on remote control and then walking off behind the amps in order to talk about football or play billiards. I'd almost prefer to see them do that. At least it would be honest."

Pink Floyd, who had been one of the most expansive, dynamic and creative live bands just a few years previously, were once more interrogated about their honesty, but for different reasons to the way Chris Welch had done in 1967, mixed in with a bit of typical soon-the-instruments-will-play-themselves technophobia.

New Musical Express journalist Peter Erskine spoke to David Gilmour about the offending *"buying this shit"* line a few weeks after Kent's in-print mauling.

"Mmm. Yeah. It is possibly a sneer, but not at the audience as a whole, but at the type of adulation bands like us get," said Gilmour. "I mean I think there is something wrong with people needing hero figures like that, thinking that rock musicians have all the answers.

"We've always said that we don't believe in that whole number, but it's very hard to get away from the image people put on you."

Regarding the group's lack of improvisatory flair, Gilmour made it clear that the days of their unfettered onstage explorations had come to a halt and were unlikely to return. To Erskine: "I've just got memories of standing onstage farting about, plonking away on stuff and feeling terribly embarrassed for long periods of time – and looking across at everyone else realising that they were all obviously feeling the same way.

"Maybe guaranteeing that what you play is something that you'll enjoy is 'playing safe'. But I don't think we've got an intentional play-safe policy."

We will return later on to see how the group continued on this tack.

CHAPTER 7

And Did Those Feet…: Ladies and Gentleman – Lemerpal, Aker & Son

'Jerusalem' was composed in 1916 by Hubert Parry as an anthem to be sung in unison in concert, but has become so dear to English hearts it has effectively been elevated to the status of a hymn-cum-unofficial national anthem. The song has been taken up by all manner of groups and institutions from the Suffragettes and the Women's Institute to the Labour Party, as well as being sung at sporting occasions.

Although William Blake's words, written over 100 years prior to being put to music, were a small part of his canon – being the short introduction to one of his allusive, allegorical epics, *Milton* – they are beautifully succinct. Importantly, they avoid the nationalistic fervour of the seldom sung verses of 'Rule, Britannia!' and 'God Save The Queen', where Britain is the dread and envy of the world, scattering by force its knavish foes to all four corners of the globe.

Instead, 'Jerusalem', which refers specifically to England, starts by Blake asking a number of questions. Firstly he inquires if *"those feet in ancient time"* did actually walk upon that country's land? Here Blake is referring to the legend that Jesus Christ and Joseph Of Arimathea journeyed to England, their visit being commemorated by the planting of a holy thorn – which only died in 1991 – in Glastonbury Abbey.

Blake immediately crumples up the timescale, further asking if the Holy Lamb Of God was also seen in the English countryside, among the *"dark satanic mills"* of the industrial revolution, as if their belchings and outpourings that fouled this idyll were coming from vents sunk deep into hell itself. Blake also saw them as metaphors for those with closed and strictly rationalist minds.

Not for nothing was Blake described as a visionary. It's a strange and obscure first verse, seemingly rhetorical, but genuinely posing questions. But it gets its message across: that whether or not the legend of Jesus's visit is correct, or whether or not the Holy Lamb Of God was actually seen is almost immaterial, for once it has been envisioned, it becomes at least possible.

Kaleidoscope in 1967, "an absolutely amazing year to be 21 and making music in London", according to vocalist Peter Daltrey (top right). Dezo Hoffman/Shutterstock

Tomorrow using appropriate transport after releasing their single 'My White Bicycle' in May 1967. Future Yes guitarist Steve Howe is second left. Bill Johnson/ANL/Shutterstock

Fairport Convention in their UFO Club days, 1967, with vocalist Judy Dyble (centre front), who went on to work with Giles, Giles & Fripp. Pictorial Press Ltd/Alamy

Barclay James Harvest seeking out an alternative to the Mellotron, 1968. Pictorial Press Ltd/Alamy

Progressive rock is born: King Crimson deliver their epochal set to the masses at the Hyde Park Concert, July 5, 1969. Mirrorpix

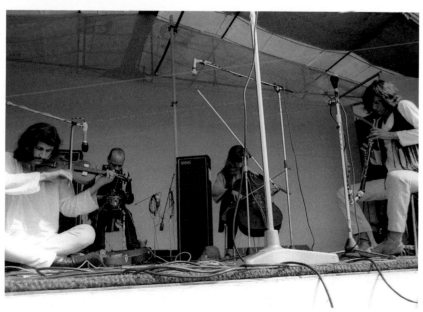

Third Ear Band play their acoustic post-psychedelic ragas at the Isle Of Wight Festival Of Music, August 1969. Ray Stevenson/Shutterstock

A publicity shot of Gracious following the release of their self-titled debut album in 1970.

One of the first and most successful bands to fuse jazz, rock and blues: Colosseum, onstage in 1970. Michael Ochs Archives/Handout/Getty

Jethro Tull in 1970, around the time of their third album, *Benefit*. ZUMA Press, Inc./Alamy

The Moody Blues onstage in 1970, having made the transition from washed-up Sixties pop group to progressive rock "cosmic gurus". Pictorial Press Ltd/Alamy

Soft Machine surveying the venue for their next gig, the Royal Albert Hall, where they became the first "pop" group to play at the Proms on August 13, 1970. Keystone/Stringer/Getty

Centipede's 1971 double album, *Septober Energy*, needed a gatefold sleeve to accommodate a group shot of the 50-piece ensemble, described by founder Keith Tippett as "the most progressive group of the era". NearTheCoast.com/Alamy

The Curved Air line-up that recorded *Second Album* in 1971, which reached number 11 in the UK charts, and the single 'Back Street Luv', which reached number four. Mirrorpix

Arthur Brown's Kingdom Come in 1971. The group had been taking LSD together, but surely no one at Polydor would have suspected. Jorgen Angel/Redferns

John Peel at the annual Reading Festival where he DJ'd throughout the Seventies. Keystone/Getty

This leads to the second verse, full of imagery from the Book Of Revelation. Here Blake writes the lyric in the first person and therefore each singer, by singing it, is making their own proclamation that with their own *"bow of burning gold"*, *"arrows of desire"*, *"chariot of fire"*, and their ceaseless *"mental fight"*, they have both the purity of vision and physical strength to actually build this new Jerusalem here in England's gentle *"green and pleasant land"*.

Blake was not smugly saying that England is great; more that we can make it great, but it's going to take huge reserves of physical and mental strength and will be hard won ground. To hear such powerful spiritual yearning put into verse and sung en masse to the heavenward trajectory of Parry's melody makes the scalp rise, even if some of the singers might not have really considered what it was they are singing about.

The song has been arranged many times depending on the context and the particular musical forces involved. Parry's original arrangement of his own swelling tune is spare, heartfelt, but not showy. Sir Edward Elgar's orchestration, the one that is sung yearly at the Last Night Of The Proms, carries a feeling of Edwardian pomp and grandeur – of which he was a master – but is also coloured with a typically Elgarian deep longing. Then there is the 1973 version by Emerson, Lake & Palmer.

Keith Emerson plays a variation on Elgar's introduction on Hammond organ, then Carl Palmer introduces his new stainless steel drum kit by launching into a thundering two-bar roll across seven tom-toms.

Greg Lake's rich choirmaster's voice calms things down a little, but as the song progresses we get mighty gong crashes, snare drum breaks, more tom-tom bombardment and Emerson adding progressively more ornamentation, including pseudo-baroque trumpet fanfares on his synthesizer.

If Parry's version feels, in its atmosphere, like a graceful, unostentatious parish church and Elgar's is like Westminster Abbey, then ELP's is like a Spanish Catholic monastery church, gaudy and opulent with gold, polished marble in clashing colours, and lavishly carved ebony and stone. But then one can't help thinking that if you're going to storm the gates of heaven, you'd be wise to deploy everything at your disposal.

To those who label the group as vulgarian Visigoths, sacking this national treasure as they have done with so many pieces from the classical repertoire, it's something of an abomination; but to the ardent fan of the group it's an eminent jewel in their crown. As usual, the truth – or in legal parlance, a "reasonable" viewpoint – lies somewhere in between.

Emerson, Lake & Palmer were formed in early 1970. Appropriately for the start of the decade, it was a time of change, with flux in the line-ups of the emerging progressive rock groups, particularly around Emerson and King Crimson guitarist Robert Fripp.

Emerson was still in The Nice, but had met Greg Lake at the Fillmore West in December 1969 where the first incarnation of King Crimson played one of their last shows, as drummer Michael Giles and multi-instrumentalist and principal composer for the group, Ian McDonald, had announced that they were about to leave. Jimi Hendrix had shown an interest in working with Emerson, but it appeared there was no longer room for a guitarist in The Nice, even for him.

Emerson had approached Lake to work with him in The Nice – they certainly could have made use of his vocal abilities – but Lake decided to stay on in King Crimson. In discussions about the future of the group, Robert Fripp had told Lake that he would now be in charge of the musical direction and so Lake decided to leave towards the end of the recording of King Crimson's second LP, *In The Wake Of Poseidon*, in April 1970 and join forces with Emerson and drummer Carl Palmer as Emerson, Lake & Palmer. The musical combination of Emerson, Lake & Palmer then piqued Fripp's interest. He enquired about working with them in some capacity, but nothing came of it. Fripp was also asked to join Yes after guitarist Pete Banks left that year, but he declined.

While in The Nice, Emerson was already known for arranging classical pieces for a rock group, while Lake, the guitarist turned bass guitarist with the commanding voice, had been used to longform compositions with King Crimson. But what about the less well-known twenty-year-old Palmer, who had played with Arthur Brown and, most recently, in the hard rock band Atomic Rooster? It turned out that he had followed The Nice with interest, and this new post was exactly what he had been looking for.

"I come from a classical background," says Palmer. "My grandfather was a professor of music at the Royal Academy; his brother was a classical percussionist; their mother – my great, great grandmother – was a classical guitar player, so I've always been interested in that. One of my first jazz albums was one of the [early Sixties] Jacques Loussier Trio's *Play Bach* series, so having a band that wasn't guitar driven, that was keyboard driven, that was looking at classical adaptations, I always thought was a great way to go."

Emerson, Lake & Palmer's rise was meteoric and they were labelled one of the first supergroups. This was basically journalese for a band of fairly high-profile, proven musicians. But Emerson, Lake & Palmer made it into a lot more than that. If they had not actually been any good or the chemistry hadn't been right then they wouldn't have lasted the initial flush of interest, but the group's flash, dynamic music was soon picking up fans in their legions. Which made it doubly annoying for the naysayers.

For many journalists, being in a blues or a rock'n'roll group was all about "paying your dues", as if the musicians were serving an apprenticeship towards achieving some kind of authenticity. Emerson, Lake & Palmer completely sidestepped all of that. They were also almost brazen in their desire – with a great deal of success, it must be said – to seduce punters by a mix of technical ability and flamboyant stagecraft. Soon a new journalistic genre term – "technoflash" – would be applied to the group, principally in the *New Musical Express*: and it wasn't meant as a compliment. Palmer was all too aware of the view that some had of the group.

"We were kind of born with a golden drumstick in our mouths," he admits. "We were successful from the second concert. We played Plymouth Guildhall, and then the 1970 Isle Of Wight Festival and we were an international success. It went from nothing to something overnight."

Their set at the Isle Of Wight in August 1970 was introduced by the MC Rikki Farr, both tautologically and with notable inaccuracy, as "their first debut performance ever".

A contingent from *Melody Maker*, namely Chris Welch, Michael Watts, Richard Williams and Mike Plummer, went to the festival. The journalist who wrote this section (presumably Welch) is not identified, but one could understand his defensive use of humour, enjoying the show as his colleagues presumably rolled their eyes heavenwards: "Despite the mutterings of the underground press, there were one or two people who enjoyed Emerson, Lake & Palmer's set. There was, for instance, some guy at the back of the crowd, who managed to make his voice sound like several thousand people cheering.

"It's quite likely there are some of the rock fraternity who don't approve of Keith adapting classical themes, displays of virtuosity and a touch of showbiz. They wore bright clothes. They let off two cannons in the penultimate number. The arrangements were long and adventurous. There were no long blues guitar solos. In fact, they were wide open to criticism."

Nothing if not ambitious, during their set the group performed a version of Modest Mussorgsky's *Pictures At An Exhibition*. It had been composed as a piano piece in the 1870s based on paintings by the composer's friend, compatriot Russian artist Viktor Hartmann, but was never orchestrated. Others have had a go, the most performed version being the orchestration by Maurice Ravel. Being unfinished meant it was ripe for interpretation and it soon became finished in the ELP way. At this time the group's debut album had still not been released, so this was quite a statement of intent. They also played a selection of Nice and King Crimson pieces, with their version of Dave Brubeck's 'Blue Rondo A La Turk' renamed 'Rondo'.

Emerson, Lake & Palmer's self-titled debut album arrived on Island Records in late 1970. 'The Barbarian' is a dramatic opener with Lake's fuzz bass introducing Emerson's strident organ theme. It's a taut, high-energy affair with the keyboard player going on to engage in a series of calls and responses with the rhythm section. A piano interlude, urged on by Palmer's speedy brush work, leads back, via a mighty gong crash and fuzz bass, into a restatement of the main theme. The track climaxes with Emerson's repeated staccato five chord sequence spurring on Palmer to finish with a thrilling, hyperspeed snare and cymbals white-out before the final chords.

It was a powerful calling card, and all their own work. Except it wasn't. Although credited to Emerson and Lake, all the musical material was taken from a short, fiery piano piece, *Allegro Barbaro* by Hungarian composer Béla Bartók. The bass guitarist explains the situation.

"Keith came in with this piece of music one day and played it to us and I thought, 'That sounds interesting; very fierce.' When it was done I said, 'Well what do you call it?' and he said 'The Barbarian'. And this sounds awfully naïve but it's true, when it came time to do the credits, they just wrote out who wrote the songs and that was that. Then the record comes out and it was a big hit.

"So one day our managers at the time, a company called EG Management, were in their office and the phone rang. This lady came on the phone and said, 'I believe you may have inadvertently infringed my husband's copyright.' So they said, 'What?' She repeated what she had said, and they said what's your name? And she said, 'Mrs Bartók'. So they said, 'Fuck off,' and put the phone down. It sounded like Mrs Beethoven to them – 'Mrs Handel? Mrs Tchaikovsky? Don't think so'. The next day they get a phone call from [music publisher] Boosey & Hawkes and it was Mrs Béla Bartók [Ditta Pásztory-Bartók, b. 1903]. And she had inherited his copyright.

"Then Keith owned up that he had lifted it from *Allegro Barbaro* and he just didn't bother to tell anybody. Of course we put it right and made sure that she was paid fairly and on all future copies of the record it was properly credited. But in those days, to us, classical composers were dead a long time and it wouldn't really occur to us."

The centrepiece of the first side – which remains one of the most impressive twenty minutes the group recorded – is 'Take A Pebble'. It begins with Lake's ballad-like tune, with Emerson playing sympathetic piano and Palmer on tympani. This leads into a section rather like the drummer's beloved Jacques Loussier and his jazz trio readings of Bach. Here Palmer plays with brushes, and Emerson's left hand sets up something between a Bach ground bass and a boogie-woogie, with a top-line melody that has a frilly, almost Mozartian delicacy.

Lake's acoustic guitar interlude is followed by a looser recapitulation of the "Loussier" theme. The group's three-way chemistry is apparent. Lake has often been damned with rather faint praise as a bass guitarist, but here his rhythmically fluid, melodic and improvisatory playing shows a great deal of flair. The song became a perennial live favourite.

The side closed with 'Knife Edge', again credited to Emerson and Lake, and also roadie Dik Fraser who wrote the lyrics, which depict a romanticised future dystopia very much in the mould of early King Crimson. The song pivots on a three-note motif, which Emerson had also filched, this time from Leoš Janáček's *Sinfonietta*. The Czech composer's estate made moves to sue the group as the piece, composed in 1926, was also still in copyright. Reparations were made.

If 'Take A Pebble', with its Bachisms, and 'Knife Edge', with its appropriated Janáček themes, showed how a rock group could play the classics, it also demonstrated how restricted in choice a group was unless they rearranged the compositions.

Emerson quite skilfully reconfigured the themes of Bartók's *Allegro Barbaro* for rock trio power-play, but most classical music wasn't rhythm driven, and drums – the driving force of a rock band – were generally used for punctuation. 'The Barbarian', then, was a vast improvement on The Nice noodling away politely beside an orchestra to popular classics.

Side two was sketchier, with Emerson's keyboard showcase 'The Three Fates' and Carl Palmer's 'Tank' lacking the animated group playing of side one. Lake's 'Lucky Man' – an acoustic song that had been written for King Crimson but rejected by the group – closed the side. An attractive, but rather simplistic reminder that ultimately money cannot save you, it closed with dramatic bleeping and whooping sounds rearing out of the mix that the masses had first heard at the Isle Of Wight Festival – the Moog synthesizer.

Emerson also plays synthesizer on 'Tank'. There its glossy textures are bedded into the rest of the instrumentation, but here it is dramatically forefronted. To the many who had never heard its like before it was a startling sound.

Experiments had been taking place with electronic or synthetic sound generated from electric currents, and oscillators and filters, to produce tempered signals since the beginning of the 20th century. High-profile 20th-century composers such as Karlheinz Stockhausen and György Ligeti had used electronics and tapes in pieces like *Kontakte* (1958-60) and *Artikulation* (1958). In the UK, working in a different context, sonic pioneers in the BBC Radiophonic Workshop like Delia Derbyshire and Daphne Oram produced some amazing sounds. But their production relied on tape manipulation and edits, which was a painstakingly slow process.

The first time this kind of pure electronic sound entered mainstream UK culture in a big way was Derbyshire's 1963 theme for the BBC TV science fiction series *Doctor Who*, which allied the disturbing thrill of hitherto unheard sonics to a beautiful tune. It sounded so eerie and mysterious then that despite numerous updatings in the TV show's long history the original has never been bettered.

That year, working in isolation, Don Buchla in California, and Robert Moog in New York, both invented a solid-state modular synthesizer. The idea was to produce an instrument that was at least reasonably portable. Moog designed the first operational model in 1964 and thereafter — and perhaps a little unfairly — his name became synonymous with the synthesizer, rather like Hoover with vacuum cleaners, and by 1970 a few groups had bought these large and expensive items. Keith Emerson recalls when he first heard its futuristic sound on record.

"I went into a record shop in London and someone said, 'Hey Keith have you heard this?' It was [synthesizer pioneer] Walter Carlos's *Switched On Bach* [1968] and I listened to it and just went, 'Wow!' My father used to work at the telephone exchange at Worthing and he played a bit of piano, and I saw this instrument and I thought, 'It looks like a telephone exchange and makes this amazing sound, so that I've just got to get this, partly to impress my dad.'

"I told them [at Moog] who I was, that I'd been in The Nice and was just getting this new band together. I asked about sponsorship. They said that as The Rolling Stones and The Beatles had paid for theirs, they didn't see why I shouldn't pay for mine. The Moog arrived with no instructions, not even, like with a Norton motorbike, how you could kick start it. I ended up going to see Bob Moog in Buffalo quite a lot."

Emerson might not have been the first to record with a Moog synthesizer, but he was determined to make the instrument his own. When he was interviewed in the music press, his comments that he could make the sound of trumpets and strings got him into trouble with the Musicians' Union.

The Musicians' Union was a powerful body at the time and were basically fighting for the rights of musicians who, as they saw it, would otherwise have been paid to play on the recordings. Emerson must have upset the MU in a major way as he was apparently banned for a year. This seems rather absurd when one considers that the church organ has its own stops that were designed to imitate – or at least emulate – a host of wind and stringed instruments.

Emerson used both a keyboard in conjunction with the door-sized Moog patchboard – the "telephone exchange" – and a ribbon controller. This was a metallic strip, which, like the fingerboard of a stringed instrument, gave a different note depending on at which point along its length the player put their finger.

In this respect it was similar to the Ondes Martenot, an electronic instrument, dating from 1928, with both a keyboard and a slider that changed the pitch, which was used to dramatic effect in Oliver Messiaen's *Turangalila Symphony* (1948).

In March 1971, ELP recorded a live version of *Pictures At An Exhibition* at Newcastle City Hall, but it was held back by Island and released in November 1971 at budget price, a few months after their second studio album, *Tarkus*, which went to number one in the UK.

Emerson's onstage antics with the Moog ribbon controller invited comparisons with Jimi Hendrix, for like Hendrix's feedback-drenched rubbing of the guitar neck across the speakers and mike stand, these interludes, with their bleeping, buzzing and helicopter-like noises, were quite thrilling in their sheer newness. Listeners were experiencing sounds that they had never heard before.

Ever the exhibitionist, Emerson was keen to exploit its sonic potential in conjunction with his own anatomy and rubbed it between his legs, and up where the sun don't shine, prompting some critics to surmise that he preferred it to leading brands of toilet tissue. It was fun of sorts, but there was something rather unedifying about it all.

All this was displayed on the big screen as part of the poorly edited *Pictures At An Exhibition* film, with all manner of visual effects employed in post-production to try to beef it up. It was recorded at the Lyceum, London, in 1970 and did the rounds of provincial cinemas from 1972–4, supported by videos that the Strawbs made to accompany their 1972 album, *Grave New World*.

He had the respect of his peers, winning the keyboard section in the 1971 musicians' poll in *New Musical Express*. The front cover of the issue was a photo of him sweating and grimacing, engaged in the extra-musical activity of climbing atop his battered Hammond to mete out yet more punishment.

"I know my stage presentation doesn't harm what I'm playing," Emerson told Penny Valentine of *Sounds*. "It can't, I'm too involved in the music. Even if I was standing on my head the music still comes out the way I want it to."

Sections of ELP's interpretation of *Pictures* took it a long, long way from the original, with the group re-arranging its dramatic themes and adding much self-composed material. 'The Old Castle' utilises Palmer's drum rhythm from the finale of 'Tank', while having little to do melodically with the Mussorgsky piece, and the ferocious 'The Curse Of Baba Yaga' was written by the group. A significant section of 'Blues Improvisation' was lifted from 'Interplay', a 1962 composition by jazz pianist Bill Evans, but credited to the three group members. Considering that Evans lived on until 1980 in a heroin-addicted state and could probably have done with some practical help from the royalties, ELP's cavalier attitude towards compositional credit rankles here.

The encore for *Pictures* was always 'Nutrocker' by B. Bumble & The Stingers, an alias for musician, svengali and purveyor of quality pop trash, Kim Fowley. ELP's choice was tongue-in-cheek as Fowley's song was based on 'March Of The Toy Soldiers' from the score to Tchaikovsky's ballet *The Nutcracker*. The album reached number three in the UK charts.

Taking a break from rockin' up the classics, Emerson, Lake & Palmer's second album, *Tarkus*, comprised mostly original material, but introduced some musical DNA from neo-expressionist Argentine composer Alberto Ginastera (1916–83). But rather than lifting sections from his compositions, Emerson's instrumental sections in 5/4, 5/8 and 9/8 on the twenty-one-minute title track – 'Eruption', 'Iconoclast' and 'Manticore' – were informed by the agitated, rippling rhythmic patterns of Ginastera's *Piano Sonata 1* Op. 22 - 2nd Movement: 'Presto Misterioso'. 'Eruption' also bears more than a passing resemblance to Dave Brubeck's 'Blue Rondo A La Turk' – again – but this time in a brisk 5/4.

Emerson explains how he fell under Ginastera's spell: "I was at Burbank in California in 1970 with The Nice, just before I formed ELP, and NBC grabbed into the idea that it would be great to get rock bands together like Jethro Tull and The Nice, and mix it with Ray Charles, Daniel Barenboim and Jacqueline Du Pré, Jerry Goodman of the Mahavishnu Orchestra, all to be conducted by Zubin Mehta in a TV movie called *The Switched-On Symphony*.

"I remember being down in my dressing room and waiting to come up and do my stuff and I heard this storming piano, and the pianist's name was João Carlos Martins from Brazil. I watched this guy play and I went, 'My God, this is the most incredible work I've ever heard.' He came down in the dressing room and had the score, which looked like someone had splurged ink all over it. I said, 'Hi, my name's Keith,' very timid, like. 'What was that you played?' and he said that it was a new piece by Alberto Ginastera, who was his teacher.

"Back in England I found the recording of Martins playing it, and went down Bond Street into [music publisher] Chappell's and they actually had a copy of Ginastera's piano concerto. I looked at it and it looked like I had seen in Burbank; it was just a blur of notes. I remembered my music teacher's words, 'Don't play all the stuff that people know, play something completely different.' I thought, 'Well this is completely different.'"

Tarkus was given a mixed reception but the title track was the group's most original and coherent piece to date. Maybe its chart success partially explains the backlash, but in the letters page of the *New Musical Express*, there were a number of conflicting views prompting the rather quaint headline: "Tarkus – Tripe Or Greatness?"

Some letter writers, who had naturally assumed that ELP were the heirs to The Nice, had apparently lost their bearings with this new work. With hindsight this is hard to understand as the title track, with its combination of Lake's songs, Emerson's syncopated, Brubeck- and Ginastera-inspired links and some fiery, spontaneous group playing – particularly on 'Stones Of Years' and 'Mass' – is a potent piece of work.

Tarkus has spuriously been described as a concept album and, like the first album, side two is patchy, with about sixteen minutes of short songs. These include two novelties in 'Jeremy Bender' – about a man who becomes a nun – and 'Are You Ready, Eddy?' a take-off of Little Richard's 'Ready Teddy', albeit with a reworked tune. It sings the praises of engineer and producer Eddy Offord whose work on the album is worth celebrating, and as with his work with Yes, he creates a vivid, spacious sound. Both these tracks are filler and of the more serious stuff, 'Hymn', which starts off predictably with Emerson playing an excerpt from a Bach organ piece, represents the absolute nadir of songs questioning organised religion. It finds Lake singing like a ham actor, over-stating his lines in which he asks, with a sneer, how could God exist if he managed to lose *"six million Jews"*.

Caroline Boucher wrote in *Disc*: "Keith has always found thinking up titles for his music difficult. 'With *Tarkus* I went through all sorts of Greek mythology books to think of a name for this animal and I didn't come up with anything. Then suddenly we were driving home from a gig one night and I said Tarkus. And the others said Tarkus? and that was it. I don't know how the word came into my head. The nearest word I've seen to it is the Jewish word for arse.'" ("Arse" in Yiddish is "Tokhes".)

Trilogy followed in 1972, and without anything topping the side-long *Tarkus* suite, it's a far more consistent album. At the time of writing, *Trilogy* has been available for over 40 years and forms a cornerstone of progressive rock. But back in the day, no one knew how long this was all going to last. Emerson also said this to Caroline Boucher: "I write my music with a view in mind that it will be valid in 10 or more years' time. I can't be that presumptuous about my music to say whether it will be valid or not.

"I'm pleased with it [*Trilogy*]; it's a lot different from *Tarkus* and I think there's something in it for everybody. It goes from country, a bit of ragtime piano, I wrote a fugue, Greg does another acoustic guitar number much on the lines of 'Lucky Man', a bolero I wrote, ballads, heavy rock − whatever label you want to stick in there. We asked Salvador Dali to do the album cover but he wanted 50,000 dollars!"

Emerson's apparent diffidence brings the then newness of progressive rock into sharp perspective. The way he describes it makes it clear that even with the commercial success ELP had gained thus far and their undoubted ambition, there was no masterplan in place and in an era of musical flux, who knew how tastes might change?

It also seems odd that Emerson was selling it like there's something in it for everybody, as if the dads and mums who liked James Last would dig it, and the younger brother or sister who liked T. Rex might find something there. He needn't have worried.

'The Endless Enigma (Part One)' starts with eerie Moog signals transmitting through primordial space. This ushers in a quicksilver trio section led by piano, then organ, and then the ensemble rise up into one of the group's most anthemic songs. The aforementioned piano fugue is a dazzling little gem, which leads back into the looming architecture of 'The Endless Enigma (Part Two)'. The lyrics of this song were surely influenced by the non-sequiturs and illogicalities of folk songs like 'Nottamun Town', as Lake sings of a play whose parts were all played, but the play was not shown. And it was performed to an audience, but each audience member stood alone. Enigmatic, indeed.

As Emerson said, Lake's 'From The Beginning' is one of his most sweetly melodic acoustic tracks. It was released as a single in the US and reached number thirty-nine. The country element to *Trilogy* is another jokey song, 'The Sheriff', the tale of an outlaw, which ends with a pistol shot that cues in some speedy ragtime piano. 'Hoedown', which became a live staple, is a condensed suite of music from Aaron Copeland's 1942 ballet, *Rodeo*, and crackles with energy as a group performance.

The bolero Emerson mentioned is 'Abaddon's Bolero', rather oddly named after the ultimate exterminating angel cited in the Book Of Revelation as the controller of an army of locusts. But the piece is more benign than its title would suggest, at first sounding like a Disney army marching into view to a tune not so far from the old American marching song 'The Girl I Left Behind Me', but getting darker and denser as it progresses, with keyboard lines overdubbed and Lake's bass becoming more percussive. He also plays Mellotron here, an instrument rarely used by the group. The album went to number five in the US charts and three in the UK, and that wasn't due to the wide demographic that Emerson had predicted, but to a burgeoning, mainly young male fanbase who were enjoying this new style of music that was opening out before them.

At the time of *Trilogy*, Emerson, Lake & Palmer's popularity was going through the roof, but what was the essence of what they were bringing to music in the early 1970s? Emerson offers this candid view: "All I can say is that Greg Lake, Carl Palmer and myself wanted to do something that was completely unique from what other bands were doing at that time. Of course we could have written a whole load of music that attracted women, like Led Zeppelin did. We weren't really into it for that. The music came first and we worked damned hard at what we did because we loved the music – it wasn't a case of going out and pulling chicks, getting groupies. If we did, we did, if we didn't it wasn't important. What was important was getting the music played and played right."

BRAIN SALAD SURGERY
Original label: Manticore
Producer: Greg Lake
Recorded: June–September 1973
Release date: November 1973
Chart position: 2 (UK), 11 (US)

In 1973, Emerson, Lake & Palmer acquired a disused cinema in the North End Road area of Fulham, London, as a rehearsal space, setting their instruments up onstage. They had used a lot of studio overdubbing on *Trilogy* so the idea was to rehearse the next album, *Brain Salad Surgery*, basically as a live set so that it would be easier to record and for the three-piece band to transfer into a live context.

In breaks from live work, Emerson had been writing a lot of music, especially for the album's centrepiece, 'Karn Evil 9'. "In between going back home, mowing the lawn, and saying 'Hi' to the wife and kids, I'm not sure how I managed to write all this down, but I wrote it all on manuscript paper and presented it to Greg and Carl," Emerson says. "The first part of 'Karn Evil 9 First Impression' used a lot of counterpoint and that worked well. We used to occasionally make music up from blues jams, which was quite good fun, but I didn't always think it was satisfactory. I was generally the instigator of the music, but Carl would suggest putting in a gong crash and Greg would maybe add some power chords or suggest lines on the Moog."

Palmer recollects the process rather differently. "There was a basic structure laid out and then we'd play through all the ideas, and we'd exploit it to the full," he says. "Most of it was in a pretty embryonic form when we started playing it and we found out what worked and what could be put together to make a piece of music. It all had to be developed."

The album was recorded in Advision and Olympic Studios with Lake on production duties. None of the musicians remember much about the studio sessions, as, due to the fact that they were well rehearsed and ready to go, these were over relatively quickly. "It's probably the most inventive album that we made," Palmer confirms. "But you don't realise that at the time you are making it as you are so wrapped up in it."

Compared to the brighter, more open sound of *Trilogy* and *Tarkus*, *Brain Salad Surgery* is tougher and darker. Lake agrees and thinks that this could be down to a particular factor: Eddy Offord, who had engineered their previous albums was absent, and so duties fell to Chris Kimsey and Jeff Young.

"Firstly, every engineer has a palette," says Lake. "And it's amazing how different a group can sound in different studios. Secondly, *Brain Salad Surgery* is almost a live recording done in a studio: the sound was quite raw and quite ambient."

The album opener is the group's take on 'Jerusalem'. It was released as a single in Europe and the USA, but the UK version was effectively banned by the BBC. The organisation was noted for its paternalistic attitude in rooting out drug and sexual references in songs, but in an extraordinary move, 'Jerusalem' was effectively banned on grounds of taste.

Lake: "I can only assume that the motive for banning it would be that when we covered it we were blaspheming something cherished by the nation. We did it as well as we could and there was no mockery about it. You either like it or you don't like it; there was no reason to ban it. But that was the BBC in those days – they were very bigoted."

'Toccata' finds Emerson leading an adaptation of the fourth movement of the Ginastera piano concerto that he had first heard back in Burbank. He had established a friendship with Alberto Ginastera and his wife Aurora, who was a cellist, and got the composer to endorse the group's version. He was quoted on the album insert: "Keith Emerson has beautifully captured the mood of my piece."

While it remains the group's most adventurous classical cover – collectively they really inhabited its spiky, forbidding landscape – it also featured a section played on synthesised drums.

Palmer had recently commissioned a stainless steel drum kit, etched with hunting scenes, that was so heavy it was a problem to move around. If you've got the money and are trying out new ideas, these things happen, but that was little consolation to the two roadies who were needed to manhandle the bass drum. He explains the synthesised aspect of this new kit: "'Toccata' was one of the first tracks that ever featured an electronic drum solo and these were electronic drums that I had specifically made for me. They weren't being manufactured anywhere in the world and I had someone develop me a system. People wondered where are all these sounds were coming from and didn't relate it to me playing and triggering the drums."

Palmer used a pedal, The Mitigator, to switch to mikes on the drums that could trigger a series of preset sounds, which he could further alter with an octave divider. The results were impressive, like an early version of Syndrums, which were commercially produced three years later. Still, this innovation might have been better used in a different context, as it drives a wedge into the piece.

Next up is a Greg Lake song, 'Still You Turn Me On', one of his most affecting acoustic ballads, with a chorus etched with wah-wah guitar. Again, like 'Lucky Man' or 'From The Beginning', it was an interlude of calm in an intense album. Lake explains the song's sentiments. They sound like he's addressing a woman in the audience.

"Only nominally," he says. "When I think about the lyric, it's looking at faces in the audience looking up at me and you can see in their faces that they want to be you. When the audience looks up on the stage they see a star, but when he gets home he's just like them. A star is a perception, so it was that concept that I was trying to voice in a romantic way."

'Benny The Bouncer' is, like 'Jeremy Bender' and 'The Sheriff', an example of what Emerson calls the group's "nonsense songs". It is also the first one to feature lyrics by Peter Sinfield, the former King Crimson wordsmith. In this case Lake, in a yobbish voice, describes cartoonish violence at the *"Palais De Dance"*, giving the album a light relief, of sorts, where it isn't really needed. Lake was born in Poole, Dorset, and grew up in Bournemouth, and here he harks back to his early days playing in West Country venues in the mid-Sixties with The Gods.

"The thing about 'Benny The Bouncer', like it or not, it was actually a story," he explains. "When I was very young I used to play shows, sometimes at Salisbury City Hall, and there was a bouncer there and he was fucking huge: he must have been six foot two or three. He never did anything because no one would ever dare say anything to him. But he is Benny The Bouncer and the Palais De Dance is Salisbury City Hall."

Lake's former King Crimson bandmate Robert Fripp served his apprenticeship playing in dance bands in Dorset, and has this to say about the clientele at some of their gigs in the county's pubs and dancehalls: "One thing I learned from working at the Burdon Ballroom, Weymouth, when the Fleet were in, was that if someone hits someone else, the blood hits the floor before they do. It was not a sophisticated world, Dorset in the early Sixties."

It seems inconceivable that 'Benny The Bouncer' would have been preferred over the track 'Brain Salad Surgery', which appeared on a free flexi-disc given away with *New Musical Express*. It would have been a perfect fit for the album but, alas, was recorded shortly after the album sessions.

All the above are like the hors d'oeuvres to the blow-out main course of *Brain Salad Surgery*, the near thirty-minute, three-part suite, 'Karn Evil 9', which finds the group at their most inventive. Lake feels that Emerson's music was "a perfect platform" for the lyrical concepts he had been hatching up with Pete Sinfield. The first section of the 'First Impression' – as the constituent parts are titled – is a prophetic proclamation with Lake issuing warnings and describing ominous portents, visions of a future *"age of power"*. But right from the rehearsals in the cinema, Lake had in mind the idea of theatre, a unique performance, something happening in real time. He also notes that Sinfield's family had a connection to the circus.

"There's a character, like a ringmaster who [welcomes his friends to a never-ending show]. It's slightly cold," he explains. "There's a wry smile that goes with it."

Once we have accepted this rather sinister invitation, we are presented with a surreal parade of exhibits and performances, including the heads of bishops in jars, a single blade of grass and a car with a bomb inside. And alongside these peculiarities, a mule and "*seven virgins*" promise some particularly transgressive entertainment.

While the subject matter is threatening, rather than the feeling of inexorable doom evoked in a King Crimson song like 'Epitaph', there's a comic book boldness to the imagery and a dark humour, which draws the listener in as an eager spectator.

The music is fittingly spectacular, charged with energy and momentum. It evokes Bach, Bernstein and boogie woogie, woven through with Emerson's extravagant synth lines. Palmer navigates its complexity with a single-minded intensity, while Lake reminds us of his pre-bass-playing roots with his lead guitar lines.

The purely instrumental 'Second Impression' begins as an intricate piano trio – again somewhat akin to Jacques Loussier – which is played so hyperactively that one wishes they'd taken their collective foot off the gas just a bit to let the music breathe. The group then hit one of their trademark pseudo-Latinate grooves – similar to parts of 'The Three Fates' and 'Trilogy' – which, with its distant snatch of 'Speedy Gonzales' vocals, sounds like music heard emanating from a houseparty in the backstreets of a sci-fi *barrio*. But its main inspiration had come from a different continent.

"I had been on holiday in Trinidad and I got this crazy sound on the Moog, which sounded quite like steel pans," says Emerson. "Carl really got into the rhythm of that one and it was a little more light-hearted than the serious mood of the other Impressions." A slow, sparse section follows, a nocturne that evokes eerie, empty streets, but this is a brief respite before the initial piano theme kicks in once again.

The 'Third Impression' is Emerson, Lake & Palmer in excelsis, seven minutes of the group at their most concentrated, and an onrushing rollercoaster of rich musical ideas. But lyrically, its sci-fi themes require a suspension of disbelief.

Back in 1973, personal computers were extremely rare and hugely expensive. Computers were associated with the military, government organisations and large corporations and were devices that most people didn't understand.

In the Seventies, no one knew where computerisation might lead, but there was some concern that in the fast-approaching future the increasing "intelligence" of these machines might take away people's jobs. At the time hippie culture was intent on re-establishing lost links with nature apart from – or in begrudging parallel with – advances in industrialisation and technology. In this respect computers were anathema.

Back in the Fifties and Sixties, computers were inextricably linked to a sci-fi vision of a future in which expressionless people walked down antiseptic corridors wearing identical suits. Then there was HAL 9000, the spaceship's computer in Stanley Kubrick's 1968 film, *2001: A Space Odyssey*, who, becoming sentient, turns against his masters. It was all fiction, of course, but HAL represented how the unnatural, impersonal and purely logical computers might act in a potentially threatening way.

Nowadays, this kind of reasoning seems quaint and anachronistic, but it's against this background that Lake, like William Shatner in *Star Trek*, battles against his spaceship's rogue *"bridge computer"* in this final section of 'Karn Evil 9'. One also needs to bear in mind that co-lyricist Sinfield had started work as a computer programmer. With his voice electronically distorted, Emerson, as the *"perfect"* computer, challenges his human creator with the barked-out final line of the song. Lyrically the track now seems a tad ridiculous or at least very much of its time. Lake will have none of that.

"Pete and I got onto the idea of a world where computers actually take over from people, and the more we thought about it, the more sense it made. It was prophetic," he says, referencing the computer's declaration that *"I am yourself"*. "I predict that it won't be so long before computers will have almost a genetic capacity for knowing their owners, and the more control it would take, the more of your life it would consume. Never a truer word was spoken. As the first step along the way, we have already become cell phone dependent."

To add to the album's futuristic themes, *Brain Salad Surgery* arrived in one of the most spectacular album covers of the era. The front depicts a skull pierced with horizontal rods set within a kind of metal housing. A cut-out circular portal shows half of a woman's face beneath. Opening up the two halves of the cover revealed the full woman's face. She is like a beautiful corpse, her eyes closed, with braided hair and painted in deathly grey. The woman is Li Tobler, partner of Swiss artist H. R. Giger, whose disturbing, beautifully wrought biomechanical paintings caught the attention of Ridley Scott, who commissioned him to set design his 1979 film, *Alien*.

"The title of the record was retro-fitted," says Lake of *Brain Salad Surgery*. "It's got nothing to do with the content of the record. As is the album cover, but it just somehow held together well. Of course, when you retro-fit something – the artwork of *Tarkus* was also a case of retro-fitting – it sort of automatically gets some of the record's genetic imprint. Even if it wasn't connected, it is now and it represents the music."

There was a very strange element of synchronicity in all this. The group had thought of using the title *Whip Some Skull On Yer*, a rather reductively biological description of oral sex and, as a variation on a theme, the final title, *Brain Salad Surgery*, is a slightly more surreal black American slang for fellatio.

"We had a record company called Manticore Records and the guy who was running it in America was a black guy called Mario Medious," Lake explains. "We said, 'We've got to think of a name for the album,' and he came up with this name, *Brain Salad Surgery*, so we said, 'What is that?' It sounded so intriguing.

"The guy who ran Manticore [ELP's record label] in England was a Swiss guy called Peter Zumsteak," Lake continues. "We were looking for someone good to do the album cover, and he said, 'There's a great artist in Zurich called H. R. Giger. Maybe he would be interesting.' We must have seen some of his work in a book and so we said, 'Let's go and meet him.'

"So we flew over to Zurich to his house and it was the most bizarre experience. It was like a nightclub. He just had UV lights, so it's dark, and Giger's house is full of horror, with sinister-looking sculptures and terrible pictures of rows of burnt babies. The dining table and chairs look like they are thrones, and are made of black ebony. The backs of the chairs are all made up of skulls, one after another. He himself, of course, is just a sweet, gentle person. It's a beautiful example of where the artist's vision is not actually him."

There has been some speculation as to whether or not the shape beneath the woman's mouth, which on the cover is just discernible, was originally, and quite fittingly in the circumstances, a penis.

"It *was* an x-ray of a penis," Lake confirms. "Giger's, not mine, I hasten to add. I can't remember how much of that was coincidental, but it all just hung together really well." This was considered just too outré and was virtually airbrushed out. "With all the albums that frontage was important," adds Emerson. "I think the unique work of H. R. Giger put the final stamp on *Brain Salad Surgery*. The amalgamation of the artwork and the music really made it."

Reactions to the album were mixed, but by this time Emerson, Lake & Palmer had largely given up on press support. It was a smaller world in the Seventies and the music press ostensibly had more power than they do now, but then ELP had more power than the press.

Lake: "The interesting thing is it made absolutely no difference; the journalists would slag us and the people decided who they liked. I think it was at the Royal Festival Hall where we decided to put in our concert programme a scathing review by John Peel, who said we were 'a waste of talent and electricity'. It had become almost de rigueur to knock ELP."

The attitude that Lake expresses is justified. Why worry about sniping journalists when you have sold millions of albums to people who love your music?

By 1973 Emerson, Lake & Palmer were, in Lake's words, "already huge". Another point of critical entry for the rock press was the amount of hardware the group deployed onstage. This was all played by, or transmitted the playing of, the three musicians. But to journalists brought up on "honest" rock'n'roll music, this was seen as a kind of affront and claims were made that it was automaton music, which, considering that it was basically just a load of instruments and amplifiers, makes little sense.

US journalist Lester Bangs, writing in *Creem* in 1974, in an article titled "In Blood Feast Of Reddy Kilowatt! Emerson, Lake And Palmer Without Insulation", voiced what some saw as the dehumanising effect of technology in rock music, which took it further into the realms of spectacle. He wrote: "What really makes ELP a dinosaur potentate is the sheer scale of the noise they emit... This is robot music mixmastered by human modules who deserve purple hearts for managing to keep the gadgets reined at all."

Quite how it was "robot music" was never fully explained, and was unusually glib for Bangs, but other writers had a similar technophobic reaction when faced with such a stage line-up of hardware. But in the end it all had to be played by human musicians.

The article was syndicated to *New Musical Express* under the headline "Crazed Power Demons Of The Energy Crisis", following power cuts and the three-day week in 1973 and problems with the supply of crude oil from the OPEC states. It implied that Emerson, Lake & Palmer's usage of electricity was somehow imperilling the entire national grid.

In spring 1974, ELP embarked upon a lengthy world tour, titled *Someone Get Me A Ladder*, which yielded a triple live album with an appropriately elongated title, *Welcome Back My Friends To The Show That Never Ends... Ladies And Gentlemen, Emerson Lake & Palmer*.

The album was recorded at the Anaheim Convention Center in California and Palmer feels that this was the brief period when the trio were in the Big League with the likes of The Who, Pink Floyd and Led Zeppelin. But the opening track, 'Hoedown', came out at such a lick, it sounded like the normally drug-free group were peaking on amphetamines.

"I've long since realised the speeding issue about ELP; some of the tempos are too fast," Lake admits. "But in some ways that frenetic energy was one of the good things about the band. Because when we came onstage and opened up, people used to almost fall over because of the intensity, and the speed it's coming at you is so fast and hard, your brain can't handle it."

On the tour ELP headlined a one-day rock festival, the California Jam, held on a speedway track in Ontario, California. "That would have been the highlight of that era," says Lake. "That was where we staged the flying piano. I believe there were about 600,000 there. The audience stretched as far as the eye could see. It was biblical."

If ELP's shows had always been bombastic, the flying piano took their showmanship onto a new and rather dangerous level. In a flouting of all things health and safety, Emerson's piano and stool, with the keyboard player (hopefully) secured, were raised on a hydraulic stand and spun round, taking his knife-wielding, Hammond-humping showmanship onto another level. "Well actually by that time I'd achieved my pilot's licence and I was pretty efficient in doing aerobatics," Emerson quips. "Originally it was a five-foot drop. I can handle that, although probably not if I've got a 400lb piano landing on me, but it's rock'n'roll. When I looked at where I was going to be, which was right over the heads of the audience, there was a drop of a further twenty feet and I thought, 'Well, if I go out and people don't remember my music, they'll fucking remember this!'"

Chris Welch of *Melody Maker* describes the group's place in the rapidly developing spectacle of progressive rock: "When you went to see one of these bands like ELP you really got value for money, because you'd get laser beams and smoke and dry ice, and the musicians seemed like supermen compared with the three guitars and drums beat groups of yesteryear."

But their rise to fame and fortune had been achieved at a cost and by the end of 1974, the endless touring that had helped them break America had taken its toll, and so they did the sensible thing – which many groups don't do – and took some time off to recharge. Except in ELP's case, this move proved disastrous.

In The Goodies' 1974 annual, the TV comedy trio made a number of musical references, one being that Emerson, Lake & Palmer had split up and reformed as Lemerpal, Aker & Son. Although that wasn't strictly the case, when the group came back on the scene a few years later, things had changed irrevocably.

CHAPTER 8

Kick out the Jams to Jerusalem: Genesis

Back in 1966, a group of songwriters – Peter Gabriel, Anthony Phillips, Tony Banks and Michael Rutherford – were schoolboys just embarking on their A-level studies at Charterhouse school, near Godalming in Surrey. The public school was a conservative seat of learning, designed to turn out young men who would be equipped to rise to the upper echelons of the armed forces or the civil service. It was certainly not geared towards producing pop songwriters.

Gabriel claims that he has always had an affinity with the visual rather than the textual and after he had completed some tests, his career advisor, who could recognise that he looked lost, suggested that he might consider the idea of becoming a photographer or a landscape gardener.

Charterhouse was an environment in which even playing a guitar was frowned upon as subversive. Gabriel has said how, being born in 1950, he was at the key adolescent age for the music of the 1960s to exert a massive influence on him, particularly psychedelia, British beat groups, soul and blues.

"All those things were part of my education. And as an English boy growing up initially in a public school, [music] was the one place I felt really alive and my own man," Gabriel recalls. "I was lucky enough to see Otis Redding at the Ram Jam club in Brixton in 1967 and in my head it still stands as gig number one because of his extraordinary voice and his warmth and the vitality."

Michael Rutherford experienced a moment of epiphany when he first heard The Kinks' 'You Really Got Me' in 1964, listening to Radio Luxembourg under the bedcovers: "That guitar riff was the first really exciting riff I'd ever heard. The Shadows didn't quite get to this level of energy and grit. I wasn't a very good guitar player at the time and I was encouraged that you could make a song work on simple chords."

The four songwriters had initially thought in terms of producing material for others rather than being a group themselves and had sent demos to a number of record companies. But although their idea of becoming something like a home counties answer to Holland-Dozier-Holland or Leiber & Stoller went by the wayside, their demo attracted the interest of music biz svengali Jonathan King, who paid £10 for them to re-record some of their material in a better studio.

"There came a certain point when you realise that no one else is going to do it, and people said, 'Why don't you do it yourself?'" Banks recalls. "So at that stage we were 17 or whatever and we tried to do a pop album with a little more going for it."

Under King's direction, the teenagers signed to Decca as Genesis, but without really scrutinising the small print, and their horrified parents were relieved that they could extricate their sons from the contract, as they were technically still minors. They redrafted the contract and signed on the group's behalf for a year. Genesis recorded the singles 'Silent Sun' and 'A Winter's Tale' with school friend Chris Stewart on drums, and then John Silver took over on the group's 1968 debut album *From Genesis To Revelation*.

At this point their music was a tad derivative and the album sold poorly. The group also found Decca difficult to deal with. Gabriel remembers that, "We used to go to Decca, give our name at the door, and the man at the desk would phone up and say, 'The Janitors are here to see you.'" The group also never received reliable sales information. Gabriel: "Our sales figures seemed to fluctuate rapidly too – we'd be told a record had sold 1,000 one week, then 2,000 the next week and so on; then later they'd say it had sold a total of 649."

Undeterred they shifted their focus and in 1969, Genesis decided to go professional, securing enough backing from friends to purchase amps, instruments and a PA. But they were soon running up debts and one agency advised them to "give up" without even hearing their music.

Soon things turned around and Genesis received interest from Island Records, The Moody Blues' Threshold label and renewed interest from King. In the end they signed to Tony Stratton-Smith and Gail Colson's newly formed Charisma label. They had supported Charisma band Rare Bird, whose keyboard player Graham Field had handed a tape to producer John Anthony.

The group wrote and rehearsed a new batch of material between October 1969 and February 1970 at a cottage in Wotton, Surrey, owned by the parents of their friend and de facto road manager, Richard Macphail. John Mayhew, who had played with Steamhammer took over from John Silver on drums; Banks played keyboards and guitar; Phillips was on guitars and dulcimer; Rutherford on bass guitar, guitar and cello; and Gabriel on vocals, accordion, flute and bass drum. The group went into Trident Studios with John Anthony producing in the summer of 1970 to record their second album – but really their debut album proper – *Trespass*.

As songwriters, Genesis had been influenced by pop and soul, but were beginning to make something more original, spurred on by developments they heard in the music around them.

"*From Genesis To Revelation* was not a success and it gave us a chance to reassess what we wanted to do," says Banks. "Peter and I decided that maybe we did want to play live and see how it went, and wanted to do music that was a little more sophisticated. We had been shown the way by The Beach Boys and The Beatles and, in terms of structure, groups like Procol Harum, and we were quite into Fairport Convention as well. Then the King Crimson album [*In The Court Of The Crimson King*] came out and set a bar for what you might be able to do within some quite complex music – and some quite simple music, actually – done in a grandiose style with elaborate drumming. We found that exciting, so that gave us impetus as well."

The most dramatic song on *Trespass*, 'The Knife', was inspired in part by 'Rondo' by The Nice with its "bouncy rhythm" and as a work-in-progress it was actually called 'The Nice'.

'The Knife' took shape as a lengthy, multipart composition on the theme of doomed rebellion. The songs on the album had a far more individual flavour now, with Banks's organ and Mellotron giving it all a grander sweep and John Mayhew contributing the "elaborate drumming".

The group were rocked by Phillips' decision to leave, but the guitarist didn't enjoy playing the same songs live every night and was subject to stage fright. They also decided that now was time to part company with Mayhew and try to find a drummer who was more of a writer and would be more creative with his own parts. Although Mayhew himself has since said that he wasn't technically up to the job, on *Trespass* he certainly gives a good impression of someone who is, particularly with his bombastic breaks and dramatic snare rolls on 'Looking For Someone'.

His place was taken by Phil Collins, an impressive 19-year-old drummer with a solid and technically flexible jazz and rock-inflected style. Collins had trained as an actor at the Barbara Speake Stage School and as a child had appeared as an extra in films including The Beatles' *A Hard Day's Night* and *Chitty Chitty Bang Bang*. He could also sing and in 1969 had made an album, *Ark 2*, as part of Flaming Youth.

Genesis tried out a couple of new guitarists, the second of which, Steve Hackett, was welcomed into the fold. But he familiarised himself with their music in an unorthodox way.

"They answered my ad in *Melody Maker*," Hackett recalls. "I'd heard of them, but I didn't know what they sounded like. I went and listened to *Trespass* in a booth, as you could do in the old days, on vinyl, in W.H. Smith on the corner of Sloane Square.

"We went down the basement – this was my brother [John] and I. Pete Gabriel had suggested we check out a track called 'Stagnation' and straightaway we were intrigued by the sound of the band, and we couldn't quite pin down the instruments. It turned out later that it was a combination of twelve-strings playing.

"The style of early Genesis often sounded like a cross between guitars, keyboards and harps, and it gave the band a certain otherworldly character, and sometimes one of the twelve-strings would be put through a Leslie cabinet, which would give it a slightly more keyboard-like quality. Genesis in the early days had this impressionistic air about them – something indefinable, but magical – and I was an avid twelve-string player already, so I think we were lucky to find each other."

Hackett had also been hugely impressed by King Crimson and was struck by the possibilities opened by their startling and "rather frightening" new music. He was also very impressed by the original approach taken by his new band.

"I was aware that Genesis could be built into a killer ensemble team, if we headed for precision and got somewhere near it," he says. "But we also had that slightly feminine, fey quality." The new line-up worked on fresh material at Tony Stratton-Smith's house, Luxford Manor, near Crowborough in Sussex and they went into Trident Studios again with John Anthony in August 1971. He was also introduced to the band with the information that songwriting credits were split five ways, so as long as a musician sang or played on a piece they would receive a credit.

Trespass introduced the group's narrative songwriting style, which encompassed both fantasy and satire, and their remit was expanded further on *Nursery Cryme*. 'The Return Of The Giant Hogweed' lampooned the panic, fanned by the media, caused by the spread of these plants with their enormous stalks surmounted by giant umbels that reached a height of over three metres – like a sci-fi version of cow parsley – whose toxic sap could cause serious skin burns. The giant hogweed had originally been discovered in Russia in Georgian times and had been brought back to Britain for decorative planting, but had long since spread and was now viewed as an invasive species. Gabriel recasts these plants as malevolent, Triffid-like creatures.

On 'The Musical Box', eight-year-old Henry Hamilton Smythe has been beheaded by a croquet mallet wielded by nine-year-old Cynthia

Jane De Blaise William. But summoned by the tune of 'Old King Cole' that is played by her musical box, he returns in spirit form to the bedroom of his assailant. Henry manifests and begins to age unnaturally quickly. With a lifetime of desire coursing through his body he attempts to bed the girl, but her nanny thwarts the bearded child and destroys him by hurling the box at him. These sinister lyrics resonated with the writings of Edward Lear, Lewis Carroll and the macabre imaginings of Arthur Machen, as well as the American writer Edward Gorey's compendium of Gothic tales, *The Hapless Child*.

'The Musical Box' begins with another "otherworldly" mesh of twelve-string and electric guitar and flute, but also exemplified a developing dynamic in the group, when this meditative pastoral approach could suddenly cut into high-velocity sections with repetitive, arpeggiated keyboard lines.

An even more dramatic keyboard cavalry charge in this style – like Bach's "sewing machine" music – cuts into 'The Fountain Of Salmacis' and for the beginning of 'The Return Of The Giant Hogweed', Banks and Hackett had developed a dense, unison demi-semiquaver line.

"With keyboards you cross the two hands which makes it sound like you are playing twice as fast as you are, and you get some great rhythmic parts," Banks explains. "It's done in classical music but it really lends itself to pop music because you can kind of play the hi-hat part in sixteenths or faster than that and it wasn't too difficult to do, but it meant that the drummer could play more round it."

Hackett is generally regarded as the originator of the tapping or hammer-on style, where the guitarist uses their picking and strumming hand to play percussively on the guitar neck, which effectively gives two notes in close succession. This technique has since been used by countless rock guitarists and forms the basis of the superfast "shredding" style.

"I was using the fretboard more like a keyboard, tapping on one string, while Tony was trying to sound like a guitarist," says Hackett. He had a Hohner Pianet (electric piano) put through a fuzz box, which produced an interesting sound in itself – and the two in harmony produced that intro, and much of the colouring of early Genesis, where again, you're not really sure what's guitar and what's keyboard."

The humour in the group's music was most overtly stated on 'Harold The Barrel', a dark and perverse piano-led tale of a *"Bognor restaurant owner"*, who, having clearly lost his senses, cuts off his toes and serves them up to a customer, before fleeing, climbing to a ledge and despite attempts to talk him down by his mother and a "Plods chorus" – a group of policeman singing *"We can help you"*, like D. P. Gumby from *Monty Python's Flying Circus* – he jumps to his death.

This was the first song on which Gabriel took on different character voices. There's a stylish and particularly English daftness about it: a hint, maybe, of Gilbert & Sullivan or the humorous songwriters, Flanders & Swann.

"That's very much it," says Banks. "That was Peter's lyric – and we always liked that comedy kind of thing, although Flanders & Swann were very much a period piece; I'm not sure that a lot of their humour stood up later on. The lyric is really silly, but it has enough drama in it and the fact that the guy at the end jumps off is wrong in a way, but it works rather well."

A dramatic closer to *Nursery Cryme*, 'The Fountain Of Salmacis' is closely based on a poem by Ovid from *Metamorphoses*, Book IV, in which the nymph Salmacis tries to seduce the boy demi-god Hermaphroditus to the extent of attempting to rape him while he is bathing in the stream. She calls out to the gods that they shall never part and in the original poem, they answer her wish in a way she could never have envisaged, by melding them together, *"a single body with a double sex"*.

Hermaphroditus then curses the waters so that anyone else who enters them will meet a similar fate, emerging *"supple, unsinew'd and but half a man"*.

Hackett recalls that he was trying to "fly above" the lyrical ideas with his playing and the song ends with his soaring, lyrical solo before the final swelling Mellotron chords.

Although Genesis could be seen as somewhat fey, as Hackett noted, they subverted the standard rock'n'roll sexual clichés of groupies and jailbait, exploring stranger and stranger sexual backwaters as the Seventies rolled on. Banks wrote the lyrics to this song with Gabriel and explains the context.

"We were pretty repressed sexually," Banks admits. "We had been to British public school, all male, and although we had sisters, we were extremely bad with women. We were really shy and ill at ease so we had no idea, and our concept of women was really based on *Playboy* and stuff. Peter did find a way around it and he came out with these sometimes slightly weird things."

In amongst all this, the genteel, wistful 'For Absent Friends' feels like a postcard from a bygone, semi-rural England, popped into the pillar box after a church service to catch the first post on Monday, and offers a brief window of order in among these strange goings-on.

John Anthony had attended a 1970 London gallery show of upcoming young artist and record sleeve designer Paul Whitehead, and thought he would be perfect to work with Genesis. He firstly designed the cover to *Trespass*, a photo of a painting of what looks like a scene from Ancient Greece with a knife slashed through it. Charisma had liked it so much that Whitehead was given free rein for *Nursery Cryme*, and the result was one of the closest fusions of music and imagery in progressive rock.

Typically, Whitehead would absorb both the album's music and lyrics, so as not to put too much of his "own stamp" on the artwork. He would then meet the group armed with a bag of art books, in this case on Magritte, De Chirico, Bosch and Brueghel. De Chirico inspired the sense of perspective, which is given by the bold stripes in the mowed lawn outside a large country pile, on which Cynthia is moving around on shoes with spoked wheels, leaving a number of lopped-off heads in her wake. Now she has stopped, staring at the viewer, while brandishing her croquet mallet.

"We focused on 'The Musical Box' as the standout track on *Nursery Cryme* and Peter told me the story behind the song," says Whitehead. "Its setting was a sadistic and somewhat menacing Victorian nursery, with an atmosphere not unlike *Alice In Wonderland*. *Nursery Cryme* was quite shocking because it was before all the slasher horror movies. I have often been told that Cynthia's eyes seem to be not those of a child – they have an adult maturity about them."

The nurse from 'The Musical Box' can be seen using the same mode of transport. A lone statue stands on the lawn and an older man in a tweed suit is pictured, hunched, playing a quiet solo game of croquet, but again with a human cranium rather than a ball.

"When I finished the painting I presented it and they loved it, but we all agreed it didn't look old enough," says Whitehead. "So I dated it 1871 and varnished it with some marine varnish, which was the colour of honey, and put it outside to dry. Of course every flying insect in the neighbourhood decided to [land] on the wet varnish. I was horrified when I discovered it, but once again we all agreed that it just added to the aged look and we left all the insects."

On the inside cover the lyrics, together with Whitehead's visual interpretations, are presented in an unusual way.

"I bought a Victorian photo album from a junk shop because I liked the look and the decorative elements, and suggested to the band that we treat each song as if it were an item in an album. This enabled me to create a unique illustration for each song and gave listeners something to think about as they read the lyrics."

"That was 'The Fountain Of Salmacis' and it's the first time I've seen Genesis live with the Mellotron and I must say it vastly adds to the sound," said Andy Dunkley when presenting the BBC *In Concert* session, recorded at the Paris Theatre, London, on March 3, 1971, with Genesis following a set by Max Merritt & The Meteors.

Hackett had loved the sound of the Mellotron used by King Crimson. A studio model had been used sparingly on *Trespass* and he had lobbied for the group to acquire one in advance of the recording of *Nursery Cryme*, reckoning that its sound would transform the group. In fact, Genesis bought a secondhand Mk II model from King Crimson.

Hackett describes that it took four people to carry the iron-framed instrument – "like pallbearers". There were also the inevitable tuning problems when playing live.

"You go with the flow with the Mellotron, and you forget your idea of what a conventional orchestra [sounds like]," says Hackett. "It's almost as if the sound of an orchestra was flown out into space and then received on another planet – it's lost a lot of the hi-fi qualities that we associate with the source sounds, and the bottom end, but something else happens – you get this alienated quality."

Dunkley also referred to Gabriel as the group's "court jester" and the singer obliged with a stream of consciousness monologue to introduce 'The Musical Box', which deviates greatly from the song's subject matter, to the extent of including a reference to the much loved and much imitated TV rugby league commentator Eddy Waring.

Nursery Cryme was released in late 1971, and in these early days the group were working hard to get some kind of a name on the gig circuit, but sometimes venues were sparsely attended and the band's occasionally fey and feminine acoustic sections were met with indifference by an audience wanting to drink beer and boogie.

Peter Gabriel was the epitome of the thoughtful, diffident person who comes into their own onstage and his "court jester" monologues were the first signs of the teenager who never wanted to appear live beginning to grow into his role. But then necessity was the mother of invention.

"It began really when we were playing bars where no one would shut up or pay any attention," says Gabriel. "And then every time we got a slight bit of interest we'd got thirty-six strings of two or three twelve-string guitars that took about ten minutes to tune, so everyone looked at this poor prat in the middle, who was the singer without any instruments to hide behind, and so I thought I'd better come up with something."

FOXTROT

Original label: Charisma
Producer: Dave Hitchcock
Recorded: August–September 1972
Release date: October 1972
Chart position: 12 (UK)

Charisma Records had put Genesis on the 'Six Bob Tour' of 1971 with label mates Lindisfarne and Van Der Graaf Generator – with Bell & Arc appearing on some of the dates – as a musical package to grab some attention. It was so called because the UK moved over to decimal currency about halfway through the itinerary.

Nursery Cryme had unexpectedly taken off in Italy and so in early April 1972, Genesis embarked on a tour of the country, playing the 10,000-capacity Palasport in Pesaro and headlining theatres like the 800-seater Teatro Mediterraneo in Naples on April 19. But returning home, live opportunities were often less glamorous, as proven on May 5 when they entertained the customers of The Red Lion in Leytonstone. "It was a schizophrenic existence," Banks recalls.

Charisma, meanwhile, were hoping that all the group's promise would bear fruit with their next album, *Foxtrot*. Studio sessions began in August 1972.

Banks: "The real problem with the *Foxtrot* session was that Charisma wanted us to lighten up a bit and use this producer Bob Potter."

Potter had engineered for American producer Bob Johnson who had produced and mixed Charisma label mates Lindisfarne's 1971 number one album *Fog On The Tyne*. But Potter and Genesis didn't get on. "He didn't think we should have that bit at the beginning of 'Watcher Of The Skies', for example," says Banks. "And so we realised he wasn't the man for us."

The "bit" to which Banks refers is a magisterial solo Mellotron introduction lasting a minute or so, a kind of overture presenting some of the song's melodic material, which remerges briefly at its conclusion. Played largely in a heavily syncopated 7/4, the song was the most dynamic group composition so far and live, Banks's intro would elicit cheers from the opening chord.

'Watcher Of The Skies' was largely composed by Banks and Michael Rutherford – although in accordance with the group's collective songwriting policy it is credited to all five members. The lyrics were written on a hotel balcony in Naples, from which vantage point the city appeared quiet and deserted. This brought to mind Arthur C. Clarke's novel *Childhood's End*, which signified the metamorphosis of the human race into its next stage of development. "The other part of it was The Watcher from Marvel comics, who was a being who could observe what was going on but could take no part in it," Banks explains. "Some aspects of the lyrics are alright, but I don't think it was our finest hour in the way that they fit with the music. But it's a good intro, anyhow."

After Potter left, David Hitchcock was brought in as producer. He had produced Caravan and their manager Terry King had introduced him to Tony Stratton-Smith, and the two socialised in London music venues like the Marquee. He explains his role overseeing the project.

"They had been in five days and got one backing track, and they had another five days to finish the album, so I was parachuted in. We were booked into Studio 2 at Island. I preferred the sound in Studio 1 and it became available so we moved.

"We changed engineer, because I didn't think the engineer was the right one for them in terms of sounds and attitude. I got in a guy called John Burns – he really put a lot into the album and went on to produce their next three albums.

"I was there to get a good recording out of the band, to represent them on record as excitingly as possible. My role with Genesis was to try to work out what was in their heads and make it feasible to get onto tape, to cram it all in – I think it was eight-track we were working on – and there was so much to fit in there it was more a logistics exercise.

"It was not an easy session. There was a lot of tension in the group," Hitchcock continues. "Tony Banks said to me during the sessions that if the album didn't make it the group were going to break up. Whether that would have actually happened I don't know. There was a lot of anxiety and a lot of pressure trying to get things done and an awful lot to get done in a short space of time."

'Time Table' has a more straightforward structure, with grumbling Mellotron brass in the chorus and a cleanly articulated guitar hook. Lyrically it's a kind of memento mori.

"It was a song I'd had around for quite a while," says Banks. "It's just about the passage of time. I like the idea that something that seems new and shiny one moment, take it fifty years down the line and suddenly it's all shabby and finished."

'Get 'Em Out By Friday' is a Gabriel lyric and the song was typically composed and recorded before the singer added all his vocals. Although some group members have opined that it's a little congested lyrically, it was one of his most affecting tales in song, a mocking, satirical look at unscrupulous property developers working in the London overspill "new towns" of the late Sixties and early Seventies – in this case the Essex town of Harlow. In the song, older housing is pulled down to make way for new development with elderly residents having their rents increased, then being repeatedly visited by the sinister *"Winkler"*, who offers them a cash pay-off and a relocation into a tower block. He plays upon their gullibility, telling them that it's all in the *"interests of humanity"*.

Gabriel then flips the action into a kind of sci-fi scenario laced with absurdist humour, announcing that *"Genetic Control"* have decided to limit people's height in order to cram more of them into new, smaller, more profitable units. Ultimately he advises the property developers that the next step after amassing worldly goods is to *"invest in the church"* to ensure a comfortable afterlife.

The closer on side one of *Foxtrot* is Hackett's 'Can-Utility And The Coastliners', its title a loose pun on King Canute. Gabriel's dramatically declaimed verses of the lone figure commanding waters to retreat leads into a vocal and instrumental episode of panoramic acoustic guitars with Mellotron backdrops and Rutherford's sonorous bass pedals – which he would often use in concert when playing six or twelve-string guitar – ending on a section of tricky unison organ and guitar lines.

Hackett: "It's very interesting rhythmically, once it got into the kind of fusion side of it, where you've got folk meets jazz drumming, meets classical influences. The hybrid that the band was capable of is certainly embodied in that song."

Another Hackett composition, the formal solo guitar piece 'Horizons', opens side two. It starts with the opening lines of the prelude of *Cello Suite No. 1* in G Major by J. S. Bach.

"It was the first thing that I'd ever really completed for six-string acoustic steel," says Hackett. "I was also thinking of a short piece that William Byrd wrote called 'The Earl Of Salisbury', that I recorded many, many years later – a piece written for virginal."

After that refreshing palate cleanser comes the main course, the 23-minute suite, 'Supper's Ready'.

"Peter was the best lyric writer in the early days of Genesis. [And for 'Supper's Ready'] he felt that he wanted – and we agreed – that it should be one person's idea all the way through," says Banks. "But when he came up with the title idea 'Supper's Ready', I thought, 'Oh no, it should really be something epic,' and 'Supper's Ready' was so un-epic."

But the very appeal of 'Supper's Ready' is how the full meaning of its apparently humdrum title is ultimately revealed as being epic on a cosmic scale.

Hitchcock had produced Caravan's 1971 album *In The Land Of Grey And Pink*, with its eight-section, twenty-minute track, 'Nine Feet Underground' and gave some sage advice. "They thought that they had to play it from note one to the end in one take, which was going to be pretty demanding and I showed them other ways of doing it – how you could record it in segments and how you cut them together in a master track. Or record them and mix them separately and cross-fade them into one another."

The opening scene, 'Lovers' Leap', begins with a trademark mesh of guitars, with Rutherford playing cello, and lyrically focuses on a suburban couple at supper time. But things soon become uncanny as the woman's face appears to change, which pertains to a paranormal event experienced by Gabriel's wife, Jill, which the singer witnessed. Then a procession of seven shrouded figures are seen moving across the moonlit lawn, one bearing a cross, while Gabriel sings of his partner's blue, angelic *"guardian eyes"*.

'Supper's Ready' continues filmically, like an obscure drama in which the director presents just enough tantalising clues – mainly biblical and from ancient history – to make you feel you can maybe follow the narrative, and so we are led into the first full band section, 'The Guaranteed Eternal Sanctuary Man'. He is someone that Gabriel describes as a *"supersonic scientist"*, someone who has fooled us all. But he is also a messianic figure who commands us all to look into his mouth, knowing that the children will *"walk inside"*.

In Revelation 19:15 is the passage, *"From his mouth comes a sharp sword with which to strike down the nations, and he will rule them with a rod of iron."* Afterwards there is a brief snatch of the lullaby 'Rocking Carol', but this time sung by a group of children, who are themselves rocking to sleep and nurturing a *"little snake"*, a symbol of both evil and the fall from grace.

This leads us onto 'Ikhnaton And Itsacon And His Band Of Merry Men'. Just to complicate matters, the title specifically refers to the Egyptian pharaoh Iknaton, or Akhenaten, who attempted to deviate Egyptian religious practice from polytheism to the worship of Aten – or the sun. His attempts were ultimately unsuccessful, and so maybe, ultimately, it's a con. Get it? But what's happening on the ground, so to speak, is an Armageddon-style conflict between the forces of good and those from *"The West"*. As the western border of the Holy Land is the sea and the unknown, so in biblical terms the West is the place of darkness, where the sun sets, and was often used to represent evil and death.

Hackett launches off into a searing solo, before landing back on another of his demi-semiquaver unison themes with Banks's organ. So pumped up is Gabriel as narrator of the extensive carnage, that he has to be sedated and then compelled to activate his *"prayer capsule"*.

In the respite after the battle comes 'How Dare I Be So Beautiful?' – its title carrying echoes of the scurrilous rugby song 'Why Was He Born So Beautiful?' To a muted two-chord keyboard accompaniment, the victors climb up a gory mountain of *"human flesh"* onto an Eden-like Arcadia and spy Narcissus pondering himself by a pool, his body stamped *"Human Bacon"*, but who ultimately, as the legend goes, turns into a flower. *"A flower?"* Gabriel asks rather camply, and after a comedic pause we enter 'Willow Farm'.

'Willow Farm' was originally a stand-alone song that Hackett has described as "like a psychedelic 'Teddy Bears' Picnic'". And indeed, the four descending chords that lead into the vocal – here played by Banks on Mellotron brass, and sounding particularly ugly and banal – are almost identical to the children's song. But Gabriel describes a kind of halfway house to the afterlife, peopled by grotesques, including the unforgettable image of Winston Churchill *"dressed in drag"*.

Gabriel yells the bus conductor's cry of *"All change!"* with sound effects of a whistle and a slamming door and suddenly we're in a different world, a brisk, staccato piano section – in a way that echoes McCartney's middle "bus" section in The Beatles' 'A Day In The Life' – a completely different tune with images of bodies morphing between male and female form. In this section it sounds like Gabriel's voice is being sped up. But for the female part, he wanted to sing after having inhaled helium, so it was Hitchcock's job to procure some.

The lyrics also hint at a potential for growth and transformation, as all those at the Farm are metaphorically *"under the soil"*. One senses that 'Willow Farm' may well have been touched by the absurdist influence of Spike Milligan.

Gabriel: "I think that in the time that I have been alive Milligan has been the most important philosopher because he's changed the way people think. And I think that capacity to jump from one thing to another and see the humour in it is a God given thing. And Milligan begat Goons, which begat Python, which begat modern humour."

After an interlude of sweet guitars and Gabriel's flute comes a brief section of stomping 4/4, over which he describes the ominous swarms of the guards of Magog, the satanic dragon emerging from the sea and bringing down fire, and a pied piper leading the children underground to escape the mayhem that is set of follow. It references this part of Revelation:

"20: 7 When the thousand years are complete, Satan will be released from his prison;

"8 and will go out to deceive the nations in the four corners of the earth, Gog and Magog, to assemble them for battle. Their number is like the sand of the seashore. [In this case Gog and Magog represent the hostile nations of the world, although they can also represent physical beings.]

"9 And they marched across the broad expanse of the earth and surrounded the camp of the saints and the beloved city. But fire came down from heavens and consumed them."

All these ominous portents bring us to the 'Apocalypse In 9/8 (Co-starring The Delicious Talents Of Gabble Ratchet)'. On this instrumental section, Banks's organ solo is crisply articulated, but has an eccentric air about it, with its manic arpeggios going back and forth over melodic material and his obsessive, slowly rising patterns cranking up the tension. It feels as if the curious Gabble Ratchet – surely a lesser-known character from a Spike Milligan script – had sneaked up into the organ loft of his local parish church to let off steam, thinking no one was listening. Banks describes how it was all put together: "Mike had this idea of playing the bass pedals followed by a guitar chord – boom-ching, boom-ching – and I said it sounded exciting, but I thought we should make it repetitive. I said if you can play an E on the bass and you only play an F sharp and a B above, then I can play anything I like on top of that, and it would be great. And so between them, Phil and Mike developed the riff.

"I just played all sorts of things, with an almost Keith Emerson pastiche at the beginning, playing through slightly more sinister chords. I didn't worry about the 9/8 at all, I just played in whatever time signature I wanted and we would occasionally come back together. Phil would float between the 9/8 that the guitar and bass was playing, and what I was playing."

The ending is spectacular. Banks: "Basically I had these two chord sequences. One was a slightly unusual chord change from F sharp minor 6 to A minor 6. Then Pete did his *'666 is no longer alone'* lyric on top of it – at the time I didn't think there was going to be a vocal, but it ended up like that – and is probably one of the strongest moments in Genesis's music.

"At the end we did this big thing that I always wanted to do, which was to play the chords C and D with the E bass," Banks explains. "Having played most of the thing in E minor you then go to a big E major chord making it very serene. The way that it evolves into that *'brand new tune'* chord sequence over the top of that riff, which by that time had become totally hypnotic, it's just an incredible moment."

During this exultant section Gabriel also exhorts the seven trumpets that herald the apocalypse to blow some *"sweet rock'n'roll"*, with a mention of Pythagorus writing the lyrics of that *"brand new tune"* in blood, adding to the welter of imagery.

The 'Lovers' Leap' theme re-emerges to an orchestral snare drum roll and a churchy carillon of tubular bells as the returning Gabriel looks into his lover's *"guardian eyes"* once again.

He exclaims how he has travelled far, but he is back now and makes the bald declaration that everything's going to *"work out fine"*, which takes us into the section 'As Sure As Eggs Is Eggs (Aching Men's Feet)'.

That sounds glib in a way – and by this point, anyone unable to maintain their suspension of disbelief would have long since bailed out – but as a figure of speech "as sure as eggs is eggs" means a certainty, and it also echoes the views of the 14th-century Christian mystic and anchoress, Julian of Norwich, who wrote that "All shall be well, and all shall be well, and all manner of thing shall be well", a guarantee from the seer that, through time, all deeds will inexorably lead to a positive spiritual outcome. T. S. Eliot also used this phrase in his poem, *Four Quartets.*

Surely the 'aching men's feet' in question are those of the subjects of William Blake's poem, 'Jerusalem', who *"In ancient time/Walked upon England's mountains green"*. For this is where we are heading.

The music of 'The Guaranteed Eternal Sanctuary Man' remerges, slower now, with more majesty, as the two lovers are reunited with the ignition of their souls producing their own light show, in a metaphorical (positive) last judgement or ascension, or their passing into another world, as an angel standing in the sun proclaims this to be the *"supper"* of the *"mighty one"*. Onstage Gabriel would appear delivering these lines in a white suit like some showbiz evangelist.

Which takes us to Revelation 19:17: *"Then I saw an angel standing in the sun, and with a loud voice he called to all the birds that fly directly overhead, 'Come, gather for the great supper of God'."*

With Banks's insistent Mellotron chords and Hackett's guitar skywriting lines in the stratosphere, Gabriel puts in a terrific, raw vocal performance, his slightly cracked, hoarse voice belying his soul roots as he evokes visions of the *"new Jerusalem"*.

Onstage Gabriel ended up static, holding a fluorescent tube vertically and if practical he would be slowly hoisted into the air. While this ascension was taking place, just as on the album the music fades out – the antithesis of a pseudo-symphonic ending – leaving the stage in silent darkness, as if this bizarre pageant, teeming with its weird characters, its violence and beauty and nonsense, had just drifted gently away. At the end of the lyrics printed on the album is one word: *"(CONTINUED)"*.

"Whatever anybody thinks, we never took ourselves very seriously, even when we were being intense," Banks says. "We knew when we'd gone a bit too far with the whole 'Jerusalem' bit at the end, but the music lent itself to it and you'd take it to a certain extreme, and not be self-conscious about it, just do it, and it works. It's a very uplifting piece, it's got some wonderful imagery and the end part is such a strong emotive moment."

'Supper's Ready' is panoramic, embedded with nuggets of arcane knowledge, obtuse, witty, absurdist and in a way, completely preposterous. It's epic while constantly undermining its own epic-ness and it's also full of music of great invention – and some good tunes. It can mean as much or as little as the listener wants. But if 'Jerusalem' by Parry and Blake could slot in as the new British national anthem, 'Supper's Ready' is surely the unofficial anthem of progressive rock.

And it's not just a progressive rock rollercoaster ride through the Book Of Revelation. Hackett has other ideas about its meaning: "I think both that track, and many of the aspects of *The Lamb Lies Down On Broadway* two albums later, had something about the lyric that owed a bit to Dostoevsky – the redemptive qualities of those journeys and sojourns.

"I completely underestimated the appeal of 'Supper's Ready', all the people I expected to hate it loved it," Hackett continues. "And fortunately, because I thought it was only a matter of time before Tony Stratton-Smith said, 'Well, that's it boys, it's been nice working with you, but your contract is hereby terminated: don't call us, we'll call you.' On the contrary, he felt that *Foxtrot* showed the breadth of the band, and said many nice things about the band, and my own contributions towards it."

Such were the prevailing tastes in 1972, that rather than getting more commercial success by toning things down, in the case of *Foxtrot* it came by Genesis pushing further out. The album charted at number twelve in the UK.

Meanwhile, for those who enjoy puzzles and allegories, Paul Whitehead's cover yields at least as many as the cover of *Nursery Cryme*, despite the group giving it something of a lukewarm reception. A woman with a fox's head stands on a melting iceflow on the sea, while four deformed huntsmen on horseback have stopped on the seashore with an attendant pack of foxhounds sniffing at the incoming tide. Whitehead explains his creation: "The four horsemen are the four horsemen of the

Apocalypse from 'Supper's Ready'. The huntsman crying is death on the pale horse. The guy with the Pinocchio nose was supposed to be a Nixon kind of character, a politician. There's an alien, and famine and pestilence. The building on the far left is a Holiday Inn. I put that in because in those days they were just beginning to tour a lot and I saw an endless stream of hotels in their future. There are also remnants from *Nursery Cryme* – like the cover in the distance, and a croquet mallet and some hogweed floating in the sea."

Back in 1972, in terms of progressive rock, 'Supper's Ready' ticked all the boxes. Apart from its strong tunes, and adventurous arrangements and playing, there was a hip "otherness" about the group, an eccentricity and a sardonic sense of humour with Peter Gabriel the increasingly charismatic frontman. There was also something quite clever about Genesis, which was droll without being smug.

Rock fans have always liked the idea of the somewhat messianic star who knows more than they do – or at least makes a convincing impression of doing so – and Gabriel's name already had angelic import. Some fans were even seen at concerts with the words *"Human Bacon"* written across their foreheads in reference to Narcissus in 'Supper's Ready'.

Onstage Gabriel differentiated himself from his largely sedentary bandmates – who, in Hackett's words, became visually, at least, like his "pit orchestra" – through his between-song monologues and other gnomic utterances. He had now got himself a unique haircut, shaving a few inches into the centre parting of his lengthy tresses and with kohl-lined eyes and striking good looks he looked like the leader of some newly sprung up cult.

He has admitted the influence of Spike Milligan and how some of his ideas had manifested themselves in *Monty Python's Flying Circus*. And now young fans would be doing the *"a flower?"* routine and other extracts of 'Willow Farm' at break time alongside *Monty Python*'s 'Dead Parrot' sketch.

Foxtrot was clearly the album that put Genesis on another level and was generally well received in the press. Writing in *Sounds*, Jerry Gilbert said: "Lyrically and musically *Foxtrot* comes across as a total mind trip, with imagination and musical ideas being allowed to run wild and in turn stretch the imagination of the listener. Genesis have taken a lot of chances, but these days they have the full courage of their convictions to back them up. They're in a territory all of their own and picking up supporters all the way – I hope that this outstanding album receives the patient, repeated listening that it deserves."

Gabriel began to add more to his personal onstage performance, adopting masks and costumes. What kicked off this trend was a show soon after the release of the album, in Dublin on September 29, 1972, when the band were understandably shocked by him disappearing during an instrumental break and re-emerging wearing one of his wife Jill's red dresses and a fox's head. The group may have had an inkling that he was up to something, but not all the details.

"I certainly wasn't always upfront about everything because you'd end up having these endless debates and I'd think, 'Oh, fuck it, I can't be bothered,'" says Gabriel. "There was a silence when I walked out on the stage in this outfit. I think that very few people had seen a man in a dress at that point and certainly not one wearing a fox's head as well."

"The red dress came after the cover and when Peter debuted it, it was a complete surprise to the band," says Paul Whitehead. "I saw them quite often in the early days around London and the South, and Peter was always very interested to hear any feedback, particularly concerning the staging and visuals. In those days Peter was a somewhat awkward and self-conscious mover, he took some dance lessons and got better but it was never his strong card. The other members of the band always insisted that it was all about the music, and considered the theatrics a distraction from the music. In retrospect I don't think that Genesis would have caught on as quickly as they did without the theatrics."

Gail Colson of Charisma Records recalls: "In the beginning poor old Genesis got so much flak from going to Charterhouse. It was awful. It all turned, presswise, when Peter put the fox's head on and they were on the front cover of *Melody Maker*."

This well and truly opened the dressing-up box, with a giant flower mask for the *"a flower?"* section, and a sort of red box-like head and cloak combo for the *"guards of Magog"* section. Gabriel also donned bats' wing headgear for the character of The Watcher. The rock theatricality of Genesis was, in its own way, like glam rock for aspiring Heads.

Hackett remembers that musically speaking, the group were also beginning to turn into something special: "When we first got our own light show, which was on the cusp of 1972 and 1973, the band were something of a fairy tale coming to life. We managed to look and sound like nothing else on Earth. The band sounded mighty – you had something that was like a spooky version of church music, mixed with the syncopation of big band stuff, and all of the instruments sounded weird and wonderful, and you had [someone who was] nothing like a straight lead singer."

After the success of *Foxtrot*, its successor, *Selling England By The Pound*, released in August 1973, was more of a fantastical overview of these sceptered isles. On 'Dancing With The Moonlit Knight' Gabriel upped the pun quotient from the title down. In the song he juxtaposes banal scenes of consumer society, of burger-chomping masses, with the dance of grail knights of the *"green shield"*. This was the name of trading stamps acquired from petrol and other retail purchases, which were stuck into books that could eventually be redeemed for catalogue goods.

Both this song and 'The Cinema Show' feature complex instrumental sections, the latter a Banks outing on his recently acquired ARP Soloist synth. The song begins with pithy observations of a modern Romeo and Juliet starting their day and thinking ahead to their Friday night date after work. Another sexually unusual figure wanders in from the background drama, Father Tiresias from T. S. Eliot's 1922 modernist poem *The Wasteland*, in which he is described as an *"old man with wrinkled dugs"*.

Banks explains another hermaphroditic character's presence within the story: "Well, he changes sex, actually, from one to the other and the question was – very 'deep' stuff – who got the most pleasure out of sex".

Father Tiresias's speech within the song ends with the enigmatic proclamation that there is more earth than sea. 'Which means nothing at all," Banks admits. "But it makes people think. It's just fun playing with words."

Genesis scored an unexpected hit with 'I Know What I Like (In Your Wardrobe)', which went to number twenty-one in the singles charts a number of months after the album had been released. It reflects Betty Swanwick's cover painting of a recumbent gardener in an ornamental garden taking a lunchtime rest from his duties.

Gabriel came into his own on 'The Battle Of Epping Forest', a cartoonish gangland battle saga that would have made an entertaining comic strip, its storyline full of dodgy geezers, protection racketeers, a clergyman turned pimp called The Reverend, an effete art student and many more. As a story it's like an updated Ealing Comedy, although rather congested lyrically, with a plethora of creaky puns, as when judge refers to The Reverend as a *"robbing hood"*.

Speaking of creaky puns, the most affecting song on the album is 'Firth Of Fifth', a Banks and Rutherford composition that consists of three hymnal verses, with an instrumental section before the third.

Banks: "I don't think it's a very good lyric, it's got a few images in it which are quite nice, but it's kind of floppy, if you know what I mean; it doesn't say too much. Musically the song is one of the things I'm most proud of from that era, and I love the guitar, the way it takes over the melody in the second half is one of the strongest moments of Genesis."

Two verses in, after Gabriel's pretty flute theme, comes the instrumental section to which Banks is referring. Here, Hackett takes up the flute theme on guitar, slows it down and turns it into something spectacular. Hackett can hear in his own flourishes and bent notes something of the melismas of Indian music, or the effect that Eastern scales had on the music of early 20th-century French composers like Claude Debussy and Erik Satie.

"I'd just got an Echoplex, and I was using a Hi-Watt amp, and nine times out of ten I could get a high F-sharp to sustain with feedback if I was placed in the right spot," Hackett explains, "and I think Tony loved the fact that I played his melody over and over again. I'd visualised a bird flying above the sea, a very high-wheeling guitar solo." That might sound fanciful, but if ever a guitar solo sounded like a bird wheeling high over the sea, then surely this is the one.

Ahead of the group's 1973 tour Gabriel talked to Barbara Charone of *New Musical Express*: "I've been having conversations with my mask maker. I gave him a copy of the lyrics to the new album… I've found it helps to go over the words with him, trying to get pictures from the words, conceptions of characters.

"We also have a guy working for us on stage designs. We explain what effects we'd like, with lighting and all. On this tour we'll be using a screen for backdrop projections. All these things," he stresses, "help to create the fantasy we work under."

Gabriel goes on to explain that in his view, film, art and music will someday merge and that the idea of a Genesis show is to transport the audience into fantasy, and that they would ideally like to have their own portable theatre to enable them to do this. He also commented that some people thought the group were derivative.

"They think we ripped off Yes's music, Alice Cooper's visuals, and we came up with Genesis. And just because I was dressing up, people assumed I was imitating Bowie. But the thing is, the characters I play are things talked about in the lyrics. Bowie's a great writer, but I don't always think his costumes are relevant to his music."

The fact that three of the current line-up had gone to Charterhouse was never quite forgotten and prompted one notorious headline in *New Musical Express*: "Public Schoolboys – Can They Rock'n'Roll?"

This came from a particular type of rock'n'roll fundamentalism born out of the Sixties underground, which envisaged a classless society and one that should do away with privilege. Which is a fair point if you are arguing against the old school tie network in business, but Genesis went against all peer pressure and parental expectation and effectively became outsiders. No, they didn't fit the romantic stereotype of salt-of-the-earth rock'n'rollers. But was that even relevant?

Hackett, a mere grammar school boy, has these views: "Well, there was a certain animosity, you know – what are these nobs doing out there on a jolly jape for an afternoon, surely they're dilettantes? But music should be assessed on the quality of ideas."

Another criticism levelled at Genesis was that they played everything live essentially the same as they did on record, as if that signified a certain sterility and lack of rock'n'roll spontaneity. This was exemplified by *Genesis Live*, an attractively unglossy recording that was released shortly after *Foxtrot*. Improvisation was certainly limited in the music of Genesis, but Banks explains why, in the era of jamming and elongated soloing, this was band practice: "We always felt that interminable guitar solos that all sounded pretty much the same were not where we wanted to go, so if we had solos they tended to be structured, written pieces of music as much as the songs. 'The Cinema Show' [keyboard solo] was written as a melodic musical piece."

If the group's music might have been somewhat predictable in concert, their choice of support on their 1973 tour, Ron Geesin, was anything but. "The infamous first gig was at Glasgow Apollo, in October," Geesin recalls. "I thought, 'I'll do a non-entrance tonight'. I went on with a white coat looking like a stagehand or a doctor. The audience got very unrestful and started shouting, and that was it – I'd lost it from the start. I lasted about 20 minutes out of the half hour, torrents of abuse coming from the audience, and the place was in such uproar at the end that Genesis didn't go on.

"The group looked extremely pale when I came off; even Peter Gabriel under his white make-up. They cancelled the gig and gave everyone their money back. The next night was Manchester and I knew what to do, and I flattened the audience before they had time to move; and the rest of the tour was a great success."

Writing fantasy novels or making fantastical films already had a considerable history by the Seventies. The musical fantasy that Genesis embraced was not always well regarded, but then rock'n'roll and pop music was usually anything but social realism, and had generally erred towards fantasy elements anyway, rather than assiduously chronicling accounts of the day-to-day or cold hard facts.

That said, Genesis did take the rock'n'roll lexicon into strange climes. As Banks admits, once you start writing songs about Ikhnaton, "You are in real trouble". Anyway, leaving that argument to simmer on the back burner, it's time to go even stranger and become immersed in progressive rock's ultimate fantasy tale, *The Lamb Lies Down On Broadway*.

The idea of writing a concept album had been hanging around Genesis for quite some time, but the differences in the group members' approach were such that Mike Rutherford suggested an album based on the children's novella *The Little Prince* by Antoine De Saint-Exupéry. Although the book's story includes a wise fox, which would have saved on the costumes budget, it would surely have been a disastrous move.

One only needs to compare that to what was actually released to understand the tensions that were operating within the group. This time Gabriel insisted that he wrote all the lyrics to give the double album thematic consistency, whereas other group members, Banks for one, were insisting that he didn't. But Gabriel won through.

The album has been described as being like a sort of latterday *Pilgrim's Progress* or another *Alice's Adventures In Wonderland*, while the all black-and-white photographs on the sleeve – this time designed by Hipgnosis – recall some of Orson Welles' cinematography for *A Touch Of Evil* and his version of Franz Kafka's *The Trial*. There are some parallels between the structured anti-logic of Kafka's novel and Gabriel's story of Rael, a Puerto-Rican teenager. Rael's journey begins on Broadway within a kaleidoscope of American cultural imagery, but soon spirals down the proverbial rabbit hole into a dark subconscious world full of threat and paradox, with yet more poetic and mythological references, like the Lamia, who are female creatures from Greek mythology via the poetry of John Keats. The songs are highly visual with some of their imagery inspired, in part, by Chilean film director Alejandro Jodorowsky, who into the 2000s, Gabriel still hoped might direct a film version.

Received wisdom is that progressive rock can be epitomised – according to something I heard on the radio at the time of writing – as "a twenty-minute flute solo followed by lyrics about hobbits", of which there are no examples, and more seriously that "progressive rock fans loved twenty-five-minute tracks", of which there were hardly any. Over time, received wisdom habitually grows to be less and less accurate. Take Led Zeppelin. Some strongly dislike the group for being constantly priapic cock rockers, whose every song is about shagging, except for those that are about hobbits – and probably one or two that are actually about shagging hobbits. After the first two albums there is very little overtly sexual imagery. On their 1975 double album *Physical Graffiti* two of the tracks, 'Custard Pie' and 'Trampled Underfoot', employ bluesy sexual metaphors, while 'The Wanton Song' and 'Sick Again' deal fairly directly with sex and desire.

The Lamb Lies Down On Broadway is, however, chock full of sex – and weird sex at that. Rael brags of his fights and sexual conquests, but his heart begins to grow hairy, a metaphor for a hollow threat of rape, but which in fact leads to him having to consult a sex manual on how to make love to a woman, which he attempts with little success. He later meets the Lamia of the pool and after symbolic lovemaking they die and Rael eats their flesh. He then joins the colony of Slippermen who have become hideously deformed after similar experiences with the mythical snake-like females. They have also ended up with giant testicles and things get worse when Doktor Dyper cuts off Rael's penis, which is then put into a tube and stolen by a raven.

If the story of *The Lamb...* owes a debt to the insights of psychologist and writer Carl Jung, it seems that he's metaphorically slugging it out with sex-obsessed Sigmund Freud.

Brian Eno made a brief appearance, treating Gabriel's vocals on 'The Grand Parade Of Lifeless Packaging' – credited as "Enossification" – while 'Silent Sorrow In Empty Boats' with its simple, ascending six note sequence with distant Mellotron choir was unlike anything Genesis had attempted before and resembles the still life moods Eno would conjure up on his forthcoming album, *Another Green World*.

Prior to recording, the group had decamped to Headley Grange in Hampshire, the old workhouse also used by Led Zeppelin, to rehearse and work up some ideas. A short extract from these sessions known as "The Headley Tapes" runs at the end of 'In The Cage' on side one.

Starting with one of Banks's most famous cross-handed, seemingly double-speed piano lines in the intro of the title track, the album features some of the group's most adventurous music. Collins, playing an expanded kit with racks of percussion, is particularly inventive throughout. Some of the sections like 'Fly On The Windshield' and 'Silent Sorrow In Empty Boats' were semi-improvised. 'The Waiting Room', in which Rael awaits, fearful of the appearance of the *"Supernatural Anaesthetist"* aka Death, is largely a free improvisation but full of clanking, crashes, twitchy echoed guitar notes and meowing synth played through a wah-wah pedal or similar filter.

"The first time we ever did it we were at Headley Grange and so we said, 'Let's frighten ourselves,'" Banks recalls. "It was dusk and it was a pretty creepy place anyhow, and we played it and it was absolutely fantastic, but we didn't record it because we had nothing there. So every time after that we were trying to capture that moment, but never really did."

It's a shame that this particular path was left to grow over as the group showed that when they collectively improvised, it added an edgy and exciting new dimension to their sound.

The stage sets for *The Lamb Lies Down On Broadway* were spectacular with two levels for Gabriel to run around on with a radio mike, and slides projected onto screens to emphasise the story. Gabriel's stage persona went from the short haired leather jacketed character of Rael to being picked out by lights within a swirling cloth lantern during 'The Lamia', to the Slipperman costume, with its inflatable testicles and a massive head, the inner acoustics of which made microphone placement difficult. He also used constructions like giant shadow puppets to cast shadows during 'The Waiting Room'.

It was a spectacular piece of music theatre, but the group experienced technical difficulties on most nights. Banks: "I'm very proud to have been involved in it, because I think it was quite a revolutionary thing to do, but I don't honestly ever think it truly worked. There were always technical problems every night, which was depressing. I remember once Peter got wrapped up in the thing that was twirling around him in 'The Lamia'."

One of the problems about playing the album live in its entirety was that the opening two sides of the album are stronger than side three and four. Unlike the cathartic end of 'Supper's Ready', there is lyrically an odd, cryptic resolution where Rael and his brother John, who has shadowed him throughout the narrative, change faces, signifying a destruction of one character or part of self to let the other one live on. The last song, 'It', with soaring guitar lines from Hackett, is lyrically dense but difficult to read.

The album was released in November 1974, the month that the tour started in the USA. The problem for audiences was that many hadn't even heard the music that made up the ninety-odd minutes of each concert.

It was a long haul, into May 1975, and morale wasn't helped by the fact that Gabriel had told his bandmates that he was intending to leave after the tour.

"It was a downer and the tour sort of petered out," says Banks. "We were supposed to do Toulouse as the very last show, but we cancelled it because the attendance looked like it would be very poor so the last show was the Palais de Sports in Besançon, and that was not very well attended and very low key."

Hackett has similar memories. "Even when we were doing what's lauded now as one of the finest prog rock albums of all time, *The Lamb*

Lies Down On Broadway, at the end of having toured that for six months straight on the road, carrying our own huge production around – or so it seemed at the time, but it was quite small by today's standards – we were in the hole for £250,000, which was extremely depressing. So we came to the end of that, and then we lost our lead singer – a double, bitter blow."

As Genesis had operated as a songwriting collective, that Gabriel got so much more attention than the other musicians and had come up with the concept for *The Lamb Lies Down On Broadway*, had caused a degree of tension in the group. But then how could they replace him?

Reporting on the news when it was released in August, *Melody Maker* journalist and long-time Genesis supporter Chris Welch wrote a rather sombre, valedictory piece with this as the summation: "While we keep talking, perhaps unfairly, of Genesis in the past tense, the departure of Gabriel is certainly an end of an era both for the band and British rock."

Welch's view that Gabriel's departure marked the end of an era was prescient, but as we shall see later on, all this gloom and despondency was misplaced, and both Genesis and Gabriel flourished in a way that no one could have predicted.

CHAPTER 9

Swings and Roundabouts: Yes

On November 26, 1968, Cream, one of the most revered groups in the UK, waved goodbye to their brief and somewhat tempestuous career with a farewell concert at the Royal Albert Hall, London. They had briefly defined the zeitgeist with their mix of pop, psychedelia and heavy blues. The support groups were a young Irish blues-rock trio, Taste, led by guitarist Rory Gallagher, and something quite different, a hot young band called Yes. Their name was as cool as flashing a peace sign and they carried all the post-psychedelic positivity that it implied. This made one audience member, *Melody Maker* journalist Chris Welch, an instant convert.

"They brought together such an unexpected range of influences from folk to jazz and rock and made it all sound so new, fresh and attractive," he would write in his book *Close To The Edge: The Story Of Yes*. "They were already playing advanced arrangements. Here were songs that stopped and started with nerve-shattering suddenness, paused for reflection, and then stormed back with all guns blazing."

These first stirrings of a new kind of rock music as purveyed by Yes chimed perfectly with the journalist's own tastes.

"It hadn't occurred to me that anybody wouldn't like it, because it struck me that this is what we'd all been waiting for," Welch says now. "Rock was being taken seriously, the musicians were getting better and better. I always wanted to see the music improve and be more satisfying. So I couldn't see any argument with it, personally."

Here was a group who mixed original songs and cover versions in a way that nodded towards American group Vanilla Fudge and some of Deep Purple's radical reinventions, but in a way that felt more holistic, and different again. "They had the vocal harmonies, clever choral arrangements, and what with Bill's jazzy, inspired drumming, it sounded like a compact little jazz big band to me with a West Coast feel as well," adds Welch.

Guitarist Peter Banks and bass guitarist Chris Squire had played together in the psychedelic band The Syn in 1967 and soon after became bandmates in the group with arguably the most quintessentially twee English psychedelic moniker, Mabel Greer's Toyshop.

Squire was put in touch with a singer from Accrington, Jon Anderson, who possessed a distinctive natural alto voice. Anderson had served time in The Warriors and had briefly been in The Gun, leaving just before they had a hit single with the hard rocking 'Race With The Devil'. The Gun's self-titled debut album sleeve artwork was the first commission by upcoming young artist Roger Dean, who would soon feature prominently in Yes's story.

At the time, Anderson was serving drinks at La Chasse, a well-known musicians' watering hole on Wardour Street in Soho. He had worked on the family farm near Accrington since the age of 15 to help his ailing father, and had had a job delivering bricks. He told Welch: "Being in a working class area of Accrington, you work for a living. You don't become an artist. You don't paint. For me it was a fight to get away from that sort of situation. I didn't want to end up all my life driving long distance lorries or delivering milk."

When Anderson and Squire first met they realised that they shared a love of Simon & Garfunkel, Fifth Dimension, The Beatles and The Byrds, and sketched out the song 'Sweetness', a sophisticated pop ballad with unexpected twists and turns. Squire had been a choirboy in his youth, initially having no interest in rock'n'roll, and although his voice lacked the character of a lead singer, his pitching was spot on and his vocal lines sat well with Anderson's, with Banks making up the harmony trio.

Understandably, Anderson wasn't keen on being the singer in a band with a name destined for ridicule and Banks came up with the name Yes. They drafted in a precocious teenage drummer, Bill Bruford, who had grown up with jazz, via an advert in *Melody Maker*, and also Tony Kaye who had planned on becoming a concert pianist, but gravitated towards jazz and then towards R&B in his teens. He cited Family, from his hometown of Leicester, as a particular influence.

Welch's fellow *Melody Maker* journalist Tony Wilson wrote the sleeve notes for Yes's self-titled debut album on Atlantic: "At the beginning of 1969, I was asked to pick two groups who I thought would make it in the following year. One of my choices was Led Zeppelin. A bit obvious perhaps, but then we all like to back a winner occasionally. The other was Yes."

Yes's debut gives the listener an idea of what they were like live. 'Looking Around' and 'Harold Land' are particularly strong songs with Kaye's punchy Hammond organ complementing Banks's dextrous, freewheeling guitar lines. 'Sweetness' was included, and their version of

Lennon and McCartney's 'Every Little Thing' from *Beatles For Sale* (1964) is another of the standout tracks, given momentum by Bruford's onrushing snare drum figures, with no clue given as to what song is being covered until two minutes into the instrumental intro, when a casual reference to 'Day Tripper' eases us into the first verse.

Big, distorted bass lines had been the driving force of mid-Sixties pop songs like The Nashville Teens' 'Tobacco Road' and The Spencer Davis Group's 'Keep On Runnin', but it was still a time when bass guitarists were often left to do the donkey work. Chris Squire's bass had an unusual trebly edge that cut through, snarling, in the chorus and keyboard break of 'Survival'.

The genesis of his bass guitar style had come about in bizarre circumstances. One day, when he was feeling a bit off colour, he was offered a tab of homemade acid, which he gratefully consumed. Back in 1967 when he was in The Syn he would enjoy taking LSD at psychedelic clubs like UFO when "it was fun and great and colourful", but this expected pick-me-up triggered a seriously bad trip. Squire later found himself in Fulham hospital without any idea where, or even who, he was. Such were the risks of taking acid in the late Sixties. After being discharged, Squire ended up staying in his girlfriend's flat for months, still feeling mentally frazzled and afraid to venture outside.

But in an unexpected by-product of this psychedelic dabbling, Squire practised playing his Rickenbacker bass all day, expanding on the probing, melodic lines of Paul McCartney and the flamboyant approach of John Entwistle, whose distorted bass would sometimes become the lead instrument in The Who. During this hermetic period he forged a highly individual style, admitting: "I learned to do a few tricks of the trade that other people hadn't done before."

Mark Williams of *International Times* gave *Yes* a very positive review, concluding: "They'll appeal to pop audiences and progressive freaks with equal effectiveness." But disappointingly, *Yes* failed to chart.

For a headlining concert at Queen Elizabeth Hall in London in March 1970, Yes decided to expand their horizons further by showcasing some new material with an orchestra. Mark Williams again reviewed proceedings and as well as being unimpressed by the sound, he was critical of the second half of the concert in which the group presented new material. They seemed to Williams like a youth orchestra who "lacked any empathy with singer Jon Anderson's music arrangements. They were all dressed up as hippies and bopped around with suitable enthusiasm, but (a) they could rarely be heard and (b) when they were audible, they seemed to be playing schlock arrangements."

The follow-up, *A Time And A Word*, recorded in late 1969 and released in 1970, had an orchestra on some of the tracks, most notably on their version of 'No Opportunity Needed, No Experience Necessary', a cover of a song by American singer-songwriter Richie Havens, which started off audaciously with the semiquaver string arpeggios of Jerome Moross's theme to the 1958 Western *The Big Country*.

This made a dramatic opening statement, but on record as well as live, the strings feel like a bit of a cheesy garnish spread over a feisty group performance. The same applies to 'The Prophet', with its hippieish lyrics and a token musical quote from the first main theme of 'Jupiter' from Gustav Holst's *The Planets*. The group were rushing into what was de rigueur at the time and not doing it particularly well, while losing some of their early promise along the way.

A clearly disenchanted Banks was unhappy with the orchestra and other musical matters besides, and was asked to leave. He went on to enjoy some success with another group with a memorable name, the shortlived Flash. Tony Wilson's metaphorical punt on Yes being the next big thing seemed in jeopardy and although the album charted at number forty-five in the UK, Atlantic were seriously considering dropping what had once seemed to be a hot property, but was now cooling in a rather unappealing way.

Their new guitarist was Steve Howe who had shown unusual invention in the psychedelic group Tomorrow, then with the shortlived Bodast, whose record label had gone under.

"It was Peter Banks that I was replacing, so I had something of a template of what player they wanted," says Howe. "But what I wanted to do in the band was contribute, and partly the reason that the band stopped doing covers was because I said that a band should only play its own music."

As well as Howe's skills on guitar he could also sing, and like Squire, although he was not lead singer material he could hit the notes and so the Yes three part harmony approach was maintained.

"We were all trying to move up a gear," Howe recalls. "We were looking for songs with depth. Any intro that was under two minutes we thought, 'That can't be long enough!' So we enjoyed that sort of flamboyance and reckless turning away from convention. We didn't want to be ordinary or similar or bluesy or rocky. We always used to try to deny that we were a rock band."

This more concentrated approach to their compositional process produced some spectacular results with *The Yes Album*. A young recording engineer Eddy Offord co-produced the album with the group in

Advision studios in autumn 1970. Offord gave the album a vivid, panoramic sound, with each instrument distinct, but mixed together beautifully to give it considerable heft.

While 'No Experience Necessary, No Opportunity Needed' had quoted *The Big Country*, on *The Yes Album*, 'Yours Is No Disgrace' kicks off with a bass, guitar and drums unison part that clearly nods back at the syncopated 4/4 of the film's opening theme. Kaye joins in with his Hammond organ chords given a corrosive edge by being used in conjunction with a rotating Leslie speaker.

Already in this opening section it was clear that everything had indeed gone up a gear and Squire's bass sounded like nothing else at the time. He had taken Yes's new-found freedom and flown with it, and was playing with an almost arrogant swagger. But far from being hollow grandstanding, Squire's performance is full of subtlety and nuance. His double speed figures gnaw thrillingly into Bruford's incisive drum groove and then he takes off into spiralling melodic lines that complement Howe's spangly country-style finger picking.

We are only about a minute and a half into the song when it all slides down to a single organ chord, the band drop out, and the Yes harmony trio come in, but we have already heard a significant rethink of rock bass playing, a veritable low-end Rickenbackerama. When the song's juggernaut momentum abates in the slow sections, Squire's bass line – somewhere between a jazz walking bass and a Bach bourée – is as memorable as the vocal melody.

Anderson's approach to writing lyrics had changed to a more abstracted style, with a very personal use of syntax. 'Yours Is No Disgrace' has a lyric that ostensibly carries on the ideas of 'Harold Land', of the hapless soldier stuck in a combat zone, lost in circumstances he cannot win. It had been partly inspired by the ongoing Troubles in Northern Ireland although it also finds Anderson referencing Caesar's Palace and admonishing the venal human race.

"By the third album, I had found a very loose way of writing, using words more for the sound rather than meaning," says Anderson. [As on 'Yours Is No Disgrace', with the opening line and a] *'flying, purple wolfhound'* – they all made sense to me."

'Yours Is No Disgrace' is a dazzling piece of work, but it also signposted the future in that it does ramble somewhat in the instrumental sections. Howe: "With 'Yours Is No Disgrace', we expanded it, we improvised and I was given the chance to extend solos a bit like I used to do in a crazy way with Tomorrow, but with Yes it was more concise. But there was always a different sound going on onstage."

The Yes Album was unequivocally Yes's major statement so far, reaching number four in the UK charts and sneaking into the American Top 40. 'Starship Trooper' was a collective effort and is divided into three sections – as was the hip thing to do at the time – and each part is very different: 'Life Seeker', by Anderson, is the big anthemic opener; 'Disillusion', a brisk acoustic section written by Squire has harmonies reminiscent of Crosby, Stills & Nash; and after a brief reprise of 'Life Seeker' we are into 'Würm', a three-chord guitar refrain – originally from Howe's Bodast days – that gradually builds to a crescendo with Bruford subtly adding to the intensity of his playing. It all peaks with sonorous organ bass pedals and Howe breaking into a double-tracked solo in his lyrical but angular style.

Interviewed in 2009, Howe said: "In the Seventies, everything had to do with psychedelia. It may have quit as a fashion in 1968, but I was still a psychedelic guitarist in my mind. I would not play blues clichés for love nor money."

Then Tony Kaye was sacked. It has been said that he was given his marching orders for his reluctance to play synthesizer, although he had played it on *The Yes Album*. There were allegations from Squire that Yes had to change the keyboard player because of Kaye's tendency, when on tour, to bring women back to the room that he shared with Howe, and the resultant disturbance. If that is true, it is one of the oddest reasons that any musician has been sacked from any group. He went on to play with Badger whose debut *One Live Badger* was recorded in 1973, when the group supported Yes at the Rainbow Theatre, and was co-produced by Jon Anderson.

It transpires that Rick Wakeman, then in the Strawbs, had already been tapped to be Kaye's replacement. Bruford was not impressed and told Welch: "It was definitely a case of ambition and there was no loyalty at all. The scent of success was in the air, and now it was a pack of hounds in full cry."

This gives the implication that behind Yes's benign, hippie exterior, Anderson, who had always been assertive when dealing with gig promoters in the early days, had a steely, careerist vision of furthering the group. Rather than investigating all that as a cold case, it's best to move on and welcome Wakeman into the fold. As mentioned in Chapter 5, he had been invited to play with David Bowie full time but he chose Yes as there would be no limitations on what he could contribute.

The next Yes LP, *Fragile*, was titled with regard to the stability of planet Earth. This idea was referenced on the cover artwork, by Roger Dean in his first commission for Yes, of a stylised planet with a chunk of it sheared off, while fantastical bird-like sailing ships navigate the sky.

The idea was that each member would compose a solo piece, which, although veering away from the united front that they had shown on *The Yes Album*, worked surprisingly well, as these were all short sketches and gave some light relief from the three striking long tracks, 'Roundabout', 'South Side Of The Sky' and 'Heart Of The Sunrise'.

In 1971 Wakeman had signed a deal with A&M as a solo artist and was published by Rondor, a different company to the rest of Yes. Due to these complications, he wasn't able to have his name down as a composer with Yes until it was sorted out, even though he had contributed to a number of songs on *Fragile* – the first time Wakeman met the group in rehearsal prior to actually joining them, he helped them finish off 'Roundabout'. Yes's manager Brian Lane told him that they would make it up to him, but he never received any further royalties.

Wakeman also remembers Howe presenting the group with a short, melodic guitar line and Squire with a fast semiquaver bass run of a few bars and when the latter was asked if he had any more, he said: "No that's it." Together these two elements went on to form the basis of the first section of 'Heart Of The Sunrise'.

"I'd written 'Heart Of The Sunrise', then I heard Chris [Squire] and Bill [Bruford] weaving a great riff one day in the studio," remembers Anderson. "I suggested they modulate to a different key, then do a jerky stop/start idea, very Stravinsky-ish, then play in another key. By then Steve had joined in, and I suggested to Rick to create an orchestral sound [on Mellotron] rising out of the riff, then join in. We had so much harmony at that time. The song expanded and that became the key to real Yes music."

"That *was* the key to Yes," Howe assents. "It wasn't that we took a song by Jon or me and played it, we took the parts that we thought were best and we arranged it and took parts from other people to make it more interesting, so the input of ideas was at a very high level for a rock band. We were doing what other people were doing, but in our own way and trying to get our own individual sound.

"Prog is about influences merging in an indescribable sort of way, the folk, the blues, the rock, the jazz, the classical – in my case flamenco – but not being allowed to dominate."

In all this inspired fitting together of puzzle pieces, on 'Heart Of The Sunrise', one of the group's most revered compositions, there is a surfeit of ornamental instrumental elements. But the main song – which sounds like something that might have been written by Jimmy Webb – is so strong it can withstand such decoration.

'Roundabout' also has its fair share of ornamentation and comprises around fifteen edits. Like most tracks on *The Yes Album*, it is basically an elongated, souped-up pop song mixed with many other musical delights. Anderson's lyrics had moved even further away from literal meaning but are rich in imagery. They were the subject of much scrutiny and some derision, but then putting it all into context, one doesn't normally go to pop or rock music for instruction or meaning.

Bill Bruford gives this assessment: "I was never fussed about Jon Anderson's lyrics because to me they were vocals with phonetics. I wasn't after literal meaning. I didn't really care if the mountain came out of the sky and stood there or not, because the words had enough information for me in their sound and rhythm, which is all that this drummer needed. Were they any 'good'? I don't know. What did they mean? Their meaning for me was rhythmic, sonic and expressive. Their meaning for you might have been something entirely different."

'Roundabout' begins with Howe's ruminative acoustic guitar solo but is exceptionally funky in places, courtesy of Squire's commanding bass and Bruford's crisp snare and thumping kick drum, with Wakeman playing some rippling organ lines around these figures. The song careers into a dramatic bass riff with Bruford's subtle but relentless snare drum patterns and cymbal punctuations, leading to one of Yes's most thrilling three-part harmonics, with Wakeman weighing in with dramatic organ punctuations. Then a final verse and chorus, a glorious a capella section and it all resolves beautifully with a few closing acoustic guitar lines.

This mix of big tunes, thunderous rock'n'roll oomph and finely wrought arrangements made up Yes's most emphatic statement to date. It was released as a single in edited form in the US in 1972 and reached number thirteen in the *Billboard* charts. Piecemeal composition or not, Yes were certainly onto something. If any one song could be picked to represent all that is exhilarating about progressive rock, this has to be on the shortlist.

Yes went on tour in the USA in 1971 and momentum was building. *Fragile* reached number four in the US *Billboard* charts and number seven in the UK. Richard Cromelin wrote this in his *Rolling Stone* review: "Gorgeous melodies, intelligent, carefully crafted, constantly surprising arrangements, concise and energetic performances, cryptic but evocative lyrics – when all these are present Yes is quite boggling and their potential seemingly unlimited."

But as Yes were transcending their initial status as support act at UK colleges and were beginning to take their place in the vanguard of progressive rock, Bruford noted a competition between groups, an "arms race" to acquire more gear and to put on more impressive shows. "We should not underestimate the influence of the other bands in the immediate proximity," he says. "We watched ELP, we listened to Led Zeppelin, and we thought, 'Why are they doing so well?' The answer was frequently technological: 'They've got a PA; we haven't. Who's got a Hammond organ? Can we afford to ship one? Has Rick Wakeman got a Hammond?'

"There was a lot of competition. We played with the other bands of the day and I'd be in the wings listening to all of them. We were concerned with what other musicians were doing and how well they did it – or not.

"We thought, 'They're doing that so we'll be different. The Nice are pretty good but they haven't got three-part vocal harmony. We can sing whole songs in harmony, fantastic, just like The Beach Boys.' We would think along those lines; what have they got and what can we do that's different?"

And when you got the instruments there was the small matter of mastering them, especially with synthesizer technology, which was still in its relative infancy and still rather unpredictable.

"It was the end of the era when the musician was ahead of technology," says Wakeman. "As there were no preset keys you spent hours trying to get your own individual sounds, so what you had in your head is what you created, not the other way round.

"Keith Emerson and I have laughed about it. We got [synthesizers] in the early Seventies and you'd spend weeks trying to get the sound you really liked. And then when you got it you nurtured it because it became yours. The problem was when you turned it off you had lost it again and you had to keep finding it."

The recording of *Close To The Edge* commenced in February 1972. The group then went on tour and rehearsed in the basement of Una Billings' School Of Dancing in Shepherds Bush, London, in May, before the final sessions took place the following month. But the transition from rehearsal to studio was far from smooth. They'd had a month in the studio to record *Fragile*, but sessions for the follow-up were taking longer.

Yes were starting to make a lot of money for Atlantic, and Bruford notes that the group were allowed to work without record company interference: "Tom Dowd came down to the studio during *Fragile* or maybe *The Yes Album*; he was Atlantic's big arranger and a wonderful guy.

And he just sat quietly at the back at Advision for about forty-five minutes or an hour and didn't say anything, then just got up and left quietly, the implication being 'We'll just let these guys get on with it, there's nothing much to add'. Which I thought was really nice, really open."

But the adage that work expands to fill the time available was beginning to apply and when Chris Welch visited Advision during the *Close To The Edge* sessions, he found a group in the throes of what he called "studio stupour". He recalls hearing a thud as a fatigued Eddy Offord, who was by now regarded as a sixth group member to the extent that his photo appeared on the album sleeve, somnolently slipped from his chair at the mixing desk and hit the floor. In Welch's view: "It seemed that only Steve Howe and Jon Anderson really knew what *Close To The Edge* was about and only Chris Squire and Eddy Offord could pull it into shape. As for Rick and Bill – they seemed like innocent bystanders."

Yes's compositional process could also become chaotic, with the musicians forgetting what they had done the day before, suddenly realising that the song in question needed a link from A to B, and at times changing their minds about what they had previously come up with in rehearsals.

But despite all this, *Close To The Edge* had a far more unified feel than *Fragile*. Anderson explains the Yes process in full flow from a more positive viewpoint: "I had started working very closely with Steve. We had a lot of the nuggets of songs before we went in the studio, and I had a dream of creating a large work. So with the great talents of Bill, Chris and Rick, it was inevitable that the music would take over, and it did on many levels.

"I look back and remember Chris and Bill working out very different riffs and ideas, really helping to magnify the music, and Rick was constantly coming up with musical ideas. The wonderful engineer Eddy Offord was a big part of the free thinking that went on at that time; it was truly magical each and every day. We had amazing harmony as musicians and friends for that album. It wasn't hard, yet it wasn't easy. It just was incredible to be there."

Wakeman: "*Fragile* was the perfect forerunner to *Close To The Edge*. It taught us a lot about each other, how we could work together, how we could play together and how we could actually make something like *Close To The Edge*."

The side-long title track found Yes slipping their moorings and sailing out into the unknown. After an intro of birdsong and ambient sounds –

which required an enormous tape loop to be snaked around the studio – the first two minutes of 'The Solid Time Of Change' are astonishing. Although composed, the group instrumental sounds like an improvisation with no discernable chordal foundation. Howe's angular guitar lines veer crazily, tracked by Squire's hyperactive bass and Wakeman's high-velocity, skittering keyboards, while Bruford explores the rhythmic possibilities on offer with idiosyncratic cymbal and snare figures, and full kit rolls. Occasionally it stops dead and Anderson punctuates the pause with a short, exclamatory *"Ah!"* This was rock music that had left behind the blues scales and the cover versions and, briefly, sounded like nothing we'd ever heard before.

Following on from this comes a series of sumptuous melodies over further servings of taut grooves from Squire and Bruford – who has noted that they were both fans of Sly Stone. 'I Get Up, I Get Down' is a hushed middle section with a vocal call and response between Anderson, and Squire and Howe, with Wakeman playing huge church organ chords. His Hammond organ solo in the high-speed ensemble section that follows feels a bit perfunctory, like someone practising scales. But it climaxes with an exultant re-emergence of the main vocal tune, then fades to birdsong.

"The message there is that Yes found a medium of twenty minutes and felt really at home in it, really comfortable," says Howe. "With 'Close To The Edge' we weren't being indulgent, we were [tying] together a suite of music. It contains about four songs in there, at least but then multiple instrumental approaches, so twenty minutes was just a ball of fun."

Their painstaking approach was ultimately vindicated. *Close To The Edge* took longer than planned, with takes prevaricated over, much splicing together of tape and all hands on the mixing desk. Certainly the group were struggling at times and mistakes were made. At the end of the title track, the last verse can be heard to have a slightly more reverby ambience. It was a great take, but not the one they had actually intended to splice in. Another near disaster came when the group who had, in a rare display of unanimity, decided on a particular take, but couldn't find the section of tape and in something of a panic went outside into Gosfield Street where they recovered it from the bins where it had been taken by the studio cleaners.

Side two features two ten-minute songs. 'And You And I' mixes acoustic strum with towering Mellotron themes on the 'Apocalypse' section composed by Squire and Bruford, while 'Siberian Khatru' sees Yes's rock dynamic working in a new space. They might have begun to disappear into their own world, but that was partly the beauty of it: big chunky riffs, a harpsichord solo from Wakeman and interludes packed with glowing vocal harmonies. Apparently, "Khatru" means "What you wish" in Yemeni, not that that information is a key to unlock its lyrical secrets.

This distancing from the tack taken by most rock groups was reflected in the cover art, now a vital part of the group's aesthetic. Roger Dean's visual creations had a symbiotic relation with the music within. An airbrushed green cover with the new Yes "bubble" logo opened out to reveal a stunning inner gatefold, a painting with Chinese and Japanese influences, of a geomorphologically impossible plateau, from whose island-dotted top, water pours off in all directions.

This is the image, complementary to the music, that helps imbue *Close To The Edge* with an enduring magic. Bruford's view on the album is that "it remains a classic of the genre. I don't know how we managed it but we somehow got lucky. To this day it seems to have the perfect form, and form is everything."

Even prog-agnostic journalist Nick Kent concedes that: "*Close To The Edge* is the greatest prog rock — with all the clichés attached — record ever made."

Shortly before the final sessions for *Close To The Edge*, Andrew Tyler from *Disc* had gone to see Yes in rehearsal at Una Billings' School Of Dancing. Firstly he went to meet Squire who talked about the group's upcoming touring schedule starting at the end of July, including some big American concerts.

When they got to the rehearsal space Bruford was there playing drums and some piano, then Anderson arrived and jokingly told the drummer he was fired. Bruford then enthusiastically spoke to Tyler about how he was "very happy" and that "there's plenty to do and absolutely no limit to growth".

That may have been true, but it wasn't to be in Yes, as Bruford quit on July 19, 1972, to join King Crimson. This came as a considerable shock to the group, but after an epiphany seeing King Crimson at the Marquee in 1969, his heart had been set on eventually joining. He had previously spoken to Crimson guitarist Robert Fripp, but had been told that he was "not ready yet". Now he evidently was. On leaving Yes he writes: "It is the obligation of every artist to exercise his or her higher sensibilities for as much of the time as possible, and with Yes I knew I could go no further."

Bruford's replacement was Alan White, who knew Offord and had even sat in on one band rehearsal when Bruford had to leave early. White had played in all manner of contexts from sessions to stints in Ginger

Baker's Airforce and The Plastic Ono Band. He was keen and was drafted in almost immediately.

Yes's manager Brian Lane was intent on penalising Bruford as much as possible for the inconvenience he had caused them and despite White learning the live set in a few days, some concerts had to be rescheduled. Amazingly, the pragmatic, level-headed Bruford agreed to make a substantial cash payment and relinquished 50 per cent of his royalties for *Close To The Edge* to White.

Touring ran through until April 22, 1973, during which time the group recorded the triple live set, *Yessongs*. Clearly there was more to be said than could be fitted onto a single forty-minute live album, but a *triple?* The compulsion towards making grand statements had clearly taken hold. "It was the time of the long shows," says Wakeman. "In 1971 when we were on tour in America there might be five bands on and we would start at the bottom of the bill and you played for twenty-five minutes while people were coming into the auditorium, then maybe The J. Geils Band and then maybe Ten Years After would get an hour. But within the space of two years, bands were basically doing most of the show, if not all of it, and doing two to three hour sets."

Having recordings of entire shows at their disposal there were discussions about what could be left off. There was even an idea, eventually nixed – that they might release a double album and a bonus live album six months later.

"I remember Roger Dean coming to the studio and us having a chat," says Wakeman. "He said, 'If I can do a triple cover I could gel the whole thing together.' He played an integral part in making it as one."

The fold-out artwork for *Yessongs* – released in March 1973 – was like a portable art gallery of Dean's landscapes of imagined worlds. Bruford featured on one previously recorded track, but the rest of the cuts had the incumbent White. His style was more overtly rock than Bruford's. Whereas his predecessor sat tight on the beat, White's approach was slightly looser, more rolling, and drove the material from fractionally just behind the beat, with a flatter drum sound. His propulsive style navigated the material's complexities with ease. Or as Anderson describes his style: "More rock'n'roll, harder, wilder."

"Live albums at that time didn't particularly sell," Wakeman notes. "But that sold absolute shedloads. It's far from the best live that we ever played. It's awful [sound quality], sixteen track, but then that was cutting edge. You have to think of it like an old 78 – how did they record that back then? Then it sounds pretty fantastic."

In early 1971 Yes were on about £25 per week, which was a low but liveable wage. By 1973, when the royalties for *Fragile* and *Close To The Edge* started flowing in, Wakeman was taken by surprise. "I remember I had a little terraced house in West Harrow, straight onto the street – two up, two down – which I loved to bits and then Yes started really earning some money. We were told, 'Go buy a house,' and I said, 'I've already got a house.' And this accountant – I didn't know what accountants were – he said, 'Well, let's pay your mortgage off.' I said, 'Well, the house is £4,500 and the mortgage is £4,000 and I pay £30 a month.' He said, 'No, no, that's no good, you've got to spend £30,000.' I said, '*What?*'"

Wakeman bought a house in Gerrards Cross, Buckinghamshire. "I always remember [the estate agent] saying, 'This is the breakfast room.' I said, 'What's a breakfast room? You have a room just for breakfast? We've got a kitchenette and a lounge in our little house.' And there was a dining room *and* a breakfast room. It was a new world and we couldn't really take it seriously. And society wasn't really ready for us. They were ready for the pop stars because in a way the towns liked the pop stars. If you were Cliff [Richard] or a pop star at the time, that was cool, but if you were one of those rock people, that was very iffy."

The keyboard player recalls being a "beer and skittles" man. He was in the darts team in his local pub and people would come up to him and talk about music, and he'd be taken aback by the extent of his fame. But he felt a bit adrift as one of Middle England's *nouveau riche*. "I remember a woman knocked on the door and said, 'I'd like you to sign the petition about the fish and chip shop in Gerrards Cross.' I said, 'Brilliant, we normally have to go to Chalfont St Peter to buy them.' She said, 'No, it's to stop it!' Ah, right. I don't fit here do I?"

But he was soon wondering how he fitted into Yes. And one can only wonder what Wakeman's darts team and the wider populace of Gerrards Cross made of Yes's next step, *Tales From Topographic Oceans*.

TALES FROM TOPOGRAPHIC OCEANS
Original label: Atlantic
Producer: Yes & Eddy Offord
Recorded: Summer–autumn 1973
Release date: December 7, 1973
Chart position: 1 (UK), 6 (US)

Tales From Topographic Oceans remains one of the most controversial and divisive albums in the whole progressive rock catalogue and it is still seen by some as an icon of Seventies self-indulgence, with its four twenty-minute songs spread over four sides of vinyl.

To those critical of the group it was one giant step too far: their melodic nous had been degraded into long, meandering structures that sagged from the weight of their portentous, yet unfocussed, musical and philosophical ideas. Put bluntly, the group were starting to disappear up their own collective pipe.

And what did the title mean? The album had first been mis-reported in the music papers as *Tales From Tobergraphic Oceans*, which didn't help. But oceans aren't topographic except for the physical features of the ocean floor. Or did Dean's cover, with its shoal of fish swimming in a giant bubble past a Mayan temple indicate that, y'know, the sea is the land, the land is the sea and everything is everything else? Quite possibly.

Those not kindly disposed towards Jon Anderson's lyrics had problems getting past even the first of the four titles of the side-long tracks, side one being 'The Revealing Science Of God: Dance Of The Dawn'.

If doubters hadn't already fallen at these hurdles, reading the sleeve notes presented a new challenge. According to Anderson the whole thing was inspired by a footnote in Paramahansa Yogananda's *Autobiography Of A Yogi* (1946). The footnote describes four Shastric scriptures that cover religion, art, social life, medicine, music and architecture. This looked suspiciously like a case of cultural magpie-ism that yielded a sort of *Reader's Digest* of Hindu mysticism, a "one size fits all" philosophy purveyed by a rock band, but one that was rendered incomprehensible by their style of lyric writing. If ever an album casually requested a huge leap of faith from its listeners it was *Tales From Topographic Oceans* and it was one that many refused to take.

Ever since *Fragile*, Yes had represented for some a kind of hippie transcendentalism, where they positioned their music in a fantasy world of their own creation. To fans who craved breathing in this kind of rarefied atmosphere, that was exactly what it was all about, while others ended up with progressive rock altitude sickness. The arrival of *Tales From Topographic Oceans* made it open season for rock'n'roll fundamentalists in the music press to engage in some serious Yes baiting.

They also got wind of the band's exploratory dietary regimes, although Yes rather defensively claimed that they weren't strict vegetarians. Back then it was assumed that real rock'n'rollers thrived on whatever dried-out pies or greasy meat products were left in the heated trays of a motorway transport café, with chips and baked beans the only vegetables, rather than enjoying organic wholefoods. It caused much amusement and was another reason why Yes weren't like the rest of us. Anderson was aware of all this and says: "[It] never bothered me at all. Most of it was silly."

King Crimson percussionist Jamie Muir had spoken at length to Anderson about *Autobiography Of A Yogi* at Bruford's wedding reception in March 1973. In the Sixties and Seventies, Hindu mysticism had made a significant input into hippie culture, and *Autobiography Of A Yogi* was essential reading for those interested in such matters. George Harrison had received his copy from Ravi Shankar in 1966 and Paramahansa Yogananda is one of the life-size cut-outs assembled on the front cover of The Beatles' *Sgt Pepper's Lonely Hearts Club Band*.

The way that Anderson conveyed his creative methodology in the sleeve notes for *Tales From Topographic Oceans* was far from clear, especially regarding the influence of the "Shastric scriptures" on his lyrics. Shastra is a Sanskrit word for a treatise on, or rules around, practice, ritual and teaching methods within different areas of knowledge in the arts and sciences. In Buddhism, shastras are commentaries on the sutras written by Buddha.

Lyrically, *Close To The Edge* had been partly influenced by *Siddharta*, Hermann Hesse's 1922 novel concerning a journey to self-realisation, but this wasn't mentioned at the time. Basically, if Anderson hadn't written these notes there would have been less opprobrium heaped upon him, especially as they caused considerable misunderstanding.

It was all rather confusing and unnecessarily so. That particular footnote in *Autobiography Of A Yogi* was simply a jumping-off point for lyrical ideas, and Anderson is clear now that the album was never meant as a kind of accompaniment to these particular scriptures. "When we created *Close To The Edge*, which was a lyric from Steve, I always thought it was 'Close to the edge of realisation,'" says Anderson. "But in *Tales…* I just used the concept of the four movements – Revealing, Remembering, Ancient, and Ritual – not the teachings of the Shastric Scriptures, even though they played a big part in my own understanding of life, and eventually my learning of meditation."

Howe recounts the group's inexorable drive towards this grand statement. "We'd done *Close To The Edge*, that was an eighteen-minute opening side. So we thought, 'What the hell, we'll do four of those and call it *Tales From Topographic Oceans*!' I could argue that we were being totally defiant. We were saying, 'Look we don't really mind what you think, this is the time when Yes have got to expand.' And it had been such a progression from *Yes*, *Time And A Word*, *The Yes Album*, *Fragile* and *Close To The Edge*. We were just trying to top ourselves – the only thing left was a double album [*laughs*] and we had a ball.

"At that point if we'd had CDs we might have thought about even longer periods. It was fortunate in a way that records were only about twenty-two minutes long before they started to sound really crap."

Wakeman has bemoaned the fact that the group were now writing to fit the format. But with hindsight it was, perhaps, just as well that the brakes had been applied by that format. The first piece that the group worked on in rehearsal was 'The Revealing Science Of God', which initially ran to twenty-eight minutes. "It was far too long," Howe admits.

Howe and Anderson famously came up with the basis of the album in one epiphanic, all-night songwriting session. Demos that have come to light in recent years show surprisingly stiff early run-throughs before the musicians were really playing the music. But compared to the creative free-for-all of *Close To The Edge*, the *Tales From Topographic Oceans* sessions had a rather different atmosphere.

"When we created larger forms of music from then on, it was generally based on ideas that I would conjure up with Steve," says Anderson. "And as time moved on everyone got used to that concept. 'Let Jon explain what he's thinking, and we will musically work it out,' dear Chris would say and he was always there, helping to sort out the ideas that popped into my head. I was blessed to have such open musicians around me, and I was most always a step ahead of everyone, knowing what to try next. But when I came unstuck, someone would figure out a new musical step to take, for which I'm forever grateful. It took everyone's commitment to make it work. And sadly, there wasn't the same collective 'harmony' as we had creating *Close To The Edge*."

Howe also recalls that a certain amount of motivational management was necessary. "When [Jon] had said enough and his voice was sore, I took up the gauntlet and said to the guys, 'Let's do that again, let's work this tune up,' because Rick and Chris and Alan, bless them, weren't so enthused by the music. That was a show of strength. We had already written 'Roundabout' and 'Close To The Edge' so we were quite confident as writers, but we still wanted their input."

In his short time with the group Wakeman had threatened to leave on more than one occasion. He has a quite different view on perceptions of the album's gigantism. "That was a difficult time. Because if a band is earning so much money that it can do anything it wants, that power is really dangerous," he admits. "We had an interesting situation with *Topographic Oceans*. From pre-orders we already knew we had a number one album. We had enough material for an album and a bit, so it was a matter of either reducing it or adding to it and the vote went in favour of adding to it. But most of the additional material was made up in the studio – and it was a lot of padding.

"That annoyed me because I said, 'Listen guys, there are some great melodies on here, some great sounds, what's all this crap that's going on there – a percussion thing?' It was a mixture of everyone banging drums, which seemed like an eternity. I remember when we did it I was going, 'What the fuck's all that about?' They were going, 'That's another six minutes, lads!' And I'm going, 'No, no, no, no, no, no, no.' I ended up really hating the album because of that and things were black and white then, and the more I said I hated it, the more they said they loved it."

Wakeman spent time during the sessions hanging out with Black Sabbath who were recording *Sabbath Bloody Sabbath* next door, both drinking beer with them and adding keyboards to the album. "Playing on *Sabbath Bloody Sabbath* and being with the guys was brilliant for me. That was the period when Yes was thinking that it was divine, almost, and it needed divine intervention. And that, for me, was going over the road to Studio 4 and being with Sabbath. That was sanity."

Howe is reluctant to be drawn back into what he sees as a "boring" old debate: "In Yes, when a musician would say, 'Oh I don't think this song is working,' the answer was always, 'That's because you haven't found anything.' That was really in your face so you couldn't jettison a song by saying, 'Oh I don't really like this,' until the invention of your own parts. So if Rick is not happy, he didn't reach that goal."

But the difficulties of making the ambitious album seem to have impinged on a number of levels. What does Anderson think now of this eighty-minute creation?

"It's a very hard question to answer," he replies. "I would keep getting swayed by critics and such, thinking nobody's perfect. With Yes it was always like climbing a mountain. Sometimes you need to drag people up or at times they drag you up. Music is like that; all art is like that."

For their UK tour of autumn 1973, in an uncompromising display of self-confidence, Yes played the then unreleased double album in its entirety as almost the entire show. This was sung onstage by a man wearing messianic white, who talked to the audience about his concept of God, while accompanied by a keyboard player sporting a glitter cape who looked like a cross between the Phantom Of The Opera and Liberace.

Some audience members and critics found it too much to take and even Chris Welch thought it bordered on oppressive. Howe offers a different view: "The tour was amazingly successful when we played the whole thing. Then we started dropping side two and dropping side three because of fear, almost. We were slightly chickening out. Thank God we didn't do that straightaway."

Wakeman's idea of chickening out was to consume a chicken biryani onstage at the Manchester Free Trade Hall, when a misheard comment to one of the road crew involved him receiving a takeaway order mid-show. Although not the most outrageous thing to have ever happened onstage, in terms of a gastronomic metaphor for Wakeman's relationship with the rest of the group's health-conscious diet, it was a pretty good one.

Before choosing to record at Morgan Studios in the nondescript north London area of Willesden, there had been much discussion of finding a rural studio. Getting rather carried away by the whole venture, Anderson had wanted to record it at night in a forest. As a joke, manager Brian Lane arranged for a picket fence, some hay bales and a couple of cardboard cows to be brought into the studio. This information leaked out to the press, causing much hilarity.

Tales From Topographic Oceans was released in December 1973, by which time Yes had been voted as number one in the *Melody Maker* readers' poll, above even Led Zeppelin. The album reached number one in the UK charts and number six in the US. Reviews were mixed. Chris Welch was unsure about the album, writing: "In the face of marvellous musicianship and obvious sincerity, I can only say that the music is more of a worry and test of endurance than a transport of delight."

So, finally, after all that, as we emerge blinking from this historical labyrinth out into the daylight, what is the album actually like?

Yes fan Chris Ball remembers his reaction to the album: *"I was just 16 when* Tales *was released and back then getting a new album was something that only tended to happen on birthdays and at Christmas. Still being at school the only money I had was what my parents gave me (50p a week) plus what I earned doing the odd bit of strawberry picking or whatever, and 20p of that weekly income went on twenty No. 6 cigarettes. With the cost of an album being about £2.50 you didn't splash the cash on just anything.*

"In those days I never bought an album without hearing it (or at least a bit of it on Alan 'Fluff' Freeman's Saturday afternoon radio show) first. However, a new Yes album was an exception. This would be an eagerly awaited Christmas gift. I don't actually recall whether I had to wait 'til Christmas or not but I do remember sitting down to listen to it all. Four sides!

"Back then there was time to put the record on, sit down, light a fag and inspect the sleeve. Not a word remained unread — I don't think I have EVER read anything on a CD 'sleeve' — and it was examined in minute detail. There was the classic Roger Dean artwork that said what laid within was going to be great.

"Generally, it was all a bit of an anti-climax. Where was the new 'Roundabout', the new 'Heart Of The Sunrise', the new 'And You And I'? Overall I was not too impressed. It was always the albums that I didn't like much at first that ended up being my favourites. This one grew on me more and more and I now regard it as an absolute classic, and still gets a regular airing."

Looking back, it feels that all the hoo-ha the album stirred up was more specifically relevant to the time. Now it's harder to imagine what all the fuss was about.

The accusation of longueurs, which was at the centre of contemporary criticisms of the album, doesn't seem so much of a problem now. Sonic Youth's fourteen-minute 'Trilogy' on their 1988 album *Daydream Nation* didn't cause such critical frothing and groups in the so-called post-rock milieu of the late Nineties and 2000s like Tortoise and Godspeed You! Black Emperor released critically acclaimed albums with tracks that meandered over the twenty-minute mark.

Instead, *Tales From Topographic Oceans* contains some of Yes's most lyrical, melodically strong music and some of their most exploratory and dark instrumental passages, cut with acoustic and impressionistic near-ambient interludes. And rather than poring, furrow-browed over the meaning of the lyrics, it's far more satisfying to think of them as word paintings that complement the music.

'The Revealing Science Of God: Dance Of The Dawn' starts with vocal incantations before the whole group kick in with a spectacularly convoluted Howe guitar theme that recurs throughout the album. It's episodic and constantly shifting, but there's space in the music for the melodies to breathe and as Howe says, the twenty-minute length sits just right.

"We were being accused of [being indulgent] but to us, there were some lilting moments when it was just wonderful," says Howe. "On side one I'm playing a very warm sound and I'm just kind of rambling, and then Jon comes in and sings, 'They move fast/They tell me'. Side one happens to be a very glorious track. It's also a forewarning of what's coming – it's a kind of overture to things that go on in the whole album."

'The Remembering: High The Memory' is the most tightly arranged side, starting with a number of song sections with luminous vocal harmonies, cut with propulsive bass–led sections and atmospheric passages coloured by Wakeman's synth and Mellotron.

"Jon had the idea that we would go out into this space where it would be like the sea, and rise and fall," says Howe. "And I got the picture pretty straightforwardly, some nice minor chords, some major seventh chords, some nice changes."

For someone who was apparently disengaged in the process, Wakeman makes some crucial contributions to the album. Whereas his organ and synth solos can sound rather rattled off, his ensemble playing weaves into the texture throughout, and his Mellotron chords give a spectral otherworldly feel.

The song ends with a spectacular reprise of one of the initial vocal themes pivoting on Anderson's *"Alternate view..."* refrain in an echo of the finale of 'Close To The Edge'.

'The Ancient: Giants Under The Sun' also nods to the opening of 'Close To The Edge' in a series of speedy, percussion-led rhythm patterns overlaid with Howe's exploratory guitar lines. These are interspersed with strident verse sections and a recurrent, crunching on-off two-note motif. It achieves calm with a striking solo acoustic guitar section that segues into a duet with Anderson. Howe explains what happened in rehearsal: "Side three was a highly experimental track, but we knew we were going towards this beautiful song at the end, so we thought we were really going to have some fun. We sat in the rehearsal room and all [made] this mayhem: there were two [rhythmic and melodic] things going on at once that were completely different, but every now and then they met. That was the whole purpose of what we were doing, that I was flying off in this hemisphere and suddenly we were all together again."

'Ritual: Nous Sommes Du Soleil' finds the group briefly running through a series of themes and then into the 'Nous Sommes Du Soleil' song, before taking off into an instrumental section with Squire cutting loose on bass guitar. Then into the percussion section that so irked Wakeman. There is a reprise of the 'Nous Sommes Du Soleil' song, with Wakeman playing some sparse, delicate piano, before a final instrumental surge with Howe reintroducing the theme that opened the album, and it all ends peacefully, with gentle Mellotron exhalations.

"I am immensely proud of it," says Howe. "Not just for what I did, or the fact that I wrote it, but for what Yes did with it."

Tales From Topographic Oceans represents the highwater mark of the creative wave that drove progressive rock. It was inevitable that a group would tackle something of that scale sooner rather than later, but then it didn't initiate a spate of cerebral double concept albums. And for that we should also be grateful. In an admittedly statistically non-significant vox pop among younger friends, some of whom weren't born when it came out and are therefore unencumbered by this historical baggage, most regard it highly.

Wakeman was unhappy with the way that the group was going and left Yes in 1974 in acrimonious circumstances, to pursue his solo career. He had released *The Six Wives Of Henry VIII*, and *Journey To The Centre Of The Earth* reached number one in the UK album charts just as he quit (see Chapter 5). But he would return as we will find out later.

"Yes was democratic, but if it had been a government there would have been a lot more resignations," he says now, adding: "I can look back on it now with a smile."

CHAPTER 10

Stand up and Be Counted: Jethro Tull

Years before the enormous and comprehensive choice that consumers of music enjoy today, fans would often have to base their decision of whether or not to buy an album on listening to a single song. By the end of 1968, the progressively inclined blues fan wanting something a bit more adventurous than run of the mill British blues, who chanced upon Jethro Tull's 'My Sunday Feeling' played on John Peel's *Night Ride* radio show, or listened to it in a record shop booth as the opening track of their debut *This Was*, was likely to be hooked. It was often the case that at this point you would basically decide to like an album: your new discovery. The rush you get from hearing a new group for the first time can make you an instant fan. It would be interesting, albeit impossible, to know how many copies were sold on the basis of this track alone.

'My Sunday Feeling' is a rolling blues of pop-song length, shaped by Mick Abrahams' gritty rock guitar and Ian Anderson's jazz-informed flute. His vocals sound like they were recorded in the next room, but the whole thing swings, courtesy of drummer Clive Bunker's jazzy syncopations and huge pressed rolls. It was, if not radical exactly, then certainly something ear-catching, fresh and limber. And from that track onwards, Jethro Tull's career trajectory would, for the next four years at least, be an ever-steepening upward curve.

Ian Anderson started out as vocalist and guitarist in the early Sixties in a Blackpool school band, The Blades. He also played harmonica and then graduated onto flute so as not to assume the workaday role of rhythm guitarist. Through many upheavals and line-up changes the young group finally settled upon the name Jethro Tull – after the 18th century agriculturalist who invented the seed drill. In 1967 they signed a management deal with Chris Wright and Terry Ellis and recorded a single for MGM in early 1968, 'Sunshine Day' b/w 'Aeroplane'. A misprint meant that this came out under the even less sexy name, Jethro Toe. Although it was an undistinguished single and an inauspicious start, the group, comprising Anderson, Bunker, Abrahams and Glenn Cornick on bass, developed at speed and were, as one might say at the time, a "hit" at the 8th National Jazz & Blues Festival at Kempton Park Racecourse near Sunbury in Surrey.

Derek Boltwood of *Record Mirror* reviewed their set in a peculiar terse style of reportage. "They started with B. B. King's number 'Rock Me Baby' with Ian Anderson on harmonica. Next came Roland Kirk's 'Serenade To A Cuckoo'. This time Ian on flute playing in the Roland Kirk fashion of humming into the instrument whilst playing. A very exciting effect which left the fans wanting more. His sense of humour and wild abandonment endeared the group to the crowd. Closing number by Jethro Tull featured drummer Clive Bunker on 'Dharma For One'.

"A great ovation followed for this virtually unknown group. A great chant of 'We want more' echoed around Kempton Park. Unfortunately, once again missiles were thrown because the fans were deprived of a very good group. But schedules must be kept."

It's sobering to note that the throwing of missiles, which became a nightmarish fixture of the Reading Rock Festival throughout the Seventies began so soon after the Summer Of Love. That unsavoury business aside, the group's mix of jazz, rock, blues and folk was a perfect fit for the late-Sixties zeitgeist.

Anderson was an unorthodox frontman, a scruffy, greatcoat-clad hairy, shod in a pair of manky old plimsolls, but this outsider anti-image made him stand out from the pack. *This Was* was a competent calling card with originals, 'Serenade To A Cuckoo' and the blues instrumental 'Cat's Squirrel', first recorded by Doctor Ross and which had also featured on Cream's 1966 debut album, *Fresh Cream*. Ian Anderson has this to say on the album: "*This Was* was a very unadventurous collection of blues-derived material, a cheerful, slightly home-grown, very middle-class white boy English blues, but it was a foot in the door. When I named it *This Was Jethro Tull*, people said, 'You can't do that,' and I said, 'Yes I can, because the next one is not going to be anything like this, that's for sure.'"

The front cover is a striking photograph of the group made up to look something akin to grizzled, sexagenarian agricultural labourers surrounded by dogs. It carries no title or information, all of which is on the back of the sleeve. The design is credited to Anderson and Terry Ellis.

"I said, 'It may not be convention, but it's a bit more interesting,'" Anderson recalls. "So they went along with it and looking back I'm amazed that they did. But I managed to persuade Terry Ellis, our manager, that it was worth a shot from a marketing perspective. Teasing is commonplace in advertising now, so you have no idea of the product or the brand until the pay-off punch line. Back then it was just something you didn't do."

It worked, and through their irreverent and humorous anti-style, Jethro Tull hinted at a kind of old weird Englishness, an eccentric image that would carry them throughout their career. *Stand Up* (1969) was the first album of all original Ian Anderson songs, and this time the cover was a woodcut portraying the group as something like extras from a Grimm's fairytale. Opening the gatefold sleeve, one was greeted with a cardboard pop-up of the musicians waving their arms as if rising up from the pages of a children's book.

Artistically the album was a considerable step on from *This Was* and commercially it achieved five weeks at number one in the UK charts. Abrahams had left to form the even less glamorous Blodwyn Pig, and with Martin Barre the incumbent guitarist, 'New Day Yesterday' is an opening track with all the attention-grabbing brio of 'My Sunday Feeling'. It's better produced, though, with more heft and has a kind of mutated twelve-bar structure, rhythmically ebbing and flowing with Anderson's harmonica wails and flute solo. Overall, the album is a beguiling, eclectic affair with Eastern influences showing on the acoustic 'Fat Man', while 'Bourée' is a pithy, concise, coolly exercised Bach cover, one of the best of progressive rock's classical adaptions, featuring some deft interplay between Anderson's flute and Cornick's fluent bass.

On *Stand Up*, Anderson's songwriting was becoming more personal and characterful, particularly on the acutely observed 'Back To The Family', which reads like a young man's diary entries chronicling an escape from day-to-day pressures and back to the sanctuary of the family home, and the particular problems that in itself creates. On a similar tack, 'For A Thousand Mothers' is a poignant lyric about the problems facing late-Sixties youth, when their expanded ambitions draw them away from familial expectations. It was like a more assertive companion to The Beatles' 'She's Leaving Home' from *Sgt Pepper's*, a troubled, but ultimately exultant song riding out on an agitated 6/8 rhythm.

The album's successor, *Benefit* (1970), was generally tougher in its guitar figures, particularly on the complex structure of 'To Cry You A Song'. Jethro Tull's initial foray to the States included an appearance at the Newport Jazz Festival and proved a turning point in the group's career. The transatlantic trip also informed Anderson's songwriting.

"My experiences in the USA made me very uncomfortable. There was a lot of violence, a lot of weird stuff going on," he recalls. "So *Benefit* was sometimes reflective and sometimes a bit darker, but overall a more riffy kind of an album. You could structure a song out of simple repeating motifs, riffs, without going very far beyond that." It reached number four in the UK charts.

In between their albums, Jethro Tull had, what was on paper, an unlikely parallel career as a singles group. The singles charts in the UK had always shown the record-buying public as loving standard pop fodder and taking extremely gauche novelty songs to their collective bosom, but also harbouring a liking for adventurous oddities. And at the dawn of the Seventies, their increasing appetite for the new and the strange was born out by record sales.

Much has been made of the fact that 'Living In The Past', released in 1969, was in a 5/4 time signature — and was surely indebted to Dave Brubeck's 1959 composition 'Take Five' — but it was a near-perfect pop moment with a melody of such easy nonchalance that it reached number three in the singles charts. 'Sweet Dream' followed (which peaked at number seven); then 'Witch's Promise' (number four); and best of all, 'Life Is A Long Song' (number eleven), an expansively orchestrated detailing of the day-to-day with the bittersweet pay-off line, that the tune always ends too soon.

This run of hit singles from 1969–71 was more than many a grinning, coiffured pop group could muster. Everyone who had a current single hoped to get exposure on BBC TV's weekly chart-based show *Top Of The Pops* and as soon after release date as possible, as it was viewed by millions. An appearance could mean instant chart action and accelerated sales.

Sensing a possible sea change in buying habits, the show's producers accommodated a short-lived album slot in 1971, during which the audience of grooving teenies were stopped in their tracks to respectfully watch more "progressive" groups, including Fairport Convention, The Moody Blues and the Strawbs, the latter featuring keyboard player Rick Wakeman running a paint roller over the keys while miming to the fabulously grim 'The Hangman And The Papist'. Most of the studio audience were doubtless impatiently counting the seconds away until the likes of T. Rex or Chicory Tip appeared onstage.

It was never going to work as a long-term format, but Jethro Tull appeared on their own terms as idiosyncratic purveyors of pop music. For 'Witch's Promise' Anderson was now wearing his checked frock coat and striped multicoloured flares, looking like a raggle-taggle troubadour from non-specific times past, brandishing his flute, rolling his eyes and gurning at the camera in a way that cried out: "I'm a bit mad, me."

"With the advent of bands like Fleetwood Mac and The Nice being on *Top Of The Pops*, it had this element of subversive defiance about our ilk being on there, but we weren't very good at playing the game," Anderson reflects. "You were asked to do a rehearsal in the way that you would perform in front of a live audience, and that was rather difficult if you weren't used to doing that sort of thing.

"I wasn't very good at that, and it was probably through self-consciousness and embarrassment that I sleepwalked through the rehearsal and leapt around during performance and the cameras were not prepared for it, so I was rather in and out of frame for my own good."

It was, indeed, all over the place and, with hindsight, slightly embarrassing. But it only added to Jethro Tull's weird allure, for back in 1971, being weird was hip. Anderson never thought the group would have a long tenure as a singles band, but he saw his ability to write short songs that could become chart hits as a valuable parallel to their album releases for as long as it lasted. And these idiosyncratic forays into the mainstream could only help raise the group's profile.

Ian Anderson's early songs carried the exuberance of a young man, together with an appealing kind of insouciance. On Jethro Tull's first single 'Love Story', from 1969 (which got to twenty-nine in the UK charts), he uses a folky refrain of going back each morning to see what his love is up to, thinking that she might be *"picking roses"* or even *"painting the roof"*. On 'Inside' he's on a less quirky excursion, going off to see his friends, including one who was often mentioned in song, Jeffrey (Hammond, who would soon join the group). He is flat broke, but who cares when he's just consumed such a great cup of coffee. It was naïve but full of optimism.

This kind of freewheeling song has great charm, but it was not an avenue that Anderson was willing or able to explore at length: "If you are me, you can't write about yourself as that is just incredibly boring. The majority of pop lyrics since the beginning of time have been obsessed with self. Pop music is the audio-selfie, in that you might be interested in how they are feeling today and their latest state of romance or lack of, and that is considered enough."

But one of the overlooked songs in the Jethro Tull catalogue, an outtake released on the *Living In The Past* compilation and clocking in at under two minutes, is the acoustic 'Just Trying to Be'. It's a poignant statement, which Anderson likens in its sentiments to 'Sad Lisa' by Cat Stevens. It is addressed to a woman who is trying to make her way in the world, away from parental domination and expectations.

"When you lack the skills you stumble upon things, simple expressions, which resonate far more easily with regular folks and that moment probably never comes again," he says of the song. "As you go through life you become more sophisticated and enjoy, revel, in language and vocabulary, and things that people haven't said before. I think you can only write that song in your early twenties."

One could say that Anderson's skills for expressing such direct sentiments, although something he appears to view now as rather naïve, even juvenilia, were, in their own way, potent examples of the songwriter's art. But by the time he was 23 years old, Anderson's mode of expression through song was becoming less personal, and a lot more observational and wide-ranging.

The group's 1971 album *Aqualung* saw Jeffrey Hammond replacing Glenn Cornick on bass and the addition of keyboard player John Evan (née Evans), both of whom had played in The Blades back in Sixties Blackpool. Evan had also played in a pre-Jethro Tull line-up in 1967 called John Evan's Smash. The album was divided into two sides titled 'Aqualung' and 'My God'. Anderson maintains that it isn't a concept album, so we will call it an album of two side-long song cycles with some of these songs allied along similar themes.

The titular character is a down-and-out, who appears leering after schoolgirls on the title track, his clothes and demeanour described in unforgiving detail by Anderson and his wife Jennie, who co-wrote the lyrics. The main guitar theme of 'Aqualung', "a riff par excellence" as Anderson describes it, is harsh and dramatic. This unsavoury portrayal is suddenly cut with reflective acoustic passages where Anderson sounds empathetic, even sad, when describing the old man's miserable existence – and so the song see-saws in mood.

This disreputable character crops up again, peering lasciviously through the school railings on 'Cross-Eyed Mary', a song about a schoolgirl who is either a prostitute for pocket money, doing the sex act for *"a song"* (i.e. very cheaply), or is being groomed. Her reward is to be taken by some *"leching grey"* to one of Hampstead's less swanky restaurants to dine on *"expense accounted gruel"*.

Blues and rock'n'roll have a long history of songs where the prize is "jailbait", a girl who is legally under the age of consent, like Chuck Berry's 'Good Morning Little Schoolgirl' and 'Stray Cat Blues' by The Rolling Stones. Gary Puckett & The Union Gap's song 'Young Girl' was a UK hit for the American group in 1968, but its lyric, ostensibly of a romantic mismatch, held a much darker meaning as the protagonist finds out that the girl is under age. Clearly torn, he yells out in anguish that she should leave, before he has time to change his mind.

In the US, the Seventies phenomenon of under-age groupies made the name Sable Starr familiar to readers of the music press. When interviewed, she boasted of illegally having sex with a veritable who's who of rock stars while under 16 years of age. How much of this was a post-Free Love teenage rebellion against the mores of "straight" society, whose limits and strictures were not universally agreed with across the world anyway, and how much of this might have been prompted by problems in her own background is moot and some way beyond the remit of this book.

Anderson is fully aware that a song like 'Cross-Eyed Mary' is a "touchy area". But then the lyrics of some 21st-century death metal groups or rap artists that revel in graphic violence and the most soul-sapping misogyny are considered by some fans to be "cool".

"As always it fits into a historical period," he says. "I think that we could sing certain things forty years ago and it was OK, but it wouldn't be OK now, just as there are things that people would say now that would not have been OK forty years ago. So we live in this ever-changing social context, and we have to find out what is the best way in any given period of time to express these things."

Anderson mentions the song 'Fiddle About' from The Who's *Tommy*, which was informed by author Pete Townshend's own alleged experiences of abuse as a child. In this scenario "pervy" old Uncle Ernie sneaks in to Tommy's room to physically abuse him. "It's not something that people would feel comfortable with now, but then it had a cheerful innocence," Anderson notes.

There is nothing romanticised or cheerful about 'Cross-Eyed Mary', either now or back then. Again a riff-based song, it's hard-nosed, ugly, with Anderson's dry, hoarse vocal sounding like it is fuelled with disgust.

The light relief on *Aqualung* is 'Mother Goose', an acoustic song with Bunker's hand drums, Barre's recorder refrain and a lovely folk-infused melody redolent of Pentangle, but lyrically full of allusion and allegory. In it, the narrator walks around Hampstead Fair, interacting with a carnivalesque cast of characters, including Johnny Scarecrow, the *"Chicken Fancier"*, a group of foreign students and a bearded lady.

By this point the love songs, the groovy, youthful outlook, the high times hanging out with friends was now turning sour as Anderson was observing more, looking for subjects other than himself in his songs. And it wasn't always a pretty sight.

'My God' is a bold railing against the man-made proscriptions of organised religion, but the grimmest song on the record is 'Locomotive Breath'. Musically it's broadly structured on a twelve-bar blues over an on-the-beat fuzz bass pulse. In this respect, it draws on the lineage of train songs in the blues. Some pianists would find work on trains entertaining the passengers and the rolling momentum of what would be called boogie-woogie was in itself influenced by the train travelling on the track. Meade Lux Lewis's 1927 recording 'Honky Tonk Train Blues' is a prime example of this genre.

But after Evan's ruminative piano introduction, 'Locomotive Breath' feels like we are on hot rails to hell. Barre's staccato guitar chords accent this nightmarish journey as the *"all time loser"* is on a one-way trip, grabbed by the balls by his nemesis, watching his children deserting him, bailing out from the speeding vehicle, and humiliated by viewing his *"woman"* being bedded by his best friend. He even consults *"Gideon's Bible"*, but to no avail as God has made off with the brake handle, so we're off at full speed to oblivion.

Whereas 'Life Is A Long Song' has a feeling of wistfulness and a sigh of resignation at our brief allotted span, on 'Locomotive Breath' that span is horribly shortened. The song has been played to lighter-brandishing stadium crowds for decades, but is one of the few truly nihilistic songs in the progressive rock canon.

Anderson describes this song and 'My God' as "youthful, rather angry, letting the bile rise to the surface." And from *Aqualung* onwards his writing became ever more earthy, with a lyrical lexicon in which *"balls"* would join *"snot"*, *"sperm"*, *"pants"*, *"panties"*, *"jockstraps"*, *"excrement"*, *"toilet seats"*, *"VD"*, *"breaks wind"*, *"whores"*, *"blackheads"*, *"foreskin"* and references to bed wetting, chamber pots and masturbation, as well as musings on the existence, or not, of the Deity.

He was beginning to assume more and more the image and role of the court jester, the minstrel, the observer of follies and foibles, who holds up a cracked mirror to society. It felt at times like he was describing modern-day equivalents of the figures in paintings by Brueghel, or the caricatures of Hogarth and Gillray.

"Writing in a more observational way satisfies my personality and my creative efforts are likely to be more usefully brought to bear in songs that are more observational," he says. "It's portraiture, but putting people in a landscape, and the people who are unlike you are much more interesting than the people who are."

THICK AS A BRICK

Original label: Chrysalis
Producer: Ian Anderson & Terry Ellis
Recorded: December 1971
Release date: March 3, 1972
Chart position: 5 (UK), 1 (US)

Ian Anderson has described Jethro Tull's 1972 album *Thick As A Brick* in a rather tongue-in-cheek manner as the mother of all concept albums, a reaction to what was going on round him, adding: "If you look at the history of that time there were a plethora of rather ridiculous, over-the-top concept albums." But were there? He cites Yes, Genesis and Emerson, Lake & Palmer, none of whom had released a concept album at the time and only two of these groups would release a concept album in that decade: Yes with *Tales From Topographic Oceans* in late 1973 and Genesis with the cinematic *The Lamb Lies Down On Broadway* in 1974.

In fact, most progressive rock concept albums arrived after *Thick As A Brick*. Even Gentle Giant's *Three Friends*, which marked the very different lives of three former school chums, was released in April 1972.

Rather than it being a commentary on the concept album, to set the record straight, *Thick A Brick* was actually, in factually, incontrovertibly the first major fully fledged progressive rock concept album. Many have thought it disingenuous of Anderson to say that it was a spoof concept album, but it was clearly that, too. *Aqualung* had certain unifying themes, but this was the real deal, a continuous forty-odd-minute musical and lyrical narrative, only split into two tracks due to the constraints of the LP format.

Anderson wanted *Thick As A Brick* to be a "mind boggler" and it was. Before you'd even put the album on the turntable, it was a unique proposition, as the disc came wrapped within a parody of a parochial local newspaper, the *St Cleve Chronicle & Linwell Advertiser*, dated January 7, 1972. The front cover ran a story on Gerald Bostock, also known as "Little Milton", an eight-year-old boy who had apparently written an "epic" poem, *Thick As A Brick*, that he had submitted to a nationwide competition, promoted by The Society Of Literary Advancement And Gestation (SLAG). But after reading the poem on a BBC TV Young Arts programme, complaints had poured in and "A hastily reconvened panel of judges accepted the decision by four leading child psychologists that the boy's mind was seriously unbalanced and that his work was the product of an 'extremely unwholesome attitude towards his life, his God and Country.'"

There was also controversy over the usage of a four letter word, "G_ _r". In another story, he was implicated in a 14-year-old schoolgirl's pregnancy scandal. This poem – the lyrics to the album – were printed on page seven.

To those who loved to pore over album sleeves, this unwieldy package was a treat, a satire on what made provincial England tick. The twelve-page newspaper, with its local stories, small ads and sports news, is a droll, inspired pastiche. It was like nothing any group had attempted before. To compound it all, Gerald Bostock is credited on the album label as a co-composer with Anderson. Rock music has never been a great vehicle for irony and for years later, some people contacted Anderson enquiring after Bostock.

Arriving in this package, *Thick As A Brick* was clearly conceived as a spoof. But then the musical contents, although shot through with humour, were also the progressive rock version of high art. With hindsight it feels like Anderson had, rather cleverly, managed to have his lavishly decorated cake and eat it.

"I wouldn't deny that for one minute," he admits. "It was absolutely about playing it both ways and having a bit of a buffer in terms of people's reaction to it."

The album is introduced by Anderson as narrator in uncompromising fashion: "The opening lines with that little acoustic guitar pattern, that was written probably in a hotel room in America somewhere – that first minute or so was all I had, so I knew how it was going to begin with those words, *"Really don't mind if you sit this one out"* – total rejection to the audience, saying if you don't like this then fuck off [*laughs*]. That was the sentiment; a rather dangerous way to start an album, but in a way, throwing down that kind of gauntlet was part of it."

This opening address continued to the prettiest of acoustic guitar and flute embellished tunes, with the exceptionally jarring lyric, *"Your sperm's in the gutter, your love's in the sink"*. Bearing in mind that the core audience was in their teens to early twenties, this was an excitingly obscene start to an album. No one had ever talked about this stuff so bluntly on record before. The narrator then notes that his love he feels *"is so far away"* and it becomes clearer that this is an adult talking about reliving the youthful history that has helped shape him. The lyrics defy easy analysis, but unfurl as a tale of a young man's rites of passage and the passing down of knowledge, responsibility, and the sins – and virtues – of the fathers through the generations. Or at least that's one interpretation.

"It was all, on the face of it, over-the-top stuff, but lyrically speaking, what was lying underneath that was a very real tale of the pre-pubescent misunderstanding that children could have of the adult world that they were soon to enter. It was about those emotions, and those confused ideas and ideals," Anderson explains.

"If you were growing up in the post-war era you got comics like *Lion* and *Tiger*, not the innocence of *The Dandy* and *The Beano*, but the next generation of stuff that still talked about 'Jerry' and national and racial stereotypes in ways that would be entirely unacceptable today, even in Nigel Farrage's local pub.

"There was a lot of parental and peer-group stuff that was going on that was both racialist and confused about sexuality, and was full of stereotypes and dangerous portrayals. And so for children growing up in the Fifties and Sixties, there was a lot of confusion as things became, in the latter part of the Sixties, very liberated, and we started to address sexuality, women's rights, anti-war sentiments, that would have been unthinkable in the years before. And suddenly, a young male, an adolescent, is playing a part in that youthful society that is being told it has to change the world.

"So that was what lay behind the lyrics of *Thick As A Brick* but it was all being presented as a spoof, down to the newspaper. It was all meant to be [Monty] Pythonesque fun. I think it mirrors very closely and very carefully the mood of the day in British humour."

Musically, the album was far more adventurous than anything that Jethro Tull had attempted before. Drummer Clive Bunker had departed and was replaced by Barrie Barlow, another former member of The Blades. Whereas Bunker excelled in a jazzy style, Barlow was a formidably tight, dense and punchy rock drummer. In the spirit of the band's Ye Olde English Eccentric image, he was now known as Barriemore Barlow, complementing the bass player's name, which had grown into the absurdly double-barrelled Jeffrey Hammond-Hammond. Guitarist Martin Barre was unusual in this respect in that his middle name really is Lancelot.

In the section that begins when Anderson announces that a *"son is born"*, the playing is at high velocity, with Hammond organ flourishes from John Evan, and Barre's guitar and Hammond's bass lines in one-note-per-beat sixteenths leading into a shuddering unison passage that brings to mind the unison section in King Crimson's '21st Century Schizoid Man'. The first side features acoustic interludes – including a delicate section with celeste and piano that sounds like the nursery rhyme 'Three Blind Mice', band improvisations and martial sections with Anderson running through a list of *"comic paper idols"*, the heroes of the young protagonist.

It's only on side two that it thins a little in terms of inspiration. Right at the end there is a reiteration of the opening acoustic section, bringing it, in a slightly unwieldy way, full circle.

Although the music was unprecedentedly complex for Jethro Tull, it was put together on the hoof. For all its ambitions, *Thick As A Brick* was, significantly, recorded before some groups were allowed the luxury of taking whatever time was needed to record an album. Anderson reckons it's a moot point whether it would have necessarily have been any better if he'd have had the mixing and editing facilities of today and could have pored over the structure. But one of the main aspects about recording in the early Seventies is that you still had to think, work and make decisions quickly.

In preparation, the group's work regime was centred on The Rolling Stones' rehearsal studio in Bermondsey, London. One might assume that this would be a well-appointed facility, but Anderson describes it as "a dive. It was a derelict, damp and nasty cellar with a loo and one big room." Anderson would get up early, have two or three hours to write a few minutes' worth of music, then take the tube from his north London flat and meet the band there. In the afternoon and evening, they would rehearse the new parts, consolidate what they had already learned, and then Anderson would head off back home to compose some more.

Nowadays Bermondsey offers a range of bars and restaurants catering for all tastes, but back in 1972, the Borough of Southwark had yet to be regenerated, let alone gentrified, and some of the areas by the Thames, which now command high property prices, were little more than a wasteland of derelict buildings. And the catering was definitely more basic.

In 1997 guitarist Martin Barre looked back to a culinary experience delivered by someone who sounds like they might have stepped out of the background of one of Anderson's songs: "My biggest memory of learning it was going to the café for lunch, Rosie's Café down the road. It was dreadful food – pie, chips, mushy peas and pie and custard – but it was served by this huge woman, whose hygiene was definitely questionable, who had a moustache and a beard and her apron was spattered in blood and dirt. It was incredibly hot in there, everybody smoked and the windows were steamed up.

"When we started recording *Thick As A Brick*, we didn't know that the end would be a concept album," said Barre. "I think it just started life as another Tull album and we learned the music in the way that we learned the music for *Aqualung* and *Benefit*, but it developed along the way mainly because we were splicing the bits of music together in a way that would be continuous. I don't think we were ever aware of what direction the music would end up going in – it was just something that we did on a day-to-day basis."

In about two weeks or so they could play the piece top to bottom and the backing tracks were in shape by the time they took it to Morgan Studios, where they spent about ten days recording the album. This was quick work, with a number of first takes deemed good enough to be included.

Martin Barre: "It was very live in as much as that everything was put down other than flute and vocals."

Ian Anderson: "I probably wasn't singing all the lyrics then as I'm always a bit embarrassed about my lyrics and prefer to work alone when I'm recording my vocals. By the time we made *Thick As A Brick* there was a bit of a plan in my head as to how it should all sound and how it should all fit together, but it wouldn't have been easy to share with anybody else, not that they wouldn't have understood, but I'd find it difficult to talk about things that were a bit personal and which I'd rather play close to the chest."

During one overnight session, at 6 a.m., Anderson rallied the troops, saying: "Let's go outside and go for a run."

Barre: "We were so tired. It was dawn, getting light, and we trotted about ten yards up the road and realised that was about as far as we could run, and went back and carried on."

Chris Wright and Terry Ellis had now formed the Chrysalis label, which was distributed by Island. Terry Ellis was credited as the producer of the record, but had more of an executive role now. Anderson reckons that Chrysalis were a bit uncomfortable with what was delivered to them musically, but ultimately they were supportive. They were also "appalled" by the idea of the newspaper, but there was one to write and it took at least as long to produce as the album did to record. It was mostly written by Anderson and Hammond, with contributions from John Evan.

There are references to *"building castles"*, sometimes by the sea, in the lyrics and one of the stories in the paper is of St Cleve local, Mr Derek Pith (39), a competition-winning sandcastle maker, who had decided to give up his hobby due to his impending nuptials with Angela De Groot (17). It was all supremely silly, and meant to be so, but odd clues like this piqued the interest of the fans searching for meaning.

Notices in the press for *Thick As A Brick* were mixed, erring towards the negative. In the US, John Swenson of *Crawdaddy!* wrote, rather patronisingly: "It provides another aspect of the group for Tull's extant legions, and thus justifies itself, and it will undoubtedly impress an awful lot of dull minds with the superficial grandiloquence of its scope... Jethro Tull ought to think about coming down from the clouds to do their next one."

Dave Marsh of the notoriously irreverent Detroit magazine *Creem*, came up with this bizarre take on the album: "Jethro Tull may think they are making art, which is something that isn't of much use in the 20th century in the first place, but it looks from here as though they are only making an ultra-sophisticated lounge music for the post-lunar space age."

Statements that art wasn't of much use at the time and how this could possibly be described as "lounge music" are both perplexing, and exemplify how Seventies music journalists could resort to making these kind of sweeping "hip" proclamations without feeing the need to actually explain them, let alone justify them.

Melody Maker's Chris Welch was more positive: "There is not quite the same doomy quality that *Aqualung* had; the ideas flow in super abundance, making me suspect this will receive similar if not greater acclaim. An intense level of performance is maintained throughout this long work."

Looking back with a year's grace, former − and future − fan Charles Shaar Murray of *New Musical Express* offered a considered criticism of the album: "As a Jethro fan of some standing, I was thoroughly disappointed. Ian Anderson had long before proved his real skill at writing short, compact, witty, pointed songs − so what in the name of Yuggoth was he doing presenting a forty-minute epic poem with musical interludes? God knows. Various points in *Thick As A Brick* contained flashes of the Jethro of yore, and there were some inspired instrumental passages, but even the immaculate production couldn't save the hideous thing from collapsing under its own excess of weight."

There were positive reviews alongside the negative, but ultimately the fans voted with their wallets: the album went to number one in the US *Billboard* Charts and number five in the UK. No one would have heard anything quite like it before, and so if the writers − who are busy people and whose quotes I'm using here could have come from hastily written copy after two or three listens − had had more time to digest such a groundbreaking album, then their views may have been different. Maybe not. But the press were now primed for Jethro Tull's increasing ambitions, and the overall critical view of the equally ambitious *A Passion Play* would be almost universally negative. And with hindsight this is much easier to understand.

A Passion Play is basically a concept album about a recently deceased person (Ronnie Pilgrim) and his journey through the afterlife. This has come to light more recently, but at the time it came across like an ill-thought-out mystery film, where the audience is fed cryptic clues as if they all fit together, but at the completion of the puzzle some pieces don't quite fit and others seem to have become lost, leaving everyone scratching their heads.

And, indeed, the album was intended to be made into a film, but that venture fell through, although video footage was shown during the group's live shows. The album has its many champions and was again number one in the US and number thirteen in the UK. It was also critically savaged.

Lyrically, *Thick As A Brick* was at least partially comprehensible and poetically quite attractive. *A Passion Play* presents some interesting imagery, but is less comprehensible. But all that could be forgiven if the music had been of better quality. There were times on *Thick As A Brick* when its complexity seemed a tad gratuitous. But that was nothing compared to its successor, where everything feels over-ornamented in a way that both fails to serve the song-sections and produces a huge accretion of detail that quickly becomes wearisome. Some parts are impressive – the 'Overseer Overture' in particular – but if ever a Seventies progressive rock album warranted a panning for being over-wrought, this is the one.

It includes a faux children's tale, 'The Hare Who Lost His Spectacles'. This was meant to serve as light relief – and its chamber ensemble backing is quite sweet – but the recitation, with its groan-inducing punch line, that all along the hare had *"a spare pair"* delivered by Jeffrey Hammond in a toe-curling, exaggerated comedy Northern accent, makes one so glad it's over that for a minute or two, it's actually a relief to be plunged back into more of the brain-curdling bombast.

But why was it all so indigestibly over-egged? Ian Anderson offers these views: "It's a pain in the arse," he admits. "There is just too much going on, but it was done with a cheerful innocence. Not only I, but members of the band, would come up with ideas of layering things and complex rhythms that were demanding on the ear. We all got carried away and as a record producer, I should have had more discipline and taken a bunch of stuff out of the arrangements.

"But it was difficult to tell enthusiastic musicians in a band to 'just play 4/4 drums through this [section].' You feel like you are hampering somebody and taking something away from them, because they want to be creative and do something interesting.

"But I would be the first person to say – and I knew this early on when we started playing it live on stage – there is too much stuff happening; it's too incessant. There are sections where the music opens right out, and there are quiet and rather stark passages that are slower and more open but when the band come crashing in it does tend to get a bit daunting." He also picks out his "bloody saxophones" as something the album could have done without.

Anderson's relationship with the music press always seemed uneasy, especially around this time, but now appears to have become rather ameliorated through the passing of time.

"It wasn't uneasy on my part," he asserts. "It was just that people understandably couldn't be supportive if they didn't like something that you did or they felt that your time had come and gone, and they shouldn't be in hock to your record company or you just because you were pals.

"So for example Chris Welch of *Melody Maker* decided that he'd be supportive of us, but had to be seen to be an independent mind, dish out some bad reviews and not be tarnished with the idea that you were somehow a tame journalist."

Steven Rosen of American magazine *Circus* spoke to Anderson in 1975, by which time Jethro Tull had been generally accepted back into the critical fold. But it exemplifies the power of music journalists who could dish it out and then retreat back to their bunkers. One needs to recall that he was, at this time, only a young man thrust into the spotlight and trying to make sense of the dichotomy between huge sales and negative reviews.

"If somebody says, 'I think your music is shitty,' that's like saying, 'I think your wife's a whore,'" he told Rosen. "And I get very angry when people say that behind my back or via the unassailable media of the press. Because I'm not in a position to defend it and I won't be brought out or taunted by public criticism into answering it back in the same medium."

Record companies spent a considerable amount of money taking journalists on press junkets in the hope of good reviews. Chris Welch recalls being flown to Tokyo in 1972 by Island Records to see Emerson, Lake & Palmer, where he saw the rivalry between progressive rock's rising stars at first hand: "We arrived at the Hilton Hotel in Tokyo and just as we walked in – Keith [Emerson], Carl [Palmer] and myself, and a photographer – through the other glass doors came Ian Anderson and Jethro Tull. They were playing a concert in Tokyo that night, and because we were at the Hilton, Ian Anderson took one look at them, said, 'I'm not staying at the Hilton with ELP,' turned around and stormed out. They walked out and booked themselves into another hotel. It was exactly like *Spinal Tap*."

Welch's album review of *A Passion Play* and assessment of Jethro Tull's live show were both critical, but seem fair and considered. Speaking to the journalist now, there is no sense that he suddenly felt obliged to mete out a panning. Fellow *Melody Maker* writer Chris Charlesworth offers a second opinion: "I sat next to Chris Welch during *A Passion Play* at the Empire Pool. We were both bored stiff. The audience was bored too, and were making paper darts out of the programme and flying them around."

What happened next was the single most bizarre outcome of a clash between the music press and a group. Jethro Tull announced their retirement.

Jethro Tull's manager Terry Ellis told Rob Partridge of *Melody Maker* that his charges were retiring due to the "abuse" that they had received from critics.

"I say abuse and I mean abuse – it certainly wasn't fair criticism. In a lot of cases critics have been taking advantage of their unassailable position to be abusive.

"Ian Anderson is extremely brought down by it all. When he reads in the music papers '*Passion Play* is bad' he feels terrible, his life is music. The abuse is psychologically wearing him down and he feels it's not fair to perform under this pressure."

At the time fans didn't know what to make of it. This hugely popular band suddenly seemed revealed as a bunch of cry-babies because some people had the temerity to point out to them that *A Passion Play* was such a towering folly.

"This gave the impression that the band had broken up and I was somehow responsible," Welch explains. "The *MM* ran a 'shock' front page news story about the decision. It wasn't until some years later I learned that the story had been the result of a deal between *MM* editor Ray Coleman and Tull manager Terry Ellis, without reference to me. My feelings about it all? Well, I was surprised the editor felt greater loyalty to the music biz than to his staff but at least I hadn't upset Peter Grant and Led Zeppelin and caused them to 'break up'. That could have been rather more awkward."

Anderson had been cited as being part of the perpetrators of this story, but he puts the blame squarely on Ellis and Coleman and opines now that the whole scam was "ridiculous".

So, as we know, Jethro Tull didn't split up in 1973. In fact, their popularity was rising exponentially. At the time in the US the only bigger band was Led Zeppelin. Even now this is difficult to comprehend. The *Aqualung* material was full of heavy guitar riffs, but with *Thick*

As A Brick and *A Passion Play* they had served up two idiosyncratic, extraordinarily complex albums. And live there was the Old English Loon aspect about them – notwithstanding the fact that Anderson is Scottish – with the band camping it up, and Anderson clad in tights and a codpiece standing on one leg playing the flute, serving up comedy routines.

But the group did tailor their jokes for American audiences. Jethro Tull fan Voot Zombo recalls seeing them play the Inglewood Forum, California in June 1972: *"I attended the* Thick As A Brick *show and as my memory serves me, the skit went like this: Tull was killing it, playing the album complete from start to finish – I can't remember exactly what part they were on, but they were cooking along nicely – when the sound of a telephone ringing is heard through the house PA system. Everyone in the band immediately stops playing so the only sound is the telephone. Mr Anderson walks over to a phone that is sitting on a stool on stage, that had appeared while I wasn't paying attention, and he answers it.*

"He turns his face to the crowd and announces loudly, 'Is there a Mr Mike Nelson in the audience? Mr Mike Nelson. It seems there is a fish on the line!' And he drags out the word fish so it sounds like 'fisssssssssh'. Just then the band members begin playing again at exactly the place in the song where they had stopped and carried on as if nothing had happened.

"About two minutes after this is when the wetsuit-wearing roadie, complete with scuba tanks and flippers, walks slowly out on stage and picks up the receiver, assumedly to speak to the fisssssssh.

"I'm guessing Anderson had been watching reruns of the old TV show Sea Hunt *that ran from 1958–1961. It starred Lloyd Bridges as the crime-fighting scuba diver, Mike Nelson".*

When they performed material from *A Passion Play*, John Evan, who liked a drink, would piss into empty beer cans backstage. On one occasion he was due to come on during 'The Hare Who Lost His Spectacles' and hop about dressed in a hare suit, but unfortunately, one of the cans had fallen over, soaking his comedy hare's head in his own urine, a fact he only realised when he put it on.

One could imagine this might have gone down well as a bit of a lark in Britain, but in the US? They certainly had a different take on the group. Some thought that Anderson was called Jethro Tull so they shortened his name to "Jet". Their knowledge of 18th-century British agrarian history was understandably found wanting. "Thick as a brick" was a quaint colloquialism, like "thick as two short planks" to signify someone of limited intelligence. But something seemed to gain in the translation.

Martin Barre has this to say on Jethro Tull's enormous stateside popularity: "I don't understand it either. You look at the Americans and think what do they want? The Doobie Brothers, The Allman Brothers – these are real American bands. But that's what made our career over there. It was something different and something innovative. I think all musicians are looking for something different for inspiration. They are very quirky, the Americans. They love Monty Python and Benny Hill because it's really zany and different to anything they'd do."

In 1975, UK journalist Nick Kent was flown over as a guest of the group to LA to "witness how huge they had become" and see them playing four nights at the 20,000-seater Felt Forum. Kent was an odd choice as he had no particular affinity with the group, although he got on well with Anderson.

He recalls the experience: "It was so bizarre, because it was so English that even English people would have been hard-pressed to get a lot out of it – but all these Americans kids just ate this stuff up.

"I just don't understand how Jethro Tull, and a lot of those prog rock groups, managed to attract an audience of millions of dumb American kids on downers who just want to hear a forty-minute drum solo and throw a bottle at the stage. And those people went away satisfied.

"I understand what you're getting out of Ted Nugent, or stuff where it's just like being beaten to death with a sonic battering ram. But when they're playing Elizabethan madrigals and doing a Monty Python sketch in between, why 20,000 young people would sit there in the Seventies and applaud wildly for that was an absolute mystery to me.

"The Americans in particular seemed to think about Jethro Tull and Yes – 'Wow, this is DEEP, man,'" Kent continues. "I remember when I was spending time with Jethro Tull, that their American press office were, 'Yeah, man, that Ian, he's deep.' It was like, 'It's deep music; those guys, they're deep,' that's all they'd say. They couldn't define exactly what the depth of the man consisted of, but, 'He's deep, you know – he's a deep, deep dude.'"

We will catch up with Jethro Tull in a later chapter.

CHAPTER 11

From a Whisper to a Scream (Including Lighthouses): Van Der Graaf Generator

A soul aficionado vocalist, a cathedral organist, a free jazz sax player and a psychedelic rock drummer walk into a bar. No, it's not a joke, but there is a punch line. For collectively the musicians in question made up one of the most original and volatile groups of the Seventies – Van Der Graaf Generator.

Van Der Graaf Generator was formed by Peter Hammill and fellow student, Chris Judge Smith, at Manchester University in 1967. The name was one of a list that Judge Smith had compiled, his own favourite being Zeiss Manifold And The Shrieking Plasma Exudation. This tinge of wackiness ran through the music, with the group's onstage props including a typewriter and burning drumsticks.

In the post-psychedelic landscape of 1968, pop impresarios began actively looking for something that was a bit more 'happening', and the combination of the duo's songwriting skills and Hammill's distinctive voice – and pop star looks – caught the attention of Mercury Records executive, Lou Reizner. And like so many young trainee pop stars Hammill, who describes himself then as "an idiot 19-year-old", duly signed on the dotted line without perusing the contractual details as carefully as he might. "It was the chance to make a record. That's all anybody wanted," he explains.

Once signed to Mercury, Hammill and Judge Smith met Quincy Jones – who told them that they needed more rehearsal – but nothing quite prepared them for meeting Graham Bond. Bond was hired by Mercury in a sort of advisory capacity. "So he was Minister Without Portfolio – as if Graham Bond could ever have a portfolio," says Hammill. When interviewed over thirty years later Judge Smith, unsurprisingly, remembered their first meeting well: "He was wearing a psychedelic mini dress and pink tights. He was a corpulent guy and he had his long greasy hair covered in red poster paint. He looked like one of those mud people. He was surrounded by a sea of carrier bags, each decorated with the Viet Cong flag. He just sat there with snot running down his chin and Lou says, 'Hi guys, this is Graham Bond. He's gonna be your musical director.'"

Bond took them to a warehouse in South Kensington. It was ostensibly a rehearsal space, but at the height of his Aleister Crowley obsession – he was convinced that he was the son of the 'Great Beast' – Bond had installed his keyboards, but had also brought in an altar and black candles, and had painted a pentagram on the floor. Hammill wrote a couple of songs using Bond's organ, but apart from this his influence was slight.

"He was a pretty wild chap," Hammill recalls. "I didn't meet him that often, but he gave me advice in a very avuncular way, which when it came down to it was, 'Do what you believe in.' This is probably not what Mercury Records were hoping he would say to anybody coming into his orbit."

Hammill had been given his very own Crowleyesque 'Do What Thou Wilt' mandate from Bond, but in a situation of increasing complexity, Judge Smith left the group and the subsequent line-up ground to a halt in June 1969 after all their gear had been stolen. His band now dissolved, Hammill was still signed to Mercury and was due in the studio to record *Aerosol Grey Machine* the following month, ostensibly as a solo album, but with the musicians from the defunct group hastily reassembled as a backing band.

Tony Stratton-Smith, of Charisma Records, managed to extricate Hammill from his Mercury contract – as he was the only one of the original group who had signed – and the album was later released under the Van Der Graaf Generator name (although initially only in the USA). Stratton-Smith was an avid fan and part of the reason he formed Charisma Records with Gail Colson was to release Van Der Graaf Generator's music. Initially, they were the label's flagship group.

By 1970, Van Der Graaf Generator had consolidated into a five piece comprising Hammill, drummer Guy Evans, David Jackson on saxophone and flute, organist Hugh Banton and Nic Potter on bass guitar.

Many musicians who flourished in progressive groups had graduated from playing soul and R&B, and many had grown up with jazz and classical music. But in Van Der Graaf Generator these individual influences stood out more boldly than usual and when they slammed together, sparks flew.

Drummer Guy Evans's parents had a jazz band, The Joe Evans Orchestra and, as a boy, he would go to sleep listening to them playing at dinner and dance nights in a venue across the road, The Swan Hotel in Yardley, east Birmingham. He also helped his father set up for afternoon rehearsals for shows at Chesford Grange, Kenilworth, and would be allowed time playing on the kit of the drummer, Ted Chandler, with some of the band musicians joining in. Chandler gave him his first lessons, but thereafter he was self-taught. He joined Van Der Graaf Generator after a brief spell in the US psychedelic group The Misunderstood when they were based in the UK.

David Jackson was classically trained as a flautist, but once introduced to his older brother's saxophone and experiencing the thrill of playing jazz, his perspective changed. "I had my first experience of being an outcast at this time," Jackson has said. "There I was making as much noise as possible on what was considered to be the 'Devil's instrument', and at the same time I was refusing to take up my destined post as head flautist in the all-important school orchestra." Jackson often played soprano and tenor saxes simultaneously in the manner of Roland Kirk, which gave the sound of a one-man horn section. But Jackson's approach was different. He was one of the first rock proponents of electric sax, amplified with pick-ups and effects, which gave his characteristic harsh, dry sound.

Guy Evans says now: "Dave was coming from a straighter classical background and lots of jazz; very out-there jazz. You'd go round to Dave's, he'd offer you a cup of tea and put on [John Coltrane's] *Ascension*." But rather than try to emulate Coltrane's lengthy explorations to the outer limits, he kept his own lines terse and finely etched.

Hugh Banton had been a budding organist at Durham Cathedral and he brought a wide-reaching array of ecclesiastical lines into the group's music via his Hammond and Farfisa organs, his playing incorporating both the free-flowing lines of J. S. Bach and the atonal crunch of Olivier Messiaen. He was also adept at modifying his instruments – later in life he built organs for a living – and, particularly inspired by Jimi Hendrix, he made and customised effects units to expand the instruments' tonal and timbral possibilities.

Vocalist Peter Hammill wrote the majority of the music. He had his first musical "wow" moment singing Handel's 'Hallelujah Chorus' as a boy treble chorister. Later he experienced an epiphany hearing Martha & The Vandellas' 'Dancing In The Street' blaring out of a Derby record store. "That snare sound, and exactly that off the beat, it was clear there was something different here," he says.

The teenage Hammill loved the British beat groups and became a devotee of the raw blues of Howlin' Wolf, Muddy Waters and John Lee Hooker. Hammill first had a go at songwriting in earnest when he wrote a batch of blues songs in his mid teens, but realised that compared to the gritty experience that had fed into the songs of those who had inspired him, these were, at best, flimsy creations.

"I was away at boarding school, so I was this classic lost soul, really," Hammill explains. "While my adolescence was taking place in Derby, going to Derby Locarno, I was the geek who couldn't dance, spoke funny, disappeared for three quarters of the year, but still wanted to come and see Herbie Goins." As a teenage mod he made "a vague effort towards the suit and a vague effort towards the haircut, because this was the East Midlands triangle of Leicester, Nottingham, Derby, which was the surviving continuous line of mod-dom and soul music."

The 18-year-old Nic Potter had been drafted in to replace the original bass guitarist, Keith Ellis. This was at the insistence of Evans who had played with him a couple of years before in The Misunderstood.

This line-up recorded the group's first "proper" album *The Least We Can Do Is Wave To Each Other*, in early 1970. Although Stratton-Smith loyally stuck with the group, Hammill suspects that he was more taken by songs like 'Afterwards' on *The Aerosol Grey Machine*, with its atmosphere of post-coital languor undercut by doubt, and all set to a hymnal tune, with Hammill's striking voice peaking at a gorgeous falsetto. But this album was the first test of the new group's mettle and was Hammill's first foray into writing adventurous longform songs like 'Whatever Would Robert Have Said?' and 'After The Flood'. He would become progressive rock's prime exponent of this song format and this stretching-out seemed fitting for his lengthy lyrical narratives. His voice also expanded its remit, from soft susurrations to a harsh bark, and travelling further up through the scales, to a controlled scream.

"A band who I don't think are given enough credit are Procol Harum, the first to do an extended longform piece, 'In Held 'Twas In I' [on *Shine On Brightly*, 1968]," Hammill says. "I remember thinking, 'Oh, it's possible to do that – have it quite dramatic with lots of sections, and cover lyrical moments and riffs.' I'm not sure that it influenced me per se, but it was pretty rad for them to do, because I suppose they were reacting against 'A Whiter Shade Of Pale' at the time – against success.

"Having said that, a lot of the psychedelic, underground and progressive longforms were pretty bloody noodly. And that didn't and doesn't interest me. But if it's a kind of a trip along the corniche with dashes in and out, and lots of things happening pretty quickly, *that* is a thing that interests me."

In Van Der Graaf Generator the songs were never padded out. Solos were generally brief and designed to serve the music. In Hammill's parallel solo career, which ran from 1971's *Fool's Mate*, the songs were generally shorter, but Van Der Graaf songs had a cinematic quality that often landed them around the ten-minute mark. *The Least We Can Do Is Wave To Each Other* is also the first overt example of what Hammill calls the group's "scary stuff". This was basically encoded in their dynamics, which could suddenly switch from an ominous build-up, to bursts of ferocious energy, like a musical "boo!"

"The nature of the line-up lent itself to bombast and blast and so on," says Hammill. "We felt that this is our territory, let's see how far we can take it. And just as with films, with scary stuff, you have to have the real blast, but there is also the anticipation – there is something coming, it's going to happen any moment.

"We had our pastoral moments but they were generally the calm before the *sturm und drang*. The bit that interested us – the 'Aaaarrgh!' – was exciting stuff, and, for what it's worth, nobody else was doing it in any sphere."

This all carried on through to the next album, 1971's *H To He Who Am The Only One*. Potter left halfway through the recording of the album. "I was actually very young at that point," Potter explained. "I was not ready for what was coming, the intensity of the vibes surrounding the group at that time, the madness of the intensive touring."

Hugh Banton was on hand as back-up bass guitarist and also played organ bass pedals. The lengthy 'Pioneers Over c' was their most adventurous song to date, a sci-fi tale of lost space travellers. Whereas David Bowie's Major Tom ended up floating off into the void in his *"tin can"* on the 1969 single 'Space Oddity', the travellers on 'Pioneers Over c', having surpassed the speed of light – which is signified as 'c' – have become the *"lost ones"* in an equally disturbing scenario in which time, space and existence are all swirled into a limbo of everything and nothing, of being and non-being. As with many of Hammill's songs at the time, a suspension of disbelief is required, but it contains some imaginative insights.

'Killer' is the song where the group's soul influences become most audible. Hammill has said that he thought they were "bleedin' obvious", but in a straw poll conducted among a number of seasoned Van Der Graaf fans, not a single listener had spotted them. In this respect, context appears to be all and they were hiding in plain sight. Before the vocals come in, close your eyes and imagine a Stax horn section blaring away, but instead of Otis Redding, Hammill steps up to the mike to belt out a metaphorical tale of isolation and loneliness.

Guy Evans has this to say on the track's genesis: "Nobody else had this recollection – but it's a strong recollection of mine – that 'Killer' originated from a cynical conversation that we were having about prog and how to put together, from a box-ticking, focus group point of view, a successful prog hit. We had all these criteria: it would have to be about some mythical creature, it would have to have fast complicated bits, it would have to have an anthemic bit that people could remember. It would have to have a couple of fuck-off solos. And that was the result."

The track dates, in part, back to the era of Chris Judge Smith, who is credited as a co-composer with Hammill and Banton. But no matter how it was created, the results are spectacular. After the chorus, the first of these solos finds Banton playing his organ through a Fluid Sound Box, an Italian contraption that was designed to emulate the doppler shifts – the "whoosh" – of the rotating Leslie speaker, which was often used in conjunction with electric organs at the time to give a more "churchy" sound. But the Fluid Sound Box's failure to sound like a Leslie was, in fact, its strength. Instead, as exemplified on 'Killer' it produces a groaning asthmatic effect, like a kraken that had been dragged ashore and is giving out its last baleful bellows. The second solo features Jackson skronking furiously.

The most remarkable aspect of the song was that it was a portal into, in Hammill's words, "the aggression and chaos" that the group could produce on stage. Under Banton's solo, Hammill's piano and Evans's drums career around and only just keep in time. Evans has this to say about their live shows and the combination of the players' idiosyncratic styles: "There were all sorts of places that we could meet, but if things went somewhere unknown then it wasn't a problem for us – you knew what you were embracing."

Tony Stratton-Smith organised the 'Six Bob Tour', which ran from the end of January until the beginning of April 1971, with Van Der Graaf Generator, Lindisfarne and Genesis on the same bill, with Bell & Arc on some dates. Van Der Graaf were generally headliners, with the opening spot shared between the other two groups. It was an effective showcase for the nascent label, although Lindisfarne were on their way to becoming one of the most successful British groups of 1972.

"Lindisfarne and Genesis were very good at being crowd pleasing, but somehow we never really made that much of a priority," Hammill notes.

There has always been a disparity between what fans think touring must be like and the actuality. By 1971, Van Der Graaf Generator had made some critically acclaimed albums and were among the brightest stars in the progressive rock firmament, so surely they must have had some creature comforts laid on? Evans puts that record straight in regard to touring in the UK.

"It was mainly B&Bs," he says. "But it was a luxury to have any accommodation at all – if your gig was under £100 you couldn't afford it; you'd just came back. They would have to be prepared to let you come back late and also serve breakfast late if it was a late-night job.

"There were a couple of legendary ones. There was one in Leicester called the Stansbury Hotel, run by a couple of gay guys, a real pair of old queens. They were fantastic. Whatever time we came in they would open up the bar. We often ended up not going to bed at all – it would just go straight on to breakfast.

"And then there was Mrs May in Plymouth. She used to put up bands who were playing at The Van Dike club. Everybody was in the same dorm. She had a tarantula mounted on cotton wool in a tacky circular gilt frame that she kept on her living room wall. She would warn the inevitably late arrivals that she would unleash it if anyone failed to make breakfast.

"She took pride in listing all the groups who'd stayed there, but like Irene Handl, she would get it a bit wrong. 'Oh, last week we had Yes-Yes' – that was Yes – 'and The Havens', which was Richie Havens."

In May 1971 Van Der Graaf Generator went on a month-long tour of Germany. Surely this must have been more of a rock'n'roll junket: some sightseeing, playing live to adoring fans, and then drugs and pulchritudinous fräuleins as part the aftershow? That would certainly beat working – if it had been like that.

Hammill retrospectively chronicled the tour on the song 'German Overalls', which opened his second solo album, *Chameleon In The Shadow Of The Night* (1973) and in a letter published in a book of lyrics and writings, *Killer, Angels, Refugees* (1974), under the chapter heading 'Audi'. In that missive he describes how an obsessive female fan cornered him in the group's dressing room and begged for him to give her a child. It didn't sound like too much fun.

Evans: "It was that bad and that good in terms of being life transforming, and a rite of passage. We did twenty-three cities in twenty-eight days on no money in this incredibly slow bus that looked like an ice cream van. The company was called Kosmos Tours; it had a logo on the side.

"We were almost starving. There weren't wages. They used to give us extremely lowly per diems – and we were always waiting for this money to be wired through to some bank in some strange German city. There would be some screw-up, it would arrive the day after we'd left there or wouldn't come at all, or there would be problems with currency fluctuations. There's a line in 'German Overalls' that Hugh spends his last mark on coffee and cheese, and that was true.

"There were all sorts of things going on – drugs were involved. There was one particularly hairy expedition to the very top of Ulm Cathedral spire aided by extreme Afghan black and chillums, and God knows what else."

The mixture of malnourishment and the side effects of a voracious appetite for strong drugs was not a healthy one. And worst of all, the group were not going down well.

"People look at Van Der Graaf as if we had a completely trouble-free passage through things," says Hammill. "We were touring with Jackson Heights and Audience. Lee Jackson had been in The Nice and so had more public cred than we had. They had their bits that were designed to get the audience going and we didn't. We'd done half a dozen shows and we were going down appallingly. It was grim."

Part of the reason why Hammill disassociates the band from the rest of the progressive rock groups, especially the ones who would put on a show, a spectacle to wow the audience and to make the stage some kind of "shrine", is that with Van Der Graaf it was a riskier business. "With our shows, for better or worse, out of every five, two on average were appalling maelstroms of sound – organs and fuzz boxes akimbo, sheets of feedback from the sax, the vocalist's voice had gone because he's just been shouting for two days – [two would be good] and one would be fantastic." Or in Evans's words, in concert the group was an "unstable entity" that could at times go "utterly liquid".

"We had played in Ulm and we were about to set off for Tübingen," says Hammill. "I went out walking in the morning and I came across Guy sitting by the river. It was the time that the American forces were there and we met an American deserter, which put our worries in perspective to a certain extent. Guy and I sat there and summoning up that spirit of Graham Bond, I just went, 'Well, it's crap isn't it? But what else can we do but the very best that we can and front it out?' And certainly in our attitude, Guy's and mine, that was a watershed moment. That's what we did and we never looked back."

But the Tubingen gig held its own problems. Since the riots and student unrest that had swept across mainland Europe in 1968, the group noticed a shift in the attitude of German youths, some of whom had become particularly radicalised. The idea that music should be free and be independent from the corrupt capitalist record industry was all very well from the consumer's point of view, but even for those radical times it all seems exceptionally naïve. Suddenly there was a fire at the back of the gig, fighting broke out and agitators were banging on the doors chanting: "Free music, free music, free music…"

Going up the vertiginous spire of Ulm in a heightened state was one thing, but in a classic case of "out of the frying pan and into the fire", Evans and Jackson decided to take up an offer to briefly get away from it all.

Evans: "After the gig in Tübingen, Dave and I were invited back to the home of some of the audience. The next day we had a day off and they came and got us, and drove us out to a really deserted farm in the middle of nowhere, down a dirt track. When we got there the place was full of guns: serious guns, shotguns, sub-machine guns, grenade launchers, at which point we were given the opportunity to take acid and go and shoot wild boar. We were wondering how we could refuse it and how the fuck we could get back with our lives."

The drummer's recollection of how they escaped the nightmarish proposition from these Baader-Meinhof Group affiliates is understandably hazy, but he was relieved to get back to the relative safety of the Kosmos Tours van for the next leg. In the van, Hammill was busy writing some new music, a massively ambitious song called 'A Plague Of Lighthouse Keepers'. "Maybe that's what was keeping me sane," Hammill muses. "On the other hand maybe that [German tour] experience was feeding into the work at that point."

PAWN HEARTS
Original label: Charisma
Producer: John Anthony
Recorded: July–September 1971
Release date: October 1971

By 1971 the idyllic pastoral childhood reveries of UK psychedelia were long gone, although an idiosyncratic and warped view of Englishness was brewing up in the music of fellow Charisma band, Genesis. But with their fourth album, Van Der Graaf Generator turned all that over into its horrible inverse. The milk of human kindness that had flowed benignly through songs like 'Auntie Mary's Dress Shop' by Tomorrow or the more recent 'Golf Girl' by Caravan had become sour and horribly curdled.

The album's inside cover shot captures that tone perfectly. Keith Morris's image is of the group in the beautiful garden of a rambling country pile, Luxford House near Crowborough in Sussex, a 16th-century listed building rented by Stratton-Smith. But rather than portray a pastoral atmosphere – with, say, the band sprawled out on the lawn, smiling, getting it together in the country – it shows David Jackson carrying a football, wearing boots and spectacularly short flared trousers in full sail, striding towards the rest of the group, who are standing on a table. All are wearing black shirts and giving Nazi salutes. The image had been shot using infra-red film so that colours are distorted, with the vegetation turned shocking pink, and flesh tones near-white and drained. So what exactly was going on?

For the rest of the shoot, Morris had photographed the group playing a game they had invented for their amusement during breaks from rehearsals for the album: Crowborough Tennis.

"In Crowborough Tennis the ball was thrown. You bounced the ball on the table and your opponent(s) had to catch it before it hit the ground, then return it from wherever they caught it," Evans explains. "Exchanges were all about trying to get close to the table so that you could either bounce the ball a great distance or just clip the edge of the table and send the ball to the ground before it could be caught."

In a way it was just a bit of looning about, not so far removed from playing croquet on the lawn. Except that the group had started talking about a huge statue of Nazi stormtroopers that they had seen in Kaiserslautern on their recent tour, which they had been shocked to see still standing, and re-enacted it for Morris's benefit.

"He said, 'I know this is going to take a good deal of thinking about, but I think this is the image,'" says Hammill. "So in the end we decided that was to be the image and trusted that our sympathies wouldn't be taken to be in the wrong place. We didn't get a lot of grief on that. But we could have done."

The group rehearsed the album in the barn, with sessions starting at night and the musicians slowly adopting a thirty-six-hour clock.

"At night those different spirits rule and that bucolic country atmosphere was not ours," Hammill says. There was a supposedly haunted portrait in one of the rooms – alongside a sword that Manchester United manager Matt Busby had given Stratton-Smith when he was a sports reporter. The house was apparently haunted in a number of areas, but Hammill never witnessed any apparitions. Stratton-Smith later claimed that through his music, Hammill had caused a manifestation of a presence in the house. "I'm not saying that I wasn't personally responsible for it, but I can neither confirm nor deny," Hammill says now, clearly amused at the accusation.

It all seems a bit tongue-in-cheek and somewhat over-the-top – music so extreme that it can conjure up some kind of minor daemon, albeit briefly. But *Pawn Hearts* is quite unlike anything that was produced at the time, and its three long, dark, uncanny songs, played and sung at times with a ferocity bordering on mania, invite such notions. The soundworld, like the cover shot, is malevolent, garish and grotesque, with Hugh Banton's treated keyboards sounding positively diseased. This was the apogee of the group's "scary stuff". It's probably as near an aural approximation as you can get to what it actually feels like to drop a tab of acid and go off, heavily armed, into the German countryside to shoot wild boar.

When I spoke to Hammill in 2016, I mentioned that on hearing *Pawn Hearts* for the first time in a friend's living room on a lovely summer's day, probably just turned 15 years old, I left feeling both thrilled and deeply disturbed at what I had just heard, as some of it had been so horrible. "Yes and deliberately so," he laughed, apparently delighted. "That's great isn't it?"

Back to more sober analysis, *Pawn Hearts* was recorded at Trident Studios in London with John Anthony as producer. Anthony had worked on their two previous albums and his layering of the instrumentation, which is denser than on previous offerings, is done with skill, so as well as it having a mighty heft, it never sounds cluttered.

Although essentially Hammill's composition, 'Man-Erg' is typical in having group input. Based on lengthy, piano-led verses and choruses of a hymnal quality, the song's title is a play on sorts of "horse-power", but its energy comes from an internalised personal struggle between good and evil.

Hammill: "It's quite unusual for that era in that it does have that fairly standard verse-chorus, it's just the middle eight in this particular case is where it goes a little bit wonky. We wanted to go somewhere more interesting than just playing a straightforward tune."

The "wonkiness" in this case is a lurching 11/8 riff honked out by Jackson's saxes and driven like a wedge through the middle of the song, with Hammill pushing his vocal range to the extreme. After a sedate middle passage with two verses of a different melody, the final verse is gradually overtaken by a reappearance of the 11/8 riff with the ensemble hitting a grandiose, pseudo-symphonic ending.

"The Van Der Graaf process of working was often that the stuff was written from point to point, but there were always gaps, and that was the arrangement responsibility, or to be fair, often HB's responsibility to meld things over," Hammill explains. "Or all of us saying, 'We've just got to get from here to there and that is the fun of arrangement.'"

'Lemmings' is a more complex song than 'Man-Erg', an alarming parable of mass self-destruction. After the two verses and choruses there is

213

a middle section that incorporates a series of *musique concrète* elements, tapes that Hammill and Banton brought to the studio, which were then looped and varispeeded. In the background, there are sounds of people murmuring and howling, and also a slowed-down recording of an electric razor. Another slowed-down recording of a bottleneck travelling up a guitar cues the lurch into the 'Cog' section, an explosion of barking sax and distorted organ lines.

"It was quite deliberate and very much the warped accumulation of our experiences, because it is, again, a soul horn section in the hall of mirrors," says Hammill. "It's an *almost* traditional sound, not particularly loud, but it's got a nasty element in it."

Just as soul was a potent force in Van Der Graaf's music, Hammill has identified his tendency to write these kind of lopsided riffs as stemming from his love of John Lee Hooker, specifically his idiosyncratic timing and warping of the twelve-bar blues template into figures of erratic bar lengths. But still, whatever would John Lee have said?

There are improvisational sections before the final verse and a delicate, completely free improvised coda, with Jackson playing one of the main vocal themes dolefully on flute.

Weighing in at over twenty-three minutes, 'A Plague Of Lighthouse Keepers' is a series of episodes, written in first person, by Hammill in the role of the lone lighthouse keeper in his *"isolated tower"* who, after witnessing ships wrecked on the surrounding rocks and with his light dying out, has difficulty separating the real goings-on off the coast with his turbulent inner visions. The narrative, of sorts, reads like a macabre, Poe-like short story.

"Maybe a bit more movie than short story," Hammill suggests. "It's impressionistic rather than thought through, I would say, although it does have direction and vector.

"I honestly don't remember what the original idea was. My brother gave me a book on lighthouse keepers some time later, which was quite interesting," he continues. "It was just whatever was buzzing around that young man's brain at the time. And even if I had the initial workings in front of me, which I wouldn't as they were on scraps of paper, and scrawls, I probably wouldn't understand the thought process behind it."

Hammill again invited the other group members to contribute to the structure as well as the arrangement, and so Banton and Jackson produced the sheets of keyboard sea mist and foghorn blasts of 'Pictures/ Lighthouse'.

Evans composed a piano section, 'Kosmos Tours', which was based on a typically idiosyncratic drum figure of triplets he had seen Ringo Starr play on TV in the Sixties. "It was drumming on a piano keyboard," he says. "The centre of my figure is on the A flat and moving it out from there." He is joined on it by Banton's spiralling synthesizer lines.

One of the prime cinematic moments that pictures the calm before the *sturm und drang*, is the contemplative section called '(Custard's) Last Stand', which ends on a long, eerie organ chord that fades and swells back up. The comparative peace is suddenly destroyed by 'The Clot Thickens', a hideous, carnivalesque section that veers, initially from 5/8 to 9/8 to 7/8, as the lighthouse keeper, either literally or metaphorically, struggles for life in the heaving sea, the details screamed out by Hammill.

It then shifts into a sardonic, convoluted riff, that's something-or-other in eight time. But ultimately time signatures are less important than the thrill of hearing the musicians doggedly grappling with the material, as if they are trying to keep balance on a ship that is listing from side to side, buffeted further by Banton's Mellotron and synth gales. Merciful release for the drained listener comes as 'A Plague Of Lighthouse Keepers' ends in relative peace with the chorales of 'We Go Now', to music composed by Jackson.

"It was new, it was very exciting," says Hammill of 'The Clot Thickens'. "That mad fairground macabre stuff wasn't around beforehand. So at the time it seemed a completely rational thing to do. And it felt a little bit extreme, but within the job description of being in a group at that time.

"But I have to say we did find it fun to do, and it might also have something to do with the drug experience and drug world at the time. Having given the impression so far that everything was entirely rational and thought out, we were pretty out there, which is why we were making music that was pretty out there."

Evans: "It was an easy album to make because it was an album of discovery. The two big playing pieces are 'Lemmings' and 'Man-Erg', and we'd really got those played in. Side two, 'Lighthouse Keepers', was an experiment on our part. We recorded it all in bits and didn't hear it until John Anthony edited it.

"Recording all of those [separate parts] was a delight, because you weren't going into the studio knowing that it had to be a really representative version. The sections were quite disparate in their feel, and it was a case of getting absorbed in each particular thing. So in terms of energy it wasn't that demanding, it was pleasurable."

Pawn Hearts was about as far away from 'Afterwards' as one could get. Hammill can't remember Charisma's response to the album, but says: "I suspect there was an element of gob being smacked."

Gobs would have been smacked further had the group stuck to their original idea of making *Pawn Hearts* a double album, with individual tracks by group members. Those that have seen the light of day are certainly challenging. Jackson chipped in with a brief, pithy jazz tune, 'Ponkers' Theme', but Evans's 'Angle Of Incidents' is a free jazz blast with real time and backwards drumming, and some wild playing by Jackson, with slowed-down voice and smashing glass. Banton's 'Diminutions' is a creeping, dissonant keyboard piece, which brings to mind Messiaen at his most delicate, or the cloudy, spectral forms of a György Ligeti composition like *Atmospheres*.

The group also intended to record some live-in-the-studio tracks for a fourth side and made 'Squid/Octopus', a formidable eighteen-minute reworking of 'Octopus' and 'Giant Squid' from *The Aerosol Grey Machine* played in the edge-of-the-seat style of *Pawn Hearts*. They also recorded a version of George Martin's 'Theme One', the original of which was the theme for the BBC Radio 1 *Friday Rock Show*, which was released as a single, the Italian version coming in a fetching "Nazi salute" picture sleeve in March 1972. A German version shared the same label catalogue number, but, unsurprisingly, substituted the Crowbrough shot with a less contentious group photograph.

Part of the reason that the solo tracks had been agreed was a kind of deal for having '...Lighthouse Keepers' on the album. Banton, for one, had been initially wary about an album with just three songs. But with the extra recordings abandoned, that is exactly what came out. Hammill is almost certainly right when he says it was "probably the stranger and the stronger because of that."

"After this we'll change radically, I feel. We've arrived at the point we were aiming for," Hammill told *Melody Maker* after the album's release in October 1971.

Reviews of *Pawn Hearts* were understandably mixed. "I have to confess complete ignorance of precisely what Van Der Graaf Generator are trying to achieve," was the bemused response of a writer credited as BM in *Disc & Music Echo*.

But one particular mass response that bemused everyone including the group, was that *Pawn Hearts* reached number one in the Italian album charts.

This prompted another three Italian tours as well as British dates, with the group playing bigger venues through louder PAs, with more riots and tear gas. Charisma Records had, in Hammill's, words shown a "benign tolerance" to the group, but the flipside of this benign tolerance is that "they didn't know that we were feeling we were on a raft being buffeted about without anybody being in control."

Van Der Graaf Generator first split in May 1972. It would be tempting to suggest that *Pawn Hearts* was like a musical black hole that inexorably sucked in its demented creators, snuffing out the band's existence, but the facts were more prosaic.

In Italy, even with their new-found stardom, it was still a case of getting to the town, finding a poster, then trying to locate the promoter, venue and hotel. The group weren't making much money and Charisma were increasingly wary about their tour support, and so Van Der Graaf Generator broke up, even though some Italian promoters tried to tempt them into carrying on playing live with a stand-in for Hammill. But enough was enough for all concerned – that was a crazy idea. However in the fall-out from *Pawn Hearts*, as Evans says, the musicians really felt that they were going mad.

"It was everything," he explains. "It was the madly structured or unstructured lifestyle. It was being catapulted into an insane level of celebrity, the Italian thing. It was a bit like being in The Fall in Van Der Graaf, that sort of feel to it, then suddenly being where you couldn't cross the street and you had riots going on at your gigs – that was insanity. And the big crowds, big venues and big PAs... I kind of felt uneasy about it a lot of the time – probably fuelled by quite a lot of dope."

With the group's demise, Hammill continued as a prolific solo artist. He had released his debut, *Fool's Mate*, in 1971 just before the recording of *Pawn Hearts* began. It's hard to think of two more different albums. *Fool's Mate* is piano- and acoustic guitar-based, and definitely in the introspective singer-songwriter mode, although it was recorded with a little help from his Van Der Graaf friends. He went on to release a series of stylistically diverse solo albums, *Chameleon In The Shadow Of The Night* (1973), *The Silent Corner And The Empty Stage* (1974), *In Camera* (1974) and *Nadir's Big Chance* (1975). All of these featured the group as session players and two of the songs, '(In The) Black Room/The Tower' and 'A Louse Is Not A Home', had been written for Van Der Graaf Generator who had already played them live.

"The solo dictates of the solo artiste brook no democratic debate, so they are slightly different to the way they would have been if they had been actual Van Der Graaf recordings," says Hammill. "But they weren't going to be recorded if they weren't recorded by me."

Evans: "When the band was in full flow, the situation with that was that Peter still writes all of the songs. Certain of us got credit at the time on some of them. But in terms of song, themes, lyric, it's the Peter Hammill Show still and that caused a certain amount of friction, because we knew damn well that the energy and the full impact of the music came out of the band, and wasn't just the Peter Hammill Show.

"When we got to doing Peter's stuff, it was, 'There's nothing to fight here, we are being paid session fees, it's Peter's album,' so you're not thinking about the politics of it at all."

Relations remained cordial and Hammill recorded in commercial studios with the band members, but he had also made a perspicacious move. His early experiences with Mercury had been instructive and so, partly inspired by Todd Rundgren's home recordings for *Something/Anything*, he purchased a TEAC four-track reel-to-reel when such a piece of gear was expensive but necessary. "I had an inkling that the music business might not wish to have me on its roster forever, and therefore I'd better get a means of production," he says. Few people were doing this type of recording and on album sleeves he referred to these home recordings as being made at "Sofa Sound".

Before we leave Hammill and Van Der Graaf – for the moment at least – by the early to mid-Seventies Hammill was well established among fans as a pretty heavy duty artist, writing about existential concerns like love, sorrow, loss, leaving, isolation, hope and death, and in a particularly dramatic way. The book *Killer, Angels, Refugees* was published in 1974, with claims on the cover notes made for his lyrics being "literature".

Hammill can be quite self-critical about his early lyrics, but to some of his Seventies fans, typically impressionable young men, it was like he had looked into the very abyss and was relaying his findings. A friend witnessed a solo Hammill concert in the late Seventies and heard one acolyte shout out: "Hammill is Jesus!"

"Oh yeah, horrid, horrid," Hammill says now. "I have always done my best to put my hand up and say, 'I am just groping around for things, I don't have the reason, I'm not a philosopher or a leader in any way.' The entire process of writing songs is 'I don't know, but sometimes it looks like this; or viewed from this angle it looks like this'.

"What happens with the stuff when it leaves my hands is not my concern and what the audience's relationship with it is a relationship with the work but not necessarily with me. Neither I, nor, I'm sure, anyone you've ever interviewed, goes through their life being THAT PERSON, in capital letters. Or if they do they must be in serious trouble."

CHAPTER 12

"Plus... Tubular Bells!": Mike Oldfield & Virgin Records

In 1972 teenage guitarist and multi-instrumentalist Mike Oldfield began recording his debut solo album. It would eventually grow into a forty-nine-minute suite, on which he played most of the instruments himself.

Overdubbing had been a common studio device ever since the advent of magnetic tape, but no one had used it to this extent before and Oldfield's 1973 album, *Tubular Bells*, was made up of hundreds of overdubs. On the face of it *Tubular Bells* must have seemed to some like a typical statement of Seventies grandiosity, a haughty "beat that" challenge. But its genesis could not have been further removed from those notions.

Oldfield was born in Reading in 1953 and had two older siblings, Sally and Terry. Home life became particularly difficult when their mother was rather mysteriously sent away for a while. It was later revealed that she'd given birth to a child with Down's syndrome who had died in infancy, and she returned home heavily medicated and in a state of acute psychological distress. To try to escape this painful situation, young Mike would habitually shut himself in his room practising guitar and by the age of 12 he could play with considerable facility.

"I used to write these little songs. They weren't very good at all, but then I would make long instrumentals on steel-stringed acoustic," Oldfield recalls.

On the cusp of his teens Oldfield played folk clubs with his vocalist sister. They formed a duo called The Sallyangie, and recorded one album, *Children Of The Sun*, which was released in 1969, the year in which they split. Oldfield joined Kevin Ayers And The Whole World in 1970, playing bass and guitar in a line-up with modern classical composer David Bedford on keyboards and jazz saxophonist Lol Coxhill.

Oldfield shared a flat in Tottenham, north London, with Ayers, who had been experimenting with tape music on a two-track reel-to-reel recorder. Ayers disbanded The Whole World in 1972, and left the tape recorder at Oldfield's disposal, and the teenage guitarist also borrowed Bedford's Farfisa organ and started recording in his room. He remembers spontaneously playing a keyboard motif that he now recognises was influenced by Terry Riley's 1969 piece, 'A Rainbow In Curved Air', on which Riley plays electric organ and harpsichord, and percussion.

"There are many times when out of the blue a little tune or motif or harmonic progression will appear in my brain and I'll go, 'Ah thanks!' It certainly made me feel more like a messenger than a composer, passing something on rather than doing it myself," says Oldfield. "It's a very strange feeling.

"[With] *Tubular Bells*, I just sat down and played that little introductory piano motif; I didn't have to work it out. 'Oh, that's nice, I'll just play that loads of times, then.' And then I added a bass, which I didn't have to think about. I had to do a bit of homework, like, 'Where can I go from there? Alright, I'll do a little key change and have a nice tune going over the top.'"

Whereas Riley delivers a top line of dazzling speed, Oldfield plays a recurrent motif in 15/8 as a basis for a number of counterpoint melodies. In effect it's split into one bar of seven followed by a bar of eight, and it's the slight irregularity of the figure that captures the imagination and makes it the most memorable theme on the album.

Oldfield took the first demo recordings of his intricate instrumental music to EMI, who initially seemed interested but never got back to him, and to CBS. "They thought I was crazy as it didn't have any vocals, it didn't even have any drums. And I gave up then," Oldfield told the BBC in 2013. It looked as if the album was going to require a specialist outlet.

Serendipitously, an ambitious young entrepreneur, Richard Branson, was in the process of expanding his business interests. In 1968, aged 16, he had launched a new magazine, *Student*, but ultimately it didn't bring in enough advertising revenue for it to remain viable. Since 1970 he had been running a record mail order company, Virgin – initially out of a public phone box – which had a whiff of the counterculture about it, of sticking it to big business. Virgin offered discounts of 10–20 per cent on the commercial price of all albums, with advertisements in the music papers stating: "Virgin have never sold a full price record."

In 1971, Branson and his business partner Simon Draper decided to also open record shops, firstly in a first-floor premises at the downmarket, eastern end of Oxford Street and then at Notting Hill Gate, where there were bean bags to sit on and if you were lucky you might be able to get some of their free vegetarian food.

But along with this hippieish approach, Virgin was doing good business and with the help of a loan from his Aunt Joyce – which came with stiff repayment interest rates – Branson bought a 16th-century country pile in Shipton-On-Cherwell in Oxfordshire, and began renovating it as The Manor, claiming it to be Britain's first residential recording studio.

Branson, Draper and associates had been talking of starting an independent record label and in 1972, after playing some sessions at The Manor, Oldfield handed engineer Tom Newman a reel-to-reel demo of his solo music. He was captivated. A meeting with Branson followed and a deal with Virgin was agreed.

Virgin's arrangement with Oldfield was that he would record Part One of *Tubular Bells* – which is simply side one of the LP – at The Manor in autumn 1972. He then became a temporary resident at the sixteen-track studio and recorded Part Two in studio down time in the spring of 1973.

Before Oldfield started recording the album he gave a list of instruments that he needed Virgin to hire in, including acoustic guitar, Spanish guitar, concert tympani, glockenspiel and mandolin.

All the electric guitar on the album was recorded using a Fender Telecaster that had previously belonged to Marc Bolan, and Oldfield borrowed a Telecaster bass. In terms of effects pedals, the oddity was the Glorfindel Box, a homemade effects unit, which was named after an elf in J. R. R. Tolkien's *The Lord Of The Rings*, and whose creator gave it to David Bedford at a party, who then passed it on to Oldfield. Although somewhat unpredictable, as its best it gave his guitars a smooth sustain.

John Cale had been recording at The Manor and when the session ended, Oldfield noticed a set of tubular bells being removed and asked for them to be left for use on his work-in-progress. For the end of Part One Oldfield had a repetitive bass line to which more and more instruments are gradually added, each taking turns in the spotlight playing a ten-bar melody before dropping down into the mix.

Vivian Stanshall of The Bonzo Dog Band had been recording at The Manor and Oldfield asked him to be the "master of ceremonies" on the final section. Early run-throughs were disastrous, with Stanshall having problems with his timing, but ultimately he sounds fully in control, introducing each instrument in his trademark plummy tones. The section climaxes with his dramatic announcement, *"Plus... tubular bells!"* and they clank out the tune.

Oldfield found out that when he played the bells with standard mallets, they didn't cut through the way that he had wanted. This gave rise to a fractious all-night studio session trying to give them more presence without unbalancing the mix. In the end the desired metallic clang that can be heard on the record came from playing them with a standard claw hammer.

There are no actual songs on the album, but it's not without vocals. Part Two begins with an exquisite mosaic of electric guitar harmonics, acoustic guitar, piano and organ, with snatches of wordless vocals. This leads into a Celtic-style melody with skirling guitars underpinned by tympani. That in turn segues into a section featuring another guest musician, Steve Broughton of the Edgar Broughton Band on drums, which offers some absurdist light relief with Oldfield as Piltdown Man. Named after an early 20th-century hoax in which human and other primate remains were presented as a composite "missing link", it finds Oldfield bellowing in some made-up ur-language, made more guttural by slowing down the recording.

Steve Broughton plays drum kit on this part, and elsewhere Jon Field of Jade Warrior plays flute. Lindsay Cooper, ostensibly a jazzer who had played everything from free improvisation to stints in the ship's band on the Queen Mary, features on double bass.

Oldfield had a pragmatic approach to the vocal choruses, with his sister Sally accompanied by Manor manager Mundy Ellis appearing as "Girlie Chorus". The "Nasal Choir" who hum on side one comprise a number of the Manor kitchen staff, while engineers Tom Newman and Simon Heyworth sing in the "Manor Choir".

Part Two's climactic 'Sailor's Hornpipe' was initially a different version, playing in the background while an audibly inebriated Vivian Stanshall took the listener on a late-night guided tour of The Manor, but that joke would surely soon have paled.

Oldfield's sensitive disposition had been further shaken by an incident when he was 17 and living alone in a Pimlico flat. He experimented with LSD and had the dreaded bad trip. He told the BBC: "People didn't look at all recognisable and looked like biological machines, and it completely disturbed me. At the time it was like the end of the world for me. It scared the life out of me. It made me retreat even more into my music. In a way music was more real than normal reality."

Newman has memories of Oldfield being technically well up to the task of making *Tubular Bells*, but finding the realisation of his composition an overwhelming experience. He told the BBC: "Mike was a mental wreck, when he was making it. He was walking around with his eyes wet with tears nearly all the time. He was in a terrible state. What was going on in his head was eternal and beautiful. My heart went out to him."

After hearing the tapes of the album in early 1973, Branson tried unsuccessfully to arrange its release through an established label. He was also left wondering if he had made the right decision to launch Virgin Records with an experimental album with no lead vocals. Virgin released *Tubular Bells* on May 25, 1973, a week after Oldfield had turned 20, along with *Flying Teapot* by Gong, but the former was officially first in the label's catalogue as V2001.

The album was the quintessential sleeper. Although many reviewers latched onto it, it was initially more of a cult release and it reached a healthy number seven in its initial chart run. John Peel praised it effusively and played it in its entirety on his Radio 1 show. Then it re-entered the chart and eventually reached number one for one week in October 1974, by which time it seemed that everyone had a copy.

The album's success was helped by its opening theme being used as the soundtrack music to William Friedkin's notorious horror film *The Exorcist*, which came out in late 1973. But the reason it became such a phenomenon was due to more than this exposure, and more than the novelty of the boy genius Oldfield playing nearly all the instruments. There was something about *Tubular Bells* that resonated with listeners to an unusual degree.

Without a particular lyrical subject the album could potentially mean all things to all people. The cover features a stylised convoluted tubular bell hovering above a summer seascape and the music really feels like the soundtrack to a sunny day by the sea. And who doesn't like that?

As Oldfield says, he essentially viewed music as more real than his troubled "normal" reality and so he poured his heart and soul into *Tubular Bells*. The result is an evocative, colourful sound painting in which the listener can lose themselves, but one of emotional substance rather than just a series of pretty musical scenes.

With the success of their inaugural release, Virgin were naturally hoping to get Oldfield to tour, but although he had done so with Ayers, *Tubular Bells* was such a personal statement that he absolutely hated talking about it to the press, let alone wanting to tour it. "The night I finished it I didn't want to know about it as it was such a big thing and I'd got it out of my system," he recalled. The one showcase concert that he felt obliged to do – in June 1973 at the Queen Elizabeth Hall, London – almost ended in a no show. Branson had only stopped Oldfield pulling out at the last minute by promising him the keys to his vintage Bentley. Despite some tuning and cueing problems the musicians received a standing ovation.

Oldfield appeared looking reasonably relaxed on the BBC 2 arts programme *2nd House* in November 1973, leading a line-up that included musicians from new labelmates Gong (Steve Hillage on guitar, Pierre Moerlen on percussion) and Henry Cow (Fred Frith on guitar, Tim Hodgkinson and John Greaves on keyboards), with the Stones' Mick Taylor on lead guitar and Terry Oldfield on flute. The piece had been slightly rescored – for example, there is an oboe part played by Karl Jenkins, then in Soft Machine – and the assembled company did it justice.

"No one thought that *Tubular Bells* was going to be a big record or a hit, it was just thought of as being a very interesting thing," says Hillage. "The Queen Elizabeth Hall concert went really well and afterwards we also thought the record might do well. It really captured the zeitgeist.

"Next year, of course, there was the *Orchestral Tubular Bells* concert. Mike dropped out at the last minute and Richard Branson had to ring round various guitarists. I deputised at the Albert Hall and did it again in Glasgow and the other person who he got to deputise in Newcastle was Andy Summers.

"The more challenging aspect was that the night before, Gong had done a gig at the Melkweg in Amsterdam, where large amounts of hash smoking, et cetera, occurred, so I was in an interesting state of mind when I rolled up to do it. But it made my mum very happy – she came and she was very proud."

Virgin was such a cool label to begin with. Roger Dean, well known for his groundbreaking sleeve artwork with Yes, designed the company's logo on the record labels and he also designed the artwork for their carrier bags, an indispensable fashion accessory for young poseurs to be seen with on the street.

The company's attitude came through with the sleeve information: "In Glorious Stereophonic Sound. Can also be played on mono equipment at a pinch." In the bottom left-hand corner of the back cover, in barely legible text, is a parody of the standard notice that the record can be played on a mono record player provided that it is fitted with a stereo cartridge. Virgin's take on that was the less reverent: "This stereo record cannot be played on old tin boxes no matter what they are fitted with. If you are in possession of such equipment please hand it in to your nearest police station."

But there was more to it than establishing an alternative to buttoned-up formality. In 1973, problems with the oil-producing OPEC cartel started off the oil crisis and the subsequent vinyl shortage, and so many companies were trying to cut costs by using recycled vinyl, including melted-down leavings from the pressing process. In fairness to Virgin, they walked it like they talked it and having listened to crackly and inferior test pressings of *Tubular Bells* on recycled vinyl, they decided to use the higher-quality virgin vinyl, which was usually earmarked for classical pressings, for their flagship release.

The Virgin roster grew apace. Gong's *Flying Teapot*, which came out on the same day as *Tubular Bells*, was seen as a bit less their baby since the group were still technically signed to the French label BYG/Actuel, which had been set to release it, but through financial problems had effectively ceased to operate. It dramatically raised the profile of the Anglo-French group in the UK.

Steve Hillage had already signed a solo deal with Virgin after his showings as a guitar hotshot, songwriter/composer and vocalist with Uriel, Egg and Khan, who released the excellent psychedelic-cum-progressive album *Space Shanty* on Deram in 1972.

Virgin were soon synonymous with a certain strand of progressive rock, both cerebral and psychedelic. They signed the uncompromising Henry Cow and two of the most significant German groups of the era, Faust and Tangerine Dream.

Tangerine Dream, who signed to Virgin in 1973, had recorded the semi-abstract and austerely beautiful *Atem* for the German Ohr label, which DJ John Peel proclaimed as his favourite album of 1973. "Gong did three or four gigs with Tangerine Dream in France before we signed with Virgin," Hillage remembers. "They built up the psychedelic synths, the electronics and then we'd go on and take it over the edge in our unique way."

They went on to record *Phaedra* for Virgin, a vast billowing kosmische soundscape of electric pianos, Mellotron and all manner of keyboards running through effects and an early use of synthesizers hooked up to sequencers as a pulsing rhythm track. It was released in 1974 and again caught the zeitgeist, reaching number fifteen in the charts.

Virgin mail order had been pivotal in making German imports available in the UK and they made an audacious attempt to make German group Faust into a household name by releasing an album, *The Faust Tapes*, for the price of a single, then 49p. A dazzling collage of material made up of twenty-six tape edits, it ran the gamut from charming ditties to idiosyncratic instrumentals to searing machine noise. In total it sold over 100,000 copies and so became the most avant-garde album in virtually all of those collections.

Following an arrangement with BYG records, Virgin drummed up interest in their new signing Gong by reissuing their 1971 album

Camembert Electrique, also for the price of a single. Virgin's image at the time was unimpeachable. This bunch of businessmen hairies gave you the hippest music that you didn't even realise you wanted, and sometimes for next to nothing.

Other early Virgin signings included Hatfield And The North, a kind of Canterbury Scene supergroup, and two uncompromising modern blues singers and visual artists, Kevin Coyne and the American Captain Beefheart, and in 1974, ex-Soft Machine drummer and singer, Robert Wyatt whose debut Virgin album *Rock Bottom* became one of the most critically revered of the decade.

Hillage recalls that Gong founder Daevid Allen, the former Soft Machine guitarist, was excited about the possibilities that he saw with Virgin: "Daevid was buzzing about the fact that we were going to be part of this new record label. We were all excited about it," he says.

But this honeymoon period was not to last long. Although the company appeared to be tailor made for the early Seventies, one could flip the argument around and say that Branson would have probably been astute enough to have made money in whatever cultural milieu and in whatever decade he operated. Rumour had it that he knew little about music and his favourite song was allegedly Cliff Richard's celebration of a certain state of independence, 'Bachelor Boy'.

Virgin eventually dropped the "Virgin has never sold a full price record" statement of intent. They continued casting around for innovative artists, not least because this was the absolute heyday of the non-mainstream group, where a significant chunk of the record-buying public were actively seeking out something different, as had been proven by the success of *Tubular Bells*. And the rather more outré stuff found a home on a subsidiary label, Caroline Records. One example is a split album with keyboard player Steve Miller, formerly of Delivery, and saxophonist Lol Coxhill on different sides called *"The Story So Far…" "…Oh Really?"*. One of Coxhill's tracks is a twenty-two-second nod to his former Whole World bandmate entitled 'Tubercular Balls'.

One can't help but also feeling admiration for Virgin taking a punt on Bedford's avant-garde orchestral work *Star's End*, which, even though it featured Mike Oldfield on electric guitar as well as Henry Cow drummer Chris Cutler, was hardly likely to race up the charts.

"They were thinking, 'This is hip, this is cool, this is good for us,'" says Cutler. "It wasn't until *Tubular Bells* sold six million copies that they knew which path to follow. Before that they were still casting about to find something that would dig them in."

Cutler puts forward an idea of what was informing Virgin's choices and how his group became signed to the label.

"Richard Branson realised that the record business was making him money, and he was smart enough to delegate A&R decisions to people who knew something about music – because Richard himself didn't really know or care. And the people he chose – Jumbo Vanrenen and Simon Draper – liked the Soft Machine. Intelligently, they chose to not compete with the big boys but rather to corner the market in something they could have a virtual monopoly in, because no one else was in the game. So they chose the Soft Machine. That's why they signed Gong very early on, and tried to get Robert [Wyatt] who said no at first, but signed up later. They also went after Kevin [Ayers] and didn't get him either [until 1976]. Next they approached everyone in Kevin's band [*The Whole World*]: Mike Oldfield, they got him, David Bedford, him too – and then Lol Coxhill.

"We sent our demo to lots of labels. Virgin showed an interest. Then they asked the people they knew what they thought – these people were Daevid, Robert Wyatt – who we all knew since he'd come to one of our Explorer's Club concerts – as had Virgin's Simon Draper; and NME journalist Ian MacDonald – with whom most of the band had been at Cambridge. So all our referees were people we knew. That's almost certainly what tipped the decision in our favour. They liked the demo – and then they got the endorsements."

But the avant-garde progressive rock party soon went rather flat for Henry Cow. Although Virgin artists were visibly working on each other's projects, there was no "all for one, one for all" label camaraderie. That was not the group's problem, though. Despite Virgin having their alternative kudos, they weren't some groovy patrons of the arts or a philanthropic benevolent society: they were a business that needed to make money.

Cutler notes that the atmosphere when recording at The Manor was fairly unpressurised. But then it's not as if all the bands were on mates' rates and they would receive a bill for studio time. Many musicians in the Seventies simply signed whatever contract they were handed and hoped to make hay while the sun shone, which is why a startling number made next to no money or ended up in debt. The recording, advertising, promotional and mysterious "tour support" costs were just that: costs to be paid by the musicians. One particular musician who had signed to Virgin in the Seventies died in the 2000s still owing the company money, although the debt was posthumously written off. Henry Cow tried to be realistic and knew when to bail out.

"We were fairly careful," says Cutler. "We didn't let it get out of hand. And we got out of most of the dependencies early – so we weren't doing tours with the Virgin Agency and we weren't taking money from the label except studio costs, which was not money we got but money they paid themselves [for The Manor]. After a while, they lost interest but at the same time we were blocked from any other alternatives, so we needed to get ourselves out of the contract to move forward.

"We went to a lawyer and he said the only other contract he'd seen like ours was drawn up by the American mafia. 'They are billing you for absolutely everything, then taking 60 or 70 per cent off the top, so you'll never get a penny,' he said. In the end we got out by insisting that Virgin honour the contract they'd written. We went to the office and said, 'Here we are – ready to make our next album, which, according to our contract, is already two years overdue, so we need a month at The Manor.' They said, 'We can't give you a month at The Manor, we can give you two weeks at a cheap studio somewhere else.' We said, 'It says here we get a month in a first class studio.' They still refused. We said, 'Does that mean you're breaking the contract?' They said they were, so we were free. Of course, they still own our publishing, and we'll never get that back, so we weren't that clever."

Back in 1974 Oldfield recorded a follow-up, *Hergest Ridge*, named after a hill in the English-Welsh borders near where he had moved to escape from the rockstar life that was waiting for him. He demoed the album at his home, The Beacon, but recorded it at The Manor, with Bedford arranging some strings. A different Lindsay Cooper guested on oboe, this time the (female) musician from Henry Cow. One of the backing vocalists, Clodagh Simmons, had been in the cult Irish folk rock group Mellow Candle.

Hergest Ridge reached number one that autumn, but was then knocked off the top spot the following week by a resurgent *Tubular Bells*. As Oldfield told the BBC: "There was pressure to do the big one. I didn't realise I'd already done the big one."

Although nothing that Oldfield did subsequently chimed with the zeitgeist like *Tubular Bells*, both *Hergest Ridge* and *Ommadawn*, which reached number four in 1975, contained some sublime moments. There was a Celtic feel to some of melodies, like the soaring woodwind lines at the beginning of *Hergest Ridge*, which sounds like an Irish air. This was mirrored in the high recorder and keyboard lines used on *Ommadawn* and made most overt by Paddy Maloney of Irish traditional group The Chieftains, who plays a gorgeous song-like melody on Uilleann pipes on the second side. Overall, its themes were more fully developed than on

Tubular Bells. Oldfield then took his time coming back with *Incantations* in 1978, which was rich with tuned percussion that brought to mind Balinese gamelan and some of the contemporaneous minimalist compositions by American composer Steve Reich.

"They had *Tubular Bells*, which was fantastically successful and then the next album *Hergest Ridge* was very successful, but on the back of *Tubular Bells*, and got critically attacked," says Oldfield. "*Ommadawn* was very, very well received critically and that sold pretty well and then I had this *Incantations* album, which I wasn't really into, to be honest – it took me three years and my heart wasn't in it."

By this time, Virgin had changed their focus completely and Oldfield was one of the handful of initial signings who had been retained by the label, as we shall see later on.

CHAPTER 13

Sock in Opposition: Henry Cow

In 1971 drummer Chris Cutler was looking for a group to join and together with Dave Stewart, the keyboard player with Egg, he hit upon the idea of forming a Rock Composers' Orchestra. This ensemble was The Ottawa Music Company, which they envisaged as a pool of musicians playing each other's compositions as well as cover versions. Mont Campbell and Clive Brooks, the bass guitarist and drummer of Egg respectively, were also members, as were vocalist Barbara Gaskin and guitarist Steve Hillage.

After three concerts, Cutler joined Henry Cow, shortly after they had won DJ John Peel's Rockertunity Knocks contest. This had simply involved sending in a demo tape, which Peel then played on his *Top Gear* Radio 1 show. Henry Cow had been formed back in 1968 at Cambridge University by guitarist Fred Frith and keyboards and reeds player Tim Hodgkinson. Initially they played music that was exploratory, but also whimsical and eccentric – as demonstrated by their choice of group name – and then spent some time as a drummerless, and rather rudderless, trio.

The new group line-up of Cutler, Frith, Hodgkinson, saxophonist and winds player Geoff Leigh, and bassist and pianist John Greaves decided to make a serious go of it, and decamped to London.

Henry Cow then set up their own performance-cum-concert series, *Cabaret Voltaire* and *The Explorer's Club*, where they would appear with special guests, because, as Cutler says: "We had assumed – correctly – that no one would want to book us." Most members of Henry Cow joined The Ottawa Music Company and when they played at one of Henry Cow's *Cabaret Voltaire* nights, the company swelled to twenty-two members.

In spring 1973, Henry Cow landed a deal with the nascent Virgin Records and were shipped off to record at the label's sixteen-track studio, The Manor, in Shipton-On-Cherwell. Mike Oldfield was still on site and he engineered for a bit when Tom Newman was indisposed.

With their 1973 debut album *The Henry Cow Legend*, Henry Cow raised the bar in terms of compositional complexity and musicianship. It was clearly the product of a rock group with particularly eclectic tastes, and these have been confirmed as including Soft Machine, Sun Ra, The Mothers Of Invention, Miles Davis, Lifetime, Ornette Coleman, The Who and early Pink Floyd. Cutler is a fan of Who drummer Keith Moon, while Frith has cited Pink Floyd's Roger Waters as one of his favourite bass players.

Unlike some of the groups whose classical influences were along the more comforting lines of the Romantic 19th-century composers, Henry Cow's came more from astringent 20th-century modernists like Schoenberg, Bartók and Stravinsky. But along with this embracing of dissonance and atonality, their music had a considerable tonal melodic content, and veered from loose and jazzy to intricately structured. And just as they relished rock drama, they were equally adept at free improvisation.

One thing that stands out is the ease with which the group negotiated complex time signatures. The album opens with the Zappa-esque brass theme of 'Nirvana For Mice', which Fred Frith has since revealed that he composed by drawing on ideas of chance put forward by John Cage: "I used playing cards to generate pitches and durations, then listened to what I had, and set about framing it in the language of a rock band – beats, chords. Once I had the framework, I wrote a countermelody to bind it together."

Rather than being an acolyte of Cageian philosophy, Frith was simply being inquisitive, seeing how it might work in his music. And rather than the anti-melodic intervallic leaps that one might expect from such a ploy, Frith emerged with a strong, even whistleable tune. The guitarist describes the middle sections as "jamming over a riff in time-honoured rock fashion". But in full spate, the group played with freedom and with an elasticated sense of timing. The composition ends in a thrilling passage with Leigh and Hodgkinson playing a staccato unison saxophone passage in sixteenths.

Henry Cow rehearsed assiduously to get to this level of collective empathy, as Cutler explains: "We'd improvise for a couple of hours, rehearse the written material and then spend some time experimenting with additive rhythms, poly-rhythms and cycles. We'd think of numbers and play every variation and internal subdivision imaginable, dreaming up different possibilities and then running them with or against one another, until we could all feel all of the rhythms at once and not be distracted by whatever else was going on."

The album is actually quite accessible for those who like a bit of a challenge. Newman's engineering gave the group's material a colourful and vivid sound, and although it has complexity, it also has more of an organic flow than might be expected from some of the compositional methods employed.

'Teenbeat Introduction' is a group improvisation that slowly builds into the dynamic 'Teenbeat', where, after a short pastiche of R&B brass, it gearshifts through different episodes and themes, alighting awhile on a sort of mutated bossa nova beat.

Tim Hodgkinson's 'The Nine Funerals Of The Citizen King' was inspired by Situationist texts and is another memorable melody. The only song on the album, it also references early 20th-century modernist writer Gertrude Stein's line *"A rose is a rose is a rose"* from her 1913 poem *Sacred Emily* and she is referred to as the *"mumma of Dada"*. The song manages to be both literate and also rather goofy. The album was released in August 1973 as V2005, the fifth album in the Virgin catalogue.

The members of Henry Cow were trying to expand their soundworld both through the use of effects units and also through applying novel techniques to their playing. Cutler had a compact drum kit augmented by a small pair of bongos on a stand, but during live improvisations he would introduce objects like stones and pieces of wood and metal onto the kit. He played perched high on his stool, cheeks sucked in, arms waving balletically, sometimes just clipping the bell of a cymbal or landing a rimshot on the snare. Presumably he was influenced by players in the UK free improvisation scene?

"I didn't go to a lot of improvising gigs back then," Cutler replies. "But I must have been aware of what was going on; and it was in the air that you would try to find different ways of getting unusual sounds out of a kit; everyone was experimenting with everything."

Frith was the first guitarist to bring the techniques and approach of free improvisation into rock, if not exactly into the rock mainstream. As well as using numerous effects pedals, he played with a glass prism and attached crocodile clips to the strings to alter their harmonics, and for his "stereo guitar", Frith also divided the guitar neck with a capo and added another pick-up at the nut end.

"I suppose I would have to consider myself a pioneer in some way or another, but it doesn't quite fit," Frith says. "Because coming from the rock background that I did, I feel as if the use of the rock guitar in The Velvet Underground, Zappa – especially in his recording of the guitar –

Jeff Beck or Pete Townshend... they were all doing things that for me were new and exciting."

Beck and Townshend brought their own innovations, but they were still linked to a blues tradition, whereas Frith brought an approach to guitar playing that was coming from somewhere completely outside that.

"I was a failure then," he jokes, "'cos I certainly have a blues base. I guess I was experimenting in a slightly different way. And also it begs the whole question, 'What is rock music anyway? What category are we actually in?' In those days, improvisers didn't want anything to do with me; I was a rock musician. And rock musicians were, 'This isn't really rock music, this is some sort of avant-garde shit.' So we weren't exactly accepted in either world."

Frith told Ian MacDonald of *New Musical Express* in 1973: "The basic difference between us and most other groups in our situation is that their music is contained by them – in other words, they write music which they can already play and, to that extent, they're strait-jacketing themselves from the start.

"What we've done is to literally teach ourselves to play through the medium of the group by composing music which we could not initially play."

Cutler confirms it as a "kind of spiral of technique", with the musicians coming up with solutions to problems they had set themselves, the results of which might then appear in improvisations, which in turn would inspire new compositions.

UNREST
Original label: Virgin
Producer: Henry Cow
Recorded: February–March 1974
Release date: May 1974

Chris Cutler has said that artist Ray Smith's mixed media "paint socks" on each of the Henry Cow album covers reflect the mood of the music within. So after the colourful one on the cover of *Legend* ("Legend" = "leg-end". Geddit?), the sock on the cover of *Unrest* looks like it had too much black in it to go with a brown suit and too much brown to go with a black suit, and was therefore thrown away onto a patch of estuarine mud. Correspondingly, the album has a bleaker, darker mood. Saxophonist Geoff Leigh had departed, and had been replaced by Lindsay Cooper on bassoon, oboe and flute, who Cutler had met while she was playing in the folk rock group, Comus.

Cutler: "One of the reasons Geoff left was that the music was getting more complicated and austere, and less loose and jazzy. And one of the reasons we didn't get another sax player is that we wanted to sound less 'normal' and find our own musical language. Certainly Lindsay's instrument – and Lindsay herself – influenced the way things moved, because she didn't play loosely and her way of improvising was informed more by contemporary music than jazz."

Unrest opens with Fred Frith's good-humoured, if knotty, 'Bittern Storm Over Ulm'. He admits to borrowing the bass line from The Yardbirds' 1965 track 'Got To Hurry', a filler instrumental written by Giorgio Gomelsky that uses a generic twelve-bar R&B walking bass in a brisk 4/4. John Greaves has fun deconstructing the timing, his bass moving around crab-like across the beat, visiting all the notes eventually, while adding more inflections in between. Sax and bassoon join in at the end playing the theme generated by the bass, like a mutation of a punchy R&B horn section. It's a piece of musical drollery, but one that works convincingly – and, at under three minutes, very succinctly.

Greaves's 'Half Awake/Half Asleep' starts off with his lyrical piano introduction before shifting into gear with a two-bar bass figure over which the group play a long, non-repeating line – again, this is melodically rich material that flows through a number of metre changes without obvious contrivance. The individual lines begin to loosen up and diverge in an improvised mid-section, where the "one" gets buffeted by terse, epigrammatic phrases and Cutler's eccentric clattering, with all the activity ultimately resolving itself in Greaves's piano coda.

Frith's 'Ruins' became a perennial live favourite and was an example of how their "finished" compositions could in fact remain as works-in-progress. It was also an example of music that demanded Henry Cow stretch themselves yet further, causing Frith to be critical of his own xylophone and violin playing on the recording.

That said, 'Ruins' stands as some of the most striking twelve minutes of rock music from the early Seventies and ends a side of impressive compositions.

The structure of 'Ruins' is palindromic and is in part based on the Fibonacci number series that dictated the proportions of the golden section.

"Compositionally my main sources of ideas were Messiaen, especially in the palindromic construction of rhythmic phrases in the middle section, and Bartók," Frith has noted. "Or more specifically, a biography of Bartók that I was reading that talked about his use of the Fibonacci Series. This led me to explore those numbers—it's a fifty-five-beat sequence, and some of the harmonics used the Fibonacci numbers if I remember rightly."

Fibonacci numbers are derived from adding the previous two integers together, so it goes 1, 1, 2, 3, 5, 8, 13, 21, 34, 55 and so on. As with his Cageian experiments that led to the opening of 'Nirvana For Mice', Frith was doing this as someone who was just curious as to how it would translate into his own music. Music dictated by chance methods or from number series is interesting in regard to the theoretical methodology that created it, but put simply, if it doesn't sound any good then it is only interesting in that regard.

And a piece ostensibly in a 55/8 time signature – although practically speaking it would be broken down further – don't mean a thing if it ain't got that swing. As Cutler says: "Of course these numbers – as numbers – are not essential to the music's reception, but they do make the process of composing and performing interesting – and fun."

The piece starts off with a high keyboard drone, and sparse sax and oboe fanfares that are very reminiscent of Stravinsky's 1920 composition, *Symphonies Of Wind Instruments*. It's the sort of music that could have been used in a Seventies TV history programme to underline the sudden dramatic appearance of church gargoyles gurning out from weathered walls. The fact that the piece was only titled after it had been rehearsed suggests that it evoked similar thoughts in the imagination of the composer.

The form is fairly clearly palindromic in terms of its structural blocks. An introductory theme with xylophone leads onto the first 55/8 section. Anyone thinking that their mind would be totally blown by the deployment of such a time signature will actually hear a line seesawing erratically on bass and piano chords, and punctuated mainly on two, three and five, as Frith and Hodgkinson play noisy solos on guitar and keyboards.

The very middle section has more of a chamber feel, with unison violin and bassoon figures answered by unison xylophone and bass figures, which sound very similar stylistically – and are of similar length – to the unison marimba and guitar lines on Captain Beefheart's 'Golden Birdies' from *Clear Spot* (1972).

The second time around, the 55/8 section is arranged for piano with dancing counterpoint oboe and violin lines and the whole track suddenly blossoms into a beautiful and all-too-brief guitar, organ and bass harmony theme before ending on a string drone – and then more wind chorales that fade into the wintry mist.

A significant number of albums over the years have been ruined by deadlines, too few quality ideas and too much filler, but *Unrest*, short by nearly twenty minutes, was filled up in some style with necessity proving, as usual, to be the mother of invention.

"Lindsay had just joined the group and we didn't have enough material to make an album," Cutler says. "She'd also just had two wisdom teeth removed and couldn't rehearse for about a fortnight, so we decided, based on our experience of working on *Legend*, that we'd just generate music in the studio. We made the whole of the second side of *Unrest* that way. So Lindsay was really thrown into the deep end."

Side two opens with Frith's 'Solemn Music', a minute-long oboe and guitar chamber piece. It was the only thing that survived from music that the group had made for a production of William Shakespeare's *The Tempest*, directed by John Chadwick, which had been performed at the Watford Palace Theatre. Oddly enough it shares a similar feel to the Third Ear Band's music for Roman Polanski's film of *Macbeth* that was released in 1971. It acts as an overture to the extraordinary music that follows.

On 'Linguaphonie' we are immediately plunged into a disorienting soundworld of electronic drones, the churning low notes of Cooper's bassoon and Greaves's bass, prepared with clothes pegs, while Frith's guitar spills out sourly and then chirps like a cricket. Meanwhile, Cutler offers some tentative, fragmentary percussion utterances. Everything feels unstable. Then come the nonsensical French lyrics, which all rhyme and are enunciated in a very deliberate way so as to emphasise their absurdity.

Cutler calls this the group's comedy song and the title refers to *Linguaphone*, a Seventies correspondence course involving cassette tapes that purported to be able to teach you to speak a foreign language *tout de suite*. It also punningly refers to the way the singers intone on Karlheinz Stockhausen's *Mikrophonie II* (1965) – which also happens to be based on the Fibonacci series. Furthermore it brings to mind the hoots and screams of György Ligeti's 1962 vocal piece, *Aventures*, which is in itself an absurdist exercise.

Cutler explains how the piece was put together: "In the case of 'Linguaphonie', the basic material came out of an improvisation that didn't have a lot of form. It was Lindsay humming that gave us the clue. I think we had a picture of someone in the living room doing the hoovering and thought, 'Right, we're in comedy mode.' And that was the key to all the other decisions we made on that track.

"First we doubled her voice, then John played what she sang on the bass – with clothes-pegs damping the strings – and then Lindsay did the same with bassoon harmonics, to make a thematic connection. After that the chants went in, because we wanted to focus on the vocal idea. After that we added and subtracted things until the piece sounded as if it had been composed – which, after the fact, it had been. Most of side two was put together that way: listening to what we had, cutting stuff out, sticking things together, overdubbing and then mixing."

The "comedy" nonsense recitations begin to break down, like a language class that has got out of control, leaving the voices occasionally barking out vowels, like *"Oh!"* and *"Eeh"* in guttural disruption, as the atmosphere becomes increasingly tense and sinister. Then a pause, an electronic pulse and on cue someone emits a massive scream, with Frith coming in with maximum squall and Cutler flailing around for all he's worth. More breathless cries and instrumental outbursts and then it's all calmed slightly with overdubbed brass themes. This brief section is called 'On Entering The Hotel Adlon'. All in all it's one hell of a scary comedy routine.

Following that, 'Arcades' is a terse, sparse exchange of lines on sax, winds and guitar that sounds like a composed chamber piece, seemingly with a nod towards Anton Webern, but was actually an extract from a longer improvisation.

The most inspired piece on side two is the closer, 'Deluge'. It was made by running a forty-foot tape loop around the studio of a wonderful piece of playing by Cutler, like heavily deconstructed jazz, with flashes of superfast cymbal work and twitchy snare clicks punctuated by long pauses and Greaves's sparse, dollopy bass. Cutler notes that the friction on all the bottles and cans that it was looped around made the timing slightly erratic.

Gradually, more instruments are added as sparse punctuation and a strange, melancholic drone starts up in the background, which is in fact the glorious bass, keyboards and guitar section at the end of 'Ruins' played at half speed. It's very affecting and in Cutler's words: "It starts very youthful, fast and optimistic, lots happening, lots of energy, and it slowly turns into something sad and tragic."

The album ends with a few lines of a Greaves piano song and then a few seconds more of eerie drone before the run-out groove.

Unsurprisingly *Unrest* didn't chart. Some people don't think that it should be called progressive rock because it sounds so unlike most other progressive rock, but that is surely why it is absolutely quintessential progressive rock. And for all its supposed difficulty and the group's curious ways of working, *Unrest*'s autumnal lyricism is particularly haunting.

Henry Cow found an unlikely champion in *New Musical Express* journalist Charles Shaar Murray, who admitted in a 1974 interview-based article on them that he was generally more au fait with groups like Mott The Hoople, but when he had decided to take the plunge himself and listen to their first two albums, *Legend* and *Unrest*: "I found myself enjoying it so much that I was convinced that I'd misunderstood it."

This highlights a perennial problem with so-called difficult or inaccessible music. Just as one visitor to an art gallery might stand in front of an abstract painting and enjoy it for what it is, another might become agitated and frustrated, exclaiming: "Yes, but what does it *mean?*"

When speaking to Murray, drummer Cutler came out fighting when the word "inaccessible" was used to describe Henry Cow's music: "That's a word that *NME* journalists like to use, actually, in conjunction with 'determinedly', which implies that we made it that way on purpose. Bit of a nerve, that, in terms of our aims and intentions. 'Inaccessible' doesn't mean a thing when you think about it. It just means that they find it hard to listen to, thereby being responsible for a lot of other people not listening to it..."

Looking back, Cutler has this to say now about the music press: "I think we had a few friends – critics who liked us, but even they would say things like, 'It's great but only a few people will understand it' – which may or may not have been valid, but didn't help. We thought what we were doing was accessible to anyone who could be bothered to listen."

But one feels that Cutler took so strongly against those sorts of comments about their music in print, partly out of frustration and partly because he knew that, as far as most people were concerned, it was far easier to politely decline than to put aside time to listen to Henry Cow. Any territory they had gained within the music business had been hard-won ground. And as mentioned in the previous chapter, their relationship with Virgin quickly soured.

But Cutler's idea that there was no reason why an audience couldn't enjoy Henry Cow's music was born out by the attention of Jakko Jakszyk, currently of King Crimson, but then a schoolboy fan: "I'm 14 and a guy I know at a theatre group says, 'You've got to see this band, they're brilliant. They're called Henry Cow.' I go and see them and I'm completely smitten. I think it's extraordinary. They play what seems like one piece because they string it all together with improvisation and I'm blown away. I become a complete Henry Cow Head and I keep going to see them, and eventually everyone at school says, 'If Jakko asks you to go and see a band called Henry Cow, don't go. It's absolute fucking rubbish; it's not even proper music.' So I find myself at the age of 13 or 14 going to see Henry Cow on my own.

"The guys in the band come on and they start waving to me – there's that kid on his own. And that's another reason for going: the band know who I am. They play at St Albans Art College and it's fantastic and I love it, and I'm walking back up to the high street thinking, 'I've no idea how I'm going to get home, I've missed my last bus.'

"A van pulls over and Chris Cutler gets out and says, 'Are you all right, what's the matter?' I said, 'I've missed my last bus home.' And he said, 'Really? Where do you live?' I said that I live just outside Watford and he says, 'Hang on a second,' goes into the van, and comes out and says, 'We'll give you lift home. We're going to eat first: do you want to come with us?' We went to an Indian restaurant and it was the first Indian meal I've ever had – the first curry I ever had was bought for me by Henry Cow.

"They drive me back home to Croxley Green, where I was living with my parents and I say, just out of courtesy, 'Do you want to come in for a cup of tea?' And they say 'Yeah, alright.' My parents are asleep upstairs, I'm in some semi-detached house in Croxley Green and I've got my favourite group in the living room drinking tea."

But although they were clearly a friendly lot, there was something intimidating about every aspect of the group. The ugly name, the "difficult" music, and a left-wing stance applied to a largely apolitical music scene – in which many punters thought that politics were just basically rules dreamed by a bunch of unenlightened squares – all contributed to making them outsiders. Even Fred Frith's capacious peg leg trousers – which looked like they had come from a charity shop suit several sizes too large for the guitarist – were seen as subversive in the heyday of the loon pant.

A good example of their position in relation to the prevailing musical climate is their notorious – and for most owners, least played – side of the 1974 *Greasy Truckers* live double album. It's a series of uncompromising, largely improvised pieces driven like a wedge between contributions from Gong, Camel and Global Village Trucking Company. "It certainly sorted out the sheep from the goats," Cutler laughs.

Cutler was often the group's spokesperson in interviews and was dubbed by one journalist "the most argumentative man in rock".

"I was very opinionated then, because everything seemed more black and white to me than it does now," he explains. "We [Henry Cow] were permanently in a state of struggle, not only with the conditions of our existence, the kind of ecology of being in a group, but also with our instruments and the music we were playing – and each other.

"It often was pretty grim; we'd fight a lot. So we were in a pretty highly aroused condition and that probably made us seem far more elitist and argumentative than might have actually been the case. But we did have a kind of political agenda in those days."

After *Unrest* Frith demonstrated his extended techniques on a highly regarded album *Guitar Solos* on Virgin's Caroline subsidiary in 1974.

In an unexpected spin-off, the *New Musical Express* ran the Guitar Book, a weekly pull-out supplement that dealt with chord tutorials, interviews with the likes of Jimmy Page and Robert Fripp, and with Fred Frith writing each week about great guitar performances. No doubt many teen guitarists across the land wondered: "Who's Fred Frith?"

In 1974, Henry Cow also met Slapp Happy, a trio based in Germany, comprising an American vocalist, guitarist and wordsmith Peter Blegvad; a British keyboard player Anthony Moore; and a German singer Dagmar Krause, via new Virgin signings Faust and their svengali-cum-producer Uwe Nettelbeck. "They came over, the three of them, and we got on like a house on fire, and then we played on their album," says Cutler.

Faust had played on Slapp Happy's debut album *Sort Of* (1972) and its follow-up, which Polydor rejected. Virgin got the trio over to re-record their second album at The Manor. Geoff Leigh, freshly departed from Henry Cow, plays saxophone on that album, with Faust's Jean-Hervé Péron on bass, a string section lead by Graham Preskett and, among many others, Ottawa Music Company member Jeremy Baines on sausage bassoon, or rackett.

For their next Virgin album, *Desperate Straights*, Slapp Happy were backed by Henry Cow, with the sleeve displaying a split credit. 'Bad Alchemy' was co-written by Blegvad and John Greaves and shortly after, Slapp Happy officially joined up with Henry Cow for *In Praise Of Learning*. But this particular inter-group alchemy was not to last for long. The brief 'War', which had been recorded in the sessions for *Desperate Straights*, was the only significant compositional contribution by Moore and Blegvad, although both played on the album. Their quirky, neo-cabaret songs had no place next to daunting new compositions like Tim Hodgkinson's fifteen-minute 'Living In The Heart Of The Beast', and although asked, Blegvad had been unable to come up with lyrics for that song. With the two less than keen to play live, even with Slapp Happy, they slipped out of the picture leaving Dagmar as the Henry Cow vocalist.

There are two group improvisations on the album, 'Beginning The Long March' and 'Morning Star', but although seething with detail, they feel cluttered and unfocused compared to their equivalents on *Unrest*.

Dagmar looks back on the merger of the two groups: "[With *Desperate Straights*] Slapp Happy was saying goodbye. We were tortured on all sorts of different levels, in personal relationships and maybe artistically, wondering which way to go. It was OK, but showed the schizophrenic situation we were all in.

"Henry Cow were keen to do something with Slapp Happy, so they took over a bit. At the time it all made sense, but the dynamic with Henry Cow had changed everything. Slapp Happy was really something else and to bring the two opposites together was exciting as a thought, but it didn't have longevity."

In Praise Of Learning was recorded at The Manor and released in May 1975. It was on the demanding music of the two big songs, 'Living In The Heart Of The Beast' and 'Beautiful As The Moon... Terrible As An Army With Banners' that Dagmar's remarkable voice came into its own, encompassing a wide range of expression from light and airy, especially in her upper register, to stern and severe.

'Living In The Heart Of The Beast' addresses people enslaved by a capitalist system that will only see them as *"coinage"* and only good for *"hollow exchange..."*

'Beautiful As The Moon... Terrible As An Army With Banners' is based on Cutler's lyric texts – used for the first time in a song – which exhorted *"workmen"* to *"seize the future"*, although it surely wasn't intended that the revolution would be monosexual.

The album's title comes from Bertold Brecht and the sleeve carries a quote by realist filmmaker John Grierson: "Art is a hammer – not a mirror." The fact that Ray Smith's sock cover was bright red against a red background was more than coincidence. But although Grierson's quote immediately feels dramatically destructive, like the hammer on the communist flag, he saw it to be a force for good, representing construction and industry.

"We were consciously left, but we were not aligned to any particular party," says Cutler. "Our analysis of things was basically Marxist, or wanna-be Marxist, or more-or-less Marxist, and we acted accordingly."

Cutler has always been interested in the application of critical theory, in which one would take an art form and examine the social and ideological forces – both current and historical – that were involved in producing it and which might generate its success, or serve to constrain it.

"There was a lot of inflated nonsense about [progressive rock] being a real art form, but without any theory behind it," says Cutler. "And without theory all you have is opinion and shopping." Which is, of course, what most music consumers are happy with. This only spurred Henry Cow on to further question the role of music beyond its just being a commodity – to question its use and the way it reflected society.

After *In Praise Of Learning*, in spring 1975, *Melody Maker*'s Steve Lake interviewed Cutler, Frith and Dagmar. The atmosphere was somewhat confrontational and Lake noted that during the interview, "Marxist theorising is settling like thick fog". He admitted he had done his "damnedest to get out of this encounter", but because he had mistakenly claimed the group had split up, they insisted that he should be the one to hear their new album. And so they arrived with a tape.

Cutler was brimming with positivity, albeit couched in very un-rock-musician-like terms: "The status quo must be threatened because it's the status quo. It's things as they are that are keeping us in the rotten awful state we're in, and instead of moaning about it and saying how dreadful and terrible everything is, it'd be better to get some perspective on it and get hold of some dialectical materialist attitudes and do some work."

The article feels like it was written by a man who was rather weary and browbeaten by the meeting and although there is some humour in the exchanges, one of Cutler's last quotes is, "I embrace the apocalypse of the Revolution".

The new six-piece group was captured at its peak on the double album, *Henry Cow Concerts*, which was released on Virgin's Caroline subsidiary in 1976. One of the highlights is an extract from a concert at London's Drury Lane Theatre from 1975, which features Robert Wyatt, duetting with Dagmar on 'Bad Alchemy' and 'Little Red Riding Hood Hit The Road' from his 1974 *Rock Bottom* album. Wyatt played a few concerts with the group in 1975, including an open-air event at the Piazza Navona in Rome, but access problems and lack of facilities in general made playing live a bit of a nightmare for someone in a wheelchair. "It could have lasted much longer if I could have dealt with it physically," Wyatt says. But he enjoyed his time with the group, and both Fred Frith and John Greaves contributed to his 1975 album *Ruth Is Stranger Than Richard*.

"Henry Cow would sit round discussing, for hours, the meaning of what they were doing and the relationship between new music and new politics, and all that stuff," Wyatt recalls. "I remember absolutely nothing of that [in Soft Machine], nothing whatsoever. I am rather envious of Henry Cow. I thought, 'Gosh I could have hung around having conversations with musicians if I'd known musicians like Fred Frith and Chris Cutler earlier.' I'm glad we did the concerts. I think Henry Cow were a lovely bunch of coconuts: thoughtful, original and genuinely a progressive rock band."

The best example of Henry Cow humour was in their stage sets around this time. Compare them to Yes's 1975 stage set: they would venture onstage with their smart, almost glammy togs into an environment marked out by glowing fluorescent perspex blobs with giant illuminated mechanical crustacea threatening to consume drummer Alan White and keyboard player Patrick Moraz.

By contrast, Henry Cow's stage set consisted of easy chairs and old-fashioned standard lamps, like a Fifties parlour. Ray Smith would occasionally accompany them on the side of the stage doing the ironing. There was little concession to glamour.

"We wanted to be completely self-sufficient," says Cutler. "We thought it was charming, memorable, funny, suitable." And a satirical poke at some of the stage sets and huge lighting rigs that were beginning to appear at rock concerts? "Actually, yes, but intentionally, no," he replies.

So what was the main musical difference between Yes and Henry Cow?

"[Yes] is very male music," says Dagmar. "It's dazzling, but I don't really go for the dazzle. We weren't part of that prog thing; at least I wasn't aware that we were in that. Although our music was different, it was very different to that sort of music as well. Our music was more down to earth it seems to me – although that sounds quite funny, doesn't it?

"But nobody tried to dazzle anybody and that's something to do with the fact that there were always at least two women in the group after I joined, at best three. So there was a different slant on the whole [thing]. We were certainly some kind of avant-garde rock'n'roll with a hint of left-wing politics attached."

The third woman to whom Dagmar refers is cellist and bass guitarist Georgina Born, who replaced John Greaves in 1976. Greaves went on to make the eccentric, inventive avant song cycle *Kew Rhone* with Peter Blegvad, which was released in 1977, before joining National Health the following year.

Only a handful of women musicians specifically worked in progressive rock in the UK in the 1970s, and three of them were in Henry Cow: Dagmar, Lindsay Cooper, Georgina Born, Annie Haslam of Renaissance, Sonja Kristina of Curved Air, Gilli Smyth of Gong, Miquette Giraudy with Steve Hillage, and Barbara Thompson of Colosseum. That was pretty much it. Now, many media commentators love to lump decades together culturally and behaviourally and have a good old laugh at those unsophisticated times, as if we haven't got sets of contemporary problems that are just as bad but slightly different. Taking the commonly held notion that the Seventies was a decade when impossibly Neanderthal views on sex were rife, did Dagmar ever get any disparaging comments when singing and playing piano with Henry Cow?

"Gladly not; I never experienced that," she replies. "I think guys liked the fact that there were some women to look at in the band while listening to the music that appealed to them... I'm making a joke now [*laughs*]. There was a big feminist movement going on at the time and certainly the mini skirt went out of the window. We didn't dress to kill at all. We dressed with two boots firmly on the ground. Make-up had gone out of the window as well. We were in working clothes. Nothing titillating. I knew what I was doing, I'd like to think, so you'd better take me seriously!"

In 1976, released from Virgin, Henry Cow survived by playing concerts on mainland Europe, because they got far more work there and were more appreciated. In the spirit of getting on and organising rather than bemoaning their lot, they formed Rock In Opposition with a number of groups in mainland Europe who were all obliged – or forced by circumstance – to do things differently and distributed each other's records, organised tours for each other and promoted festivals, thus bypassing the whole music business structure.

The organisation was launched with an inaugural concert at the New London Theatre, Drury Lane, London, in March 1978 with Stormy Six (Italy), Samla Mammas Manna (Sweden), Univers Zero (Belgium) and Etron Fou Leloublan from France. Cutler liked the idea of being for something rather than against it, but Rock In Opposition was a good slogan and showed a certain strength. Although the organisation didn't last long as a formal entity, affiliations have continued and Rock In Opposition festivals are still run to this day.

Cutler recalls that in order to survive the vicissitudes of the music business the group had to be organised. In that respect there were regular minuted band meetings and a lot of discipline. And while they might have participated in breathing exercises to become focused before a concert, Cutler rejects that they adopted Maoist ideas of self-improvement, saying these weren't in their lexicon. Stories emerge of the group being quite an ascetic bunch, so were there ever any drugs around?

"Everybody has to answer for themselves on that, but personally I tried to avoid them," he says. "Was it banned? No, but there was no overt obvious drug taking going on, nor much talk about drugs or where to get them when we arrived at a venue. Drugs was pretty much a non-subject.

"In Henry Cow, if people took drugs they took them quietly and discreetly and in their own time. And not before a concert, although that loosened up towards the end when it was perfectly acceptable to drink a few glasses of wine. Initially there had been a rule of no stimulants before a gig because we had to have our wits about us."

Partly as a result of the "spiral of technique" that Henry Cow were generating, the compositions were becoming more difficult. Cutler remembers that some of the challenges they set themselves were too high and they didn't always play them well enough. There were some problems with Hodgkinson's twenty-minute composition 'Erk Gah'.

"Musically speaking I don't think anybody ever criticised anyone else for anything, or said, 'Play it like this', or 'that's too simple' – until we came to the very end and were about to record 'Erk Gah'," says Cutler. "I think it was Lindsay and Georgie and maybe Fred who called a meeting to say we shouldn't record 'Erk Gah' with Tim's texts. The problem was specifically the text, not the music. But that was the only occasion I remember on which something was said that was overtly proscriptive. We discussed music and performance all the time of course, and there was general criticism, especially when we felt things were getting stale or repetitive, but always in general, rather than specific terms."

Cutler was asked to re-write the text but left it unfinished.

It wasn't all down to one song, but 'Erk Gah' showed how far the group had gone in a few years. It employs a twelve tone or serialist approach with intervals that sidestep simple melody. Its dry, forbidding structure was a long way from the more tonal music of the first two albums.

Hodgkinson has explained his approach in composing the piece: "Twelve tone. Atonal. Where could you go with it? This was going to be dry, astringent, angular, with no compromise towards rock music. Given all this pretension on my part it's amazing how the group managed to possess and inhabit the piece. Seeing his part at the first rehearsal, Fred uttered the immortal words 'Erk Gah' – which is how characters in Don Martin cartoons express shock and dismay. This became its provisional title, then its working title… I suppose the way the piece unfolds to the listener is closely connected to the process of me learning what I could do with this approach – but I never thought that was a bad thing, and I wish more music sounded like it had just been discovered."

Henry Cow split in 1978, after releasing *Western Culture* on their Broadcast label. It's a dazzling selection of shortish instrumental pieces. Hodgkinson had felt that the recent songs put forward by Frith and

Cutler were not really Henry Cow material, so they formed The Art Bears with Dagmar and these songs appeared on their debut album, *Hopes And Fears*, yielding two related releases in that year.

Dagmar: "I'd had conversations with Chris that I was fed up with long pieces and I felt like singing songs again. I found a kindred spirit in Chris, as he had written some song lyrics and Fred had written some tunes."

"The approach was different in the sense that there were three of us and we decided on song form. We didn't have to go through the process of meeting and lots of discussion to decide on one thing. It was, in a sense, more organic, smaller scale and, to me, a natural follow-up to Henry Cow. [The Art Bears' 1979 album] *Winter Songs* I absolutely adored: the whole process of making the record was magical."

In early 1978, as a curious teen, I saw Henry Cow play a concert at the Arnolfini Arts Centre in Bristol and a free gig, in both senses of the word, in Bristol Cathedral the following day. The latter was a completely improvised performance with players moving around, making use of the space. It was like nothing I'd ever witnessed before. Afterwards I recall slightly nervously talking to a genial Chris Cutler as he was packing away his kit, barefoot, wearing considerable flares. I noticed there was a tree painted on one of his tom-toms. I also passed by Fred Frith sitting on the floor in one of the aisles, next to his xylophone, hunched, motionless, with his head in his hands, as if overwhelmed. I thought it impertinent to tarry and moved along, probably thinking something along the lines of, "Wow, *heavy!*"

CHAPTER 14

Knights in Beige Terylene on Acid: The Moody Blues

"'GI-NORMOUS' is the only word to describe The Moody Blues' present status in America," wrote *Record Mirror*'s Keith Altham in 1971. "They have reached the kind of heights there which are only enjoyed by vintage groups like The Rolling Stones and The Who."

This turnaround was remarkable. The Moody Blues were now selling out huge arenas, whereas only a few years previously, the group had appeared to be on its last legs.

The Moody Blues formed in Birmingham in 1964 and made a name for themselves on the R&B circuit. They were one of many groups who saw authenticity in the blues and even backed Sonny Boy Williamson when he came over to the UK. But in 1970, drummer Graeme Edge referred to their early music thus: "We started realising that we weren't being true to our own heritage. We were English and we didn't know anything about the blues, so the best we could offer was third-hand."

The group had scored a big UK hit in 1965 with 'Go Now', which had been a US hit for American soul singer Bessie Banks the previous year, but they had failed to capitalise on its success and were starting to drift. By late 1966, guitarist, vocalist and songwriter Denny Laine and bass guitarist Clint Warwick had both left, and Justin Hayward and John Lodge were drafted in. They joined Edge, Ray Thomas on harmonica, vocals and flute, and Mike Pinder on vocals and keyboards. But in the fast-moving Sixties, with their suits and R&B covers, the group seemed out of time and the two new members were no doubt wondering how long it would be before they would be scouring the small ads in the back of *Melody Maker*.

Matters came to a head in March 1967, when after a concert, one of the attendees and his wife berated the group for being "rubbish" and ruining what otherwise could have been a good evening. In the van on the way back home, the group were understandably deflated, but Edge, asleep in the back on top of the PA, suddenly awoke and, experiencing some kind of epiphany, piped up that they were indeed rubbish and their music and image were both in need of a serious rethink.

At this point The Moody Blues also owed money to Decca from advances, and their contract was about to expire, but luckily they had a champion in Hugh Mendl, an A&R manager, who was setting up the label's progressive subsidiary, Deram. Mendl offered them the chance to record a rock version of Dvorak's *Symphony No.9: From The New World* with an orchestra for the debt to be waived. This extraordinary idea for a money spinner was conceived as a way of showcasing a new stereo recording technique developed in Decca's studios, known as Decca Panoramic Sound. This involved running two four-track stereo tape recorders in tandem. The term was shortened to Deramic Sound, which, shortened further, gave Deram.

The idea was shelved and the story has since been disputed by recording engineer Derek Varnals. But importantly the group received the green light for another Deramic Sound recording, a concept album chronicling a typical "day in the life", *Days Of Future Passed*, with orchestral sections written by Peter Knight.

Comparisons to The Beatles' *Sgt Pepper's* were way off the mark. But at the time *Days Of Future Passed* was something relatively new and reached number twenty-seven in the UK Top 40, and, astonishingly, reached number two in the US when re-released in 1972. A single from the album 'Nights In White Satin', gave The Moody Blues their first Top 20 hit since 'Go Now'.

In Search Of The Lost Chord followed in July 1968. The cover design is remarkable. The painting on the front has some humanoid entity manifesting from out of a subterranean cavern – which contains a skull, a giant human foetus and some strange cloaked figure with a number of heads – and rising up into the sky. So far, so far out. But on the back cover, we are met with a collage of group photos which look like a bunch of grinning squares modelling for the men's casual wear pages of Grattan's mail order catalogue.

Pinder stands resplendent in a sand-coloured pullover and beige slacks, while Hayward, as the token pretty boy, wears a leather jacket and a tight orange shirt that appears to have shrunk in the wash and has ridden up, revealing a saucy glimpse of navel.

Thomas sports a kind of a rugby shirt – never a good look for any musician in any age – but in his individual portrait shot he wears a red high-collared frock coat with frilly dress shirt, sculpted hair and 'tache, all of which gives him the look of some gigolo–cum–dandy predating Peter Wyngarde's TV role as playboy Jason King.

On Pinder's individual portrait he goes for a casual jacket and cravat, his thinning hair brushed in a comb-over, giving him the look of an RAF officer on leave. Neither the group nor Deram Records appeared to have any idea what audience they were aiming for. But appearances can be deceptive. The Moody Blues were also party animals, frequenting the West End musicians' hangout The Scotch Of St James with the likes of Keith Moon and Jimi Hendrix. And with the exception of the abstemious Lodge, these men had been taking LSD.

'Departure' finds Graeme Edge declaiming a poem with imagery of flowers bursting through tarmac towards the sun, synaesthetic sensations of hearing the grass sing and how this can all bring us closer to God. An upward arcing glissando of electronics and we're straight into the driving psychedelic pop song 'Ride My See-Saw', with Lodge's stratospherically high falsetto and Hayward's nimble guitar work swathed in Pinder's Mellotron strings.

For 'Dr Livingstone I Presume', Thomas metaphorically dons a paisley pith helmet and details a series of explorations and strange meetings, interspersed with a chorus with the existential message that we are all *"looking for someone"*.

'House Of Four Doors' is a musical guide through the titular dwelling with each door creaking open to reveal a new musical episode. Ray Thomas's 'Legend Of A Mind' is another multi-part song, this time a paean to notorious LSD advocate and countercultural guru Timothy Leary, with the chorus, *"Timothy Leary's dead"*.

Speaking in 2013, Thomas recalled their friendship: "We got on really well with him, we spent a lot of time at his house. He was a great guy, like a mischievous Irishman. And had a very good sense of humour. Timothy was always great company. I wrote the song 'Legend Of A Mind' about him and the way he used the *Tibetan Book Of The Dead*. It was really tongue-in-cheek."

In the song Leary is relocated in good old late-Sixties Blighty as a man who is metaphorically in charge of amusements on the pier, with its swooning Eastern strings played on Mellotron and cello and Thomas's flute adding to the musical exoticism. It was the most individual and complex song the group ever attempted.

On 'Best Way To Travel', Pinder advises us that the best way to travel is by thought, acting this time as a kind of psychic bus conductor on a stoned journey through astral projection. As the album nears its end we are told that to find the lost chord is our *"life's hope"*, and that the name of the chord is *"Om"*. That's it – meaning of life all sorted.

The Moody Blues are often cited as being in the vanguard of progressive rock and they might have been if they had carried on this tack, but the album is essentially an oddity in their canon. It's eclectic, experimental and full of good tunes – all the group were talented writers – but although they refined their sound they never really pushed themselves out like this again.

As The Moody Blues had sought to change their musical style, so they were also keen to become more independent in the studio. And they also tried to establish a relatively autonomous position within Decca.

They had set up their own label, Threshold Records, under the auspices of Decca, in 1969. All their first seven albums were principally recorded in Decca studios and with their growing success they negotiated with Decca chairman and former financier Sir Edward Lewis to be able to have exclusive use of Studio One in Decca's facility in West Hampstead, in north London.

Hayward recalls the pivotal meeting between the group and Michael McCarty: "We went to see him and he said to us, 'I don't know what you're doing, but it's jolly good, so go and carry on and do it.' We said, 'No one will interfere with us then?'

"And he said, 'No, no, no! Not at all. Just go in and do what you want.' And we thought, 'That's bloody great. That's what everyone dreams of!'"

Released in 1969, *On The Threshold Of A Dream* found The Moody Blues artistically consolidating and exploring metaphysical and existential issues with an easy-going melodic style. Ray Thomas's 'Dear Diary' and the slice-of-life sketch of a quiet English late-Sixties Sunday afternoon, 'Lazy Day', evoke a similar sensibility to some of the material written by The Kinks' Ray Davies, but the sentiments feel comparatively banal.

The opening Edge poem, 'In The Beginning', deliberately misquotes René Descartes' maxim, "I think therefore I am" and features an everyman character arguing with a computer, an example of Sixties fear of a depersonalised sci-fi future taken over by the things, until Pinder comes in at the end of the recitation as the cool Head, advising the listener to continue *"thinking free"*.

Tony Clarke was the first producer to establish himself as a specialist in psychedelic and Seventies progressive rock. His input as a producer and arranger and someone who encouraged the musicians to experiment was such that The Moody Blues seriously considered making him a sixth member of the group. With Pinder's Mellotron an integral part of their sound, they were referred to – tongue-in-cheek – as the world's smallest symphony orchestra. *To Our Children's Children's Children*, released in

1969, had a psychedelic feel, with a multitude of overdubs of instruments including harp, oboe, celeste, sitar and synthesizer all set within a slightly hazy, reverby soundworld.

With their facility for melody and the grandeur of the Mellotron, not forgetting their albums' surreal cover art, by 1970 The Moody Blues were chiming perfectly with the times, particularly with American audiences. Their hippieish "aware" lyrics were like not so distant cousins of those of the thoughtful, introspective singer-songwriters of the time, which were becoming popular both in the US and the UK. In 1970 Mike Pinder was saying, "We like gentle, smooth music" and bassist John Lodge backed him, adding, "We don't like anything that grates the ear."

The Moody Blues' early trips over to the States were originally hallmarked by long drives between gigs, poverty and poor accommodation until, in Thomas's words, you are "tired and ill [and on] the verge of collapse".

But by the end of 1970 and into early 1971, US tours on the back of the big selling *A Question Of Balance* – which went to number one in the UK and three in the US – helped transform the once uncool, impecunious band into one of the biggest in the world.

It took until 1973 to see the full ginormosity of the enterprise. By then The Moody Blues were flying around the USA in their own private jet, a refurbished Boeing 747 with living areas, bedrooms and an in-flight organist, which was called the Starship.

In 1971 Keith Altham also wrote: "The Moodies have shattered every attendance and percentage record by a British group in America, having sold out every auditorium on a three-week tour from Chicago Ampha Theatre to the Miami Sportatorium which was the largest rock concert ever seen there. That was the night the promoter came on stage and asked them if they would like to do a second house to the 10,000 people outside who could not get in."

Sid Bernstein, who had booked The Beatles into Shea Stadium, was co-promoting the tour and claimed that The Moody Blues' reception at a concert in Orlando was "almost god-like". One newspaper review headline proclaimed, "And The Gods Came Down From On High" and Keith Altham mentioned their "unique cathedral-like sound" and their "peaceful mind music". This level of fame drew some nutters out of the woodwork, as Altham noted.

"The only bad apple in San Antonio was a character called 'The Queen' who had suffered a traumatic experience following the last Moody Blues concert when Ray looked at him in the front row of the audience and his tooth fell out.

"The freak decided this was a sign – a portent of the end of the world, no less – and sat out by the freeway for 50 days until their current visit, predicting the end of the world on their next appearance."

Hayward tried to make sense of this kind of adulation when looking back in 1986: "Probably the biggest misconception about the Moodies is that we're all sort of cosmic gurus sitting on some mountain somewhere and just come down occasionally to do tours and make records. I think a lot of that came from the fact that when we first went to America in 1967, we just happened to be playing in San Francisco when the whole Flower Power thing was going on and we got caught up in it and our reputation was born from that."

All this quasi-religious talk of rock gods, cathedrals of sound and the group's guru-like status can be traced back to the way they came across on *A Question Of Balance*.

After the lavish arrangements of *To Our Children's Children's Children*, The Moody Blues were keen to take a different direction on *A Question Of Balance* and record songs that would be easier to replicate onstage. The result is a more focused, punchier sound. The album was released in August 1970 in their most surreal sleeve yet. Painted by Phil Travers, it depicts a beach scene with the sky above the sea full of chaotic imagery.

'Question' kicks off proceedings, one of their most memorable songs and a hit single despite it being almost five minutes long. Beginning with fast acoustic strumming, Lodge's high backing vocals and mobile bass, and Pinder's Mellotron looming ominously in the background, it lyrically sets the tone of the album. It pitches a tone of protest, on behalf of those who question authority about the pointlessness of war and was specifically prompted by what was happening in Vietnam at the time. Hayward points out society's ills in a general way that anyone could agree with. The middle section is a slow love song with Hayward seeking redemption, someone to change his life, looking for the *"miracle"* of love, and singing like he really means it. Then there is a recapitulation of the initial theme, which fades out leaving the song's question unresolved but the listener filled with hope.

Pinder, who was by this time apparently into the "New Wave" Christian movement, then comes in with a question of his own, the impossible to answer 'How Is It We Are Here?' This is followed by Thomas's 'The Tide Rushes In', which destroys his *"castles"* and amplifies the feeling of uncertainty. Graeme Edge's 'Don't You Feel Small?' follows, addressing a feeling that we all have from time to time.

Lodge's 'Minstrel's Song' sounds rather like a happy-clappy trendy modern hymn along the lines of 'Lord Of The Dance', as he exhorts us to listen to the minstrel who "*sings of love*".

Hayward's 'Dawning Of The Day' tells us that a sense of self-realisation will come when you start to be yourself and he reaches out with an offer of comfort and salvation, assuring the listener that the group are trying their best "*to find you*".

Pinder's 'Melancholy Man' is a tale of a "*very lonely man*", who, when faced with the chaos of the world, just needs to keep believing and he will receive enlightenment.

The album ends with Graeme Edge's 'The Balance'. It's a story, recited by Pinder, of a man on a journey who came upon an orange grove and rested, tasting a fruit – all couched in a pseudo-biblical way. The man then achieves a state of enlightenment, like Buddah under the Bodhi tree, in which he realises the "*magnificent perfection*" around him and that he is now "*in balance*". The man learns compassion and the album effectively ends with the starting point of a new journey – with the refrain that you must "*open your heart*".

Part of the album's magic is that The Moody Blues seem to speak directly to the listener and include them in their concerns. They sided with the listener saying, yes it can be difficult, but our records are always here as your friends. Their advice is to just open your eyes, just realise and all shall be well. One can see exactly why so many fans saw them in a religious kind of way, with the group bestowing their blessings on adoring crowds.

John Mendelsohn referenced all this in a particularly sarcastic view of the album in *Rolling Stone*: "… Their heady, thoughtful, eminently poetic lyrics just cannot be topped when it comes to important stuff like the universe and man's plight and so on." He goes on to suggest that the listener will be moved to "store this album within the cardboard shrine that houses your Nam myoho renge kyo scroll."

In *Let It Rock*, Simon Frith wrote: "The Moodies' art is to build a portentous superstructure on a meagre structure – they always sound important and it's difficult to say why."

This is a tad unfair on a group who delivered a simple message of hope in their music to fans, some of whom then looked upon them like the titular character in the Monty Python film *Life Of Brian*.

If you are looking for a religious experience, you will have to look somewhere other than a four-minute rock song, but the erroneous "guru" label stuck fast to The Moody Blues, as did that of "progressive rock pioneers".

They produced some memorable moments in the Seventies like the sublime pop rocker 'The Story In Your Eyes' and the epic ballad 'Isn't Life Strange', but they also produced some complete clunkers. Thomas's 'For My Lady' is a cringe-inducing middle-of-the-road pseudo-sea shanty that sounded like something that middle-of-the-road singer Roger Whittaker would have left well alone. Likewise the old advice to not act with children or animals was shown to also apply to songwriting on those subjects by Lodge's 'Emily's Song', a pretty but exceptionally mawkish ode to his baby daughter, and 'Nice To Be Here', on which Thomas describes a band of animals playing music in a woodland glade.

Hayward recounted in 2013: "One guy in Texas spent weeks standing virtually naked on a street corner telling everyone we were the true messiahs and that we would ultimately save the world with our music. Then he met us, changed his mind and told everyone that we were false messiahs."

Sometimes you just can't win.

CHAPTER 15

The Moody Poor Man's Blues: Barclay James Harvest and Renaissance

In late 1967 an Oldham band, Barclay James Harvest – who had grown out of the Blues Keepers – were in the unusual and enviable position of having a patron, local fashion entrepreneur John Crowther, who knew guitarist John Lees' older sister. Crowther had bought Preston House, a semi-derelict farmhouse in nearby Diggle and in an all-for-one, one-for-all show of commitment, the group – Lees, keyboard player Stuart "Woolly" Wolstenholme, bass guitarist Les Holroyd and drummer Mel Pritchard – moved in en masse. "We all more or less quit our jobs and threw holiday pay and final pay into a pot, and with this help we were going to write the hit single and that was going to get us off and running," Lees recalls.

Crowther hawked a demo tape around record companies and Barclay James Harvest were briefly signed to Parlophone, for whom they recorded a single 'Early Morning' in April 1968, but it failed to show in the charts.

Although most people associate the group with their Seventies heyday, Barclay James Harvest were active in London from early 1968, playing at psychedelic club Middle Earth on support slots to Pink Floyd and to groups from the freakier wing of the underground like Pink Fairies and the Edgar Broughton Band, as well as with Genesis and Led Zeppelin in 1970.

With that hit single remaining elusive, they began to explore more personal musical avenues. Initially they played in a melodic, folky style and experimented with chamber ensemble instrumentation such as tenor horn, oboe, recorder and cello in the studio and onstage. "It was progressive music," says Lees. "They called it underground, there were a few names for it, but the whole point was that we were trying to do something different that married the [classical and rock] genres together."

When the group went into Abbey Road to record 'Early Morning', they acquainted themselves with the studio's resident Mellotron, which Wolstenholme played on the single. They then hired one from a keyboard shop in Derby, which they eventually purchased, and which became a hallmark of their quasi-orchestral sound.

But in the questing spirit of the era the group were determined to work with an orchestra. They had met up with Robert John Godfrey at the Roundhouse in December 1968 and befriended Andrew King and Peter Jenner, managers of Pink Floyd and the men behind the management agency Blackhill Enterprises.

"I was always hanging about their offices," says Godfrey. "Then I got a chance to meet Norman Smith of EMI with the possibility of going to work for EMI as a junior record producer, but what in fact happened was that I was encouraged to go work with Barclay James Harvest."

Barclay James Harvest signed with Blackhill Enterprises, who promoted the Hyde Park Festivals. They were booked to play there with the Grateful Dead in September 1969, which could theoretically have given them a King Crimson-style breakthrough, but that particular date was cancelled. Blackhill also got them a deal with EMI's as yet unnamed new subsidiary label.

"We used to go in and bum albums off [label director] Malcolm Jones, and they were talking then of forming a label for our kind of stuff, for underground or progressive music," says Lees. "He asked for people to give ideas [for names] and Woolly and I wrote 'Harvest' down for him. When they said that they were going to call it Harvest, he said that your album will be the first album to go out on the label, but it wasn't, it was The Pretty Things' *Parachute*. Ours was somewhat later on."

Godfrey had recently left the Royal College Of Music and had had his head turned by the likes of *Pet Sounds* and *Sgt Pepper's*. Like many of his classically trained peers he was looking for a new direction.

"I didn't like the preciousness of classical music in the way it impacted on society," he says. "Because it seemed, in spite of the fact that the upper classes are mainly dunderheads and philistines, the perception was, particularly from the working-class point of view – and I mention that because Barclay James Harvest were completely that – that the well-to-do were all going to the theatre and the opera, and [were] cultured. And of course it couldn't be further from the truth. Having been brought up in a family like that it was all about cocktail parties, going to hunt balls, getting plastered and shagging other people's wives. It had nothing whatsoever to do with how the working classes perceived the toffs."

Godfrey was keen to bridge the gap between pop, rock and classical with arrangements that had integrity. He moved into Preston House – which Lees left as he deemed it too squalid – and worked with the group, arranging material for their 1970 debut album *Barclay James*

Harvest. He mentions 'Dark Now My Sky' with its "raging orchestra part" as indicative of the synthesis he was striving for. "I was trying to create within the music the drama that you get from classical music," he says.

By contrast he was less enamoured of Norman Smith's strings on the already somewhat fey 'Mother Dear', on *Once Again* (1971). "I would have done a completely different arrangement for that but Norman Smith felt that it was just simply too bizarre and so he did a pop arrangement – a completely awful, mediocre piece of shit as far as I was concerned, although I certainly didn't say anything at the time. It would have been better just recorded really nicely without all that on it."

Godfrey's arrangements are finely wrought creations that at times feel more like they should be standalone pieces.

"The arrangement I did for 'Galadriel' on the second album [*Once Again*, 1971], that's quite Benjamin Britten-esque in a way. It isn't a pop arrangement."

Godfrey conducted the Barclay James Harvest Symphony Orchestra, as they were called, when the group played at the Royal Albert Hall in July 1970, and had hoped to join the group as an official member, but they parted in acrimonious circumstances. Lawyers were involved in a dispute over his role in the group and money owed.

Barclay James Harvest were one of the first rock groups to tour with an orchestra, from early 1971, with arrangements mainly by Godfrey and Martyn Ford. The latter had taken over as conductor and arranger – most notably orchestrating Wolstenholme's 'Moonwater', which was released in 1972 on *Baby James Harvest* – but things were not as grand as they might have appeared on the surface.

"It was a disaster," say Lees. "It was a [London-based] student orchestra who were really hard to work with. We needed to pay for extra rehearsals when they weren't up to speed."

Lees recalls that their budget dictated that the orchestra would get smaller as they played further away from London. John Crowther withdrew his support as the venture virtually bankrupted him, souring their relationship, but the move had its benefits.

"It probably made the group, because then we had to pay for it all and that meant gigging for as many days as we could every week for a year and a half to two years doing universities, clubs and colleges," Lees explains. "And that gave us a name and really cemented our career."

The guitarist's song 'Galadriel' from *Once Again* is one of the few in the entire progressive rock canon that references J. R. R. Tolkien. But the lyrics deal with notions of youth and hope and seem to have little to do with the elfin princess.

However this was typical of the group's lyrical approach. Many of their peers wrote lyrics that didn't seem to mean much in particular, but were presented as if they meant a lot. And despite their image of grandiose pastoralia, Barclay James Harvest were one of the few progressive rock groups who engaged in social commentary, and addressed specific issues, even politics, albeit rather elliptically at times.

"I'm fortunate in that I can explore my anxieties and fears in songs," says Lees. "But there was always a caveat with me that I don't really want to ram it down anybody's throat: if you get the lyrics, then great; if not it still stands up as a song."

Lees' '1974 Mining Disaster' references the Bee Gees' 1967 single 'New York Mining Disaster 1941' and updated it to reflect the miners' strike that brought down Edward Heath's Conservative government, although Lees was keeping his cards close to his chest about exactly what he thought.

Holroyd's 'Negative Earth' chronicles the ill-fated Apollo 13 mission set to a swooning melody, while Lees' 'Child Of The Universe' and 'For No One' are statements against war and for peace and universality. On his song 'Everybody Is Everybody Else', Lees plays with the hippieish idea of the phrase as a rather woolly expression of a kind of groovy totality, and turns it around so that it reads the way that most people are more likely perceive it, that the human race is a great featureless mass until someone stands out.

"Everybody is everybody else until you need someone to help you, y'know? It's a very interesting proposition. Everyone's a loner until they need a helping hand, until it pertains to you," Lees says.

'Mocking Bird' and 'Dark Now My Sky' were inspired by the book *Silent Spring* by Rachel Carson, which puts forward dire environmental warnings. "I can remember that book had quite a dramatic and anxious effect on me," says Lees. "'After The Day' is about nuclear war, Armageddon."

By *Everybody Is Everyone Else*, their first album for Polydor, released in 1974, the hard-working group had developed into a tougher proposition with dramatic, anthemic songs fuelled by Lees' incisive rhythm guitar and keening lead lines, cut with vocal harmonies with Holroyd along the lines of Crosby, Stills & Nash, particularly on the bass guitarist's song, 'Poor Boy Blues', a folksy tale of hard times and a companion track to Lees' 'Mill Boys'.

Half of the songs from *Everyone Is Everybody Else* fed into *Barclay James Harvest Live*, released in 1974, a big-selling double album that broke into the UK Top 20. It seemed that while some were looking the other way, the group had developed into one of the more powerful and dynamic live acts of the day. And Polydor A&R saw their potential.

This was music of high drama, epitomised by the live version of 'Summer Soldier' from *Baby James Harvest* (1972). Live, the song swells up into huge instrumental chorus melodies played on Mellotron and guitar, and further whipped up by Mel Pritchard's drumming. A dextrous and incisive player on record, onstage he came into his own with enormous rampaging breaks around the kit crammed full of snare and tom-tom rolls that seemed to launch out on a wing a prayer, but always landed back just in time. It was a tremendously exciting style, somewhere between classical percussion crescendos and Keith Moon. On an expanded 'Medicine Man' Wolstenholme plays a fizzing, aggressive synth solo.

Despite "selling out gigs for fun", the size of the venues and the cost of the PA, lights and road crew meant that Barclay James Harvest were only breaking even towards the last few shows on a tour. "That's one of the reasons we went into Europe where you could get more bums in seats and justify the cost of the show," says Lees.

Few UK groups at the time were based overseas, a notable exception being the progressive space rock group Nektar. For most UK progressive and other rock bands Germany had been a place to tour and make a bit of money on the club circuit. But Barclay James Harvest turned all that around in spectacular fashion. Throughout the Seventies they played bigger and bigger venues.

Touring took its toll on Lees who suffered an "anxiety breakdown" due to overwork and the group had to pull out of some German dates in July 1977.

"We had to reschedule the tour and went back, and it just went ballistic," says Lees. "I remember when we did the Düsseldorf Philipshalle, it seats about 5,500 people and they've got a curtain so they can make it into a smaller theatre. It started off that they had sold 900 tickets, but on the night we got there it sold out so they had to keep opening the curtain to let more people in and after that, every gig we did was just packed. On one of the later tours we sold a million tickets in Germany alone." Towards the end of the Seventies at German festivals, Barclay James Harvest were playing way up the bill from the likes of Dire Straits and The Police, and by 1980, they played to close to 200,000 people outside the Reichstag in Berlin.

Barclay James Harvest released their eighth studio album *Gone To Earth* in 1977. "On 'Hymn' we are producing, from a simple beginning, this huge climactic number, with what appear to be massive brass and strings, which was in fact just us using synthesizers, Mellotron and guitars," Lees says. "'Sea Of Tranquillity' was an orchestral thing that Woolly had done, so there is quite a level of sophistication creeping into the arrangements when you get to *Gone To Earth*."

One might assume that this would be exactly the sort of musical sophistication that would have been anathema to new wave groups and particularly the music press at the height of punk. But punk didn't make such a big splash in Germany and Lees admits that he was largely oblivious of events in his homeland.

'Hymn' feels literally hymnal and religious, but in common with many of Lees' lyrics it's metaphorical in that it also deals with the deity-like importance that hard drugs can assume in an addict's life.

"I was vehemently against any kind of drug use so [I said] there has to be a spiritual high rather than a drug-induced high and the commonest reference at the time to that was Christianity," Lees says. "So it was posing the idea that if you want to see any sort of god, see it in a different way."

In one snide music paper review that stuck in Lees' mind, Barclay James Harvest were referred to as "the poor man's Moody Blues", mainly through their use of Mellotron. This prompted the guitarist to write 'Poor Man's Moody Blues' on *Gone To Earth*, which comes across as a droll pastiche of 'Nights In White Satin'.

"Musically it might sound similar but it's not the same," Lees asserts. "Justin [Hayward] could have taken umbrage at the reference, but he's been a gentleman and said that [The Moody Blues] are the rich man's Barclay James Harvest, which is perfectly true. But it was a compliment to him really in a backhanded way.

"I've always been fine with constructive criticism, but this just seemed a destructive thing to say. And so I penned a song. Wish I hadn't. It's haunted me ever since. The Greeks use it as a wedding song. When they have the first dance they play 'Poor Man's Moody Blues'. How that figures I do not know!"

As Barclay James Harvest had begun to play more in Germany, that country's audience formed a peculiarly strong bond with the group that Lees finds hard to understand. But they became massive there and while *Gone To Earth* reached number thirty in the UK charts, in Germany it peaked at number ten and stayed in the album charts for 197 weeks. As of 2011 it is ranked number six in the list of longest-running albums in the German charts.

Although Barclay James Harvest might have been dubbed the poor man's Moody Blues, in Germany at least, they were just as enormous.

Family on the set of _The Old Grey Whistle Test_, 1971. Michael Putland/Getty

Dave Stewart, keyboard player of Egg – who went on to play with Hatfield And The North and National Health – pondering a tricky transition from 5/4 to 13/8 in 1971. Fin Costello/Getty

Bob Harris on the set of _The Old Grey Whistle Test_, the BBC TV music show that he hosted from 1972 to 1979. Alan Messer/Shutterstock

Studio sessions for Yes's 1971 album, *Fragile*, the first to feature Rick Wakeman (far right).
Michael Putland/Getty

Strawbs in the studio in 1971, scrutinising the recordings of *From The Witchwood* with the soon to depart Rick Wakeman (far right). Photoshot/Retna

Van Der Graaf Generator onstage at the Reading Festival, June 27, 1971, shortly before the recording sessions for *Pawn Hearts*. Michael Putland/Getty

Matching Mole in 1972 proving beyond argument that progressive rock was not beholden to any notions of glamour. Cuneiform Records

Emerson, Lake & Palmer at the *Melody Maker* Awards 1972. They were voted Best Group by the paper's readers and also won in individual categories. Mirrorpix

The Notting Hill-based "Hindu Grateful Dead", Quintessence, take a break from their meditation, 1972. GAB Archive/Getty

Procol Harum in 1972, gearing up for the opulence of their *Grand Hotel* album, which was released the following year. Brian Cooke/Getty

Gryphon, the band described by *Melody Maker* journalist Chris Welch as "the 13th-century Slade", demonstrate their crumhorn section in 1973. Brian Cooke/Getty

Composer, keyboard player and arranger David Bedford, who introduced an avant-garde sensibility into progressive rock, pictured here in 1973. Rob Bull/Getty

Bass guitarist and vocalist Richard Sinclair, who started out in Caravan in 1968, onstage with Hatfield And The North in 1973. Gijsbert Hanekroot/Getty

Hawkwind in 1973 performing the *Space Ritual*, with dancer and "art project" Stacia Blake (centre). Studio Canal/Shutterstock

Although it featured none of the original group members, this is the 'classic' line-up of Renaissance that recorded *Ashes Are Burning* in 1973. Brian Cooke/Getty

Traffic in concert featuring the line-up that recorded the 1973 double live album *On The Road*. Brian Cooke/Getty

Mike Oldfield overdubbing in the studio during sessions for *Hergest Ridge*, 1974. Gijsbert Hanekroot/Alamy

Both groups have been labelled as symphonic rock, a term that, as mentioned in Chapter 5, brings this writer out in a bit of a rash. But moving on, another group who have been labelled thus are Renaissance.

When The Yardbirds split in 1968, guitarist Jimmy Page formed The New Yardbirds or, as they became better known, Led Zeppelin. But vocalist Keith Relf and drummer Jim McCarty wanted to go in a completely different direction and make music with a more subdued pastoral flavour that drew on classical and folk ideas as well as rock, and reflected their liking of Fairport Convention, Tim Hardin, The Incredible String Band, Judy Collins and Joni Mitchell. Relf plays guitar and sings alongside his sister Jane who had casually mentioned, almost jokingly, that if his new group ever needed a girl singer to give her a call. Louis Cennamo plays bass and John Hawken, formerly of The Nashville Teens plays piano and harpsichord.

Keith Relf explained to Richard Green of *New Musical Express* in 1970 that what prompted him to leave The Yardbirds was what many fans loved about them: "I was more interested in the music, but the fans just stared at Jimmy and Jeff [Beck]. I had always really wanted to play guitar but this wasn't what I was looking for.

"We want people to listen to our music. We're not loud or heavy or a bunch of ravers, so it should be easier for people to listen."

Released in 1969, the album *Renaissance* confounded a number of expectations as it was very different to The Yardbirds. To satisfy promoters who saw that group's name as still worth dropping, they initially went out as Keith Relf's Renaissance, which resulted in them ending up on mismatched bills with groups like The Kinks.

Green described them as "gentle but forceful", and there is certainly a muscularity to the playing, particularly McCarty's drumming. 'Bullet' is a lengthy bluesy groove, but the majority of the material carries more of a chamber ensemble feel. They released a single, 'Island', but with their otherwise lengthy songs, Renaissance were clearly an album band and with their debut had delivered one of the first statements in the progressive canon.

Renaissance recorded a second album *Illusion* in 1970, but before it was released in early 1971 there was a reshuffle. Jane Relf had left and the post of female singer had become vacant.

On New Year's Eve 1970 the group held an audition to find a replacement. Bolton-born Annie Haslam was one of the hopefuls; she bought a copy of the album and learned it thoroughly. She was especially taken with the lengthy, episodic 'Kings And Queens' and Jane Relf's "gorgeous voice". She was asked to sing 'Island' and on New Year's Day 1971 they called her with the news that she had got the job.

Haslam came from a family of singers. Her father was an amateur comedian and singer, and her older brother Michael Haslam had been managed by Brian Epstein in the early Sixties and recorded a couple of singles with George Martin. Annie sang for fun until her brother's girlfriend said she ought to take it more seriously and have voice lessons so she could master the technical aspects of singing.

She was taught by opera singer Sibyl Knight who transformed her voice into a remarkable instrument – pure toned and with a bit of grip to it, but without the operatic yell that some classical singers adopt, and a five-octave range. "I'm a coloratura soprano. I only realised that when he told me," she says.

Haslam entered and won a number of talent competitions and joined a group, The Gentle People, who played supper club type gigs. "The guy who played the guitar said, 'Annie, you are wasted here, your voice is different. I've just seen an ad in the *Melody Maker*.' And it was for Renaissance. I'd never heard of them."

When Haslam joined, initially singing lead vocals with Terry Crowe, formerly of The Nashville Teens, the group went straight over to play some concerts in Germany. At that time both Relf and McCarty, who had both been at the audition, were ostensibly still members in that they intended to have writing and production input. But both soon dropped out of the picture, so by the middle of 1971, there were no original members left. And by 1973 after much coming and going, Renaissance comprised Haslam, John Tout on keyboards, Jon Camp on bass, drummer Terence Sullivan and guitarist Michael Dunford, the line-up that endured throughout the Seventies.

Released in 1972, *Prologue* was considered by the new Renaissance line-up to be essentially the group's first album and carried their new confident stamp. That said, they also expanded on the style of the original group on a song like 'Kiev', which had been written by the departed McCarty, with lyrics by Betty Thatcher, who remained the group's main wordsmith. With its big balladic structure and a brisk middle section it shared some similarities with Emerson, Lake & Palmer's 'Take A Pebble', although Tout's direct quoting of the stern, portentous – and very well known – *Prelude In C Sharp Minor* from the five *Morceaux De Fantaisie* by Rachmaninov (aka *The Bells Of Moscow*), feels a bit heavy-handed when compared to the rest of his playing, which found him absorbing and synthesising classical influences into an elegant and individual style.

The group's main signature was the relationship between Tout's keyboards and Haslam's voice, and because he favoured piano in the vocal sections and Dunford played acoustic guitar, that combination gave them a lighter, less bombastic sound than many of their peers.

They were hard to classify. In 1974, when interviewing Haslam, Jerry Gilbert of *Sounds* was rather groping for descriptors. He wrote: "In a folk-rock band such as Renaissance her voice appears to be a product of the folk tradition rather than anything else although she denies any familiarity or affiliation with folk music right down the line."

The new Renaissance carried on the parent group's penchant for lengthy songs with strong narratives. Did they feel obliged to make their statements on a grand scale?

"No, I don't ever remember us saying things like that," Haslam says. "It was just very exciting. Betty Thatcher who was the main lyricist was a brilliant poet. Usually Betty might give a poem to Mickey [Dunford], although it did work the other way round – sometimes Mickey would give the music to me and I would write the words to the music.

"But more often than not Betty would come up with these amazing stories and you can't just do it in a three-minute song, so they had a lot more depth and meaning. 'Carpet Of The Sun' [from *Ashes Are Burning*, 1973] is beautiful and it doesn't need to be any longer than four minutes because it's just a simple song about the sunshine. But 'Mother Russia' [from *Turn Of The Cards*, 1974] is about the book *One Day In The Life Of Ivan Denisovich* by Solzhenitsyn. So straightaway you think that's got to be a big song."

Although Renaissance theoretically ticked all the progressive rock boxes, they were always more popular in the USA than in the UK, where they were comparatively overlooked. DJ Alan Freeman was a big fan and 'Mother Russia' was a favourite on his Saturday afternoon Radio 1 show.

"Looking back on it all, I would absolutely say that our career was focused on making it in America," says Haslam. "We did go to Germany and Italy in the early days, but once we started going to America, that's where we were working all the time.

"We were one of the pioneering bands, definitely, of prog rock. We were one of the earlier bands who were trailblazers, I guess, and I think we were all, managers included, not quite sure how to deal with it early on."

The manager in question was Miles Copeland who by 1974 had got the group a US deal with Seymour Stein's Sire label. And a demonstration of how well this strategy had worked was the double album *Live At Carnegie Hall*, recorded in 1976.

Renaissance had often used strings and orchestral arrangements on their albums. Haslam explains that some of her vocalese onstage was less scatting and more singing instrumental lines like clarinet or horn parts from the albums to compensate for the lack of orchestra. "I was the missing link," she says.

But on this showcase set they were backed by the New York Philharmonic. The album reached number fifty-five in the US charts and it's a bit of a mixed bag. Whereas 'Carpet Of The Sun' sounds like superior orchestrated pop and 'Mother Russia' is a powerful mini-epic, the band also displayed some lapses in taste like doubling the length of 'Ashes Are Burning' to twenty-three minutes to accompany lengthy pianistics from Tout and a bass solo by Camp that is superficially impressive but, typical of the era, goes on for far too long without really adding anything to the song. Of course this is a view derived from the benefit of hindsight and from listening to it on record, not as it was played before a typical Seventies audience, who were clearly lapping it up.

Given that, as previously noted, received wisdom has it that the Seventies were the irredeemable dark ages as far as sexism was concerned and there were only a handful of female musicians in progressive rock groups, how was Haslam treated?

"The attitudes were definitely positive, there was no doubt," she replies. "It was a sad thing, but in the Seventies... I'm not going to mention any names but some of the women singers were so horrible, very competitive.

"It was never a band where we would come offstage and they would say, 'Wow, you did a great job tonight.' And I think there was a little bit of jealousy there as well. Any woman onstage is going to get a lot of attention, so that did unfortunately cause a few problems. It was mainly in the band really, I don't remember [anything] in the press.

"Those were still wonderful times that I'll never forget but there were times when I wasn't very happy being the only woman on the road with so many men. And I wasn't one to go and sit in a bar after a show or on a day off, as alcohol isn't good for the vocal cords. John Tout and I used to mess around if we had a day off sometimes, but it got me down a lot."

The big breakthrough for Renaissance in the UK came with their 1978 single 'Northern Lights', which reached number ten. The lyrics, by Betty Thatcher, were arrived at from conversations she'd had with Haslam about her feelings of isolation while on tour.

Haslam's partner Roy Wood, who'd registered numerous hits with The Move, Wizzard and ELO, had some helpful ideas regarding the song's production.

"Roy helped enormously because when we had done 'Northern Lights' my vocal was great, but something was missing," she recalls. "He said, 'Why don't we treble-track your voice through the whole song?' We did that and it changed it completely, gave it that commercial sound."

But even with this commercial boost, which propelled the album *A Song For All Seasons* to reach the UK Top 40, like so many groups at the end of the Seventies, the changing tastes of both the public and record companies in terms of music and image derailed their career.

"The next album we did we were encouraged to write something more commercial, so we came up with [the single] 'The Winter Tree'. It was left too long before that came out because that was another great commercial-sounding song. Then we started to lose our way after that musically and it just fell apart, really."

After disappointing sales of 1979's *Azure D'Or* the group were dropped by Sire. Haslam, Camp and Dunford soldiered on with some new recruits, but it's not an era that Haslam looks back on fondly.

"We blew it with *Camera Camera* [1981] and *Time-Line* [1983]. The fans didn't accept them. They were songs that anyone could sing, so what's the point? The winning formula had been my voice and the five musicians at that time. *Camera Camera...* all you have to do is look at the cover!"

CHAPTER 16

Divertimento No.1: Notes on Drugs

Psychedelia was the first and most overt meeting between drug usage and Western culture. The inspiration behind it was the mind-expanding quality of LSD-25 and so, unsurprisingly, its usage fuelled some powerful and strange creations across the arts.

These were either produced directly from tripping participants, or more likely from those who were keen on exploring the idea of mind expansion, of connecting with the unconscious, without having necessarily having to set aside eight hours for "dropping a tab" which might result in them laughing hysterically before embarking on a journey through a state of seeming nirvana or rattling around on a nightmarish psychological ghost train ride. It carried certain parallels with surrealism, which was also about exploring and unlocking the potential of the unconscious mind.

The progressive rock era from 1969 onwards was less closely associated with drugs, although groups like Gong created the *Radio Gnome* trilogy of *Flying Teapot*, *Angel's Egg* and *You*, all released in 1973 and 1974, in which the Pot Head Pixies played a significant role. Songs like 'I've Bin Stone Before' and 'You'll Never Blow Yr Trip Forever' more than hinted at their recreational activities.

Caravan's 'And I Wish I Were Stoned', a lament on the running-out of one's stash, was pitched in a way that was even oddly moving. Guy Evans of Van Der Graaf Generator said, jokingly, that in terms of enthusiastically smoking brain-bendingly strong hash, most groups "couldn't keep up with us", although there was no reference made to this in any of their music.

My research has uncovered recreational drug usage among progressive rock groups to have been widespread, but generally pretty moderate. Ian Anderson of Jethro Tull and Robert Fripp of King Crimson were almost completely abstemious – Fripp noting that he might enjoy a glass of sherry on occasion. Keith Emerson offers this explanation: "We didn't do drugs. We were very sensible in that regard. If we had three weeks off, then I probably did dabble with something up the nose just as a bit of fun, but I don't do that any more. You've probably seen me [onstage] with a bottle of cognac on top of the Moog, but that was mostly full of water, it was a spoof. It was a bit like a prop, like Janis Joplin used to go on with a bottle of Southern Comfort. No, there was just no way we could do that. Try playing *Brain Salad Surgery* when you are out of your fucking box!"

But some groups who played less intricate music displayed a ferocious level of consumption. The great exemplar of the stoned musician was surely Richard Michael Davies – or Dik Mik to his fellow cosmic travellers – who played synthesizer and audio tone generator for Hawkwind. His modus operandi was to turn up to the gig stoned, make bubbling and whooshing noises for the duration, without having to hit any particular cues, then go backstage and get even more stoned.

Some of my school friends had tried LSD, but knowing and rather fearing my own hyperactive mind, personally that was a definite no-go area. Hearing reports of cowering teenage trippers seeing red hands coming out of TV sets reinforced that view.

But from a listener's point of view, smoking hash, the most user-friendly and easy to acquire drug, went very well with the more atmospheric strands of progressive rock, as the cannabinoids enhance the detail and the texture of the music, making it an intense and immersive experience.

During one particular session with various members and friends of a certain Reading-based neo-progressive band at the end of the Seventies, I witnessed the stoned gathering displaying their love of their favourite group via some impromptu singing, to the tune of Sammy Cahn and Jimmy Van Heusen's 'Love And Marriage', *"Drugs and Genesis/Drugs and Genesis/Go together like cunts and penises"*. It's hard to argue against that degree of enthusiastic fandom.

All this might now prompt a response of "so what?" In the 21st century, the laws have been relaxed so that carrying a small amount of cannabis will result in little more than a ticking off. But this is now and that was then. Apart from using hash or weed to enhance one's private listening, in the Seventies just getting hold of the stuff gave one a feeling of being an outlaw, engaged in countercultural activity, which strictly speaking it was, because it was illegal.

Back then possession was a far more serious offence with the possibility of a hefty fine or a custodial sentence. In 1967, in the infamous drugs bust at Keith Richards' Sussex home, Redlands, Mick Jagger was given a four-month prison sentence for having four amphetamine tablets legally acquired in Italy, and Richards got a year for allowing cannabis to be smoked on his property, but they were almost immediately released on bail, and escaped jail. That same year, the well-known activist, underground figure and co-founder of The UFO Club, John "Hoppy" Hopkins, who presumably could not afford such a powerful legal team, was arrested for possession of cannabis, described as a "pest to society" by his trial judge and sentenced to nine months' imprisonment.

It's still difficult to understand how changing your mental state by the ingestion of relatively harmless non-addictive (untaxed) plant extracts in a way that didn't adversely affect anyone else was thought of as being serious insurrection by the establishment. But the consumption of the (heavily taxed) and addictive drug, alcohol, and the social problems that came with it, was a part of British society. And so that was OK. Clearly the law was a braying ass. And so to smoke dope was one for the counterculture, and a firm two fingers held up to the establishment.

Mont Campbell was the bass guitarist and vocalist with Egg, and he ended up getting busted for possession of cannabis by the police. "You had to go to court and the whole thing, but now you get a spot fine," he says. "I was in fear of being apprehended by policemen and told to empty my pockets."

This sort of (founded) paranoia permeated the dope smoker's world, with rumours that if you talked about "dope" on the phone someone might be listening in, and so alternative names, like the imaginative "rope" were used instead. The police force obviously had nothing like the manpower for that kind of surveillance, but although it was an urban myth, the feeling lingered, that just because you were paranoid, it didn't mean they weren't out to get you.

The effect of all this was that smoking dope – or taking other drugs – became a badge of honour. Hence at concerts in the Seventies by exploratory songwriters and avowed smokers Roy Harper and John Martyn, some Head, in an act of solidarity, would inevitably step up from the audience and hand the artist a joint mid-set.

The paternalistic BBC would try to seek out any drug references in pop songs that might be played on Radio 1, which resulted in Mungo Jerry's 'Have A Whiff On Me' – the B-side of their 1971 single 'Lady Rose', and based on an old American blues song – being banned for referencing cocaine, even though that reference would have gone past most people. But their huge 1970 hit 'In The Summertime', with its reference to having a drink and a drive was deemed perfectly acceptable – until it was used in a 1978 Public Information film, *Drinking And Driving Wrecks Lives*.

Being out of it was cool – to an extent – as well as being fun, as it showed an individuality and a fighting spirit, albeit that of a person who was a bit too befuddled to actually fight. Some blame must be laid at the door of the American comedy duo Cheech & Chong. At times they were amusing, but their seemingly endless and ultimately enervating dope references were the Seventies dopehead equivalent of contemporary comedians who say "fuck" to elicit a cheap laugh.

Which brings us onto a Seventies archetype: the dope bore. One who vividly sticks in the mind was a person I witnessed at a Roy Harper gig at Guildford in the late Seventies, an older, rubicund fellow, with a West Country accent and a big frizz of blond hair. He left the assembled company in no doubt about the extent of his intoxication, as if it were, of itself, interesting to other people.

"Oi'm so fuckin' stoned," he said through a village idiot grin. "Oi'm so fuckin' stoned." He stopped for a while, smiling, and then continued. "Oi'm so fuckin' stoned... I hope the police don't come as oi've got a big lump of dope in me pocket," he expanded. There was no wit or insight, no attempt at repartee – that was his basic vocabulary for the entire evening. Even at that tender teen age I was pleased that I wasn't like him. Mind you, it has to be said that a lot of music does actually sound pretty good when you're fuckin' stoned.

CHAPTER 17

In Search of Space: Arthur Brown and Kingdom Come

"The Crazy World Of Arthur Brown were supposed to tour the USA in 1968 supporting Jimi Hendrix, but Soft Machine ended up doing it instead," Arthur Brown recalls. "Chris Stamp from Track Records came up to me to explain, 'Well, I showed Hendrix the photos of your fire helmet and make-up and he said, "I'm not going on with that, man,"'" So that was that."

But if the flamboyant guitarist with a penchant for setting his guitar on fire onstage felt he might be upstaged by the equally flamboyant singer who had a penchant for donning a flaming headdress, he certainly admired his labelmate's work. Hendrix even helped the Track Records publicity campaign that made Brown's single, 'Fire', a hit in America that year. While the label founders, Stamp and Kit Lambert, managed to get it some airplay on AM – initially as a novelty record – and then on FM radio, Hendrix helped by taking it around the black radio stations. "He was 30 per cent of the reason it became a hit," says Brown. "He said, 'Play this motherfucker!' They thought I was black because I had the make-up and because I was singing in a style that they didn't associated with white singers, and they all went, 'Wow!'"

Back in the early Sixties, Brown was reading Philosophy at Reading University. He played bass in a jazz group, who specialised in Mingus tunes and also performed at local folk clubs. Brown was inspired by a wide range of singers, including Elvis Presley, Little Richard, Howlin' Wolf, Ray Charles, opera singer Beniamino Gigli and Welsh singer and comedian Harry Secombe.

After a number of false starts, by late 1965 he had assembled the blues-based group, The Arthur Brown Set, and they decamped to Paris, securing a residency at a club, The Bus Palladium.

"It was a very wild club," he explains. "The audience were completely berserk on various substances, stage diving, and I started to bring in the theatre there – mime and stuff like that." Life at The Bus Palladium was tough, with the group playing three sets a night and six on a Sunday.

When boredom set in they engaged in improvised comedy skits. At this point Brown had never witnessed the theatrics of the likes of Screaming Jay Hawkins and Screaming Lord Sutch, but he had plenty of ideas of his own.

"I once saw an album cover where Solomon Burke wore a crown and a cloak and thought, 'Oh that's pretty cool,'" he recalls. "The hotel we were staying in was rather decadent, shall we say, with ladies of the night. After one party they had left a crown with candles in it outside my door. I put that on and with make-up to black out my teeth, the effect on the audience was astounding."

Brown returned to England at the end of 1966 with the idea of opening a club that would run on similar lines called The Crazy World Of Arthur Brown, but was unable to raise the necessary money.

But in 1967 Brown looked set to make a big break into the pop mainstream. He had been co-lead singer, with Clem Curtis, of the UK-based multi-racial soul group The Ramong Sound. They became The Foundations and were due to sign a record deal with Pye, which was to kick off with the recording of a single, 'Baby Now That I've Found You'. But Brown declined to sign the three-year contract, feeling that his heart was more into developing a personal experimental approach to music. The single went to number one.

His new group took the name The Crazy World Of Arthur Brown, and with them he expanded the striking theatricality that he first introduced in Paris. But initially, audiences had no idea what to make of it. "I thought, 'Well the only way they are going to understand is if I make them aware of different kind of characters, so that's when I started with the masks and the robes.'"

Brown appeared onstage as if he were about to lead some nameless ceremony. He would cast off his robes to reveal a torso streaked in body paint while he danced as if possessed. "It was so strange for its time that we got about five gigs in the first year," Brown admits. "And it wasn't going down very well."

Undeterred, Brown pushed this angle even further by wearing the fire helmet. This was a homemade metal crown set on a leather skull cap with a container for petrol and a pair of petrol-soaked horns that he would set alight. Sometimes he also wore a metal visor. This was a dangerous business as it could become painfully hot and sometimes Brown burnt himself or set fire to his hair.

Eventually the group caught the attention of manager and publisher John Fenton. Brown recalls that Fenton told Stamp and Lambert, who also managed The Who: "This you have to sign. You've got The Who into opera and this guy is doing performance art."

"Pete Townshend appeared at one of our gigs," says Brown. "And he told me, 'Well, I was trying to persuade Track to book the Bonzo Dogs and we lost them, and so I'm going to make sure we don't lose you.'"

Townshend took the group into The Who's Ramport Studios and onto his own Eel Pie Studios to record the demos. Somewhere there is a tape of Townshend playing the rhythm guitar on 'Fire'.

"He took Stamp and Lambert the demos and that was it," says Brown. "They came down and saw the fire helmet and all of that, and said, 'Oh, right!'"

The group consisted of Brown, organist Vincent Crane and drummer Drachen Theaker. After recording the basic tracks for the album, *The Crazy World Of Arthur Brown*, Crane's classical training came in useful for the brass and string arrangements.

The predominant lyrical theme of the album is fire. Born during an air raid on his hometown of Whitby on the Yorkshire coast in 1942, Brown identifies this imagery with his troubled youth. "My family was pretty torn apart by the war," he says. "There were a lot of arguments and emotional shit."

Brown's father Peter, treasurer of the Yorkshire Conservative Party, was in many ways anything but conservative. He was telepathic – to the extent that the local police asked him to help in murder cases – and also practised meditation. "I was about 12 or 13," recalls Brown, "and one day I came home and my father said, 'I know you are having a hard time with the family. I've brought someone here who will help you clear your mind.' This man taught me to make my mind not be ruled by the passions that came in. It gave me an independence to deal with all that [other] stuff.

"By the time of the album, I thought, 'Well I want to do a journey about someone going inside themselves, as opposed to down Route 66. Fire has got two aspects: one, it's going to burn and hurt; or two, it's going to be a source of light and joy and warmth.'"

'Fire' is essentially an R&B stomper with extravagant Hammond organ runs and Brown's menacing vocal performance culminating in a inferno of screams. It was one of the most startling singles of the Sixties, and a hit in the UK and the USA. The album also includes the darkness of 'Prelude/Nightmare', the psychedelic ballad 'Child Of My Kingdom', and showstopping covers of James Brown's 'Money' and Screaming Jay Hawkins' 'I Put A Spell On You'. It clearly established him, under the fire helmet, make-up and robes, as one of the UK's foremost blues and soul singers.

Brown feels that the group were fortunate in having Lambert and Stamp working for them, as they were "geniuses of promotion", especially with respect to 'Fire'. He also recalls that they told both himself and Hendrix that their audience would grow with them so it wouldn't do them any good to repeat themselves. But their long-term thinking was veering in a different direction. Brown recounts when this was revealed, mimicking Lambert's upper-crust tones.

"I had Kit call me into his office. Looking me in the eye he said, 'Arthur, Chris and I have been talking. Now, this underground – a flash in the pan. What we want you to do is shave off your sideburns and your beard, and wear a little bit of a wig, because you need thicker hair and we think we can make you as big as Tom Jones or Engelbert [Humperdinck].' I said, 'Kit, what will I do when I go down the underground clubs?' He said, 'Oh, you wear false sideburns and beard. You glue them on.' I couldn't believe it! They knew I wanted to be part of the underground, so that was their idea of compromise."

It could never have worked. Not so long before, Brown had written to a friend from Reading with these uncompromising sentiments: "What needs changing is the whole of the approach to life, all the attitudes to work, all the attitudes to what make a worthwhile society and our band are going to do whatever we can to bring about that change."

Over the years Brown and Hendrix kept in touch; The Crazy World… and The Jimi Hendrix Experience shared bills at a number of gigs and festivals. In 1969 Brown received a tantalising offer. "We were going to form a band together, Hendrix and I. We had meetings and he wanted to have the Experience with Vincent, because he wanted to expand. He wanted projection screens and tapes of Wagner playing in the background. But when Vincent had to go into a mental institution that was the end of that idea. And I decided that I'd got my own trajectory."

But despite his brief brush with international stardom, Brown's "trajectory" was a constant search for purpose, both musically and spiritually. Like many at the time, he had absorbed esoteric musical influences from African to Egyptian to classical music, and explored spiritual teachings. He had also expanded his mind in various ways over in the Haight-Ashbury district of San Francisco, spending time with the likes of Jerry Garcia of the Grateful Dead. After blowing one's mind it was time to find a path to follow.

In 1969, The Crazy World… decided to give communal living a go. Brown looked through the property advertisements in *The Times* and found a farmhouse to rent in Puddletown, Dorset, on the estate of Ilsington House.

"I was dealing with musicians who were off their heads and I took acid and started smoking pot, and that changed my whole thinking about how a band should be run," Brown says. "I wanted it to be more of a cooperative thing with everyone, including the manager and the roadies [getting] paid the same, but it didn't work."

Rather tired of having a scripted show, The Crazy World... recorded a completely improvised album that year, which induced horror in the record company and was shelved until its release twenty years later as *Strangelands*. It's an experiment that probably needed to be undertaken, but didn't work. The group followed it with a series of improvised gigs. "Half of which were dreadful," Brown recalls.

Brown's confrontational approach caused controversy at one 1969 show. After the Paris riots in 1968, the Communist Party organised a series of concerts featuring Soft Machine, Pink Floyd and The Crazy World..., to show, in Brown's words that they had "the youth under control". Brown took this opportunity to not only call for revolution from the stage, but he did this while performing naked, drawing some rather unwelcome attention from the armed police.

With last year's troubles still fresh in the mind, this is exactly what the Communists had hoped to avoid. Brown and his then manager, Giorgio Gomelsky, were asked to see the party heads Philippe and Francois Mettrani.

"They said, 'Arthur we respect that you are an artist, but if you feel that the performance can reach the people without you having to sing naked, we have already lost one of our seats on the local council.' I didn't want to kow-tow to anybody, but decided we could do what we did without all that."

Back at Puddletown, Brown found himself at a crossroads. He and his wife had decided to move from the farmhouse into the servants' wing of Ilsington House to get some space. "The experiment of living together was successful in terms of making me realise that I don't want to do it," he says, laughing. "I mean, I want to talk to people with whom I might have a sensible conversation." Although there was some money coming in from gigs and the group got on surprisingly well with the locals, the social living experiment foundered because the publishing advance that had been paying the group's wages was running out.

Brown found himself at a crossroads and was wondering whether or not to go to a retreat to the Kagyu Samye Ling Buddhist monastery in Scotland or form another band. His idea to solve the dilemma was to take mescaline. "Bound to give you the right choice isn't it?" he says, wryly.

He went into the paddock outside Ilsington House and saw: "A huge angel about forty foot high, with a sword made of light and a breastplate. And when you see a creature that big that is in a way a living creature, you go, 'Aaaaagh!' and somehow without any real logical argument, I knew, 'Oh well, it's the band.'"

Brown moved back to London and assembled the band, Kingdom Come. They only made three albums but the records were three of the more imaginative offerings from the emerging progressive rock era. The group rehearsed almost obsessively for three months in a warehouse in Covent Garden, swapping phrases in what Brown has called a "musical pass the parcel". The driving organ sound of The Crazy World... was allied with guitar and synthesizer, in music of greater complexity.

Brown explains that the concept of *Galactic Zoo Dossier* – released in March 1971 – is partly autobiographical and was also informed by the chaos and violence he had witnessed in the USA in 1968.

His idea that the album's narrative is about a "free spirit sent down almost like a prisoner to the earth and subjected to society's shit" is exemplified on a song like 'Night Of The Pigs', but there is also a redemptive feel to Brown's wonderful vocal performance on 'Sunrise'.

In the Seventies, Ivor Kallin was a fan of Arthur Brown and *Galatic Zoo Dossier* in particular. He writes:

"My room in my parents' house in Strathbungo was wee, and not centrally heated, but my walls were insulated, from floor to ceiling, with photographs, posters and reviews from the NME *and* Melody Maker. *And pride of place went to the poster of a crucified Arthur Brown, taken from the record sleeve of the astonishing* Galactic Zoo Dossier. *Had I kept it intact, the package would be worth £100 on eBay, but music exists in an exalted space beyond commodity.*

"Two problems with posting the poster: one, it meant I had no access to the lyrics on the back, thus causing me to write them out on a piece of card, which I still have in the gatefold sleeve. The other problem was that it made my parents feel a bit uneasy, seeing their good Jewish son displaying a Christ-like figure on his wall. Galactic Zoo Dossier *struck me as a radical record, dark and metallic, those scary deranged bug-eyed passport photos gracing the cover. Mr Brown had spent time studying music and dance at a Gurdjieffian seminary and the lyrics conveyed a connection with my then interest in Gurdjieff, and then anarchism, [offering] an anarchist critique of contemporary materialist society.*

"And what a voice the guy has. One of the finest in all of the recorded music I've ever heard. There may be finer, but I ain't heard it. Up there with Beefheart. Such strength, such soul and screams only matched by Diamanda Galas. This is a mighty strong and disturbing dossier, unlike anything heard since."

Nic Roeg's 1971 film, Glastonbury Fayre, shows Kingdom Come's live show in all its absurd and macabre pomp, with Brown in death-mask face paint and embroidered wizard robes. Drummer Martin 'Slim' Steer hunches over his kit in a tight black-hooded satin jumpsuit, as does Michael Harris over his keyboards, while guitarist Andy Dalby, dressed as a sinister circus clown, stalks the stage. Bearded and bare chested, bass player Desmond Fisher is also facially painted up. Down in the audience, punters hastily retreat as, in flagrant disobedience of all things health and safety, three large wooden crosses at the front of the stage are set alight. Indoor shows featured Brown draped over a giant cross in a nightly mock crucifixion.

Things got less aggressive but even freakier on the following album *Kingdom Come*, released in 1972. The band had been taking acid together and it shows in the cover shot of Brown as a bishop, another band member dressed as an alien emerging from a coffin and another with a demonic ram's head. The music was more democratically composed by the stoned musicians and, in Brown's view, was: "rather sloppy. It was kind of loose, with some nice images and some flowing bits of music and a very, very theatrical performance." This involved the musicians appearing onstage as traffic lights and giant telephones. The idea of the traffic light that wouldn't go green on 'The Traffic Light Song' was used as a metaphor for the hung-up members of straight society.

Kingdom Come is a bit daft and scatological in places, but like *Galactic Zoo Dossier*, the way it jump-cuts across musical and lyrical subjects is particularly impressive, and its satires on society carry a whiff of Frank Zappa. The two had met in the States and although Brown concedes he might be an influence, he asserts that his own satire was less direct and more to do with inference and innuendo.

Released in late 1973, *Journey* was something quite different: a reaction to the complexity of the group's previous two albums and to progressive rock in general. "I particularly wanted something that would sound like our version of a string quartet," Brown says. "We thought, 'We are going to go forwards, but what we want is a thing where each of the instruments has equal value.' Everything got simplified. I wanted to simplify my life."

To prepare for recording the album, Brown put the brake on his acid intake and made a drastic change of diet. "A Druid fellow told me that the people before the Christians purified the will by doing apple fasts, where you just live on apples. I did it for about ten days."

Journey sounded quite shockingly stripped down and unlike anything else around at the time. Martin Steer had gone AWOL and in his place they decided to use a Bentley Rhythm Ace drum machine – played by Brown – which in a groundbreaking move was the only percussion on the album. Its mechanistic minimalism combined with Victor Peraino's synthesizers predates Eighties synth pop, while 'Triangles' feels like a not so distant cousin of 'Art Decade' on David Bowie's 1977 album *Low*. And it's no surprise that Gary Numan has declared himself a fan of the record.

"No one had used it to that extent," says Brown. "Sly Stone had experimented with [a drum machine] in the studio but not as a band member. It was just the idea of, 'This is a new direction. What on earth can we do with it?'" To this end they gave the drum machine a name – "Ace Bentley".

The opening 'Time Captives' starts with a single bass drum pulse, which metamorphoses into a slightly more embellished rhythm. Andy Dalby plays one note on guitar, while Peraino's Mellotron and synth fanfares give the song a monumental grandeur.

Like Hawkwind and like other musicians before him, Brown was also in search of space, in order to escape from both the turbulence of society and his own personal mindset, which he had depicted in the previous two albums. This felt like more a journey into expansiveness and inner peace. Instrumentally *Journey* feels clean and cool, but it featured some of Brown's strongest material and most impassioned vocals.

"We even got to open for Duke Ellington in Belgium," he reveals. "In certain places it was viewed as a very cultural thing as it was embracing the new technology but putting it in a form that was easily approachable, even if it was strange for some people."

Drum machine technology was still at a formative stage and Brown had to operate this new piece of kit manually, even for the rhythmic acceleration in 'Time Captives' and the sudden time changes on 'Gypsy', on which the high-velocity, tinny, synthetic drums seem to pre-empt the recordings of the New York duo, Suicide.

"On one hot sweaty evening at The Marquee there was a lot of moisture in the air and the synapses of the drum machine started operating themselves," he says. "I couldn't do anything, I just stood back and the band did their best to try to keep up.

"For 'Time Captives', we had black velvet with transparent cylindrical plastic helmets with lights in and we would all march on and then it would go into everything from projections of Tibetan design, [paintings by William] Blake, and then there would be strobes, so it was a light show that mirrored the music, it was kind of elegant rather than the older kind of lightshow from the underground, which was more the oil slides and everything flooding into each other. That seemed to reach something good, but it never reached what I was looking for."

Brown then felt compelled to move on and leave the group. Originally intending to travel to India, he made a stop-over at the Institute Of Continuous Education at Sherborne House in Gloucestershire – run by J. G. Bennett, a disciple of the Armenian philosopher and mystic George Gurdjieff – in 1973, the year before Robert Fripp went there after having disbanded King Crimson. Bennett wanted Brown to found a dance academy for the Gurdjieff movement, but instead he went off to study Sufism in Scotland and travelled to Turkey.

Brown returned to record *Dance* (1975) and *Chisholm In My Bosom* (1977) but although they featured some spirited vocal performances, they came nowhere near to *Journey*'s originality.

It's difficult to tell how much influence *Journey* has exerted on other artists or whether they just eventually caught up with what Kingdom Come had been doing in 1973, which leaves the album standing alone like some strange monolith.

CHAPTER 18

In the Garden of England: The Birth of the Canterbury Scene

Ye goon to caunterbury – God yow speede,
The blisful martir quite yow youre meede!
And wel I woot, as ye goon by the weye,
Ye shapen yow to talen and to pleye.

Geoffrey Chaucer, *Canterbury Tales: The Prologue*, lines 769-772

Journalists and fans alike have perennially been drawn to the idea of scenes, of movements, of an outpouring of music from a certain geographical area, where musicians are somehow bonded by their proximity to one another and that their music therefore embodies a collective sense of place and time. And none more so than the Canterbury Scene of the Sixties and Seventies.

One explanation is that it evokes a peculiar modern idyll, a juxtaposition of the genteel, well-to-do English city steeped in history coming up against a new kind of post-psychedelic Englishness. Seen through certain lenses its towering cathedral, taverns and ancient side streets carrying echoes of the bawdy verse of Geoffrey Chaucer and the grand tragedies of Philip Marlowe, with the River Stour flowing past sequestered urban locales and out into sun-dappled water meadows, could be transformed into some kind of culture-meets-counterculture freaks' playground.

But, alas, as with most idylls, it was never quite like that. The abiding memory of Kevin Ayers – of The Wilde Flowers and Soft Machine – was of being beaten up outside The Beehive pub in the city in the late Sixties for having long hair.

"I can remember Canterbury being talked about in the early Seventies," recalls composer Andrew Poppy, then a teenage bass guitarist based in Gillingham. "But I wouldn't be able to describe a scene or style. There were all sorts of Hell's Angels bands and pop bands and hippie bands playing in the city."

The notion of a thriving, artistically rich music scene in Canterbury in the late Sixties is generally accepted now as being essentially fallacious. Most of the musicians who were, at least symbolically, part of that scene, have said that there was never much of a kinship among the Canterbury groups. But by name it exists still, as a metaphysical construct, or simply a groovy idea that has grown in importance over nearly five decades, so it definitely exists in some form, and with musicians knowing and playing with each other and some moving from group to group, there was an exchange of ideas.

The one incontestable fact is that the group that spawned this "scene" was The Wilde Flowers, who formed in 1964/5 and from them came Soft Machine, Caravan, Matching Mole, Hatfield And The North and National Health. Also related were Uriel, Egg and Khan, while other affiliates include Gilgamesh and even, rather tenuously, Henry Cow and Camel.

To try to corral all those groups together seems, on the face of it, a fool's errand, but even now there are intuitive ways of connecting them. Among the threads that run through their music is a melodic pop-song sensibility, and although they might have been influenced by, and in their earlier days, covered, American soul and rock'n'roll tunes, lyrically they were far removed from anything American. Instead, their lyrics typically involved intimate, day-to-day observations expressed in the vernacular, with a few word plays thrown in, yielding a peculiarly English style of whimsy and eccentricity.

This ranged from the gentle to the defiantly strange, and at times it harked back, lyrically, to the likes of Edward Lear and Lewis Carroll. Richard Sinclair, who had played in The Wilde Flowers, Caravan and Hatfield And The North, displayed a penchant for that very English pleasure of a restorative cup of tea, which was particularly refreshing when slaking a thirst gained from the dehydrating effects of smoking marijuana.

Musically they displayed a collective penchant for jazzy time signatures and other metric complications, and the employment of fuzz organs that ran from the drifty and bucolic to the scorching. This combination was of its time, but its appeal has endured.

However it's clear that a core group of musicians defined the scene rather than the cathedral city somehow exerting a deterministic influence over musicians' musical activities. For example there was no comparable scene associated with Norwich, Durham or St Albans.

An unlikely focal point for the early scene was Wellington House in the Kent village of Lydden, which is situated between Canterbury and

Dover. Robert Wyatt's father George Ellidge – he later took his mother's surname – was unwell, suffering from multiple sclerosis, and the family had moved from Bristol into the fourteen-room Georgian building in the late Fifties. Wyatt was already a precocious student at Simon Langton Grammar School For Boys in Canterbury. He was clearly intelligent in a way that was at odds with academia and had a cocky disregard for authority, exemplified by statements like wearing his blazer inside-out.

To help pay for the house, Wyatt's mother Honor took in foreign students and other lodgers, including young Australian Beatnik Daevid Allen and American drummer George Neidorf, who gave Wyatt his first drumming lessons. It was a place where ideas were exchanged – Wyatt's parents were politically left and culturally more enlightened than most – and jazz LPs, many brought in by Allen, were played along with his father's penchant for 20th-century composers like Webern and Bartók. Wyatt had been learning violin but swapped it for trumpet, and there were jam sessions in the house with Neidorf on drums and Allen on guitar.

The open, musically and intellectually stimulating environment of Wellington House was a rarity at the time and so understandably it acted as a magnet, attracting the hip kids of the area.

Kevin Ayers went to live in Wellington House in the early Sixties, where he also encountered regular visitor and former Simon Langton boy, keyboard player Mike Ratledge. He recounts the story: "I was just out of boarding school. I lived rough in London for a year, as I'd left home, then I got busted on a phoney drugs charge, where a policeman puts his hand in your pocket and pulls out a package and goes, 'Hello, hello, what's all this?' I couldn't even possibly have afforded what he was bringing out of my pocket. So I was put on remand in jail for two weeks and fortunately the judge threw it out of court, but then he said I had to leave London. I had to go to the country – like in a Western.

"I met with Robert Wyatt, Mike Ratledge and Daevid Allen and I thought, 'Hey, these people are interesting; these *other* people aren't in the least bit interesting.'

"They introduced me to jazz, which I thought was utter nonsense at the time. I hadn't a clue. I mean, I'd never played anything. The only record I remember was *The Sound Of Music*, which my parents used to play. But we suddenly found a mutual interest in poetry, modern American writing, classic French writing. I started learning when I came out of school.

"So these people were my tutors, my inspiration: I wanted to be like these guys. I said, 'OK I will learn to play guitar.' And it took me two years. But I did it because I liked the people and wanted to be part of the scene, that very small scene, which has since been called the Canterbury Scene, which spawned Caravan and other people."

Wyatt has few good memories of the period, not least because his father was suffering from a terminal illness. He had, in his words "a very, very unhappy and unsuccessful time at school in Canterbury" and felt desperate about leaving school with no prospect of university and having no idea where he fitted into the world.

Both a self-confident and self-effacing youth, Wyatt experienced a teenage crisis and made an unsuccessful suicide attempt over Christmas 1961, swallowing a bottle of painkillers that his father took for his multiple sclerosis. Into 1962, he cooled off for a few months in Deià, Majorca, with a friend from his mother's side of the family, the poet Robert Graves. As an unconventional careers advisor Graves was a godsend to the troubled teenager, encouraging him to be himself and achieve his potential, particularly as a musician. The poet referred to him as Batty, short for Batterie, and Wyatt occasionally sat in on drums at gigs in the island's clubs, which he viewed as his apprenticeship. Ayers and Daevid Allen also went over to visit. They were entranced by the island and both went back to live there in subsequent years.

In 1963, when George Ellidge died, his son Robert was playing in his first proper gig, in the Daevid Allen trio, which actually consisted of four musicians: Allen, Wyatt, Ratledge on piano and Hugh Hopper on bass. They played at London's Establishment Club where their shambolic, strange sets proved exceptionally unpopular with the clientele – Ratledge was described as playing a mix of Bill Evans and Cecil Taylor. Poet Mike Horowitz also guested on some other dates but the group didn't last long.

Back in Canterbury the following autumn, former Langtonians the Hopper brothers were assembling a R&B-cum-beat group, which became The Wilde Flowers. Having been only partly successful at avant-garde jazz, Wyatt and Hugh Hopper decided to have a crack at pop music.

The Wilde Flowers formed in late 1964 and lasted until 1969. Typical of many groups of the time they played cover versions, but on the night their set list might have featured songs by Mose Allison, Willie Dixon and Nina Simone, together with The Byrds, The Who, some Dylan, James Brown, even Manfred Mann's 'Pretty Flamingo' and jazz tunes by Thelonious Monk. Kevin Ayers even got to sing Bukka White's Forties blues song, 'Parchman Farm'. This was an adventurous mix, and more or less from the off, they also began to write their own material.

Their line-up interchanged between Kevin Ayers on vocals, Robert Wyatt on drums and vocals, Hugh Hopper on bass guitar and Brian Hopper and Richard Sinclair on guitars. Later on Richard Coughlan took over the drums, Wyatt took on lead vocals and Pye Hastings joined on guitar and vocals. The group made their debut on January 15, 1965, at The Bear And Key Hotel in Whitstable and went on to play at venues like Toft's in Folkestone – "One of the country's most leading and famous clubs" – as their flyers proclaimed, the Starlight Ballroom in Herne Bay, and pubs and college venues in Canterbury.

Future Caravan mainstay Pye Hastings was a few years younger than Wyatt and friends, but recalls the lure of the artistic environment of Wellington House and how it led him to join his first group.

"When I joined The Wilde Flowers I was living in Canterbury. However, I went to Pilgrims Boarding School in Lydden, and periodically we were allowed out into the village. This is when I first heard Robert playing his drums in the front window of Wellington House. I remember thinking, 'What a racket.' I did not play any instrument at this time but clearly had opinions. Little did I know then that I would be joining Robert and the rest of The Wilde Flowers some years later.

"I got to know the band through Kevin Ayers who taught me my first guitar chords and it wasn't until Kevin had quit the band that I got the invitation to join by the band's leader, Brian Hopper.

"I loved playing with The Wilde Flowers. My first gig was a 'Battle Of The Bands' at Dreamland Ballroom in Margate. The line-up was Brian and Hugh Hopper on lead guitar and bass respectively, me on guitar and backing vocals, and Robert on drums and lead vocals. Needless to say I was terrified but we came in joint first. The grand prize was a day's free recording in a local studio, which of course was just some guy with a Revox Tape recorder and a couple of mikes."

The group made a number of studio demos, but never released any recordings commercially. When Wyatt left The Wilde Flowers in 1966, he had decided that having tried to play mutated versions of jazz standards with poetry and also pop music, the groups he was in weren't particularly good at either and in his own words "we had to make up our own sort of music".

But the circumstances in which his next group, Mister Head, were formed were some of the strangest in all the strangeness of the Sixties. It was 1966. Daevid Allen was in his home in Deià, Majorca, and had taken LSD and was envisioning the village of Deià as it had been 400 years ago. In the trip he saw Kevin Ayers and a friend called Blind George in different guises, but somehow recognisable to his heightened senses, and a third character, a "black-wigged Spaniard with an aristocratic jaw". Allen's partner Gilli Smyth appeared in the vision and told him: "You will be taken to the temples in the Andes where the ancient music from Atlantis is played and that is what you will bring back."

After also having a vision of Robert Graves, suffused with light, proclaiming, "Another day another death", Allen staggered out into the garden where he saw – in reality – Ayers and George and "met the newcomer who I knew had come to help us out as he had four hundred years earlier". This was the aristocratic Spaniard, who was actually a rich American called Wes Brunson.

Ayers introduced his guest to Allen with: "This is Wes, he's from Tulsa and wants to put money into a band." "I know!" Allen exclaimed and started laughing. Allen later recalled: "I knew it to be serving a future spiritual and cultural need."

All of which certainly beats putting an ad in the back of *Melody Maker*. And the bizarre quality of the story's introduction carries on in the subsequent chain of events. Brunson was an optometrist, allegedly thinking himself an incarnation of Christ, who was clearly conflicted between being a successful businessman and wanting to take on the Timothy Leary dictum of doing the absolute opposite, to "turn on, tune in, drop out".

"He sold spectacle frames and he was embarrassed about how much money he was making by it," says Ayers. "And he heard Daevid and myself playing together and maybe Robert as well, and said, 'You guys are the future. I'm going to give you money to get a band together.' And do you know what? He did. We went back to England and lived in my girlfriend's house, and these thick bundles of letters would come through, each with a hundred dollar bill to buy equipment to get started."

Initially the group was called Mister Head in a tongue-in-cheek recognition of Allen's psychedelic vision and although the increasingly eccentric Brunson was soon out of the picture, Allen later immortalised him in the song 'Stoned Innocent Frankenstein' on his 1971 solo album, *Banana Moon*.

Mister Head comprised Ayers on guitar and vocals, Wyatt on drums and vocals, Larry Nowlin on guitar and Allen on bass, but soon changed their name to Soft Machine, after author William Burroughs' novel, which was also a description of the human body. Allen, who has always classified himself as a "reconstituted beatnik" rather than a hippie, had collaborated with Burroughs back in 1961, while living in the Beat

Hotel in Paris, accompanying the author in live performances with an early version of the Daevid Allen trio and with American minimalist composer Terry Riley, and so gained his permission.

Wyatt's mother, Honor, had left Wellington House and moved into a house in Dalmore Road, West Dulwich in south east London, which was soon full of the extended Soft Machine family. She was friends with the mother of Bill MacCormick and his elder brother Ian as both were teaching assistants at Dulwich College Preparatory school. The two teenagers were regular visitors.

"We lived in West Norwood so going to school meant going past the house where the band lived and rehearsed, or I arranged so it did," says MacCormick. "So we started popping in and Robert's too polite to tell you to fuck off, so we'd sit there and drink tea and listen to his records and wander into the front room downstairs where all the Soft Machine's kit was and poke things and hit things, and generally not know what to do with them. At that point he was in his early twenties, so he was pretty generous to let some 15-year-old public schoolboy oik with his school uniform to wander in and sit there with all these longhaired types and attractive young ladies and babies, and strange smells and all sorts of things going on." MacCormick recalls going to a party at a "Sufi-run place in Kingston".

"It was the first time, I believe, that they played under the name Soft Machine," MacCormick says. "And my brother and I went along to this bizarre house with rambling gardens and ponds, streams and little temples.

"It was Allen, Ratledge, Ayers and Wyatt and there wasn't a stage, [they were at the] end of a room pressed up against a window and they performed things like 'Love Makes Sweet Music', and that was the first time that I'd seen a rock band, it was about 1966, I was about 15, my brother was about 17 or 18 so that was it: the slippery slope."

In 1967, Soft Machine and Pink Floyd were viewed by many as the twin leading lights of the underground, particularly as they played at the movement's epicentre, The UFO Club. But to the wider public Soft Machine remained on the periphery of the psychedelic scene, as although they had made a high-energy single, 'Love Makes Sweet Music', with American producer Kim Fowley in 1967, a number of recordings with producer and svengali Giorgio Gomelsky made that year – ostensibly demos – were never released or further worked on due to a dispute over payment. And so, like Tomorrow, their debut album was delayed until 1968. To compound the delay, Mike Jeffrey and Chas

Chandler, the group's managers, were rather preoccupied with the big star on their books, Jimi Hendrix.

In the summer of 1967 Soft Machine had a residency in the south of France where they played in a giant tent in Saint-Aygulf designed by Keith Albarn and advertised by posters saying "Dansez! Freak Out!" And you could do both at a Soft Machine performance, with the most spectacular mix of the two being 'We Did It Again' a two-chord exercise in repetition – sounding almost exactly like an avant-garde version of The Kinks' 'You Really Got Me', that they would play for anything up to an hour.

As it turned out, there was a little too much freaking out for local tastes and noise complaints curtailed their residency. But this trip to France inspired the then-59-year-old American writer Arnold Shaw's rather fanciful and less than accurate sleeve notes for their 1968 debut album, *The Soft Machine*. A romanticised take on the freewheeling Sixties that would even have looked a bit overcooked when the album came out, Shaw's text painted a primary-coloured picture of a fresh new culture powered by the freedom of youth, in which, if the scene got stale in London, you'd all just put on freaky hats, grab some beads, pack a few pairs of tie-dye Bermuda shorts and groovy shirts, jump into a paisley Mini Moke and drive on down to le Sud De France and create an art happening.

In many ways this was fairly close to what happened. Soft Machine made their way down in a yellow bandwagon, but cancellation of their initial booking could have spelt disaster for the impecunious group, only they moved on to St Tropez where they played a show in the town square and a gig entertaining local hipsters at Brigitte Bardot's private party, where they played 'We Did It Again' for forty minutes to what Allen described as "an ecstatic 'in' crowd..."

They also ended up providing the opening music for a version of Picasso's surrealist play *Desire Caught By The Tail* in a tent in the town.

Allen recalled: "Suddenly we were the avant-garde of intelligent rock. We were soon invited to stay at luxurious beachfront houses, with the best food, wine, hash and cocaine."

It was during this trip that the group came across 'pataphysics for the first time, something which became linked with the group. 'Pataphysics was dreamt up by French author Alfred Jarry in the late 19th century, a kind of spoof science in which logic is redefined and all viewpoints have equal validity. Put into a brief "idiot's guide" – which, one assumes, would be as 'pataphysically valid as any other guide – 'pataphysics is, in Jarry's words "the science of imaginary solutions" and "the law governing exceptions". In it, science's apparently immutable laws are scoffed at. To Jarry, they are merely "the correlation of exceptions albeit more frequent ones... which reduced to the status of unexceptional exceptions, possess no longer even the virtue of originality." 'Pataphysics was, he said, "the greatest of all sciences".

"I wasn't drawn to Jarry and 'pataphysics from reading about it," Robert Wyatt explains. "I think we were chosen to be 'pataphysicians before I knew what it was. Later we were playing in Paris, and some representatives of the College Of 'Pataphysics came to the concert. A very venerable old member of their group heard it for about five minutes, thought we played the most incomprehensible and appalling music he had ever heard, gave us his blessing and gave us certificates.

"So we are officially Petits Fils Ubu – Ubu's grandchildren – and in our case it gives us the right to lead the marching band at the front of the victory parade of the 'pataphysical movement. But nobody who gave it to us thought to explain it any more than you would explain a football match to a teddy bear mascot."

More practical problems arose when, in late summer of 1967, Daevid Allen attempted to get back into the UK, but was refused entry at Dover and was shipped back to France where he jumped a train to Paris and spent some time in the country assembling his new musical project, Gong.

Ayers recalls that when they got back home: "We went on the road and we were lucky to get six pounds each a night, up and down the M1 and all points north."

He also met Hendrix: "Jimi liked what we did, especially some of my earlier songs with some weird time signatures. He said, 'You're weird, man.' And *voila!* There we were on the Jimi Hendrix tours to the USA – two of them. It put Soft Machine on the map."

Soft Machine carried on as a trio and recorded their debut album in New York City on their first trip to the USA in the spring of 1968. Wyatt had thought the group "suburban fakes" when they mingled with the countercultural druggies at UFO, and in the States he saw a level of racism and street violence that shocked him as a sheltered Englishman. The album was produced by Tom Wilson, who had worked with both Bob Dylan and The Velvet Underground, but from all accounts, he wasn't exactly crackling with enthusiasm for the project and spent a considerable amount of time on the phone to his girlfriend. The album has some potent moments with 'Hope For Happiness' showing the group off at their poppiest and 'So Boot If At All' more experimental and meandering. 'We Did it Again' was there in a manageable form.

The most striking feature of the group's sound was Mike Ratledge's Lowry Holiday Deluxe organ fed through a fuzz box. Apparently, if Ratledge took his hands off the keys for any length of time the instrument would start feeding back. But the distorted sound that he gets on 'Lullaby Letter' is on the edge of breaking up, and a combination of that visceral sound and his manic high-speed approach makes it one of the most thrilling keyboard solos on record.

The other aspect is Wyatt's drumming, which on this track is equally adrenalised, hyperactively swinging, but with rock propulsion, something like a cross between Keith Moon and Elvin Jones. The one thing that lets it down is that Kevin Ayers' bass is out of tune throughout the album, its pitching problem accentuated by distortion. It still stands as one of the most adventurous albums of 1968 and Soft Machine sounded like they were heading somewhere else – and fast.

Quite where they were going on the tours of America supporting the Jimi Hendrix Experience was another matter, with dates being added to cope with the demand to see the American guitarist, who was making a name for himself in the UK, so that their travel itinerary looked like random zig-zagging across the map, with long drives as well as air flights leaving everyone exhausted. On the first tour, Ayers had been like the proverbial kid in a sweet shop, helping himself to booze, drugs and women. But for the second he adopted a strictly macrobiotic diet and an ascetic lifestyle, preferring to retreat to his hotel room to read.

"Sometimes I was so weak from the macrobiotic diet – brown rice and veg – that I actually had to be helped on stage and still played a ninety-minute set. It's because you don't eat any protein. Your hair falls out; your libido falls to zero. I just did it at the wrong time of my life. It's a total detox diet. But to try to and combine that with live gigs fronting for Jimi Hendrix for five or six nights a week was weird [*laughs*]."

It was weird indeed and at the end of the tour Ayers had had enough. In many ways the other musicians thought of Soft Machine as Ayers' group in that he was the main songwriter, but as well as not taking well to touring, he could see that the music was heading towards what Ayers has called "rehashed jazz", adding: "I think what I was doing was too simple for them and what they were doing was too complicated for me; it was something I was not equipped to do." He decided to take his talents elsewhere, but with no hard feelings.

The band broke up again with Ayers selling his bass to Noel Redding and going out to Majorca to rethink things. Wyatt, on the other hand, was the recipient of one of Mitch Mitchell's kits and hung out in New

York State then in Laurel Canyon writing and recording a batch of new material in downtime at TTG Studios in Los Angeles.

Hugh Hopper, who had been a roadie on the strength-sapping US tour, was drafted in on bass and they recorded *Volume Two* at Olympic Studios, London, in spring 1969.

Hopper was a phenomenal bass player, rhythmically rock solid but as lithe and mobile as a dancer. *Volume Two* finds Wyatt writing in what was becoming his characteristic style, delivered in the vernacular, and observationally clear and philosophically direct to avoid cliché. It was both "no bullshit" and full of wry humour. And in doing this he could make the humdrum seem something special as it was framed in a song. The album starts with a grand theme on 'Pataphysical Introduction', after which Wyatt recites the *"British alphabet"*.

Hopper's muscular fuzz bass riff follows, ushering a new group style with Brian Hopper playing sax lines that are sort of jazz by default, as they are just as much like big-band or soul horn sections' interjections. And in a reprise of 'Pataphysical Introduction', Wyatt delivers the alphabet backwards.

"I just decided that singing the alphabet backwards was a 'pataphysical activity," says Wyatt. "Some people get very upset by art that doesn't make sense to them – I never had that problem. I never saw what was the sense that modern art wasn't making."

Although Wyatt was not directly influenced by 'pataphysics, his lyrical worldview incorporates elements of absurdity and has also been called Dadaist, but some of it comes from more unlikely sources. "I felt empathy with the whole anarchic movements in culture at the turn of the century as being a reaction to the pompous certainty of the people who run the world. They seem mad but they are so certain," Wyatt says. "There were also some completely daft comedians who came through music hall – Tommy Cooper is an example."

The album is a seamless medley, which came from the group's live shows. Side one is called 'Rivmic Melodies', for which Wyatt had sketched out his song sections on his West Coast sojourns in 1968. But Soft Machine were advised that they would earn more royalties, especially for compositions and for radio plays, if each section was given a title, which gave rise to some rather ridiculous examples like 'Hibou, Anemone And Bear'.

The highlight of the album is 'As Long As He Lies Perfectly Still', a touching tip of the hat to Kevin Ayers, which drolly weaves a number of his song lyrics into a vocal melody backed by some luminous fuzz organ lines by Ratledge.

Mont Campbell, who was the bass player in Egg, picks it out as a favourite. "It's a heterosexual love song between one man and another. It was amusing but you could tell there was a huge sense of loss and sadness for what might have been and that comes across in that chord sequence that just repeats, but it's genius."

Soft Machine changed stylistically with the double album, *Third* (1970), with its four side-long tracks containing some austere monumental themes. Was there a feeling in the group that this was being presented as a kind of grand statement?

"I don't remember any group discussion on the matter, but jazz and classical records were like that anyway," says Wyatt. "Thinking back, in the case of the instrumentals, the length simply derived from the fact that the written parts were sort of a launch pad for solos. I don't think we thought there was anything distinctive about that. After all, we'd all been listening to Coltrane records up to his death in 1967. Personally, I don't remember ever paying to go to a rock concert, buying any papers or magazines on that subject, or buying more than one or two records by rock groups, so except when we shared the stage with others, I didn't follow what they were doing, and can't remember the sort of zeitgeist career consciousness that question implies."

The influence of Terry Riley can also be felt in the flickering, multi-tracked varispeed tape section that bookends Mike Ratledge's 'Out-Bloody-Rageous'.

Hopper's composition 'Facelift' demonstrates his burgeoning interest in tape manipulation and is a collage of live recordings from the Fairfield Halls, Croydon. The group's furthest foray into a kind of ersatz jazz – which saw the introduction of Elton Dean on sax and saxello, and flautist Lynn Dobson – is Ratledge's 'Slightly All The Time'. Hopper plays a particularly elongated theme, a sort of walking bass that trips over itself, quickens its pace and at times slows to look around, shifting metres with ease while always beautifully in time. Wyatt also plays with a highly personalised approach that at times finds him concentrating on just snare or just hi-hat, then launching off into extravagant forays around the kit.

Wyatt's composition 'Moon In June', had originally been composed as a musical letter home to his wife Pam and their son Sam, written on the East Coast and demoed in Los Angeles. For the album it was recorded solo with a full band instrumental coda.

Just to show how times were changing, Soft Machine appeared at the Proms at the Royal Albert Hall on August 13, 1970. Composer Tim Souster had gained a position of trust with BBC TV, which recorded and filmed the concert, and he chose a running order of Terry Riley's

Keyboard Studies, his own *Triple Music II* and 'Out-Bloody-Rageous', 'Facelift' and 'Esther's Nose Job' by Soft Machine. Some of the notices from classical critics were sniffy to say the least, and Wyatt recalls nipping outside for a cigarette and then having some difficulty persuading the security to let him back in as he was due onstage.

By the time of *Fourth*, released in 1971, Soft Machine had completed their shift to a style that was more electric jazz than the long mutated rock riffs on *Third*, although these did still appear, with themes balancing the freer sections, particularly effectively on Ratledge's composition 'Teeth'. The guest musicians included Marc Charig (cornet) and Nick Evans (trombone) from The Keith Tippett Group, Alan Skidmore (tenor sax) and Caravan's Jimmy Hastings on bass clarinet and alto flute. Even in the more lyrical moments it's quite austere with Ratledge's fuzz organ sounding less psychedelic when run up against the horn section, and band member Elton Dean's hard-edged playing. Wyatt's high-energy style fits well. Or so it seemed.

Wyatt had meanwhile recorded a solo album, *The End Of An Ear*, on which he explored the use of tape loops. It came out in December 1970 and on it he credited himself as an "out of work pop singer currently on drums with Soft Machine".

At the time Bill MacCormick was playing in Quiet Sun with keyboard player Dave Jarrett, drummer Charles Hayward and guitarist Phil Manzanera. He recalls Wyatt coming over to one of their rehearsals. "He was falling out of love with the band and he was also beginning to unfortunately drink rather a lot. Robert was always an alcohol man rather than a dope man. Cigarettes, fried eggs and drink would be Robert's ideal diet.

"One totally dismal evening he turned up and brought the entire rehearsal to a standstill, with gloom oozing out of him, basically because the band was his, but he no longer felt part of it."

This combined with onstage tantrums, including walking out of one gig at the interval, and tension between himself and the group was increasing, partly because he felt that they were moving away from what he wanted to do musically and that his songs were being phased out. Unwittingly he had set that particular ball in motion by inviting in extra wind players (Dobson, Charig and Evans) for a BBC Session from 1971, who essentially played his vocal lines on some of the previously recorded material.

But although the group moved towards free jazz on *Fourth*, while in Soft Machine, Wyatt also played with free-improvising ensembles The

Amazing Band and Symbiosis, as well as with Keith Tippett in his pioneering large ensemble, Centipede, so he was no stranger to this style of music.

But communication between the musicians was deteriorating and Hugh Hopper has admitted that "Mike and I couldn't stand Robert's singing". This all came to a head when they asked Wyatt to leave. "The things they had to put up with – my vanity, my gross alcoholism. Let's just call it quits," Wyatt said in 1994. But he was devastated by his dismissal.

MacCormick: "Robert had gone to school with these people, this was a significant part of his growing up and his life, and I think everyone underestimated the importance of it to him."

It's hard to convey the intensity of feeling that can be produced by playing in a group unless you have done such a thing. The chances of making any money are slim and if you are serious about trying for some kind of longevity, if you don't have the "all for one, one for all" mentality you won't even get through the first set of privations. Relationships within groups can be – without any exaggeration – as intense as within families, with the members sometimes even more reliant on each other.

A *Melody Maker* news piece put Wyatt's departure down to "a difference of musical opinion". If only it had been that simple and clear cut.

Fuelled by his continuing depression and alcohol consumption, Wyatt made another suicide attempt. But nothing if not resilient, he soon got a new group together.

Wyatt has a singular view on progressive rock. As a boy he grew up in a household where Beat poets and avant-garde composers and painters were a part of the fabric of his life, but his love of complexity and experimentation was also cut with a striving for a more direct form of expression that would begin to manifest itself more over the coming years. As he said in 2003: "The underlying ideology of the kind of rock I was involved in was that we started out simple and we got dead clever. But I was brought up with dead clever and since then I've been trying to get really simple."

So what does he say now on Soft Machine experimenting with structure? "I think you're talking about someone else here," he replies. "We went on the road as a support band for most of 1968. We came back and there was this other thing of these bands doing loads of complicated fiddly arrangements with lots of written bits in and I suppose these are the things you mean.

"It's very hard playing drums, and bands I was in did tend to stretch themselves, so the moment you became comfortable with playing a certain way they pushed it harder, so it was harder to do. So that takes up your time. You are trying to concentrate on the music, just playing what happens.

"It can be a difficulty for writers, because you are looking at an overview of things and relating them in some way, but the people in the middle of it aren't doing that. I don't remember at all, prog rock. When I first heard it I thought it possibly meant programme music. That's what 'prog' meant to me: illustrative music.

"The adjective 'progressive', when I last heard about it, was a term that meant a tendency to move to the left and a more egalitarian society economically. I don't see any connection with that and prog music."

And as for the Canterbury Scene: "Daevid Allen is from Australia and Kevin Ayers from Malaya. I don't know how near Canterbury those two are – not very. And anyway I was born in Bristol and went to live near Dover in the Fifties.

"I think there's an exaggerated sense that people have a control over what they play, what their voices are like, what their sound is. I don't know much about the other musicians who are called [Canterbury Scene]. I don't have their records. I get on well with the ones that I meet. I can't think of any particular agreement or shared sensibility or even shared experience, or anything particularly, to be honest."

Which just goes to reinforce that writers and listeners can have a very different perception of the music to that of the musicians who make it. But Wyatt was working within a milieu that was ostensibly rock and whose artistic scope was progressing, and so we won't let that derail us too much.

His new group was called Matching Mole. The name looks ostensibly like a rather whimsical and English moniker, but it was a nod back to Wyatt's former group, a translation into French of "Soft Machine" being "Machine Molle".

As well as Wyatt, Matching Mole consisted of Dave Sinclair from Caravan on keyboards and Phil Miller on guitar, who had played in Delivery with Carol Grimes and had been recommended by a "mutual friend". On one of Wyatt's gigs with Symbiosis, they were supported by Quiet Sun, and the school-uniformed lad who had dropped by Dalmore Road, Bill MacCormick, was now a grown man playing some excellent bass guitar. And so he was drafted in.

Initially they tried out a number of songs including George Harrison's 'Beware Of Darkness', Gil Evans's 'Las Vegas Tango' – which had appeared on *End Of An Ear* – and Caravan's 'Nine Feet Underground'.

"I was very, very keen that we should learn to play 'Moon In June', but he wouldn't have it no matter how many times we started playing it," says MacCormick.

The album feels very much like a Wyatt solo album, although Miller chips in with the lengthy 'Part Of The Dance'. It's far more coherent than *End Of An Ear* and contains two of Wyatt's most memorable songs.

'Oh Caroline' – co-written with Sinclair – starts with a matter of musical metacommentary, which finds Wyatt explaining that David Sinclair is on piano and he is playing on "a drum" for our entertainment.

But overall it's far from emotionally detached and Wyatt goes on to proclaim his love for Caroline Coon, the writer and activist, with whom he had just ended a short, intense relationship. Wyatt also doubts the efficacy of what he is singing, but warns his subject that he will be annoyed if she deems it *"sentimental crap"*, aware that his love song might be misconstrued, yet he is keen to state that although they have parted, he loves her still. It's a beguiling serenade, made more poignant by being riddled with such self-doubt.

The apex of this self-referential style of writing is 'Signed Curtain'. It's an almost hymnal piano ballad, but which the writer can't fill with anything but a pencilled-in structure. So he sings that this is the *"first verse"* over and over and then later the chorus is announced, but then Wyatt isn't even sure of that and thinks aloud that it might, in fact, be just be another part of the song. There is an element of droll humour, of hip novelty in the proceedings, but in the signalled *"key change"*, the song reaches a denouement that is both harmonically and lyrically unresolved. It finds the songwriter shrugging his shoulders and admitting that he has lost faith in what he has written as it won't help him reach the song's subject or the listener, and that the exercise is essentially futile. Suddenly the joke isn't funny any more.

The reason the song is called 'Signed Curtain' is that at the end he reverses a chord sequence from Hugh Hopper's composition 'A Certain Kind' on *The Soft Machine*, which gave the idea for the phonetic pun 'A Curtain Signed' and finally 'Signed Curtain'.

Wyatt was renting a flat in St Luke's Mews in Notting Hill, just around the corner from Basing Street studios, with Phil Miller as his flatmate. Without beds and with just matresses on the floor it was a rather unglamorous band HQ. Miller recalls playing sides of albums by Miles Davis, Miroslav Vitous's *Freedom Jazz Dance* and Eric Dolphy on the

Dansette, with Wyatt paying particular attention to the playing of Jack De Johnette and Billy Cobham.

In the "progressive" spirit of the era Matching Mole developed at a pace. Miller had been into guitarists Jimmy Reed and Eddie Boyd, but was also listening to Ornette Coleman. He says: "I think you know blues isn't where you are quite going to end up, but it's a stepping stone." Miller was clearly fascinated by the complexity and language of jazz and admits he was at the start of a lifetime search for new harmonic possibilities. He was already developing into a singular player.

"Phil, I thought, was always challenging himself. His melodic sense and his ear are just different from almost everybody else that I have heard," says MacCormick.

"A uniquely fresh ingredient, I thought," says Wyatt.

MacCormick was the youngest band member and admits that he only initially picked up the bass to play the Quiet Sun material. He had been influenced by Jack Bruce and Charlie Haden, Stravinsky and Messiaen, but he had little knowledge of rudiments. He notes that, "with Matching Mole you could do what the hell you wanted and if you put it through a fuzz box it would be even better."

Dave Sinclair was more keen on songwriting and arranging than playing some of Matching Mole's looser music that slipped in the space between jazz and rock, and he soon left.

The new keyboard player was Dave MacRae, a New Zealander who was very much into exploring new possibilities. Miller recalls the sense of excitement when Wyatt and MacRae first played together at St Luke's Mews.

"Robert, what a great drummer," says Miller. "He was very imaginative. When Dave MacRae first came to play as an introduction, I was sitting downstairs and the amount of ideas that Robert came up with was phenomenal. You could hear that Dave MacRae was taking him to a step beyond, sometimes where he couldn't quite go, but he would never stop. And Dave was completely open to it."

The title of Matching Mole's second album, *Little Red Record*, was derived from Chairman Mao Tse Tung's *Little Red Book*, which contained philosophical sayings, and was published to accompany the Chinese Cultural Revolution.

The cover of *Little Red Record* is a painting of the group in the heroic pose of a Chinese Communist Party poster. At the time it carried a frisson of controversy and seemed to caricature Wyatt's left-wing views, although he wasn't to join the Communist Party for another decade or so.

"That wasn't our choice," Wyatt clarifies. "It was entirely decided by record company executives. I was thinking more along the lines of the [children's book] *The Little Red Engine* than the *Little Red Book*. I'm not a Maoist; I don't think I ever was. I mean, I didn't mind it, I just thought it was rather sad to give Dave MacRae, the gentlest man, who would lose sleep over swatting a fly, a machine gun and tell him to go liberate Taiwan. I thought that was a bit insensitive. He didn't care at all. If you want a better indication of what we were like at the time, it's David Gayle's sleeve notes – just a serious fantasy."

On 'Gloria Gloom', Wyatt wonders aloud whether making music is a better course of action than fighting for a socialist world.

"I was much more interested in that at the time," he says. "But I have never had the slightest thought that anything I did would make the slightest bit of difference."

Little Red Record featured some songs with Wyatt putting his vocals to the compositions of other band members, most notably Phil Miller's 'God Song'. On it, Wyatt seems exasperated and somewhat sad having to play by *"impossible rules"*, which culminates in an irritated, sarcastic *"Well done, God!"*, questioning the deity in a way that reflects some branches of Judaism where God is taken to task for the injustices of the world.

If MacCormick thought of himself as being something of a dilettante as a bass player, Brian Eno, then still with Roxy Music, had no such reservations and played his VCS3 synth at the opening of 'Gloria Gloom' in a whale-song-like section of long falling notes, but his presence rather rankled Dave MacRae.

On 'Gloria Gloom' and some other tracks there is some – rather irritating – background chat by Der Mütter Korus, which was band friend David Gale, Alfreda Benge (Wyatt's girlfiend) and her friend, the film actress Julie Christie (as Ruby Crystal). Christie's presence in the studio made MacCormick think of his teenage picture collection of the actress. "Gloria Gloom" was Christie's nickname for Benge, while Benge's for Christie was "Flora Fidgit".

Robert Fripp produced the album, but Miller was less than impressed with his input. "When he was mixing Matching Mole's *Little Red Record*, he wouldn't let anybody else be there," says Miller. "He made it sound as small as possible – a really horrible mix, compressed into a thin band with no bloom on it."

In concert, Matching Mole were a match for Soft Machine in terms of invention and they were a particularly powerful unit. But MacCormick remembers that the magic wasn't necessarily always on tap.

"We very much an on-the-night band. At times we could be absolutely awful and unfortunately we tended to do that on high-profile moments like the Reading Festival. We weren't even bad enough to boo – they just went to sleep. It was like, 'Something has happened for the last forty minutes but we're not quite sure what it was.'"

By contrast they supported John Mayall at Greens Playhouse in Glasgow and the blues audience loved them. "I know it was a great gig because I can't remember anything about it," says MacCormick. "I got back to the dressing room absolutely shattered. And we were all just grinning hugely at each other."

But the group's management were dysfunctional to the point that MacCormick, who was holding down a job as a civil servant earning £20 a week while living with his parents, was contributing to the rent at St Luke's Mews. The band made a maximum of £25 a week each but there was often a shortfall. One can see from a CBS promo shot that Matching Mole were never going to make it in the glamour stakes. Miller, with his dark curly tresses, looks quite presentable, but MacRae, balding, bespectacled and wearing a psychedelic poncho, comes across like an eccentric music teacher. MacCormick appears rather worryingly thin; while unshaven, grinning and quite possibly inebriated, Wyatt looks like the sort of person you would dread coming to sit next to you on a bus.

Despite some good notices, including one in the *New Musical Express* by MacCormick's brother, Ian MacDonald – "He described us as world class!" says MacCormick – the group split up, with Wyatt beginning to feel the strain of being the leader of a group on the poverty line.

In early 1973, Wyatt had gone with Alfreda Benge to Venice where she was working for a couple of months on the set of Nicolas Roeg's *Don't Look Now* with Julie Christie and Donald Sutherland. Benge had bought her restless partner a keyboard, called a Riviera, from an Italian toy shop to keep him occupied and he had written a number of songs.

A new version of Matching Mole was soon mooted. Henry Cow guitarist Fred Frith was briefly in the frame, but meetings with MacCormick, saxophonist Gary Windo and Francis Monkman, who had previously played keyboards in Curved Air, looked promising. The group played some gigs together as WMWM in 1973.

All seemed set fair for the new Matching Mole, with interest from the newly formed Virgin Records. After a band meeting on June 1, 1973, Wyatt told MacCormick about a party up in Maida Vale at the home of poet and artist June Campbell Cramer aka Lady June.

"He said, 'Are you going to Lady June's party?' And I said no, it was too far to come, and I went home and the rest is history. The unpleasant thing being that I was phoned on Sunday morning – I had forgotten about the party – and was told that Robert had fallen out of a window. Alfie's flat was on the 21st floor, so I thought he was dead. And so I was amazed when I heard that he was in hospital. I thought, 'What did he do – bounce?' Then I had appendicitis in sympathy and was in hospital the following morning."

Wyatt had broken his back and was taken to Stoke Mandeville Hospital. The fall could well have been fatal if he hadn't been so drunk and so had landed on the ground in a relaxed manner.

Wyatt survived but was now a paraplegic, a terribly cruel blow for one of the UK's most gifted and imaginative drummers. The first thing he said to his distraught mother, Honor Wyatt, was apparently: "Don't worry, Mummy, I always was a lazy bastard."

Wyatt and Benge were the recipients of friends' generosity. Pink Floyd and Soft Machine played a benefit concert for Wyatt at the Rainbow in November 1973, and the following year Julie Christie bought them a wheelchair-accessible ground-floor flat in Twickenham. And despite this catastrophic turn of events, Wyatt was about to produce the best music of his career.

CHAPTER 19

Can a Wyatt Man Sing the Blues?: Rock Bottom & Ruth Is Stranger Than Richard

In all the interviews since his accident, Wyatt has acknowledged the physical problems it has caused him, but has kept up a positive, sometimes slightly sardonic line on the subject, concentrating on how it was beneficial to his artistic growth.

"In the early Seventies, I always imagined that I would be a drummer in a group, so the difficulty was finding musicians who were unique and different from each other, but also compatible," Wyatt says now.

"I could do that on specific pieces of music, but it's very difficult to do it for a band with lots of material if it's going to have any longevity. But the problem for me was solved by breaking my back and not being able to be a drummer, and not being able to be in a group any more. Suddenly, with one bound I was free."

By 1973 there had been a number of high-profile rock deaths. Some were messy and drug-related, like Jimi Hendrix; or invited conspiracy theories, like Jim Morrison; or murder mystery intrigue, like Brian Jones. There were the inevitable romanticised notions that they had died for rock'n'roll, or some such. Then there was the cold, hard, unglamorous fact that Stone The Crows guitarist Les Harvey was electrocuted onstage in 1972. Wyatt survived, but he was a young man with a new set of problems to face.

And what's still astonishing is that after such trauma, with *Rock Bottom*, Wyatt came back with one of the most original, groundbreaking albums of the decade.

ROCK BOTTOM
Original label: Virgin
Producer: Nick Mason
Recorded: February–May 1974
Release date: July 26, 1974

"After I had the accident we were stuck for somewhere to stay, and one of the people who helped was Delfina Entrecanales, who had a farm in Wiltshire around a village called Little Bedwyn," says Wyatt. "There were some disused farmers' cottages there. So when the recording van came up it parked in a field behind and put cables through the windows, so it wasn't really soundproofed – a few donkeys and tractors going by are on the tape, but you won't really hear them. I did a few things there. It was a bolthole for me and Alfie to try and sort ourselves out, when I was trying to get used to being paraplegic." The rest of the album was recorded at Virgin's The Manor studio at Shipton-On-Cherwell and CBS Studios in London.

Rock Bottom begins with 'Sea Song', and although one is wary about putting too much emphasis on the influence of Wyatt's recent trip to the lagoons of Venice, the sound is lush and fecund, washed with bright aqueous greens and blues, with the Riviera organ adding a tremulous reedy sound to his piano and voice.

"When I'm working on music there is a kind of visual thing, and I do have a sense of landscape, vaguely, and a choppy chord sequence with a rocky landscape and colours, and so on," says Wyatt. "But on the whole it's self-referential."

The song addresses a sea creature, a kind of anthropomorphised combination of fish, porpoise and whale, a transient playmate, but one the singer finds difficult to relate to in human terms. The lyrics are cryptic, and may well refer to Alfie. They are oddly moving with pictorial imagery a long way from Wyatt's characteristic matter-of-fact observations. His phonetic scat singing on the coda, over a synthesizer refrain, sounds more engaged, more passionate than any such previous excursion.

'A Last Straw' is another song about the sea, with the participants cartwheeling into the water to play, as if in escape, an observation made more poignant by the singer's recently limited physical capabilities. This song felt most closely related to Alfreda Benge's original album cover drawing of children playing by the sea, with Wyatt, here, peering up, sub-aquatically, through the *"seaweed tangles"*.

'Little Red Riding Hood Hit The Road' bursts out with a thrilling explosion of Mongezi Feza's overdubbed trumpet – the "hard, bright, no bullshit tone" that Wyatt loved. He plays flamboyantly on a hand drum, accompanied by a breathy, gasping vocal line, giving the feeling of forward motion and hyperventilation, with backwards tapes flickering past in its wake.

And in what is probably a unique structural device, when Wyatt's long, snaking vocal melody finishes, it's played backwards, and then he sings another verse to the melody of the backwards version. Then, in all the mayhem, Ivor Cutler recites an absurdist poem, with references to Terry Gilliam's animations on *Monty Python's Flying Circus*, about lying in the road along with a hedgehog, trying to trip up passing cars. It's a strange adrenalised ride and fades into a reverbed cloud of trumpets, a sonic corona with a metallic sheen, at the song's close.

Lyrically the song is disturbing. There's a vivid feeling of pain, with Wyatt's vulnerable man-child's voice sounding under duress. It's full of unresolved emotional currents.

Ian MacDonald went on to link *Rock Bottom*'s subject matter with the aftermath of Wyatt's accident when he was in Stoke Mandeville Hospital. In the *New Musical Express* review he wrote: "(Factual note. People with spinal injuries aren't given painkilling drugs for the first couple of days after their accident in order to facilitate the doctors' diagnosis of the seriousness of their complaint.)"

As he continues, in the vernacular of the time, "*Rock Bottom* is a heavy album." Heavy, indeed: no rock musician had ever invited the listener into this sort of world of genuine pain before. Except that none of the above is strictly true. Although recorded after the event, the songs had been written by the ambulant Wyatt in Venice before his accident.

"I thought that was wonderful," says Wyatt on MacDonald's review. "He had found out that the things that he said it was about hadn't been intended at all. But I thought that was perfectly legitimate. You put out half a bridge and the other person builds half a bridge to meet you if they want to, and between you, you've got a thing that means something."

'Alifib' features the refrain, *"Alifie my larder"* and Wyatt delivers edge-of-consciousness phonetics like *"No not nit"*. It also sounds like a lullaby, featuring made-up words like *"wossit"* and *"landerim"* and the appearance of characters like a *"water mole"* named *"Burlybunch"*. Musically the Riviera drifts through the song with Hugh Hopper's impossible, double-speed bass solo trilling away. "It was his idea and it was lovely," says Wyatt.

The song segues into 'Alife', a stranger, darker song based on a rotating four chord sequence with Wyatt's spirited hand drum playing and a sax solo by Gary Windo that starts with semi–coherent spluttering and mixes melody with ugly barks, as Wyatt, in less innocent voice, runs through the lyrics of 'Alifib' once more.

And at the end of the song Alfie – Alfreda Benge – makes an appearance, speaking in a similar child-language, reciting some of Wyatt's lyrics in a mocking way. She calls him a *"soppy old custard"* and informs him that she's not his larder but is, in fact, his *"guarder"*. It's dreamlike, but it still sounds like a child's world under threat.

"Certainly the child thing is accurate," Wyatt agrees. "The disconcerting thing, the myths that end up as fairy tales are adult tales inventing symbolic characters and places to represent the world you live in, which can be a very spooky and scary place where you are trying to find somewhere comfortable, but there are nightmarish possibilities around the corner. Both these things go together – the search for a simple homely feeling and the desperation of avoiding an alienated painful one."

The final song, 'Little Red Robin Hood Hit The Road', finds Wyatt's keyboard and Mike Oldfield's skirling lead guitar blending together. This one is set in the Garden of England but this time the moles are lying dead inside their holes. Laurie Allen's martial drumming gets looser and careers around and as it all fades down, Fred Frith enters playing the sort of viola lines you might hear emanating from a school practice room. Ivor Cutler then reappears for another recitation, still bursting car tyres with his pal the hedgehog and destroying his TV with a phone receiver. He concludes with a laugh like a reaction to a joke that hasn't been told. Or has it? It's hard to say.

Wyatt notes that the album's vivid production, by Pink Floyd drummer Nick Mason, contributes to its success: "He was very good at watching out for the dynamics of things, which is a Floyd skill, how things are placed and where, and both he and Mike Oldfield were very helpful on the record in terms of putting the details into a context."

One of *Rock Bottom*'s strengths is that it feels like the listener is drawn along in a sort of narrative, no matter how cryptic or non-linear it might be. Wyatt gives his view.

"I tend to see things in two bits, that's how nature works, there's a binary thing about life, two parts that are not the same," he says. "I liked it with singles where you had the A-side and the B-side and the relationship between the two always interested me. On an LP you had these two twenty-minute chunks. They have a relationship between each other. I can't say what they are, but it is important to me and is true on *Rock Bottom*."

Wyatt performed the album and more at a concert at the Drury Lane Theatre on September 8, 1974 – his last solo concert appearance to date. Richard Branson managed to convince the reluctant Wyatt that a number of musicians wanted to play live with him, while telling said musicians that Wyatt wanted to play with them.

Two days later he made an appearance on *Top Of The Pops* to promote his single, 'I'm A Believer', a Neil Diamond song that had been a hit for The Monkees, with a backing band including Nick Mason on drums and Fred Frith on violin. Although a fine version of the song, the recording process for the TV programme had been excruciating. Richard Branson had bought a new wheelchair for Wyatt, but this form of transport was not deemed appropriate for a pop singer. Looking back in 1994 Wyatt said: "There was this geezer [producer Robin Nash] there saying, 'Could you sit on something else? Wheelchairs don't look well on a family entertainment show.' I just exploded, the whole atmosphere frightened me. I just thought I was losing control of my life."

Wyatt followed up *Rock Bottom* in 1975 with *Ruth Is Stranger Than Richard*, a darker, but equally haunting set. He revives an old Wilde Flowers number 'Slow Walkin' Talk' as 'Soup Song', a kind of boogie woogie number with its nightmarish lyrics written from the standpoint of one of the ingredients of a soup, hoping that although he will be consumed, he will leave the diner doubled up in pain with a *"tummy ache"*. Gary Windo's saxophone solo sears like acid reflux. The ironically titled 'Team Spirit', based partly on 'Frontera' from Phil Manzanera's 1975 solo album *Diamond Head*, finds the protagonist gaining recognition and acceptance by being kicked around the muddy ground like a football, which, some commentators felt, invited comparisons with Samuel Beckett.

"I thought it was a bit disjointed compared with other things I've been aiming at and indeed it is," says Wyatt of the album. "But in terms of the individual pieces on there... for example the Fred Frith piece with him on piano and me on voice ['Muddy Mouse' and 'Muddy Mouth'] was such a wonderful bit of music and I really enjoyed working out lyrics for it and singing it. I enjoyed George Khan's tenor solo on 'Team Spirit' and Gary's [playing] on the funny boogie woogie bluesy thing ['Soup Song']."

It was to be Wyatt's last solo album of the decade.

CHAPTER 20

Pilgrims' Progress: Caravan

After The Wilde Flowers broke up in 1967, bass guitarist Richard Sinclair and his organist cousin Dave Sinclair formed Caravan in 1968 along with ex-Wilde Flowers guitarist and singer Pye Hastings, and Richard Coughlan on drums. After all the pop, blues and soul cover versions, times had changed and in the spirit of the age, Caravan wanted to explore what they could do, although as Hastings says: "We had no clear direction to follow."

Caravan's early retreat to the country was less the pursuit of some kind of romantic idyll and more a result of poverty. They had rented a house in Whitstable, but when the money ran out the group moved further inland, pitching tents for a while outside the village hall in Graveney and rehearsing, even sleeping in the hall.

Their self-titled debut album *Caravan*, released in 1969, found them playing a mixture of post-psychedelic pop and starting to write longer compositions like 'Where But For Caravan Would I?' Although let down by Tony Cox's rather cavernous production, *Caravan* contains some quality material and 'A Place Of My Own' reputedly became adopted as something of a mod come-down song, a soundtrack to a return to reality as the daylight intensified and the drugs started to wear off.

Hastings was unaware of this usage of his song.

"'A Place Of My Own' was the very first song I wrote and was just a bit of escapism," he says. "It seemed I was endlessly living in bedsits or sleeping on people's floors, and I was fed up with the whole thing."

Caravan got into their stride on *If I Could Do It All Over Again I'd Do It All Over You* (1970). They had been moved to Decca's Deram label – initially a pop label now a progressive subsidiary – on which they benefitted from a clearer, more present production sound, courtesy of manager Terry King, with Sinclair's reedy organ to the fore. We associate that drifting, meandering style of playing with sunshine, space and open landscapes, and Sinclair was closer in feel to Rick Wright's bittersweet Farfisa organ lines on Pink Floyd's 1967 song 'The Scarecrow', which dances across the soundscape as if sketching out some lost Arcadia, than to Mike Ratledge's more aggressive outbursts. Maybe the late Sixties and early Seventies is long enough back in time for this sound and style to have become its own archetype. Or more likely that the sound itself harked back to something more ancestral, like the piper playing his tune across the fields as described in folk song. But there is no doubt that the sound of an electric organ on a reed instrument setting subjected to some form of slight distortion is singularly evocative.

In terms of the Canterbury sound, there were some stylistic links with Soft Machine. Richard Sinclair has stated: "Soft Machine are the main reason why Caravan started. I thought that Kevin Ayers was super on bass – really good melodies, a real step forward."

"I don't think any of us thought we were part of any specific [Canterbury] scene," says Hastings. "We were just two bands amongst many getting on with the job we all loved – playing music."

Both bands, however, were keyboard-led which did create a different focus. When you add the offshoot bands like Matching Mole and Hatfield And The North, who had a similar keyboard dominance, you arguably have a real case for a distinctive movement or sound.

"The distinction for Soft Machine and Caravan came from the employment of jazz structures and chord sequences," says Hastings. "This possibly caused the music to stand out from the rest of the field, and so the title was duly pinned."

Another link between the groups was Pye Hastings' highly pitched man-child voice, which shares a timbral overlap with Robert Wyatt's. In Caravan Hastings shared vocal duties with Richard Sinclair – another candidate for the Voice Of Canterbury. Wyatt, in turn, admits to being influenced by Sinclair: "What a lovely voice, it's so true. He came from a musical background; his dad was a musician. He was younger than us and always used to sing in tune, which I thought was pretty avant-garde at the time, and actually I learned to do the same. A musician that he liked even when he was a teenager was Nat King Cole, who *nobody* listened to in the Sixties. Singers like [Cole] so much because he's so in tune, so accurate."

One of the more remarkable songs on *If I Could Do It Again...* is 'And I Wish I Were Stoned'. Sung by Sinclair and Hastings it's an attractive tune that sounds like it's shaping up to be some kind of post-psychedelic love song, but the chorus gives us a different perspective as Hastings passionately tells us that he wishes he were stoned out of his mind. When drug songs were often wrapped up in code and allusion, this was unusually blatant. A reputable source suggests that the group took acid together and it looks like smoking hash was pretty high up on the band's list of hobbies.

"There is no doubt that dope smoking has produced some catchy songs – albeit fuelled by paranoia and possibly even self-obsession, but let us say that some of Caravan were more enthusiastic dope smokers than others," Hastings reflects. "Of course we all did our bit in trying to keep up the trend of experimenting with dope, thinking it would bring enlightenment and brilliant new ideas for songs, but you can't fight against what your body tells you, particularly if you don't smoke, like me, so I gave up the challenge and quite quickly fell off the Dope Train."

The highlight of *If I Could Do it Again...* is 'Can't Be Long Now/Francoise/For Richard/Warlock'. Starting with a lengthy muted section with Hastings singing somewhat diffidently, it segues into 'Francoise' on which they hit a seesawing, almost Latin keyboard groove. Hastings' sharp, incisive rhythm playing gets more animated as the song progresses, while Sinclair's melodic bass dances around Coughlan's crisp and occasionally flamboyant drumming, with Sinclair's keyboard lines sitting on top. Auxiliary member Jimmy Hastings – Pye's elder brother – is featured more in the spotlight. An accomplished jazz musician who had worked with Humphrey Lyttelton, his sax playing adds an extra dimension to their music and he plays a fine solo here.

This exhilarating track ends with a series of dramatic riffs, and stands as one of progressive rock's early highpoints. Like Soft Machine, Caravan liked to run their material as medleys – maybe "composite compositions" might be a better descriptor. Rather than extending music by jamming, this was a way of simply putting structural and improvisational elements together.

Back then length was impressive. Running times were often not included on the cover, which would prompt young fans to get a paper and pencil and check their wrist watches, viewing it as a particularly good result if the track lasted over ten minutes. That the track generally referred to as 'For Richard', clocked in at over fourteen minutes was viewed as a bonus. It was essentially a way of measuring how far you had travelled from pop convention.

Caravan's tendency to switch to irregular time signatures added an extra frisson to their music. Apart from songs in 3/4, or waltz time, almost all popular music was essentially in a regular metre, from standardised twelve-bar blues to rock'n'roll, ballads and pop songs. Dave Brubeck showed on 'Take Five' (1959) how you could make a tune in 5/8 move along nice and easy, and as such he was a big influence on progressive rock thinking. Keith Emerson took another Brubeck tune from the same year, 'Blue Rondo A La Turk', which was in 9/8 and 4/4, and flattened out the kinks, playing it in four time as 'Rondo' with The Nice and Emerson, Lake & Palmer.

Into the Sixties, people were listening to music from Asia and Eastern Europe, where these sorts of time signature were an intrinsic part of its structure. And while in that decade Indian scales and the hip usage of the sitar expanded the language of rock, the metric complexity of some Indian classical music, which consisted of a number of different rhythmic cycles as part of a work's "super time signature", takes some unravelling and study, and is not easily translatable en masse to rock music. But switching between metres is, and to the listener the playing in ragas gives a feeling of liberation, in which the musicians have a fluid, seemingly telepathic, relationship with each other, which also appealed to free jazzers.

Hastings recalls Brubeck as being an influence on Caravan, but that the band were particularly "blown away" by another jazz musician, American trumpeter Don Ellis. Ellis had played with the likes of Charles Mingus and Eric Dolphy and studied ethnomusicology at UCLA in the early Sixties, which prompted him to form the Hindustani Jazz Sextet in 1964. Ellis, tellingly also a drummer, made irregular time signatures his trademark, and The Don Ellis Orchestra recorded an album *Live In 3²/₃/4 Time* in 1967, a droll way of writing 11/8. Another 1967 album *Electric Bath* was a landmark jazz/rock crossover and includes music inspired by Eastern European rhythms.

"It seemed to open up a whole new way forward," says Hastings. "Of course you only have to listen to Indian music to see where these influences and timings really originated. Still, it was all new to us and so very exciting that we had to get our heads round it somehow."

This sort of relationship between rock and a certain style of jazz was vital to Caravan. But it's not all about counting. When Don Ellis isn't being ostentatious with his odd time signatures, he has the ability to make you forget about the fact that some pieces were in, say, 7/4, because they had strong emphasis on the two and the four, like a rock'n'roll backbeat, and the other three beats can take care of themselves in a little shuffle. This took jazz into new directions, but conversely when this approach was transferred to rock music this gave it a rhythm that might not have swung like jazz exactly, but at least seemed to do so. And having absorbed all that, you could also play, like Caravan, in four time but make it sound more subtle and syncopated.

David Hitchcock was working for Decca in the A&R department and so was the first point of contact between Caravan and the record label, and although he didn't produce *If I Could Do It Again…*, he recalls some of the medleys would be cross faded or spliced together and in one case another novel time signature was introduced by unusual means: "The engineer with his razor blade didn't quite get it right, so in the middle of a whole sequence of 11/8 there's one 10/8 bar."

Hitchcock describes how he came to be a producer for Caravan, Genesis, Camel, Renaissance and Curved Air: "I was going to leave to go to the newly independent RCA and Hugh Mendl [head of A&R] said, 'Why don't you stay here and be a producer?' I said, 'I've never been in the studio and never done any recording,' and he said, 'It doesn't matter, that's what you've got engineers for.' For a certain style of production he's absolutely right, you go in there and say, 'This is what I want to hear,' and the engineer is there to make that real, as a cameraman will for a film director." Hitchcock was for a while the house producer at Decca, going freelance in 1971.

In late 1970 he produced Caravan's album, *In The Land Of Grey And Pink*. Released in 1971 it featured their longest medley, 'Nine Feet Underground', which weighed in at just short of twenty-three minutes.

Many writers and musicians have identified the tendency for the smokers of marijuana to write longer songs that take more time to make their point. It might be coincidental, but 'Nine Feet Underground' fits those criteria. It feels very much like the sort of piece of music where the listener could roll up a big one, get their first hit, drop the needle, then sit back and enjoy the gently rolling post-psychedelic pastoral landscape which takes around twelve minutes to substantially change its mood – by which time they probably wouldn't be particularly bothered about identifying the point of transition between sub sections 'Dance Of The Seven Paper Hankies' and 'Hold Grandad By The Nose'.

On 'Golf Girl' a jaunty trombone and flute accompany Sinclair's tale of meeting a girl on a golf course who is selling cups of tea and a subsequent romantic attraction between the two, as Mellotron figures drift by on the breeze and the band lollop along in a good natured manner. This sunny vibe runs through all of the first side with more references to drinking tea on the title track.

Released in 1972, *Waterloo Lily* had a different mood. Steve Miller formerly of Delivery was on keyboards. He adds a slight sense of jazziness on electric piano, but the title track carries some heavier, rockier riffing. Again the album is produced by David Hitchcock, but this time Sinclair's bass is up in the mix, like a lead instrument. The perennial live favourite, 'The Love In Your Eye/To Catch Me A Brother/Subsultus/ Debouchement/Tilbury Kecks', shifts around through strings, oboes, flutes and trumpets, a nifty Miller electric piano solo and a feisty Hastings wah-wah guitar solo on its twelve-and-a-half-minute course.

The group were less of a commercial success than many would have imagined. In June 1972, Andrew Tyler from *Disc* travelled with them to Digbeth Civic Hall, where they played to a rather disappointing crowd of about 140 people. He wrote: "They open with 'Waterloo Lily' – about a London slag and the things she gets up to. They'll need a few minutes to warm up. They follow with 'Place Of My Own', a not very impressive tune, but the piano break brightens it up.

"They come together nicely on 'Nothing At All'. It roams all over the place hopping in time and space, halting, moving into a gallop and, yes there's melody.

"But what they do lack is charisma – that unfathomable quality that inspires young men to roll up their shirt sleeves and [bring] young ladies into orgasmic relief."

It was beginning to look like Caravan might have failed, both in these metaphorically carnal tasks, and more generally when Sinclair and Miller absconded leaving just Hastings and Richard Coughlan as band members. But they then assembled one of their strongest sets, albeit with a title that is such awful wordplay that it almost mitigated against it being highlighted in this book. That said, both that title and the subject matter of 'The Dog, The Dog, He's At It Again', with Hastings singing the praises of the sexual act, suggested that Tyler might well have been wrong. But enough already, as they say.

FOR GIRLS WHO GROW PLUMP IN THE NIGHT
Original label: Deram
Producer: David Hitchcock
Recorded: Summer 1973
Release date: October 5, 1973

Despite this "mass exodus", Hastings was determined to carry on. He and Coughlan auditioned a number of keyboard players but none were deemed suitable and so Sinclair came back as a session player. John G. Perry was drafted in on bass and Geoffrey Richardson on viola.

Richardson recalls travelling by train with some friends from Winchester Art College down to see Caravan in Southampton in 1970, buying *If I Could Do It All Over Again...* then going to a pub and poring over the sleeve notes, but in the process getting so drunk they missed the band that, unbeknown to him, he was going to join two years later, and finished up staggering back to Southampton station.

"My audition with Caravan was in August 1972 out at Graveney village hall which was on the marshes and a beautiful place," Richardson recalls. "I was thinking, 'Where am I? This is a lovely place to work, this is not a cramped rehearsal room in the East End of London.' And that is where Caravan was born, more or less, where they rehearsed their first album and they all lived in tents in the fields outside. There was an idyllic thing going on."

He recalls that the range of the viola seemed ideally suited for these songs. He once tried playing the violin at a Caravan concert because he always carried the two instruments around, but it didn't work very well. "I remember Richard Coughlan saying, 'What the fuck was that row you were making? Well don't.'"

Considering how well Richardson integrated into the group and his contributions to *For Girls Who Grow Plump In The Night* (Lord, that title!), it's surprising to learn that a number of fans didn't much like the viola either. "I'd get the odd grumble, like, 'Why couldn't Jimmy Hastings be in the band? Why do we have the viola?' People were very grumpy about it at the outset. I'd love to have heard the original group live and I know that my incarnation from 1972 on is different, and I respect people's opinions on that."

Listening to *For Girls Who Grow Plump...* it's evident from their lengthy opening medley, 'Memory Lain, Hugh/Headloss', that there is a new tightness and energy about the group. It starts off with choppy, funky rhythm guitar and Coughlan, in particular, plays tight and fast and rides off on some lavish drum fills. As a composite composition it has more coherence than any of the group's past efforts.

Hastings had effectively taken the reins off the group and taken on the responsibility of being the single vocalist, and where at times in the recent past, his voice had been so light it felt like it would float away completely, he now sang with more authority, in a slightly lower register. The track features Rupert Hine on synthesizer, and a horns and wind section of Jimmy Hastings and other top players like trumpeter Henry Lowther and Tony Coe on clarinet. The orchestral arrangements are by John Bell and Martyn Ford – who had worked with Barclay James Harvest and who also conducts.

"We had a tour lined up so we took the new tracks on the road and ironed out all the bits that didn't work," says Hastings. "We then returned to the studio and recorded the whole thing in a couple of days. This is one of the reasons that I think it works. Add to this, the relentless talent of producer David Hitchcock who constantly suggested that this song or that would go really well with a brass section or even a full orchestra backing. We of course went for it with a vengeance."

Hitchcock was clearly growing into his role as producer: "My deepest relationship was probably with Caravan – where I would start putting ideas across about types of songs and time signatures to use, styles of arrangement," he says. "But I was not there to make the David Hitchcock sound, even if I could think of one. I was there to get a good recording out of the band, to represent them on record as excitingly as possible, and also it was getting interesting in terms of what you could do in the studio."

Richardson remembers the sessions fondly: "It was the first time that I had been in a recording studio. I found myself in Chipping Norton Studios, Mike Vernon's place, in January or February 1973, a residential studio, with Dave Hitchcock and Caravan smoking drugs and drinking and playing music and having a great time."

'C'Thlu Thlu' is full of gnarly blues riffs, and is a droll and creepy account of the monstrous entity from the tales of H. P. Lovecraft relocated into a nocturnal forest scenario where it menaces those who wander in. 'Surprise Surprise', by contrast, is another strong Hastings vocal performance sung to a robust pop tune.

The album ends in grand style with 'L'Auberge Du Sanglier/A Hunting We Shall Go/Pengola/Backwards/A Hunting We Shall Go (Reprise)'. The track includes a theme from Mike Ratledge's 'Backwards' from Soft Machine's *Third*, the orchestral arrangement amplifying its melancholic melody.

"I think ['Backwards'] was Dave's suggestion," says Richardson. "And I thought, 'That's going to be hard to play because that's proper jazz, a melody with strange chords,' but it all works."

'A Hunting We Shall Go' is in 19/8," says Hitchcock. "I'd been listening to Don Ellis's stuff which had a piece in 25. Dave Sinclair came up with the idea of incorporating 'Backwards' as the middle section before going back to the 19/8 riff. That track had strings, horn and a brass section."

"It's a very important record in many ways, absolutely pivotal," says Richardson. "It was Pye reinventing Caravan. And I think it was a transition for Caravan because we had Martyn Ford's orchestral arrangements, which we hadn't done before and then *Caravan And The New Symphonia*, the next record, was live with the orchestra. It was a very important record and it had good tunes on it too."

Caravan And The New Symphonia was again arranged by Martyn Ford, who had become used to the group's musical language, and it's an experiment that works well. Caravan made three further albums in the Seventies, *Cunning Stunts* (1975), *Blind Dog At St Dunstans* (1976) and *Better By Far* (1977), all creditable releases, but they felt more like a consolidation of a style and with a little less of the exploratory spirit that their work had shown earlier in the decade.

CHAPTER 21

Counting out Time: Egg

In 1968 four pupils of the City Of London School formed a group, Uriel. They comprised Steve Hillage on guitar, Mont Campbell on bass and vocals, drummer Clive Brooks and keyboard player Dave Stewart.

"When we first got together we were only interested in replicating what we knew at the time, which was blues, Hendrix, Cream and those bands that to us were composed of gods," says Campbell.

The group recorded a demo in 1968, paid for by Campbell's parents, which included a rock version of Gustav Holst's *Saturn*. Uriel secured a residency at The Ryde Castle Hotel on the Isle Of Wight that summer, playing on their own during the week and supporting bigger bands at weekends.

In their set they played predominantly cover versions – including 'Flower King Of Flies' and 'Daddy, Where Do I Come From?' by The Nice – but when they played at the Middle Earth club, DJ Jeff Dexter advised them that they needed to write their own material. Campbell did write some tunes for Uriel and the group loosely modelled themselves on a cross between The Nice and Soft Machine.

Middle Earth had moved to the Roundhouse, and Paul Waldman and Dave Howson who ran the club – and who Uriel were surprised to find out were quite straight-laced – made overtures towards managing them, but instead, now known as Egg, they signed with Decca in mid-1969, to record for their progressive subsidiary Deram.

They were also offered a one-off deal by Zackariya Enterprises to make a kind of post-psychedelic improvised album, but as they were under contract to Deram they briefly reformed as Uriel, recording *Arzachel* in one session and releasing it in June 1969, with all the group members going under assumed names.

Campbell's songwriting expanded in scope and he wrote a number of pieces for Egg's self-titled debut album, released in 1970. "I had one eye on the music and one eye on the admiration," he says. "But I was too musically over-educated to be a rock musician."

As a music student Campbell had been tutored in French horn and piano, and one of the pieces that exemplified what could be an uneasy relationship between rock and classical music was a composition that took up all of side two called 'Symphony No.2'. It's an engaging piece, like The Nice in places, mirroring their tendency to stick in a classical theme when it might well have been better left out – like the rather pat quote from Grieg's *In The Hall Of The Mountain King* in the first movement.

The third movement was replaced by the electronic piece 'Blane', because it used a direct quote from 'The Augurs Of Spring', the first rhythmically animated section of Stravinsky's *The Rite Of Spring*, and both band and record label were confused as to whether or not it was still under copyright. But what about the title, 'Symphony No.2'? Was it ironic or was it serious?

"It was very, very pretentious," Campbell admits.

Was he seeking approval from the classical establishment or presenting his music as a form of defiance?

"Both things are seeking approval," Campbell replies. "But in my emotionally immature state I couldn't distinguish between what I could do and what other people could do, and I thought that because I was doing it, it was probably as good, but in a different way, perhaps. I lacked discrimination.

"I never knew if what I was doing was any good, because there was never any feedback," he elaborates. "No one said, 'That's a really good song, Mont', so I was in freefall, I thought, 'Maybe this is no good; maybe I should do something more impressive or more sophisticated.' I didn't lack ability. I lacked self-knowledge; I lacked self-confidence."

All that said, Campbell did write some top-quality material, often generously credited to 'Campbell, Stewart, Brooks'. An early piece like 'While Growing My Hair' was a wry commentary, delivered in his warm baritone, on the disjunct between the fusty establishment and the new hairier youth who were all striving to be one of *"the few"*. It's a sobering thought that Campbell and Stewart were still 19 when the album was released; and Brooks only 20.

Another song, 'I Will Be Absorbed', deals with the mercurial nature of the creative process itself. Keyboard player Dave Stewart notes: "Mont drew inspiration from mainstream classical music. This gave him a harmonic sensibility that few rock writers of the time possessed.

"The lilting 9/4 rhythm of the verse supports a pleasant slightly jazz chord sequence, but it's the chorus that really catches the ear – a beautiful uplifting series of open voiced major seventh and minor seventh chords, played in a syncopated 7/4 rhythm. For the instrumental section

Mont wrote a dramatic 13/8 progression based on a chordal riff. Though these chords are simple triads, they change very quickly and some are played over a bass note in a different key. This was totally new to me and when Mont played it to me on piano it took a while to get my head around it."

The Polite Force, released on Deram in 1972, is a mature-sounding record, starting off with the droll and evocative 'A Visit To Newport Hospital', about Uriel's residence at the Ryde Castle Hotel, with a lyric about trying to avoid both skinheads and the police.

"They weren't Isle Of Wight skinheads, they came down in droves from the East End of London," Campbell explains. "That was their holiday destination. We were dope-smoking barefooted long-haired layabouts and we were an object of suspicion to the law. Steve Hillage and I were in a tent – we had pitched it late at night – and we were woken up by a policeman looking in and saying, 'Excuse me, you are on the Shanklin crazy golf course, could you please move your tent?'"

Stewart says: "I think it's important to stress the influence of the psychedelic movement: Uriel & Egg were very keen on making a mindblowing racket, hence tracks like 'Blane' and 'Boilk', which divide opinion even today. That approach came totally naturally to us, and was an important parallel to the complex note-based compositions."

As a title, 'Blane' came from Campbell practising yoga in a chemically enhanced state and making the observation that the blood had run into his brain, but only managing to utter "blane", much to the amusement of those present.

The 'Blane' that appears as the substituted third movement of 'Symphony No.2' acts as a wedge driven into the piece and was a mix of processed keyboards and electronics including the sounds of the audio tone generator – an oscillator-based instrument with a knob control that changed frequencies and allowed a choice of waveforms. Originating in school physics laboratories, a version could be built at home with a moderate amount of technical skill. Dik Mik was another early exponent, playing one in Hawkwind.

"Boilk", taken from a comic strip in *The Beano* is, like "Pow" or "Bam", an onomatopoeia, albeit a rather surprising choice to represent the sound of a sinking ship. 'Boilk' first turned up on *Egg* as a minute or so of Mellotron and cut-up tapes. But the 'Boilk (incl Bach: *Durch Adams Fall Ist Ganz Verdebt)*' on *The Polite Force* weighs in at over nine minutes. It's more of a constructed collage, a mixture of *musique concrète* elements, including recordings of running water, backwards tapes, chimes, speeded-up percussive noises, creaky Mellotron and a fuzz organ solo, which ultimately softens in tone, bringing it all to a more ecclesiastical conclusion. Stewart has said: "It's thought of by some as the bummer track on an otherwise great prog album."

'Long Piece Number Three' – renamed from 'Symphony No.3' – took up the whole of side two and was a quite mind-boggling procession of different time signatures, played with the group's typical precision. Did Campbell think that this kind of metric complexity was in itself progressive?

"Well, I suppose I was quite happy to be labelled progressive and for me that was what progressive would have meant," he replies. "In my mind I was thinking that I was a fuck of a lot more progressive than any of these other imitation people who were posturing rather than writing music. That's not a valid point at all and I'm not justifying myself, but that is what I was thinking."

American composer Aaron Copland had been played *The Polite Force* by a friend and Campbell was horrified to find out his assessment of the music: "[He said] We were 'counting freaks'. It took me years to get over being told that! 'How can he say that? What's so different between what he's doing and what we are doing?' He was right – that's what we were."

But out of this interest in metres came a single, 'Seven Is A Jolly Good Time', in 1971. Basically a kind of Young Persons Guide To Time Signatures, it's a very witty piece, complex but also something of a sing-along. It could have been a hit single... Couldn't it?

"It was never going to be a hit," Campbell avers. "It could have been a very good song, it's similar to the Thunderclap Newman [single, 'Something In The Air'], but it was too badly recorded for one thing. We had Pat Bowland, our A&R man from Decca, overseeing the session and I don't know how he got that job. He got us into Decca, which was great, and we made a couple of records, but as a producer he didn't know his arse from his elbow. Having said that, the B-side 'You Are All Princes' is one of our best tracks ever."

There were stories, perhaps apocryphal, of signs put up at Egg gigs saying, "NO DANCING".

"I don't remember," says Campbell, clearly amused. "It was probably a joke. No one danced at Egg concerts, they just sat there in their greatcoats."

Does he have any thoughts as to why the Egg audience, and that of progressive rock in general, was so sedentary, so male?

"It was a sort of boffins' area," he replies. "I think some women were interested, but because being in a band was very much one of male display, the women might not have liked the music or they may have loved it, but they just went with the flow of that kind of phenomenon."

Egg split in 1972 and so Campbell resumed his musical studies. "I'd already decided not to be in rock music," he says. "I wanted to be a bit more part of ordinary society. And I had an idea of developing my French horn playing. I found out that I was not cut out to be an orchestral musician. I just wasn't a very good performer and I was more interested sitting in an orchestra listening to what everyone else was doing than concentrating on what I was supposed to be doing."

But the group had left a lot of their favourite material unrecorded and so reformed to make *The Civil Surface* for the Virgin subsidiary label Caroline in 1974.

"I think with the three main pieces on *Civil Surface*, 'Wring Out The Ground, Loosely Now', 'Germ Patrol' and 'Enneagram', I was trying to make proper compositions, not just things joined end to end. I tried to learn from what Aaron Copland said."

'Enneagram' is a complex piece with overlapping metres on which, for example, Campbell runs a section in 11/8 with one in 4/4, keeping them going until they get back in synch. Apart from its complexity, over its nine-minute length it also gained a cumulative rock clout.

"Yeah, it's a pacey piece, we played it very fast and tight," Campbell says. "We played it a lot, and we were pretty slick, but it's just a lot of stuff going on fast. To many people I think it would not have had a whole lot of meaning.

"Some things have an emotional punch – I'm thinking of delta blues or some of the West African kora and ngoni music and singing. They are not just playing in order to play impressive licks, they are playing something that is very heartfelt and even the fast and furious Bulgarian music, which suffers from virtuosic overrun, comes from a genuine expression of something – it has emotional power. But I think our music suffered from a lack of emotional content."

Stewart has a different view on 'Enneagram': "Live, it was a showstopper, its powerful attacking passages contrasting with the quiet, almost child-like sub-theme and the floaty 'pool' section. Heavily written but with improvisational sections that made it different every night, this was Egg's most original piece."

There are also a number of Stravinsky influences in Egg, particularly the combination of driving rhythms and internal complexity exemplified by the first movement, 'Danse', of the Russian composer's *Four Etudes For Orchestra* (1928). "I was very consciously referring to that when I wrote 'Nearch'," says Campbell. The piece features Lindsay Cooper from

Henry Cow on bassoon and is a far more convincing cross-pollination of rock and classical music than casually quoting Grieg.

"That's why I thought Stravinsky was so good because he was closest to the gutsy feel of a rock band, if you think of *The Rite Of Spring* and 'The Dance Of The Adolescents', a lot of the music would not have been a million miles from what we were trying to do."

So given that Egg and Uriel were all basically Londoners, does Campbell mind that they are viewed as being a part of the Canterbury Scene?

"We were very influenced by Soft Machine, so that pulled us into that gravitational orbit, if you like. Steve Hillage had a Canterbury connection [as he went to university there], so we went there quite a lot to see him and to do gigs there and hang out with the students in their days of protest. So I don't see anything wrong with being lumped in with that lot. Also we were quite self-consciously English.

"Egg was an anomalous band," he continues. "It was not rock music as it should be. Rock music is meant to supply a musical service or product to a grateful, or anticipating public. But we had no public, really, and the people that became our public, our one hundred devoted fans, did so out of some kind of perverse kind of desire to try to understand what we were doing, and bless them for it."

CHAPTER 22

All Roads Lead to Homerton: Hatfield And The North and National Health

Hatfield And The North was first mooted as a potential group name by keyboard player Mike Patto, who had seen the legend on road signs on the M1 leading out of London. This piqued the interest of his drummer friend Pip Pyle, and Hatfield And The North formed in 1972. Initially they comprised Richard Sinclair on bass guitar and vocals, and Dave Sinclair on keyboards – both ex of Caravan – Pyle, and his friend since childhood, guitarist Phil Miller, who had played in the recently disbanded Matching Mole.

Pyle had played in Delivery with Miller and his keyboardist brother Steve, and with Carol Grimes on vocals. The young group backed American blues artists like Otis Spann and B. B. King as a pick-up band when they toured the UK, but they had more wide-ranging ambitions.

Delivery split in 1971 after which Pyle joined Gong, having been introduced to Daevid Allen by Robert Wyatt. Pyle went off to France to "learn about the joys and horrors of communal living and further my investigations into the effects of strong mind–altering drugs on music". He played on *Camembert Electrique*, but like most Gong drummers his tenure was short lived.

Dave Sinclair had also played briefly with Matching Mole and only played a few gigs with Hatfield – one with Robert Wyatt guesting on vocals – and found the music rather too loose and unpredictable. He left in early 1973.

Alan Gowen was seriously considered as his replacement. A prodigiously talented musician and composer, he had formed Gilgamesh, who had released a self-titled album in 1972. Gowen remained closely allied to this axis of musicians and wrote a double quartet piece that the two groups played together on two occasions in November 1973. But in his audition he was passed over due to his lack of gear – an upright Hohner piano which, according to Pyle "unfortunately sounded awful". Dave Stewart, ex of Egg, also auditioned, and with his ability on electric piano, organ and synthesizer – and audio tone generator – he got the job. Richard Sinclair recalls the effect of him joining.

"It was clear that we had the makings of a good band and Dave brought both structure and detail to our often uncontrolled mayhem, and was keen to work on arranging our material as well as bringing in some great compositions of his own."

The group started off playing arrangements of Miller's Matching Mole compositions, like 'Lything And Gracing', 'Part Of the Dance' and 'Nan True's Hole', but soon amassed a repertoire of new material that they recorded in late 1973 and into the New Year, for their debut album *Hatfield And The North*. For fans of the likes of Soft Machine and Caravan, Hatfield And The North ticked all the boxes. In Sinclair they had an exceptional vocalist who seemed to flourish after leaving Caravan – where he had shared vocal duties with Pye Hastings – by being the only singer in the group. As a bass guitarist his playing was always poised and richly melodic, even when slaloming through some tricky rapids. Pyle was a dextrous and imaginative drummer and although as a rhythm section they didn't exactly swing in the strict jazz sense, with their ability to play around the "one", they rather implied swing.

Miller was an avid student of the guitar and had a particularly enquiring mind about how harmony and melody work, and how chords can be voiced. Again he played with a jazz feel, but one expressed within an individual language that avoided cliché, and he could deliver a blistering rock lead guitar solo when required.

More so than Egg and Caravan, even Soft Machine, as a unit Hatfield And The North had a rare melodic and rhythmic fluidity, giving even their more complex compositions an exhilarating joie de vivre.

Richard Sinclair: "There were some similarities for me between Caravan and Hatfield in that at the beginning we were just friends, getting together with an equal interest in writing and living together. However, it soon became clear that with Hatfield there were more possibilities, which is what I wanted from the music at the time. Hatfield required four times the effort and was four times the fun. I wanted to be in a touring band with the people I was living with, which was made possible when Dave Stewart joined."

The group's debut album also demonstrates their schoolboyish sense of humour, no more so than on 'Big Jobs (Poo Poo Extract)'. On that short track and on its companion piece 'Big Jobs No.2 (By Poo And The Wee Wees)', Sinclair demonstrates a debt to Robert Wyatt's observational approach to lyrics, his meta-commentary, as does Pip Pyle who wrote a significant amount of the lyrics. By way of introducing the album he sings, that the musicians will try to make the album *"sound nice"* and that, whatever, it should be *"a laugh"*. Later on, after the high drama of Pyle's relentless riff-based instrumental composition 'Shaving Is Boring' — in syncopated 6/8 — dies down, we shift into 'Licks For The Ladies', on which Sinclair sings that it's time to sing *"a sober song"* after all the clamour that has preceded it. It's full of everyday stuff, with the obligatory references to drinking tea.

Sinclair's wordless singing of the melody line — as on Miller's 'Aigrette' — and his improvised vocal "bubbling", with a mouth-produced wah-wah effect, both owe a debt to Wyatt. He acknowledges his friend's influence from Sixties Canterbury.

"Robert appeared and sung me a whole Charlie Parker solo, and just hearing the human voice sing the melody like that was completely liberating."

Wyatt sings as a guest on Miller's composition, 'Calyx', wordlessly duetting with Sinclair. "Because it's only got nine chords to it and it has a definite tonal centre, you know where it's going to progress, where it's leading to each time it comes around," says Miller. "That's quite nice if you're jamming on chords as it's got its own resolution points. It's a simple piece and there isn't a lot to learn, but you can do so much with it."

The Stravinsky influence that was prevalent in Egg is present on some of the staccato melodies of Stewart's 'Son Of "There's No Place Like Homerton"', with sax punctuations by Geoff Leigh who had just left Henry Cow. But it's particularly apparent later on in a theme in four time with contrapuntal lines and a strong emphasis on the first beat of the bar — again like parts of *The Rite Of Spring* and the 'Danse' movement of *Four Etudes For Orchestra*. It comes as no surprise, then, to find out that the rather austere melody in question was a fragment composed by Mont Campbell. But this track also had its feminine side, literally, in the shape of the vocal trio, Barbara Gaskin, Ann Rosenthal and Amanda Parsons under the name The Northettes. In the middle of the piece they sing a song section in gorgeous three-part harmony along with Leigh's flute.

The first Hatfield And The North album stands as a dazzling, melodic collection with some pretty serious playing in places, and even the daft humour contributing to a sense of bonhomie. It was, however, transcended by their second effort.

THE ROTTERS' CLUB

Original label: Virgin
Producer: Hatfield And The North
Recorded: January 1975
Release date: March 1975
Chart position: 43 (UK)

The Rotters' Club represents the apex of the whole Canterbury approach and of a particular strand of progressive rock that avoided bombast and was musically rich, with inspired ensemble playing, tunes of pop-song potency and good vibes aplenty.

The group had released a single, 'Let's Eat Real Soon', in 1974 in which writers Sinclair and Pyle present a paean to food, the singer declaring himself *"vitamin enriched"* and *"absolutely wholesome"*.

Made from similar ingredients, 'Share It' opens *The Rotters' Club* in breezy and melodic fashion. It's another Sinclair/Pyle composition and this time deals with generosity. And however one wants to analyse it, one of the most striking aspects to *The Rotters' Club* is that it exudes a sort of sonic glow and always feels like a fresh sunny day in June.

The album was recorded and produced by the group at Saturn Studios, Worthing. "The studio was pretty cheap and cheerful," says Miller. "We had been rehearsing pretty religiously. 'Underdub' was fairly new, but Dave was such a whizzo at it all, he never played a wrong note on it once he knew it – I never really heard him stumble over the changes, ever. Dave is a natural musician. He's a hell of an organ player – not many people had that choice of sounds and that facility. In the old days Dave was always fiddling with his Hiwatt amp, knob twiddling to get more middle, all the time tailoring sound, all the various textures and voices."

Both 'Lounging There Trying' and 'Underdub' are concise Miller pieces – rather like 'Aigrette' from the first album but with remarkable serpentine melodies that barely repeat, but which have such presence that they are the sort of pieces that you'll find yourself whistling, then wondering how you managed to remember them.

"I always sang my tunes in those days," Miller explains. "I'd just put the chords down and sing to it and tried to play what I was singing, [although] I might elaborate and change it around thereafter.

"I suppose I was trying to get into playing over bebop changes and of course you can only understand it if you've got a melody that works with it – that's the way of proving how these set of chords can work. You can make the chords just work on the voice leading at the top of [each] chord, but that will spell out some very, very basic melody.

"We were all living together in those days and Richard Sinclair was a great ally. He's got a fantastic ear and is a very good guitarist, and his idea was you've got to sing what you're playing in order for it to really mean something."

'Underdub' has Stewart on electric piano and Jimmy Hastings from Caravan on flute doubling the "singing" line, with Stewart on electric piano.

"There was no better flute player in England at the time than Jimmy Hastings," says Miller. "He was another person with perfect pitch. You gave him a part [and he would start playing it] as he was going over to his music stand."

Just as Stewart would explore noise with his 'Blane' excursions, so Sinclair would do the occasional wah-wah fuzz bass freakout, as on 'Shaving Is Boring', and he gives a slightly more restrained version on 'Chaos At The Greasy Spoon'.

'The Yes/No Interlude' borrows its name from a popular Fifties and Sixties TV quiz show, Take Your Pick, during which section the host Michael Miles would ask the contestants questions and they would have to avoid saying either "yes" or "no". If they did they would be gonged off. It's a dynamic composition with an organ theme and a riff-based middle section punctuated by Hastings' sax stabs and Miller stepping on his Big Muff fuzz pedal and letting rip in grand style.

In one section the angular riffing drops out, creating a sudden lightening in mood with Stewart playing a deliciously phrased electric piano section, and Pyle scurrying around the kit.

"Dave's a very good orchestrator," says Miller. "He's able to make these dramatic scene changes and make them work. It sounds natural as well – when he wanted something to change, a new sonic scenery is set. Dave's always got an idea and he's got it now, rather than leaving people to their own devices and trusting they will get it together. I think that happened a bit with Richard – it could be rather inhibiting."

This is followed by another Pyle composition, 'Fitter Stoke Has A Bath'.

Again it's based on a memorable melody, vocal this time, that doesn't repeat until a simple three-chord refrain after a couple of minutes, then Sinclair does his vocal bubbling sound to emphasise Pyle's assertion that he is drowning in the bathroom, while The Northettes coo wordlessly like a mentholated breeze. It brings to mind the lengthy lines on Robert Wyatt's Soft Machine composition, 'Moon In June', and another connection is that both songs address Pam Howard. Wyatt sang to her from his bolthole in New York State on the original 1968 demo of that song, and by the time of 'Fitter Stoke Has A Bath', she was the partner of Pyle, who had become the stepfather to Wyatt's son Samuel. Pyle's lyrics are a self-deprecating look at his apparently *"groovy"* life, with a nod towards his domestic set-up with Pamela *"looking elegant"* while she is *"writing prose."* The side ends with Sinclair's 'It Didn't Matter Anyway', one of his loveliest creations, a couple of bittersweet verses, and a simple, melancholic shrug of the shoulders as he walks away, leaving Hastings' flute and Stewart's synth weaving around each other.

Side two begins with 'Underdub' and then leads into Stewart's four-part composition, 'Mumps', which takes up the rest of the side. The first part is titled 'Your Majesty Is Like a Cream Donut (Quiet)'. It comes from a *Monty Python* sketch, a parody of Oscar Wilde's witty aphorisms, in which Wilde, James McNeill Whistler and George Bernard Shaw accuse each other of insulting the (non-specific) king, with some ludicrous similes. Wilde comes out with "Your majesty is like a big jam donut with cream on the top", then accuses Whistler of having come up with it.

Whistler awkwardly responds: "What I meant is that like a donut, your arrival gives us pleasure and your departure only makes us hungrier for more."

With so few TV channels, *Monty Python* was hugely influential. "Musicians loved *Monty Python*," says *New Musical Express* journalist Nick Kent. "If you hung around with Led Zeppelin, Robert Plant and his roadie were always doing *Monty Python* routines, in any given situation. And I think this must have been true with most groups, whether it was the dead parrot skit or whatever. You would hear this over and over and over and over again."

"Pip and I, especially, loved *Monty Python*, and Dave, although I'm not sure he had a television in those days," says Miller. Which might explain the slight mis-titling. Presumably there was a desire to counterbalance their cerebral musicianship with humour?

"I find that less successful, the humour in Hatfield," says Miller. "I must admit I think Frank Zappa did that much better. The humour was often in the clever writing, in the notes."

'Your Majesty Is Like A Cream Donut (Quiet)' seems an odd choice of title for such an unassuming yet gorgeous little piece, with no drums and led by Stewart's electric piano, with The Northettes contributing wordless vocal harmonies.

This leads into 'Lumps', which begins with a turbulent ensemble introduction and runs through a series of episodes, some with The

Northettes adding the sweetest of textures, and Sinclair sings a passage about letters with a number of endearingly daft puns about treading *"upon a B... "* and *"...upon the C"*. 'Your Majesty Is Like A Cream Donut (Loud)', this time featuring the whole band and with smooth fuzztone organ and guitar playing the melody in unison, ends the album with a glorious sonic sunset.

One criticism that could be levelled at the group's recorded output is that it lacked the power they could generate live, and Pyle is not always well served by the light drum sound of *The Rotters' Club*.

"The albums sound pretty and have a fairly controlled atmosphere. The gigs, though were something else," says Stewart. "There was a lot of improvisation – we would play the head of the tune a couple of times and then launch into a blow based on the bass line – which might be in some elusive metre like 9/8 or 13/8. Being of tender years and rather headstrong we often played too fast, too loud and too much, especially me, but out of it came some moments of staggering musical bravado where you think, 'Blimey did we really play that?'"

Like Soft Machine and Caravan, Hatfield favoured medleys of numbers in concert. But rather than them accreting into compositions, their medleys might find them reordering their albums and hopping from section to section in a seamless flow.

There was also a certain amount of japery onstage with the group suddenly veering into 'The Laughing Policeman' or some other old chestnut, or a 'Blane'-type electronics piece with scat singing. On one live recording that has emerged since the group split Stewart plays Campbell's fragment from 'Son Of "There's No Place Like Homerton"'. And each time around Pyle smashes a plate. He might also destroy garden gnomes. No one could ever accuse them of being precious.

What does Miller think of *The Rotters' Club* now?

"As a whole it really does hold up," he replies. "I do like it and when we had done it, it was a good effort. It's a shame we couldn't have gone on and done some more."

But although Sinclair had initially been enamoured of the group set-up, that perennial problem, lack of money, came into play. Hatfield And The North were on the hip Virgin Records, but as with many groups, the honeymoon period was soon over, as there was little money coming in, and they broke up in the summer of 1975. Miller delivers a post-mortem: "I think we were about to [break into something bigger], but with personal reasons and some musical reasons – quite a bit to do with music – it came to the natural end of its existence. But I [wish] we'd had the ability to pull it together and say, 'Come on, look, let's have six months away and each do some different things, but let's keep the goodwill that we built up with Virgin and the public.' Because there was a fair bit of that.

"We played mostly in England and Holland – a couple of gigs in Germany, in France maybe ten a year. The next year we had a decent date sheet that was beginning to fill out. But you fall out with people eventually. Things were not right in the band. It was just about our personalities inter-reacting. Richard had his own idea of what he wanted to do and I think he was getting frustrated with his input into Hatfield, and realised that he wasn't going to get as much of a say as he would like, therefore it would probably be a good idea if he had his own band. Which was fair enough. And there wasn't enough money in it to support his family. I didn't have a family so was much more free and easy."

In Jonathan Coe's novel *The Rotters' Club*, published in 2001, in a scene set in 1977, the character Richard tries to get his friend Doug to come and see National Health, saying they are a "new band: sort of hippy intellectual stuff. Most of them used to be in an outfit called Hatfield and the North."

National Health might have been essentially like Hatfield And The North with a new bass player, but initially it was a bit more complicated than that. The group formed in 1975 at the instigation of Dave Stewart – who was, to all intents and purposes, the group leader now – and featured Gilgamesh's Alan Gowen on keyboards, Phil Miller and Phil Lee (also from Gilgamesh) on guitars, Mont Campbell on bass, vocalist Amanda Parsons and Bill Bruford on drums. After King Crimson disbanded in late 1974, Bruford was looking for work.

"It was not so easy, I had to read parts. Right there is the selling point for me, an opportunity to learn," says Bruford. "I'm going to enjoy getting my teeth into that. Don't care who's in the audience, don't care if I'm getting paid a lot of money or not, but if there's some purpose musically for my being there, that will be the governing factor."

That line-up recorded some demos including Campbell's 'Zabaglione'. Miller recalls that after a tour in February 1976 the group did an audition for Island Records. "They said the girl singer's got to go – they thought it was unnecessary for some reason – and you've got to get rid of one of the guitarists. Then they start telling you what to play."

The group recorded a Peel session in February 1976, playing Campbell's compositions 'Paracelsus' and 'Agrippa' plus a Stewart composition, 'Excerpt From Lethargy Shuffle And Mind-Your-Backs Tango'. Then Campbell, now something of an enigmatic figure, mysteriously went back into the wings. He was drawn toward the teachings of Armenian philosopher and mystic George Gurdjieff and also the Subud movement.

"The Subud movement is about direct experience through active surrender, so it's like meditation, but it's kind of dynamic meditation," he explains.

"I found National Health too incompatible with my spiritual aspirations. I thought, 'This is deadendsville.' I had thought at first, 'Oh this will be good' – Dave asked me if I wanted to join and we never lost contact. I think we admired each other without realising why. So I produced some music, which I was very happy with and which had integrity. But then after going nowhere at a very slow pace for a year I thought that I could be doing something better with my life, more satisfying – which I didn't do, but I thought I could."

Miller was impressed by Phil Lee's ability to sight-read complicated charts, but recognised that he was more of a spontaneous jazz player and this new music was more composed. He left and Steve Hillage came in to help out.

Bruford played live with the group on a February tour but by March 1976, as nothing seemed to be happening, he had left to tour with Genesis. He did, however, play on a couple of Peel sessions that year, with Hillage stepping in for Phil Lee. And Bruford went away having learned something important.

"They had wanted it to be written music, they wanted it to be instrumental and they wanted it to be rock music. And that was a blueprint for my band, Bruford," he says.

National Health recorded their debut album in 1978, with a core line-up of Stewart, Miller, the returning Pyle and bass guitarist Neil Murray, with Alan Gowen on keyboards, Jimmy Hastings on flute and clarinets, Amanda Parsons on vocals and John Mitchell on percussion.

The opening 'Tenemos Roads' – over fourteen minutes in length – has some of the Hatfield spirit about it, although it's more expansive. There is a lengthy opening section in 3/4 with crunchy organ chords and Amanda Parsons featured as lead singer as compared to her backing-vocalist role with The Northettes. Stewart is the single author of the two-part 'Borogoves' and co-composed 'Elephants' with Gowen, which is also over fourteen minutes long and quite dauntingly complex. Gowen was the sole composer of 'Brujo', a more melodically open piece, starting with a sublime mosaic of keyboards, guitar, flute and vocals. "His writing was more in a jazz sense, less pernickety, but just as intricate [as Stewart's]," says Miller. "'Brujo' was a very nice piece. It was very sophisticated harmonically, National Health. Dave was a wizard with chords, as was Alan."

Miller had no writing credits on the album and was basically playing parts, and while he notes that "playing the part as written sometimes is the best way", he wanted to stretch himself more.

"They were very prolific writers," he says. " Every day there's a new part put in front of you, but there isn't a need for you to write more, which can be a bit suffocating. It makes you technically proficient, [but] it doesn't broaden your ear out."

Of Queues And Cures appeared in the record racks in December 1978 on the Charly label with no advance publicity. Amanda Parsons had become uncomfortable singing with the group's volume, so the line-up was whittled down to a four-piece. Murray left, stylistically branching out to become a member of Whitesnake, and was replaced by John Greaves, formerly of Henry Cow. The album was recorded at Ridge Farm in Dorking, engineered by Benj Lefevre who had worked with Led Zeppelin and The Rolling Stones. The result was less austere, more muscular and approachable.

National Health had been on tour with Steve Hillage that year, during which they showed that, like Hatfield And The North, they were far more powerful live. "When you go out and play to a rock audience, whether you like it or not you are influenced," Miller notes. "But I like all that, I come from the blues and that had its heavier moments. If you'd played it in Ronnie Scott's you'd play it with more nuance."

When National Health came to record, the only piece that hadn't been fully played in was Greaves's composition 'Squarer For Maud'. On record this includes a recitation by Peter Blegvad who had been with Greaves in Henry Cow and Slapp Happy. Georgina Born, also ex of Henry Cow, plays cello on a number of tracks, with Jimmy Hastings and other wind players also guesting.

Writing credits were shared around, with Miller contributing 'Dreams Wide Awake', which features a spectacular organ solo from Stewart, and Pyle chipping in with 'Binoculars' – sung by Greaves – which he wrote about his children watching violent television programmes. 'The Collapso', another Stewart composition, has a Caribbean-flavoured tune, with Selwyn Baptiste playing steel pans. Miller's guitar themes sound like George Martin's 'Theme One', and Stravinsky wasn't left out of the party either, with a quote for his 1945 pseudo-jazz piece, the *Ebony Concerto*. Stewart's expansive 'The Bryden Two-Step (For Amphibians)' opens and closes the album.

The group fell apart in strange fashion the following year. Greaves had also made an album, *Kew. Rhone.* with Blegvad in 1977. It's a song cycle of the most cerebral kind, expanding on the duo's work in Slapp Happy and featuring vocals from Lisa Herman. It felt a bit like a musical equivalent of a cryptic crossword that one keeps picking at and never solving.

National Health were supposed to be playing it in Italy, with some dates booked, but Stewart was not keen on the idea, and less so on the band attempting to outvote him, so he left and joined forces with Bill Bruford in the group Bruford. National Health continued to play live, with Gowen returning, until the keyboard player's untimely death in 1981.

CHAPTER 23

The 'What I Was Doing was Too Simple for Them and What They Were Doing Was Too Complicated for Me' Blues: Kevin Ayers and Soft Machine Post-Wyatt

After leaving Soft Machine, Kevin Ayers enjoyed a fabulously erratic solo career throughout the Seventies, producing a body of work that was so stylistically diverse that as a solo artist he had as wide a musical remit as The Beatles' *White Album* from 1968.

On his 1969 debut album *Joy Of A Toy* he was joined by avant-garde classical composer David Bedford on keyboards and arrangements, whose input was crucial in making the album one of the high water marks of the British post-psychedelic milieu. His piano playing ranges from pellucid on the balmy, dreamy 'Girl On A Swing' to splintered and dissonant at the conclusion of 'Oleh Oleh Bandu Bandong', while his exquisite wind and string arrangements, with Paul Minns of Third Ear Band on oboe and Paul Buckmaster on cello, illuminate 'Eleanor's Cake (Which Ate Her)' and 'Town Feeling'. "I approached it from a classical point of view, using the themes that the voice was singing as part of the texture and voicing the chords very classically in the strings," Bedford says.

Ayers was instructed by Harvest to form a band and take the songs on the road. "Kevin said, 'Right, join the band,'" says Bedford. "So that's how I ended up joining a rock band. Remember, Schoenberg said there is still a lot of music to be written in the key of C major when he was at his most revolutionary. I'd got used to playing in the key of E major because that was Kevin's favourite key."

Ayers called the band The Whole World, and their 1970 release, *Shooting At The Moon*, is a particularly exploratory album with whimsical songs alongside a tape collage of chopped-up group playing and classical recordings, and also a couple of rather uncertain sounding excursions into free improvisation. "Yes, there were a few of those and we used to do a few of them live too, but they would always lead to something," says Ayers. "It would go back to a song or it would be a break. It was just something you threw in – another colour."

Their performances could be inspired, or shambolic, as when they supported Pink Floyd at Hyde Park in 1971, which has since been released on CD. "Well, the Hyde Park concert is absolutely atrocious. We're all out of tune," Bedford says. "But for some reason, it was a wonderful, sunny day and it didn't matter."

The Whole World even played the mantric exercise in repetition that Ayers wrote for Soft Machine, 'We Did It Again', with Lol Coxhill reciting his 'Murder In The Air' playlet and the track ending up as an dissonant mash-up. It seemed that The Whole World could either be brilliant or total chaos.

"That's exactly right," Ayers assents. "A lot of it was chaos and very often too much wine was consumed – not just by myself. But there were some blissfully inspired moments, some of which I think have been recorded. Certainly there were times when I finished a gig, when I thought: 'Wow, that was so good. It's not going to get much better than that in terms of inspired lunacy and people picking up on each other.'

"[The Whole World] had moments of great self-indulgence and in Soft Machine, too. It wasn't so much free improvisation as noise – playing around with noise. But there was some structure to it. Upon listening back to it about once every ten years, with a wry smile I think: 'How did we get away with that?'"

Ayers' 1971 solo album, *Whatevershebringswesing*, starts with the orchestral 'There is Loving/Among Us/There Is Loving', which encompasses big brass themes and the odd frisson of scribbling, atonal strings. It then goes to 'Margaret', a subtle love song with wah-wah guitar, then onto 'Oh My', a sort of Noel Coward pastiche, and the side ends with the churning, ugly tape loop rhythms of 'Song From The Bottom Of A Well'. Ayers plays a shrieking guitar solo that earned comparisons with Lou Reed's excursion on The Velvet Underground's 'I Heard Her Call My Name'.

"I hadn't even heard that then," says Ayers. "It was just a spur of the moment sound. I turned a Vox AC50 [amp] up to distortion point and just whacked away. The only person I acknowledge using some stuff from is Hendrix; some of his rhythmic link-ups."

A BBC 1 *In Concert* recorded in 1972 shows the group in their element, with an orchestra and songs occasionally breaking out into a heavy-handed skank. Ayers had lived in Jamaica and other Caribbean islands, and was a fan of the music.

"Everything from calypso back to ska and the origins of reggae," he confirms. "But I usually use it in a quite tongue-in-cheek way because I know I'm a white man trying to sing black music, which rarely comes off. I loved it, but I wouldn't even try to pretend I'm good at it."

Ayers recorded *Bananamour* (1973) for Harvest, and *The Confessions Of Doctor Dream* (1974) and *Sweet Deceiver* (1975) for Island, returning to Harvest for *Yes We Have No Mañanas (So Get Your Mañanas Today)* in 1976. With his almost unfeasibly good looks and ability to write melodic songs, he was groomed for being a pop star, but as his material became more straightforward it also lost some of what made it great in the first place. There were rumours in the press that his sojourns to foreign climes made him unavailable for work and effectively avoiding success.

"It isn't fair because it's not true," he asserts. "What I used to do was when nothing was happening I'd say, 'I'm not going to hang around, I'm going to go sit in the sun and write some more songs.' Blackhill Enterprises, always used to say, 'He's never around to work,' and it's absolute bullshit. I was always prepared to go out and work, it's just that there were long gaps of doing nothing.

"I was very involved in enjoying my youth. And in between working, I never liked hanging around the rock'n'roll scene, going to the right parties and talking to the right people. Also, I suppose I've always been a reluctant star. I found people's adulation somewhat embarrassing and disproportionate to what one is doing."

But he was certainly seen as a bon viveur, even appearing in *NME* in a consumers' guide to wine. Geoffrey Richardson of Caravan, who would go on to play on *The Confessions Of Doctor Dream*, recalls the first time he encountered Ayers in 1974 when the group were on their way up to play in Manchester.

"We were in our Volkswagen bus driving up Cricklewood High Street going up to the M1. We pulled up and Pye [Hastings] looked down at a taxi that had pulled up alongside and said, 'Christ, it's Kevin!' We opened the window and he wound the window down and there was Kevin with an acoustic guitar, a very attractive woman and a bottle of champagne in the back of a black cab. I said, 'Where are you going?' He said, 'The Friars, Aylesbury, old boy.' He was going all the way to Aylesbury in a black cab. That was completely bonkers. I thought he was really exotic, I have to say."

By way of contrast, Soft Machine took quite a different tack after Wyatt left. On *Fifth* (1972) they drafted in Australian drummer Phil Howard who played in a dense, free jazz style. He left after the first sessions, which comprise side one of the album, and was replaced by

John Marshall who had played in Ian Carr's jazz rock group, Nucleus, with Roy Babbington – also of Nucleus – guesting on double bass. This time out Elton Dean was the sole brass player. Stylistically the music was close to that of *Fourth*, Wyatt's last appearance with the group.

A major change came on *Six* with the arrival of Karl Jenkins, also from Nucleus. As well as playing keyboards and saxophones, he also played oboe, which was an unusual instrument to use in a jazz rock context. More importantly, he brought a more melodic and structured approach to the music.

The first disc of the two-LP set was recorded live in 1972. It featured a version of Mike Ratledge's 'All White' from *Fifth* and a number of short punchy tracks. But the studio side was quite different in feel, with Jenkins' 'The Soft Weed Factor' moving in a poised and regal manner with a repetitive, near-minimalist treatment of the melodic elements. Ratledge's 'Chloe And The Pirates' also steers away from the freer jazz elements of the previous two albums, with Jenkins' oboe to the fore, and it fades out in a haze of gently oscillating tape loops, with flickering backwards keyboards, again evoking Terry Riley. The most striking piece is Hugh Hopper's '1983' with its ominous main theme played on low piano notes, with cymbal splashes overlain by more tape loops. After contributing this composition, Hopper left the group to be replaced on a permanent basis by Babbington. *Seven* (1973) was a consolidation with more of Jenkins' concise and memorable tunes and riffs epitomised by the speedy, convoluted 'Nettle Bed', with Ratledge playing a rippling synth solo.

By 1975's *Bundles*, Ratledge's influence had shrunk to two compositions, and the complexion of the group changed with the arrival and brief sojourn of guitarist Allan Holdsworth, who had recently played with Jon Hiseman in Tempest. In 1975 *Melody Maker* journalist Karl Dallas introduced them as "an exciting new band just making the rounds, which is receiving well deserved attention for its tight ensemble playing and creative soloing", as they were, by now, completely unlike the original Soft Machine.

John Marshall underlined this difference by saying, about the history of the group: "Originally it started off, I don't know if it was a rock band but there was no jazz in it and there didn't seem to be much rock either. It was what was known as progressive, which always made me laugh because if ever there was a misnomer, that was it."

Regarding Jenkins, Dallas neatly summed up his role in this most recent incarnation of the group with: "Though currently he doesn't play more than one solo in the set, plus a sort of interlude on grand piano when the sound permits, Karl Jenkins is an essential piece of the five-piece interlocking jigsaw that is Soft Machine."

Holdsworth mentioned to Dallas that the group asked him to play the violin and compose for the instrument, "but I get nervous about it". Ratledge meanwhile told the journalist, regarding future plans: "If I knew what we'd be doing in two years' time, we'd be doing it now." Not much as it turned out: both he and Holdsworth left after *Bundles* was released.

In 1976, the new Soft Machine line-up of Jenkins, Babbington, Marshall, saxophonist Alan Wakeman and guitarist John Etheridge, who had played in Darryl Way's Wolf and who joined the group on Holdsworth's recommendation, were reviewed favourably, if somewhat drolly, by *New Musical Express*'s Barry Miles when he saw them at the Hammersmith Palais in that summer. He wrote: "It is so hard to write about a group who have no vocalist and who don't announce titles. Things happen on stage though: John Etheridge stomping off across the stage stretching his lead as far as it would go. It's dramatic stuff. The Softs play at speeds that have to be measured in mach numbers. John Marshall must be one of the fastest drummers in Britain and Etheridge is just ridiculous, throwing out leads and catching them dozens of beats later, just when you thought he was never going to tie them all in. It's a real juggling act."

Softs, which featured this line-up, had just been released, the album epitomised by Jenkins' composition 'The Tale Of Taliesin' which has a typically big formal main theme which then cuts into a high-speed middle section with Etheridge doing just as Miles described, before they revisit the initial theme. Soft Machine recorded the poorly received *The Land Of Cockayne* in 1981, by which time the group was essentially Jenkins and Marshall augmented by session players, including Holdsworth on guitar – but still no violin.

CHAPTER 24

Divertimento No.2: Notes on Fashion and Youth Tribalism

In the Sixties, the prevailing design aesthetic of consumer items, from lampshades to crockery to soft furnishings to clothes, had shifted from the old and traditional to the modern, and this was further embraced into the Seventies. The trademark design of the decade was bolder, more colourful, and confident in its newness.

The thirty-somethings and middle-aged, who may have been intimidated by goings-on in the Sixties, began to keep up with the times: hair touched collars; sideboards became longer on those who were keen to be seen to be "with it", in the vernacular of the time; pink shirts and floral ties became accepted wear for work; there were even the short-lived matching shirt and tie sets, with the tie made out of the same material as the shirt.

Shirts were becoming fitted and pleated, losing the lengthy tails of their more voluminous antecedents, with the option of button-down collars curving out and away from the body of the shirt to accommodate a big knot tie. Kids would spend time fashioning a thin, bedraggled school tie into as big a knot as possible, tied loosely with only a few inches of the wide front part of the tie visible, the other twelve inches or so surreptitiously tucked into the shirt. Just as they do today.

While such styles became mainstream, in the Seventies everything in youth fashion became yet further exaggerated, both vertically and horizontally − wide lapels, long collars, hugely flared trousers, Oxford bags, platform shoes − as fashion carried on in a symbiotic relationship with the outrageously dressed stars of early Seventies glam pop and rock. There was also a distinct feminisation of men's fashion.

For example, some photos of Carl Palmer from the Seventies show him wearing what looked like a woman's coat. But then it was cool for men to look a bit "fem".

This reflected and fed into many young mens' attitudes towards women. While they were not practising a hippie-ish variant of courtly love exactly, it found them subtly influenced by feminism, and unconsciously setting sail towards the concept of the New Man, which became established in the Eighties. Looking macho felt old fashioned and a bit ridiculous. Similarly, peers who told women what to wear or tried to control them in other ways were thought of as jerks, relics of a bygone age.

Richard Ball shares his teenage voyage through the fashions of the Seventies.

"I can't decide what it was that attracted me to my Afghan coat; the look of it or the smell. But one day I popped into Chelsea Freak (one of the trendier Norwich shops) and there was a rack full of them and their unique scent even managed to overcome that of the incense that was burning. I tried one on and decided that I looked cool in it. Plus, it complemented the other gear that I was wearing; loon pants and an orange t-shirt covered in stars, and clogs. But maybe the coat would be a step too far.

"I'd recently taken the leap from wearing clothes that my parents had bought for me to being able to buy my own with my pocket money and my meagre earnings from collecting glasses in a local pub at the weekends. The loon pants were the first items in my hippie wardrobe, and I'd started with a pair of purple ones. I liked the look of them with their huge flares and complete absence of pockets or belt loops. Plus, as a teenager I was almost terminally thin and the low hip style worked well on a skinny frame.

"I had a black pair that I wore for school and kept the more exotic coloured pairs for socialising. As far as tops were concerned, these were mostly brightly coloured and styled, and my most extravagant one was my red flared-sleeve, scoopneck t-shirt, that I wore without a trace of self-consciousness.

"My father was in the armed forces and very straight-laced. But somehow, despite his strict approach to parenthood, he never gave me a hard time about the clothes that I wore, even though I was getting to look more and more like the long-haired freaks whom he would deride incessantly as we watched Top Of The Pops, so it was with trepidation that I walked into the house in the Afghan.

"The response from my father was nil. I don't believe he even commented on it. Analysing it now, I think he'd given up on me by that time. The long hair, love-beads, aviator shades, bedroom choked with incense and freaky music playing had probably put me down as a lost cause, and this was just one more step on the road to perdition."

Another Norwich emporium that was a magnet for the curious youth was Head In The Clouds, which is, at the time of writing, amazingly still trading and boasting the title of "Britain's Oldest Headshop".

In the Seventies, the range of stock was severely limited compared to today's items. The window display consisted of chillums, metal hash pipes, king size Rizla papers and other smoking paraphernalia, and once inside there were trails of incense smoke wafting up towards the blue ceiling with its painted clouds, while the walls carried a rather crudely wrought landscape showing a Cruxifixion scene on a green hill.

Their other wares included a box of second-hand records and racks of cheap Indian clothing, jewellery, bells and various items of hand percussion, and bamboo flutes for twenty pence. As a gauche teenager, it was a hip and slightly intimidating place to hang about in and just pretend you were a freak for a half hour.

Then, most teenagers were simply waiting for hair to continue its slow creep over ears and collar without parental intervention. And once it did, then style often became a thing of the past. Compare actors in contemporary TV and film dramatisations of the Seventies with vintage footage of teens and twenty-something longhairs, and the modern interpretation often looks too styled, for what was most hip was a sort of non-style, just letting your hair do its own thing for as long as possible, and with only some cursory and reluctant trimming by either sex.

But there were a few exeception. Feather cuts were initially associated with "skin birds" – girls and women who hung around with skinheads – but they soon became more mainstream. The male skinhead's hair typically stopped at a number three cut, rather than going right down to the wood, but still looked dramatically different from the prevailing trends. They favoured a combination of tailored Ben Sherman shirts, straight, Sta-Prest trousers, sometimes with a tonic effect, and Dr. Martens bovver boots.

Suedeheads were a less well-defined sub-species, but they were more conventionally smarter, their hair slightly longer, and favoured Crombie coats, parallels and loafers. In the 21st century both haircuts would look like standard issue, but then, in amongst the prevailing trends of longer hair, they looked provocative.

The feather cut was also adopted by some men, most spectacularly in the platinum blond barnet of guitarist Mick Ronson, who played with David Bowie from 1970–73. Bowie himself sported the dyed orange Ziggy mullet cut. To see a youth sporting such a hairstyle, particularly in the village of Brundall near Norwich, was both a shock and a talking point.

But some Seventies youths went that step further to emulate their heroes. Kevin Derbyshire was one. He tells the story:

"The year: 1972. The place: Norwich. The day: a grey Wednesday. The time: 8.15 a.m. The scene: Bryan Derbyshire is feverishly administering Falcon hairspray to a comb-over he has recently created on the head of his son.

"Was this a bizarre Seventies middle-class ritual, like cheese fondue parties or wearing floor-length sweaters? No, this particular librarian was attempting to camouflage the action of his errant son, who had shaved a rectangular chunk out of the front of his hair in order to emulate Peter Gabriel of Genesis.

"Why I had done it is the subject of some speculation, even by me. I was very keen on Genesis and Peter Gabriel in particular for a short spell, but I had other 'fave raves' who lasted longer, Led Zeppelin, Pink Floyd and – most avidly of all – David Bowie. Come to think of it, given what subsequently happened in response to this fairly mild fashion faux pas, it would have been difficult to have turned up at school with an orange Bowie coiffure and wearing a knitted hot-pant suit.

"Why was I keen on Genesis? Well, I was an immature, excitable – we didn't have 'ADHD' in the Seventies – and narcissistic 14-year-old with no inclination to work hard in order to 'get on'. Convinced I was precious by my doting post-war parents, and written off as a deadbeat by my grammar school teachers, I had acquired an alarming egotistical streak combined with a chronic lack of confidence. It hadn't escaped me that Peter Gabriel was eliciting adulation, not to mention making a good living, from spouting nonsense, confusing adults and wearing silly clothes: all attributes I had in my skill set. Overlooking the musical talent and, no doubt, relentless hard work that had got Mr G. to where he was, I probably felt this was a career I could aspire to.

"After leaving home my first action, of course, had been to un-comb the comb-over. Combined with the slight headwind from my cycling, the Falcon hairspray had actually reinforced the hairstyle by the time I reached the school gates. Loping into the classroom with a carefully rehearsed nonchalance, I enjoyed my fifteen minutes of fame – the titters, the whispered insults all being translated in my mind into awe and reverence.

"Mr Howard was a disciplinarian with little tolerance for the indulged generation who had not experienced military action, National Service or even rationing. Lean and thin-faced, his slick black hair was subject to a short-back-and-sides for which, in the early Seventies, he would have needed to seek out an old-school barber that catered to the requirements of the old, the ex-military and the ex-convict.

"He wore his black teacher's gown with a swagger missing from the less committed members of staff. He would swing round with a flourish to confront any hint of dissent in the ranks, grabbing the sides of the gown, bestowing him with a fleeting resemblance to Peter Cushing in one of the Hammer horror movies popular at the time.

"When I entered his maths class, I caught him by surprise, but he ignored my hair, and lack thereof, for the whole lesson. When he finally drew me aside after the class, he meekly enquired whether it was the result of an accident. With a level *of pride, I made it plain that it was entirely deliberate, although I stopped short of wasting on him an explanation of the ethos of Peter Gabriel and Genesis.*

"Mr Howard's swagger and flourish visibly returned, accentuated by anger that he had been duped into feeling uncharacteristically compassionate. Having mentally scoured the rulebook, which he almost certainly knew off by heart and had possibly had a hand in writing, his anger only increased when he realised that the crime of 'unconventional shaving of parts of the head' had been omitted. With a swirl of his black cape, he vanished, but not before thundering, 'Well, shave your upper lip before you start shaving your head!'"

The moment that glam rock first broke is the subject of some conjecture, but for argument's sake let's say it was with T. Rex's performance of 'Hot Love' on *Top Of The Pops* in the early spring of 1971, with Marc Bolan clad in satin, his cheeks speckled with glitter. That was the world of pop, but some of the progressive rock musicians found that adopting the flasher, brasher style of dress that had come with the advent of glam reflected the increasing ambition and scale of their musical presentation.

From Yes, Rick Wakeman and Chris Squire were kitted out like the models in a fashion show who wear the more outré creations that demonstrate the designers' vision and cause the controversy, but those that no one would ever be expected to actually buy or wear: Squire in his frock coats and above-the-knee, cream suede pirate boots, or fur boots which gave the impression that he was metamorphosing into a yeti; Wakeman swanning around in his glitter cape and silver jumpsuit.

"It was a strange period of time because we weren't pop stars," says Wakeman. "Pop stars were those who went on *Top Of The Pops*... I was going to say, 'dressed in silly clothes...'"

It was essentially showbiz and even some of the group's fans agreed that it looked a little tacky. More reflective of the tastes in clothes of the young progressive rock fan were groups like Pink Floyd, who, fashion-wise, had abandoned the psychedelic dandy look even before Syd Barrett left the group in 1968 and now wore the "what you see is what you get" jeans and t-shirt combo. This was the sort of "honest" look that showed you were serious, and not in thrall to the dictates of fickle fashion, although in Floyd's case, any sartorial shortcomings were more than compensated for by lavish light shows, onstage projections, flashpods, exploding model aircraft, a monstrous inflatable pig and, ultimately, a giant wall.

This group's nondescript dress sense was informed by the hippies; a kind of "natural" look. And it put one in a tribal grouping. Musician and

Seventies music fan Ben Waters was one teenager who adopted this kind of 'anti-style'. He recalls the era:

"'Our' bands were *Edgar Broughton Band, Groundhogs, Stackwaddy, Skid Row, early Jethro Tull, early Hawkwind – nothing too arty farty or posey. We hated ELP, Genesis and all that art school crap. We thought Deep Purple and Led Zeppelin had sold out. We inherited freedom and self-expression from the hippies, but it was kind of an antidote to 'peace and love, man', flowers and bells. We wanted something more rebellious. We wanted more of a riot, get involved and change things rather than just smile and give someone a flower.*

"We might wear tie-dye t-shirts, but they were just the simple three-button granddad shirts – we didn't go in for frilly shirts and kaftans, just simple clothes.

"The greatcoat was very useful. It had big pockets to stash all your stuff, you could button it up to the neck if it was cold. You could sit on it, you could even sleep in it. It felt that not only did you have a coat, you had a blanket, a mat and a storage place all in one.

"At school the teachers tried to stop me wearing it, so my mum went to the school and said it's a perfectly good coat, it's not offensive, it keeps him warm, I'm not buying him another coat. At that time we had one teacher who was quite an authoritarian guy who would wear a pink jacket with big black buttons on it the size of old pennies, flap pockets, a paisley tie, fawn trousers, orange socks and a frilly yellow shirt. I was in the cloakroom putting on my greatcoat ready to go home and he came in dressed like this. He looked at me sneerily and said, 'Waters, you look ridiculous.'"

For artist and writer Edwin Pouncey, the greatcoat was also an object of desire.

"Being a devoted fan of The Nice in the late Sixties I was heartbroken when I read in the weekly music press that they had decided to call it a day. Keyboards player Keith Emerson had joined forces with King Crimson bass player Greg Lake and Atomic Rooster drummer Carl Palmer to become the ultimate prog rock super group Emerson, Lake & Palmer. While part of me mourned the loss of The Nice, the thought of one day witnessing ELP (as they later became universally known) sent a thrill of excitement through me. I didn't have long to wait.

"As part of their grand opening UK tour ELP were to play at Leeds Town Hall on October 1, 1970, with support from The Farm and Wishbone Ash. I was determined to be there to see these rock gods in action, but what to wear for the occasion? I couldn't possibly turn up wearing the suit I wore for work, and such trendy fashions as tank tops and loon pants (as advertised in the back pages of Disc & Music Echo*) were beyond my means. But perhaps the other prog rockers' staple – a greatcoat? I selected a dark navy one from the Army and Navy store – cheap, well made, a near perfect fit and it would hide my severely uncool*

suit. As I needed a new winter coat this seemed to be the ideal solution. The one worry, however, was if my parents would approve of my purchase.

"In an attempt to remedy this problem I drew a picture of said greatcoat in the sketchbook that I always carried with me and chanted a prayer of acceptance, convincing myself that if I gave the coat talismanic powers my parents would be dazzled into letting me keep it. Whether this amateur bit of magick worked or not I could never tell, but on seeing it they actually congratulated me on making a wise choice. 'That will last you years, lad,' my father said to me warmly – and did I detect a tremor of regimental pride in his voice as he helped me on with this sturdy blanket of a garment? Maybe not.

"Whatever, I went to see ELP properly kitted out, and they were as fantastic and thrilling as I had hoped they would be – sweating it out in the front row wrapped in my new military greatcoat that was almost as heavy as the music being played."

Into the mid-Seventies, one classification of the situation was that we had "the hips" and "the smooths". There was a certain degree of overlap – the two factions hardly went at each other with bike chains – but you generally knew which side you were on. The smooths were into disco, wore high-waisted bags, patterned big-collar shirts, smart shoes and had long, but styled hair. Some smooths even went to Wigan Casino and danced to Northern Soul, an alien world that few of the hips knew anything about. As far as the hips were concerned, the smooths seemed too happy to lap up what they had been offered by mainstream music.

The hips modelled themselves on having more anti-establishment leanings, although as both existed within a middle-class milieu, these differences were rather theoretical. The hips had all grown up listening to soul music, especially Tamla Motown, but just as so many musicians got fed up with playing soul and R&B and wanted to make their own music, so to the hips, disco and the airbrushed soul of groups like The Stylistics didn't really cut it. The line had to be drawn somewhere.

Those of a hippieish persuasion wished to distance themselves from the music of the smooths, which seemed, at least to a certain breed of teenager, a bit fake, too bound up with the lineage of naff pop music. The hips, meanwhile, sought a kind of apartness or otherness in their music. The idea was to be different from all that chart stuff.

And if there might be any doubt whose side you were on, you could always dabble in a bit of posing. "Poseur" was a favourite Seventies word for anyone adopting an ostentatious stance in order to get attention. If you were a teenager, then what better device to use than the LP sleeve that could be recognised at thirty paces? Of course one could have put it in an inconspicuous plain carrier bag, but where was the fun in that? If you carried it around in a transparent plastic sleeve, that was OK, but it made you look slightly needy. The best compromise was the transparent record shop bag. Subway Records in Basingstoke, where I moved to from Norwich, recognised the potency of this kind of self-identification by producing a transparent bag, with a discreet red trim and the Subway logo, so that onlookers realised that you had hung out at one of the few hip places in Basingstoke, and you had just happened to "score" an album when you were there.

But then you also had to carefully choose the LP sleeve to be displayed in the bag. Something like *Tubular Bells* or *Dark Side Of The Moon* only numbered you as a consumer. If you wanted to be seen as a bit of a Head or freak, then maybe Gong's *You* or King Crimson's *Red* should be on display. Those who were keen to cultivate the mad, bad and dangerous-to-know poetic image – at least until they became a trainee quantity surveyor – might offer something like Roy Harper's *Lifemask*. Those brandishing Syd Barrett's *The Madcap Laughs* might be bracketed in a similar way. Using these criteria, anyone showing off The Velvet Underground's *White Light/White Heat* needed to be given a wide berth until they had been positively vetted.

The idea amongst young males, who were those most readily wearing their heart on their sleeve in this manner, was that this was also some kind of – possibly completely misguided – mating display. Surely wandering around with a copy of Van Der Graaf Generator's *Pawn Hearts* in a transparent bag would attract the perfect partner eventually?

I recall walking back from school one afternoon holding a copy of Edgar Froese's *Aqua*. It had a cool sleeve and at least it wasn't Tangerine Dream's *Phaedra*, which – yawn – everyone had. But then the album wasn't actually very good. Two girls were walking behind me on the way home and I recall some conspiratorial chat taking place. One came up beside me and said: "Can I borrow that Edgar Froese album?" I assented and rather awkwardly handed it over to her.

They dropped back behind me, giggling. It was hard to tell if they were either laughing with glee at having borrowed such a hip album from such a handsome, cool dude, or laughing at the fact that anyone could be such a doofus as to be carrying around an Edgar Froese album, thinking that it might impress a girl. I received it back a few days later with a cursory, disinterested "thanks". I was none the wiser. At least she hadn't scratched it.

Just as the American youth, mentioned back in Chapter 1, took to rock'n'roll while probably living as conservative a life as their parents, so, essentially did the teenage hips. By the Seventies, things had moved on culturally, but in the haven of your bedroom, bedecked with posters of characters from *Lord Of The Rings*, and the free posters of Yes, ELP and Genesis that came in the middle pages of the weekly music paper, *Sounds* – all viewed with an orange light bulb, while listening to some cool sounds – one was staking out a small corner of a different world. You could always be a weekend hippie, looning around when the chance presented itself, as opposed to those who genuinely pursued alternative lifestyles. And this, perhaps, was the cultural heartland of the progressive rock fan.

And just as Seventies youth liked to differentiate themselves in these sub-genres, there was also the psychologically complex need to demonstrate your individuality to your parents.

Teenage Seventies progressive rock fan David Trevor-Jones offers these views: *"My mum listened to classical music, but my dad didn't listen to music at all except Welsh male voice choirs and military bands. My mum used to go upstairs and listen to Mozart and think I was just trying to impress her and assert that what I was listening to was just as valid, just as important. And you were always going to proselytise, especially at that age because what you are listening to and what you are getting off on is important, and you want to spread the word.*

"My parents dismissed the music that my sister and I were listening to as incomprehensible pop stuff. So what we were looking for was an acknowledgement of validity – it's not rubbish."

And yet there was also a place for another musical subdivision along the lines of sibling rivalry.

"My sister went from The Osmonds into disco soul," Trevor-Jones continues. *"I found Barry White unlistenable, while she felt the same about Genesis. We were on different musical planets."*

Elain Harwood was a teenage King Crimson fan in what was a male-dominated world. She writes: *"There was an exciting boyishness to it, lyrics and all, a whiff of rancid clubs, black leather and, to a 17-year-old, sex. It meant I could talk about music to the most anoraky boys in school, or rather in the dank darkness of its nearby pub on a Friday night – especially those limp-haired youths desperately trying to form their own bands – though it left my girl friends bemused.*

"King Crimson introduced me to the Mellotron, Robert Fripp, Bill Bruford, Jamie Muir et al, to Dylan Thomas and Tom Phillips. It certainly didn't lead to sex. Instead it was my first venture into becoming one of the boys, and from that I've never looked back."

Being weird and different was also like an eye-catching mating plumage, an alternative to alpha maledom – at least in theory – although that was, again, by no means guaranteed to work in attracting a mate. For a young male progressive rock fan, and generalising wildly here of course, your object of desire would most likely be a Seventies "hippie chick" with a similarly unkempt mass of hair, generous flares, or a flowing dress, perhaps Indian, maybe clogs and a cheesecloth top, like a dreamy updating of a painting by Burne-Jones or Waterhouse.

Your average young male who fancied himself as a bit of a freak was likely to have thought it cool to wear scruffy clothes. Some of these anti-fashionistas took things to extremes, figuring that the more band names you wrote on your desert boots in ball pen and the more patches on an item, the clearer it became that you didn't kow-tow to mainstream tastes. Trousers were embroidered, ripped, painted on and defaced, sometimes even with the inclusion of unusable zips sewn into a trouser leg.

In this respect there was a far greater overlap than is usually acknowledged between the fashion of a certain species of youth in the early to mid-Seventies and those who embraced the DIY ethos of punk later in the decade. Some were no doubt one and the same.

CHAPTER 25

Surrey Super Novas: A Brief History of Gracious

Gracious were one of the quintessential progressive rock groups of the early Seventies, but ironically they are also one of the least well known, as they only enjoyed a couple of years in the spotlight, recording two albums, *Gracious!* (1970) and *This Is… Gracious!!* (1972).

Gracious formed in 1967 out of a Weybridge-based school group called Satan's Disciples. The original line-up was Mark Laird on bass guitar, Alan Cowderoy on guitar, Martin Kitcat on keyboards and Paul 'Sandy' Davis on drums. Robert Lipson, formerly of Rush Release, then joined on drums allowing Davis to concentrate on vocals. Gracious played songs written by Davis and Kitcat, which were in a similar vein to The Beatles and The Moody Blues. In 1968 the group landed a support slot on tour with The Who.

Under the auspices of veteran producer and film soundtrack writer Norrie Paramor, Gracious recorded a session engineered by his associate Tim Rice. Two tracks from the session were issued as a single on Polydor in 1969, 'Beautiful', backed with 'Oh What A Lovely Rain'.

Gracious began to take a more progressive direction. While this had the effect of alienating them from Paramor, Brian Shepherd of the nascent independent label, Vertigo, signed them up in 1969 after seeing them play live. With the group's move into more demanding music, bass player Mark Laird left and was replaced by Tim Wheatley, who had been serving as the group's driver and roadie.

As well as releasing the two albums, Gracious played at the Isle Of Wight Festival in 1970. They undoubtedly possessed the quality to have had a longer career, but succumbed to a number of factors, most notably the struggling rock band's most pernicious foe, lack of money.

I met Cowderoy, Lipson and Wheatley at Lipson's Camden home on a pleasant June afternoon. It was a particularly entertaining interview, and I decided that the best way to preserve the atmosphere of the reminiscences and the banter was to let them tell their own story.

Mike Barnes: You mention that you played in Germany in 1968 as Gracious when you were still teenagers. What was that experience like?

Tim Wheatley: That was when the band went pro and everyone gave up their jobs. I was actually the road manager at that time. Most British bands did the air force bases, but we did the clubs. We had three two-week books, one at the Star Club in Hamburg, one at the Starpalast in Kiel up on the Baltic. We ended up in Munich at the PM Hithouse. We called it the Shithouse. There was also a one-off show at Geesthacht on the way from Kiel to Munich.

Robert Lipson: At the Star Club the woman behind the bar was a hooker and we were like little kids.

Alan Cowderoy: When we arrived the owner of the club was watching porn projected onto the curtains and it was some sort of weird old black-and-white film, with everybody moving all across the frame like a Laurel & Hardy film, with someone twirling his moustache and wanking at the same time.

We arrived on Christmas Eve and he said, 'Who are you?' We said, 'You've booked us.' He said, 'No I haven't.' He didn't really want us there. Initially we were supporting Freddy "Fingers" Lee, who had a glass eye. His piece de resistance was doing a somersault and ending up on his head playing the piano, and his glass eye dropped out and they were kicking it around the stage.

RL: We started at six at night. It was an hour on and an hour off, and it ended at midnight. We couldn't just play our forty-five-minute set and so we started to hone our skills – *lots* of blues.

We went to a place in Kiel and the guy there had a fixation about 'In The Midnight Hour'. Did he have a gun – or is that my imagination?

TW: Yes he had lots of guns. He had bullet holes in the windscreen of his car.

RL: He said, 'When I pull my gun out you play "Midnight Hour".' We said, 'Sorry, we play our own material.' He said, 'You don't understand' and took this gun out, and we were in. God almighty! It was a fantastic learning curve. I don't regret a minute of it.

TW: The choice of accommodation: you either slept in the cellar with the boiler and it was boiling hot, or you slept upstairs and it was freezing cold. We were there over New Year and it was so cold, it was just ridiculous.

RL: Then we came back and started playing our three-minute pop stuff and chronologically we got a recording deal with Norrie.

Up until recently, Norrie Paramor had had more number one hits than anyone else ever: Helen Shapiro, Cliff, The Shadows. That whole roster: you look it up, it's un-fucking-believable. This was an absolute darling of a man. Tim Rice worked for him and he signed us up. We recorded two or three of our songs with Tim producing.

Later we sat him down and played him some much more "underground" music, longer pieces and he said, 'Listen guys, I can't do anything for you. It's not in my area, but be well and I'd be happy to help you wherever I can, and we'll keep the publishing.'

MB: I'm interested in what seemed a fairly rapid expansion of styles. Talking of the newer "underground" piece you played Paramor, you had a track 'Opus 31: A Choral Symphony'.

RL: It's not pretentious in any way!

TW: In early '69, I replaced Mark Laird who was the bass player and the first thing I did was 'Opus 31'. That was the start of the evolution from pop to prog. Bits of it were still very poppy, but it brought in different influences.

MB: I located a letter to *Top Pops* magazine from your manager David A Booth dated September 9, 1969: 'I spent a very pleasant afternoon one day last week listening to a group called "GRACIOUS" perform a new symphony called 'Opus 31'. The work lasts fifty minutes and tells the story of the four seasons, a sort of modern Vivaldi, in fact that's what made it so nice – it was an up-to-date baroque. I think it would make a very good film, using the instrumental parts to describe the story. Also, with a good light show they could make an excellent TV show (London Weekend or *Colour Me Pop* producers please note)!'

AC: I think Martin Kitcat brought in the classical element and Sandy would have the harmonies and that melodic thing, and we'd have more of a groove, a bit of blues, as it was that kind of hybrid. I'm not comparing us specifically with Crimson but they had that progressive thing and that collision with jazz and rock that hadn't really been done before. In our way there was that kind of collision but on a much smaller scale. I don't remember that we were influenced by anybody, we just created this pompous, proggy kind of area. And so we had to have a concept.

We were pushing for something that had a broader vision and something that engaged more than just your melodic sense – it engaged your mind and your heart and made you think a little bit more.

RL: Some drugs took over and we started to extrapolate. And then we did a double bill with King Crimson at the Beckenham Mistrale Club. [King Crimson guitarist Robert] Fripp came into our dressing room and said, 'We want to do the middle section, can you do the first bit and you can close it?' We said, 'Yeah.' So we go and play our three-minute nice little pop songs. They came on and did '21st Century Schizoid Man' and that was the end of that. I'm not kidding. I don't think I have ever been so blown away by a band ever. Fuck! Not only can they play, but what are these songs? And the timing? And they had this simple but very effective light show.

AC: Their performance was so extraordinarily good that we made some feeble excuse that water had been spilt on our plug board and we couldn't play the second set.

RL: [*Reading diary*] 2/12/69 Vertigo offered us a deal because we played Klook's Kleek with Keith Relf's Renaissance. We got £5.

AC: I think Island wanted to sign us. Island had a better legacy at the time. We were a bit more excited about signing for them, but as it turned out we signed for Vertigo.

RL: It was quite something, one of the first bands to be signed to Vertigo. The same weekend as Juicy Lucy.

TW: We were chuffed to bits. There was lots and lots of talk about us going to tour the States.

Released in the spring of 1970, *Gracious!* is a remarkable debut album from the cover inwards. The gatefold sleeve, designed by Barney Bubbles, is on textured white cardboard featuring a slanting greyscale exclamation mark. The track listing and recording details are on a white back cover and the inner gatefold has a garish pop art painting-cum-collage.

Once past the memorably melodic 'Introduction', the track titles look exceptionally portentous, but 'Heaven' has its pastoral moments and droll chorales, in which a multi-tracked Davis asks if the listener has a *"clean mind"*. The music is impressionistic without being overly ornamented. A dissonant keyboard solo introduces us to 'Hell', which ends up in a bar-room scenario. 'Fugue In D Minor' is a pseudo-classical keyboard confection that leads into the lengthy, episodic 'The Dream'.

TW: When we stepped into the Philips studio in Stanhope Place, that was the first time I went into a recording studio.

RL: But you were very cool. I absolutely freaked because, live, you could fuck up – you got past it, on we go. We went in and started with 'Introduction', I think, and stuff didn't work. [Engineer] Hugh Murphy was not a delightful man.

AC: We should have had some pre-production time with him in a rehearsal room, not just turn up.

TW: All we'd done was work live and hadn't any thought of how this was going to work in the studio.

RL: I don't think the record company had heard any of these songs, they had been to see us live, so it was just delivered to them. It was idiotic!

AC: Now everybody would be going, 'We've invested in this, so play us what you've got.'

MB: Had you given them any shorter tracks for demos?

AC: Nothing. We hadn't done any demos. We were recording in the building where they were, but no one came down and said, 'Can we hear what you are doing?'

MB: 'The Dream' is nearly seventeen minutes long. Was it recorded live or in sections?

AC: We wanted to do it in sections, but the producer, without telling us, obviously thought, 'I can't spend all fucking day doing this,' and said, 'Just play it like you play it live,' and that's what we had to do. A few overdubs, but that was essentially what it was.

RL: We'd started recording stuff and it sounded terrible. We had to change things that had worked fine live. It was very unnerving. I can only speak for me, but I was never happy in the studio, I was always very uptight.

MB: But it had originality about it. There seems to be quite a bit of wry humour in 'Heaven' and 'Hell'.

RL: There was a lot of humour. We'd just got a Mellotron, so for us playing 'Heaven' with those strings was just orgasmic. That was Sandy and his Catholicism coming out with *"Do you have a clean mind?"* I thought it was a bit trite. But there were bits of them that I enjoyed. The 'Hell' riff – fabulous, you could really go for it, it was lovely.

[*To the others*] Do you remember going to Shel Talmy's place in Hyde Park Mansions in Knightsbridge, with speakers about as big as those windows? That was the first time we'd heard the album. With the second album we were involved lots more, but with the first album they told us to fuck off and they'd do it all, Roger Wake and Hugh. There was no time for mixing; we had so much on.

MB: The album got some high-profile attention from Kid Jensen on Radio Luxembourg.

AC: When that came out there weren't many radio programmes that would play it, but somebody said that he was going to play a track off the album, so we all tuned in and he started playing 'The Dream', which was the longest track on the album and he played the whole number.

RL: We did an interview – we did a whole Gracious programme, which was kind of... *"What?"* Kid Jensen did that with a couple of other bands but not many. It went to number two in his chart.

MB: Was there any pressure to be commercially successful?

AC: There was a little pressure or we wouldn't have recorded [the 1970 single] 'Once On A Windy Day'.

RL: Live we didn't do it like the single. If you listen to that Isle Of Wight set, it's an eighteen-minute piece with a jazz section in the middle and a soaring guitar solo that went on for seven minutes! Then we go back to the song again and the [Mellotron] strings start quietly – it's all nicked from Crimson, obviously – and it gets louder and gets louder. Some moments were magical and when we got it right, fuck me...

We were going to record it like that but they said, 'No, we are going to cut it to three and a half minutes.' We knew it wasn't going to sell, but it had nothing to do with us. So there was a bit of pressure.

AC: [At the Isle Of Wight] The Mellotron wouldn't work. It'd gone out of tune. It was the first time that we'd ever played 'Super Nova', although we'd rehearsed it to death. It wasn't too bad. Unfortunately no one had ever heard it, so we got away with it.

TW: The audience were in the sort of mood that if a dog had walked onstage and farted it would have gone down well. Everyone was completely zonked by then, they just wanted some entertainment and were happy for anyone to be up there.

[We watch a DVD of the Gracious 1970 Isle Of Wight Festival performance.]

RL: The Mellotron has come in four bars late, he's on the wrong bit. So he's fucked it up before we've even started. I'm surprised we got anywhere from here. [*Drums come in*] Not nervous at all, am I? I sped up 80 per cent! We're on this huge stage. Tim's right near me as is Alan. Martin's miles over there.

TW: The Mellotron packs up in a minute and Martin's crawling inside it.

AC: We were filmed and when Martin was taking the back off his Mellotron and was trying to fix it, the cameramen thought that was all part of the performance, like Keith Emerson sticking knifes into it. The generator kept going down and not giving us a constant power supply of 240 volts. The Mellotron was very temperamental.

RL: We should have gone on mid-afternoon, but we got there late and went on last. It was a Wednesday or a Thursday – the festival was on for four or five days. It was dark and all that I could see were a couple of fires that seemed about a mile away.

Jimi Hendrix, that was a disastrous gig. The Who were fine, but it was the same kind of sound. We haven't spent any money on that DVD except getting it synched. The Who spent a lot of money on it and it's gone out as *The Who At The Isle Of Wight*, the whole set, and it sounds as empty and as out of tune. The pictures are great but the sound was abysmal.

We left during Jimi's set. We had more pressing business, like playing at Toff's in Folkestone for £15.

TW: I went to the Isle Of Wight Festival in 1969 as a punter and it wasn't remotely anywhere in my mind that a year after I would be playing there. We did some other festivals that year: we played twice at Plumpton, the free festival and the jazz and blues festival. We played with Family down there.

AC: In the book *The Last Great Event: The 1970 Isle Of Wight Pop Festival*, by Chris Weston, there are three pictures of Gracious playing but they are credited as Black Widow. This will be corrected when they reprint one day.

Away from the heady heights of the Isle Of Wight, like many groups of the era, Gracious had to pick up work as and when it was offered, which resulted in some marathon drives.

TW: We lived in Surrey and we got a gig in Glasgow, drove there and back in one night.

AC: There wasn't enough money for us to stay overnight.

RL: We used to do a lot of silly ones; they didn't plan it properly. We did a couple of nights with Fleetwood Mac. Peter Green in his white robes and the three guitar players. Some of the rhythms that they got into!
 We played with the Floyd a couple of times, Family. I remember watching [Cowderoy's] face. He was always cleaning and putting his guitar back in its case, but Family's guitarist Charlie Whitney had a double-necked Gibson SG and when they were packing the gear he slid it – not in a case – into the top of the van. I thought, 'What the fuck?'

AC: It was very exciting for us, but there weren't many outlets for our kind of music and we needed to be touring more heavily. It was Friday night and Saturday, then there would be a gap for a couple of weeks. We'd rehearse every day, but with the live thing we needed to be more visible.

RL: It was hard to put us in dances really, although we did lots of university things.

The group recorded their second album *This Is... Gracious!!* in the summer of 1971 with Hugh Murphy again engineering. Although the album is a more vivid recording of a more confident-sounding group – including the side-long piece 'Super Nova' that they had played at the Isle Of White Festival – the cracks had quickly started to appear and Gracious had split by the time it was released. Hence it was shunted out on the Philips International Series, which included a number of compilations with the generic *This Is...* title.

RL: On the second album [Wheatley] and I were loving Chicago – he was Mr Funk. One of the songs is called 'CBS' as Chicago were on CBS. There was a brass sound on the Mellotron and [Martin Kitcat] picked it up quite quickly, but that was our input. Todd Rundgren was a massive influence, The Nazz 'Open My Eyes', Spooky Tooth, lots of them, so [Sandy Davis and Kitcat] would take some of our ideas, but we were never acknowledged. We evolved this track. Without us it would be an acoustic guitar and a [Hohner] Pianet.

TW: A track like 'CBS' was as just as much us as them. [Davis] had come with a ditty and we turned it into something else.

MB: Was 'Super Nova' recorded all in one go like the long tracks on the first album?

AC: I can't really remember but I think we did it in sections. Although we did all the harmonies live, Sandy overdubbed them in the studio. But the biggest problem was getting the right sound from the Mellotron. And we were constantly arguing.

TW: The tensions wouldn't have gone if we had continued, they would have become more enhanced. The three of us were certainly pulling in a bit of a different direction musically.

RL: Interestingly, I think it would have really come unstuck if we'd been successful. None of us were making any money, but to see them with ten times more dosh than us would have bugged us as they had the writing credits. We can blame lots of things but in the end we have to say it was about us. We can say that we didn't have the right management.

AC: We *didn't* have the right management.

TW: We didn't have enough work; our management weren't very good at that. Our manager was a dentist.

RL: Not a good dentist, either.

AC: Yes, but then people start to quit the band.

RL: Yes they do – that would be me. It's not that I wanted to be rich, I just wanted to pay the bills. We just weren't making enough money and it all started to fall apart, which was a great shame.

We were good, but I was the weakest link in the band. That's OK, but that meant, like the Floyd, I led the way in the evolving – I can't play in 19/4 time, but I can do this. When I was leaving we got Andy McCulloch in who had played on [King Crimson's] *Lizard*. I thought, 'Fucking hell, this is like getting Billy Cobham in.' As he put his kit up, I got a wry smile on my face because there's a lot he can't do and the reason he can't do it is because he hadn't evolved it.

AC: The best bands aren't necessarily the flashiest musicians, but together they evolve their own style.

TW: You could also say [that about] Ringo in The Beatles. Our band would never have been what it was without Robert.

Gracious officially disbanded on the August 5, 1971.

RL: After we split up we did a Marquee reunion gig the next year, April 6, 1972, and it sold out in minutes. It almost broke my heart. But there was no money.

AC: After that I signed on the dole.

CHAPTER 26

What's Sauce for the Goose: Camel

When Camel formed in Guildford in 1971, guitarist Andy Latimer had previously played in The Brew with bass guitarist Doug Ferguson and drummer Andy Ward – who also had a brief stint in The Shades with blues and boogie pianist Champion Jack Dupree, when aged 16. DJM records showed an interest in the young group's demo, but they ended up backing the label's singer-songwriter, Phillip Goodhand-Tait, on his 1971 album, *I Think I'll Write A Song*, and were dropped by the label shortly afterwards.

In their search for a new identity they put an ad in *Melody Maker*, which was answered by keyboard player Peter Bardens, who had played in Them with Van Morrison and in the short-lived Shotgun Express with Rod Stewart, Peter Green and Mick Fleetwood. In both age and experience, Bardens was the senior member, and in deference the group were initially named Peter Bardens' On, but soon changed their name to Camel.

Latimer's early influences included The Beatles, The Beach Boys, The Shadows and the blues. Bardens had already played with some major figures in soul and blues, but wanted to stretch out, and suggested that the band play some pieces in a style like the Latino rock group Santana. This idea also appealed to Latimer in terms of a platform for his own playing, but the guitarist felt that they should explore their roots. Having been a boy chorister he enjoyed the transcendental side of classical music. "I was adamant about it sounding as English as we are and was trying to interject some kind of Englishness or European [elements]. We were very bluesy and yet we ended up doing this English-style music – it was quite bizarre how we found ourselves in this position."

Like many groups in the early Seventies, Camel were given the chance to develop their signature style. On their debut album, *Camel*, released on MCA in 1973, this transition is apparent from the opening song 'Slow Yourself Down', written by Latimer and Ward, which has a Santana-ish groove with drums augmented by percussion, swelling organ lines and a blow-out guitar solo, whereas 'Mystic Queen', written by Bardens and sung by Ferguson, is more indicative of the style that Camel would pursue, in both songs and instrumentals that were song-like in structure. These often include passages in five or seven time – or six time as in the instrumental 'Six Ate', with rolling rhythms that at times are reminiscent of Caravan, a group who Latimer acknowledges as an influence.

As was the order of the day, they also stretched out live, an example being the sixteen-minute neo-psychedelic excursion – with just a few of those Santana influences peeking through – 'God Of Light Revisited', recorded at London club Dingwalls in 1973 and released on the *Greasy Truckers* double album.

Camel's next album, *Mirage*, was released on Deram in 1974 and before the stylus hit the vinyl, the most striking thing about it was the cover, which utilised the design of the cigarette pack by American tobacco manufacturers, Camel. If the group had just helped themselves to the design they would surely have been stomped upon by big legal boots. But Camel's star was in the ascendant, and so their manager Jeff Jukes had had a bright idea of how to secure sponsorship from the company's European wing.

"He told us that we were going ahead with it, but we were getting a little uncomfortable with it," says Latimer. "What happened is that four guys from Switzerland came into the studio and were asking us questions like, 'Have you got a title for this song?' And we said 'No,' and they said, 'Why don't you call it '20 To The Pack'?"

Jukes came up with the idea of mini promo packets of three cigarettes with the names of the album tracks on the reverse side. There were mooted plans of girls walking up and down the aisles at gigs selling cigarettes. The band became desperate to stop this ill-considered and potentially embarrassing promotion from happening.

The sleeve went into production in Europe, a striking image of the Camel cigarettes camel, standing in front of the pyramids, distorted as if in a heat haze, as befitted the title. Over in the US the Camel marketing executives were chary about the idea of tying their cigarettes to a young English rock group as they were specifically aiming their product at the older smoker, so they pulled the cover and the US version of *Mirage* came out with hastily rendered sleeve artwork featuring a rather anomalous dragon.

Coughing through these obfuscatory clouds of Camel smoke we find that *Mirage* was a step forward from the group's debut and the album in which their identity was forged. 'Freefall' is an object lesson in how to compose a flowing song in a variety of time signatures that lacks any contrivance. The song begins with a muscular and punctuated 4/4 verse with some melodic guitar lines from Latimer and a second memorable theme in 6/8, including some bars in 5/8, spinning out of the verse. Crucial to its success are the deft rhythmic manoeuvres of Ferguson and Ward – the latter an especially elegant and empathetic player – and while flamboyant, Bardens and Latimer are never superficially flashy. On the instrumental 'Supertwister', Latimer's lyrical flute becomes the lead instrument in lieu of a voice.

Although the group had three vocalists, the singing was serviceable without being particularly strong. The highlight is the closing track 'Lady Fantasy'. As its name suggests, she is a young man's fantasy figure, a remote, unattainable romantic archetype, with the lyrics just keeping on the right side of mawkish. The ideal accompaniment would have been to dreamily stare at "art" postcards by popular Seventies photographer David Hamilton which featured soft-focus images of languid young women, Seventies updates of Pre-Raphaelite ideals of beauty. The three-part song features a number of affecting vocal and instrumental passages including a dramatic charge to the close.

One track in particular, 'Nimrodel/The Procession/The White Rider', pointed the way to their next LP, the concept album *Music Inspired By The Snow Goose*. Although not mentioning Hobbits as such, it's one of the few progressive rock tracks that references J.R.R. Tolkien's novel, *The Lord Of The Rings*. Frankly, it's surprising that there weren't more, due to both the book's popularity in the Seventies and the fact that it referenced an imagined and unheard musical tradition, with numerous songs laid out in the text that served as lyrical material for many a teenage bedroom guitarist who had a few chords and a yen for producing something fantastical.

Latimer explains the roots of the song: "We'd all read *Lord Of The Rings*, like everyone does, and I'd written 'The White Rider' on *Mirage* and that was inspired by Gandalf, and all that stuff at the time [*laughs*]. And as we were doing it we said, 'Wouldn't it be a good idea to make an album based on a story?' So then we all went round trying to find a good book to base it on."

On that subject, Swedish keyboard player Bo Hansson scored a hit with his *Music Inspired By The Lord Of The Rings*, which had been released in Sweden in 1970 and was re-released on Charisma in 1972. Although the cover art brought to mind all the posters of characters from the book who, disappointingly, were depicted in a way that didn't look anything like you had imagined, the music was particularly evocative and the album went gold in the UK.

MUSIC INSPIRED BY THE SNOW GOOSE
Original label: Gama/Decca
Producer: David Hitchcock
Recorded: Early 1975
Release date: April 1975
Chart position: 22 (UK)

By 1975 it had become de rigueur for progressive rock groups to have written either a concept album, or at least some kind of side-long suite. Latimer doesn't remember there being any pressure or obligation to make a concept album per se, but he does recall that Camel had been thinking about doing something with an orchestra, following forays into this area by Deep Purple, The Moody Blues and Caravan.

Peter Bardens had an idea of writing music inspired by *Siddharta*, the 1922 novel by German author Hermann Hesse, a work that had been taken up by the counterculture as a kind of Buddhist *Pilgrim's Progress*. The book they finally agreed upon was Paul Gallico's 1941 novella, *The Snow Goose*. With all ideas of making the first concept album on smoking now far behind them, in the summer of 1974, Latimer and Bardens hired a converted farm building in Devon and headed out west to write the music.

"I can't recall exactly where it was now, but we noted it was quite near the River Camel," says Latimer. "It was such an idyllic place, we were young and Pete and I would just go and sit up on the hills and talk about what we thought about *The Snow Goose*, and where we were going to take it.

"We saw more possibilities in *The Snow Goose*, it was more defined," continues Latimer explaining the group's choice. "There were only three characters and both Pete and I had a clear idea about where we wanted to go musically, so it was an easy task in a way. At the time it was a very powerful story and quite inspiring."

Its main character, Philip Rhayader, is a semi-disabled outsider who lives in a lighthouse on an Essex marsh. He strikes up an unlikely friendship with a teenage girl, Fritha, centred around their rescue and rehabilitation of an injured snow goose. The subject matter was a perfect fit for the Seventies with its themes of the still relatively recent World War Two and of transcendental spirituality. In the story Rhayader dies helping to bring troops back over the Channel in his boat during the evacuation of Dunkirk. The snow goose is a wild animal whose first instinct, once well, is to fly away, but as Fritha releases it she feels that it represents Rhayader's soul living on, as it soars high above with the flocks of other snow geese. It was made into a compelling short film for BBC TV in 1971 starring Richard Harris as Rhayader and Jenny Agutter as Fritha, although the group hadn't seen it when it was first broadcast.

On *The Snow Goose*, the characters are portrayed by particular musical themes. This device had been used before in classical music, Sergei Prokofiev's 1936 composition *Peter And The Wolf* being the prime example, and that approach works particularly well on this album.

"We wrote quite a lot of pieces for each character until we found what we thought was right," Latimer explains. "It's enjoyable to listen to the album and read the book at the same time, because it takes about the same time.

"We started recording and in the middle of it, we had a three-month tour of America. So we had a lot of time to think about the piece and when we returned we rewrote several of the things because we weren't happy with them."

For the initial sessions, the group went into their label's own Decca Studios in London to record the album. It was one of those recording studios that still kept its corporate science lab look, peopled by technicians wearing white coats. The label's groups could use their studios for an agreed duration, but they had to be careful not to go over budget.

Producer David Hitchcock, who had worked with Caravan and Genesis, and whose services the group had specifically requested, noted that into the Seventies, with more tracks available to record on, there was a general trend towards an elongation of the recording process, which was not guaranteeing a superior end product. "Albums were taking weeks to do," he says. "Bands would rehearse in the studio, they would write in the studio. It was incredibly tedious."

Without mentioning names – and not pointing a finger at Camel – Hitchcock also notes that the cannabis-based drugs of the day were contributing to a general lack of focus while recording. With little pressure upon them, the musicians' mental processes gradually decelerated to the more comfortable, slower pace of the drug high.

"You could noodle away quite happily, think it was good, then go back to it and think that it doesn't really cut it, does it?" says Hitchcock. "No, do it again. Then three hours later everyone's stoned again. With four-track you had to be incredibly disciplined as you had to bounce down and tracks would be locked together for eternity so you had to be not too hung up if it wasn't exactly right."

During the Seventies, technology developed at a faster pace than before and from then onwards there has been an unspoken pressure to use the latest studio hardware or you would sound old fashioned. And so groups and producers became beholden to technology and their engineers' desire to use it.

In Camel's case, the sessions for *The Snow Goose* got bogged down around the drum sound. Latimer feels that Andy Ward was often ill-served by the gaffer-tape-dampened sound that was used when recording his drums, just to make sure there were no intrusive rings or rattles: "I'd say, 'Nobody's going to hear that when we play and that's what you get when you hit a drum kit.' But they were set in their ways and so you got a very dead drum sound."

Frustrated by the way things were going at Decca Studios, Hitchcock abandoned the sessions and moved the group to Island Studios in Basing Street, west London, although Latimer recalls they later returned to do some mixing at Decca. The group recorded all sixteen pieces with the band playing live, then they kept the best rhythm section track, with keyboards, guitar and other overdubs being added later. This was standard at the time in a quest to achieve maximum separation and eradicate mistakes, but looking back, Latimer can see flaws in this approach.

"You would often be in the studio on your own trying to come up with a solo and it was very difficult to capture any sort of emotion as you aren't playing off anybody. It's a strange environment and often clinical. And that's the way you did thing in those days, you wanted to be as perfect as you could, but I do think you could lose the plot sometimes."

Hitchcock also found some difficulties with the group's interpersonal relationships. "Pete Bardens wasn't the easiest person in the world to get on with, and he and Andy Latimer were often at loggerheads," he recalls.

"From the start, Peter and I had a love/hate relationship," Latimer admits. "We worked really well. We wrote together and it was a very special partnership. We conceded to each other's wishes – when we saw that somebody had the bit between their teeth, we'd let them go with it. We fell out on things like live performances, and recordings could be a little awkward at times, a little tense and a little stressful. But we were working as a band quite well at that point and I think it was generally quite harmonious."

For the orchestration, producer David Hitchcock approached the composer and arranger David Bedford.

Bedford's arrangements are typically sympathetic, but also pithy and unsentimental. He makes his mark with a striking Stravinsky-esque wind quartet on 'Friendship' and scored a female alto voice to drift hauntingly across the repetitive guitar arpeggios of 'Preparation'. But mostly the orchestrations are subtly woven into the music, only really breaking out more dramatically on 'La Princesse Perdue' towards the end of the album. The parts were played by the London Symphony Orchestra.

"Pete and I were very happy with David Bedford's arrangements," says Latimer. "I think they worked really well. I wasn't knowledgeable about such things and it was a bit of an ego boost hearing your music played by an orchestra.

"It was a strange album in as much as we recorded all the parts separately, so we didn't really know what we had until we edited it all together in the studio. That was the first time we'd heard the thing from start to finish. And we were all really pleased with it."

The guitarist put forward the idea that the album should come out with the book text, but Gallico was having none of it and his lawyers tried to stop the album's release. One of the reasons that he gave for this negative stance was the group's perceived link to Camel cigarettes. "He was anti-cigarette smoking, which I find interesting because every picture I've seen he's got a pipe in his mouth," Latimer observes.

The main reason for his antipathy towards Camel's album was that unbeknown to the group, Gallico was also working with musician and songwriter Ed Welch – who'd had a minor hit single in 1971 with the single 'Clowns' – on what his estate still calls the "official" album of *The Snow Goose*, with narration by Spike Milligan, which was released in 1976. "Of course at the time I thought ours was better," says Latimer. "But Spike and Ed Welch did a great job, although I don't particularly like narration. We had discussed using narration, but people get fed up listening to someone say the same lines. But music can hold your attention time and time again." To get around the copyright problems it was released in May 1975 as *Music Inspired By The Snow Goose*, with the first three words in a significantly smaller font.

Music Inspired By The Snow Goose may have no lead vocals, but it is a mix of short song-like sections full of colour and melody, with no superfluous jamming or padding. Even Latimer's spectacular solo on 'Rhayader Goes To Town' is of a part with Bardens' organ and synths. The album reached number twenty-two in the UK charts and raised Camel's profile to the extent that they were voted best newcomer in the *Melody Maker* poll of 1975, despite having been extant for four years.

After its release, Camel played some concerts in Holland and while the fans liked their earlier music, they gave a less than enthusiastic reaction to this new material, and so Camel had to re-arrange the material for playing live as a four-piece. They played a showcase at the Royal Albert Hall in London in October 1975 with the LSO and, typically for this kind of project, the orchestra were less than enthusiastic about playing with a rock band.

The Albert Hall concert was recorded and eventually came out on *A Live Record* in 1978. To get it ready for release a studio session was booked for some orchestral overdubs. There had been problems with feedback on the mikes when getting the balance between the orchestra and the group due to the quality of the sound system. Latimer also recalls that the French horn players, especially, seemed to be getting bored, and were sometimes playing out of tune. Listening back to the live recording, he discerned one particular onstage discussion.

"You could hear two brass players chatting when the music was going on and they didn't have anything to do, and they'd be saying, 'Are you going down the pub afterwards,' and 'How much longer is this going to go on for?'"

Hitchcock recalls one exchange during the subsequent studio session. "We were setting up in the studio and one of the orchestra said, 'But we've already recorded this.' I said, 'Well, you got it wrong so you've got to do it again,' which didn't endear me [to them]."

Following *Music Inspired By The Snow Goose* – which Camel played on BBC Radio 1's *In Concert* and on *The Old Grey Whistle Test* – the band went back to the group format, including some tracks for their next album *Moonmadness*, which contained a few actual songs, and like its predecessor ended up selling enough albums to go silver.

Reviewing the album in *Melody Maker*, Chris Welch, tried to define what made the group so potent and so popular. He noted that it "swung sturdily", but picked up on a certain "sweetness and light" about their "freewheeling" sound, a certain "airy feeling" that he had some trouble pinning down. And understandably so, as it has more than a hint of a particularly English "otherness" about it.

Camel's mooted affiliation with the Canterbury Scene came from the fact that as well as having at least some musical ideas in common with Caravan, they were joined in 1977 by Richard Sinclair, former bass player and vocalist with Caravan and Hatfield And The North, which had some wags referring to them as Cara–mel. Apparently, Doug Ferguson had been less than enthusiastic about the group exploring further metric complexity – which, considering some of their earlier tracks seems a bit hard to understand – but Sinclair's addition gave the group a brilliant lead singer and a formidable bass player in a single package.

The combination first recorded on 1977's *Rain Dances*, one of their strongest sets. They were also joined by ex-King Crimson and Kokomo saxophonist and flautist Mel Collins. Mention sax and people immediately think "jazz", but Collins was just as much a rock reeds player. Some diehards were unsure about his inclusion but he gave the group a new dimension. Brian Eno made an unexpected appearance on the album playing synthesizer on the track 'Elke', which also featured a harpist. But despite such pellucid pastoralia, Latimer and Bardens were at it again and almost came to blows in the studio.

Young *New Musical Express* journalist Paul Morley made these comments on 1978's *A Live Record*, which he felt exemplified Camel's "English, extreme, synthesized folk music".

"Ultimately, despite their perfect technical abilities, the group's stumbling block is their naivety. The flawlessness, flashness and tightness of the music can easily overwhelm the basic immaturity of the constituents. Camel, again typically for this loose, imprecise hybrid music, are like gifted children: writing a novel with superb prose, taut plot manipulation but possessing no experience of an outside world, so therefore unconvincing."

Morley was approaching the music from a completely different tack to that of Chris Welch, but his tempered criticism, in its own way, also recognises what made them hard to pin down, and their otherworldly, slightly detached "naivety" that he highlights, contributed to what made them so appealing to many. "A sort of blues band with classical leanings" is how Latimer describes them. It wouldn't be too far of a stretch to compare *Music Inspired By The Snow Goose* to some of the British tradition of 20th-century Light Music. If that seems like damnation with faint praise it's not meant to be, as leaving aside the novelty pieces and stirring marches, that approach to making music yielded some beautifully orchestrated pictures-in-sound.

Camel carried on beyond the end of the Seventies, which, chronologically, is outside the remit of this book. In some cases groups that had ridden the wave that had risen so high at the start of the decade found themselves creatively beached, lacking impetus and ideas. But Camel had hit their stride at this time and had enough of a following to sail through the changing attitudes of fans and the music press that came with punk, without much of a problem. But another major factor was a change in attitudes within the record companies, which were now scrutinising the accounts books rather than taking a punt based on the idealistic notions of unfettered expression and hoping that brought in an adequate return as they had done before.

Latimer: "We had a lot more leeway in [the early Seventies], when the record industry in general gave most bands a free hand. It wasn't until they realised that there was a lot of money to be made and then it started coming from the top of the record company to the bottom: 'We want you to do something that will sell. We want a hit single; we want something that's commercial; you've got to do something with your image.' All that stuff came about, I would say, in the late Seventies. And to make concessions to that pressure, we had some half-arsed attempts to do hit singles on *I Can See Your House From Here* (1979), and it didn't work."

CHAPTER 27

So-Called Journalists: Seventies Rock in the Media

Into the Seventies the role of music papers had expanded from delivering chart and industry news to becoming essential adjuncts to the music scene, their contents absorbed each week, discussed and argued over. With an expanding market and circulations on the increase – at least for the larger papers – their role increased in importance.

Music journalists were becoming a lot more than reporters, and the sometimes rather perfunctory reviews and articles of the previous decade had expanded into more individual and opinionated writing, and more in-depth profiles of musicians, and reviews of their music. Publications did more than just reflect the tastes of their readers, as some journalists effectively set themselves up as tastemakers, provoking strong reactions as a result. Their influence has never been greater than in that decade and their young readership had their favourite music journalists as well as their favourite groups.

Melody Maker was historically the musician's paper. If you wanted to buy new or second-hand musical gear, read a review of gear or instruments, or wanted to take out a classified ad for a new bass player or singer, *Melody Maker* was your marketplace. The paper also had an extensive gig guide and was a mail order emporium with advertisements for faded denim jackets, loon pants and other fashion items du jour.

Chris Welch joined the paper in 1964 and recalls his first day: "They took me to the pub and said, 'You know the *Melody Maker*'s going to close? The circulation's rubbish; it's only selling about 14,000 a week.' Might have been a bit more, but it was very low."

Welch first used the term 'progressive rock' in those pages to describe Cream in 1967, and in the Seventies he was basically the *Melody Maker*'s main progressive rock correspondent.

"When I was first enthusing about progressive rock, we didn't use that phrase all the time – it was just 'current bands'. I have a feeling that phrase was used rather more later. We were lucky to be on the ground floor discovering these groups who then became enormously successful and gave *MM* a huge circulation.

"It hadn't occurred to me that anybody wouldn't like it, because it struck me that this is what we'd all been waiting for: rock was being taken seriously and the musicians were getting better and better," says Welch. "I always wanted to see the music improve. So for me, bands like Yes, ELP and Jethro Tull were the cream, the best of what rock could produce.

"And [in the Seventies] these bands were so successful they were winning *Melody Maker* readers' polls and touring the world, selling gold and platinum albums. The editor was pleased that I knew them all from their previous bands, so I could get interviews with them, no problem at all. We had instant access, so to speak, and then you whizzed off to go with them on tour. It was like a honeymoon period."

By 1972 *Melody Maker* was selling a hefty 200,000 copies a week. Editor Ray Coleman had taken over in 1969, replacing Jack Hutton who left to launch *Sounds*, taking several *MM* writers with him. Coleman re-staffed *MM* largely with journalists from provincial papers, most of whom had written about music as well as covering general news stories; among them Richard Williams, Roy Hollingworth, Michael Watts and Chris Charlesworth.

But *MM*'s layout felt a tad functional and uninspired – also like a newspaper – and in Welch's opinion its cover looked like the *Daily Mirror*. It certainly didn't appear that design aesthetics were a high priority. "We had a problem with that," Welch admits. "There were attempts to revamp. Designing the paper was a mammoth task and to be honest I don't think anyone was up to doing it. We didn't have an art editor. People came up with ideas and the editor rejected them all."

Welch recalls that there were more staff than freelancers – around ten – working on the paper, but due to its sixty-four pages, things always got frantic when it went to press. "It would drive the subs and the editor of the day nuts, really, trying to bring all the articles together in time to meet the print deadline. There were terrible rows with freelancers who'd had their work cut to make way for late advertisements. It's all coming in at the last minute on type written sheets of paper, which have to be subbed then sent off to a printer's by motorbike messengers. People were working up to midnight, going mad, chain smoking."

In this more album-oriented age, when Welch was assigned to review the singles, it was a task that he appeared to approach with a certain disdain for the subject. The page was particularly entertaining, but the reviews at times bore no relation to the single in question.

"Singles were still important but there were so many of them and a lot of them were terrible," Welch explains. "And so I thought that at least I could make it funny. It did get a bit surreal. The editor, Ray Coleman, used to get a bit miffed at times, so I would include some serious reviews as well."

Melody Maker moved out of London to Sutton for a while, but while musicians would often drop into the office, they didn't make the journey out of London. Coleman decided it was essential that they moved back into town and in Welch's words, "managed to secure a run-down, beaten-up old shed in Southwark which was just across the river from Fleet Street, in Meymott Street. It was a terrible building – it looked like a Nissan hut on a bombsite – but at least it was ours and wasn't so far away. It was freezing cold in the winter. We had our own open-plan room there. We always had one small cubicle for playing music in. When we started we only had an old-fashioned record player, like a Dansette, but they did actually buy us a hi-fi."

Richard Williams joined *Melody Maker* in 1969 and became assistant editor. After a spell in A&R at Island Records, he returned as editor from 1978–80. He also wrote for *The Times*. How did writing about music for newspapers differ in terms of the editorial brief?

"The only direction I ever had from the arts editor, a very nice man called John Higgins, an opera fan, was '300 words', '350 words' – that was it," says Williams. "So I could write about King Crimson, or Laura Nyro, or more obscure things because he didn't really know the difference. There wasn't any real interest in what I was actually writing about – as long as they had something with rock or jazz in it occasionally, that was fine."

With hindsight, although *Melody Maker* was regarded as being a bit staid, it covered a far more adventurous range of music – including outré jazz, free improvisation and American minimalism – than any of its rivals.

"The thing I can't stress too strongly is how much freedom there was writing for music papers at the beginning of the Seventies," says Williams.

In 1970 Jack Hutton and Peter Wilkinson, formerly of *Melody Maker*, founded *Sounds* and for many, its main selling point was the free poster in the centre of the magazine, which was printed in colour from 1971. Not all of the transfers onto newsprint were of the best quality – the close-up of Yes guitarist Steve Howe playing live was a slightly out of focus melange of hair, teeth and a guitar headstock – but those depicting Keith Emerson in prime Hammond-humping form, a white-suited Greg Lake playing lead guitar, Hawkwind, The Who, Andy Powell from Wishbone

Ash, Alice Cooper, Tony McPhee of the Groundhogs and Genesis adorned many a teenage fan's bedroom.

The front pages of the music press in the early Seventies invariably carried a dramatic news story relating to tours, new albums or bands splitting up, or – in the case of The Beatles – reuniting. "There was a lot of competition on that score," says Chris Charlesworth, who was *Melody Maker*'s news editor in 1970. "I had to try and beat *NME* and *Sounds* to be first with the news. We prematurely split a few acts, much to their surprise."

Elton John, interviewed for *ZigZag* in 1973, proved himself to be a dedicated reader of music papers. "Apart from *ZigZag* I read *Let It Rock*. I read them all really but the weeklies are pretty mundane. There's another new rock'n'roll paper coming out of Harrow [*Fat Angel*]. Of all the weekly papers *Sounds* has probably got the best editorial staff – Steve Peacock, Jerry Gilbert, Penny [Valentine], Martin Hayman.

"I used to be very hostile to the press, although they're generally improving. Even so, *Record Mirror* is dreadful – it's just nothing. *Melody Maker* seems the best value for money but I'm not keen on all those instrument surveys, which just seem to be fill-ins. I think *Disc* is improving. I like John Peel's singles reviews." Valentine was one of the few female music writers at the time and worked for Elton John's press department from 1973 until 1975, when she founded the short-lived music magazine *Street Life*.

New Musical Express, which carried adverts on its front cover, was viewed as *Melody Maker*'s unhip cousin in the late Sixties, and into the Seventies it was having something of an identity crisis.

In January 1972 a young journalist who was then still a student, Nick Kent, began working for the underground magazine *Frendz*, based in Portobello Road. He was given his chance there by Rosie Boycott, who went on to edit feminist magazine *Spare Rib* and *The Independent*, but he soon realised that the magazine was not long for this world and it only lasted until August. Kent was headhunted by Nick Logan, who was then deputy editor of *New Musical Express* under Alan Smith, and became a contributing freelancer in 1972. Kent was joined by new recruits Charles Shaar Murray, who had contributed to the infamous *Oz* 'School Kids Issue' in 1970, and Cambridge University graduate Ian MacDonald, who was drafted in as assistant editor.

By then *NME*'s sales figures of around 60,000 were dwarfed by *Melody Maker*'s 200,000 weekly circulation. Kent notes that it was still trying to push its role as a pop paper, while also trying to cover progressive and heavy rock, a combination that was not working, as the two camps weren't compatible and, if anything, their audiences were pulling apart from each other. With a new team in place, the idea was to give the paper a new identity, and they had only twelve issues in which to do it, or it would fold.

"When Murray and Ian MacDonald and myself came in, it became more rock orientated, and was far more irreverent. We mistrusted prog and very often were belittling," says Kent. "The *NME* overview was, 'Its sell-by date elapsed around 1971, and it really needs to be brushed under the carpet now.'"

That said, the paper's remit widened to include jazz pages and some articles about musical equipment. And there was space for progressive rock groups as the *NME* wasn't about to cut out that chunk of potential readership, and throughout the Seventies there were in-depth pieces on ELP, Yes, Genesis, Pink Floyd, Jethro Tull and more. The difference was that these groups that were treated with greater respect in *Melody Maker* could never be sure if they were going meet with an ally or a smiling assassin. There had always been a symbiotic relationship between music papers and groups, especially those who generated advertising revenue, but that relationship was often put to the test.

Melody Maker's Chris Charlesworth explains why that paper's approach was largely respectful. "Because of *MM*'s long history of being a musician's paper it was more likely to support something like prog rock because we always had the attitude of interviewing a musician about their skills and talents and what sort of instruments they used, rather than who they voted for in the election."

Even writers who liked the progressive bands could muster up some frank, even confrontational, lines of questioning, forcing the musicians to justify themselves, which could make for compelling reading. This more combative attitude – by no means limited to *NME* but something of their trademark – largely contributed to a cagey relationship between bands and press, and rather than wanting to have fawning critics validate their work, some groups, Pink Floyd particularly, were renowned for being press shy.

Similarly Ian Anderson of Jethro Tull tended to get defensive and made asides about critics in some of his songs. That said, he was unaware that Tull's manager Terry Ellis engineered the scam with *Melody Maker* editor Ray Coleman – as detailed in Chapter 10 – that the group were splitting up after Chris Welch's review of their 1972 album, *A Passion Play*.

There were always accusations in the press of "build them up and then knock them down". But looking back it feels more like once the enthusiasts who championed a band had their say, there was always someone more negatively inclined lurking in the wings waiting to put the metaphorical boot in.

The journalists were in a greater position of power, but realistically they weren't going to turn a band's fanbase against them. But they might influence a few floating voters. And some, Nick Kent particularly, numbered several rock stars among his drug buddies, and looked more like a rock star than some of those he interviewed. And rather than the *NME* going down the pan after twelve issues, its circulation shot up to around 250,000 per week. Did he have a feeling of power, that he could influence taste?

"Well, I probably did at the time. The writers would like you to believe that it was selling a quarter of a million copies a week because of the standard of writing. But Nick Logan told me that [in 1972] *NME* had quadrupled its sales figures within six months, and that IPC, who owned both *Melody Maker* and *NME* at the time, had done a survey amongst this new readership to find out what the magical 'X' ingredient was that was making them buy so many more copies. And they said that, basically, we don't read the paper, we look at the photographs. The only thing we read diligently, every week, is the gossip column on the last page.

"They've already got their own opinion. They want to read an interview with David Bowie, and they will quite purposefully miss out the paragraphs where there aren't actual direct quotes from Bowie himself. So my reaction was, it's like being a musician and being told a quarter of a million bought your record last week, but no one's listening to it.

"So in order to get them to read, I became far more flamboyant, in my style of writing, in my style of dress, in my style of behaviour. You know, going to extremes gets results — it's just a fact.

"The music press at that time viewed things like an ongoing party," Kent continues. "And the question was, what were you bringing to the party? Were you going to bring musical talent to the party? Were you going to bring some kind of shock value that was entertaining to the party? Were you going to be funny, like a court jester? Then you could hang in there and do your thing for a while. But if you were just going to stand in the corner and moan, then you could fuck off."

Kent paints a picture of the *NME* office as being an uninspiring place rather than the den of iniquity that some writers have described, with maybe someone having the odd surreptitious hit on a joint and someone taking amphetamines to meet their deadline.

Chris Welch noted a similarly light usage at *Melody Maker*, as well as a fair amount of after-hours drinking. But out in the field, things were quite different.

"There was a lot of temptation. I was offered drugs all the time by musicians and record companies, not British record companies who were very like the BBC – all very establishment," says Welch. "But in America I remember being offered cocaine by a record company, thinking that they could get you to write nice reviews about their acts. It was all there, but I'd already been through the drug scene in the Sixties and seen how horrific it could be for musicians. If you let people know you weren't into drugs, they wouldn't bother you after a while."

Barry Miles had been a major figure in the Sixties counterculture in London, founding Indica Books and Gallery, and Europe's first underground newspaper *International Times* in 1966. But into the Seventies these independent publications, like *Oz* and *Frendz*, were coming under criticism. A letter published in the *Oz* 'School Kids Issue' in 1970 noted that: "The Underground Press seems to be getting straighter with each issue." Even Miles admits: "They had been going for some time and had become a bit tired, certainly the earlier issues of *IT* and *Oz* are far more exciting and interesting than the Seventies issues of both papers."

Miles had spent a lot of the early Seventies in the USA and began contributing to *NME* on his return to the UK in 1975.

"[In the Seventies] underground press people like Nick Kent, Charles Shaar Murray, [photographer] Penny Smith, Mickey Farren, myself, all needed to pay the rent and with the demise of the underground press, we went to work for whoever would pay. The controversial side of *NME* was restricted to sometimes being rude about Bryan Ferry. When I was there it was not permitted to mention drug taking or to use any four letter words. About as far from *International Times* or *Oz* as you could get, but this was expected. It was owned by IPC and they were only interested in making money.

"Nick Logan was a clever editor, allowing the outspoken staff to go so far but not so far as to in any way threaten IPC profits. When I suggested articles on payola, buying records into the charts; connections to the mob; violent behaviour by thug managers like Don Arden, Nick was not interested. He was there to plug the latest product and get advertising, and *NME*'s reputation for being a bit outspoken helped this."

Maybe the reason that some of the rock'n'roll fundamentalist writers gave progressive rock such a bad press, made jokes about the groups, or –

the much-used failsafe – labelled them as "pretentious" was because they didn't know what to write about the music?

"Very, very few rock critics know anything about music theory, and even fewer can actually read music, so they simply did not have the vocabulary to write about the new music that was being made, particularly by bands like Henry Cow," Miles concurs. "I gave it a try, but I was not trained in that area either. Back then none of the papers except possibly *MM* had anyone competent – Richard Williams, for instance, was an exception.

"The people at *NME* who thought rock should return to its roots were probably encouraged by Nick Logan to be controversial. There was a bit of working class tomfoolery as well; it was always fun to put the boot into public school boys because then, as now, they ran the country."

In the Seventies the radio options were limited outside the BBC. There were the commercial pirate stations Radio London, whose offices were in the West End, but which broadcast from a ship anchored off Frinton in Essex, and Radio Caroline and Radio North Sea International that broadcast from various locations off the coast.

If you could find Radio Luxembourg – and find out what was being broadcast that evening – you might be able to find some progressive rock, even live recordings of, say, Emerson, Lake & Palmer, as long as you didn't mind sitting with your hand on the dial as the signal disappeared then remerged through hissing clouds of static. For those in tuning distance of London, Capital Radio also had the option of a weekday evening slot featuring progressive and non-pop sounds, *Your Mother Wouldn't Like It*, presented by Nicky Horne, who would play entire sides of new albums.

If you wanted to listen to album-based or non-chart rock music on the BBC *Sounds Of The Seventies* on Radio 1 was the place to go. It was broadcast on weekday evenings. The format was of a different programme every day with DJs including Bob Harris, John Peel – whose show was still called *Top Gear* as it had been in the late Sixties – Mike Harding, Stuart Henry, Pete Drummond and Alan Black bringing their own personal slants to what was played.

"We were a sort of enclave, a troublesome advance party of this extraordinary album music," says Harris. "There was a particular atmosphere that was prevalent at the BBC. It was the time of *Monty Python*, it was the time of pushing out the creative boundaries. The way that programmes got realised onto air was very unstructured and very casual. If you had an idea about a show you could sit down with your producer or put your head around the door of the Radio 1 controller, sit down and say, 'I've got this great idea for a show.' [They might reply] 'Oh, we've got a gap in ten days, why don't you put it out.' In that way it was a very creative time."

It was also the place to hear different versions of groups' music and maybe exclusive material through their sessions specifically recorded for the BBC. Soft Machine recorded a version of 'Moon In June' for a session for John Peel's *Top Gear* in 1969, for which singer and drummer Robert Wyatt changed all the words of the song to describe the process – the acoustics in the studio, the tea machine down the corridor, how the songs had expanded in length since the group last recorded for the programme, while noting the programme's quality and recommending it even in spite of its *"extraordinary name"*. In 1973 Hatfield And The North recorded a beautifully crafted spoof *Top Gear* jingle as part of their session.

Harris notes that sessions were a necessity back in the Seventies as the Musicians' Union stipulated that in an hour of broadcast there could only be twenty minutes' needle time – forty minutes when the programme expanded to two hours – and the rest had to be made up by sessions, for which the musicians were paid.

Sounds Of The Seventies was an even greater starter of discussions than the weekly arrival of the music press, with kids at school comparing lists of tracks that had been played the previous evening and how they had rated them.

There was also an *In Concert* on Saturday early evening with either one or two groups playing live. When Pink Floyd appeared in 1971 to premiere as yet unheard music from *Meddle* – 'Echoes' and 'One Of These Days', plus 'Fat Old Sun' and the unreleased 'Embryo' – it was recorded off the FM radio broadcast and soon circulated as a bootleg LP.

Harris's thoughtful, unassuming delivery couldn't have been further from some of the daytime Radio 1 DJs, who adhered to the Radio 1 playlist – which was heavy on lowest common denominator pop – and who delivered their banal humour and corny catch phrases in an exaggerated manner through what sounded, over the radio, like a fixed cheesy grin. This approach was exemplified by Tony Blackburn.

"I was a Peel protégé and John had introduced this more natural, casual form of presentation," Harris explains. "I took my cue from his show, *The Perfumed Garden*, on Radio London and I was very fortunate because John and I became very good friends and he kind of championed me at the BBC.

"[*Sounds Of The Seventies*] went completely against the grain of the idea that music is light and fluffy, that it's completely disposable and it doesn't have any underlying meaning of any description. There was an adage at Radio 1 that held fast for many years. That was 'ratings by day, reputation by night', which I think is great."

Blackburn even suggested that the place for *Sounds Of The Seventies* was on Radio 3, the classical station. "There's no doubt that as a breakfast show host in the Seventies, [Blackburn] was very uncomfortable about this new strand of music," Harris says.

Peel was already something of a legend by the start of the Seventies from his shows *The Perfumed Garden* on the pirate station Radio London, and *Night Ride* and *Top Gear* on Radio 1. Peel was vocal in his denunciation of progressive rock excess and pretension – Emerson, Lake & Palmer in particular – and was an early fan of punk and reggae and used to play all sorts of oddities through the Seventies including folk, free jazz and old rock'n'roll. But he had actually been one of the first DJs to champion Genesis and Yes, and had commissioned sessions by groups like Gong, Egg, and Gentle Giant and even Phil Collins' jazz rock project Brand X in 1976. But he generally erred away from the bigger progressive rock groups as the decade progressed.

There was something both endearing and avuncular about Peel. Although he spoke in a near monotone and with a slightly mannered air of I'm-here-as-a-DJ-but-I'm-not-playing-the-DJ-game – especially in the early Seventies – he was exceptionally articulate and was possessed of a droll wit. It appeared that the BBC didn't really know what to do with him, but he remained perennially popular. He has opined that being voted as best DJ in numerous music paper polls throughout the Seventies might well have kept him in work. Interviewed in 1987 by his producer John Walters, Peel mused on his popularity in the Seventies when other poll winners were Yes, Genesis, Jethro Tull and the progressive rock big hitters.

"It was always a complete mystery to me how that happened, because you'd have thought that the people who voted for all of that stuff would have voted for anybody rather than me," Peel said. "Or that perhaps they were voting for me as kind of a good thing – they liked the idea of it, but didn't listen to the programmes at all. Because you felt they couldn't have done, to have [also] voted for all those people like Yes and ELP."

Into the Seventies Alan "Fluff" Freeman surprised those who had perennially associated him with the Sunday chart show, by playing mainly progressive and hard rock on his Saturday afternoon slot. He also replayed some of the *Sounds Of The Seventies* sessions. His show was delivered with a slightly tongue-in-cheek camp drama. Freeman would read out listeners' letters like, "Mike in Basingstoke writes in, 'Dear Fluff, please play more Camel, Caravan, Van Der Graaf Generator, Gong and Gnidrolog.' Mmmm, that's taste there, Mike." He would also habitually signal the playing of his beloved Emerson, Lake & Palmer, with a snatch of Handel's *Hallelujah Chorus*, before announcing, "And now... the very royal ELP".

There was little time allotted to music on TV in the Seventies. In the Sixties there had been *Juke Box Jury*, *Thank Your Lucky Stars*, *Ready Steady Go* and *Oh Boy* – and *Colour Me Pop*, which ran from 1968–69. The concept was that each programme would concentrate on a particular album. The first one was on the Small Faces' 1968 album *Ogden's Nutgone Flake*.

Rowan Ayers, the father of Soft Machine founder Kevin Ayers, used to produce *Late Night Line-Up*, a magazine arts programme with some musical content. Ayers was keen to expand its music side and produced a programme called *Disco 2* – originally titled *Line Up's Disco 2*, whose name referred more to the disc itself than the discotheque – which ran from January 1970 to July 1971.

Tommy Vance initially presented the show, and Richard Williams made his first TV appearance as an occasional presenter. The programme's success led on to *The Old Grey Whistle Test* which was envisaged to feature album bands who were unlikely to make it onto *Top Of The Pops* and whose singles were unlikely to interest the compilers of the Radio 1 playlist. Williams was chosen by the show's producer Mike Appleton to present BBC 2's new flagship rock programme, which must surely have been a dream come true for any young journalist.

"Mike Appleton wanted a kind of *Melody Maker*-type journalist to front it, so he asked me to do it. And I did it until I couldn't stand doing it any longer," says Williams, laughing. "The first thing it became famous for was Focus, who were on one of the early shows. It was only watched by a couple of hundred thousand people, but they were basically a couple of hundred thousand *Melody Maker* readers. So a lot of them went out the next day, and astonished Polydor Records by asking for the Focus album. And I hated it – because it was exactly the kind of prog that I really didn't like, you know – sort of twiddly twiddly. I thought they were awful. And I hated effectively being a frontman for that sort of thing.

"I mean, it was great when John Martyn was in the studio, or Dr John, or Curtis Mayfield – somebody that I respected. I interviewed Ornette Coleman once on it and that was rather a proud moment."

374

The studio was small with no set dressing, just a functional space in which the artists played live, to give it a sense of authenticity away from the gaudy – if low-budget – glitz of *Top Of The Pops*.

The pay for scripting and presenting to show was only £20 a week, rising to £30, but Williams left for reasons other than his dislike of the music. "I thought the show needed somebody just a bit louder than me, somebody with a bit more oomph. Instead, Appleton went off and got somebody who was even quieter than me. I mean, I spoke at a normal volume, but Bob Harris whispered! But he obviously fitted the sort of West Coast singer-songwriter side much better than I did. He was more comfortable with that."

Harris never had the intention of getting into TV, but Appleton was again looking for someone with a journalistic background – Harris had been involved in the founding of the London listings magazine *Time Out* and had some limited broadcasting experience, and in the spirit of the time was just kind of slotted in.

"What I tried to do on *Whistle Test* was to take my approach on radio across onto television – the intimacy, that one-to-one thing," says Harris. His pay had gone up to £40 per week and it was BBC policy that all bands and artists appearing also received a fee. He remembers that for an early appearance, Elton John received £38.50.

But if you were a progressive rock fan, although *Whistle Test* was pretty much your only chance to see any, there wasn't a great deal of it on the show. And looking back on clips, not all the choices were the most exciting. It's a reminder that there was plenty of indifferent music in the Seventies, especially the sort of lame soft rock/boogie/pub rock bands – a lot of which ended up on the show.

"When people began to think back at *Whistle Test* they began to label it as a prog rock show, because as we were there in the early Seventies, prog must have been a staple diet, but it wasn't," says Harris. "We actually didn't have as many prog rock bands on as perhaps one would have expected. It wasn't, however, like there was a massive catalogue of prog rock bands who were available at that time. Bands like Jethro Tull, ELP and Yes were the staple diet, but then once you'd gone through Barclay James Harvest, Trapeze, possibly The Moody Blues, Caravan, Camel, it's not like there were many prog rock bands selling millions of albums.

"When I was first on the programme, the show was coming out of a tiny little presentation studio behind the lift shaft on the fourth floor, a weather studio called Presentation B. It only had eight microphone points. But when we got down to TC5 the *Top Of The Pops* studio in late

1974, all of those problems went away because there was a massive mixing desk and hundreds of mike points.

"But by the time we had got down there, that massive initial flush of prog rock begun to fade and there weren't so many bands. We were massive supporters of Yes but we just didn't have the facilities to accommodate them." Over the years the show featured film clips of Yes performing live, interviews with Rick Wakeman, Chris Squire and Jon Anderson, and music from their solo projects, but not the group performing live in the studio. And when Harris says that it was difficult to accommodate the bands he was not exaggerating, as apart from its limited microphone points, Presentation B was only ten by seven metres, and to get the band, the mixing desk, the cameras and the presenter in there was a bit of a squeeze.

Although Harris was softly spoken, he shocked the audience in 1972 by publicly dismissing Roxy Music at the height of their hipness, when they were there in the studio. What caused that? "I took exception to Roxy Music," he replies. "It wasn't even anything to do with the music, but I did a Radio 1 *In Concert* with them a few weeks before they came in to do *Whistle Test* and they were so arrogant, they were deeply unpleasant – Bryan Ferry and Brian Eno to an extent. I really, really had a problem with their arrogance and particularly towards their fans. I know that people saw them that night, and me saying 'I don't like this band' and then hearing 'Virginia Plain' and going 'What the hell was he talking about?' But they didn't know the backstory, and I still stand by that."

It was also noted by a number of Roxy Music fans that the group were clearly miming and this was meant to be a live music show. "That was totally to do with the lack of facilities in the studio," says Harris. "The way it worked was that if we couldn't cope with the size of a particular band they would go away and record a supervised recording session to put down the backing track minus whatever instruments could be played on the show. The backing track would be running and you would have a live lead guitar over the top of it and lead vocals, so some of the instruments would be live, but not necessary all of them. You could say that all the performances you saw were exclusive to *Whistle Test* but all were not live – it was impossible to stage it."

Some of the music presented on *Whistle Test* was just an album track with an accompanying video, or more likely, old film clips matched up to the music by *Late Night Line-Up* film critic Philip Jenkinson. This low-budget approach did yield some magical moments, particularly when Mike Oldfield's *Tubular Bells* was premiered on the show to footage of

Alpine skiers in black and white taken from the 1931 film *Der Weisse Rausch*, which starred Leni Riefenstahl.

In 1972 Harris was presented with the award for Best TV Show for *The Old Grey Whistle Test* at the *Melody Maker* poll awards. Harris was also voted number two DJ behind John Peel.

The demands of being *The Old Grey Whistle Test* presenter – as well as a radio DJ – eventually took its toll on Harris. "In the early years, *Whistle Test* was on the air for forty-two weeks of the year. There was an eight to ten week break in the summer to go over to America to do filming, then we brought everything back and did the next series. Every programme was live. It was a very demanding schedule. So by the end of the Seventies I felt burnt out by it, quite honestly, and needed to step back and get away from it all. So the last show I did was the New Year's Eve programme from 1979–1980, where I introduced Blondie at the Apollo Glasgow."

CHAPTER 28

Divertimento No.3: Funny Foreigners

In Sixties Germany the Nazi party had been banned, but their ideology still permeated society in a subtle way, with prominent ex-Nazis known to be working in German corporations that were household names. The country's youth, who'd had no role in that terrible episode of history, wanted none of it and rebelled against the old order and the culture in which it had been birthed.

This sort of dissatisfaction was felt across mainland Europe, giving rise to the May 1968 student riots in Paris and violent protests by the 68er-Bewegung student movement in Germany. At its most extreme it provoked the formation of militant groups like the Italian Marxist-Leninist organisations The Red Brigades and in Germany the anti-capitalist terrorist organisation the Baader-Meinhof Group.

There was an overlap with the German rock scene. Producer and left-wing intellectual Uwe Nettelbeck – best known for promoting and producing Faust – allegedly had links with the Baader-Meinhof organisation. One night Amon Düül II vocalist Renate Knaup came home to the communal house in which she was living to find the fugitive Andreas Baader sleeping in her bed.

Without wishing to trivialise the differences, in the UK the north London-based Angry Brigade, active from 1970–72, carried out a number of bombings, mainly aimed at property. The group's mastermind, Jake Prescott, later said that he realised he was the only one who was actually angry.

Nettelbeck was known and respected by the German branch of Polydor. There was a lot of money in the record industry in 1970, but even now it seems amazing that in their desire to find a "German Beatles" Polydor trusted Nettelbeck to the extent of footing the bill for an unknown band to be installed in a studio in a converted schoolhouse near Wümme, in north Germany, and left to their own devices. Faust had access to a top engineer in Kurt Graupner, and Nettelbeck would occasionally report back on progress, while the band lived naked, grew their own dope and tomatoes, and experimented with sound.

'Why Don't You Eat Carrots?', the opening song on Faust's self-titled debut album, starts with brief snatches of The Beatles' 'All You Need Is Love' and The Rolling Stones' 'Satisfaction', which are almost immediately swamped by a great electronic splurge, like a casual rejection of British solipsistic hedonism and hippie-dippy idealism. It was also the nearest Faust got to what Polydor had wanted. From then on it sounded like a deliciously off-kilter marching band playing a tune that soon morphs into a crazy bierkeller singalong with synth signals raking around and around like a lighthouse beam, cut with interludes of speech and solo piano. It was this innovative way of editing, initiated by Nettelbeck – rock re-envisaged as *musique concrète* – that really set the group apart. That and the fact that the album was released on clear vinyl in a clear plastic sleeve, bearing an x-ray of a clenched fist, the like of which no one had seen, making it one of the most prized items of 1971.

Like British progressive rock, this new German music was a rediscovery of the musicians' roots. But the big difference was that it was on a much more personal level and was all about forming a new means of self-expression, about making a fresh start. So rather than exploring their musical heritage and tradition like the British groups, they basically rejected both German tradition and the rock'n'roll culture of the USA and the UK.

Cologne-based group Can were formed in 1968 of musicians from the fields of romantic classical, avant-garde modernism – bass guitarist Holger Czukay had studied with Karlheinz Stockhausen – and free jazz, all of which they deliberately discarded. These trained musicians were on a mission to pare their music down to some kind of ur-rhythm and one or two notes. On some tracks on their 1971 double album *Tago Mago*, keyboard player Irmin Schmidt – who had potentially been concert pianist material – goes as far as playing almost nothing.

But realistically, no one can just suddenly re-emerge completely sui generis, and in terms of rock, Can did acknowledge the influence of groups like Velvet Underground and Pink Floyd. Although probably coincidental, Can's song 'Yoo Doo Right' from their 1969 debut *Monster Movie* is based on the same two bass notes as Floyd's 1968 song 'Careful With That Axe, Eugene'.

Another prime example of Seventies German musical rebirth was Neu!, the Dusseldorf-based duo of Michael Rother and Klaus Dinger. As a teenage guitarist, Rother was particularly influenced by Jimi Hendrix, but as a German living through this period of societal unrest, he could see no future playing Anglo-American rock or jazz. "Suddenly I knew I had to be different," he says. His idea was of a new European music with a "European feeling about harmony and melody that lay underneath". Neu! – "New" in German – had a pared-down approach both instrumentally and structurally. To make sure they didn't use hackneyed chord changes, 'Für Immer' is largely based on one chord. Their music had a significant amount of melody but was essentially all about momentum and forward motion towards a metaphorical "vanishing point on the horizon". The subtext of their yearning for escape from the past to something new, was inescapable and was enforced by their exclamation mark.

The UK Common Market referendum of 1975 showed that having joined in 1973, voters were keen for the experiment to continue, but psychologically and perceptually the UK was still isolated from mainland Europe. Arguably it still is today, not least after the 2016 referendum, when a small majority voted to leave the European Union. But back in the 1970s it was more so: many people wouldn't even have travelled abroad. This geographically insular mindset differed from that of young people across the Channel and this new German music became commonly known as "krautrock", which was at best a snappy, albeit clumsy, piece of journalese and at worst, with its World War Two connotations, a rather dismissive lumping together of many exploratory, radical takes on rock.

Except that commonly held view is not strictly accurate. As well as it being a term that was rarely, if ever, used in common parlance, "Kraut Rock" was first used in 1971 in the headline of an advertisement by a German company Popo Managements in *Billboard* magazine, both to offer an inroad for Anglo American bands into the German market, and to promote their roster of bands and their label, Bacillus Records, in the UK. They defiantly inverted stereotypes with the lines, "When you think of Germany, you don't exactly think of rock. Oumpa-oumpa, right?" and "Just drop by and listen to one of our albums. They'll blow your lederhosen-ideas to bits and pieces". The Virgin mail order company used the term "krautrock" in late 1972 to describe the albums that they were importing from Germany, but subsequently dropped the term in favour of "German rock". Which is what it was called by most people in the UK.

Faust disliked the label so much that they re-appropriated it for the opening track, 'Krautrock', of their 1973 album *Faust IV* on Virgin Records.

But krautrock caught the ear of fans who craved more extreme kicks than could be had from British progressive rock. It was born out of cultural turmoil and so had an edge that British music could rarely match. British youth were not used to being presented with new music of such quality from mainland Europe, and this German progressive music was suddenly regarded as the coolest thing among teenage "Heads" trying to out-weird each other.

It took on an exotic quality. Germany isn't far away, but in the early Seventies many of these groups' albums, on German labels such as Brain and Ohr, were not distributed within the UK and so were only available on import. The media that disseminated information on, or music by, these groups was so small in comparison to what we have today and so focused on the UK and the US, that news only leaked out sporadically. This only served to heighten the mystery and prompted queries along the lines of: "Who was that amazing German band that John Peel played last night? I didn't catch their name? Did anyone tape it? Where can I buy it? What, just on import? Blimey, is it that expensive?"

Duncan Fallowell was the first British music journalist to go to meet Can and he wrote a tantalising article on the group in *Melody Maker* in October 1971, which incorporated a brief overview of the German scene. It was significant enough to be reproduced as the liner notes for the UK version, on United Artists, of Can's 1971 album *Tago Mago*, to try to put the music in some kind of context for the listeners, most of whom would probably know nothing whatsoever about Can or any of the other groups that Fallowell mentioned.

And some of this music sounded like it had come from another planet. Keyboard-based Berlin group Tangerine Dream's 1971 album *Alpha Centauri* found them escaping from the repressive culture of their homeland via metaphorical space travel.

In 1973, Tangerine Dream's austere, haunting *Atem* was John Peel's album of the year and they signed to Virgin, becoming a high-profile group with their 1974 album, *Phaedra*. Its synths, sequencers, Mellotron and treated keyboards stirred up a warm, beautifully recorded bubblebath for the mind, with textures ranging from sumptuous to spectral. It reached number fifteen in the UK album charts.

Dutch group Focus also enjoyed significant commercial success in the UK. Their albums *Moving Waves* (1971) and *Focus 3* (1972) were most closely linked to British progressive bands, with their jazz and classical feel but with rock dynamics, and the group had in Jan Akkerman an exceptional lead and rhythm guitarist. They also scored two hit singles in the UK charts. 'Hocus Pocus' (1971) was built on a base of heavy rock riffing and flamboyant drumming, while keyboard player and flautist Thijs Van Leer stole the show with his scat singing and stratospheric yodelling. 'Sylvia' was more serious, a song without words, a beautifully constructed melodic instrumental.

The main point about 'Hocus Pocus' is that in its rather absurd yodelled lines it was having a poke at what was seen to be naff about a lot of mainland European pop and rock. It felt like those over the Channel just didn't "get it" somehow and they so often built poor replicas of American and British pop and rock. Even their easy listening was awful, exemplified by James Last's mind-numbingly bland orchestrated medleys of popular tunes.

Back in Blighty there came the naïve realisation that "Hey, they have progressive rock groups in Holland as well". And then someone would come into school with albums from the suddenly hip Netherlands by Kayak and Alquin. They had bands in Italy as well (Banco, PFM – with lyrics by Peter Sinfield, ex-of King Crimson on 1973's *Photos Of Ghosts* – and Le Orme, who had Peter Hammill write the lyrics to *Felona And Sorona*, also from 1973); in France (Magma, Ange); in Finland (Wigwam, Tasavallan Presidentti); even in Japan (Stomu Yamashta).

Although the music press was instrumental in widening the appeal of foreign groups in the Seventies, that residual hangover from World War Two was set deep in the British psyche. John Cleese and Connie Booth's script for the BBC 2 *Fawlty Towers* episode, 'The Germans', showed this resentment bubbling up from Basil Fawlty's id through the cracked veneer of "We're all friends now" with excruciating brilliance.

Even in the liberal music press, this parochialism could border on xenophobia. One can only assume that *NME* journalist Ian MacDonald was less than impressed when he saw that some bright spark of a sub-editor had given his perceptive 1974 piece on Can the headline 'We Have Ways Of Making You Listen', presumably to be read aloud in a comedy German accent.

There was also a jealousy of the Germans, who had been defeated in the war but whose economy was booming, particularly in the areas of manufacturing and technology.

Kraftwerk – their name means "power plant" in German – had surfaced in Dusseldorf in 1970. Essentially a duo of Florian Schneider and Ralf Hütter, they initially experimented with both conventional instrumentation and found sounds, their rhythms coming from drum machines, real drums, and echoed flute and keyboards.

The group hit their stride with the synths and sequencers of *Autobahn* (1974), with Wolfgang Flür drafted in on "electronic percussion". The album reached number four in the UK albums chart. The side-long title track was a sonic evocation of car travel – including synthesised car horns and doppler effects – and an edited single charted at number eleven in that year.

Ralf Hütter claimed that as part of krautrock's ongoing reinvention, Kraftwerk were typical of a new generation seeking new electronic sounds, as he told American journalist Lester Bangs in *Creem* in 1975. By now they had been joined by a second electronic drummer, Karl Bartos; had uniformly short haircuts; and were dressing in anonymous middle management suits, while peddling a whole impersonal "music of the machines" schtick.

When Bangs asked if the machines could ever start playing the musicians, Schneider replied: "Yes. When it gets up to a certain stage, *It* starts playing... it's no longer you and I, it's *It*."

Bangs even asked Schneider if they intended to provide a musical "final solution"? Crass and offensive though that question undoubtedly was, Kraftwerk also played up to the notion of national stereotypes.

Hütter told him: "We want the whole world to know our background. We cannot deny we are from Germany, because the German mentality, which is more advanced, will always be part of our behaviour."

Kraftwerk were provocative with their arch, eccentric, almost comic-book android severity and always played it dead straight, but much of their music revealed itself to be quite charmingly droll and tongue-in-cheek. Evidently the German sense of humour was also far more nuanced than we had realised.

CHAPTER 29

A Jazzy Collection of Antiques, Curios and Battered Ornaments: Colosseum, Greenslade, Pete Brown and Centipede

In the Seventies many UK jazz groups moved more towards jazz rock, which feels, subjectively, more like an extension of jazz rather than the hybrid style of progressive rock. There is some overlap of course, particularly with groups like Isotope and Nucleus, but it's an area that deserves its own book. So this chapter focuses on some examples of jazz musicians who crossed over into progressive rock.

COLOSSEUM

As a young semi-pro drummer, Jon Hiseman played with UK jazz luminaries like Ronnie Scott and Tubby Hayes. And together with saxophonist Dick Heckstall-Smith, he played in a trio version of the groundbreaking jazz and R&B group, The Graham Bond Organisation, which he joined in 1966, replacing Ginger Baker. While he had enjoyed the sense of freedom that Bond instilled in the musicians in his group, both he and Heckstall-Smith absconded in early 1968 due to Bond's erratic behaviour while trying to quit heroin, and after a brief spell with John Mayall's Bluesbreakers they were both looking for something new.

They formed Colosseum in 1968 and the band's initial line-up also included Tony Reeves on bass, James Litherland on guitar and vocals, and Dave Greenslade on keyboards, with whom Hiseman had played in semi-pro outfit The Westminster Five. No one else really sounded like Colosseum. Hiseman was only 25 at this point but he and the group already had a wealth of experience to draw on.

"Dave Greenslade had come from three years playing with Chris Farlowe [in a band] with Albert Lee, one of the greatest blues and country rock guitarists. Dick Heckstall-Smith was one of the best modern jazz saxophone players of his era," Hiseman explains. "I had played with all the great British jazz stars by the time I got to play with Graham Bond. So we had a very special pedigree, which nobody else had.

"I had a very clear idea of what I wanted: rock rhythms, jazz solos and two- or three-part harmonies," Hiseman continues. "We take for granted jazz solos are played over rock rhythms these days. That was not so at the time: jazz was played in jazz clubs and rock was twanging guitars."

Greenslade – who also had experience buffing up his soul organ lines playing with Geno Washington – doesn't recall this idea being spelled out to him as such, but the chemistry between the players was immediately apparent.

"We met at St Matthew's Hall, in Elephant & Castle," says Greenslade. "We had no idea what we were going to play – and we just started getting sketches and things together. First piece I think we ever played was 'Those About To Die', which is on the first album.

"In 1968–69 there was a big musical pot, everything was being thrown in by these young, mainly white guys in London. And, depending on the combination and preferences of those few people in each group, out came something new every time."

Colosseum's debut album, *Those Who Are About To Die Salute You*, released on Fontana in 1969, glanced back at Hiseman and Heckstall-Smith's time with Bond with a version of his 'Walking In The Park', but took that already potent mix of jazz and R&B into new directions. It's a little quicker, with stop-start interjections giving it a greater sense of dynamics. Hiseman's virtuosic drumming adds to the excitement with an incisive backbeat punctuated by sudden explosive snare and tom-tom rolls.

'Beware The Ides Of March' rather cheekily starts with a fantasia on Procol Harum's 'A Whiter Shade Of Pale', alights for a while on Bach's *Toccata And Fugue In D Minor*, and there's also a half quote of The Rolling Stones' 'Satisfaction'.

'Backwater Blues', a cover of the Leadbelly song, has Hiseman nibbling away at the rhythm and engaging in a musical dialogue with the soloists rather than playing standard slow blues-rock figures.

On the title track, the rhythms are more overtly jazz. Hiseman's drumming is elegant but at times swings fast and fierce, showing his love of Dave Brubeck drummer Joe Morello and the more intense, physical approach of Buddy Rich and Elvin Jones.

Valentyne Suite was the first release on the Vertigo label – the progressive subsidiary of Philips – in November 1969, the title track taking up all of side two, a kind of musical elongation was de rigueur at the time.

"We simply came up with a series of ideas and linked them together, and suddenly it was the whole side of an album," says Hiseman. "It was called this in a most unlikely fashion, really," Greenslade explains. "I was going out with a girl called Val and it came into my head about Valentyne and I rather pretentiously called it a suite. Mostly my hands were on the first two sections; Dick composed the third section. But we used to kick the whole thing around in rehearsals, so all the arrangements were done by the band."

The side-long title track, especially Greenslade's sections, was different from their more jazz- and blues-fuelled music, with a baroque feel to some of his prominent keyboard lines. "My mother was a great singer, and sang in a church choir, and every Easter I would go with my brother and my father to hear Handel's *Messiah*," says Greenslade. "So I wasn't just into Tubby Hayes and Dave Brubeck, I enjoyed Handel and Mozart, and Vaughan Williams in particular."

Arranger Neil Ardley, came up with a big-band arrangement on 'Butty's Blues' and strings on 'Elegy'. "In fact, we even did some live dates with the jazz orchestra," Greenslade recalls. "Playing Los Angeles with a big band was marvellous and I wish we'd done more of that."

'The Machine Demands A Sacrifice' features lyrics by Pete Brown, and is a bluesy pop song with vocal harmonies by Greenslade, which fades into a section of mechanistic percussion, the "machine" with which Hiseman is credited on the sleeve.

Valentyne Suite went into the UK charts at number fifteen and the success of this new hybrid of rock, blues, R&B and jazz prompted a new seriousness in the way it was presented.

"We walked into Brunel [University] into this big hall where we were told the gig was going to be, and there were rows and rows of chairs, and a big stage," says Greenslade. "I thought, 'No, no, they've taken us to the wrong hall, there's probably some club at the back here.' I was assured, 'No, that's where we're playing.'

"That was one of our first experiences of having a totally sat-down, silent audience, packed, waiting on our every note. I thought, blimey, the atmosphere has really changed from the sweaty Marquee and the Flamingo – which is a milling-around crowd and very vibrant – to suddenly what appeared to be a concert hall."

The group recorded *Daughter Of Time* in 1970. The line up was in transition during recording with Dave "Clem" Clempson coming in on guitar, Mark Clarke on bass, Chris Farlowe on vocals and Barbara Thompson on saxes and flute. Despite this it's still a strong set, although its running time was bolstered by the eight-minute makeweight, 'The Time Machine', a live drum solo rather clumsily edited with a few bars of ensemble playing during the fade in and about thirty seconds more at the end.

Colosseum Live, recorded at Manchester and Brighton in 1971, has some tremendously energetic, well-played – and long – versions of studio cuts and some unreleased music. And Clempson, Mark Clarke and Farlowe were singing in three-part harmony.

"On the album we play 'Tanglewood '63' with vocal harmonies with no words, and songs like 'Lost Angeles' and 'Skellington' are what I set out to do. But it took me three years to get there," Hiseman says.

Sadly, that was also the end. Colosseum were a high-profile group, but Clempson accepted the offer to join Steve Marriott in the already commercially successful Humble Pie, which precipitated the band's break-up in 1971.

Hiseman formed Tempest with guitarist Allan Holdsworth, Mark Clarke and later Ollie Halsall, a kind of progressive/hard rock hybrid, which was rather less than the sum of its parts. Tempest ran for a couple of years and in 1975, Hiseman formed Colosseum II – more in the jazz fusion category – with guitarist Gary Moore and keyboard player Don Airey.

Producer and former Colosseum manager Gerry Bron suggested the group – initially called Ghosts – do some studio recordings and was so impressed that he offered them a deal on his Bronze label as long as the Colosseum name was used somewhere. Hiseman: "I rang all the guys who said, 'Go for it.' I called it Colosseum II but in terms of the original Colosseum, it didn't really deserve the name."

GREENSLADE

By autumn 1972 Greenslade had formed the band Greenslade, with bass guitarist Tony Clarke from Colosseum, Dave Lawson from Samurai and Web, and drummer Andy McCullough, who had played with Fields and King Crimson – a busy, technically brilliant player and not dissimilar to Hiseman in his approach. It was less jazz influenced than Colosseum and if anything, carried on from Greenslade's compositions on *Valentyne Suite*.

"When I formed Greenslade, I'd never heard of the term progressive rock," says Greenslade. "I wasn't saying, 'Right chaps, let's form a prog rock band'. It was just a natural progression with a different kind of line-up from Colosseum.

"All my colleagues in the music business said I was mad, and it would never work, because there wasn't a guitar player. But it suited the kind of music that was in my head, and I was writing an awful lot after Colosseum. I had a small studio, and therefore I could multi-track, and play all the keyboard parts. But onstage I couldn't do that so I thought, 'Right, I'll find another keyboard player and I'll make sure he can sing.' And I found Dave Lawson, who was a great player.

"And so each of us were playing at least three keyboards. It must have been a nightmare for the road crew – six keyboards in a band – and they weren't small and portable in those days. We used to swap about. I played the Hammond quite a bit, and a Fender Rhodes. Then I bought an RMI, an American electric piano and an ARP synth. Dave had a lovely ARP, and we wrote for all these voices."

In fact, their two-keyboard-player front line gave Greenslade a certain hip cachet. Their debut, *Greenslade*, arrived in a Roger Dean album cover in 1972 and was a fresh-sounding combination. Dave Lawson's hard-edged voice cuts through the instrumentation on 'Feathered Friends', but although the songs were melodically and rhythmically complex, the instrumental 'An English Western' finds the musicians knitting together, typically playing for the composition rather than indulging in grandstanding keyboard wizardry.

"I never got into that big ego trip thing of, 'Does the band look alright behind me?'" Greenslade says. "I didn't feel like that at all. I'm not a frontman, I'm a musician and I play with other musicians."

On *Greenslade* all the music was written by Greenslade and the lyrics by Lawson. The follow-up, *Bedside Manners Are Extra*, showed a growing rapport between with the musicians.

"It's always been said that your second album is the most difficult," says Greenslade. "The first one went down very well, and it was quite a breath of fresh air in some ways. But we topped it with *Bedside Manners Are Extra*. We started to write some really good stuff together, Dave and myself. We all started to really feel the groove of Greenslade – what it was, what we had – and I think it manifests itself on that second album."

The group recorded only two more albums together, *Spyglass Guest* (1974), which reached number thirty-four in the charts, and *Time And Tide* (1975). Given their togetherness on their second album, did the fact that, at times, the two keyboard players worked separately, recording all the keyboards on their respective compositions, start to undermine group solidarity?

"If we played them on stage, then all four of us would have to be involved. But in the studio, if the composer's got his own arrangement in his head, and his own ideas to do it, why shouldn't he do it? And the other guy could have the afternoon off. And no one was very precious about it."

Greenslade were never going to be flash rock stars but they gained a degree of commercial success and toured across Europe and the US – then just disappeared.

"I had a great band but things changed a bit as we went along, and I had real management problems," say Greenslade. "Quite a well-known management company, but they weren't really interested in [the band], they were interested in the money that came in, and it got in a bit of a muddle. I tried to get away from them and go to a more suitable stable, but they wouldn't let me go unless I paid lots and lots of money, which I didn't have. So I had to break the band up after three years."

PETE BROWN

Pete Brown had been performing his vivid, Beat-influenced poetry since the early Sixties, often to jazz accompaniment and most notably with The First Real Poetry Band, which included guitarist John McLaughlin, Binky McKenzie on bass and Laurie Allan on drums. The group never made any commercial releases although they recorded some demo sessions.

Brown had been writing lyrics for Cream since 1966, but he decided that he wanted to sing with a band and so, in 1967, he went to visit his friend Graham Bond. "I took the songs over and had some melodic ideas to sing to him. And he said, 'I want you to join my band,'" Brown recalls. "We were both living in a fantasy world at the time. I said, 'I'm not really a singer.' He said, 'Well you just did.'"

But that line-up of the Graham Bond Organisation with Dick Heckstall-Smith on saxes and Jon Hiseman on drums was about to split up so nothing more came of it.

"I was hanging out at Middle Earth chasing girls and stuff, and this friend of a friend of mine said, 'Look I've got an opportunity to produce some tracks, could you put a band together? I've got free time at Polydor.'

"I got this incredible band together: McLaughlin and Phil Lee on guitars; Binky McKenzie and Danny Thompson on bass; Heckstall-Smith; [trombonist] John Mumford; a great keyboard player called John Mitchell, he was an organ scholar at Oxford and a first rate guy; Laurie Allan on drums; and another singer who was much better than me and I was friends with at the time, a songwriter called Graham Layden – he used to work with the Liverpool Scene.

"We did a couple of rehearsals with that line-up and got a few people to come down. I remember one A&R guy came down and said, 'Yeah, but it's just a bunch of jazz has-beens.' This was 1967, before Pentangle, before Colosseum, and before Mahavishnu Orchestra."

But at that stage, Brown found it intimidating singing against such formidable players. Instead, he opted to go "lower down the scale" in his search for musicians. Only he was unhappy at what he found there. "I started off with something that was pretty rough. We did a few gigs, and I realised that I was used to people who were very, very good and I couldn't really hack it."

Brown formed another phenomenal group, the Battered Ornaments, who numbered in their ranks free jazz saxophonist and flautist Nisar Ahmed "George" Khan, and young hot-shot guitarist Chris Spedding.

Lyn Dobson played sax with them for a time, and their original drummer was Jamie Muir, who was also a free improviser and would go on to play percussion with King Crimson on their 1972 album *Larks' Tongues In Aspic*.

"He had very good chops and his timing was good," says Brown. "But on the kit he was more like a free jazzer. He was a very interesting guy, but I wanted something a bit more regular."

Early live performances of Pete Brown & His Battered Ornaments featured Graham Laydon doing vocals with Brown, and a dancer called Romy, who was friends with Sonja Kristina of Curved Air, who could also sing.

"Originally I got someone on keyboards called Mick," Brown recalls. "He could play a bit, but he'd taken way too much acid. In rehearsals he'd gradually take his clothes off. Eventually he'd be sitting there with no clothes on at all playing the organ, so I realised this wasn't going to work. I tactfully suggested we'd got somebody else in mind and that I didn't think this was going to work, but we'd really like to hire the organ from him."

Brown then drafted in Charlie Hart on organ and violin, and Pete Bailey, his road manager and percussionist from The First Real Poetry

Band. Bailey was 44 years old and the prodigiously gifted drummer, Rob Tait, was only 18, giving the group a remarkably wide age range for the time.

They recorded a demo, which ended up with Andrew King of Blackhill Enterprises, who along with Peter Jenner became their manager and agency. The group recorded a single on Parlophone, 'The Week Looked Good On Paper', the first song that Brown had written for Bond, and then Blackhill got them a deal with EMI's progressive subsidiary, Harvest.

"The Harvest label formed as a tax loss by EMI as they were making too much money, then they got the Floyd and Deep Purple and realised they were making too much money again. I'm sure they signed people like me because they thought it was going to lose enough money to justify it."

Initially, Pete Brown & His Battered Ornaments rehearsed in Brown's small Fulham flat. "I got served with this wonderful summons, which said: 'You are charged with creating a disturbance with a musical instrument, to wit, a band.'"

The group spent a lot of time on the road travelling and sleeping in their converted army ambulance.

"The Battered Ornaments was quite a popular band in Britain. It is quite British in lots of way," says Brown. "We had a kind of act. I used to do things like destroying toilet brushes and I had a false hand that came off: things to compensate for me being a crap singer."

Being signed to EMI, they recorded most of their debut, *A Meal You Can Shake Hands With In The Dark*, at Abbey Road, although Brown was aware they were not the company's top priority. "Every now and again you'd have a call from a studio booker saying, 'You know you've got that gig in Peterborough? Well, if you came in after that for a couple of hours you could do some recording.' You'd walk into the studio in a semi-coma, having given your all and then be obliged to do it again."

Even for EMI's progressive Harvest label, *A Meal...* was a particularly adventurous and curious creation. "Originally it was meant to be more of a modern R&B band, but the organ got repossessed and so that meant it changed its flavour," says Brown. "I suppose you could pitch it somewhere between Soft Machine and Pentangle. One of the main influences on it was definitely the Albert Ayler record *New Grass*, a combination of funk and free jazz. I'd worked as a poetry and folk duo with [guitarist] Davy Graham, and I incorporated folky elements into things like 'The Sandcastle'."

'Dark Lady' is ostensibly a straight-ahead soul stomper, but is galvanised into something else by Khan's ferocious sax interjections and Spedding's skidding slide guitar. On 'Station Song' in particular Brown's vocals are poised and evocative. He could hold a tune, and even though his range and expressive ability are somewhat limited, his delivery is always charismatic, full of energy, and fits into the music's spontaneous sprit. He is, however, dismissive of these early performances.

"I was a fucking awful singer," he says. "There's a whole thesis you could write about poets who couldn't sing," he says. "Dylan, Leonard Cohen, Patti Smith – a whole syndrome. Most of them were doing things with very simple three- or four-chord backings, which made it a lot easier for them. What I was doing was not that at all, I was trying to do something very complex and be part of a band."

The standout track is 'The Politician', a radically different version of the song Brown wrote with Jack Bruce for Cream. Brown begins with a savagely satirical, semi-improvised rap on the sleazy doings of the MP. Khan steps in with a visceral tenor solo, and what could have been an R&B jam, more or less, is urged on by Tait's high-velocity stickwork into an instrumental tour de force. The song's subject is cast in the role of the bluesman-seducer and Brown piles on the grotesquerie with references to the politician's *"hideous sores"* and his desire to deposit his files *"in your drawers"*.

But the end of Pete Brown & His Battered Ornaments came in the oddest of ways. They had a place on the bill with The Rolling Stones at the 1969 Hyde Park Festival, which also launched King Crimson. But in a coup orchestrated by Spedding, Brown was ousted two days beforehand. "It would have done me a lot of good, probably, but didn't do them a lot of good," says Brown, and the group played an instrumental set with a couple of numbers sung by Spedding.

Most of the follow-up album, *Mantle-Piece*, released later that year as The Battered Ornaments, had already been recorded so Spedding re-recorded Brown's vocal tracks with his own, highlighting his own limitations as a singer. Unsurprisingly, the band soon folded. But Brown had already moved on. "I thought, 'I'm not going to give up,' and formed Piblokto almost immediately."

Pete Brown & Piblokto included Tait and guitarist Jim Mullen. They recorded *Things May Come And Things May Go But The Art School Dance Goes On Forever*, which included material that The First Real Poetry Band had demoed in 1967. The title track shows Brown's compositional ability and has an intricate structure, which bass guitarist Roger Bunn and keyboard player Dave Thompson explore with relish, while on the stand-out song 'Golden Country Kingdom', Brown's lyrics are rich in imagery, cryptic and ornate. The group recorded *Thousands On A Raft* before disbanding in 1971. Brown then joined up with Graham Bond to form Bond & Brown, releasing *Two Heads Are Better Than One* in 1972. He continued recording throughout the Seventies, although he became so disenchanted with the way the business promoted punk that he "gave up" for a while.

CENTIPEDE

Even though the Seventies was an era when it seemed that anything might be possible, Centipede – a fifty-strong big band of jazz, free improvisation, classical and rock musicians, who made the double album *Septober Energy* for RCA's Neon label – was an extraordinary one-off.

By the end of the Sixties, the young exploratory jazz pianist Keith Tippett was leading his own group. King Crimson guitarist Robert Fripp came to see them play The Marquee and invited Tippett and other musicians from the sextet to play sessions on the group's albums *In The Wake Of Poseidon* (1970), *Lizard* (1970) and *Islands* (1971).

Tippett was a major figure in breaking down barriers between jazz and rock in the early Seventies. In 1995 Robert Wyatt had this to say on the pianist: "A West Country bloke with a great big heart and completely unlike the Old Boy Network jazz mafia that was the London scene at the time. He listened to everybody, was open-minded, never put anybody down and one of his things was to get all these different musicians from different genres together."

His early session work had been enormously varied, from playing with André Previn, to upcoming folk artist Shelagh McDonald, to backing comedian Charlie Drake. And, as Tippett pointed out when I initially got in touch with him in 2014, his studio work with Crimson only represented about sixteen hours out of his career, and as Centipede were the most "out" progressive musical project of the time, the group warranted a place in the book. He then explained the genesis of Centipede's 1970 album *Septober Energy*.

"I thought, 'I'm going to write a piece encompassing all the people that I know.' Many people thought it was kind of crazy, but it was accomplished, because unless you dream, you can't achieve anything," Tippett says.

Or, in other words, if you are going to do a mates' project, make sure you have plenty of mates who can play a bit. And Tippett did. He began writing the piece, and when the music was taking shape he started recruiting musicians, with Fripp as producer. "I started ringing around saying, 'Listen, I'm putting this fifty-piece band together. If I can actually get it off the ground, will you be in it?'

"I knew Ian McDonald and I was married to [vocalist] Julie [Tippetts]. Her brother-in-law Brian Godding was in the Blossom Toes and through him I knew Brian Belshaw who was the bass player. I knew Mike Patto and Zoot Money through Julie and Boz Burrell. Everybody in that band, with the exception of a few of the string players, I knew socially. They were friends.

"From Nucleus, Karl Jenkins, Ian Carr, Brian Smith, John Marshall; [from] Soft Machine there was Robert Wyatt; Mark Charig, Nick Evans and Elton Dean were in my sextet and Centipede was formed just before they played with the Soft Machine; and an old friend from Bristol, Larry Stabbins [on sax]. Then you had the [South African] musicians from The Brotherhood Of Breath and Chris McGregor's Blue Notes: Mongezi Feza and Dudu Pukwana. Paul Rutherford from the London Jazz Composers' Orchestra... So there was quite a diversity in musical backgrounds, even within the jazz musicians."

News of the project got around and the London Jazz Centre Society, which was trying to raise funds to build a London Jazz Centre, asked Tippett to do a benefit concert and so Centipede played for the first time at The Lyceum on November 15, 1970, to a packed audience.

As a composition, *Septober Energy* has had its critics, but although it is a tad uneven – and gets clogged up a bit in part three – it's an inspired piece, and its sheer originality, musicality and surprising accessibility compensates for any shortcomings.

It's also imbued with the energy of change that Tippett felt at the end of the Sixties and into the Seventies. He was absorbing some of the rock music of the time – hearing The Beatles, The Rolling Stones and The Who at parties – while in jazz, players like Archie Shepp, Sun Ra and Albert Ayler were breaking through into contemporary consciousness. Then there were European composers like Stockhausen, Luigi Nono and Krzysztof Penderecki, and also peculiarly European styles of free improvisation.

Septober Energy contains free passages, some delicate and pianissimo and some pretty fiery, with linking passages of incantatory voices, with lyrics written by Julie Tippetts. There are also serpentine, complex variations on riffs with electric bass, guitars and brass.

Up until then, as Tippett says, these musicians would only have played together in a studio doing session work to back a singer, but here the rock players are expected to play on the jazz sections and the jazz players join in on the rock sections. And throughout it all, the thread of Tippett's own brilliant, finely chiselled piano lines.

"I think it appealed to jazz fans, contemporary music fans and your progressive rock and freer jazz fans," says Tippett. "There are some great solos on there, like [saxophonist] Alan Skidmore's solo on the rock section on side two and his duet with Larry Stabbins [on sax]. And Karl Jenkins on oboe.

"Robert Fripp was in the band and was meant to play on the album. He had a solo about two thirds of the way in, over the whole orchestra. It was fantastic but he was also mixing it, and ultimately we ran out of studio time. And that was a big, big shame."

"It's 70 per cent notated and architecturally directed, so that meant the musicians were either improvising within the architecture or there would be a cameo spot for a quartet, for example, that would be totally improvised. On the third side, the strings play very high with glissandi down and the voices improvise around it. That section is a very basic graphic score. They were not held to the written notes."

Although Tippett reckons that *Septober Energy* worked better when performed in concert, the studio version was essentially recorded live, with the vocals overdubbed. He still rues the fact that the fourth and final section was recorded at 10 a.m. as Boz Burrell, Mike Patto and Zoot Money had all been out partying and turned up late. Consequently their voices were all rather shot.

"What could I do? I had fifty musicians in the studio so I had to record it, but it doesn't reach the heights that it did live," Tippett says. "Naughty boys. That was naïve. We should have planned it better."

What was perhaps even more astonishing than the music itself is that RCA were right behind the concept. And as well as their established stars, they and other labels like EMI and Phillips, for a brief period, were also investing in some particularly uncompromising musicians like Mike Westbrook, John Surman, Tony Oxley, Chris McGregor and Brotherhood Of Breath.

"I had a contract with RCA and they were quite happy for me to be doing Centipede for the rest of my life. On ice next time. Or with camels," he says laughing. "They said, 'We regard you and Julie as the Johnny Dankworth and Cleo Laine of your generation and anything you want to do we will be there to support you."

This involved paying for charter flights for Centipede to play in Bordeaux. They travelled there with the RCA admin and management, and a dozen roadies.

"It was easier to charter your own aeroplane than getting individual tickets. We took off from Stansted, which at the time was only a tiny little airport. Then the signs came on that you could take off your seat belts and you could smoke. Suddenly there are these big spliffs being passed around," Tippet recalls.

"People were getting their double basses out and playing them in the aisle, a jam session at 33,000 feet. Gary Windo, the late American saxophonist, was playing to the pilot in the cockpit. You wouldn't be able to do that now. I'm sitting there thinking, 'Oh man, we're going to be busted when we land.' They're drinking wine and the band is raving all the way to Bordeaux. Then we get off and I see this customs officer and police lining up on tarmac. They just waved us through. It was like, 'Get out of here – there are too many of you to take on.'"

There were so many musicians in Centipede that they made their presence known in whatever town they were playing a concert. "We did one at Rotterdam Arts Festival [In June 1971]," says Tippett. "We were there for four days, groups [of us] playing in parks and on street corners. We'd take over a whole hotel or restaurant. People would be waiting for their food and with fifty musicians, knives and forks would be picked up and the music of the cutlery and the glasses was absolutely fantastic."

In 1994, trombonist Nick Evans recalled the perils of extra-curricular musical activity in Rotterdam: "I do remember playing with Gary Windo on the back of a low-loader lorry, which drove around the streets one sunny afternoon. I remember it because a lady threw a bucket of water over the musicians on the lorry as we passed under her third-storey window."

It couldn't last, of course, and Tippett, who once could see the heads of RCA at short notice and received wine from them for Christmas, found himself having to wait for longer in reception and the wine supply gradually drying up. By the mid-Seventies record companies were far less willing to take a punt on an intriguing art project, and by then Centipede, who only made the one album, were basically finished, although they reassembled to play the Nancy Festival in 1975.

Septober Energy was an index of what was possible into this new decade. As Keith Tippett's Ark, Tippett recorded another large-scale piece, *Frames: Music For An Imaginary Film*, in 1978, an extensive sonic panorama with thorny ensemble passages and the most gorgeous, swooning jazz tune with Tippett duetting with Stan Tracey on side three.

"I was learning an apprenticeship," says Tippett. "*Septober Energy* was a young man's work and I don't listen to it very often. But if I do, I think that it really does virtually encompass all that was happening on the popular music scene in London at that time and I'd put it up there beside anything."

CHAPTER 30

All You Need to Do Is Sit Back and Acquire the Taste: Gentle Giant

There never actually was a Simon Dupree leading The Big Sound, but for the group's fans, the prime candidate would have been Derek Shulman, the rabble-rousing lead singer in his satin shirt, tight pants, Cuban heels and sideburns. Born into a Jewish family in Glasgow in 1947, Derek was brought up in Portsmouth and although he looked more mature than his years, he started treading the boards with Simon Dupree & The Big Sound when he was only 18 years old. Also in the group were his younger brother Ray, and his older brother by nearly a decade, Phil, whose tenure in the group was telling but brief. But they started young in those days. The group had previously been called The Howling Wolves and The Road Runners, and Derek recalls times when they would play a late gig and he and Ray would get back home and go straight to school.

"There was a huge gig circuit both on the south coast and throughout England in the Sixties," says Derek. "I remember in Nottingham there were three gigs literally next door to each other and you could play four shows a night. You'd do an early evening show, an evening show and two all-nighters in the Boat Club. Back in those days that's how you got your chops down. Completely exhausting but so much fun and very important."

Simon Dupree were self-sufficient from an early age, earning their money from gigs by playing a high energy mix of melodic soul, pop and R&B, which was stylistically not so far removed from The Spencer Davis Group, with some Rolling Stones grit thrown in. When keyboard player Eric Hine was unable to make one tour in 1967, his replacement was the budding Bluesology pianist Reginald Dwight, who was just about to embark on a solo career as Elton John. They ended up recording two of his songs, 'I'm Going Home' and 'Laughing Boy From Nowhere', but they were only released in 1969, long after the group had disbanded.

Early signs of their eclectic spirit were evident when they played on *Beat Club* on German TV in 1966, when co-vocalist Ray Shulman played a French horn onstage on 'Day Time Night Time'. Although the group signed to EMI Parlophone in that year and enjoyed success on mainland Europe, it wasn't quite happening for them in the UK, for although they were selling out venues on a par with The Kinks and The Move, and getting some of their music into the lower reaches of the singles charts, they had yet to enjoy a big hit.

"Then our manager, who was my brother-in-law, said that we should really do something that was more 'commercial'," says Derek. "So he found this song called 'Kites', given to him by [publishers] Robbins Music. We thought, 'Well, it's not really our style, but to hell with it; let's go and give it a shot.' It wasn't a tongue-in-cheek version, we did it with grace and thought it might work, and it flew into the charts. In some places it was a number one single. We used Mellotron, and the sounds of psychedelia that were happening at the time. It turned into a pop hit, which changed what Simon Dupree & The Big Sound became."

With its heady scent of faux oriental exotica – gongs, koto-like twangs and the mysterious murmurings of an Eastern femme fatale – 'Kites' chimed with the spirit of 1967, but was an anomaly for the group, although they were now being photographed dressed in psychedelic garb.

But powerful forces were at work away from the statistics of hit records and chart positions. Derek reckons that due to The Beatles' influence, "in England, music drove every part of the culture; it *was* the culture".

Simon Dupree folded in 1969 and the Shulman brothers had luckily made enough money from the group to have time to consider their next step. The following year they reappeared in a new musical form. Just as the difference between early Simon Dupree and 'Kites' had been great, the difference between 'Kites' and Gentle Giant was even greater.

"In Simon Dupree we became fairly adept at our instruments – certainly me and my brothers – and we wanted to expand our musical creativity," says Derek. "And to a certain degree we were restricted by the fact that we'd had pop hits and were a pop band. And that became a millstone around our necks, actually, because we were put in shows where the screamers were there. We just wanted to show what we could do as a band, but they just wanted to hear the hits. So, firstly we looked for other musicians who would expand our own horizons. That's how Gentle Giant was born."

Derek recalls the Shulman family home in Portsmouth.

"My father was a professional musician, so instruments were generally strewn around the house – a trumpet or bagpipes or whatever – so it wasn't as if we *wanted* to be multi-instrumentalists, we would just say, 'Let me try that.' My brother Ray was classically trained on the violin and was recruited to be in the National Youth Orchestra, before he strummed it like a quasi-rhythm guitar.

"That's the genesis of why we enjoyed playing and utilising different kinds of instruments and instrumentation back when we were kids at school. There was music in the house all the time. In retrospect I thought that was normal and common, and apparently it wasn't."

The brothers' credits over Gentle Giant's albums are:

Phil Shulman b.1937: vocals; trumpet; mellophone; alto, soprano and baritone saxophone; treble, descant and tenor recorders; clarinet; percussion.

Derek Shulman b.1947: vocals; bass guitar; alto saxophone; recorder; clavichord; ukulele; percussion.

Ray Shulman b.1949: vocals; bass guitar; six- and twelve-string acoustic guitar; electric guitar; violin; viola; recorder; organ bass pedals; percussion.

Kerry Minnear, a Royal College Of Music graduate in composition, joined Gentle Giant as keyboard player for their self-titled 1970 debut and played at least as many instruments as any of the brothers. Minnear had studied with modernist composers Cornelius Cardew and Michael Tippett, as well as being an enthusiast of medieval, renaissance and Romantic classical music – which broadened things out stylistically – while Martin Smith played jazz-inflected drums and Gary Green, essentially a blues lead guitarist, took on the often challenging guitar duties.

On 'Giant' Derek's grainy, soulful voice is set in a context of Hammond organ swells and brass interjections, but the mood is now restless, unpredictable. It sounds rather like one of Simon Dupree's R&B stompers cut up and reassembled, with staccato repeated notes, dropped beats and unexpected ornamentation, linked to more reflective passages. In common with virtually every subsequent Gentle Giant composition there was a lot to take in.

Minnear's falsetto and Derek's earthier tones provided an unusually wide lead vocal contrast, together with backing vocals by Ray and Phil, whose voices were lighter than their brother's, taking the middle ground. 'Funny Ways' is a delicate song with an exquisite melody based on acoustic guitar and violin. There are some longueurs, including a rambling phased drum solo sandwiched between the West Coast vocal harmonies on 'Nothing At All', with Minnear playing piano that ranges from lyrical to avant-garde in style.

Acquiring The Taste, released in 1971, is more focused and also full of surprises. Ray has opined that it's "the purest in terms of experimentation and just being happy with the record that came out".

The sleeve is a garish pop art depiction of glossy lips and a tongue, and carries the following mission statement: *"It is our goal to expand the frontiers of contemporary music at the risk of being very unpopular. We have recorded each composition with the one thought – that it should be unique, adventurous, and fascinating. It has taken every shred of our combined musical and technical knowledge to achieve this. From the outset we have abandoned all preconceived thoughts on blatant commercialism. Instead we hope to give you something far more substantial and fulfilling. All you need to do is sit back, and acquire the taste."*

"That was my older brother [Phil]," says Derek. "He was, how can I put this, always rather upfront with his mouth rather than being selective in his verbosity. However, there were elements of truth in that statement, but it was a little pompous. We did not want to be unpopular, but what we did want to be was independent."

Released in 1972, *Three Friends* is a concept album, and one of the earliest in the progressive rock canon. It was essentially Phil Shulman's idea, and it was born of his looking back at when the family moved down from Glasgow to "a fairly working class area" of Portsmouth. Back then, streaming within the British education system came after the results of the Eleven Plus exam. Shulman gained a scholarship to Portsmouth Grammar School, while one of his best friends went to a secondary modern school and another to a technical school. As Phil said: "You were actually selected and streamed for a whole life and there was no way out of it. It's exactly what happened to me and my friends."

Having been shunted in different directions, the three friends' paths diverged, but the narrative demonstrates that the ties of youthful friendship can still be maintained. In Phil's view: "When you get into making a little album you couldn't possibly convey everything you want to say."

Gentle Giant received a mixed reception in the UK, but although *Three Friends* sneaked into the US charts at a lowly number 197, they steadily built up a following there and on mainland Europe.

Given the fact that Jewish musicians have been at the forefront of every Western musical trend – from classical, to the Second Viennese school of the early 20th century, to pop and punk music and beyond – there were very few in the UK progressive rock scene. Can Derek Shulman see, with hindsight, any particular Jewish component to Gentle Giant's music or lyrics?

"There's always a very a big emphasis certainly with Western Jews on education and thought processes and so the music had some of that. There's also some soul in there – real soul as opposed to American soul – which reflects the nomadic Jewish lifestyle of the centuries before us. Again, it's nothing to with religion at all. I'm an atheist. It's part of our DNA, there's no denying it so it has to have some outlet in our creative energies, perhaps in our focus on being excellent for ourselves, learning from each other and trying to excel. That's all part of being any minority culture."

In the Seventies, the way that bills were put together meant that "progressive" groups often shared the stage with singer-songwriters, more mainstream groups, or heavy rock bands, so open-minded concertgoers could enjoy a stylistically diverse evening's entertainment. At least generally speaking. The billing of Gentle Giant supporting Black Sabbath on a US tour in early 1972 was an exception to the rule.

One has to admire the sheer giant-sized balls of Gentle Giant to go onstage and purvey the reflective acoustics of 'Funny Ways' in front of a crowd of booze- and drug-fuelled Sabbath fans baying at the moon and restless to head-bang to 'Iron Man'. They were regularly booed off stage, but at a show at the Hollywood Bowl, Los Angeles, someone threw a cherry bomb – a large exploding firework – onstage during that number. The culprit probably thought he was up against a bunch of effete limey art-rock ninnies, but the group were made of tough stuff and Phil Shulman, who had grown up in the Gorbals in Glasgow, told his bandmates to stop playing and to leave the stage, but not before he grabbed the mike and, in a parting shot, shouted at the audience: "You guys are a bunch of fucking cunts!"

"The boo that went up after that was enormous," recalls Derek. "To this day I'll never forget it. It's not like we were asking for it... well, yes and no. Yes, it was a Black Sabbath crowd, but as far as pushing the envelope, when we came back on our own, those Black Sabbath fans would come back as Gentle Giant fans. It was a pushy thing to do and generally we would get away with it."

While they were off on tour picking up fans, being booed and occasionally being bombed, back in the UK, press coverage of Gentle Giant was mixed. Some journalists were struck by the group's originality, while others derided them for being "pretentious".

"One thing we were not was pretentious," say Derek. "And I can understand that if anyone didn't quite understand what it was about, they would think it must be crap, and so we'll slag it off. It didn't matter to us. No, it actually did matter to us, but we didn't concentrate on the UK that much and didn't want to stroke anyone's ego anyway."

Structurally, most of Gentle Giant's music is concise, partly as a result of their having been pop songwriters in the past. "It's very focused," Derek agrees. "We weren't out to do a five-minute Mellotron piece with a triangle and a bell, and pretend we were this silly orchestra, when we could say it in a couple of bars."

Gentle Giant also had no particular image – they were just a bunch of regular hairies – and the painting of the Giant holding the group in its hands on the cover of their self-titled debut, which became the band's visual signature, looked like some massively oversized hydrocephalic garden gnome: hardly sexy, hardly rock'n'roll.

John Peel was lukewarm about the group and avoided playing them, but throughout the Seventies they were championed by fellow Radio 1 DJ Alan Freeman on his Saturday afternoon show. The group retaliated towards the naysayers by releasing a best-of album titled *Pretentious For The Sake Of It* in 1977.

New Musical Express ended up referring to the group as Genital Gnat. What did he think of that?

"I'd not heard that," says Derek, laughing. "But I like it. We might do a compilation called that."

OCTOPUS
Original label: Vertigo
Producer: Gentle Giant
Recorded: July–August 1972
Release date: December 1, 1972

Octopus is regarded by Derek Shulman as one of the best albums that Gentle made. "That album is reflective of the band coming from adolescence and moving into some kind of maturity, and it has a lot of creative energy," he says.

It's certainly one of the most concentrated albums of progressive rock, with an extraordinary amount of musical and lyrical ideas crammed into its thirty-four-minute duration.

The earlier albums were rich with invention, but now a peculiar chemistry was taking place, helped on by the new drummer John Weathers, who provided a driving rock'n'roll backbeat together with a facility to elegantly navigate the complexities of the compositions, as well as being a dab hand at tuned percussion.

The label of "symphonic rock" has been ascribed to Gentle Giant's *Octopus*, but to these ears, even used loosely that term is a misnomer in describing their music. Classical music was certainly an important influence, but the contrapuntal lines within the album's eight concise tracks also sound like rock instrumentation stacked up as a form of three-dimensional chess. Only one breaks the five-minute mark.

Derek gives his views on how classical influences infiltrated their singular music: "We weren't pretending to be a classical ensemble – that

403

was the last thing we wanted to be, as we wanted to be ourselves. But it was a natural thing to do at that time. That's the background of the musicians who were in the band: Ray absolutely, Kerry absolutely and myself to a certain degree, because we were trained musicians.

"That solid backbeat could move the composition along as well as having the ability to move along the different parts. And I wouldn't say 'songs', because generally – and this is the upside and the downside of Gentle Giant – even the vocal lines weren't really vocalised per se on top of chords, they were parts of the composition. So you would hear the themes coming in different parts, whether it was a guitar, a vocal line or a keyboard line, cello or violin. It was much more classically structured than a general pop song. Even in a drum pattern you would hear a structure of a theme here.

"Certainly it was not, 'Let's get together and jam three chords.' We would do that for our benefit, for a laugh but not many songs came out of that kind of atmosphere. It was all pretty much written first."

In 1976 Kerry Minnear further explained how these written parts, and then the entire composition, would be essentially altered by group arrangement.

"The mood is chosen first by the writer. Then he gives us the parts. If I've written it, I'll give out the guitar part to Gary Green as I hear it, the bass part to Ray, try to get the right feel on the drums for John Weathers, and the vocals we leave until last. It's normally a question of reproducing what the inspiration was. After a few plays through, they start adding their own little quirks to what I have given them, so we end up with something slightly different than I intended. But that's good because we are a group and not an orchestra. We're not there to play somebody else's music, we're all a part of it. So if I write a song, I'm quite prepared for it to finish up with a completely different feel on the records than it had on my tape recorder."

Octopus arrived in a sleeve by artist Roger Dean, best known for his work with Yes, but instead of the fantasy worlds that adorned that group's sleeves, it features a rather angry looking cephalopod. The title came from "octo-opus", or a work in eight parts. The project had originally been mooted as a concept album about the group, but wisely they decided against such contrivance, thinking that to be a bit naff. But the octopus image resonated through the music, which was produced by a multitude of limbs working together and in independence.

The result is an album full of strikingly original musical ideas, written by Minnear and Ray Shulman, with lyrics by Derek and Phil.

'The Advent Of Panurge' demonstrates the singer's assertion that these weren't so much songs as compositions with vocal elements. It starts with a pretty vocal hook sung by Minnear in his high chorister's voice with a medieval or renaissance feel. The listener settles into this attractive, sweetly sung song, but it soon swings back and forth between musical motifs, with Ray Shulman's bass providing strong counter rhythms. More voices are woven into this instrumental thicket, before the introductory vocal hook re-emerges, this time sung by Derek. You can even whistle parts of it, but its construction is highly unusual.

The song was inspired by the scurrilous comic writings of the 16th-century French author François Rabelais, specifically about the giants Pantagruel and Gargantua.

"We enjoyed the classical French Rabelaisian humour, which was raucous and bawdy," says Derek. "We were interested in literature, anything that had thought processes and skills to it. It was part of our culture, part of who we were."

'Raconteur Troubadour' is a more conventional song with a kind of courtly feel to it, albeit juxtaposed with passages of Ray Shulman's speedy violin arpeggios echoed by Green's guitar, restlessly steering it into a different direction.

'A Cry For Everyone' is also based on literature, this time on the writings of existentialist philosopher – and goalkeeper – Albert Camus. It inspires an impassioned vocal performance by Derek with a replanting of soulful roots in a different soil, and features some high-speed runaway keyboard figures, and an extravagant yet brief synth solo from Minnear.

Things veer into uncharted territory on 'Knots'. The piece is based on the book by radical Scottish psychoanalyst R. D. Laing, who was a provocative figure in the Sixties and Seventies. In it he investigates a wide spectrum of emotional and behavioural ties and dependencies, through prose poems and playlets. 'Knots' has a fittingly complex structure of overlapping voices, with a refrain describing how all men are contained within *"each man"*. It has been described as a madrigal but is in more of a Modernist, avant-garde style with intricate tuned percussion interludes.

"That was very good, I thought," says Derek. "It's so not catchy, it's silly. So fucking pretentious! That's complete Genital Gnat, but I like it."

Despite having ditched the idea of *Octopus* being a concept album about the musicians themselves, the group nod back to that idea on the instrumental 'Boys In The Band', an agitated, at times fierce, multi-part instrumental, with each player shining, but within a structure, and with no grandstanding.

Octopus feels, for the most part, almost intimidatingly cerebral. 'Dog's Life', with its acoustic guitar, mini string section, synths and reed organ, has a delightful melody. It's a disappointment then that Minnear's vocals are to an extent emotionally removed, framing a tale of man's best friend; a shambling example with bad hair and teeth at that. In fact, the song is about one of the group's roadies.

"They always told us they had a dog's life," says Derek. "It was about anyone who had a gig or a job that they thought was less glamorous than they ought to have. Primarily it was about a roadie, but you could fill in the blanks."

"'A Dog's Life' was written in particular for Frank Covey, my old mate," Phil has claimed. "He's a big old dog of a chap."

But where the listener can really get an emotional hold on *Octopus* is 'Think Of Me With Kindness'. Beautifully sung by Minnear it follows a more standard verse chorus structure than anything else on the album, with odd piano interludes playing what sounds like the theme to 'The Big Country', while towards the end there is an elegiac instrumental verse with Phil playing a mellophone, a trumpet-like brass instrument but set in a lower register. It's the group's most affecting song.

To finish is 'River', a bluesy piece with a violin and wah-wah guitar hook line, with Derek singing the verse and Minnear taking vocal duties over ebbing and flowing tuned percussion and keyboard lines. The song peaks with a funky groove over which Gary Green, one of the most group-minded players in the era of guitar-led jams, finally cuts loose.

Octopus is an album that is so packed with concentrated musical incident that thirty-four minutes feels an appropriate time to take a break and let it all sink in.

Gentle Giant continued on this tack through their next few albums. *In A Glass House* (1973) and *Power And The Glory* (1974) were even more focused, but at times, as on the hyperactive 'Cogs In Cogs', this compositional density became almost suffocating. Gentle Giant's songs are so original, so skilfully wrought that they stand apart from all their progressive rock peers, but one can't help but think that just a little more space and restraint might have increased their impact.

1975's *Free Hand*, is a bit more easy going – it feels as if someone has let some air into the room. The complexity is still there, though, and no more so than on the inspired vocal arrangements of 'On Reflection', their greatest single achievement and a staple of Alan Freeman's Saturday afternoon show that summer.

Here the group's multi-part harmonies are initially heard a capella. As with many of their vocal arrangements, an initial line is joined by another singing a canon, or round. But they soon diverge into different melody lines sung simultaneously, as in a fugue. This typically only lasts a few bars before other voices join in, some in unison, and so the relationship between all the lines change again. The lyrics are about looking back on a broken relationship, and the ensemble vocals meet on a refrain of *"all around"*. The second time around, piano and glockenspiel track two of the vocal lines.

A slower second subject finds Minnear singing melancholically, accompanied by piano and recorder as he remembers the *"good things"*. The song ends with a high-energy instrumental arrangement of the verse vocal harmonies. 'On Reflection' is both the furthest point of Gentle Giant's musical exploration and one of their more accessible tunes.

Although some of their compositions may seem a bit over-egged on record, one aspect of the "Genital Gnat" brand of progressive rock that the detractors never seem to have got is that when played live through a big PA, this music, with its shifting complexity, dynamics and finely dovetailed parts was quite different to basic rock'n'roll, but it yielded a similar thrill.

While Gentle Giant were a bit of a niche band in the UK, after the notorious 1972 tour with Black Sabbath and tours with Jethro Tull later in 1972, they achieved every British group's holy grail – they broke America and were also doing well in Canada, Italy and Germany. "In somewhere like Gainesville, Florida, we'd play to about 200. But in LA at the Shrine Auditorium, we'd sell out to 6,000 people," Derek recalls. "We were enormous in Italy and Germany, where we would play 10–20,000 seaters, and sell out and do extremely well in Switzerland and Benelux. England was always sceptical about the band."

It's still a little hard to understand how such an uncompromising group could have put so many bums on seats. And also why, by 1980, they had disappeared completely. There were a number of factors. By 1977 the musical landscape was changing, with the punk and new wave bands muscling in on the commercial action – the opposition had arrived. There is no question that this "movement" did come from a genuine groundswell, the like of which had rarely been witnessed in youth culture. There is also no question that there were many bandwagon jumpers, and Derek has a point when he says that punk "did shake up things, [but] it was a marketing and corporate ploy, let there be no mistake". Just as at the start of the Seventies when progressive rock groups were signed as the next big thing, so some of these groups were now ousted from the rosters of labels who had previously been sympathetic.

Looking back in 2000 Minnear had this to say on the group's relationship to this new phenomenon. "Ray, our bass player, and his girlfriend really liked it and used to play tapes in the car all the time. We didn't feel threatened by punk, we had very committed, ardent fans and people who liked Gentle Giant weren't going to like punk. If we had been an ordinary pop band, I'd have been more worried.

"If you look at our album sales they stayed pretty steady. Personally I thought punk was quite amusing – although it offended me in terms of ethos. I'm a Christian and value generosity and helping people – not anarchy and spitting. I'm surprised that this music with no refinement whatsoever stuck around for so long. I liked a few of the songs, that one 'We're going down the pub' ['Hurry Up Harry', Sham 69]. When Gentle Giant finished in 1980 it wasn't because of punk, it was because we had lost our way musically."

But there was also an increasing corporatism in record labels, where accountants' figures were viewed with more interest than the company's idealistic promotion of groups. Maybe the audience was fragmenting, but this changing world also coincided with groups who had been together for the best part of ten years growing apart geographically, creatively and spiritually, having families, losing that all-for-one camaraderie or running dry of creative juices, or, having looked around and seen what was going on, their music becoming self-conscious in a way that they felt compelled to change.

It's difficult to summarise why, exactly, but come 1977, Gentle Giant had simplified their approach in an attempt to increase their commercial base, but became unstuck. Their music never had the lengthy grandiosity of some of their peers but *The Missing Piece* (1977) and *Giant For A Day* (1978) fell between the proverbial two stools. And although *Civilian* (1980) felt more convincing, as if they were revisiting their earlier pop roots – and had every right to do so – it found their special chemistry diminished.

With hindsight, Ray had this to say on the group's change of tack: "Well, unfortunately as the band goes on and you start to kind of do well, the pressure came from record companies and managers to do better. That always meant to soften things up and not be so experimental. Certainly there were compromises made.

"When they saw – particularly towards the end – that bands like Genesis and Yes were getting quite massive, the pressure was certainly on the business side for us to do the same. And I don't think it was ever possible for our music… the more it was compromised, the more was taken away from it. It was a matter of survival: 'Are we going to make another record? Can we keep the band going for six more months?'"

Derek has a different take on the question of record company pressure and feels that ultimately the band's fate was left more in its own hands.

"We weren't forced by any record companies to do this, but we saw Genesis having hits on the radio and that moved them from being a support band to us, to being a headliner in a big stadium. In all fairness we thought, 'We wouldn't mind some of that – why not?' We tried and the fans that liked us before said it wasn't as good, and at the same time, some of the songs didn't cut it in the pop world, so we were between a rock and a hard place. However, these were things that we didn't do under duress, they were things we wanted to experiment with in that area. Someone should have slapped us across the head and said, 'Don't try that because you can't do it.'"

There was a degree of empty bluster in punk's attitude towards the old guard. But for established older bands to get too close to their ilk seemed wrong, while mocking them looked somewhat pompous. Doing a punk parody, then, was a must to avoid.

"It's like the Edith Piaf thing, I don't regret anything – except one or two things, and one thing was recording a song called 'Betcha Thought We Couldn't Do It'," Derek admits. 'It was a tongue-in-cheek play on punk and of course we couldn't do it. That was the truth. We couldn't do punk like Johnny Rotten. And thank God! So that was certainly a bit of a pretentious statement."

That track appeared on the 1977 album *The Missing Piece* and although not as toe-curling as it might appear – it sounds more like a fast R&B song – it was hardly a career highlight.

By the end of the Seventies, Derek was both manager and lead vocalist of Gentle Giant, who had decamped to California. They recorded their final album in the last months of the decade with Beatles engineer Geoff Emerick.

Says Derek: "*Civilian* was actually a good album, going into the Eighties, and if Gentle Giant had kept going, that was the direction we could have taken but expanded. But in the lifespan of a band it was time to say, 'That's it.' Groups evolve and you become an adolescent, an adult, a senile old man and then you die. But a lot of groups don't die, they continue on life support."

CHAPTER 31

Ray Charles, the Godfather of Progressive Rock?: Procol Harum, Traffic and Family

PROCOL HARUM

For The Paramounts it was a familiar story. Like many groups – The Beatles and The Rolling Stones included – the Southend-based quartet started off playing R&B covers in 1960 when they were still at school, and eventually scored a minor UK hit with their cover of 'Poison Ivy' in 1964. Then the group, who were still in their teens, comprised Gary Brooker on vocals and piano, Robin Trower on guitar, Chris Copping on bass and Barrie "B. J." Wilson on drums. After a number of misses, the group disbanded in 1966, by which time Brooker had decided to "have a go" at songwriting.

"We didn't want to be those four smiling faces doing a two-and-a-half-minute song on *Thank Your Lucky Stars* or something, we wanted to do some different music that went somewhere; that had possibilities and experimentation."

On the cover of their self-titled 1964 EP, this was exactly the image that they portrayed, with their big grins and striped suits. But when plying a trade that was going out of fashion, those smiles become harder to maintain. It was time for a change.

After The Paramounts had disbanded, Brooker began writing new material with organist Matthew Fisher and lyricist Keith Reid as Procol Harum. Into 1967 they were producing a completely new type of pop music for the psychedelic era. "It was an expanding out and a realisation that you could, in that point in history in British music, do whatever you wanted," says Brooker. "There didn't seem to be any boundaries and if there were, you completely ignored them."

The first that the public heard of the nascent group was 'A Whiter Shade of Pale', a single released in March 1967. Procol Harum could not have dreamt of a more spectacular start. At a time when an industry figure had told Brooker that pop songs should be no longer than two minutes, forty-seven seconds to be considered for airplay – that precise timing – the song rolled on in a stately manner for just over four minutes.

It became a huge hit, reaching number one in the UK and going Top 10 in the US. This epochal song was pop as serious art music. It starts off with Matthew Fisher's organ line, one of the most memorable pop instrumental hooks ever recorded. It sounds like J. S. Bach, but the beauty of it is that it isn't lifted straight from a classical composition and plonked down into a pop song, a device long used in pop hits. Instead there have been suggestions of its origins in a number of Bach pieces – like the Air from Bach's *Orchestral Suite No.3*, commonly known as 'Air On A G-string' – but it is sufficiently different from these mooted origins to stand alone. And rather than coming over like a pale imitation, it actually sounds like a solid Bach melody.

Brooker's vocal performance is equally strong, with a weathered characteristic unusual for a young man that has a hint of Ray Charles about it. But the song's enduring mystery and inscrutability comes from Reid's lyrics, which form a stream of hallucinatory imagery – they seem to evoke the onboard entertainment of an ocean liner after the narrator's drink has been spiked. Or is it all actually the Miller telling his tale, as mentioned in the song (with its red-herring Chaucerian allusions)?

The lyrics could, of course, just be the first thing that came into Reid's head, but typical of his wordsmithery, they feel too considered to be a scribbled-down stream of consciousness.

Importantly, their striking imagery lodges in the mind and the words fit perfectly when sung, even though their meaning is obscure. And they elegantly demonstrated that meaning or even comprehensibility was not actually necessary in a song lyric. But all this had a downside, which prompted some groups in the progressive rock scene that followed to purvey a kind of portentous meaninglessness in their lyric writing.

Wilson and Trower were invited to join this new group, and they recorded a self-titled debut album that was released in September 1967. But pressure was also on for Procol Harum to record another hit, to follow up this majestic oddity with more of the same. But even the group realised that this would be nigh-on impossible and 'Homburg', which arrived later that year, was a lesser hit, but still charted in the UK and US. It has a similar mid-paced feel with a short piano line at the end of each verse that, again, evokes Bach.

On the group's second album, *Shine On Brightly* (1968), they came up with a seventeen-and-a-half-minute song suite 'In Held 'Twas In I'. The title has been called an acrostic, but in fact it comprises the first word from each of the verse sections.

"If you throw yourself back then there was a lot more freedom. Then it was perfectly acceptable," says Brooker. "It's got a lot of strange pieces that we knitted together. You can, in the end, get some kind of story out of it, but it's a bit more mythical. It starts off with the beginning of the universe, really, if that's possible. There's some Buddhist chant and it ends up going to Heaven, so it's got it all. It's even got drug addiction somewhere in the middle. It was a forward thinking idea. Pete Townshend told us once that he got the idea of *Tommy* from that piece."

Procol Harum continued to go off into a different sort of uncharted territory on 1969's *A Salty Dog* – produced by Fisher – where on the title track, Brooker's tolling piano chord crotchets are reminiscent of Brian Wilson and Van Dyke Parks' 'Surf's Up', but here Reid's lyrics tap more into a fear of the unknown, written as a captain's log of a doomed ship. Both writing teams used the sea as a vast canvas on which to express existential concerns, but while 'Surf's Up' was all towering, sun-flecked Pacific breakers, 'A Salty Dog' reeks of cold brine, pipe smoke, tar and seaweed. The album was the first to really consolidate the group's identity and style, and their use of choir and strings on the title track gives it a panoramic sweep.

1970's *Home* put the brakes on experimentation for a while, and with Fisher leaving along with bass guitarist David Knights – to be replaced by Chris Copping on bass and organ – Procol Harum had become a regrouping of The Paramounts. Around this time Chris Wright and his business partner Terry Ellis, who had started out running a booking agency, took over the group's management. They also managed Ten Years After and Jethro Tull.

"When we came on board, we believed we could reinvigorate interest in the group and sent them regularly to the US where they were signed to A&M Records and had enjoyed steady album sales," say Wright.

"They had some great songs and they reacted very well with the audience. When Robin Trower was with them he was a phenomenal lead guitarist. B. J. [Wilson] was an amazing drummer. He was considered for John Bonham's job, but he would never have made it with Zeppelin as he was too off-the-wall. Gary Brooker was a great singer."

Ellis and Wright put an advert in the *Daily Telegraph* requesting the services of a "groovy accountant". The successful applicant, Nick Blackburn, went over to introduce himself to A&M in the States. Wright called Bob Garcia, the press officer for A&M Records, who told him that, yes, he had met Blackburn: he had chanced upon him the previous night in a company office-cum-crash pad apartment in Manhattan, "stoned, naked and with a prostitute".

Although Wright went on to diversify and run a number of successful businesses, he explains the mentality of having a "groovy accountant" and coming into the Seventies music business via hippie culture: "In those days we were all part of the same thing. I didn't think the groups we worked with would have wanted to have been signed to somebody with short hair and a pinstripe suit. The whole thing about the counterculture and the hippie movement was it was all-pervading and everybody was part of it, and if you weren't part of it you were on the outside. And no one wanted to be on the outside.

"Later in the Seventies all the footballers and the mineworkers, dockers and everybody else grew their hair long because it became the fashion. But in 1969 and 1970 it wasn't so much a fashion statement, it was a lifestyle statement."

Ellis also observed that Keith Reid would tour with the group by way of justifying receiving a fee for each concert, and did things like change the set list and encores every night. Although Reid never played with Procol Harum in any capacity, his lyrics were of vital importance to the group's music, similar to the way that Peter Sinfield's helped to define early King Crimson. But Brooker notes that there was no obligation for him to set every text to music.

"I had a whole folder of Reid's lyrics that didn't get used," he admits. "Sometimes the idea was too brief and I couldn't fit it into something or it didn't spur an idea. Now and again there would be something that I liked, but there would be some words in it that I just couldn't sing. Sometimes Reid just said, 'Oh, OK,' and didn't try to change it.

"There was some epic sea story, which had a line *'And so he walked the plank'*. And I can't remember what rhymed with it now, but 'plank' is unsingable. I did try, but you cannot sing 'plank' [*laughs*]. So it never got done, that one."

On 1971's *Broken Barricades*, Procol Harum's first album for Wright and Ellis's new Chrysalis label (Chris + Ellis = Chrysalis) Robin Trower cut loose more on lead guitar, on what was to be his final outing with the group before embarking on a solo career. According to Brooker it happened organically: with Fisher gone and Copping only occasionally playing the organ, there was more space now for Trower. He also chipped in with three compositions including 'Song For A Dreamer', a paean to Jimi Hendrix, who had clearly influenced his guitar style. But the group's sales were still poor in the UK.

Procol Harum played in Stratford, Ontario, in 1971 as part of the Shakespeare Festival, and were invited to use the orchestra.

"The orchestra was there anyway and the choir was made up from the actors and actresses from the plays," Brooker recalls. "We didn't play much, just 'In Held 'Twas In I' and 'A Salty Dog', I think. But it was a tumultuous reception and a lot of people were there, and that led on to an invite from the Edmonton Symphony Orchestra.

"We just did it at the end of the tour. I wrote out the orchestrations and Trower did what he did on the recorded versions. But he never really liked the idea. You couldn't play loud when you're with an orchestra. So he had to have a tiny little amp that was a big as a radio. He did it, fair enough, and it was very impressive, but it was not his idea of what a group should be doing. So he left and we got in a new guitarist, Dave Ball."

Although the concert in Edmonton was a rush job, giving the orchestra little time to familiarise themselves with Brooker's orchestrations, Procol Harum took the opportunity of making sure it was recorded. The album, *Procol Harum Live: In Concert With The Edmonton Symphony Orchestra*, was recorded in late 1971 and released early the following year.

In Wright's view, this live album regenerated the group's career and although it only reached number forty-eight in the UK, in the US it peaked at number five and remains the band's best-selling album. The group and the orchestra integrate particularly well. Procol Harum used an orchestra on other occasions, including a show at the Hollywood Bowl in Los Angeles in 1973. But was there – other than volume considerations   ever a problem integrating the orchestra with the rock band?

Says Gary Brooker: "It wasn't the first time that it had been done, as strings were often on record, but it was our style in the sense that we made it up. But you do have limitations; you are playing to music, you are playing to a certain number of bars and the band has got to know where they are. But I communicate with the conductor, who communicates with the orchestra and choir.

"We never lacked energy from playing with an orchestra. I've always been aware subconsciously that that might happen, so we've written it and organised it so that it doesn't happen."

The following album, *Grand Hotel* (1973), is grand without being grandiose. It feels like a concept album, but although the sound is sumptuous throughout, Keith Reid's lyrical themes of opulence and decadence only really stretch as far as the title track. "I had a lot of song ideas in my head," says Brooker. "Most of the *Grand Hotel* songs are quite split-personality things that change mood. There are almost two songs in every song, like 'Robert's Box'."

"The atmospheric title track gave the writer Douglas Adams the idea for *The Restaurant At The End Of The Universe*, the second book of *The Hitchhiker's Guide To The Galaxy*," says Wright.

"We thought we'd have that big, lush sound. It wasn't all done with an orchestra but there was quite a bit. We used Christiane Legrand on 'Fires (Which Burn Brightly)' – she was a French jazz improviser, but also from The Swingle Singers who had done a lot of classical interpretations."

With Procol Harum's star in the ascendant, Chrysalis decided to throw a lavish launch party at The Plaza Hotel in New York for the album. With the group's contract with A&M at an end, it was the first album released on the Chrysalis label in America, with distribution through Warner Brothers. And in an example of life imitating art, all the invitees and the group wore black formal coats, white waistcoats and white bow ties as on the album cover. Those attending included Carly Simon, Andy Warhol and James Taylor. "There was more [of a budget] than you would think today in terms of launch parties," says Wright. "You had big billboards and things like that.

"Procol Harum were a big act and the album was called *Grand Hotel*, and so the idea of having a launch party at The Plaza and everyone dressing up for it made a lot of sense. I mean, you would have launches to suit the record you were trying to sell. OK, it was lavish and extravagant and that wasn't the norm – you wouldn't have it for most records."

After all this musical decoration, Procol Harum decided they would concentrate on being a five-piece rock group again, and after *Exotic Birds And Fruit* – another strong if more spare set, they decided to have a change. They had worked with producer Chris Thomas in Air Studios since they recorded *Home* in 1970 and in an unexpected turn of events they next worked with American producers and songwriters Jerry Leiber and Mike Stoller. Brooker had noted that they made occasional forays out of the US and had been over to London in 1972 to record the self-titled debut album by Stealers Wheel. And so they were hired.

The duo had amassed a staggering CV of songs dating back to the Fifties, and had written the 1958 song 'Poison Ivy', initially for The Coasters, which had given The Paramounts their only hit.

The sessions started to become awkward. Procol Harum would warm up with one of Leiber and Stoller's old songs in the morning as a good-natured nod to the producers. These included songs covered by The Coasters, The Drifters, Ben E. King and 'Baby I Don't Care', which they had written for Elvis Presley. Unfortunately this prompted the pair into trying to persuade Procol Harum to record some of their new songs that they had brought with them.

"It was strange because it had nothing to do with what we all should have been there for," Brooker recalls. "It was all very disruptive. But the best thing they did was 'Pandora's Box', which had strange instrumentation with a marimba. The way they had drawn out the instruments, and made them weave in and out of each other was magnificent. In fact, they made a hit out of it."

The group did record a Leiber and Stoller song in the end, one they had played in their early morning warm-ups, 'I Keep Forgetting', originally sung by Chuck Jackson, to which the composers added some brass.

Procol Harum wanted to try different producers again for their next album, which was to be their last of the Seventies, *Something Magic*. They went over to Miami at the end of 1976 to record with the upcoming sibling production duo Ron and Howie Albert. After playing them about a dozen songs straight off the plane, the group were wishing they were back in Air Studios with Chris Thomas.

"They said, 'Look Gary, you can take a piece of dogshit and you can cover it with chocolate. But when you bite into it what have you got?" We should have gone home at that point," says Brooker. "I think we were shocked more than anything. If we'd been more mercenary and sensible we would have turned round and said, 'You guys can fuck off too.' They said, shortly after that, 'We wouldn't even be here but our boat's broken.' [*laughs*]"

The brothers became less obnoxious, warming to at least some of the songs. Surprisingly they were taken by a long piece that Brooker had written based on a lengthy allegorical Reid lyric called 'The Worm And The Tree', with different instruments and melodic lines representing the characters in the story. Brooker finished off the piece in the studio and did some string and woodwind arrangements to "beef it up in places". He had never envisaged it being sung and so it ended up as musical episodes with narration, and filling all of side two.

After they had recorded *Something Magic*, the group took stock. "And when you were looking around comparing that with what else was going on, you thought, 'Wait a minute, we might have lost touch here,'" says Brooker. The Eagles had been recording *Hotel California* in the studio next door ("Their *Grand Hotel*," Brooker quips) and back in the UK it was the summer of punk.

"The punk thing was something else, because if you liked music you didn't like punk," says Brooker. "It was just a big fuck off, but luckily it died out. It wasn't progressive enough, punk. It couldn't go anywhere but down.

"After ten years, and with our tenth album we have another eighteen-minute piece. We had gone full circle," continues Brooker. "After an American tour in 1977 everyone said goodbye. We didn't even have just a couple of years off and regroup. It was just well, that's it then."

Many musicians interviewed for this book grew up playing soul and R&B. And although many turned their back on it as they realised they weren't particularly good at it – and because they sought to find a more personal means of expression – influences from soul and R&B, seeped into progressive rock, although the final product was typically quite different. But in Procol Harum's case, particularly with Brooker's vocals, those influences were overt.

Brooker has an idea why this kind of music is rarely referenced. "Music to me is about conveying an emotion and you get that from having grown up with Ray Charles and Little Richard and Sam Cooke," he says. "That thread runs through and, as you say, it's not always identified. But what's often not at the front of these prog rock bands is first-class vocals. You might, overall, get a good recording with marvellous, clever playing, but at the end of the day the vocalist has got away with quite a bit. You got it with Traffic because Steve Winwood followed that path and had grown up with those same influences and, if you like, he can be a soul singer when he wants to."

TRAFFIC

And so we welcome in Steve Winwood. Mozart defined new possibilities regarding age and musical accomplishment when he composed his first symphony at the age of eight. Steve Winwood wasn't quite so precocious, but he was channelling Ray Charles at the age of 14 as lead vocalist in The Spencer Davis Group. By the time they released their stomping R&B hit single 'Keep On Running', Winwood had reached the ripe old age of 17, and sounds rather unnaturally mature. Play Brooker or Winwood against Ray Charles and, like playing Captain Beefheart against Howlin' Wolf, the voices sound quite different, but there's still some of the same grain in there.

Following his spell in The Spencer Davis Group, Winwood formed Traffic – in which he sang and played guitar and keyboards – with guitarist Dave Mason, Chris Wood on saxes and flute, and Jim Capaldi on drums and vocals. Both Mason and Winwood played bass. Wood had met Winwood when he had sung backing vocals on The Spencer Davis Group's 'Gimme Some Lovin' and 'I'm A Man'.

Theirs is a curious, disjointed story. Traffic first came to public view in May 1967 with the single 'Paper Sun', which featured Mason playing sitar. Then, as a follow-up, they released his unforgettable 'Hole In My Shoe', which, as was mentioned in Chapter 1, set the benchmark for synaesthetic, upside-down-logic, fairy-tales-in-song. It's so quintessentially 1967, so psychedelic, that it almost sounded like a spoof even at the time.

They had signed to Chris Blackwell's Island label, and were one of the first of a roster of rock groups on what had previously been principally an outlet for Jamaican artists. *Mr Fantasy*, Traffic's debut album from that year was a mixed bag. On Mason's 'House For Everyone', he describes the titular house as being made of cheese and his bed made of candy floss. The songs by Winwood, Capaldi and Wood are less twee and sound less dated.

At this point, the group had moved into a house at Aston Tirrold in Berkshire (now in Oxfordshire), an old gamekeeper's cottage on Sheepcott Farm, which was owned by William Piggott-Brown, who also part-owned Island Records. They went there to "get it together in the country" and while it's not clear who, if anyone, came up with that exact quote, it has entered the rock lexicon. But that is exactly what Traffic did and, in doing so, they set the precedent for groups to leave the urban hubs, to clear some creative space.

Mason's lyrics made it sound like the band were living in some kind of psychedelic playpen, where reality was suspended once you had crossed the threshold. In fact it was a practical solution to the problem of how to find an affordable place to write and rehearse. They paid a total of £5 per week in rent, which was cheap at the time and the group could even play on a concrete platform outside as it was far enough away from neighbours to avoid noise complaints. And although LSD was consumed now and again, they were just as keen to knock back a few pints at the pub.

Talking to *MOJO* in 1994, Capaldi said: "I went back some years ago and it had a terrifically powerful presence. People would come and stay – friends – and you'd hear more and more stories. About the doors banging and weird things going on. And all the footsteps going in one direction."

Winwood added: "What we were doing was totally revolutionary for the Sixties. You'd never have got a rock'n'roll band in a gamekeeper's cottage in the Fifties."

One might expect 'Berkshire Poppies', a paean to rural living, to be some kind of wispy folk tune, but it looks back at the city from the country and is rendered as a raucous piano-led pub singalong.

Capaldi told Chris Welch of *Melody Maker* in 1967: "Our producer Jimmy Miller invited a few people to the studio for this one, and sixty people turned up. You can hear the Small Faces looning about. It was really beautiful."

Mason left soon after the first album was released but before 'Here We Go Round The Mulberry Bush', which became their third hit single in November 1967.

"It's because there are things I want to do and for me to do them while still in the group would hang the others up. The best thing to do is leave," Mason told Welch. "I decided ages ago. I want to do producing, and playing and travelling wastes so much time. I can get my kicks out of writing and producing."

"Dave lost his way," Capaldi told *MOJO*. "He thought we ought to jump headlong into the swimming pool of psychedelia. And we didn't want to do that. And after doing those songs he left. He just wasn't representing what we wanted to do."

Mason returned for the group's second album *Traffic* (1968) on which he actually had more writing credits, but had tempered his toytown vision into simple, witty songs like 'You Can All Join In'. This also became the title of an Island sampler released in 1969.

The band's haunted country hang-out attracted some famous visitors, including Stephen Stills, Denny Laine, Pete Townshend, Leon Russell, Eric Clapton and Ginger Baker. When questioned in 1994, Winwood and Capaldi couldn't remember if Jimi Hendrix had visited or not, although Winwood and Wood had played on a number of studio sessions with Hendrix, and Wood had guested at the last Jimi Hendrix Experience concert at the Royal Albert Hall.

David Dalton of *Rolling Stone* visited Sheepcott Farm in March 1969. He wrote: "The cottage is an hour-and-a-half from London, but it's thousand light years from Soho Square. Henley is like driving through a postcard, and then you pass through dozens of little English hamlets with names as heavy as a slice of farmhouse bread: Nettlebed, Wallingford, Uffington, Didcot.

"When we get to Aston Tirrold, we stop in at the pub to ask directions to the cottage. The owners are a friendly, florid old couple, who invite us in while the husband phones the cottage to see if we are permitted to go up.

"We cross the main road just outside tiny Aston Tirrold over a rise and dip down into the dirt track that leads to the cottage. There are really deep ruts in the road, and when it rains, it is impossible to take the upper road at all. Everyone who drives up for the first time stops here. Can this really be the road?"

Dalton was curious about Traffic's back-to-roots mentality and interest in traditional music, and asked: "Why do you think kids are getting so hung up on old things right now, like The Watersons, old clothes and stuff?"

"It's because they don't want to live through this time, they don't want to be part of it," says Chris.

Stevie: "It's like an antique thing but yet the fact that things are taken from back then and expressed now. We are using them, not just taking things."

Shortly after the piece was published, Winwood left rather unceremoniously in May 1969 to join Blind Faith, the original supergroup, which also featured Ginger Baker on drums and Eric Clapton on guitar, both ex of Cream, and Family bass player Ric Grech, who also quit as soon as asked just before that group were about to embark on a US tour to pursue what seemed like a great career opportunity. But Blind Faith only made one album before disbanding.

Traffic puttered to a temporary halt, but Mason, Capaldi and Wood joined up with organist Wynder K. Frog – who had once played with Herbie Goins & The Nightimers – as Mason, Capaldi, Wood & Frog. Shortly before splitting, the line-up inadvisably shortened their name to Wooden Frog.

By late 1969 Winwood was a free agent again and began recording ideas for a solo album. Island had already put out the presumably posthumous *Last Exit*, a ragbag of singles, B-sides outtakes and live material. But in the end he invited back Wood and Capaldi to resurrect Traffic. And although Winwood plays most of the instruments on some tracks, this began a distinct final phase of the group.

The resultant album, *John Barleycorn Must Die* (1970), comes in a sleeve with a woodcut showing a sheaf of corn, its title taken from an English folk song based on a metaphorical story of how to brew beer. And with information on the song on the back in a font like that of an old broadsheet, one would be forgiven for assuming that Traffic had made a folk rock album.

But *John Barleycorn Must Die* opens with 'Glad', a lengthy instrumental with jazz and R&B elements, which ends in a slower metre with a rhapsodic piano solo. Although it's clearly influenced by American music it doesn't sound like a pastiche and there's an expansiveness about it. Next up is 'Freedom Rider' with Winwood's ebullient bass, Wood's flute dancing through the verse, and haunting piano and throaty sax hooks. The side finishes with 'Empty Pages', which was a hit single in the US, and which is Traffic's most joyous mix of soul-infused progressive pop.

In fact, the title track is stylistically rather anomalous. It's beautifully arranged by Winwood, with a baroque mix of acoustic guitar and piano, harmony singing with Capaldi, and Wood's freewheeling pastoral skylark song on flute.

Winwood felt that Wood was crucial in helping weave together the esoteric strands that ran through Traffic's music. Although the album feels a tad unfocused, it is also an original mix of English and American roots. Winwood explained these views to *MOJO*.

"[Chris Wood] was probably the greatest influence on Traffic, in that in many ways he had the spirit more than Jim or I. He had a way of identifying certain unnoticed elements and touching on them, both musically and in his other interests. He was interested in, you know, geological make-up, earth's crust, astronomy, he'd learn about different constellations, ornithology, he was a keen bird-watcher. And then at the same time he played sax in a soul band. So he had a mixture of not only musical elements but also a way of life which really profoundly influenced Traffic."

This kind of synthesis worked brilliantly on its successor *The Low Spark Of High Heeled Boys*. In the fall-out from Blind Faith, Ric Grech had joined along with Ghanaian percussionist Anthony "Rebop" Kwaku Baah, with Capaldi swapping drums for singing and playing occasional percussion. Jim Gordon, who had been a member of Derek & The Dominoes with Clapton, was now playing the kit.

With its acoustic guitar, flute, bass and drums, 'Hidden Treasure' is a gently grooving piece of pastoralia, with occasional conga flourishes. The lyrics urge us to look beyond the everyday to find some kind of transcendence. 'Rainmaker' with its folky harmonies and entreaties to nature to allow fields of crops to flourish finds Grech playing violin.

The melodically rich title track is one the group's most brilliant achievements, and answers the critics who said that their songwriting was below par. The verse is part jazz ballad, part slow New Orleans blues based around three chords, coolly punctuated by Grech's bass and with some sweet rhythmic interplay between Gordon and Rebop. It moves up a gear into the chorus, sweetly sung by Winwood, with a further staccato piano and sax section. There follows a lengthy, slow instrumental passage based on the verse chords with piano and organ solos. At nearly twelve minutes, it just about manages not to outstay its welcome. The group are heard at their funkiest on Grech and Gordon's 'Rock'n'Roll Stew' with Capaldi on lead vocals and appropriately simmering percussion.

The Low Spark... peaked at number five in the US charts, but although the band had enjoyed regular UK album chart success, this one failed to trouble the scorers.

Traffic never matched this potent fusion again. Their following album, *Shoot Out At The Fantasy Factory* (1973), with David Hood on bass and Roger Hawkins on drums, both from the Muscle Shoals rhythm section, had the effect of producing a well-played but ultimately unsatisfactory album. The title track is based on an irresistible groove, and it was not that they had suddenly become too slick, but overall the material was simply not as strong.

Although the folk themes were not so integrated, the album delivered one lengthy oddity. Sonically it feels like it should have been named after some particular Alabama bayou. In fact, its title 'Roll Right Stones' is derived from a stone circle in Warwickshire.

After locating this haunt of ancient peace, rather than dancing around the ancient monoliths like a merry pagan, Winwood delivers the warning of the devil waiting at the *"pearly gates"* for those poor souls who have been *"mesmerised"* or have become *"insane"* as progress marches on. Rather than there being reassurance in the fact that the stones have endured, the atmosphere feels distinctly threatening, as if they are defiantly standing against the modern path that we are all taking.

The song meanders on for over thirteen minutes and although Wood's wah-wah sax solo adds an edge, ultimately it feels like a walk through the fields during which one misread the map and got lost, taking an unnecessary detour. *Shoot Out At The Fantasy Factory* went to number six in the US album charts, but again failed to chart in the UK.

Tony Stewart of *New Musical Express* caught up with Jim Capaldi in January 1973. Regarding his depleted role within the group – songwriting, playing percussion and singing a bit – Stewart described him, semi-seriously, as the Keith Reid of Traffic. To which Capaldi replied: "Almost, yeah."

Stewart was taken by *Shoot Out...*, but was aware of their commercial decline in the UK. In his review of the album he wrote: "Either it's a fresh and kicking beauty, or the final brick to be tossed in their sack to sink them. Oh no, there are no half measures for Traffic. Spend about an hour, preferably two or three or four, with this album, and rest assured you'll be hailing it as a great one."

When Stewart interviewed Capaldi a few weeks later, the resting drummer stated that it was Traffic's best album.

Capaldi told Stewart: "The reason we don't do much in England is because we don't bother much about it. Quite honestly, there's no real place to get off and do anything in England." He added: "I'd like to turn people on and educate them. But then, when they don't want to know, they very often turn round and say they don't understand it."

To blame the public for not liking them felt symptomatic of a band in decline, although there was also a sense of frustration at Traffic's commercial downturn in their home country.

The group were impressive live. After an energetic, if not so well recorded 1971 live album, *Welcome To The Canteen*, the band's second live album, *Traffic On The Road*, recorded in Germany and with Hood and Hawkins as rhythm section, was released in October 1973. The playing has more of a jazz group's improvisational facility than mere rock jamming, but some of the versions are very long. But, lest we forget, that is probably exactly what the audience were hoping for on the nights it was recorded.

In 1974 Traffic released their last album of the Seventies, *When The Eagle Flies*, which again had all the elements in place, with Wood's melodic, punchy sax lines, and Winwood expanding his sound with synthesizers. The rhythm section was now American bass guitarist Rosko Gee and Capaldi back on drums, and although Reebop guests on only two tracks, they were cooking. However, again the material feels a tad lacklustre. And once more it fared far better in the States than in the UK. But then Gary Sperrazza had this to say when he reviewed the album for the American paper, *Shakin' Street Gazette*: "This previously superb band – God, when I think of such well-developed entertaining albums like *Low Spark* and *John Barleycorn*, I can't believe it's the same band – professes to be a fusion of rock, jazz and R&B. Well, there's not enough power for rock fans, not enough drive for R&B fans and they'd get laughed out of jazz circles, unless they were considered an exercise in delicacy. Even as a 'fusion', it doesn't work as there's not enough of any single form or theme to hold [the] attention or satisfy anyone."

And although his assessment is particularly harsh, most readers would at least have been able to understand where he was coming from.

FAMILY

Ray Charles also influenced Family, specifically vocalist Roger Chapman, who has cited him as one of his two main vocal influences along with Jerry Lee Lewis. Perhaps this partly explains why, when he was approached for an interview for this book, he snapped: "Progressive rock? Don't know anything about it."

Perhaps it's also because the term has, over time, become synonymous for some with flamboyant pseudo-classical confections. But back in the late Sixties and into the Seventies there was no blueprint to follow and Family incorporated ideas from R&B, soul, rock'n'roll, folk, jazz, psychedelia, Eastern music and Western classical. Their 1968 debut album *Music In A Doll's House* is a strong contender for the title of ur-progressive rock album, and their open approach to arranging songs made them one of the quintessentially progressive groups until their demise in 1973.

Family grew up in Leicester as The Farinas and then The Roaring Sixties, playing R&B covers before they changed their name in 1966. American producer and svengali Kim Fowley had suggested that they call themselves The Family and go onstage in suits to purvey a mafia-like image, which as well as being ill-advised could potentially have invited unwanted attention.

For *Music In A Doll's House*, Jimmy Miller, who had produced the single, was slated for production duties. Instead, he had become rather distracted by working on The Rolling Stones' *Beggars' Banquet* and so Traffic's Dave Mason, who had played on the single, was brought in instead, with Miller contributing to some of the final mixes.

Mason wrote one of the songs on the album, the short, poppy and characteristically rather whimsical 'Never Like This'. When asked, in 1973, about Mason's production input, Family guitarist John "Charlie" Whitney said: "He had lots of ideas. For example 'Voyage', all those feedback violins were his idea – backwards Mellotron. You must remember that style was the thing for the time. A lot of people say that album was overproduced, and I agree that for 1973 it sounds overproduced, but for 1967 [sic] I think he was doing something that was valid."

'The Chase' features strings, hunting horns and a shout of *"Tally-ho!"* ending with the tape speeding up. Its subject matter was metaphorical, about male and female relationships, although it stops short of likening them to blood sports. "It was just a kind of hard luck love story. A chick does a naughty on the geezer. It's not a general picture, just that one type," Chapman commented.

'Me My Friend' has a horn refrain somewhere between Stax soul and Bach's *Brandenburg Concertos* with a heavily phased vocal. Typical of the album it was short, melodic and to the point.

But in common with many groups at the time, by 1969's *Family Entertainment*, they began to expand the format. "We hadn't known too much about making albums and I suppose that the biggest feeling was that we had made all the songs in little blocks," said Whitney. "And now we wanted to have a few blows – stretch out a bit."

They left behind the more obvious psychedelic tropes and with *Family Entertainment* came up with another contender for the first progressive rock album. It's certainly an eclectic set, starting with the gritty, folky musings on mortality of 'The Weaver's Answer'. Bass guitarist and violinist Ric Grech's song 'Second Generation Woman' was released as a single, although it didn't chart and Whitney explored Eastern moods on the instrumental 'Summer '67', with its swooning strings arranged by Tony Cox, which cut into passages of Jim King playing the melody on saxophone. The idea came from a tape the guitarist had heard of Ravi Shankar And The All India Orchestra. 'From Past Archives' married a baroque pop sensibility with a toe-tapping trad jazz interlude of acoustic guitar strum and clarinet, which segued into a widescreen passage of billowing strings.

Family were working without a producer per se, but in tandem with engineer Glyn Johns. Their manager John Gilbert decided to mix it in their absence, which strained their relationship. In all this musical adventure, Grech and drummer Rob Townsend had grown into a flexible, muscular rhythm section. So much so that Grech was, like Steve Winwood, poached by Blind Faith and was hastily replaced by John Weider. In a double blow, King also left in October 1969. His sax and harmonica playing and keyboards had taken a backseat, and session player Nicky Hopkins had guested on piano.

"It's sad really because such a lot of talent went to waste. It was as though he had acid in him all the time," said Whitney of King. "He was mentally fighting himself all the time; and yet I suppose that's why he played such amazing stuff."

Weider also played both bass guitar and violin, and King's replacement was John "Poli" Palmer on flute, vibes and keyboards. Palmer had been in a group, The Helions, with Dave Mason and Jim Capaldi, which came to a halt when they formed Traffic. He went on to play with Blossom Toes and the jazz/folk rock group Eclection, who performed at the Isle Of Wight Festival in 1969. Palmer had begun as a rock'n'roll drummer but also played jazz vibes, because as he says the pianos in jazz gigs often had "teeth missing".

"I knew the Family boys through Jim King, basically," Palmer explains, "because he used to pop around the Blossom Toes' house and we'd go in the garden, I'd play a bit of flute and he'd play a bit of soprano sax on a nice sunny afternoon, getting very stoned."

Although free ranging in its influences, Family's music was generally built on fairly robust blues/rock-derived structures. But they also expanded into theatrics, having jugglers and plate spinners open for them at the Royal Festival Hall in September 1969 and later, at their manager's suggestion, The Will Spoor Mime Troupe. Chapman reckoned that: "On a musical level [it] meant nothing, because that's not what our playing live was all about. I think that both those experiments showed us that we have to rely on our music to excite, rather than other things."

Palmer recalls how their idea of in-concert solo showcases had been a factor in him joining the group.

"Family did this concert in the Royal Festival Hall where everyone did their own thing as it were. And Rob [Townsend] the drummer said, 'What am I going to do?' Jim King said, 'I know a guy who plays vibes, why don't you do a little thing with him?' So I wrote a little tune and played it with Rob and didn't think any more of it. Jim got mentally fragile eventually and so he left the band. But the guys remembered me and that's how I joined Family. Serendipity, really."

Palmer describes how the group made arrangements. "It was a great environment to work in. It was just feel, basically, and throwing an idea on the wall and everyone would see if it worked or if it didn't work. As a band we knew what sounded good to us and the fact that it might be vibes and banjo didn't even cross anyone's mind as being weird. You just try something and everybody nods at one another. It's as naïve as that, really, although some people seem to think it's some sort of grand plan."

The first album on which Palmer played with Family was *A Song For Me*, released in 1970. This fluid throughput of ideas continued in the recording studio: "When we were really hot at it there was a nice feeling that everyone could put their five penn'orth in and if it didn't work it didn't matter, it only took ten minutes of studio time."

The album opener 'Drowned In Wine', would have made a strong, strummed song, but it was transformed through an inspired arrangement that encompasses edgy, unison staccato figures and a punchy, weirdly textured wind section. Originally King had played sax, but Palmer plays what sounds like a combination of soprano sax, bass recorder and some exotic reed instrument.

Palmer explains this extraordinary concord of instruments: "It was a regular concert flute, but I had a bug on the stock called a Maestro. It was for sax players and it re-coloured the instrument, and it had organ stops, like oboe or cor anglais.

"I used an oboe sound and it turned out very much like an Indian shenai. It's really a fuzz flute. Then the lads would say, 'Why don't you try and add a harmony on it?' and I got different sounds for different parts. There are probably about five or six flutes on that, but the solo is just a flute without too much on it.

"Another thing about 'Drowned In Wine', which was typical of the way that we worked, is that George Chkiantz, the engineer, was talking about something while the track was playing. It was going to be a fade-out and he leant over and said, 'I tell you what...' and stopped the tape with the echo still on. And everyone went, 'What a great ending!' So that's how the track ended in the studio and that's how we played it every time live."

As with the saxophone, if anyone plays vibes on a piece of music, people immediately think "jazz". But almost no one used the instrument in a rock context and so Palmer's playing on 'Love Is A Sleeper' completely transforms the song. "The riff is quite heavy and then [when the vibes come in] it just floats," says Palmer. "Sometimes just everyone smiles and it's like, 'That's the way to do it.'"

Palmer notes that he also used the Maestro on the vibes for the track 'Anyway' (on *Anyway*, 1970). He also started experimenting with synths. "I went a bit daft with them at the times – but we would try everything," he admits. "For instance, on one of the tracks, we ran a guitar through it, and there was no actual guitar synth available at the time. We already tried to run Roger through it, but that didn't work!

"I remember one track 'Normans' on *Anyway*, that was an instrumental and there's a piano solo and a flute solo and for the third one I didn't want to play vibes on it as it was nice and floaty and I didn't want to be too clever. And so Rog does the third solo with voice."

By this time Roger Chapman had established himself as one of the UK's most remarkable vocalists and imposing frontmen. Writing in *Zigzag*, Connor McKnight described the singer's onstage delivery as "pioneering that abandoned style" and suggested that he was performing in a way that took the approach of Eric Burdon and Mick Jagger a stage further, but which was then appropriated by Joe Cocker and Rod Stewart.

Chapman replied: "Well I think I was the first but I don't like saying that because it makes you look a bit mean." When asked if he felt abandon onstage Chapman said: "Christ, yes. I know I can get people off on it. I don't think that before I go on but I've realised that fact, because I know I'm pretty strong onstage... But it's like any musician, somebody gets into a lick and it's like a big boot up the arse. You take off from it. In a way I'm only doing what people think that, say, a drummer does. A drummer might put in a nice phrase and everyone comes flying in, but from my point of view I do it vocally. I've always thought of myself as a musician... part of the group and building with the other musicians, taking off and interacting with the other guys. So I've never thought of myself as just standing there being the singer."

While some might have viewed Chapman as a kind of rock shaman in the throes of possession, *Melody Maker* journalist Chris Welch had a different slant on it. "I used to say that Roger Chapman did 'Idiot Dancing' because he used to do all this stuff," he says. "It was at one of the big festivals. I said he has hordes of admirers called idiot fans, happy idioters. I think they liked it. Roger thought it was really funny."

Chapman has a raw voice with a heavy vibrato and he really leans on it on 'Drowned In Wine' and produces an alarmingly visceral sound. One can imagine that film footage of the back of his mouth would have revealed his uvula oscillating like a boxer's punchball. Whatever would Ray Charles have said?

Family scored an unlikely Top 20 single with the turbulent, violin-led 'Strange Band' in September 1970, and Roger Chapman's vocals burst into the UK's living rooms with full gargling intensity the following year on the single 'In My Own Time' via a startling *Top Of The Pops* appearance. Few who heard the dramatic tolling eight-chord intro, with Chapman howling along wordlessly, would have forgotten it in a hurry. Palmer recalls how the song was composed: "It was very weird, but the weird thing about it was that we didn't think it was," he says. "Charlie had some chords and a bass idea and I thought, 'That's weird,' and played some weirder chords over the top of it, and then Chappo puts that line over the top, almost like 'The [Song Of The] Volga Boatman'. That's what he heard out of the chords. If you just heard the guitar and bass you would probably recognise it, but it wasn't until everyone put their piece on that you went, 'That *is* weird!'"

The Gong collective disembark from the Flying Teapot in 1974, with Daevid Allen (looking upwards) and Steve Hillage (second from right). Michael Ochs Archives/Stringer/Getty

Keith Emerson at the Moog synthesizer patchboard that he affectionately dubbed the "telephone exchange", 1974. MARKA/Alamy

Gentle Giant collectively hanging on the telephone, 1974. Michael Putland/Getty

Peter Gabriel of Genesis in concert in 1974 in the difficult-to-mike-up guise of the Slipperman, a character from their double album *The Lamb Lies Down On Broadway*. Michael Putland/Getty

Chairman Mao scrutinises those counter-revolutionaries Pink Floyd, live c. 1974.
Nik Wheeler/Sygma/Getty

Is that an early example of team sponsorship by Guinness or just a popular Seventies t-shirt?
Pink Floyd get a half time pep-talk from a man with an orange, France 1974. Nik Wheeler/Sygma/Getty

Soft Machine founder and one of the Seventies' great musical mavericks, Kevin Ayers, at home in 1974. Michael Putland/Getty

Camel in the studio in 1975, around the time of their breakthrough album, ...*The Snow Goose*.
Estate Of Keith Morris/Getty

The Codpiece Years: Jethro Tull becoming huge in America, pictured here at the Jai-Alai Fronton Auditorium, Miami, Florida, August 28, 1975. Philip Buonpastore/Alamy

Caravan violist Geoffrey Richardson – with flares in full sail – and keyboard player Dave Sinclair at the Manchester Free Trade Hall, 1975. Simon Robinson/Alamy

Rick Wakeman (centre, with cape) and members of the English Rock Ensemble, orchestra, choir and skaters in preparation for *...King Arthur...* on ice at Wembley Arena, May 1975. Mirrorpix

The short-lived but spectacular 801 who released *801 Live* in 1976, with Brian Eno (second left) and Phil Manzanera (far right). Gab Archives/Getty

Genesis in 1977, with Phil Collins on vocals. Having negotiated Peter Gabriel's abdication, they sailed out of debt and off towards international stardom, by-passing punk en route.
Richard E. Aaron/Getty

U.K., the last progressive rock 'supergroup' of the Seventies, playing in Central Park, New York City in 1978, shortly before the departure of drummer Bill Bruford and guitarist Allan Holdsworth (far right). Michael Putland/Getty

The Enid decide to counter the threat of punk with a camp Pre-Raphaelite look. With Francis Lickerish in white and Robert John Godfrey (far right), c. 1979. Pictorial Press Ltd/Alamy

Midway through this high drama, Palmer plays a curious rinky-dink electric piano break. "It's very silly. It's very 'good time'. It's strange in another way as we thought we were being commercial with that."

Well, they were in a way as it peaked at number four in the singles charts. Palmer recalls that such a strange song getting so high in the charts seemed to be part of tangible taste change in society at the time. "People think it was a great time for music and I think a lot of it was down to the people who were looking for different things. People used to talk a lot at the time about the alternative society and that there was a different day coming with the politics – which of course didn't happen – but also in art, literature and music. The people said, 'No, I don't want three minutes, I don't want the guys to all dress the same.' So it was punter-driven.

"I can remember the fear in all the big record companies as they had got complacent and lost control for a time. A lot of smaller record companies like Vertigo were putting out stuff. They were Heads themselves, if you know what I mean. It was a labour of love for a lot of them. And bear in mind it was expensive to record a band."

Palmer is right here. Surely if this – admittedly rather brief – period of relative adventurousness had been purely industry driven, Family would not have fitted into any recognised template. But they did pretty good business in the UK with all their albums going Top 40, with three reaching the Top 10. The swaggering, funky 'Burlesque' was also a Top 20 hit in 1972. They were staples on the university circuit and the fees offered by the bigger pub venues made them still worth playing. But they never made it in the States. A tour there supporting Elton John in 1972 saw them go down like the proverbial lead balloon.

"We'd play say New York or LA and do really, really well," says Palmer. "You'd go to the Midwest and they'd... well it wasn't like they'd boo us, they'd look at us like, 'Who are this bunch of Martians?' especially Chappo, this guy going absolutely berserk. So it didn't really happen."

An altercation with US promoter Bill Graham during a show at the Fillmore West in San Francisco further impaired Family's hopes of succeeding in America.

With Palmer in the group, Family recorded the half live, half studio *Anyway* (1970) and *Old Songs New Songs* (1971), a compilation and an early example of bands reshaping their back catalogue, with a number of songs either remixed or with different parts added – including Chapman replacing King's vocals on 'Observations From A Hill'. Another outstanding bass guitarist, John Wetton joined for *Fearless* (1971) and helped make 'Burlesque' such an irresistible loping groove. This was

Palmer's last album with the group and Wetton left after *Bandstand* (1972). He was replaced by the estimable Jim Cregan, and Tony Ashton joined on keyboards and vocals for the group's swansong *It's Only A Movie* in 1973.

Some commentators claim Family were so eclectic due to the number of musicians who passed through their ranks. But looking at it in a different way the group's trajectory also changed due to the way the two main writers Chapman and Whitney were heading. The group always mixed it up style-wise but Chapman and Whitney were inexorably heading towards the more American rock'n'roll styles that they explored in Streetwalkers.

They were still coming up with inspired ideas, like the euphonium line on the bluesy, boozy 'Sat'd'y Barfly' on *Fearless*, but Palmer could see that things were changing and bailed out in 1972. He gives these reasons: "It had run its course, really. They had wanted to go into the 'good time' thing, which was fine. That mutual working off each other wasn't working so well, but it wasn't like we were at each other's throats or something; it just wasn't so easy.

"You want every tune and every album to be really good, and when it's getting harder to do, and you don't think it's quite there, it's better to just knock it on the head. It only lasted another year [after I left] and then we were finished. And it wasn't because we never wanted to see each other, but that was it, that was then, and on you go."

CHAPTER 32

Come All You Rolling Minstrels: Seventies Folk Rock

In the contemporary search for roots, the folk music traditions of the British Isles, and England in particular, have come to be held in less high regard than most other indigenous music – especially by the English. This appears to be a unique affliction. The peculiar tendency of the English is to both hang onto tradition for fear of it disappearing altogether, while playing down their native culture, feeling rather embarrassed about it, in a way that suggests the still pervasive effects of residual post-imperial guilt.

Sadly, the conclusion arrived at by some is that English folk music is somehow synonymous with nationalism. Yet, since those who wrote these vital, red-blooded songs were working people at the sharp end of the country's policies, this viewpoint is ill-informed, to say the least.

But English music has regularly resurfaced into public consciousness, the most significant time in living memory being in the folk revival of the Fifties. The traumatic upheaval of World War Two was still a vivid memory and, living in a state of post-war austerity, many went back to the tradition to examine their roots and reassess their identity.

Ralph Vaughan Williams had collected folk songs in the early 20th century, which he wove into compositions like *Five Variants Of Dives And Lazarus* and the *English Folk Song Suite*. The composer had a clear and deep sympathy with the music, which often conveyed an elegiac mood, but there was a particularly English yearning, a bittersweet longing, which is so subtle as to be nigh-on ineffable, but which his music embodied. Most classical composers have been influenced by the music of their homeland, and folk from the British Isles – to open it out geographically – influenced many composers like Arnold Bax and Arthur Moeran.

The misappropriation of traditional material – Benjamin Britten's theatrical, rather camp piano and voice versions of 'The Lincolnshire Poacher' and 'The Foggy Dew' being prime examples – had provoked a reaction among traditional singers. The singer and musicologist

A. L. Lloyd looked at the problem from his perspective as a member of the British Communist Party. Lloyd still sang English rural music but in his 1944 book, *The Singing Englishman*, he contended that much of it had lost its bite as long ago as the 18th century, when it was sentimentalised by the broadsheet ballad writers. He was dismayed how country manners and mores that had been reduced to "clodhopping bumpkin folderol" had been assimilated back into that very culture.

Aware of the growing popularity of American folk and skiffle music in folk clubs, Ewan MacColl passionately promoted English song. MacColl, who also came from the hard left, had been collecting songs in the industrial areas of northern England. Those commenting on the conditions brought about by the Industrial Revolution, he felt, were now more relevant to working people.

Folk singer Shirley Collins was a stickler for the song being sung in a way that was true to the material rather than being a vehicle for the singer. But what was to be used as accompaniment was another matter, as these old songs had originally been sung a capella. However, folk songs are made of robust stuff. In 1964 she teamed up with Davy Graham, one of the great innovative guitar virtuosi of his day, on the epochal *Folk Roots; New Routes*, which saw a fabulous tension between her pure, soaring tones and Graham's extraordinary mix of fingerpicking, Eastern scales, extravagantly bent notes and dramatic glissandi.

In 1969 Shirley and her elder sister Dolly landed a recording deal with Harvest, the newly established progressive subsidiary of EMI, "Along with Deep Purple and The Edgar Broughton Band – a lovely mix," Shirley notes. The label embraced eclecticism, but even so, the Collins sisters – Shirley who played banjo and Dolly who played piano and portative organ, a keyboard with wooden pipes, whose design dated back in design to the 13th century – found themselves on the periphery. They played at the label launch party at the Roundhouse in London in that year. "People were a bit baffled," she says. "It was very odd."

But they broke new ground with their first album for the label, the ambitious *Anthems In Eden* (1969), with its side-long suite 'A Song Story', which featured the crumhorns, racketts and sackbuts of The Early Music Consort Of London.

By the late Sixties, folk music's pastoralism had become entwined in the development of psychedelic rock, spawning groups like The Incredible String Band and Doctor Strangely Strange. In 1969, in a move initiated by bass guitarist Ashley Hutchings, Fairport Convention shifted away from the American music that had featured prominently on their early albums and, with *Liege And Lief,* showed how vital a homegrown approach to folk and rock could be. The inside of the gatefold shows illustrations of ancient folk customs, and the group's three original songs fit into the mood of the album, with 'Farewell, Farewell' based on a traditional song, 'Willie O' The Winsbury'.

As there was no template for how these tunes could be presented, and considering that this new style of British folk rock had emerged at the same time as progressive rock, it's little wonder that there was an overlap in musical style, with one feeding into another. And, in their own way, both types of music involved the musicians moving away from American influences, investigating their roots and re-establishing their individual identities. They also came up with a new way of tackling folk tunes.

'Tam Lin' is a ballad collected from the Scottish borders by American musicologist and song collector Francis Child, which has forty-two verses in its original form. Fairport Convention play a condensed version in a punchy, heavily accented 13/4 with short instrumental passages. Another Child ballad, 'Matty Groves' – a song about adultery, betrayal and murder – follows Child's published lyrics exactly, before shifting up a gear into a speedy instrumental, with guitar and violin soloing, bookended by a dramatic jig-like section which derives from Martin Carthy's arrangement of 'The Famous Flower Of Serving Men'.

Dave Pegg joined the group on bass guitar in 1970, just after Hutchings left. He had played blues guitar in groups in the Birmingham area before switching to bass and played briefly in The Uglys (with Steve Gibbons), The Exception and The Way Of Life (with vocalist Robert Plant and drummer John Bonham).

In 1967 Pegg played double bass with the Ian Campbell Folk Group who would draw crowds of 400 at the Jug Of Punch in Birmingham. "I swapped a 1962 Fender Stratocaster – which was the biggest mistake I ever made, because it's now worth about £15,000 – for a cheap Czechoslovakian double bass and I was a double bassist for about a year," he says. Violinist Dave Swarbrick – who also played mandolin – had been in the Ian Campbell Folk Group, but left to team up with Martin Carthy and so Pegg learned to play mandolin in his absence.

"As a duo they were an influence on everybody," says Pegg. "Nobody plays the guitar like Martin and he is a fantastic singer. They were doing incredible, complicated arrangements of songs like 'Sovay' with very odd time signatures, and they were so good."

After a short spell with drummer Cozy Powell and guitarist Clem Clempson in The Beast, a trio inspired by Cream, Pegg was encouraged by Swarbrick to audition for Fairport Convention – who the violinist had joined in early 1969 after playing sessions for them – as Hutchings was about to leave to form a new group, Steeleye Span. Vocalist Sandy Denny was also about to exit.

Like Pegg, guitarists Richard Thompson and Simon Nicol had come from a rock background – as had the departing Hutchings – and drummer Dave Mattacks had been in a dance band. Only Swarbrick and Denny had any sort of folk music pedigree. Pegg notes that this was all such a new venture that in lieu of electric pick-ups for an acoustic violin, Swarbrick experimented with stuffing the instrument's body with cotton wool and using a telephone mike for amplification.

"We all moved into The Angel, an old pub in Little Hadham [in Hertfordshire] and it was like a 'get it together in the country' kind of thing – Traffic had done it in Berkshire – but it was a grotty old pub with one toilet and the big skittle alley at the back room converted into a rehearsal room," Pegg recalls. "There was us lot and we got more and more roadies. It seemed that if you didn't have anywhere to live you became a Fairport roadie."

Losing a world-class singer like Sandy Denny was a blow to the group but they muddled through. "When we moved into The Angel we had a gig in about ten days' time at the Country Club at Hampstead, which was the first gig I did," Pegg recalls. "We had about an hour-and-a-half's music but there was no singer because Sandy had gone and two days before the gig it was who gets the short straw and has to sing. I'm not kidding, that's what happened. Most of it was Swarbrick and Richard, and I don't think Swarb had ever sung before in his life."

The group began working on material for *Full House*, which was released in 1971. "Swarb and Richard had become a writing team and they would come up with songs that sounded like traditional songs but they weren't," says Pegg. "They'd come up with the lyrics [together] or Richard would come up with the lyrics and Swarb would come up with the tune. They wrote some great stuff. 'Now Be Thankful' is almost like a hymn and 'Sloth' became very much a progressive rock track."

With its ominous portents of war, the brooding 'Sloth' would be stretched out in concert. "It became a big jam session piece for the band. I think the record is eighteen-and-a-half minutes. I'd do a bass solo and it would go on and on," says Pegg.

Thompson and Swarbrick's songs were peopled by curious characters who seemed to have walked out of the pages of history: the troubled Crazy Man Michael; the sinister Doctor Of Physick; Poor Will and his nemesis the Jolly Hangman; the lantern-bearing Journeyman.

The following album *Angel Delight* (1971) refers to their home – and was also the name of a popular Seventies dessert – and the group-written title track details life in the old pub and refers to an incident when a lorry crashed into the house early one Sunday morning and finished up in Dave Swarbrick's bedroom about a metre from the recumbent violinist's feet. An appearance on the *Top Of The Pops* album slot helped propel it to number eight in the album chart.

'Sir William Gower' exemplifies that the timing of jigs, reels and dance tunes could be expanded and become part of the fabric of a song. When 'Sir William Gower' was first sung, no one would have envisaged the unison instrumental lines that perambulated in a mazy manner around the vocal melody on Fairport's version.

"Those sort of things happened pretty spontaneously," says Pegg. "Dave Mattacks could read music and came up with a lot of ideas. Certainly on later albums like *Fairport Nine* [1974] Dave was very influential in the arrangements. We got 'The Hexhamshire Lass' from Bob Davenport. It would never have been accompanied before and it's got lots of stops and starts and odd bar lengths."

Picking a good rhythm was crucial to Seventies folk rock. A lot of songs were played in 4/4, but a standard backbeat didn't necessarily fit. Dave Mattacks is one of the best UK rock-based drummers of his generation and his imaginative breaks and crisp, elegant timing made him a sought-after session player. He also played with Shirley Collins And The Albion Country Dance Band on the influential *No Roses* LP from 1971, with Ashley Hutchings on bass, although some of the rhythms were a tad lumpy. Pentangle had the dextrous rhythm section of Danny Thompson on double bass and drummer Terry Cox, both of whom had come from a jazz background. Playing with vocalist Jacquie McShee and acoustic guitarists John Renbourn and Bert Jansch in an all-acoustic line-up meant that Cox, in particular, drummed with the lightest of touches.

When Ashley Hutchings formed Steeleye Span, Gerry Conway drummed on their debut *Hark! The Village Wait* (1970), but when he left, Hutchings, Martin Carthy on electric guitars and violinist Peter Knight formed the basis of a rhythmically fluid drummerless ensemble. They recruited ex-Gnidrolog drummer Nigel Pegrum in 1974, which was a mixed blessing as things became more muscular but a bit foursquare. And when the group decided to aim for commercial success with the single 'All Around My Hat', produced by Mike Batt of Wombles fame, the song's great galumphing rhythm did rather sound like an update of A. L. Lloyd's "clodhopping bumpkin folderol". It charted at number five.

Surprisingly perhaps, Lloyd was an advocate of Fairport Convention and the group used a recording of his voice onstage as an introduction when they performed their 1971 concept album *"Babbacombe" Lee*.

"Bert Lloyd was a serious folk aficionado, but he was always up for Fairport," says Pegg. "A lot of [traditionalists] could be a bit critical. But he said that it was good that we were keeping it alive – we might be young and loud, but we did folk music a great service."

A stranger musical hybrid than that of folk rock was the music of Gryphon, which mixed up traditional folk songs, renaissance and medieval instrumentals and modern compositions in those styles. "A prog/folk/medieval/classical thing" is how drummer and vocalist David Oberlé describes it.

In early 1970, Royal College Of Music graduates, bassoonist and crumhorn player Brian Gulland and multi-instrumentalist Richard Harvey, who had played in the early music ensemble Musica Reservata, were forming a group and looking to recruit a drummer.

David Oberlé recalls his first rehearsal with the then all-acoustic group: "I was completely gobsmacked by what I heard. Because having been effectively a sort of rock-stroke-jazz drummer, to suddenly be confronted with crumhorns and rauschpfeifes and lutes was a million miles away from anything that I'd ever encountered before. It put my head into a different place completely, because I liked what I was hearing, but I had to adapt not only my playing style, but also what I was playing."

With no real template as to what to play, Oberlé stripped down his kit to a floor tom, a pair of bongos, a talking drum and a couple of cymbals and played using soft-headed mallets. And while bearing in mind that drummers of yore were principally time keepers, he used a rock beat on occasions, but basically "made it up as I went along".

"It was actually very difficult playing with two classically trained musicians," he explains. "The guitarist was Graeme Taylor, who joined just before I did, and Graeme was also a very accomplished player, so all of a sudden there I was, in a situation where I had to pick things up very quickly indeed. It was a little traumatic to start with – but after about two or three months, the whole thing settled, and I could sing as well, which did help a bit.

"Basically we would take a folk song, like 'The Unquiet Grave' and 'Sir Gavin Grimbold' [on the group's 1973 debut album *Gryphon*] and probably change the tune around quite a bit, or rewrite it, and then Gryphon-ise it. So, one of the problems we had in the very early days, when we were going out playing folk clubs, was that a lot of the traditionalists didn't like it much because it didn't really follow the pattern that they understood. But just because of the sheer energy of the band, it picked up and as time went on, it became acceptable."

Gryphon were in an almost unique position in the early Seventies scene, the only other group working in similar territory being Amazing Blondel, a trio signed to Island who tapped back into the music of that period. Their individual approach made them some friends in the music press.

"A lot of the press had a real job pigeonholing us, because we didn't actually slot into anything recognisable," says Oberlé. "We had some great fans in people like Chris Welch and Karl Dallas. I think it was Chris in the *Melody Maker* who dubbed us 'The 13th-century Slade'. Which is something we've been trying to live down ever since."

Sir Peter Hall then approached the group to write music for his Royal Shakespeare Company production of *The Tempest* at The Old Vic. This became the complex nineteen-minute musical tapestry that occupies side one of their 1974 album *Midnight Mushrumps* – "mushrumps" being a word used in the text of the play. The album saw the introduction of more electric instruments.

"That really kicked the whole thing off, because all of a sudden we became sort of trendy Hampstead coffee-table type music," Oberlé explains. "It launched us into a much bigger and wider audience. As a band, we were already heavily into Yes, Genesis, Caravan – a lot of the more proggy sort of bands – and I think on *Mushrumps* a lot of those influences started to emerge."

The group appear on the cover dressed in an extravagant assortment of cloaks, capes, hats and velvet frock coats. "We were able to go and raid the costume department of the National Theatre," Oberlé recalls. "[Now] you wouldn't be seen dead wandering round in something like that, though in the Seventies, you could. And so we did."

As the music expanded in scope so did Oberlé's drum kit. "I'd got a bass drum and I'd reintroduced the snare by then, as well. So basically I was playing a kit, but standing up, with lots of percussion all over the place."

By the time Gryphon got to *Red Queen To Gryphon Three* in late 1974, the four lengthy instrumental tracks were as cerebral and teeming with ideas as ever. The early music elements and the subtlety of their instrumental interplay was maintained, but it felt like less like the product of a chamber ensemble. Richard Harvey plays synthesizer on the album and on 'Lament' he plays a thrilling, show-stopping solo on recorder.

The group were now managed by Brian Lane, who ran Worldwide Artists and looked after Yes, Rick Wakeman and Wally. "Rick went to college at the same time as Richard and Brian [Gulland], so he was very instrumental in getting us involved with Brian," Oberlé recalls.

"We took the *Red Queen* album to America when we toured with Yes [from November 1974]. That was a bit of an eye-opener for us. Having played to a maximum of about 2,000, maybe 3,000 people, all of a sudden we were walking on stage in front of 15, 20, 30,000. It went down a storm in America.

"It just worked," he continues. "Because we were so different to Yes in terms of instrumentation, there was no conflict of interest, there was no problem. And I think there was a mutual admiration between both bands for the standard of musicianship."

But it wasn't to last. Gryphon continued to tour with Yes in the UK into spring 1975 and although that pairing had clearly given them a readymade audience in the States, they had risen to the challenge and wowed the huge crowds.

But then, in a bizarre disappearing act, Gryphon just seemed to slide out of the zeitgeist. They had produced some magical music, but, admits Oberlé: "It's very difficult to keep being consistent, in terms of the material that you are producing. We were running out of steam a bit." And having made the more song-based *Rain Dances* in 1976, they were working on *Treason* with producer Mike Thorne in 1977. But Thorne had another iron in the fire.

In an odd spin-off, Oberlé ended up singing backing vocals on 'Mannequin', a song by a new Harvest signing, Wire, as Thorne was also producing their debut album, *Pink Flag*. If ever two groups were each other's antithesis it was surely the elaborate Gryphon and the minimal, austere Wire, who even some of the emerging punk audience found rather aloof and daunting.

But all this hastened Gryphon's demise. As Oberlé puts it, with punk looming on the horizon: "I think for any band that had half an eye on what was going on, this was the Sword Of Damocles."

The group had fallen so far out of favour that they did a couple gigs in 1977 where only a handful of people turned up, and broke up in that year. "Richard started kicking off his film music career, and Graeme joined The Albion Band. Everybody just legged it off in opposite directions," says Oberlé. "I got into music publishing for a bit, and I worked for the *Melody Maker* and *Sounds*, and then launched *Kerrang!*"

What is Oberlé's fondest memory of playing in Gryphon? "I think the highlight, for what it's worth, was when we played at Madison Square Garden with Yes [in 1974]," he replies. "We'd done the set and it went down a storm, and everybody in the auditorium lit their lighters. It was just amazing. And right at the back of Madison Square Garden, there was a sign going round and round that said 'New York Welcomes Gryphon'. And I thought, 'That's it. We've made it!'"

At the time of writing, Gryphon have reformed and are finding a new fanbase, and Fairport Convention have become a national institution. But the latter suffered music biz obsolescence themselves at the end of the Seventies. Dave Pegg recalls the group's apparent demise.

"Island Records said, 'Sorry, but you are going to have to go. It's just not worth it – it's costing us money.'"

Pegg remembers that when the group made *Rising For The Moon* in 1975 – "a fabulous album", which marked the return of Sandy Denny – they were given some difficult facts to digest when they went on tour to the States and met Jerry Moss, the head of A&M, which was Island's outlet in that territory.

"He said, 'We can't have you any more. I love the music but it's the worst selling act we've ever had on our label.'"

Things didn't improve when they switched labels. "We had recorded *Tipplers Tales* and *The Bonny Bunch Of Roses* for Vertigo, who were then a subsidiary of Phonogram," Pegg recalls. "In 1978 they said, 'Look, we don't want any more albums. Please don't make any more because we can't sell them.'"

"I said, 'But we've got a six-album deal with you. We've given you two albums; we're going to make another four albums. We want the money.' So the head of Phonogram said, 'We'll give you half of the money not to make any more albums.' We went, 'You're on!' We got £7,000 each, which is why we split up in 1979, because all of a sudden we were rich. It was the first time we had got any money out of the music business."

Strawbs were a group who perched for years on the borderline between folk and rock, initially playing bluegrass in the mid-Sixties as The Strawberry Hill Boys, based around Dave Cousins and Tony Hooper. They recorded an album with Sandy Denny in 1967 that was shelved at the time, but released in 1973. Sonja Kristina, later of Curved Air, also briefly featured on vocals. Strawbs were the first British group to be signed to the A&M label.

Folk music often fed into progressive rock and so it's difficult to start separating them. That also leads us onto the question, what is folk music? Take Roy Harper, who was signed to Harvest. He played folk guitar in a style similar to his friend Bert Jansch from the mid-Sixties and was a regular at London folk clubs like Les Cousins. But then how does one categorise his seventeen-minute railing against society, 'McGoohan's

Blues', from *Folkjokeopus* (1968)? Or his astonishing 1971 Harvest album, *Stormcock*, with its four lengthy, episodic songs, one of which was orchestrated by David Bedford, and his extravagant usage of massed vocal overdubbing? It certainly came out of folk, but what was it now?

I put it to Dave Cousins, the Strawbs founder, guitarist, singer and principal songwriter, that the group made a smooth transition from folk stylings to a more progressive approach.

"But we were never a folk group," he counters. "The only reason we're associated with folk groups is because we started playing in folk clubs. I played banjo, and we played bluegrass music, basically, to start with – and then I started to write my own songs, but I still carried on playing them in the folk clubs, because that was the only place I could play – I didn't play electric guitar – and that's why we evolved out of that scene."

From 1966–72, Cousins worked as a DJ and presenter for Danmarks Radio, which broadcast from the BBC so he was immersed in all sorts of different music and also had an ear for pop melody.

Strawbs signed to A&M in 1968 and recorded an album of songs they had originally sung with Sandy Denny, but here were rather overproduced by Gus Dudgeon and Tony Visconti. "Had that album come out at the time, it would probably have been the first and last Strawbs record. It was very glossy, and our singing just didn't suit a thirty-two-piece orchestra, it sounded ridiculous," Cousins says.

A&M rejected the album and asked the group to re-record it. They did so, adding some new material. "They sent us $30,000, which we spent – it was the second most expensive album after *Sgt Pepper's Lonely Hearts Club Band*," says Cousins. "It was a colossal amount, about £180,000 in today's [2014] money."

The album, *Strawbs*, was released in 1969 and chimed more with the hipper audiences. There were some elements of folk woven into its fabric, but also of rock and post-psychedelic experimentation. And like Pentangle they employed a jazzy swing on 'The Witch Once Was Mine'.

"It was picked up by the underground scene. The first review we had was by Bob Harris in the *International Times*, in the second or third edition – and it created quite a stir, because it wasn't a folk album, and it sold, in its time, 25,000 copies, when the best-selling folk album was selling 5,000 copies."

'The Man Who Called Himself Jesus' created a huge stir and was banned by the BBC as being sacrilegious. Cousins recalls that 'The Battle' caused a more positive stir when John Peel played it on his *Top Gear* show on Radio 1. "That was written about a game of chess, but it was actually reflecting on the struggle between black and white at the time in America. It was effectively observing the Civil Rights struggle between black and white, but set in a medieval battle. And I wasn't smoking anything then – it just came out of my head.

"And 'Where Is This Dream Of Your Youth' used modal harmonies. I was listening to old Appalachian banjo players and noticed that they were tuning their banjos in modal tunings, so I thought, 'I wonder what that'll sound like on guitar,'" continues Cousins. "I evolved all my own tunings. It was totally unlike anybody else."

A&M wanted another album but having gone so far over budget on their debut, Strawbs' next album *Dragonfly* was more of a chamber affair with Clare Deniz on cello. But then Cousins and Hooper were joined by Richard Hudson on drums and sitar, and John Ford on bass and guitar from Velvet Opera, who Cousins had put on at the Hounslow Arts Lab, where he arranged gigs. Also joining the group was a young session keyboard player, Rick Wakeman, who had contributed in this capacity to *Dragonfly*. Full of confidence, the new line-up recorded a live album at the Queen Elizabeth Hall on July 11, 1970, *Just A Collection Of Antiques And Curios*.

"'The Antique Suite', a four-part song, was written about a doctor friend of mine who got cancer," Cousins explains. "He went into hospital, and asked me to visit him and I didn't – I couldn't face it – and I regretted it. But I wrote a song about him, this old man lying in a room on his own with all of his old souvenirs, because he used to collect antiques, and so that song was written about a real person. But with Rick it turned into a tour-de-force."

'The Vision Of The Lady Of The Lake', although not folk per se, in its ten-minute length has the number of verses of a folk ballad and seems steeped in legend and allegory.

"I didn't set out to write a folk ballad, I wrote a song, and it just so happened that 'The Vision Of The Lady Of The Lake' was the reverse of the King Arthur legend," Cousins says. "The hand comes out of the water, but in the end he has to kill the maiden in order to survive. The creatures that arise out of the lake are the Seven Deadly Sins.

"We were out at the crack of dawn driving up to do a gig up north somewhere. There's a reservoir as you get onto the beginning of the M1, and it was shrouded in mist and I suddenly got the inspiration for a song."

Wakeman had his solo organ showcase 'Temperament Of Mind' and his busy and decorative style of keyboard playing earned him a special mention in the *Melody Maker* review of the concert, which announced him as "Tomorrow's superstar".

Cousins feels that Strawbs veered more towards progressive rock on 1971's *From The Witchwood*. The group's trademark was becoming a mixing of ancient and modern epitomised by 'The Hangman And The Papist', with its Hammond organ flourishes and medieval grit, which the group had presented to bemused teenies on the *Top Of The Pops* album slot. Wakeman's flourishes on organ, piano and celeste were less grandstanding than subtle and woven into the song.

Strawbs blended these different styles into a more individual mix on 1972's *Grave New World*. Its front cover is *The Dance Of Albion*, a painting by William Blake of a naked youth full of joy and optimism, and inside the gatefold sleeve, in silver and black, is an Atlas figure atop a pinnacle, with a rainbow at his feet and carrying a sun-like orb on his back.

After just over a year in the group Wakeman quit and was replaced by Blue Weaver, who had played keyboards with Amen Corner. It's difficult to understand this now, but such was the interest in Wakeman's virtuosity, particularly his solo spot – which had become a much-anticipated part of a Strawbs concert – that Cousins felt obliged to compensate for his departure.

"If we'd just done a straight musical show, it would have placed Blue in an impossible position," he explains. "So I devised this whole show with back-projection of film, a ballet dancer, mime artists – a spectacle, if you like – to take away the direct comparison with Rick."

Hudson and Ford had featured in the writing credits on *From The Witchwood*, and Ford's 'Heavy Disguise', a musing on fakery and deception, is graced by an ensemble arrangement by Robert Kirby, whose work with Nick Drake had particularly impressed Cousins.

"John put it down on his own but I decided I wanted a silver band. The score was so difficult, we tried it one day and the players couldn't play it. For the next session we booked the principals of the London Symphony Orchestra, and that was one of the highlights of the album."

Grave New World was released in 1972, and one of its most dramatic moments is 'New World'. The song opens with an ominous, scalp-raising twelve-string guitar and Mellotron brass fanfare. Cousins sounds particularly angry and impassioned.

"The words were written about Rick Wakeman. I was really annoyed with him because he didn't have the bottle to tell me he was leaving the band – he just left, and told our management he was leaving, and didn't even phone me up – so I was really quite hurt by that. And then he did an interview saying not particularly complimentary things about the band." In his "vindictive" lyrics Cousins refers to Wakeman's *"acid tongue"* and *"trembling spiteful hands"*.

Although no one would wish to be a dedicatee of such a song, the hymnal 'Benedictus', which is also about the keyboard player, is more circumspect. Cousins was so shaken by Wakeman's departure that he consulted the *I Ching*, the ancient Chinese book of divination, to see whether it was worth carrying on with the group, and the verses are based on text from the book. The two subsequently kissed and made up, and Wakeman played on Cousins' solo album *Two Weeks Last Summer*, which was released in late 1972.

Grave New World went to number eleven in the UK album charts and A&M decided to make a film of that title – a compilation of videos of all the tracks – which toured cinemas in 1972 on a bill with a film of Emerson, Lake & Palmer's *Pictures At An Exhibition*. It was produced by Des Cox, but Cousins would ideally like to recut it, as one of the sequences finds the group supposedly standing on top of Eros in Piccadilly Circus and there is another section that features a "woman prancing around in a psychedelic leotard".

"It was the first ever feature film made on video," says Cousins. "And it was then transferred to film, which was incredibly expensive. I went to see the film in a cinema, sneaked in when it was dark, and sneaked out before it finished. People were sitting there laughing."

But the video to 'New World' is apocalyptic. "It was one of the first things ever to use chroma key, where it was filmed against a blue screen," says Cousins, whose head appears against a black background and scenes of famine and terrorist bombings."

Strawbs exemplified what can happen when a group's balance goes awry. Released in 1973, *Bursting At The Seams* was a number two album and yielded a Top 20 single, 'Lay Down', that exemplified Cousins' love of pop, although it would sound folkish if played acoustically. Cousins' rather weatherbeaten-sounding vocals give it the characteristic Strawbs grit and he punctuates the chorus with some Who-ish power chords.

"I started to write longer guitar riffs, once I started to play electric guitar, and that's where the riff from 'Down By The Sea' came from, and again, that's evolving towards a more proggy feel. But I was fighting with the band at the time, who didn't want to do songs like that."

In its brooding power and epic sweep, that song was a precursor to what was to come, but *Bursting At The Seams* also contained its polar opposite, the grotesque singalong, 'Part Of The Union', written by Hudson and Ford. In a major miscalculation Cousins thought it best to keep this song, which was initially going to be a Hudson Ford side project (see Chapter 36), as a Strawbs track to help maintain band unity.

In the Seventies it was seen as rather cool if a progressive or heavy band got in the charts as in 1972 when Hawkwind's 'Silver Machine' went to number two to the delight of Heads everywhere. And it was fun to see Alice Cooper on the living room screen wielding a rapier while performing 'School's Out' that same summer.

But for a group to be seen to be selling out was viewed with disdain. The Strawbs had always had a hip cachet, but this most unrepresentative of singles' success almost wiped out their core audience. Not only that, Hudson and Ford would soon split to follow a successful pop career.

Cousins notes that his songs like 'New World', 'The Hangman And The Papist' and 'The Battle' were political anyway, but they were allusive and allegorical, nothing like this lowest common denominator move into Politics with a big "P".

Cousins guided Strawbs along a more dramatic tack, the big gestures that had featured on 'Down By The Sea' expanded into the elongated and complex structures of *Hero And Heroine* (1974) and *Ghosts* (1975) and Cousins looks back on these albums as representing the group's best music, although *Top Of The Pops* appearances were out now.

"[You] think the Strawbs was fun – it wasn't," he says. "In those days it was very, very powerful and aggressive. You've got songs like 'The Life Auction' and 'Hero And Heroine', which was immense, and 'Out In The Cold', and 'Round And Round', with these long, jagged riffs going on, it was a huge noise that we made."

Strawbs toured with Supertramp in 1974 – who were heading towards poppier climes – and also played in the USA with King Crimson that year. In a review of *Hero And Heroine* in *Rolling Stone* in 1974, Ken Barnes neatly summed it up: "Strawbs moved from folkier days to a lush, stately and Mellotron-dominated sound, with similarities to Yes, King Crimson and The Moody Blues. They wrote more compelling songs than the former two, and possessed more lyrical/musical substance than the latter."

This touring almost spawned a remarkable guitar duo. Cousins: "When we came back from one of the tours, Robert Fripp phoned me up and said, 'Dave, I've been thinking. How would you like to go out and do a few folk clubs, just the two of us together?' So I went over and rehearsed with him. I got my guitar out, put it in a C modal tuning, and he got his Spanish guitar out, and we went through this song a couple of times. He was fumbling around, he didn't figure out what I was doing, and put his guitar down at the end and said, 'I think you're self-sufficient [*laughs*]'. So that was that. I thought it would have been fantastic: Cousins and Fripp."

Strawbs split in 1978. Cousins reckons that due to a lack of coverage in the UK music press it seemed like they had all but disappeared before that. But in fact they were doing big business elsewhere.

"In this country, people have got no idea of how many records we actually sold," Cousins says. "*Grave New World* sold 98,000 – we managed to get the sales figures out of A&M in 1995 – and these are just UK sales figures. *Bursting At The Seams* did 78,000, I think, *Hero And Heroine* did 48,000, so it was still a big-selling record. And then *Ghosts* sold 35,000, and that was the last big-selling album we had over here.

"But in America, the albums didn't get out of the hundreds [chart placings] until, suddenly, *Hero And Heroine* spent seventeen weeks on the charts in the US, and went to number seventy-odd in the charts, and *Ghosts* spent thirteen weeks and went to number forty-five in the charts. They would have sold 250,000 to 300,000, in the USA, and we got a gold disc, which is hanging on the wall upstairs for *Hero And Heroine*, which sold 50,000 in Canada.

"We had five years of selling huge numbers of records and doing huge shows over there. The biggest show we ever did on our own was in Toronto, where we played to nine and-a-half-thousand people. People have got no idea that the Strawbs were that big."

CHAPTER 33

Divertimento No.4: Notes on "It"

"The permissive society" was a term coined in the Sixties to describe a growing trend in liberal attitudes towards the tolerance of sexual activity and expression in its manifold forms. It saw the lowering of the age of consent for heterosexuals and homosexuals – although not equally – and a less patriarchal view towards censorship of artistic pursuits. Into the Seventies, it had only been a decade since the 1960 obscenity trial of D. H. Lawrence's *Lady Chatterley's Lover* in its unexpurgated version, which had essentially been a road testing of the 1959 Obscene Publications Act.

In the 21st century, after the nine o'clock "watershed", robust Anglo-Saxon words like "fuck" and even the more taboo "cunt" can be heard on TV, and are even used in newspapers with impunity. But these were especial sticking points for the critics of Lawrence's novel.

If a written work could be proven to be of "literary merit" then it would be less likely to be considered obscene; otherwise it would be simply deemed pornography. John Cleland's 18th-century novel *Memoirs Of A Woman Of Pleasure* aka *Fanny Hill* fared less well and while it was defended as being "bawdy", the court ruled that it was pornographic in the trial of 1964, and it wasn't published in its unexpurgated version in the UK until 1970.

The way that this guardianship of public morals worked was demonstrated by the occupations of those involved with the Wolfenden Report of the mid-Fifties. The great and the good sitting on the panel included a judge, a psychiatrist and a number of theologians. Although acknowledged at the time, but not actioned, their findings eventually led to the decriminalisation of physical homosexual relations, which up to then had been illegal, in the Sexual Offences Act of 1967.

The permissive society was built on an incremental liberalisation – it wasn't as if all taboos were smashed overnight. But in 1969, thrill-seekers could see one of the first public examples of "full frontal nudity" in the sex-based revue *Oh Calcutta!*, which was considered to have artistic merit rather than just being a semi-pornographic strip show. It was created by the theatre critic Kenneth Tynan, who had caused an outrage by being the first person to use the word "fuck" live on TV, when interviewed in 1965.

But in late-Sixties and early-Seventies mainstream culture, the adjective "permissive", which effectively means "allowing", became synonymous with more and more people having "it". The British *Carry On* films had been around since 1958 and had always carried a suggestive side to their humour without ever being explicitly "blue". Initially they felt like a mix of music hall, slapstick and the bawdy humour of seaside postcards.

This peculiar British mixture of sexual repression and prurience – and ability to laugh at that combination – was, itself, "serviced" more and more by the late-Sixties *Carry On* films and into the Seventies by the TV comedy series *Up Pompeii*. Frankie Howerd played Lurcio, the slave who acted as narrator, and the innuendos got progressively ruder. One time, Lurcio, having heard of a robbery, says to a woman, Nymphia (played by Barbara Windsor): "I hear your little place has been broken into", to which she replies, in a jarring cockney accent: "I never said I was no vestal virgin."

Back then there was more of a time lag for modern notions to percolate into mainstream thought. "Full frontal" seeped into common parlance and was used to describe the occasional flash of pubic hair in films and the photographs in softcore pornographic magazines like *Penthouse* and *Mayfair*. While the latter had token articles on cars, it also contained 'Quest – The Laboratory Of Human Response', a grandly named supplement that was basically a bunch of supposedly genuine testimonies on sexual themes. American magazine *Penthouse* featured former "call girl" Xaviera Hollander as a sexual agony aunt in the Call Me Madam section answering questions from men, some of whom seemed genuinely agonised by their sexual problems. The magazine, like *Playboy*, featured interviews with musicians and some surprisingly high-quality fiction and non-fiction articles on music, photography, the occult, and of course, sex.

Back then, this freer talk of sex encompassed the indiscriminate amorality of "free love", the hippie statement of liberation that was basically a euphemism for casual sex.

A man who married young might be sexually inexperienced in terms of partners, but he was "randy" and he probably wasn't having much of "it", these days.

"The free love brigade; all those hippies – they're always having orgies. And all of them Scandinavians, they're really permissive, that lot. And as for those Swedish girls, they're sex mad, they are, nymphos, and at 'it' all the time."

If no one is on record as saying that exact quote, it was an unspoken subtext at the time. The more sexually relaxed Sweden was looked at with much "tut-tutting" and a great deal of interest. All this echoed the complaints about the American troops billeted in the UK in World War Two being "over-sexed, over-paid and over here", as if every visiting soldier from that country was running on such sociopathically high levels of testosterone that it was best to lock up your daughters, wife and mother, as, rest assured, they'd be after "it".

In the Seventies, it seemed, the general perception was there were always people who were having "it" off, having "it" up, having "it". But then it always seemed that "it" was being done by someone else.

Psychologists are invited to form an orderly queue to try to understand the Seventies preoccupation, obsession even, with breasts – tits, bristols, knockers, norks, jugs, hooters, melons – and preferably big ones. In *Carry On Henry*, Sid James wants to make sure Barbara Windsor will be an ideal bride by trying to spy on her, pre-nuptially, to get an eyeful of her knockers. The same knockers were revealed on film for a tantalising split second when her bra flew off while she was engaging in group callisthenics in the later *Carry On Camping*.

The inner temple of Seventies mammocentricity was page three of *The Sun* newspaper. This feature, inaugurated in 1970, allowed the target reader, the working-class bloke, to open his paper over breakfast to see a dolly bird flashing her jugs. "Phwoooarrrr!" Papers like the less oikish *Daily Express* refrained from going down that route, although they weren't averse to finding more subtle ways to titillate, like showing women on fashion pages modelling see-through brassieres, giving the lie to poet John Cooper Clarke's satirical poem, 'You Never See A Nipple In The Daily Express'. These were the sort of kicks one could get by opening a mail order catalogue and heading straight to the Ladies Underwear section – any photographs of models in body stockings were particularly rich pickings.

One of the prime sources of titillation in Seventies UK was the hilariously bogus naturist magazine, *H&E* or *Health & Efficiency*, to give it its full title. That might sound like a slogan akin to the Nazi ideal of "strength through joy", but it was a magazine showing photographs of naturists playing sports, lounging around and generally doing what naturists do – which included some particularly spicy "full frontal" pictures. No doubt the full benefit of this healthy lifestyle was missed by some of the lone and sedentary "armchair naturists" who bought the magazine.

Then there were the youth culture books like *Suedehead*, *Skinhead*, *Skinhead Girls* and others, written by Richard Allen, a pseudonym of author James Moffat. Quite how much Moffat, who was Canadian and 48 years old when *Skinhead* was published in 1970, could empathise with Seventies working class bovver-boy culture is a moot point, but these books were full of violence and sex, and if they were passed around the classroom at break, one only needed to hold the book up by its spine and note where the well-thumbed pages fell open to see where these sections – the good bits – were located.

In amongst all this, there was the more serious matter of the widespread rise of feminism, which was focused on the Women's Liberation Movement. Their most dramatic use of the media spotlight was the protest at the Miss World beauty competition at the Royal Albert Hall, London, in late 1970. It was essentially a reaction against the objectification and degradation of women, the competition's links with business corporations and the compère Bob Hope's links with the Vietnam War: he was involved in entertaining American troops there, as he had been in World War Two.

The movement likened such events to "cattle markets" and the veteran comedian made a clunky joke about that notion onstage when he started mooing. "I don't want you to think that I'm a dirty old man," he said, "I never give women a second thought. My first thought covers everything." Initially looking shaken when the demonstration hit the stage, Hope regained his composure, saying it had been a "nice conditioning course for Vietnam" and that the protestors must be "on some kind of dope".

They weren't, but these Women's Libbers were subject to ridicule in the male-dominated mainstream media, especially the symbolic gesture of women burning their bras as a step towards emancipation. There seemed an almost endless line of stand-up comedians with gags that commenced along the lines of: "Me wife's mother burnt her bra the other day…"

Carry On Girls (1973) was a spoof about a small town beauty contest. Only slightly more enlightened, it laughs at the ridiculousness of it all while allowing the viewer to ogle the girls. The wife of the mayor who is judging the contest, Mildred Bumble, decides she is going to burn her bra in protest. The sound of a fire engine with bells ringing is heard soon after.

In the workplace sexism was rife. Speaking in 2018 the actor Helen Mirren commented, "the Seventies were terrible for women and girls in my profession".

Gail Colson started Charisma Records with Tony Stratton-Smith in 1969, but if she is mentioned at all in that label's history, she is rarely portrayed as more than the sidekick to her notoriously flamboyant business partner.

"For years people would refer to me as Tony's assistant or secretary," Colson recalls. "I used to go to gigs and say that I was the record company and they looked at me and assumed I was a groupie. I was the MD when I was 30. Bronze Records had Gerry and Lilly [Bron], who were husband and wife, but [generally] the highest a woman could get was head of press."

She had also encountered a more physical manifestation of some men's attitude to women in the workplace in an earlier job. "There was awful lot of pinching bottoms and groping. But it was never an artist that did it. Everyone I knew who was a female in those days [had experienced it]. Even from, God bless him, Jonathan Rowlands, my first boss. I was on the phone doing reception and he got behind me and grabbed both my breasts. I'm on the phone so there was not a lot I could do, but I remember hitting my tooth with the receiver, putting the phone down and going, 'What the fuck do you think you're doing?' and slapping him around the face, and he never did it again."

This "battle of the sexes", as it was unfortunately dubbed, was a period of flux, when both men and women had their roles challenged, and many were obliged to reassess their identities. In her 1973 novel, *Fear Of Flying*, Erica Jong explored themes of sex and repression. In it she coined the phrase the "zipless fuck", meaning the option of a sexual liaison with a stranger, who you not only didn't know, but didn't want to know.

Lisa Alther's *Kin Flicks* (1976) aimed to redress the gender balance in that the sexually liberated protagonist views herself as a Don Juan character, except whereas he was erecting himself as a proud, priapic monument to his own sexuality, she gets on with her life and takes her pleasure as she sees fit. Eye-opening at the time, now it seems more commonplace. But this was a woman enjoying easy-going, non-commital "free love" on her own terms. Rather than selling herself out – feeling obliged to shag any Tom, Dick and/or Harry – she was choosing to do what *she* wanted.

The biggest pebble thrown into the pond was Australian author Germaine Greer's epochal, uncompromising book, *The Female Eunuch* (1970), which encourages women to reclaim their sexuality on their own terms, not as men expect them to look or behave. One of her central tenets is that men hate women, although she makes some extravagant deductive leaps towards this end based on evidence and testimonies from men who seem to be basically sexual misfits. She claims that the rather coy contemporary portrayal of naked women in pornographic magazines, rather than being at the behest of the censors, was because men are frightened of female genitals.

Some may hold that view, but taking that notion out of theory and into the world of actual physical relationships – and even allowing for personal bias – it's difficult to see oneself or any friends who have talked about such things in her sorry and hugely generalised portrayals of men.

To make the point further, in 1971, she appeared for the Amsterdam-based *Suck* magazine, photographed by Keith Morris in a portfolio of explicit poses that one would have only been able to get from specialist outlets at the time, as an example of "cunt power".

The idea may have seemed a potent one, to reclaim this kind of material, but ultimately, choosing to pose naked with one's own agenda is to be lost in vast sump of porn, whose "consumers" care not one jot about context, irony or feminist theory.

Greer also examines female stereotyping. The Seventies stereotypical look could be roughly summed up as cute face, slender legs, blonde hair and big knockers. But this stereotyping comes from certain sections of the media and is based on generalisations. They show us the "dolly bird", but whereas they are recognised by men as a representation, in practical terms they mean almost nothing.

You might have had a dreamy and lustful sigh over someone like the buxom and exquisitely pretty Seventies actress Madeline Smith, as a simple biological reaction, but those who would hold out for this sort of "perfection", as Greer puts it, rather than interacting with women they actually know, are a tiny minority and probably need treatment.

So rare are the women who epitomise these "desirable" physical characteristics and so removed from the reality in which people have relationships or marry, that this stereotyping exists in the media, apart from, or as an adjunct to, real life. In real life people are attracted to each other for myriad reasons that have nothing to do with seeking perfection, nor the airbrushed, subservient women who form the stereotype in *The Female Eunuch*, and who actually seem almost completely uninteresting. This also comes with the implication that men despise women if they don't fit this template. Again the argument is based on theory rather than an understanding of how men actually think.

Greer asserts that "…The feminine stereotypes remain the definition of the female sex…" But a stereotype is something that is simplistic and oversimplified, and therefore not definitive, and so although these images of stereotypically "perfect" women can be seen as negative, even insulting portrayals, they do not define the female sex for the vast majority of men. As one example, a friend sent me an unprompted email in 2018 describing his ideal woman. In it he neglected to mention any preference for physical characteristics and concluded that his ideal woman was, in fact, "a bit like a bloke".

Greer was also sex therapist for the underground *Oz* magazine. But although *Oz* had a radical political and sexual agenda, looking at it now it also feels oddly laddish, with its fair share of tits and bums, albeit mixed with radical politics and set in a countercultural context. Not like those *other* magazines.

The magazine had attracted a couple of obscenity charges in Australia before it fell foul of the authorities in the UK with its notorious 'School Kids Issue' in May 1970, which, as its title suggested was edited by school children. It featured a cartoon strip, Bear Alley, of a well-endowed Rupert The Bear – a children's cartoon character – attempting to penetrate Gypsy Granny, all of which is illustrated in a kind of sub-Robert Crumb style.

Going up against the wall for free speech to any laudable end is one thing; doing the same to stand up for something so juvenile seems bizarre. But then if you really are standing up for freedom of speech in all its manifestations, the Oz 'School Kids Issue' was part of all that.

In a display of defiance, the three editors, Felix Dennis, Richard Neville and Jim Anderson, were photographed in a humorous but defiant way, dressed up in caps, shorts, satchels and school uniforms. To certain parts of the establishment this was too much like insubordination in the ranks, and by a trio of hippies at that. They were arrested, their heads shorn and were made an example of. They were sentenced to fifteen months in prison, which, sense prevailing at last, was ultimately quashed. And all because of a sub-seaside postcard depiction of "it".

But what does all this have to do with progressive rock? Exhibit A: the novel, *Groupie*, by Jenny Fabian and Johnny Byrne. *Groupie* caused a scandal when published in 1969, mainly because it was the largely autobiographical story of Fabian, a respectable middle-class girl going off and enjoying herself sexually, initially with various musicians from the late Sixties scene. Although the protagonist was a self-possessed young woman involved in music promotion in psychedelic clubs including Middle Earth, she is very keen to be more a part of that scene by having sex with male musicians who she found far more interesting than the average guy, and to an extent defined herself in this way – like a sort of post-psychedelic camp follower.

Names are changed to protect the not so innocent and after a one night stand with Ben from Satin Odyssey, in actuality a rather less than compos mentis Syd Barrett of Pink Floyd, the bulk of the story centres on progressive rock group Family – cunningly disguised here as Relation – and her "scenes" with bass player Joe (Ric Grech) and also Grant (Family's manager Tony Gourvish).

Family's keyboard and vibes player and flautist Poli Palmer remembers her well. "I did indeed know Jenny," he says. "Although the book was written before I joined the band, my first photo shoot with them was with the band and Jenny in bed together – with shirts off – for a bit of PR for the book. Jenny was quite a shy girl. When I first joined Family, Chappo (vocalist Roger Chapman aka Spike in the book), Dr Sam Hutt (Hank Wangford) and Jenny shared a rather opulent flat in Exhibition Road, London." This place is described in the lyrics of 'Coronation' on Family's 1972 album *Bandstand*.

Groupie is a fascinating period piece in many ways, but take away the sex and the groovy trappings and it has the feel of tedious kitchen sink drama. Joe comes across as being narcissistic and selfish, while Grant is particularly manipulative and strikingly immature. For a book with so much sexual content, it's written in a flat style that is decidedly unerotic – all the getting stoned, shagging and plating (fellatio), seems oddly perfunctory. Or as Palmer puts it: "Of course, I had to read the book. After a while, the rather sexless blow jobs on each page became somewhat boring and I rather think I never finished it."

As Fabian writes: "...plating can be one of those scenes that works on an impersonal level. I mean there are some guys I would plate, but never hold hands with... My only worry was that sperm might be fattening." At which point, all but the most avid platers will be excused for feeling a tad bilious.

In an interview with *Penthouse* in 1973 Fabian was asked: "Explain why oral sex particularly goes with rock musicians?" Fabian replied: "Because it was quick, and they were always on the move and they often didn't have much time and because they were very lazy and they could get whoever they wanted. I believe now that rock musicians on the whole are bad fucks because they must have used a lot of their sexual energy on stage. They must have been using the same feeling and emotion over the music they were making as they would if they were in bed, so afterwards all you are getting is the latent ejaculation. So you might as well do it with your mouth as anything else a lot of the time. Although I was worshipping them as musicians, I had no illusions about getting great sexual satisfactions out of them."

In *Groupie* everyone seemed to be getting "it". So how much was it an accurate description of Family's sexual exploits into the Seventies? "Well, we were a prog band, which mainly played to hairy students," says Palmer. "However, there were occasions…"

Look through the lyrics of progressive rock bands and there were few overt sexual references, although in Chapter 9 it is revealed that pre-1975 Genesis songs had a greater – and stranger – sexual content than almost all their peers across all forms of rock music. An exception was Gong's Gilli Smyth. On 'I Am Your Pussy' on their 1973 album *Flying Teapot*, she made the bold declaration, *"I am your pussy… and I'm going to fuck you"*. But in the Seventies explicit sexual references in songs were pretty rare as they were likely to be banned anyway. One example of a song getting past the censors was Lou Reed's 1972 single 'Walk On The Wild Side', which references trans-sexualism, male prostitution, fellatio and drugs, namely amphetamines and valium.

In blues music some songs were startlingly explicit like 'Shave 'Em Dry' by Lucille Bogan aka Bessie Jackson (1935). She tells us that she has something between her legs that could make a *"dead man come"*. But with many, the myriad of euphemisms sounded sexier than a straightforward description. This gave us: "I need a little sugar in my bowl"; "wang dang doodle"; "I'm gonna dust my broom"; "walkin' the dog"; and of course "rock'n'roll".

Some of this blues phraseology permeated the music by British bands: On Free's 'The Hunter', Paul Rodgers had his *"love gun loaded"*, while Led Zeppelin's Robert Plant wanted his lemon squeezed before giving *"every inch"* of his love, but even in so-called cock-rock, a lot of it was down to swagger and general sexiness rather than explicit content. As noted in Chapter 8, after their first two albums, even Led Zeppelin didn't sing much about sex.

But just because you didn't sing and write about "it" didn't mean you didn't want to do "it".

In a light-hearted interview with Ian MacDonald from *New Musical Express* in 1973, King Crimson guitarist Robert Fripp explained that music corresponded with one or more of the head, the heart and the hips. He also decided that everyone knew about the group's music anyway, so it was time to expound upon extra-musical activities: "I used to get complaints from Greg [Lake]. Not directly, but I used to hear about them. You see, we shared this flat which was basically one room divided into two by a thin cardboard screen. It was, as you can imagine, not fit to live in. Anyway, Greg used to complain about the gasps and screams coming from my side of the partition and, I must admit, his women used to get on my nerves too. No comment on Gregory, just his women — but I decided to move out.

"The ensuing period of my homelessness in 1969 was one of the most rewarding of my life. I was continually thrown on the mercies and generosities of tender maidens. Oh those lovely situations. It was quite awful in one way — but quite beautiful in another.

"Of course, when one is young one has all these delusions of being the great stud and one is not interested in a harmonious relationship of giving and taking. But, I'm happy to say, those days for me are now long past and I have spent many fulfilling hours, even on this very lawn upon which I now recline, not only copulating, but involved in various other activities.

"In fact I was lying here naked one day, a young lady in attendance, when my next-door neighbour, the chairman of the Rural District Council, popped his head over yonder hedge to inform me that I had Dutch elm disease."

CHAPTER 34

She's a Rainbow: Sonja Kristina and Curved Air

Curved Air were one of the most original groups in Seventies progressive rock, but their tenure was relatively brief, and punctuated by changes in personnel and management problems. They formed in 1970 out of a group, Sisyphus, that Darryl Way and Francis Monkman had put together at the Royal College Of Music. In 1970 they morphed into Curved Air and were named after the album *A Rainbow In Curved Air* by American minimalist composer Terry Riley. Monkman had earlier played in the first UK performance of Riley's epochal 1964 composition *In C*. Monkman played keyboards and guitar and Way played violin and keyboards. At this point the rock violinist was a rare breed. "As a featured instrumentalist in a band I think I was the first one that was doing it in a rock sense, which was good for me," says Way. "It was exciting and it gave me all that breadth to make it up as I went along."

The rhythm section comprised Florian Pilkington-Miksa on drums and Rob Martin on bass guitar. The new line-up was completed by the addition of Sonja Kristina, who had played the folk circuit since she was a teenager and had appeared in the West End production of the musical *Hair*. Curved Air combined classical, folk and pop influences with an early experimental approach to the VCS3 synthesizer as a means of processing instruments and voice.

They became the first British band on Warner Brothers and signed for a $99,000 advance. The original line-up – with regularly changing bass guitarists – recorded *Air Conditioning* (1970), *Second Album* (1971) and *Phantasmagoria* (1972). After Way and Monkman left they recorded *Air Cut* (1973) with violinist Eddie Jobson and guitarist Kirby Gregory. They split and reformed with Darryl Way returning for *Curved Air Live* and *Midnight Wire*, which were both released in 1975. They disbanded after releasing *Airborne* in 1976.

What follows is based on a lengthy interview with Sonja Kristina conducted in 2014, with a few later additions, in which she chronicles her influences and musical life before and during her time in Curved Air.

Mike Barnes: The name on your birth certificate is Sonja Christina Shaw. Why is it that on the first three Curved Air albums, you are named as Linwood for your songwriting credits?

Sonja Kristina: Linwood was a name that I chose when I had my oldest son. He was born out of wedlock, and in those days that was most unrespectable, so we went away and changed my name by deed poll. And then when we came back, my mum told all the neighbours that we'd got married for the sake of the baby.

MB: Going back to the mid-Sixties, you started out playing at folk clubs, like The Swan in Romford.

SK: That was my local folk club, and I used to go along there and watch other floor spots as well as the main act. That was where everything was happening then. I had my denim jacket and jeans, and my denim sneakers. I was a beatnik! I was kind of channelling Jack Kerouac, and all that stuff.

MB: Is it true that you started playing there when you were in your early teens?

SK: Yeah, at thirteen. I started playing guitar because we were offered lessons at school – classical lessons – so I did a few of those, but then I got a book called, I think, *101 American Folk Songs*, and so I dipped into that. I'd learned to read music, because I'd had a few piano lessons, and so I was picking out the tunes, learning the chords, transposing them and finding out what the best key was for me.

We had record libraries back then, so I was listening to everything I could that involved guitars and songs, especially singer-songwriters. Buffy Sainte-Marie, I think it was in 1964 when her first album came out. Her songs were just so passionate and moving and beautiful.

Joan Baez left me cold, a bit – and Judy Collins – but Odetta was very good. 'All My Trials' was a beautiful song, so I learned that one. And Bob Dylan, I really loved his way with words.

I got a manager at 16. I asked the person who ran the folk club, who was the best manager/agent for this kind of music? And he said Roy Guest. And [his office] was right next to Cecil Sharp House where there was a big library of traditional folk music, so you could listen to lovely recordings of natural voices from the Scottish islands, Ireland, Somerset…

MB: So did you play some traditional British material in the set as well?

SK: Yes, I did, and Roy got me a spot on TV, in a programme called *Song And Story*, where I had to learn a couple of ballads. I remember doing 'The Lowlands Of Holland'.

MB: I was interested in the fact that you played a role in the musical *Hair*, which, with its hippieish ideals and onstage nudity seemed to be indicative of a change in the format. I wonder what it felt like being part of it at the time?

SK: Well, we knew that we were in something really important. It was a time of great change, and a magical time. You could say it was because of the drugs or not because of the drugs. As far as *Hair* was concerned, I wandered into my manager's office one day, when I dropped out of school, and he said, 'You should go along and audition for this, they're looking for people like you.' And he said, 'Hippies wanted, must be good movers.'

MB: From what you've said, I assume being in *Hair* must have been an influence on you as a performer with Curved Air.

SK: Oh yes, I think so, because before that I had been behind my guitar. I had done some acting at school, and I went to drama college, where we did the movement and drama. But that had all been quite static really, whereas this was working with your whole being, and that certainly did affect what I brought to Curved Air.

MB: I think Curved Air's 1970 debut *Air Conditioning* is a key album in early progressive rock. You're never quite sure what's going to happen next: the arrangement might change, or there might be different instruments, and then there's 'Vivaldi', Darryl Way's fantasia on a four-bar passage from *The Four Seasons*. It very much sounds like the start of something new.

SK: Well, it was. Much, much later on, I did a master's degree course in Post-Modernism And Performing Arts, and the thing about Post-Modernism was that it was a collage – you put things together to make something that was even more meaningful than just sticking to one genre. And so progressive rock was a collage. And it was also influenced by the freedom of jazz. Rather than just having a middle-eight solo thing, you would extemporise, and you'd have really, really good musicians, who were excited about trying new scales. Maybe they knew what they were doing then, or had just picked things up by ear. Not necessarily classically trained musicians, but people who were absorbing everything that was around.

But all the prog bands were different from each other; Curved Air wasn't like King Crimson, and neither of us were like ELP, [we were] all different kinds of music.

MB: When *Air Conditioning* came out, on the picture vinyl LP, that must have been quite a thing. I'm fairly sure it was the first picture disc LP.

SK: It came from a Dutch plant, so I think there maybe had been Dutch ones before, but in England it was the first one. But it wasn't the best quality, because the process was that the design was underneath [a laminate of] clear plastic – and I think the clear plastic was more static y than black plastic. They went onto black vinyl after they'd sold all the run of the picture discs. When it went round and round on the turntable, the coloured side was stroboscopic.

MB: On the first three albums there was a certain amount of upheaval in the bass department. Could you explain that?

SK: Rob Martin the bass player left, that was the first thing – I think that was in the middle of recording the album. He did write some good stuff for Curved Air, some of which didn't get recorded, but 'Rob One' was lovely, and I think 'Situations' he wrote the music for, too.

So then Francis played bass on some of the tracks. Ian Eyre joined us for *Second Album*, but he left because his mental health wouldn't stand up to it and Mike Wedgwood joined for *Phantasmagoria* [in 1972].

MB: I was intrigued by the fact that in the early days Curved Air supported Black Sabbath on tour.

SK: When we were touring in the States, we worked supporting Jethro Tull, we supported Deep Purple, we supported Johnny Winter, Edgar Winter, and one time we even supported B. B. King.

[Black Sabbath] was great fun. The guy that I married was Black Sabbath's tour manager, Malcom Ross. As we travelled along the road, they used to moon out of the window. They were pretty wild, and Tony Iommi and Geezer were into their black magic, as I remember.

We got a fantastic response every night. And then when we went off, Black Sabbath started with 'Paranoid'. Strangely enough, it went really, really well. And it was the first time we'd played big town halls and venues like that. It was in late 1970, early '71 – after the album was released, and it charted during the tour.

MB: On the early Curved Air songs your lyrics deal with a number of rather vividly portrayed characters, like 'The Purple Speed Queen' for instance. I was wondering if you knew anybody like that, who'd had a really bad experience with drugs?

SK: Melinda, who the song was about, was a real person, and she was a speed freak and used to inject methedrine, and then take downers to go to sleep. And I had a little flirtation with that as well, just as an experiment, really. So it was sort of autobiographical. But also, people who did lots and lots of speed would get burnt out, really brain dead, and so one did see the negative effect of speed.

Speed is a lovely feeling. I remember in the mid-Sixties that 'blues' were popular, and amphetamines, and slimming pills. I went through phases of lots of things at different times in my life. As a hippie one never thought it was wrong to experiment with drugs – it just seemed to be an adventure. I mean, using yourself as a sort of guinea pig, just to see what this does [*laughs*]. And luckily, I wasn't one of the casualties.

MB: I was having a look at some of the lyrics, and I was quite amused by 'Not Quite The Same'. I suddenly thought, 'Oh yes, I can see what this is about now.' He ends up going to the park and meeting the girl...

SK: ...And they're sitting there under the tree, wanking, yes. That was my lyric. That was on *Phantasmagoria* [1972]. A lot of them [on that album] were Francis's lyrics. On *Air Conditioning* they were mostly mine.

MB: Was 'Young Mother' [on *Second Album*] one of yours?

SK: Yeah, Darryl had a lyric for it called 'Young Mother In Style, Trying Hard To Keep Her Smile', which didn't really do much for me at all. And so I messed around with it and I sang it until I got a way of singing it that I really could feel, and then those words came to go with that feeling.

And 'Elfin Boy' was a true story. It was written for my very first real passionate lover, and I remember singing it to him. It was in 1968, I wrote it, and then it surfaced on *Air Cut*. It was a really nice version that Eddie, Mike and the others did.

MB: You were a guitarist before you joined Curved Air. Why didn't you play guitar with the group?

SK: 'Melinda' and 'Elfin Boy' had been written before Curved Air and were part of my set of songs back then. I just played guitar on those songs. I knew where I was with acoustic guitar, but I could never play electric guitar, although I did try.

When people say what Curved Air sounds like, they will quite often mention folk influences, but Darryl and Francis were so anti-folk. To them it was classical music and experimental, extending the template of what you could do with music rather than playing little songs. That's what I had been doing before I was in *Hair*.

MB: I was wondering, when the single 'Back Street Luv' was a hit in 1971, how much that might have changed the group: if the expectations were suddenly higher, and if it put you more in the spotlight as one of the handful of female musicians in the progressive rock scene and suddenly a kind of a pop star?

SK: I always had been the spokesperson for Curved Air. The other guys did the sort of technical interviews, but me and Darryl were in the photographs. Because we picked up quite a lot of press early on, so my photograph was everywhere anyway.

We'd done a TV programme called, I think, *Disco 2*, and then we had had radio play with 'It Happened Today' and with 'Vivaldi', when we were on the road.

The first album did incredibly well, so we were pretty well established. The only thing that changed was we reached a much wider audience. When we came on stage, they used to scream, which was kind of weird, especially when they're nearly all boys. But the rest of the music of

Curved Air was still getting more and more alternative, and adventurous, particularly Francis's material. He was writing long pieces.

MB: Did you get many girls who thought of you as being as a kind of role model, or someone they looked up to in that way?

SK: There was one girl in particular, called Hazel. She used to come [and see us] and go backstage, and she came to our house, which was quite unusual. I was intrigued, because she was a girl, and she was very beautiful. She was only, 15, 16, then, I think, and she had red hair in a sort of David Bowie cut. It was nice to have a girl fan – I hadn't really noticed any others!

MB: The Seventies is often labelled as a sexist decade. But did you run up against many sexist or laddish reactions to what you did?

SK: Well, no – I think laddism probably was more of a Fifties thing, actually. I was kind of protected, really, within the band. And also I'd gone to places on my own as a singer, in my teens, showing up with my guitar and being greeted by the promoter and looked after.

Sandy Denny was a big role model for me at the time. I just thought she was fantastic. I don't think Sandy got any problems, because she wasn't really a sort of a 'girly girl'.

Doing lots of interviews, the interviewers only occasionally talked about me being a sex symbol – that would obviously be *The Sun* and papers like that. 'All my men are fantastic lovers,' says Sonja Kristina. And 'I'm tired of being a sex symbol,' says Sonja. But mostly they were just fairly sensible interviews about our music and about being a band and all living together.

I also made a conscious effort to carry on the kind of *Hair* hippie ethos with the band – to break down barriers – so that we could cuddle, we could hug, one could undress in front of them, and joke about it, without it being anything more than friendly, you know? We did all live together for the entire time that the first line-up was together, which made it easier to go off to gigs.

There's a flat in Hampstead, on 87 Reddington Road. I first went there with Elaine Paige and people from *Hair* – when we were still in *Hair* – and so I remember lying on the floor there chatting to Tim Curry. I was trying to seduce him, but he said no, no, he didn't... We became really good friends...

It was a beautiful flat, there was a deck all the way around the outside of it with a great view all around London. That was where Curved Air moved into, and then we moved out of there and we lived in Lyndhurst Gardens in Belsize Park.

MB: Francis Monkman and Darryl Way tended to compose separately and had different but complementary ideas. How would you describe their respective approaches?

SK: Darryl is into very precise, organised, beautifully crafted songs and arrangements, and Francis is much more experimental – things like 'Propositions' – and then certainly a lot of the stuff on his side of *Phantasmagoria*, is really the difference. He did 'Bright Summer's Day', which was very kind of brash and throwaway, but very exciting compositions like 'Piece Of Mind'. Francis was also one of the first people experimenting with a VCS3 synthesizer; he was very advanced and progressive with sound modulation. I had one for a little while, later on.

On *Phantasmagoria* they each produced their own sides. They didn't hear music the same way. Having said that, they learned each other's songs and played in the studio. There was no bad feeling. It's just that they weren't able to collaborate further.

And when they left the band it was because they didn't want to do these American tours, whereas I loved it – it was not stressful for me in the slightest. I just enjoy going from one place to another with a bunch of handsome blokes, you know, and feeling like queen of the bandits.

MB: Was it a shock when they both left?

SK: I said to our manager Clifford Davis that this would be a good opportunity to do a Sonja Kristina solo album, but we were under contract to Warners for a certain number of albums and if we'd gone out as Sonja Kristina, we wouldn't have had access to the next advance. So we decided that it would be Curved Air and play a Curved Air set and write a new album that wasn't in a completely differently direction, but I wanted it to be more direct in a way, heavier.

The group's fourth album *Air Cut* featured a new line-up with Kristina and Wedgwood joined by Kirby Gregory on guitar and Jim Russell replacing Pilkington-Miksa on drums. Then group's new violinist and keyboard player was the 17-year-old Eddie Jobson, who had supported Curved Air as part of Fat Grapple. By way of introduction, Jobson had gone into Curved Air's dressing room at the Newcastle Mayfair to play 'Vivaldi' to Way. The new members even performed with Curved Air while Way and Monkman were still playing out their live obligations in early 1973.

MB: Martin Rushent produced the album *Air Cut*. What was he like to work with?

SK: He came along to rehearsals and gave his input at rehearsals and was very much part of the band in terms of preparation for the recording. He helped shape and bring into the world what the band should sound like.

The line-up soon split, with Wedgwood joining Caravan and Jobson joining Roxy Music. (Davis released some of Kristina's demos for a projected follow-up album along with some tracks that Kirby and Jobson recorded post-split as *Love Child* in 1990, much to Kristina's chagrin.) In 1973 Warners dropped the band. "They thought that there wasn't enough of the original band sound," says Kristina. "One change too many."

Worse than that, the group found out that both their original managers, Clifford Davis and Mark Hanau, had failed to pay any VAT on the group's income, and so they were landed with a considerable tax bill.

SK: In those days the management handled everything. You never saw any bits of paper. It was like me trying to play electric guitar. One couldn't do it. It just wasn't interesting.

MB: I understand that after you split in 1973, you worked as a croupier at the Playboy Club.

SK: Right from when I first joined Curved Air, everyone got a small salary – just enough to pay for food and stuff – and then the management paid for the rent as well, so that was why it was convenient to all live together. But it was just subsistence money, and occasionally we'd get some money to go to Kensington Market and buy some stage clothes, or whatever. We didn't get money to buy anything in our own right, or buy houses or cars or anything. You know, even with that big advance. It was $99,000, but it was never paid all at one time but depended on the contracted delivery of several albums, and then not to the individuals in the band but to the production company to fund us as they saw fit.

Well, what could we do about it, anyway? I mean, in my experience, if you get a lawyer to write all over and change things in the contract, it doesn't make any difference if they're going to rip you off anyway.

And all the rest of the advance money just went into our shows. Things began to pick up from the first album charting, but we used to have lorries with big sound systems and light shows. It was quite an expensive thing going out on the road.

When the *Air Cut* band went their different ways, all our money got cut off. I had a child to support, so I needed to get a job and I just wanted to get the most money for my time, and also to be paid while I trained. Working at the Playboy [Club], you got paid whilst you learned to cut chips, and count up to twenty-one – very fast.

So there I was, in a big dressing-room with lots of other women. I'd never been with so many women since I was at school. We had a little bow tie, and a kind of bib thing on the top, so our cleavage didn't distract the punters. And we had a little skirt, presumably so our bums didn't distract the punters [*laughs*]. And then we had these sort of high-heeled Minnie Mouse shoes, which we had to paint in the same colour as our costumes.

I was living in East Ham, and getting the night bus back at four o'clock in the morning, and sleeping until about two or three in the afternoon, and then starting all over again.

So, I did that for nine months and then I got offered my old part back in *Hair*. I remember interviewers who were interviewing me then saying, 'Don't you think *Hair*'s a bit passé?' and I said, 'No, no, it's still just as relevant' – which it was, to me, having been in the sexist nightclub croupier casino world of cocktail bunnies.

In 1974 the original line-up – with the American bass player Phil Kohn – reformed and went on a three-week tour to raise money to pay their VAT bill. This fundraising was helped by the release of *Curved Air Live* in early 1975. Sonja had split up with her husband Malcolm Ross and she met Norma Tager at a party. She didn't want to go back to her own flat, so she ended up going back to Norma Tager's place, which by an extraordinary coincidence turned out to be the top flat at 87 Reddington Road in Hampstead. She stayed there for nine months.

By now Curved Air had a new manager, Miles Copeland, who Way had been working with in Stark Naked & The Car Thieves, along with Kohn and Copeland's younger drummer brother Stewart, who had also been tour manager for the 1974 Curved Air tour. Miles Copeland released *Curved Air Live* on his own label, BTM (British Talent Management).

SK: Darryl asked, did I want to carry on with Curved Air? And I said, 'No way. Now I want to do the Sonja Kristina thing and see what I can do.' But because Stewart was in the band, Darryl managed to talk me into it. Our eyes had met across the rehearsal room and sparks flew and we were living together anyway by that time. This was very much a Darryl Curved Air. The band were really good players and everything, but I didn't have any words because since the *Air Cut* group had broken up, I'd broken up with Malcolm and I was in freefall.

For *Midnight Wire* Norma Tager helped me with the lyrics. I mumbled various stories and scenarios and she turned them into songs. She had this hip American way of writing, which I thought was really cool and Darryl liked it as well.

We got together again with Curved Air – we were offered a tour, which went very, very well. I wanted to have this [new] image, whereas before, it wouldn't have occurred to me to exploit my sexuality, because I was a hippie, and hippies didn't dress like that. Having been going around the Playboy Club for nine months, I just felt fine with that kind of image.

I designed my own costumes. I found this jewelled G-string, and jet beads across my boobs, and just a short little lace dress, and long boots and a feather cloak. I just saw myself as a sort of space gypsy.

MB: I raised an eyebrow at pictures of that outfit recently. It was pretty skimpy. Those boots look amazing...

SK: They were brocade boots, two pairs – they were gold and red, and silver and blue.

MB: I see that for *Midnight Wire* you worked with the American producers Ron and Howie Albert.

SK: Miles used various big labels for distribution for BTM. And I think we were with RCA and we rehearsed and got together a bunch of songs that the band were very happy with – it was adventurous, it had lots of character and drama and then RCA turned it down. So it was Miles's idea to get in Ron and Howie.

MB: I interviewed Gary Brooker about Procol Harum's 1977 album *Something Magic*, which they produced [see Chapter 31] and from what he said they seemed extraordinarily rude and obnoxious. How did you get on with them?

SK: It was their idea that we wrote different lyrics for some of the songs, shape them differently. We had a totally miserable time in the studio recording. They were down on everybody except me. They told Stewart that he needed to practise with a metronome. We are still trying to find the original [demo] tapes for *Midnight Wire*. Darryl's got a couple of tracks cleaned up from a cassette and it sounds just as good as I thought it did at the time.

MB: Why did Curved Air break up in 1976 after *Airborne*?

SK: We were going out doing very successful shows – town halls, colleges and unis – but we were taking our own lights and PA, and Miles was funding all of that, and the profit margin wasn't big enough for him. In terms of prog rock, he had something to do with Renaissance and then he'd got the punk bug – being American – as it was all coming across from America.

He wasn't going to pay us and so our life-blood money was cut off again. After the Miles thing we were all on a bankruptcy notice after another thing that hadn't been paid.

Stewart got Sting down from Newcastle and formed The Police, and Roy Thomas Baker was interested in doing an album with me, so he financed some auditions for my new band Sonja Kristina's Escape – which it was. It was very successful as a live band, but then the person who was managing me at the time, he didn't get a deal until after I'd stopped touring with that band. I was also doing theatre; I was enjoying my liberation. If you record it too far down the way it loses momentum and members, and gets over-produced by invading producers. It wasn't recorded at the time when it was really cooking.

The Cats in the Grove: Hawkwind, Quintessence, Third Ear Band and the Ladbroke Grove/Notting Hill Freak Scene

GETTING IT STRAIGHT IN NOTTING HILL GATE

"I was walking up the Portobello Road [in 1967] and Yoko Ono was walking down the road, and she asked me if I wanted to have my bottom on film," says Ron Geesin. "And I said, no I was too shy. I'm only an extrovert on the stage. I also thought, 'Christ! Not another avant-garde film.'"

Ono was casting for *Film No.4* (aka *Bottoms*), and the moment typified the Ladbroke Grove/Notting Hill area's reputation as a hive of creative activity. At the time, Geesin lived in Elgin Crescent off Ladbroke Grove. "There was an artistic community," Geesin confirms, "even if it was only because there were so many adventurous, creative persons in that area that you couldn't help but bump into someone if you went out."

The notorious Ladbroke Grove/Notting Hill scene of the Sixties and Seventies was the milieu in which Geesin and many other artists and performers flourished. Notting Hill is the name of the district, and the main thoroughfares of Portobello Road and Ladbroke Grove run parallel roughly north-south through the area.

By the end of World War Two, Notting Hill had fallen into decline and its imposing 19th-century terraces contained pockets of infamously bad housing, into which immigrants from Britain's colonial outposts, particularly the Caribbean, had been shunted. The influx created racial tension, which finally erupted into four days of what the press called "racial riots" in August 1958. One positive outcome was the following year's launch of the annual Notting Hill Carnival.

Cheap enough to attract drifters, artists and outsiders, in the early Sixties Ladbroke Grove became a hive of beatnik activity. By 1967, All Saints Church Hall in Powis Gardens was the venue for several key psychedelic happenings, including some of Pink Floyd's earliest shows. Local activists included Mick Farren, vocalist with The Deviants and journalist for the underground magazine *International Times*, while Glen Sweeney, of transcendental rock improvisers Third Ear Band, dedicated 'Ghetto Raga' on their 1969 debut album *Alchemy* "to all the cats in the Grove". By 1973, fantasy writer Michael Moorcock, who described his long-running fictional character Jerry Cornelius as "the coolest assassin on the Ladbroke Grove block", was hatching future collaborations with space rockers Hawkwind.

Another band based in the area, and active from late 1969 onwards were The Pink Fairies, featuring former Pretty Things drummer Twink, who came across rather like a more stoned British version of the MC5. They employed a more direct rock'n'roll approach to their peers and recorded countercultural rallying cries like 'Do It' and 'Right On Fight On'. Steve Peregrin Took, who had played percussion with Marc Bolan in Tyrannosaurus Rex, was briefly in the Fairies as a guitarist and formed Shagrat, but the band fell apart without releasing any records due to a mix of drugs and disorganisation.

In the mid–Seventies Farren was still describing the area as a "ghetto", but others were beginning to call it "funky" and "bohemian". During the Eighties the Notting Hill area underwent considerable gentrification, making it one of the first areas of London to have its image so dramatically turned around. The spaces that had once sheltered huddles of stoned freaks planning acts of countercultural insurrection had been transformed into swanky designer apartments, and property prices soared. In the 1999 film *Notting Hill*, the down at heel characters would never have been able to afford the rent for the spacious house in which they are shown as living.

Back in the late Sixties, Geesin – best known for his collaboration with Pink Floyd on their 1970 album *Atom Heart Mother* – was an experimentalist but also a focused artist and a practical man – someone who could make and mend things. He had an aversion to marijuana, and so wasn't the sort of person who relished spending hours squinting through clouds of smoke while some saucer-eyed dopehead excitedly ran through their latest sure-to-be-doomed art project. But many were.

Third Ear Band, who had saluted their fellow cats in the Grove, had been born back in 1967 out of massed free improvising sessions at the end of UFO club nights organised by violinist Dave Tomlin of the London Free School, the ensemble then being known as Giant Sun Trolley. One can only imagine what these stoned 4 a.m. jams must have been like. But after having most of their gear stolen, they settled on a line-up of Paul Minns on oboe, Mel Davis on cello, Richard Coff on violin and Sweeney on hand drums. With that kind of line-up no one else sounded remotely like them anyway, but their uncategorisable music seems to contain approximations of Indian classical music and Chinese courtly rituals, minimalist drones of Tony Conrad and LaMonte Young, and Minns was also a fan of the modal jazz of John Coltrane. They also conjured up a feeling of something deep and ancestral. On the deliberately florid sleeve notes to their 1969 debut album *Alchemy*, their pieces are described as "trance-like eclectic space trips" and "as alike or unalike as trees".

Geesin was writing library music for TV at the end of the Sixties and reputedly thought that the Third Ear Band might have a chance of their music being used for this purpose, so he facilitated a recording for the Essex Music Library. The Third Ear Band made their recorded debut in 1968 as the National-Balkan Ensemble – although no one seems to recall why they used that name – on one side of an LP, the other entitled 'Comedy Links And Bridges', that was released in 1970 on the Standard Music Library label.

The group's "saviour", according to Glen Sweeney, was Jim Haynes of the Arts Lab, an important countercultural figure who promoted them at The Crypt on Lancaster Road and they had a regular Thursday evening spot in a basement club at Westbourne Park Road.

They also appeared at the Alchemical Wedding at the Royal Albert Hall on December 18, 1968, accompanying John Lennon and Yoko Ono, who spent time onstage in a sack, a performance that they had debuted at the Arts Lab. After signing to Blackhill Enterprises they opened the July 1969 Hyde Park Concert – their debut album *Alchemy* having been released the previous month – which was headlined by The Rolling Stones, and where King Crimson so shocked the masses. They were also a fixture of free festivals and benefit concerts at the time and were happy to play for "cash, hash or crash".

In 1996 Andrew King of Blackhill Enterprises recounted working with the group on their second album *Third Ear Band* (1970).

"The band were taking acid fairly regularly. I did not realise this and could not understand what they were laughing at all the time. I think it's a fine album. Peter Mew, the EMI engineer, still remembers it as some of the weirdest sessions he ever worked on in 30 years at Abbey Road."

King went on to explain the relationship between Blackhill Enterprises, EMI and their Harvest label and this new progressive style of music at the dawn of the Seventies.

"There wasn't really anyone at EMI, except perhaps Malcolm Jones, capable of having a conversation with them. So Blackhill was always the go-between, and really Blackhill had no clear plans as to what we were trying to achieve.

"The Third Ear Band were so divorced from the normal sort of 'act', that it was always difficult to see them as anything more than a sort of strange hobby, despite the fact that they sold a lot more records than more conventional bands, [for example] Kevin Ayers. EMI went along with what we asked of them not because they supported us, but because they were frightened of missing out on something good."

The group were offered the soundtrack to Roman Polanski's 1971 film, *Macbeth*. A more disciplined approach was needed and they largely scored it while looking at the film scene by scene, as a sort of spontaneous composition. A piece like 'Court Dance' was more structured than usual and had a more explicitly medieval feel, despite there being guitar on it by new member Denim Bridges. Simon House formerly of High Tide was now on violin with Paul Buckmaster – who had been in an early version of the group – returning on cello.

The soundtrack compounds the film's dark and uncanny moods. Polanski had some specific ideas and requested one piece to sound "kind of disgusting" to accompany the witches. Composed by Buckmaster, its banal nursery rhyme tune and hideous, churning cello helps to rank it as one of the ugliest pieces of music ever written.

Steve Lacy interviewed Glen Sweeney for *Beat Instrumental* in 1971: "'I hope that we're firmly into films now,' Glen confides. 'Our next project is a vampire film in Germany!' In some ways it seems as if the Third Ear Band have followed in the steps of their fellow UFOers Pink Floyd in that they seem tailor made for soundtracks and are easing up on live work."

Apparently Sweeney was seen leafing through a yacht catalogue prior to the interview. But alas, if all mooted projects had come to fruition, there would be a lot more household names who had originated from the obscure fringes of rock music. But no German vampire film emerged and any yacht acquired from the proceeds of *Macbeth* was most likely a modest craft.

A form of the Third Ear Band existed on and off until 1993, but the core of the groundbreaking group dissipated in the early Seventies. Their records still sound unique.

THERE'S A SWAMI IN MY HOUSE – THE SPIRITUAL QUEST OF QUINTESSENCE

From the Sixties onwards many young people actively sought enlightenment, something beyond, a touch of otherness that they couldn't get from standard Christian teaching. Church Of England attendance seemed simply an obligation to be begrudgingly undertaken at the end of a long week, something that made you appear more respectable than if you didn't. You wore your best clothes while listening to stern warnings of the consequences of misconduct, delivered via sermons as dull, grey and mildewy as a damp vestry. At least Catholicism came with its bells-and-smells rituals, but go down that path and you would also be obliged to take on the less appealing side of the deal and have a lifetime of unnecessary and pointless guilt foisted upon you.

Then if you thought of expanding your spritual horizons a little, of emulating the great ranks of Christian mystics by performing some kind of contemplation – meditation by another name – you could well have been told by Christian fundamentalists that by doing so you can let in the devil. The church was part of the dead weight of history that many were trying to cast off. Not for nothing was the New Testament "rebranded", in its 1966 republishing in contemporary English, as *Good News For Modern Man*. It was accompanied by the appearance of that gently mocked archetype, the "trendy vicar", who tried to relate more to the youth. There were also musicals like *Godspell* and *Jesus Christ Superstar*, which were further ways of updating the story and teachings of Christ. It was like everyone was looking for an alternative to what they already had. But where were the real highs, the enlightenment that religion could give?

The ideas of love and peace, of 'All You Need Is Love' at its most giving and unconditional, were most closely associated with Buddhism. Many turned to a kind of pick 'n' mix of practices associated with Eastern religions, including yoga and transcendental meditation, whose popularity soared since it was known to be practised by The Beatles. This broad approach could often be a superficial flirting with esoteric strands of thought, like reading the *Bhagavad Gita* while stoned, rather than applying oneself to the rigours of practice.

Quintessence were one group that took it all particularly seriously. They had formed in 1969 as an experimental project, which put together jazz and blues rock players – Australian singer Phil Shiva Jones had played in Australia in Phil Jones & The Unknown Blues.

The group had a keen interest in Eastern philosophy and Eastern mysticism, and in 1969 they heard about the arrival in town, from Nepal, of Swami Ambikananda.

"He came over to one of the other guy's houses and pretty much laid it on the line as to what he thought the purpose of human life was, and how to attain a higher state of consciousness," Jones explains. "He made himself available to us at pretty much any time we wanted to be with him, until he became literally a full-time teacher for us, and so that expression of his teachings came through the music – he was a major influence.

"And it happened before the first album; it was leading in that direction right from the start. So the whole thing was not a gimmick, it was not show business: it was to express these, what we thought, very deep and mystical teachings, in a universal way, to as many people as wanted to hear it. And in many ways it polarised audiences: they either loved it and were fanatical about it, or it freaked people out. They thought, 'Well, this is weird; if this is a gimmick, it's sick.' And they're off. Or, 'If it's real, well, I don't know if I want to go with this.' But we had a tremendously strong fanbase, and it grew bigger and bigger over the years."

Quintessence recorded three albums for Island Records, *In Blissful Company* (1969), *Quintessence* (1970), which reached number twenty-two in the UK album charts and *Dive Deep* (1971). They then moved to RCA and recorded two more albums before splitting in 1980.

Looking back to those times, the interest in the UK in the culture of India might have been seen as superficial, viewing it in a picture book kind of way, but then there had been a long cultural cross-pollination with the sub-continent. George Harrison produced and played on a recording of chanting by Hare Krishna devotees, The Radha Krishna Temple (London), for The Beatles' Apple label. Amazingly, a single, 'Hare Krishna Mantra' went to number twelve in the UK charts in 1969 and the group even appeared on *Top Of The Pops*. They followed it up with 'Govinda' in 1970, which went to number twenty-three, and a self-titled album in 1971. The psyche of the UK singles buyer was always hard to fathom, but they embraced all sorts of novel ideas and, in a way, had been primed by the mantric singalong of John Lennon's 'Give Peace A Chance' in July 1969 – which soon became incorporated into a football chant.

And an unfortunate by-product of this interest led to earnest young orange-robed 'Hare Krishna freaks', as they were dubbed, accosting unsuspecting shoppers in town centres in the Seventies and trying to sell unusually expensive albums of chanting. Their sales pitch would inevitably start with: "Hey man, have you heard of George Harrison?"

"John Barham who was our producer, worked on the production of 'Govinda', because he worked extensively with George Harrison as well," says Jones. "So there were a few of us on a parallel path."

An indication of Quintessence's popularity is that one of their first concerts was at the Hyde Park free festival on September 20, 1969. They played the first two Glastonbury Fayres in 1970 and 1971 and headlined the Royal Albert Hall in 1971.

The group's ambition was to spread the word through their music and Swami Ambikananda, or Swamiji as Jones refers to him, went on to found the Quintessence Ashram, which still exists today, through which he sought to establish links between Hinduism and Christianity.

'Gange Mai' on their debut album is a group composition, a mix of mantraic chanting – a rearrangement of a mantra given to them by Swamiji – and blues rock. "I extend the notes – *'Gange Maaaaaai… Gange Maaaaai'* – at the beginning of the song, and then it breaks down somewhere in the middle into the actual chant that Swamiji taught us," says Jones.

The group would take fairly simple compositional ideas and extend them, earning them the nickname, The Hindu Grateful Dead. On their second, self-titled album the instrumental 'Burning Bush', with Allan Mostert playing some extravagant Hendrixy wah-wah heavy lead guitar, is followed by the devotional 'Shiva's Chant'.

"It was a jam band," says Jones. "But it had this whole Eastern influence. It wasn't heavy, hard, there was nothing violent in it, there was nothing aggressive in it – it was on fire, but it was a joyful experience. People left feeling uplifted after a Quintessence concert and we did too. There's always that energy bouncing back from the audience to you, so it takes the music even higher."

Quintessence's exoticism was compounded by the mellifluous flute playing of Raja Ram. With his long tousled hair, droopy moustache, cheesecloth smock, beads and the Hindu tilaka – the red forehead spot – he cut a hip, mysterious figure, like some psychedelic mystic who might live in a cave or meditate on the top of a pole. But things were not always as they seemed and Raja Ram was originally Ronald Rothfield, an Australian-born Caucasian mate of Jones's from his days in Melbourne.

Swamiji had given new names to the Quintessence group members who been initiated into Hinduism and so Phil Jones became Shiva

Shankhar, bassist Richard Vaughan became Sambhu Babaji and guitarist Dave Codling became Maha Dev.

Jones views this period from psychedelia to the early Seventies as a time when there was a genuine and marked evolution in human consciousness, even though it might be seen with hindsight as a relatively small step. "I think there was an innocence and a sincerity amongst the people back then, not to criticise or have narrow ideas about the possibility that there could be other ways to reach these higher states of consciousness," says Jones. "You didn't have to be part of any particular religion – or you may see that fundamental truth in all religions."

One of the ways in which Quintessence chose to demonstrate that there is a universality that links religions was when they played at Norwich Cathedral in 1971. Although it didn't spark off a series of cathedral gigs, it caused quite a stir that a psychedelic progressive rock group would play in such a place.

"Norwich was amazing. They took all the pews out and just opened it up to a Quintessence concert," Jones recalls. "It was packed, and we lifted the roof off of that church. I think it made page three of *The Guardian*. I wish it'd been filmed."

Quintessence epitomised one aspect of the Notting Hill countercultural scene in their song 'Notting Hill Gate', which appeared on their debut album and was released as a single. The lyrics enthusiastically extol the virtues of meditation.

"I think back now and how the heck did we get away with putting that in the song!" says Jones, laughing. "But I had no problem singing it, because I meant it."

Like many bands who lived in the Notting Hill area, Quintessence were involved in the local community. They played some gigs for free and Raja Ram held meetings at his house to which he would invite Swamiji, and open it to interested locals. And in all the pantheon of colourful tales of the time, no other group could lay claim to having a resident Swami in the house as in the building in which Jones lived in nearby Blenheim Crescent off Ladbroke Grove.

"I lived – I think it was at number 79 – and Dave (Codling aka Maha Dev) lived next door to me. And at one point Swamiji lived upstairs in the loft or attic apartment. So I lived on the first floor, and then directly above me was Gopala, the brilliant artist who did the Quintessence covers – so there was another shot of tremendous creative energy – and then above him was Swamiji, so it was one-two-three."

Quintessence did shows with other bands from the local area like Hawkwind and The Pink Fairies, although Jones doesn't recall hanging out much as he was "caught up in Swamiji's philosophy and the music".

Swamiji was keen that the group adhered to the difficult bit, the actual daily practice, for which sobriety was needed. They still had their fun, but discreetly and in moderation.

"We would have a joint or whatever every now and then," Jones recalls. "Being young rock stars, someone offers you a spliff, and well, you know… maybe!"

THE FINAL FRONTIER: HAWKWIND AND THE SPACE RITUAL

The Notting Hill area's most notorious denizens, Hawkwind, were a group who didn't do *anything* in moderation. They scored a chart hit in 1972 with 'Silver Machine', which was basically a rather murky live recording made at the Greasy Truckers Ball at The Roundhouse in Camden in February of that year. Bass guitarist Lemmy later overdubbed his vocals in a studio, replacing Robert Calvert's original lines.

All the band had dropped acid in the dressing room in the afternoon prior to the show, to which Lemmy added a selection of pills and powders from his portable pharmacy. In 2007 he described to Paul Moody how he had prepared himself for the gig.

"The night we recorded 'Silver Machine' we were all absolutely destroyed on dope. Me and Dik Mik especially. When it was time to go on, the two of us were stiff as boards [*laughs*]. They put my bass round my neck and literally pushed me on stage. I had two questions: 'Which direction is the audience?' and 'How many paces away are they?' They told me ten paces, so I walked forward five and started playing. But once the music started, we were electric."

Hawkwind were without doubt the hairiest, druggiest, furthest out group of the era. They took prevailing hippie attitudes and rode with them like outlaws to the further reaches of freakdom. If that sounds perhaps just a bit fanciful, in the first half of the Seventies at least, they epitomised how much the counterculture differed from middle-class mores, and as such they came across as exciting and rather intimidating to their teenage fans.

Hawkwind started out as Group X and in 1969 gate-crashed a gig at All Saints Hall in Notting Hill Gate where Clearwater Productions were showcasing some of their bands. They asked John Peel if they could play for ten minutes and he agreed. "He thought the band were great and recommended the organisers to sign us up," says saxophonist Nik Turner. "We did and got a record deal [with Liberty] and [Clearwater] were our management and our agency."

Group X changed their name to Hawkwind Zoo and then Hawkwind. Although the name sounds like it might be some kind of inter-dimensional jet stream, it actually had the more prosaic origin of describing Turner "hawking up" phlegm and breaking wind. But let's stick with the former.

The group's self-titled debut album from 1970 features an enduringly odd mix of styles, with all the material written by guitarist Dave Brock and arranged by the band. It includes two acoustic songs he had played whilst busking – 'Hurry On Sundown' and 'Mirror Of Illusion' – with more free form pieces like 'The Reason Is?' which, with its cymbal washes and vocal chorales bring to mind some of the more abstract music that some German groups were making at the time, while 'Be Yourself' is an early example of one of the group's trademarks, a simple chord structure and a chanted three-chord mantra based on the song's title, with the last syllable of each line arcing down a few semitones to give a sneering effect. The song morphs into a rotating two-bar drum pattern – akin to Pink Floyd's 'A Saucerful Of Secrets' with Turner's sax solo followed by Huw Lloyd Langton on guitar and the mysteriously named Dik Mik – or Michael Davies to his parents – adding electronics, mainly from his audio tone generator, a primitive form of synthesizer.

This was idiosyncratic post-psychedelic music and like Pink Floyd's, it was built up from simple elements. The linkage between the two groups is far from tenuous as Hawkwind recorded a demo version of Pink Floyd's 'Cymbaline' as Hawkwind Zoo in 1969. Along the way they lost Lloyd Langton, who encountered problems after taking LSD at the 1970 Isle Of Wight Festival, where Hawkwind had played for free outside the main area, partly in protest against the high admission prices and lack of facilities.

This idea of playing for free was the ultimate anti-capitalist and anti-music biz statement, and Hawkwind also played any number of benefit concerts. "Hawkwind were a band who did any gig going," says Turner. "Basically, we just wanted exposure and I found that it was also a wonderful thing to be able to help people with the music and to actually support various causes that might have been like lame ducks. I made myself accessible. People would say, 'Oh, we're putting together a benefit, would you like to come and play?' And I'd say, 'Yeah.'

"We were part of the underground and we tried to embody the spirit of freedom and self-expression and free love and free music, playing off the back of a lorry at protest gigs, Aldermaston and places like that, playing in Wormwood Scrubs and Chelmsford prison, just doing social things. I think Hawkwind were probably unique in that, as not many other bands with success did that sort of thing."

As he notes, this cost the group money and had to be budgeted for, but Hawkwind managed to put aside enough from paying gigs – and they had a pretty packed schedule – to be able to fund these altruistic activities.

Hawkwind toughened up for their next album, *In Search Of Space* (1971), which was crucial in defining the group's trajectory. Pink Floyd's early music carried a yearning to escape into the limitless and liberating expanses of a metaphorical space, but on *In Search Of Space*, Hawkwind wanted to travel to the outer limits in a customised rocket ship fuelled by acid and speed.

Dave Brock's 'We Took The Wrong Step Years Ago' is a Dylanesque protest song, played on acoustic guitar with Dik Mik now joined on the album by synth player Del Dettmar. While Brock looks back at the actions that contributed to the current state of social and environmental catastrophe, the spiralling electronics feel like they are already providing escape routes from the scene. Another song expressing similar sentiments is 'Master Of The Universe', where, over Dave Brock's timeless, near metal riffing, Turner sings in the character role of a creator figure looking down in dismay at his despoiled works.

Another song that laid the foundations for some of Hawkwind's later excursions is 'You Shouldn't Do That'. A fifteen-minute exercise in how to imaginatively deploy relentless, simple riffing, it shifts between two chords and a chorus of four. With Turner's sax to the fore, it gains a cumulative power with chanting and that disdainful downturn on the last word of lines that tell us how we are getting *"no air"* and getting *"aware"*.

Hawkwind used to hang out at the office of the underground magazine *Friends* – later *Frendz* – at 305 Portobello Road, where they met three people who would be important in shaping the group's image and future course: Robert Calvert, who wrote science fiction and worked for *Frendz* in an editorial capacity; Barney Bubbles, who was the art director; and science fiction writer Michael Moorcock, who was also involved in the editorial side. Moorcock had a stall on Portobello Road to raise money for the science fiction journal that he was editing titled

New Worlds. He also organised gigs under the nearby Westway flyover that carried the A40 into central London.

Nik Turner asked Calvert to join the band as their "space poet" and he was initially involved with putting together the concept of *In Search Of Space* in collaboration with Barney Bubbles, who created the album cover design. "Barney and Robert cooked up this story and came up with the Hawkwind Log, which was the log book of a spaceship," says Turner. "It was based on lots of mythological, philosophical, interesting theories about time travel and space travel. The ship had landed on earth and become two dimensional. The actual plastic disk was all that was left of the crew, and the log book was about their story and adventures."

This fold-out artwork with the log book inside was brilliantly put together and made fans effectively part of the group. If Hawkwind were heading out to the stars, they were taking us with them.

Hawkwind reciprocated by playing benefits for *Frendz*. The magazine's journalists included Rosie Boycott, who went on to become a major figure in the UK media. She also gave an "in" to a young writer on music, Nick Kent, who started work there in 1972.

"When I arrived at *Frendz* Hawkwind were there every day, using its premises as a meeting place to go off and do their gigs," Kent recalls. But surely having Hawkwind hanging around the office en masse must have been disruptive?

"But in a good way," says Kent. "I mean, they were far better company than… by that time, there were a lot of people in the Ladbroke Grove underground community who'd just taken too much LSD and were just floating around and not making much sense, and they were headed for self-destruction, though I was too young to realise just how bad they were. But Hawkwind were active, their life was one long adventure. They understood, in their own simple way, what the underground was all about, which was to try to live out the Kerouac dictum, that life could be a constant adventure, without having loads of money in your pocket."

Although sobriety isn't a word that one readily associates with Hawkwind, in Turner's case he tried to keep his consumption of LSD under control. After having a bad trip onstage when all the audience turned into skeletons, he decided to distance himself from it and concentrated on meditation and yoga to straighten himself out.

That year their popularity soared with 'Silver Machine' becoming a Top 10 hit in the summer. So much so that when Frank Zappa and Jeff Beck played the Rock At The Oval concert at the Oval cricket ground in September 1972, ticket sales were slow and so Hawkwind were drafted in and put on the bill as second headliners, and the concert sold out.

But before this unexpected upturn in popularity Turner had been living on the floors of friends and fans of the band for three years, and in even less salubrious conditions. "I started off living in my own van which I supplied for the band to use and then eventually we bought another van called The Yellow Wart, a TK Bedford, like a post office van and I lived in the back of that for some time with Dik Mik.

"I wasn't completely broke, I used to live quite a healthy life, really, and eat very wholesome healthy food. I just didn't have anywhere to live, which was a bit of a problem, which didn't really bother me, except I had nowhere to practise my sax."

There was a change in the group's line-up. Original drummer Terry Ollis had left to be replaced by the more powerful and straight-ahead Simon King. Lemmy had joined, expecting to be playing guitar, but Brock took on lead guitar duties and he ended up playing bass.

The new line-up was more direct and heavier in approach, with Lemmy a powerful and freewheeling bass guitarist. In late 1972 they recorded *Doremi Fasol Latido*, which carried on the space travel concept, although the album has a rather flat production sound, with King's drums sounding a tad messy. 'Space Is Deep' is lyrically informed by Michael Moorcock's novel *The Black Corridor* in which a space traveller ends up going insane from the isolation of his voyage. The album includes acoustic-based tracks like 'Down Through The Night', with Turner on flute, while on 'Brainstorm' the group revisited the hypnotic length of 'You Shouldn't Do That', but this time turned it into relentless flat-out three-chord stoner rock, which hurtles round and round like a centrifuge. Barney Bubbles' cover art is striking – a Hawkwind insignia, like a cosmic coat of arms, in silver on a black background.

Along with the electronic "whoosh", Turner's electric sax playing was one of the group's more unusual trademarks. Turner had initially learned the clarinet and grown up with jazz, but as he admits, he found it too technically demanding. He recalls that after spending time in Berlin in 1968, where he met some free jazz musicians who reminded him that you don't have to be technical to express yourself, "I sort of visualised myself playing free jazz in a rock band and that's what Hawkwind became to me."

Turner's approach was inspired by the guitar sounds of Jimi Hendrix and by the way Miles Davis had used echo effects on his trumpet on *Bitches Brew*. Sometimes his sax lines cut through, but at times they were more of a cacophonous texture. Turner explains the effects that he employed.

"I used everything, quite honestly. Somebody made me this octave splitter and I had a really brilliant Fender wah-wah pedal, which had a volume control and a fuzz box on it, and a Doppler effect like a phaser. I put the saxophone through everything, with an echo at the end of it."

Although Turner was aware of his technical limitations, his unique style was earning him a legion of admirers. He remembers going into the musical instrument retailers, Rose Morris, on Shaftesbury Avenue in London and was surprised when they offered him a discount.

"The sales manager said, 'Quite honestly 90 per cent of the people who come in here wanting to play the saxophone say they want to play like you.' And I thought, 'Oh blimey, what am I responsible for?'

"At the same time, in *Sounds* I was voted top saxophonist in Britain and number two in the world. I wasn't really that impressed, because I knew how good or bad I was, so it didn't go to my head. It made me stop reading the music papers."

SPACE RITUAL

Original Label: United Artists
Producer: Hawkwind
Recorded: December 22, 1972, at Liverpool Stadium & December 30, 1972, at Brixton Sundown, London
Released: May 11, 1973
Chart position: 9 (UK)

After Calvert had written the lyrics to 'Silver Machine', he and Barney Bubbles came up with the idea of a conceptual show with songs from *Doremi...*, *In Search Of Space* and new material. The idea was that the band were a spaceship and the audience were the energy source powering the craft on its voyage through different dimensions.

As Calvert told *New Musical Express* in 1972: "It doesn't have a plot like a traditional opera but is an opera nevertheless in the way it presents a situation. It concerns dreams people might have if they were suspended in animation in deep space. Whereas our last album concerned a journey into space, this is more about actually being there."

Unfortunately Calvert had mental health issues and was sometimes absent from the planning and also from the performances, although he appears on the album of the live show. The lightshow was conceived by Barney Bubbles, with a visual code based on the Pythagorean idea of the music of the spheres, with colours corresponding to the astrological sign of each of the group members. He worked in conjunction with Jonathan Smeeton, aka Liquid Len, and the Lensmen – Molten Mick, John Perrin and (John) Leaky Lee – who appeared at gigs with a set-up of multiple slide projectors.

They also employed the services of dancers: Jonathan Carney; Tony Carrera, a mime artist who had worked with Marcel Marceau; and Rene Laballister, an American contortionist. And for those who had wondered what that blurred pink blob was on the back cover photo of *In Search Of Space*, that was the six-foot-tall Stacia Blake, who would end the show dancing naked – something that would be unlikely to happen these days. And of course this only added to the group's attraction. But as Turner saw it, she was neither promoted by the band as a sex object, nor was she particularly a figurehead for women's issues.

"She was more like an art project to me," he says. "We became involved with her, and encouraged her to dance naked – with Barney's advice we had her painted up in body paint, rather than clothing. But being in body paint didn't amplify the nakedness, really, it detracted from it and made it more arty. That's how I saw it, really: I didn't see Stacia as a sexual sort of image. But I thought she was every schoolboy's dream – suddenly being confronted by this great sort of siren."

"People watching did not regard it as a sexual thing. Hawkwind don't attract that type of audience," said Stacia in 1971. "They reacted to my dancing as an expression of freedom. Somebody once approached me to do a pornographic film – I reacted quite violently, not physically, but verbally. I would never contemplate anything like that."

Hawkwind's approach was highly unusual at the time. The only other group who had similar ambitions were Principal Edwards Magic Theatre, a collective of musicians, poets, dancers and sound and lighting technicians – a total of seventeen over the group's lifespan – who produced one of rock's first forays into multi-media. They were championed by John Peel and recorded two albums on his Dandelion label, *Soundtrack* (1969) and *Asmoto Running Band* (1971), both of which were produced by Pink Floyd's Nick Mason, but keeping a band of that size afloat ultimately proved to be uneconomic. And while their performances had a narrative element, Hawkwind's were more about sensory bombardment.

The *Space Ritual* album was released as a double LP with a striking erotic front cover painting of a beautiful space goddess, with a third eye set in an arc above her head, and two scowling big cats in attendance, which owes something to the art nouveau paintings of Alphonse Mucha.

The cover folded out into six panels, designed by Bubbles, which again seemed to hold the key to some repository of arcane knowledge, like the Dead Sea Scrolls of space rock. The music had now morphed into full-throttle sonic hurricane, with no acoustic guitars, but with monolithic riffs, illuminated by electronics shooting by like meteorite showers and Dave Brock essentially repeating his solo on 'Silver Machine' over and over again. There are spoken interludes by Calvert delivered in a severe voice, including Moorcock's unsettling 'Black Corridor' – in which space is viewed as something beautiful, unfathomable, terrifyingly vast and impassive – and the macabre public service announcement of 'Sonic Attack'. Calvert acted as a kind of cosmic tour guide delivering a number of his own recitations, concluding with 'Earth Calling'. 'Electronic No.1' is two minutes of Dik Mik and Del Dettmar signaling electronically into outer space.

Space Ritual has such a powerful unity that it really feels like the enactment of some sci-fi ritual, such that it almost breaks the spell when audience clapping appears at the end. As well as being an icon of space rock, there's a darkness to it and a power that can be quite intimidating. This was made even clearer with the re-release on CD in 1996, which includes the hair-raising unedited thirteen-minute version of 'Brainstorm'. Hawkwind in excelsis, it's a thrilling example of monomaniacal Om-rock, including the generic Dave Brock solo, chants and Lemmy's probing, melodic bass-playing, all delivered at high velocity.

One can see why Moorcock then extended the concept by referring to the group in his novels, with the hero, Jerry Cornelius, driving around listening to Hawkwind in his car.

Teenage Hawkwind fan Ian Sturgess experienced a baptism by cosmic fire when he went to see one of the last performances of the Space Ritual. He writes:

"Seeing Hawkwind as my first live band in a tiny venue like the Top Rank in Reading in July 1973 was a mindblowing experience for a 16-year-old.

"In our enthusiasm, I remember my mates and I getting to the venue ridiculously early – about 5 p.m. – having travelled over on the train from Basingstoke. We sat on the steps of the venue for hours – me wearing the slightly unco-ordinated combo of green flares and bright yellow Brutus shirt, with a pale red vest over the top – waiting for it to open up. While we were doing so, this huge bloke sporting a black cape and a big leather hat with a feather stuck in it strode past everyone and started hammering on the door. 'Blimey,' we thought. 'He's even keener than us to get in.' We were later to discover, when he turned up onstage to make a rare appearance with the band, that this was none other than famed sci-fi author and honorary Hawklord Michael Moorcock.

"Once we got inside, we parked ourselves dead centre about ten feet from the low stage and grooved along to support band Ace, at the time eighteen months away from their biggest hit, 'How Long'. Once they'd finished and their gear had been removed from the stage, we passed the time with anticipation rising, ogling Simon King's impressive drum kit and the stacks of amps and assorted synths crammed onto the tiny stage. The DJ, Andy Dunkley, played some cool sounds and I distinctly remember 'Roundabout' by Yes being among them.

"Members of the road crew then handed out huge bunches of joss sticks to the audience so the atmosphere quickly became foggy and aromatic. Hawkwind wandered on and, after some introductory noodling, blasted into 'Born To Go' with the room swirling in psychedelic liquid light projections. Lemmy's bass locked with King's powerhouse drumming, while the frontline of synths, Dave Brock's metronomic guitar and Nik Turner's squalling echo-laden sax created a thundering sonic wash over the top. And, blissfully, it was LOUD. On tracks such as 'Lord Of Light', 'Orgone Accumulator' or the classic 'Brainstorm', their riffing would take on a mantric quality that even Can would struggle to match.

"As they climaxed with 'Master Of The Universe', they turned on a kind of electric snake that was draped across the amps, sending pulses of white light flowing across the stage. Believe me, in the days before lasers, video screens, cherry bombs and levitating drum kits, this was impressive stuff. After an encore of 'Silver Machine', part of my brain was forever lodged somewhere beyond Alpha Centauri as we staggered across the road to the railway station and back to planet Earth."

Hawkwind attempted to replicate the single chart success of 'Silver Machine' with 'Urban Guerilla' in the summer of 1973. Although Calvert's satirical lyrics had been written a year or so before, Hawkwind had played a benefit for the Angry Brigade, and while this might have passed under the establishment's radar, it was released, coincidentally, just after the start of an IRA bombing campaign and the BBC, which was notoriously twitchy about such things, had little choice but to ban the single.

Turner wishes they had released something like 'Brainstorm' or 'Master Of The Universe', since they disappeared as a singles band. "It was not a very apt subject for a pop song, so I had the bomb squad at my house and they tore up my floorboards. Every time we tried to go across the Channel, we got stopped for twenty-four hours by the customs and the anti-terrorist squad."

Things would never be quite the same again. The group recorded *Hall Of The Mountain Grill* in 1974, with Roy Thomas Baker on production duties. Dik Mik had gone and was replaced by Simon House from the

Third Ear Band on keyboards and violin. It prompted this response from Ira Robbins, writing in American magazine *Zoo World*.

"The Mountain Grill is shockingly different than its predecessors, both in sound and attitude. The general change of direction now incorporates dynamics, melody, harmony and finesse – in short, the musicalization of Hawkwind."

In 1975 the group released *Warrior At The Edge Of Time*, into which Moorcock had considerable input and the increase in musicality continued. *Space Ritual* had been such a definitive statement that the group found it difficult to match its power and scope. Lemmy was ousted from the band after a drugs bust in 1975. Calvert returned in 1976, the year that Turner was also ousted, and under the aegis of Dave Brock, Hawkwind sailed on through the Seventies and were an influence on punk, with one particular Finsbury Park longhair, John Lydon, being an avowed fan. Because for all their theatricality, their space trips and cosmic concepts, Hawkwind were at pains to be inclusive, to engage with the community, to do well by their fans, things that many groups of the era thought of as secondary considerations.

"I always considered Hawkwind to be the belt-and-braces, working men's Pink Floyd," says Turner. "Hawkwind had their feet on the ground."

CHAPTER 36

Divertimento No.5: Notes on Politics

On his 1972 composition from Matching Mole's Little Red Record, 'Gloria Gloom', Robert Wyatt sang that he had doubts about how much he should be contributing to the *"already rich"* and wondered aloud whether he was pretending to himself that making music was more relevant than the fight for socialism. But these ideas were couched as an internal dialogue and so remained questions, musings. Wyatt's more overt political statements were most clearly made on his 1982 album *Nothing Can Stop Us* after he had become a card-carrying member of the Communist Party.

But in the progressive rock scene of the Seventies, direct statements on politics were rare. In 2003, I asked Wyatt on live radio if he felt that musicians with strong political views should feel an obligation to state them in their music.

He replied: "No, I think that's really unfair on musicians. It's really hard; you're trying just to make nice records and tunes. I wouldn't dump it on musicians. What I would like is for prime ministers to stop prancing about pretending to be rock stars and do some serious politics, and then we wouldn't even have to think about it.

"[The political situation] does affect what you do, but it's ludicrous to think that it really matters – certainly what I [personally] do or don't do. People get terribly worked up about references in songs. It doesn't really change the geopolitical situation a lot either way."

Seventies progressive rock has been criticised, mainly after the event, for epitomising a disengagement of musicians from anything political. This presupposes that musicians need to reflect their times in this regard, which is a moot point. And if you are looking towards rock musicians to vivify your political opinions or provide new revelations, you should be prepared for disappointment.

Part of the reason that the music was so devoid of what could loosely be called political statement was because the musicians had grown up through Harold Macmillan's "You've never had it so good" era of the late Fifties. And despite the fact that the Seventies is often generalised as a grim decade of endless strikes, power cuts, urban blight and streets turned into vast mountain ranges of uncollected household refuse, the first half of the decade, at least, was a relatively prosperous time, with people looking towards an inviting technological future.

And as with many times of trouble and turmoil, the middle classes, who, generally speaking, produced both the musicians and their fanbase, were less affected than the working classes.

The musicians were less likely to engage directly with the audience on political terms when they were building a lavish and ornamented fantasy world that one was invited to enter into. If the musicians were anything but politicised, the same could also be said of their youthful audience, who were growing up in an era still touched by the hand of hippie and the childhood-into-adulthood idylls of psychedelia, and who were still looking for something beyond the humdrum everyday.

Crucially, for many, mainstream politics was seen as boring, run by a bunch of old fuddy-duddies, the remnant of an age that would soon be bygone. In comfortably-off middle-class UK, it was acceptable for youths either living with their parents or in higher education to pronounce themselves as apolitical, smile beatifically and flash a peace sign. At least until they had to make their way in the world.

Guy Evans, drummer in Van Der Graaf Generator, recalls a pervasive way of thinking, initiated by the hippies, which created a "whole kind of fantasy" of a separatist way of life, which required that they "get it together in the country and make our own communes". Few decided to make that jump, but that fantasy hung over the era.

He reflects on the views of himself and his peers on mainstream politics. "Either it wasn't exciting or what you thought was a dead world," Evans recalls. "There was the Profumo [scandal] and that was all a bit racy and associated with Swinging London. It was almost that a bad side of the straight mentality had been exposed. I think the naïve thing was that if we keep being beautiful and experimental and far out, then the world will catch up with us eventually."

Gong guitarist Steve Hillage remembers the arguments between a personal and a proscriptive political view towards self-improvement. "In the late Sixties, early Seventies, that was the hot debate. Do you go for inner development or do you join the revolution? There were very strong opinions on both sides. I almost had a foot in both camps. The classic argument of the politicos is if you just concentrate on your inner development, it's a selfish cop-out — you've got to be active and go and do your thing. The other argument is that OK, you've got all his activity, but that leads to a war with lots of people being killed and a dictatorship.

"Everyone found the American intervention in Vietnam to be distasteful – why can't the Vietnamese be left to sort their own future out without an imperial power going in and dictating what they should do? But at the same time if you go on a Vietnam war demonstration and are shouting 'Ho, Ho, Ho Chi Minh', it means you are on the side of the North Vietnamese in this war. How can you be protesting against a war when in fact you are taking a side in the war? That was a big thing.

"So you think, 'You are a fucking coward then. What are you doing standing here on a demonstration, go and get your gun. Why aren't you fighting?'"

Henry Cow were one of the most obviously political groups of the decade in that from their interviews and a handful of lyrics and titles, they were clearly left wing and nodding towards Marxism. But ultimately drummer and lyricist Chris Cutler saw even their political role more as activists than as sloganeers.

"We had a lot of run-ins with Cornelius Cardew in this period because of his rhetoric around *People's Liberation Music*. He was saying progressive political artists should be singing songs of struggle, the Irish question and the working class," says Cutler. "But we were taking the Walter Benjamin approach and saying, 'No, "progressive" doesn't mean propaganda, it means being in touch with your own time and relevant to your own problems, and doing something of quality.' We didn't feel obliged to be 'political'. As Phil Ochs said on [the sleeve notes of his 1967 album], *Pleasures Of The Harbor*: 'You must protest, it is your diamond duty... Ah but in such an ugly time the true protest is beauty.'"

"Phil was probably the most political of all of them, but even he came to that position – to be the servant of some political message is an abnegation, but to do something of sincerity and quality is of itself political."

Dagmar Krause was the singer in Henry Cow from 1975–78 and has since made records of music by Bertold Brecht and Hanns Eisler. She sums up her stance thus: "Not political statements, please, but let's make music where you don't fall asleep and accept the status quo: that's maybe more important. And it's important that you find your own voice. Don't preach. You have to be able to feel and examine with your head, and you have to try and come up with a good piece of music."

When progressive rock has been criticised, especially by the music press, as not being sufficiently political, the "p" word was more implied than overtly used. But the idea was that it had become detached from any sort of meaningful contemporary context and had retreated into a zone of solipsistic self-indulgence. However, that didn't necessarily lessen its relevance to the listener, as it was addressing some very different needs, and at its best it excited the imagination.

On 'And You And I' by Yes, Jon Anderson tells us that, *"Political ends"* will die and end up as *"sad remains"*, although it feels wrong to quote it out of context, especially when it's far from clear what it actually means in context. And Yes did write three political songs, which was three more than most, with 'Yours Is No Disgrace' (1970) and 'Harold Land' (1968) – both about unfortunates put into positions of conflict beyond their control – and the self-explanatory single 'Don't Kill The Whale' (1977).

Barclay James Harvest's canon seemed somewhat fantastical, but there were often elements of social comment and satire within. Released in 1974 on the album *Everybody Is Everybody Else*, John Lees's song 'The Great 1974 Mining Disaster' referenced the miners' strike in January 1974. The strikes of 1973 had given rise to power cuts, while this more recent action caused the Three-Day Week, an unthinkable state of affairs with production down and TV stations closing early to save energy.

Conservative Prime Minister Edward Heath called a general election, the Tories going forth under the rhetorical slogan "Who governs Britain?" But the results showed, surprisingly, that the electorate were more disenchanted with the government's handling of the situation than with the miners and the Labour movement, and his party lost their majority.

Barclay James Harvest's song celebrates this incident with some ambivalence and also refers to the unmarried Heath as a *"sailor gay"*. But the song is more satirical than about taking sides, as well as being a clever rewrite of The Bee Gees' 1968 hit, 'New York Mining Disaster 1941' – which was a sort of imaginary disaster song, inspired by both a real mining disaster in New York State in 1939 and the 1966 Aberfan disaster in South Wales, when a saturated colliery spoil tip slid downhill consuming a school and killing over 140 children and adults.

Lees denies any direct reference to Aberfan in his own song, but notes that the song was set against a backdrop of general Seventies industrial unrest, with wildcat strikes and the closed shop. It appears critical of the way the dispute was handled on both sides, with miners' leader Joe Gormley arguably not always acting in the best interests of the union. "It's like a reporter, both ways, both sides of the coin," says Lees. "There are the striking miners and the politicians. The Bee Gees had done 'The Great Mining Disaster…' and that was a tragedy; this was a political war. If anything was going to put you off voting Conservative, it was when Heath smiled."

Hawkwind were active within their local community, but were they ever interested in party politics? "I don't really think so," says saxophonist Nik Turner. "I suppose there was an underlying feeling of a sort of socialism with regard to Hawkwind. They were a people's band who did stuff for the people, but they didn't give it a political name at the time. We played a lot of benefits for people who were doing socially good things.

"I made myself accessible. I would just like to support worthwhile causes. We did CND benefits and protests, things about freedom. I think that Hawkwind tended to align itself with the alternative culture, an alternative attitude and a different way of looking at things, really – like underground newspapers. The underground was all about something rather political really, without saying, 'Oh, we vote for Labour.' I don't think we voted, actually."

One musician who did go into politics is Bill MacCormick of Quiet Sun, Matching Mole and 801. He joined the Liberal Party in 1973. "They were the only party opposed to nuclear power, which I was anti, both in terms of environment and civil rights," he says. A few years previously he'd had a taste of the far left when he had befriended the son of the Revolutionary Workers Party Jeremy Healey and was persuaded to go on a march.

"After I had chanted, *'Something, something, something/Nationalise the banks'* half a dozen times I thought, 'Fuck this for a game of soldiers, I don't agree with it,' threw my placard on the side of the road and went home. No doubt I'm somewhere on a list of MI5's suspicious people as a result of this one escapade, but I was always inclined to vote for the lily-livered, weak-kneed Liberals."

MacCormick retained his interest in politics and wrote a couple of features for the *New Musical Express* in 1974 – a piece on nuclear power that included an interview with Julie Christie, and one on the National Front and how they recruited from football crowds, for which he received a death threat. He says of his bandmate in Matching Mole, Robert Wyatt: "We did share some instincts, but we didn't share the analysis of what the solutions might be."

But overall, among the musicians he met, politics was something that just wasn't on the agenda. MacCormick offers this by way of explanation. "The problem can be being in a band, because you can get yourself into that sealed environment, you can cut yourself off from the world. If you were intense, serious musicians, as many were in the progressive world, it can get even more like that. That style of music did get incredibly introverted."

An album that MacCormick co wrote with his brother — *New Musical Express* journalist Ian MacDonald – and Roxy Music guitarist Phil Manzanera, *Listen Now* (1977), as 801, was influenced by events of the time. The melodic but edgy music was counterbalanced by lyrics that had a feeling of a future oppressive, Orwellian dystopia rather than some hippie vision. The album cover portraits carried a similar feeling to those on *In The Court Of The Crimson King*, but lyrically it was grittier and more to the point.

"In the Seventies it was a fairly downbeat period with the strikes and the three-day weeks and the power cuts, and the refuse collection strike in 1979," says MacCormick. "You could see that reaction from the right coming in. The NF was the extreme edge of it and that died back, but it began to solidify and concentrate around people like Thatcher and has continued to do so, and that was a particularly depressing way of looking at the world.

"That was the general mood of things in the mid-Seventies. The National Front and the IRA were at it, so that certainly influenced the lyrics to *Listen Now*. They reflected both of our pessimistic views of the way the world was going. So in that way political issues did effect what we wrote."

Robert John Godfrey of The Enid recalls his own experiences with party politics in the early Seventies. "I'm not a political person but when I was living in Brixton in 1971 I had a little fuck-buddy friend who lived locally. He was a student and was incredibly into the left wing and he persuaded me to spend a weekend at some leisure centre where there was going to be a big meeting for the young socialists and all these important people were going to come and speak. It was at a time when we were beginning to see the Three-Day Week and all of the things that were going on with the Heath government. The unions were causing trouble and there were always people on strike.

"I heard people saying that the real thing was to grab control of the trade unions as that would be a way to bring the country to its knees, get a Labour government elected and then force it to carry out Marxist policies, which is exactly what they tried to do and brought the [Jim] Callahan government down [in 1979] – the Militant tendency and all of that.

"The real problem was that the Labour Party allowed itself to be infiltrated by Marxists and Trotskyists – the glee with which they called strikes at [the British Leyland] car plant at Cowley... it seemed they were continuously on strike.

"So I was quite keen when Mrs Thatcher came along because no one else was going to do it. It needed a total bitch like that to see what was needed and that was fine. But then she went on to gerrymander the working classes by telling them they could become rich and successful like she was, and they could buy their council house and all the rest of it. We've now got a world where those decades have bred into us a new way of looking at society and that is now being questioned."

In the Seventies the Strawbs took on a singular path. Always difficult to categorise, they then scored a number two hit in early 1973 with their least characteristic song, 'Part Of The Union'.

The song was written by drummer Richard Hudson and bass guitarist John Ford during a time of trade union unrest, most notoriously at the British Leyland car plants. Workers had moved from piece rate to a flat rate monitored by men with stopwatches, and union activity had expanded in the car industry from trying to establish safe working practices in what had been a dangerous and dirty working environment, to a force behind seemingly constant disruption. Workers were called out about the most petty grievances, which rankled management, and fuelled intra-union disharmony between the moderates and the militants. In January 1970 the British Leyland chairman revealed the company's profits for the last four months as zero.

When the single was released it caught the establishment unawares and as controversial pop records have tended to do in the UK, it provoked something of a panic. "There were questions asked in the Houses of Parliament as to whether it should be banned because it was inciting riots," says the group's Dave Cousins.

Based on Woody Guthrie's unequivocal 'Union Maid', which extolled pride in the trade unions, it was transformed into a boisterous singalong. It seemed on the surface like the sort of working-class pop anthem that composer and Revolutionary Communist Party member Cornelius Cardew – who had attempted to woo the proles with lowest common-denominator knees-ups like 'Smash The Social Contract' – would have killed for.

But then its "strength in the union" message was surely being parodied by Ford as he shouted *"Out, brothers, out"* and hailed *"the factory's fall"*. This must actually have been a satirical swipe at the vindictive union Trots, who, flushed with their newly found power, would call wildcat strikes under the slightest pretext. Or was it?

Putting its hideous "oompah" tune aside, 'Part Of The Union' is a masterpiece of irony folded upon irony. Listen to it again and Ford seems to be conspiratorially intoning the lyrics in the persona of the cheeky chappy, the underdog, who the Brits tend to love. But given the inherent conservatism of the British and that even Harold Wilson's Labour government had attempted to curb union power in the Sixties, and that the miners' unions strike action had caused power cuts just a year previously, one has to ask who the hell was buying this in such huge quantities and singing along. The British have always loved a novelty song, but really!

Inevitably it was sung at union meetings, but then it appeared that the union members had walked right into the trap, singing a song that mocked them. But then they *were* strong at the time and Heath's government's inability to control them had caused the Tories to lose the 1974 general election.

Hudson and Ford had suggested releasing the single under the name The Brothers. The Strawbs' mainstay Dave Cousins was concerned that he had only recently got that line-up together and if they recorded the song as The Brothers and, as he had assumed, it would be a hit record, they might well leave.

"Well, the thing was, I didn't do any interviews for it, Hud and John did, and they just sat on the fence," says Cousins. "My view was that we should have come out being staunchly Labour and pro-union, and we'd have become the darlings of the left wing – instead of which we sort of fell through the cracks."

But in keeping with the song's equivocal message, Cousins also muddies the waters. "I certainly didn't vote socialist, or Labour," he continues, "but it was just that I thought from the point of view of making a declaration of intent, then we would have done much better to have been profoundly left wing.

"I'm not sure whether John actually thought anything about it at all when he wrote it [*laughs*] Well, I tried to add a few lines. I wanted to say *'Proud of what I am'* rather than *'amazed'*. But no, he wouldn't change anything."

That line is the crux of the song, when the narrator realises that rather than simply being proud of what the union has achieved, he is amazed at what power he now has at his disposal. Apparently, in between periods of sitting on the fence, the authors claimed that it was pro-union – probably because there was an 'r' in the month. The song's authors agreed to give a proportion of the royalties to the Woody Guthrie Foundation.

Cousins deeply regretted including 'Part Of The Union' on the album. Not only did the song's authors quit the band soon after to form Hudson

Ford, taking their new fans with them (see Chapter 32), but the success of the single had nearly wiped out the Strawbs' fanbase.

Many have said that politics and rock music don't mix, presumably to the detriment of the political message, but it can clearly cut both ways.

CHAPTER 37

Electrick Gypsies: Steve Hillage and Gong

Into the 1970s, hippies were, as their name suggested, regarded as being pretty hip. To many they exemplified a worldview that, to summarise and generalise, was set against all the mess that had been caused by "straight" society, particularly war and pollution. And as bungling, square politicians carried on in their way, the hippies represented a loftier viewpoint in spiritual terms, with an unspoken message – that we can see through you all and beyond your workaday world to grasp something greater. They were different, they were their own people and they also had more sex and drugs than the rest of us.

Even for those who lived with Mum and Dad in suburbia – rather than in a commune surrounded by young children and goats – and were maybe getting something out of their system before going into selling insurance, the idea of self-expression over conformity, being a bit different, being a bit weird even, had a great deal of currency amongst Seventies youth. For being a "straight" seemed so terribly dull.

It was a way of thinking that permeated the whole decade, an alternative for youth coming into maturity in a narrow-minded conformist society. Most teenagers would have had a puff on a joint without becoming addicted, as they had been warned they might, and so had at least some experience of marijuana's mind-altering qualities. And many Seventies kids carried on the idea of not selling out, of not just joining the ranks of suits and securing a job for life and a pension at the end of it. Instead they were searching for a way of enhancing their life, of giving it more meaning. And out of the ranks of Seventies hippies rose hippie musicians – and the woolly hatted, hippiest of all hippie musicians, in the UK at least, was the Essex-born Stephen Simpson Hillage.

As a teenager, Hillage had briefly been a guitarist in Uriel (see Chapter 21), recording *Arzachel* with them in 1969 under the pseudonym Simon Sasparella. He then secured a record deal with Deram, via Caravan's manager Terry King, from demos that he had made with Uriel keyboard player Dave Stewart when he was a student at the University Of Kent at

Canterbury. He used these as the basis for his first proper band, Khan. They recorded an album, *Space Shanty*, in 1972, and on one song in particular, 'Hollow Stone (Including The Escape Of The Space Pirates)' Hillage demonstrates his guitar skills, playing soaring overdubbed lead lines using an echo delay over a dramatic, shifting series of chords.

Into the Seventies, what was ostensibly a second wave of psychedelia was often referred to as 'space rock'; immersive music rich in colour and texture – which no doubt sounded particularly good when the listener was stoned. Khan could be bracketed in that category. But by the time the album was released, the 21-year-old guitarist found the whole business of running a band too much pressure, and while he had written the best part of another album's worth of material, he put Khan on hold awhile and went on tour with Kevin Ayers.

Daevid Allen had been resident in France and Deià in Majorca since being refused permission to enter the UK for three years in 1967 due to an expired visa. Allen's behaviour at the student demonstrations in Paris in May 1968 had landed him in further trouble.

"I dressed in a black robe, and the sort of hat that you'd wear to protect yourself in the desert, with a royalist flag on it and a very 'pataphysical attitude, and a big plastic bag full of tiny teddy bears which I handed out to all the paratroopers in a bus," Allen recalls. "They didn't know what the hell to do with all these teddy bears. They just took them, looked sheepish and started giggling.

"The students were very irritated with me as well. They said, 'What are you doing here, beatnik? Why don't you go back to your pad and get stoned?' And the normal authorities wanted to arrest me and couldn't think of a reason. I did this poem called 'I Do Not Smoke The Bananas', which was surrealist in the best sense, I suppose, as it was in pidgin French. I did it in front of a line of paratroopers on the Boulevard Saint-Germain right near the bridge.

"I was filmed by ORTF [French TV] cameras. They said, 'Stand here and do the poem, and we'll film you.' And because it had 'ORTF' on the cameras, they didn't stop us – they thought it must be some kind of news report."

Allen recorded on the French BYG/Actuel label with his partner, the poet and singer Gilli Smyth, as Gong. They produced the charming if somewhat ramshackle *Magick Brother* in 1970 and the more fully realised group record *Camembert Electrique* in 1971. The group on this album included Pip Pyle on drums and a brilliant saxophonist and flautist,

Didier Malherbe, who Allen had met in Majorca in 1968, where Malherbe was herding goats on Robert Graves' estate and living in a cave.

Ayers had been in Gong temporarily, playing live with them in 1971, when he shared bass-playing duties with Christian Tritsch. Then the group came onstage to Allen's pre-recorded tapes and featured a female juggler. Ayers also lived for a while with the group at a communal house in France.

"Daevid wrote some really good songs," says Ayers. "Gong had some excellent musicians, but it was all a bit too wacko for me."

At one Kevin Ayers show in France, Daevid Allen, Ayers' former bandmate in Soft Machine, came along to watch. Hillage had met Allen previously, but this time Allen brought the members of Gong with him to the show and at the end of Ayers' set they joined in for an extended jam.

"I just thought, 'Fuck it, this is my new band,'" says Hillage. They asked me to join and I basically just jumped ship. I was enjoying working with Kevin, but joining Gong was a fantastic opportunity. I was a fan, and I got to join my favourite [group]."

Virgin released *Flying Teapot* on the same day as Mike Oldfield's *Tubular Bells* – on May 25, 1973 – and raised Gong's profile enormously with the inspired move of also re-releasing *Camembert Electrique* (1971) for 49p, then the price of a single, and this Anglo-French musical hippie commune were suddenly one of the hippest groups around.

Hillage's role on *Flying Teapot* was somewhat limited as the material had already been written and some of it recorded. According to Allen's lyrics, *Camembert Electrique* was transmitted from the Planet Gong by the station Radio Gnome Invisible, but this new album found him formulating an entire mythos, drawing annotated characters on the inside gatefold, like the Octave Doctors, Captain Capricorn and Zero The Hero, while his cover painting depicts the Pot Head Pixies navigating the Teapot through space. Looking back, although far more sensible concepts had been ridiculed before in the music press, the fact that it was so absurd – and knowingly so – and that the whole thing was actually quite funny, ensured that Gong got through largely unscathed.

Allen gave the group members new names, so Hillage was Stevie Hillside, on "gitbox" and drummer Laurie Allan was known as Lawrence The Alien. Daevid Allen was Dingo Virgin, Christopher Longcock and a number of other aliases, while Gilli Smyth was Shakti Yoni, two Hindi words: the first meaning the divine force of feminine creative power that permeates the universe; the second the female pudendum. The best renaming was Malherbe, who was rechristened – through deliberate mistranslation – Bloomdido Bad De Grasse.

Quite apart from all this cosmic tomfoolery, Gong were a group of exceptional musicians who tackled everything from Allen's surreal singalongs to deep space group explorations. Allen played glissando guitar – a technique of vibrating a smooth piece of metal over the strings to give an unearthly high drone. Against this background wash, Hillage's lead guitar was complemented by Tim (Hi T Moonweed) Blake's synthesizer, a suitcase Synth-A used in conjunction with Revox tape recorders, which was dubbed the Crystal Machine and later Cynthia Size-A. This set-up was used in a similar way to Hawkwind, as a texture to add depth and space, and largely independent of what was going on structurally. But Gong were more mobile, lighter and more capricious than Hawkwind's relentless voyage to the stars in 4/4 time.

One of the most striking aspects of the group was singer and lyricist Smyth's "space whisper" and "loin cackle". The former style was a drifting, high-pitched echoed vocal; the second a strident, erotic, intimidating delivery often ending in screams as on 'I Am Your Animal' on *Camembert Electrique*, along with a statement of intent, that she is going to *"fuck you"*.

Hillage recalls the group living communally in a house in a wood near Voisines in the Yonne department, south of Paris. Next to the house was a converted hunting lodge where the musicians could play at any time of the day or night. "It was economically sensible," he recalls. "At times [it wasn't easy], but it managed to rumble along efficiently. I was very much focused on the music."

The drummer's stool in Gong was regularly left unoccupied. A young Charles Hayward had covered for an absent Laurie Allan – who left and rejoined a number of times – for a few weeks in June and July 1972. "It wasn't lots of screwing around, lots of drug taking, it was about sharing and working and living together so I wanted to experience that," says Hayward. "But there was a point in the evening – I say the evening, but it would normally be about four o'clock in the morning – where the day's work had been done and Daevid would make his verbena tea and take it up to his bedroom. Everyone would go to their separate rooms and you got this feeling of everyone getting cosy about not being on top of everyone else.

"I loved Daevid from outside sitting in the audience watching him on tour with Gong and Kevin Ayers. Once I was in the band, I was still in apprenticeship mode. I'm just doing what's inside this guy's head. He was leaving spaces for me but basically I had to get my own group.

"My dad came to meet me at the airport after we'd come back and he told me that he only recognised me by the fact that I was sitting next to my drum kit. I had changed. I had a few initiations when I was there, all in a compressed amount of time. It was pretty intense."

The next time Laurie Allan left, Pierre Moerlen joined. A player of astonishing dexterity, he had trained at Strasbourg Conservatoire, which left him conflicted between being, in Hillage's words, the "black sheep of the family" by playing rock'n'roll music with a bunch of freaks, and applying himself to the role of orchestral percussionist for which he had been trained. Consequently he left and returned numerous times between 1973–75 and some impressive drummers stepped in during that period, including Rob Tait, Bill Bruford and Chris Cutler.

Hillage absorbed the esoteric ideas that exemplified the hippies and those of a countercultural bent with a genuine enthusiasm. "I developed an interest, when I was quite young, in UFOs," he says. "I was an avid reader of books by Timothy Leary, Aldous Huxley's *The Doors Of Perception*, and Gurdjieff. And then Daevid was very big on his particular set of metaphors and ways of dealing with things, which was intertwined in the Gong mythology. When we were in Gong all together it was a bit like a research project, with books about alchemy, the Kabbalah and Tibetan Buddhism all mixed into a glorious cocktail.

"I was groping for ways of combining that philosophical standpoint with my music, and with Gong I kind of found that and carried on with it. I didn't do it quite the same whimsical, wacky way as Daevid – his way of dealing with it is completely unique.

"What are now called the baby boomers, we were the first post-atomic bomb generation and so you grew up from an early age with the idea that the world could destroy itself by human agency at the twinkling of an eye," Hillage elaborates. "I don't think humans in recent history have ever been in a situation like that. And put together with the economic boom post-World War Two, it left a whole new generation of people looking for something deeper."

While Allen and Smyth had gone to London to mix *Flying Teapot*, Hillage was working on new material with Blake, Malherbe, new bass guitarist Mike Howlett and Moerlen.

The album was called *Angel's Egg* and again is a dazzling mix of cosmic jamming and structured songs, together with the absurdist narrative about Zero The Hero. The album was recorded using Virgin's Manor Mobile studio at the group's house in Voisines. Some of the recordings were made during the full moon. Hillage explains why.

"Most people who are into esoterics and magic, they appreciate the time of the full moon because the tides of your psyche rise and you are open to a particular form of inspiration. The track 'Selene' is all about that. So we always used to enjoy recording on the full moon; that was when we'd do the big jam sessions. I think we did 'The Other Side Of The Sky', the first track on *Angel's Egg*, on the full moon. That's an amazing track, all one live take, no overdubs.

"We used to use it as the intro to the set. Tim would come on and play what you would call now ambient synths and we'd just come on one by one and join in until it crystallised into something."

Now credited as Sub. Capt. Hillage on lewd guitar, Hillage's input was increasing, including his solo showcase of echo guitar architecture, 'Castle In The Clouds', and he was the sole writer of a song that fitted right into Allen's world, 'Never Glid Before'. He also collaborated with Smyth on the Gallic sounding 'Prostitute Poem'.

Gong lost the house in Voisines in 1973 but moved to England where they were installed by Virgin in a new place in Witney, near Oxford. By early 1974, they were already writing material for a new album that would be titled *You*, and played some of it at a Hyde Park Free Festival in June on a bill with Kevin Ayers (with Nico), Chapman Whitney Streetwalkers, Kevin Coyne and G. T. Moore & His Reggae Guitars.

One of the songs from *You* that Gong played that afternoon, 'Master Builder', was based around a riff with a descending seven note lead-in to a nagging on-off two-note figure. "The day Gong collectively wrote that track, it came in my mind and I started singing it to myself and I thought, 'Fuck, this is great!'" Hillage recalls. "Very soon we were all playing it together. It was one of the best musical days; I was thinking, 'This is the greatest thing ever.' It was a very exhilarating and jubilant moment."

When recorded with the whole group, this riff seemed to wind around itself like a Moebius strip and although it's a bit of a stretch to call it jazz rock, it swung and was played with a jazz-like fluidity. On the album it's ushered in by 'Magick Mother Invocation', with Smyth's echoed voice sailing out into space and Allen and others incanting a mantra, heightening a feeling of ritual. Hillage's riff emerges – subtly flanged around the edges – with spiralling synths and an exclamatory solo by Malherbe. There is a sparse section with birdsong, then Allen's vocal phrases in unison with the rest of the band cut across this woodland glade. Back into the riff, Hillage plays a thrilling guitar solo and Moerlen delivers an edge-of-the-seat performance, cutting loose with drum breaks of an elegance and articulation, even at such high velocity, that is quite breathtaking.

The playing on 'Master Builder' is so ecstatic that it really does sound like the greatest thing ever. The other two big instrumental tracks are also spectacular. 'A Sprinkling Of Clouds' rides out on Blake's synth pulses, with Allen's glissando guitar painting a panoramic backdrop and on the lengthy, funky 'The Isle Of Everywhere' the way that Moerlen and Howlett drop beats, add beats and flip the beats around, seemingly telepathically, is astonishing. Overall the level of intuitive group playing on *You* is of such a high standard that few other rock groups could compete.

But Allen was unhappy. He felt that in the process of becoming such an advanced unit, Gong had lost something vital in the process. As he said looking back in 2003: "Gong was more interesting for me at that period when we were still in France rather than afterward with all the Virgin superstars, because there is something rather logical about English rock'n'roll ideas, whereas the French were onto something different. There was a whimsy and light-heartedness, a madness and a willingness to go where the English would never go."

Hillage recognises that Allen's decision was based on "his own personal and mysterious reasons". It's hard to fully understand Allen's comments except that the group, by their instrumental brilliance, rather sidelined his vocals.

Allen left Gong in April 1975 and the group continued in this line-up until the end of the year. Hillage reckons that he had written about 65 per cent of his debut solo album *Fish Rising* while he was still in Khan, but then during his time with Gong he had "discovered atmosphere and ambience" and so the material was further transformed, including lyrical contributions from his partner Miquette Giraudy aka Bambaloni Yoni. And while finishing the album in January 1975 he had been away from the group and hadn't realised that it was beginning to disintegrate, with Tim Blake also leaving amid "ructions".

After Allen's departure, Gong had played some of *Fish Rising* in concert as well as new group material. Hillage was distressed to read in the music press reports that he had ousted Allen in order to take control of the band and get them to play his material. So much so that he left the group six months later.

He played on a couple of songs on Gong's 1976 album *Shamal*, which saw the arrival of keyboard player Patrice Lemoine, with Howlett taking over vocals and more dynamic percussion work by Moerlen and Mireille Bauer, redolent of some of Frank Zappa's arrangements on 'Chandra'.

It's more exotic than spacey, but with some strong tunes and Malherbe's flute-based composition 'Bambooji' evoking sun-drenched terrain. The lyrics are as daft as Allen's, although without his absurd and occasionally ribald sense of humour they passed as rather generic hippie fare.

Further into 1976, Gong's whole ethos changed and they effectively became Pierre Moerlen's group, purveying a classy and characterful blend of groove-based jazz rock on *Gazeuse!* with Allan Holdsworth featuring on guitar along with bass guitarist Francis Moze, who had played on *Flying Teapot*, Moerlen's brother Benoît, Bauer and Malherbe on sax.

Former Rolling Stones guitarist Mick Taylor and ex-Curved Air violinist Darryl Way joined for 1978's *Espresso II* with Hansford Rowe now installed on bass. And so it continued through to the end of the decade, with Moerlen making some ill-advised stabs at vocals on 1979's *Downwind*. The group was now called Pierre Moerlen's Gong to differentiate it from some of Allen's output at the time as he was also using a derivative of the Gong name.

While all this was going on, Hillage was enjoying a time of critical and commercial success in his solo career. Going back to the cosmic keep net, *Fish Rising* had reached number thirty three in the UK charts.

Released in April 1975, the album had a similar feel to *You*, which is hardly surprising considering that recording began at the same studio in September 1974, shortly after the end of the *You* sessions, with the same engineer and largely the same musicians.

Hillage's super hippie image made him an appealing figure, far from the pop mainstream, but who wrote good tunes, could sing well enough and was an exceptionally talented guitarist. His was a post-Hendrix style, although not so overtly bluesy, but still melodic, fluent and exciting. And like Hendrix, with his use of echo and wah-wah it wasn't just the notes, it was about the sound, the glowing, ecstatic sound. And as such he was very much an alternative guitar hero.

What about drugs? One can only assume that he liked a smoke.

"I think it would be fair to say the answer is in the yes direction," he replies.

Did it help him creatively?

"I think you build up a tolerance, and having then built up the tolerance you could question if it made any difference. If you stopped taking stuff, it maybe has more of an effect. It can have an unwanted effect. I have had some mishaps."

The message of the lyrics of *Fish Rising* can be summarised as: "If we look inside ourselves and get it together, all shall be well and all manner of things shall be well." But they were rock lyrics after all and it was clear that more complex thought lay behind them. Hillage always came over as the listener's benign ally, and if he could be accused of having his head in the clouds, he might well have agreed and pointed out that it had taken him some time and effort to get it there. About his lyrics he says: "A lot of people said that it was a lot of old tosh. It was just what I felt like singing about."

Hillage certainly accepted the handover of the post-psychedelic torch that Allen had re-ignited and ran with it. The back cover of *Fish Rising* is packed with Allen-esque stuff. The group is referred to as the Sky Drunk Heart Beat Band and the fish references are done to death with Hillage recast as Steve Hillfish, and Lindsay Cooper from Henry Cow credited with playing "basoonafish". Hillage is depicted on a riverbank playing his acoustic guitar to his piscean pals.

'The Solar Musick Suite' is a paean to the sun and its *"holy mystery"* and commences with a lush, almost aquatic soundworld of bubbling synths and a rather rambling vocal line, but it gets pulled tighter by the section titled 'Canterbury Sunrise' with Hillage playing glissando guitar as an unearthly backdrop and then things really rev up with 'Hiram Afterglid Meets the Dervish'.

In its twisting, eel-like course the 'Dervish' riff is a companion piece to the 'Master Builder' riff, although slightly more complex. Hillage had contributed guitar to a briefly reunited Egg's 1974 album *The Civil Surface* and here Dave Stewart returns the compliment playing a searing, speedy wah–wah fuzz organ solo.

'The Salmon Song' finds the titular fish swimming upstream to the *"source"*, both of the river and, metaphorically, of *"love and light"* and with its billowing, echoed guitar patterns, 'Meditation Of The Snake' expands on 'Castle In The Clouds' from *Angel's Egg*.

For his next album, *L*, Hillage teamed up with Todd Rundgren. Rundgren had made the LSD-fuelled masterpiece *A Wizard, A True Star* in 1973 and was one of the few American artists who was playing what could be described as progressive rock, particularly in his group Utopia, and had since tapped into all musical points from Philadelphia to Alpha Centauri with 1975's *Initiation*, which ranged from the glorious cosmic soul ballad 'Real Man' to the half-hour instrumental suite 'A Treatise On Cosmic Fire'.

Some journalists were seeing this recording session as a meeting between two transatlantic proponents of the Aquarian Age. That idea first came into public view with 'Aquarius' from the musical *Hair*, but this idea of the New Age has since become synonymous with a kind of bland, airbrushed take on esoteric knowledge and its rather anodyne accompanying mood music. But back in the Seventies it was meant to signal a widespread spiritual change and Hillage references it in a number of his songs.

"That's a concept that's gone a bit out of the window now but at the time a lot of people were talking about a new era," says Hillage. "It was an astrological era and moved from the Age of Pisces to the Age of Aquarius, that lasts 2,000 years and all that got supplemented by the Mayan calendar so that was a bit of a damp squib and no one refers to either at the moment. The procession of the equinoxes, that's the technical term for it. It was the latter part of the 20th century, but there was no fixed date."

But the album was an artistic and commerical success. Hillage and Giraudy played with Utopia: Kasim Sulton on bass and John Wilcox on drums, with keyboard player Roger Powell. The album was recorded in Rundgren's studio in Woodstock, New York.

"I made demos and sent some in advance. We rehearsed, then got a track worked out and cut it while it was hot," says Hillage. "They were good guys."

"I was really into Todd at the time and when you work with him you get the T. R. sound. Some producers try to be a bit more invisible and put their stamp on things in a less overt way. I'd left Gong and was looking for a new musical chapter, and this was everything I'd hoped for – and the first time that I'd been to America. It was stimulating from start to finish."

The cover photo finds Hillage, eyes closed, playing his Fender Strat with blinding lights behind him as if he is about to be the subject of an alien abduction. L is a much more muscular album than Fish Rising and fairly stripped down compared to its predecessor's rich, rather cluttered soundscapes.

The centrepiece of the album is the 'Lunar Musick Suite', which starts with Hillage playing a complex figure along with Powell's speedy sequenced synthesizer. Hillage had a preference for fat snare sounds and Wilcox delivers a whomping four-to-the-bar snare beat, the drum fed by Rundgren through an Eventide Harmonizer, an effects unit that David Bowie and Tony Visconti would soon be using on Low. On L Hillage also used it occasionally in conjunction with his guitar.

This frenetic start decelerates to a middle section with Hillage's dramatic chords and typically soaring lead lines and then its mood changes, as against a spacey keyboard backdrop, Don Cherry delivers a fluttering trumpet solo, a series of acrid wisps. Cherry made his name playing with Ornette Coleman and seemed, on the surface, an unexpected participant in a progressive space rock album – on which he also adds tambura, voice and bells.

"Don Cherry was in a very early Gong collaboration as he was based in Europe and had a commune in Sweden, and he had a connection with BYG Records," says Hillage. "A friend of a friend said he'd moved away from Sweden and was in New York and I asked him if he'd like to play on the record for a few days and it was a great honour. That trumpet solo on 'Lunar Musick Suite' is fucking awesome. He's a wonderful man, a very spiritual man."

The album contains three cover versions, Donovan's 'Hurdy Gurdy Man', the mantra 'Om Nama Shivaya' – an invocation of Shiva the principal Hindu deity – and it ends with George Harrison's 'It's All Too Much' from *Yellow Submarine*. That song's lyrical themes of "take me for a trip around the universe as long as I'm back by teatime" felt by 1976 like the charming sentiments of a bygone age.

The album charted at number ten, with coordinated touring and an appearance on BBC Radio 1's *In Concert* in December 1976, during which presenter Pete Drummond enthused – in measured tones – that *L* was "one of the greatest albums of all time in the rock idiom".

Hillage's next step was particularly significant. He teamed up with Malcolm Cecil, who, with Robert Margouleff, as Tonto's Expanding Head Band, played a custom-built synthesizer set-up, TONTO (an acronym for The Original New Timbral Orchestra). Although they only released two albums under this name in the early Seventies, the influential duo went on to produce and play on albums by Stevie Wonder, The Isley Brothers, Stephen Stills, The Doobie Brothers and many more.

The resultant album *Motivation Radio* finds Hillage indulging his interest in UFOs and transmissions from other worlds. It is clearly cut from similar cloth to *L*, with Giraudy now featuring on synthesizer as well as vocals. On 'Light In The Sky' she describes the UFO she has just seen like an excited child.

But the production is cleaner, funkier, more synth and sequencer based. Joe Blocker and Reggie McBride feature on drums and bass respectively, and they were essentially a funk rhythm section. Although more direct, it did rather lack the spacey "otherness" of its predecessors.

The year was 1977, which piqued Hillage's interest in numerology, with he and Giraudy's lucky number being seven. He remembers overdubbing guitar on July 7, 1977 giving 7/7/77. He even persuaded

Virgin to give the album the catalogue number V777 and the cover includes Tarot card number seven The Chariot.

"I remember at the time we thought it would be great to do a gig maybe at Glastonbury, but we were stuck out in America still working on the album." There was a free festival at Glastonbury on July 7, 1977, which led on to the revival of the Glastonbury Festival.

"It was quite audacious to come out with *Motivation Radio* after *L*," says Hillage. "We got a kick out of that. It was provoked in part by some strange experiences we had on our big American tour off the *L* album supporting ELO. Our sound engineer at the time was massively into funk. He lived in a farm in Surrey and would have all-night parties, a bit like prototype raves, but playing mostly stuff like Bootsy's Rubber Band and George Clinton.

"We'd meet a lot of fans after the shows and so on this American tour people would be saying, 'What are you listening to Steve, what's your favourite stuff? [*in exaggerated American accent*] King Crim-San? Van Der Graaf Gen-era-tor?' I said, 'No, I'm really into Earth Wind & Fire and Bootsy's Rubber Band. And they're going, 'Steve, you're into disco? Oh Man!' I'm thinking, 'Yeah, well, what's the problem?'

"I was thinking that there was a musical apartheid going on out there: white boy rock and what white boys were supposed to play and there was all this black stuff out there and I thought, 'Sod this, I'm going to try to pull it all together,' as that was part of my musical universe at the time. That was what led to *Motivation Radio* and why I got a kick out of putting that out after *L*."

(In the context of the conversation, Hillage used the word "apartheid" quite loosely and with an element of humour, to describe a division of taste. It's only when it's put in print that it feels perhaps too strong a word to use without qualification. There was, of course, nothing to stop any musician from playing the music they wanted with whomever they wanted, irrespective of their racial background – as Hillage himself proved. And certainly by the end of 1977 it was not unusual for record collections of UK teens to include albums by progressive rock groups alongside funk bands like Funkadelic and Parliament, as well as reggae and jazz funk or jazz rock, and some punk.)

Although *Motivation Radio* was funkier and different, it wasn't *that* funky and it lacked a bit of grit. Reviews were mixed but generally favourable and it made a respectable number twenty-eight in the UK charts.

Hillage was disappointed that after he had got an "in" into the American market with *L*, this different blend of his music just didn't have the same appeal to that audience. He recalls some exceptional UK gigs with Joe Blocker and bass player Curtis Robertson, but the US tour was cancelled and so the group was forced to disband. "Joe and Curtis were still over here, so I thought, 'Quick let's get into the studio and do the other tracks,' and that's how the *Green* album happened quite rapidly after *Motivation Radio*."

Hillage and Giraudy had written the best part of two albums in the spring of 1977. They were initially called *Red*, a punchy selection of songs that became *Motivation Radio*, and another set, *Green*, that was linked more towards Mother Nature.

GREEN

Original Label: Virgin
Producer: Nick Mason & Steve Hillage
Recorded: December 1977–February 1978
Released: April 1978
Chart position: 30 (UK)

Green is important as it's one of Hillage's best solo albums and also because it came out in the summer of 1978, when punk was still in full swing, and made number thirty in the album charts. So while attention might have been diverted away from Hillage and his ilk, it proved that a space rock paean to Mother Nature and ley lines still had its place in the zeitgeist.

Hillage was largely well treated in the music papers, one assumes because although his ideas were unfashionable among the sneering classes, he was completely unabashed and put them forward with articulacy and slightly geezer-ish humour. His support for Greenpeace, particularly their Save The Whale campaign, was mentioned in the press and elicited a few good-natured jibes, including a cartoon of a whale wearing a t-shirt bearing the legend 'Save Steve Hillage'.

Hillage recalls that *Green* was released at the time that the Green Party formed in Germany and although that was purely coincidental, the party loved it and decided that it was linked to their ethos, all of which helped to make it Hillage's best-selling album in Germany by a long way. It also references sacred geometry on the cover graphics, in which meanings are attributed to certain geometric shapes.

The album was co-produced and beautifully recorded by Pink Floyd drummer Nick Mason. "He was a great person to work with," says Hillage. "He definitely put his stamp on it. Hats off." If any album ever evoked summer sunlight streaming through a lush canopy of leaves, or illuminating fronds of seaweed swaying in aquatic currents, it's *Green*. The album was recorded at Ridge Farm, Dorking and at Pink Floyd's Britannia Row Studios.

The album begins with 'Sea Nature', which is actually looser and funkier than *Motivation Radio*, with Blocker and Robertson constantly inventive in terms of nuance, and ·Hillage manipulating controlled feedback at the start together with the watery sound of the glissando guitar in the background, and Giraudy's synths bubbling up from the deep. But the sound is warmer, more radiant than its predecessor.

Here Hillage sings about devas or plant spirits and makes references to the unfeasibly giant vegetables that were grown at the Findhorn spiritual community on the east Scottish coast, which he and Giraudy visited. It must be one of the very few songs in the entire rock canon that references cauliflowers.

"We were aware of Findhorn since the late Sixties, it was quite a celebrated place," Hillage recalls. "There were pamphlets and tracts and mentions in various books. The thing about cauliflowers, and everything on *Green*, was a Findhorn reference.

"They meditatively contact the spiritual entities that are connected to the plant beings. You could say that someone who has got green fingers, who is great at growing things, has got that purely by feeling and intuition without any mumbo-jumbo about devas. But for them it worked, definitely."

'Palm Trees (Love Guitar)' finds him playing "straight" guitar and also through a Roland guitar synth. It's a relatively simple construction, with Hillage and his object of affection sitting together as the *"New Age"* grows. But it's *Green*'s most affecting song, with lovely chord sequences and some exquisite soloing.

The instrumental 'Ley Lines To Glassdom' is more guitar and guitar synth over Mason's slow, tolling echoed snare drum beats. Hillage has actually experienced the energy of ley lines, particularly when he and Giraudy went to visit Findhorn.

"Near Forres there's a mound, like Glastonbury Tor, and it's a really hot magnetic ley lines spot. We had quite close contacts with the late, great John Michell who wrote two big books called *City Of Revelations* and *View Over Atlantis*, which explore this whole area in great depth, particularly in Britain. It's very connected with Chinese spiritual philosophy – feng shui and dragon lines. In Japan a lot of people are into this concept and the Mayan Indians in Mexico, between their cities, they had very long straight roads, similar things called sacbes. It seems to be something that's pretty universal."

On 'Ether Ships', Hillage's echoed guitar lines give a near-mechanical, multi-layered, onrushing effect akin to synthesizer sequencers. He was fascinated by the mantric repetition in the music of German groups Neu!, Kraftwerk and Can.

Few guitarists were using this effect as a pulse that shaped the composition, although John Martyn employed it to great effect in the Seventies, particularly on 'Outside In'. But the one who really caught Hillage's ear was Manuel Göttsching, the former guitarist with Ash Ra Tempel who had used delays while playing in the group, but took them to a new level of sophistication on his 1975 album *Inventions For Electric Guitar*. Hillage had hung out with Göttsching in Berlin and he was an audible – and acknowledged – influence on 'Ether Ships'.

"I can relate to it because I liked playing with electronics, I like playing with synths, I always liked playing with fixed beats as well as with live musicians," says Hillage. "I find it difficult to understand why more people in the so-called progressive rock sphere didn't at least partially embrace electronic music. With an echo guitar, if you get the tempo absolutely dead right, when you're playing it you go into some kind of special hole in time and space."

The album ends with the re-emergence of the riff from 'Master Builder' that so excited Hillage, this time in a rearranged version called 'The Glorious Om Riff'.

"I had a particularly strong attachment to it and I started jamming it with Jo and Curtis and they were playing really well, so I thought, 'This has to be done.' The bottom line is I wanted to keep playing it as I enjoyed it."

Green was the last album that Hillage did in this kind of space rock style and *Open*, released in 1979, was more electronic in feel. He and Miquette Giraudy also signed off from the Seventies with an album of abstract ambient synth and guitar, *Rainbow Dome Musick*, which they recorded to be played at the Rainbow Dome at the Festival For Mind-Body-Spirit at Olympia, London, in April 1979.

Although viewed as something of a bonus release at the time – it came at a budget price – *Rainbow Dome Musick* took on a life of its own in the Nineties as a club chill-out favourite.

"When we did *Rainbow Dome…* we wanted to do a sort of neutral zone. There were all these stalls all touting their philosophical remedies. It was a bit farcical, like a spiritual supermarket," Hillage recalls. "We were making this environment for people to relax – it was the original chill-out room. We'd make sure we were fully grounded and had the right energy co-ordinates set. Set the controls for the heart of the rainbow dome!"

CHAPTER 38

The Art School Dance Goes on Forever: Brian Eno, Roxy Music, Quiet Sun and 801

In the Sixties, the influence of the British art school on pop and rock music was considerable. Although it was not the kind of schooling that would guarantee work for its graduates, it at least gave young creative types a temporary buffer against the harsh realities of the job market. And in this time they could develop their creative skills in the fields of visual art, or in the art of rock'n'roll as was the case with The Rolling Stones' Keith Richards and Ronnie Wood, Dick Taylor of The Pretty Things, Pete Townshend of The Who and many, many more.

Geoffrey Richardson, violinist and multi-instrumentalist with Caravan, had been lined up by his father for a job at the Electricity Board in Leicester, but fell in with a crowd from Nuneaton Art School and enrolled there in 1966 before going to Manchester College Of Art and then onto Winchester School Of Art.

"In the Sixties because [art schools] were independent establishments and it was not a degree course, there was so much freedom," say Richardson. "You were getting a grant, you were in full-time education and your status was pretty much the same as a university student. You were taught technical procedures, but you had to find your thing, your mojo, your theme, your inspiration. So it was inevitable that anyone interested in rock music or who played an instrument would get together."

Brian Eno had grown up in the Suffolk town of Woodbridge, near the coast on the River Debden. He attended Ipswich Art School and then Winchester School Of Art, from which he graduated in 1969. He had grown up entranced by the soundworld of rock'n'roll and doowop, but rather than trying to replicate that sort of music, he took a different tack, taking modern rock music and applying ideas to it that had originated in the avant-garde.

"I inherited Brian Eno's area at Winchester and I also inherited his chair," Richardson recalls. "Wish I'd kept it. It was an annotated chair; he had written all over it. People like him flourished at art school. But Brian was also very much at loggerheads with the staff as they were abstract expressionist painters and printmakers, while Brian was sitting there having ideas. There was a thin line between being a conceptual artist and just sitting around doing nothing, as far as they were concerned."

Tom Phillips, Eno's tutor at Ipswich, introduced the young student to the ideas of American avant-garde composer John Cage. Eno was particularly drawn towards Cage's dislike of virtuosity and his searching for "a way of living out your philosophy and calling it art".

A precocious youth who cut a foppish figure, Eno also dabbled in performance art and, as an entertainments officer, booked groups to appear at the school. Since his childhood he had been fascinated with recording and manipulating sound with tape recorders, and he was drawn to the tape loop experiments of Steve Reich and Terry Riley. He was also struck by how music could be produced by systems and processes using a limited amount of material.

"I've always been impressed by art that didn't use much to produce quite a lot," Eno says. "Mondrian, for instance, was the first painter that I really loved. I was very young, I wasn't even a teenager then, and I remember thinking, 'How can something so simple be so powerful to me?' So I was always inclined in that direction rather than the opposite direction, which might be to throw in everything and the kitchen sink. Then it's not surprising that you are impressed by the result. I like it when there isn't much there."

Being of limited technical ability, Eno thought of applying these ideas to making music that could bypass the expectations of the progressive rock era. All this might have amounted to little more than garden shed tinkering, except that in doing so he became a rock star.

Eno has said that when he got onto a Bakerloo Line tube train at Elephant & Castle in December 1970, his decision as to which door to walk through changed his life. He ended up on a seat opposite an old friend, Andy Mackay, who he had first met in 1968. Mackay was now playing in the first incarnation of a group that would become Roxy Music. Knowing of Eno's facility with a reel-to-reel tape recorder, he explained that they wanted to make some demos and asked if he would do the honours.

Mackay also had an early VCS3 suitcase synthesizer. He agreed to lend it to Eno, who was soon playing the instrument with the group and using it to alter the sound of the other instruments.

Vocalist and pianist Bryan Ferry had moved down from Newcastle to London where he had recently been sacked from a post teaching ceramics at a girls' school. He also came from an art school background and had a pop art sensibility – he had studied with Richard Hamilton – as well as a love of the glamour of old Hollywood and the suave, timeless classics of Cole Porter and Noël Coward. The group's initial guitarist Davy O'List, who had played with The Nice, was only briefly with the band before Phil Manzanera – who had initially failed his audition – took over, and the group employed a succession of bass guitarists.

Manzanera's friend Charles Hayward, who had played drums in their school group Quiet Sun, also auditioned for Roxy Music.

"There was one thing that was more like a tape piece by Eno. He had a way of getting everyone to play off the tape and play parts that went against it, so I'd pick up the pulse from the delays," Hayward recalls. "I enjoyed playing that and I think Eno enjoyed my playing on that, but I never ever heard them do it again. I'm pretty sure it was me who gave them their first ever gig, which was for the Young Friends of the Tate Gallery, for I was on the committee. Nick Serota was the chair."

Hayward was called back, but the successful applicant was Paul Thompson, a particularly propulsive rock drummer. He was a Geordie like Ferry, but had come in fresh from working as a building site labourer.

"I booked a proto-Roxy Music to come and play in the hall at Winchester for the college bop," says Richardson. "It seemed a fully formed rock group with Brian doing the PA, mixing vocals and twiddling electronics, making strange noises."

Roxy Music's demos gained them the attention of *Melody Maker* assistant editor Richard Wiliams, DJ John Peel and EG Management. EG brokered a tentative deal with hip independent record label Island, but some at the company remained unconvinced by this uncategorisable, arty, rather arch music. Label head Chris Blackwell was finally swayed when he saw roughs of the sleeve artwork to their self-titled 1972 debut album, which featured model Kari-Ann Moller, recumbent on a white surface, with some gold discs rather cheekily placed in shot, looking up imploringly and erotically at the viewer.

King Crimson's Peter Sinfield produced *Roxy Music*, and their stylistic pile-up was most brilliantly portrayed on 'Re-Make/Re-Model'. Ostensibly a love song, it has a mutant boogie-woogie-style piano verse over a driving, stripped-down four-snare-beats-per-bar drum rhythm which has something of The Velvet Underground about it. Ferry's obscure object of desire is an attractive woman he had seen getting into a car he had once owned but had sold second-hand, the backing vocals relaying the number plate: CPL 593H.

The central instrumental passage sounds like a pop art-style musical collage taped together with the joins all showing. Andy Mackay veers back and forth between R&B honking and jazz skronk, Manzanera plays abrasive non-blues figures, and Eno makes action painting synth squiggles, all three of them vying for space.

In 1972 Roxy Music had emerged somewhere between progressive rock and glam rock, gleefully helping themselves to the contents of the dressing up box. One of the most inspired images was Paul Thompson, who with a fake leopardskin sash, was presented as a glam version of a Victorian circus strongman.

Roxy Music appealed to the Heads and the teenies alike and had a Top 10 hit single in 1972 with 'Virginia Plain', a literate, witty, trashy piece of pop with a sexy synth break from Eno, who appeared to be loving it all.

The fact that there was a Brian and Bryan in the band resulted in the former just calling himself Eno. 'Eno' was actually a good old Suffolk surname with Huguenot roots – albeit uncommon outside the county – and Brian had grown up a postman's son. This was all unknown at the time and his unusual moniker made him even stranger and more otherworldly – and after all, few exotically dressed space beings are called Brian. But when he revealed his full name to be Brian Peter George St John Le Baptiste De La Salle Eno, this made him stranger still.

Eno positively flaunted his lack of technical ability, giving himself the title of "non-musician". This was a shocking admission to make in the heyday of the keyboard wizard. And while his inclusion in a book about progressive rock might seem anomalous, he was operating at a level where his ideas were genuinely progressive and influential on the development of music, which included working with some progressive rock musicians. He had already added VCS3 synthesizer to 'Gloria Gloom' on Matching Mole's *Little Red Record* (1972) while still with Roxy Music at the invitation of that group's bass guitarist Bill MacCormick, who was a friend of Manzanera's and had met Eno at sessions for the first Roxy Music album. It was at these sessions that Eno also first met King Crimson guitarist Robert Fripp.

Meanwhile, back at Winchester Art School... "The visiting lecturers thought that they could help by putting up a Quo Vadis board and scaring the life out of us, so we could see where the previous year's third year had gone," Richardson recalls. "So you had 'painter and decorator', 'dole', 'dustman' what the people were doing, all named — and then there was 'Brian Eno: rock star'.

"They said, 'Learn some practical skills like painting and decorating, because you are leaving next year and you are going to be fucked.' I remember a tutor saying, 'That Brian Eno, he's cracked it. Don't bother about post grad, the music business is the way forward, you'll not be signing on.' And by the time I had my degree show I had joined Spirogyra the folk rock group. They thought that was it, I was in the relative mainstream."

But Eno's tenure as a rock star was brief. He stayed in Roxy Music for only two albums, leaving in 1973 after *For Your Pleasure*, but in that time he made a considerable visual and musical impact, preening around onstage with ever more flamboyant costumes and make-up, his role like some glam ship's figurehead. Ferry was the traditionally handsome lead singer but Eno had the more striking image. He looked cooler, stranger, as he fiddled about with his tape recorders and produced seemingly random sounds out of his VCS3 synth.

Brian Eno left Roxy Music in February 1973 of his own volition, although relations between himself and Ferry had become difficult. He immediately set about making a solo album, *Here Come The Warm Jets*, which involved some members of Roxy Music, with MacCormick on bass and Robert Fripp on guitar, playing a particularly abrasive solo on 'Baby's On Fire'. Although some of the material is rather slight, it's a brash, flamboyant collection of songs, full of character and pizzaz, and showed Eno to be a capable singer as well, albeit with a tendency towards a rather shrill and camp delivery.

Eno toured for a while in late 1973 backed by The Winkies, taking on the role of catsuit-clad pop star, singing songs like 'Baby's On Fire' and Peggy Lee's 'Fever', while girls in the audience attempted to paw him. But despite appearances, being the centre of attention no longer appealed and live work was put on hold after the tour.

"I just got bored with it," he says. "I like reading and writing and talking, that kind of thing. And that kind of lifestyle doesn't permit much of that. I don't particularly like being the subject of adulation."

An indicator of the way things were going was an album Eno had already begun recording with Robert Fripp in late 1972, *No Pussyfooting*, which finally got released by Island in late 1973, shortly after *Here Come The Warm Jets*. If there was ever a poll conducted to ascertain what album had most disappointed expectant fans, it would surely come near the top of the list. Those who thought they might get an album's worth of '21st Century Schizoid Man' meets 'Virginia Plain' instead got an album of

513

tape delay loops, with Fripp soloing over the top. This was achieved by using two Revox tape recorders in tandem. Eno gleefully announced that the duo's follow-up, 1975's *Evening Star*, was going to be even more monotonous – and parts of it certainly were. Now regarded as a proto-ambient landmark, *No Pussyfooting* was so minimal, so unlike a rock album, that some hated it.

Robert Fripp: "*No Pussyfooting* was undermined by EG Management and Island Music, because it might have compromised Eno's commercial career out of Roxy Music. So it was not released in America – it was eventually exported years later and it was released on a budget label, HELP, in England, so it really wouldn't get much attention."

Eno recorded the more fully fleshed out, song-based *Taking Tiger Mountain (By Strategy)* in 1974, and the following year he was mixing songs with instrumental mood pieces to inspired effect on the wonderful *Another Green World*, on which he plays synths, keyboards, guitars and treated drum machines. He had such a knack for conjuring up sensual, textured, atmospheric pieces that his non-musician status looked increasingly imperiled.

He was at ease working with a host of "proper" musicians like drummer Phil Collins of Genesis and Percy Jones the bass player in jazz rock group Brand X with whom Collins also played. He would suggest ideas and let the musicians play, and then use the raw material as a basis for a track, or invite the likes of Fripp and John Cale to add parts to songs. He oversaw recordings with a disparate cast of musicians that included guitarists Paul Rudolph of The Pink Fairies and Fred Frith from Henry Cow. MacCormick also played on some of Eno's Seventies material.

"He tended to put you in circumstances with people that you had never played with before," MacCormick recalls. "I think he tried to take you out of your comfort zone in that respect, which was no bad thing.'

Eno was cropping up all over the place in recording sessions, sometimes with the deck of cards he had designed with artist Peter Schmidt, *Oblique Strategies: Over 100 Worthwhile Dilemmas*.

With phrases like "Honour your mistake as your hidden intention" and "If given a choice, do both", these were designed to be used as an aid in unblocking the creative process, somewhere between the I-Ching and the Tarot, and based on Eastern notions of coincidence and synchronicity.

So if you drew a card you could say that as it had been picked at random, it could have been any card and therefore the whole process means nothing. The alternative view is the fact that you picked that card at that time is significant in itself. That's a matter for discussion, but MacCormick recalls that on one particular occasion, during the recording sessions for Robert Wyatt's 1975 album *Ruth Is Stranger Than Richard*, its message was particularly apt.

"We were mixing at The Manor in Oxfordshire and it was a residential studio, so everyone who had been playing on it was still there," MacCormick says. "Eno isn't a fan of jazz, and there were [saxophonists] Gary Windo and George Khan, the two out-and-out jazzers, [drummer] Laurie Allan, me and Robert, and Alfie [Benge]. We were in the control room and there was a discussion between George and Gary to which, every now and again, Brian made some contribution. Robert was sitting in the studio, they were arguing over his bloody album, and I was watching him getting a bit irritable about the whole thing.

"So after a while of this going on I said, 'I think there's only one solution. Brian, have you got your *Oblique Strategies?*' [The card he drew said] 'Tape your mouths'. So I said, 'Right there we are. Nobody says another word.' Absolutely perfect!"

By early 1975 Roxy Music had recorded four albums and had four singles in the Top 20, and were one of the UK's highest profile rock acts. During a break from activities, Manzanera recorded a solo album, *Diamond Head*, a high-quality set of songs and instrumentals with contributions from Wyatt, Eno and MacCormick. 'Miss Shapiro' finds a metallic mesh of guitars ushering in Eno delivering his cryptic lyrics, full of word plays, some knowingly clunky, with *"Miss Shapiro"* found alongside *"Missa Nobis"* and *"miss a dinner"*, some striking images, which fiercely resisted logical interpretation, and a doo-wop style backing refrain of *"Shop steward"*. Along with *Here Come The Warm Jets*, it gives a – very – hypothetical glimpse of what Roxy Music might have sounded like if the other Bryan had left and Eno had taken over his role. The instrumental highlight is the majestic title track, demonstrating why with the attack and sustain, and melodic invention of his playing, Manzanera had quickly become established as one of the UK's foremost rock guitarists. And one who didn't forget his mates.

Quiet Sun formed in south London in 1970 with Bill MacCormick on bass, Manzanera on guitar, Steve Jarrett on keyboards and Charles Hayward on drums. Playing largely instrumental music with more than a passing nod at the jazzy ideas turned into riffs that hallmarked Soft Machine, they were barely out of their teens when they broke up. But in the spare studio time he had booked to record *Diamond Head* Manzanera brought the freshly reassembled group into the studio to record their repertoire.

"I think we had about one rehearsal, ran through the stuff and in the studio we did them in just a few takes, some of them were one-offs," says MacCormick.

Eno was present, coming into the studio to help Jarrett with his synthesizer and "advising and sprinkling his fairy dust over. He is just a good guy to have around in the studio, because he makes life interesting," says MacCormick.

Hearing the album, *Mainstream*, which in terms of sales was close behind Cat Stevens and Bad Company after its release in 1975, it's surprising that the group hadn't got signed up in 1971. Hayward gives these reasons.

"We hired a back room at the Fox On The Hill, Denmark Hill," Hayward recalls. "We did an audition for Hemdale, a media company that David Hemmings owned. Our concession then was that Bill bought a new pair of loon pants. I don't think we had the presentation skills, really, we were guys in roll neck pullovers. We'd lead sheltered lives and we didn't understand that a lot of it was about going to the Scotch Of St James and hanging around.

"In 1975 we were playing the same material but doing it much harder, much tougher on the record. We'd grown up and our balls had dropped. Everyone developed their ear in different ways so everyone's playing was more present."

801 LIVE
Original Label: Island
Producer: 801
Recorded: September 3, 1976, at Queen Elizabeth Hall, London
Released: November 1976
Chart position: 52 (UK)

In early 1976, during another Roxy Music hiatus, Manzanera was working on a solo project, *Listen Now*, with MacCormick on bass and vocals and his brother, the journalist Ian MacDonald, who was a lyricist on the quiet. They had recorded some sessions with Bill Bruford – which in the end were not used – and Fairport Convention and top session drummer Dave Mattacks. They were looking for a specific style and engineer Rhett Davies suggested a "brilliant" teenage drummer he had seen called Simon Phillips and he was asked to play. Curved Air keyboard player Francis Monkman had also played on the sessions. The recording was beginning to drag a bit and so Manzanera decided to have a break from recording and have a busman's holiday playing some festival shows.

Manzanera got in touch with Eno, who was asked to feature on lead vocals, keyboards and guitar – a cheap beginner's model known as a Starway. Eno insisted on a balance between technical and "feel" musicians. Lloyd Watson, who had played as support to Roxy Music and was a friend of Eno's, was drafted in on slide guitar alongside MacCormick, Monkman and Phillips. The group was called 801 after an Eno song 'The True Wheel' (on *Taking Tiger Mountain [By Strategy]*), based on a dream in which a group of female backing vocalists sing that they are "*the 801*", which is the "*central shaft.*"

"It was such an eclectic, strange collection of people with such diverse backgrounds and it worked," says Phillips. "It was a really cool set-up."

After a month of rehearsal in Island Studios in Hammersmith, the musicians in 801 had achieved a remarkable empathy. The line-up played only three gigs, West Runton Pavilion on the Norfolk coast, Reading Festival and the Queen Elizabeth Hall on London's South Bank.

"It is the only band I have ever been in when every gig we played was brilliant," says MacCormick. The idea from the outset was that it would incorporate a mix of Eno and Manzanera's material with some cover versions. MacCormick played the riff from The Kinks' 'You Really Got Me' at the end of a song in rehearsal, and so that went into the set. He also came up with the idea of playing a version of The Beatles' 'Tomorrow Never Knows' from their 1966 album *Revolver*.

'East Of Asteroid' is an amalgamation of Quiet Sun's 'Mummy Was An Asteroid, Daddy Was A Small Non-Stick Kitchen Utensil' and Manzanera's 'East Of Echo' from *Diamond Head*. This was one of the trickier pieces to play.

"One of the great treats was trying to get Brian to play in odd time signatures," says MacCormick. "'It goes like this, Brian – 1-2-3-4-5-6.' He used to get quite ratty when we would count it for him, and say 'I can't do it!'. But eventually he got it."

The group completely won over the crowd at Reading Festival, although disaster was narrowly averted when Monkman, who had been visiting his father, had got stuck in traffic and arrived three minutes before show time.

"I think the audience probably gave us the benefit of the doubt as the sun came out as we went onstage," says MacCormick. "We basked in the fact that the sun was being cheered.

"A friend of mine was there and took a lot of photographs, and because you had to be off at a certain time, there was a clock, like an old school clock, on the right hand side of the stage. A friend of mine took a lot of photographs and on one you can see it's one minute past eight."

The third concert, at the Queen Elizabeth Hall, was recorded for a live album. "We were due to play four or five festivals in France, each of which were going to be paying about five grand, which in 1976 was a decent sum of money," MacCormick explains. "And they were all going to be in the space of about ten days. The first one was going to be at Orange in the south of France, but there was a riot and [French premiere] Valéry Giscard D'Estaing banned all of them for the summer, so that was us fucked. The way that Phil made sense of it was to record the Queen Elizabeth Hall gig and release it and make the rest of the band some money."

The album opens in spectacular fashion with Manzanera's 'Lagrima' from *Diamond Head*. The solo acoustic original is transformed by his electric guitar fed through all manner of effects units and Eno's synth, which gives it a huge panoramic sweep. This high drama leads into 'T.N.K. (Tomorrow Never Knows)'. Firstly, Monkman's keyboards nibble at a few notes, followed by Watson's slippery slide guitar and MacCormick's swaggering bass lines.

This activity is resolved by Phillips' graceful, dextrous groove, which pulls it all tautly into a kind of space-funk version of the original, with Eno adding a two-note, siren-like synth motif and singing in harmony with Watson and MacCormick. In an inspired move, Monkman's lightning-fast electric piano lines reference and replicate the melodic lines of the tape loops used in the original George Martin production.

The set moved through a shortened version of Charles Hayward's 'RongWrong' from Quiet Sun's *Mainstream*, 'Sombre Reptiles' from *Another Green World*, and rearranged and souped-up versions of 'Baby's On Fire' and 'Miss Shapiro', the latter segued with 'You Really Got Me', featuring a one-note Eno keyboard line and demonstrating that he could more than hold his own as a lead vocalist in such an outfit. The album ends with Eno's 'Third Uncle', a relentless two-chord thrash transformed here into an unstoppable, high-velocity juggernaut.

801 Live was released just over two months after the Queen Elizabeth Hall concert. It might seem an odd choice for a featured album in this book, when *Listen Now*, which was finished after this flurry of activity, and released as an 801 album in 1977, is such an engaging and imaginative album.

But there is something both dazzlingly brilliant and slightly poignant about *801 Live*, which puts it in its shadow. MacCormick rightly notes that it would have been more in keeping with the time if 801 had been a jamming band. But *801 Live* is concise, exciting, brilliantly played and stands as one of the best live albums of the Seventies. Manzanera's playing is thrilling throughout and few would contest his assertion that *801 Live* is one of the highlights of his career.

It was one of the most promising projects of the whole progressive era, showing what could be achieved with a mix of technique, feel and ideas. In the free newspaper that was given out to the Reading Festival crowd, the group claimed that 801 was destined to be a "central shaft" of European music, but it was an of-the-moment assemblage when six musicians came together and showed what could be done. However, commitments meant that this version of 801 disappeared almost as fast as it had been put together, although a group touring material largely based on *Listen Now* was active in 1977.

By the summer of 1976 something new was in the air. The first, self-titled, Ramones album had been released and the group had just played in London, their goofy minimalist rock quite unlike anything that had been heard before. Meanwhile 801 was a supergroup of sorts and a late flowering of art rock, progressive rock – call it what you will – at its most potent.

Commenting on the live version of 'Diamond Head' on YouTube, Hiroyuki Takaoka wrote: "I was shocked in listening to this beautiful piece in my youth. Many prog rock listeners were seeking for [the] next stage."

As it was, the musicians all went back to their primary activities. Monkman went on to join the classically influenced all-star progressive band Sky, which also featured guitarist John Williams. They had a hit with a rock version of Bach's *Toccata And Fugue In D Minor* as 'Toccata' in 1980, which took us back to the old rocking-up-the-classics approach, which now seemed both tired and rather pointless. But such are the subtle variations in supergroups. And of course, musicians like everyone else, need to earn a living.

CHAPTER 39

Divertimento No.6: Notes on Festivals

In her 1969 song 'Woodstock', Joni Mitchell uses a device, often found in traditional folk song, where the narrator meets a traveller on the road. In this case she enquires where he is going and he tells her that he is journeying to Yasgur's Farm to make camp on the land and to set his soul free.

The traveller senses an imminent change in society and feels part of a connected network of kindred free spirits who have the idea of setting a vast, complex metaphysical machinery in motion, which will drive us all towards a better, more enlightened future.

But first, he says, we must get back to *"the Garden"*, to a new Eden, a prelapsarian idyll from which he can build this vision. The song remains an elegantly phrased and heartfelt vision of hope. The only thing that's odd about it all is that this enlightened traveller's first port of call should be a rock festival.

The Woodstock Festival ran for four days in August 1969 at the farm of Max Yasgur, near Bethel in New York State, with an estimated attendance of something like 500,000, although so many got in without paying that it was hard to be certain. The festival was billed as "Three days of music and peace... and love". There was also a lot of mud, in which some freaks frolicked, but there were no major incidents of violence, and images remain of semi-naked flower children, smiling hazily and flashing peace signs.

If Woodstock seemed like a dry run for a new society in microcosm, there were bad vibes aplenty just up ahead at the one-day festival at the Altamont Speedway in California in December that year. An audience member was stabbed to death during the set by The Rolling Stones, and other footage shows the far less tragic, but still jaw-dropping sight of Jefferson Airplane singer Marty Balin altercating with some Hell's Angels – who, in a spectacularly misguided move, were employed as security guards and given as much beer as they could drink – before being dragged offstage and beaten unconscious.

This ugly gathering has been cited as the end of the Sixties dream, but the whole idea of Woodstock was so enduring that although Altamont was the ultimate bummer, it was also registered as (hopefully) a blip in proceedings. The counterculture wasn't going to give up that easily and Woodstock continued to cast a long shadow for many years, with festivals always seen as a brief portal into a different way of being – to a soundtrack of good music – and a brief reminder of what straight society could be like if the hippies took over and ran the show.

Wind forward to Reading Festival 1976 and a fight is taking place over festival etiquette. The question is, do you stand up and watch a group, maybe dance, and at least invigorate those stiff limbs that have been set in a cross-legged position on cold ground for too long, but in doing so, knowingly obliterate the vision of those still in their sedentary position behind you and who now cannot see anything onstage? Or do you remain seated?

With no consensus, this prompted some of those who had been shouting "Siddown!" to no avail, to pelt those standing up with missiles: clods of earth, stones, empty beer cans, and beer cans that had been filled with urine so as to avoid having to pick one's way through thousands of people to the foul smelling quagmire that surrounded the overflowing urinals. These made particularly hideous missiles.

Apart from the cans, this could have been a battle between two tribes of early humanoid primates. But it was the cans that caused the damage. A young man was knocked out cold by someone hurling a Watney's Party Four can, while others had to seek medical attention for injuries sustained in this barrage.

These assailants were almost certainly the same numbskulls who had thrown similar missiles at The Mighty Diamonds the previous afternoon. The reggae music that the Virgin Front Line label was promoting might have been hip, but that was no consolation to thousands of those assembled who wanted some hard rock action. To their eternal credit, the group kept filling the Berkshire air with their sweet three-part harmonies. One puny teenaged hairy yelled "Fuck off!", while holding a Deep Purple *Stormbringer* poster aloft, which, sadly, tells its own story. And whereas the crowd's reaction might have been simply racist, such hostilities were extended in the following year to a white band who didn't fit their bill, Wayne County & The Electric Chairs.

"Siddown!"

DJ John Peel traditionally played records over the festival PA to fill the occasionally lengthy gaps between the groups playing onstage. He wrote in *Sounds* about the 1977 festival, noting that the crowd had not been prepared to tolerate the "contemporary whimsies" of the Electric Chairs and had pelted them with mud. He continued: "Sunday night at Reading is beginning to take on several ritual aspects. There are the disgraceful chants which insist that I, as compere, am miraculously transformed into a key part of the female anatomy; there is the drunken bellowing of 'Hey Jude' and 'Nellie The Elephant'; the menacing growl that follows the first bars of whatever fearful record by The Brotherhood Of Man is currently being flogged to death on Radio 1."

Yes, the crowd really did chant, "John Peel's a cunt", over and over and over and over again. At other lulls in proceedings, punters would also habitually shout out "Wally!" for reasons that no one seemed able to ascertain.

Reading started off as the National Jazz Festival and was originally staged in Richmond in 1961, before moving to a number of sites, including Sunbury and Plumpton Racecourses, and eventually finding its home at the Thameside site in Reading in 1971. In the early to mid-Seventies it put on mainly progressive and hard rock acts, but in the late Seventies it purveyed a rather uneasy mix of New Wave and hard rock, and by 1980 it had become almost exclusively a heavy rock festival.

A *Melody Maker* article, "The Metal Flies Thick And Fast", which covered the 1980 Reading Festival, referred to rival factions in the audience trampling big Party Four cans flat then spinning them at each other like Frisbees. Clearly evolution was taking place.

It's said that all the world's population could, theoretically, fit onto the 148 square miles of the Isle Of Wight. In 1970 it must have felt to the residents like that was actually happening. There had been a rock festival on the island in the previous two years, but this time it was estimated that between 6–700,000 people turned up. Due to opposition by the island's horrified populace, the organisers were only given one option and so the site was moved to Afton Down, which was overlooked by a large hill. The festival was run over five days and news spread that you could basically see it for free, albeit at a distance.

Typically, festivals like the Isle Of Wight were moneymaking concerns and their very nature attracted freaks who paid to get in and even freakier freaks, who played outside for free, and just turned up to see what was happening. One of the latter was Nik Turner, who played sax and flute with Hawkwind. These are his reminiscences.

"The day before the Isle Of Wight Festival, we told loads of people and in the morning we filled up the van. They were all fans we hung out with and who supported the band. And so we just bought a van ticket.

We were happy to ferry them across to the festival. It cost us some money on the ferry, but we just chipped in from the gig before.

"We played outside in this big inflatable dome called Canvas City as a protest because of what we thought were exorbitant prices, and the bad facilities the organisers, the Foulk Brothers, had supplied for the people. We felt quite happy about staging a protest and playing music for the people who couldn't afford to go into the festival. We didn't get paid, we didn't really ask for any money. That wasn't what it was about.

"Subsequently the fences got pulled down on the festival site. I think there were a lot of French anarchists there and White Panthers, protest groups that were going around at the time, with Hells Angels, and Mick Farren was at the forefront.

"It was a bit of a drug festival. You couldn't avoid consuming drugs because every liquid that was there had some LSD in it. Several people got freaked out by it all, but I took it in my stride. It didn't bother me – I painted myself silver and had a good time. I was in the press enclosure quite a lot of the time. Jimi Hendrix dedicated 'Foxy Lady' to me. I was the "cat with the silver face". I tried to get Jimi Hendrix to come and play with us. I invited him, but his minders wouldn't let me get near him, really.

"In the daytime we had a stage rigged up outside. We had one or two drummers playing at the same time and lots of musicians coming and going. It was an open mike sort of thing; you'd call it that now. And we had Miles Davis come and check us out, Hendrix came and checked us out as well.

"And I played on the main stage with a bunch of Brazilians I'd met, one of whom subsequently became the Minister Of Culture of Brazil, a guy called Gilberto Gil. He was part of a group of expat Brazilians who were all in exile, and we used to hang out together in London in the Portobello Road and played music together."

Poli Palmer of Family, who also played at the festival, recalls their set. "They came down from the big hill when we were playing 'Good News Bad News' and they ripped the fences all down. The stage was very high, about fifteen feet, and there was a big press area at the front of it. Because there were extra people suddenly coming in, the whole audience just came straight down and broke the press barrier. Part of me was thinking that it was really beautiful, like water lapping at a pier. We were well above it, but you could see this sea of humanity."

Family vocalist Roger Chapman made his own personal protest when he saw that *Vogue* magazine were making the most of a potential photo opportunity by snapping their models in front of the stage with Joni Mitchell performing in the background.

"I was sitting near the front with Chappo," Palmer recalls. "When he gets grumpy, he gets grumpy and he said, 'Look at that, it's fucking disgusting!' So he got beer cans and started throwing them at the photographers. People were having a go going, 'Don't do that.' Then all the people from outside the enclosure start throwing cans, and all the photographers with the expensive cameras and the models went running for the tent."

Although Altamont was a nightmare of an event, at least in California in December you are likely to get some decent weather. In the UK, that's something that can never be taken for granted. This was exemplified by the infamous Bickershaw Festival, which was staged on a poorly drained site near Wigan, one of England's rainier locales, in May 1972. What could possibly go wrong? Family were on the bill and Palmer recalls that for the band, shod in Wellington boots, the backstage area wasn't too bad. But one spectacularly ill-judged incident turned the ground into a Somme-like quagmire.

"They had this act right in the middle of the audience with a guy high diving into a big tank of water," Palmer says. "It takes a few seconds, then, sploosh, it's over. After he had done his dive, they decided they needed to get it down and empty the tank, so they just pulled the plug and all that water went over all the poor sods. It was dreadful."

Glastonbury Fair was a free festival organised by Michael Eavis in 1971, which just about got by on funding from various supporters. Its stage was modelled on the great pyramid of Giza. The entertainment came from rock groups plus a range of other performing arts including dance, theatre and poetry. Nicolas Roeg and Davis Puttnam made a film of the festival, titled *Glastonbury Fayre*, which featured David Bowie, Arthur Brown, Fairport Convention, Traffic, Family, Gong and many others. An album of music recorded at the festival was also released.

In the film, Family play a harsh and electrifying – if trebly and sibilant – version of 'Drowned In Wine', while a hippie chick, with "LOVE" written on her forehead dances, smiling beatifically.

But by today's standards the sound system at Glastonbury in 1971 was makeshift, as Palmer describes: "We had four Marshall cabs, two on my side, two on the other so you filled the space with what you had behind you. Because apart from the vocal going through the PA, there was no front of house, no mixing at all."

An attendee at Glastonbury now can arise refreshed from their tent, have a shower, decide whether it will be tofu or tempura for breakfast and then go for an aromatherapy session to get themselves centred before going to watch the bands.

Back in the Seventies at festivals there wasn't a huge amount of anything on offer. This writer can't remember eating anything other than biscuits, a lump of hash or some stodgy rice and something approximating to a curry cooked on a Campingaz stove, accompanied by a cup of tea – the only fluid consumed during the day.

Festival-going teenagers weren't necessarily the most responsible people, so there was usually an information-cum-crash tent where one could at least escape the rain and flake out in relative comfort. There were often representatives from Release, an organisation that fought against drug-based arrests on hand, who would give out information on drugs and the law, and try to help if anyone staggered in while in the middle of a bad trip.

I went to Glastonbury with some friends in 1979, when it emerged after an eight-year absence and we all slept *en plein air* in sleeping bags. We didn't even check if there was a crash tent and didn't bother with the weather forecast. But mercifully it didn't rain, as there was no Plan B. One friend admitted turning up at a festival with nothing but the clothes he stood up in, a bag of magic mushrooms and some packets of fags. Another wrapped himself in plastic and slept under a tent flysheet and emerged the next day only slightly the worse for wear.

Then there were the illegal free festivals. These were the sort of places where you might well see Hawkwind or The Pink Fairies, or the Edgar Broughton Band leading an exorcism of bad karma by playing 'Out Demons Out' for twenty minutes accompanied by can-banging longhairs.

In the Seventies, these free festivals were seen as a rallying of the countercultural clans to show the breadheads who organised paying festivals how things could still be done. This involved getting a generator and some bands to play on a space where there were literally no facilities. If the mud at Reading reached mid-calf depth and the toilets were unspeakable, there were at least toilets. But as Joni Mitchell said, this was all about going back to the Garden, and Adam and Eve didn't have facilities. But then neither did they run the risk of being beaten up by policemen after experiencing some dubious entertainment.

A young David Parker went to the Windsor Free Festival in 1974, which was illegally set up in Windsor Great Park. He lives to tell the tale:

"I was immediately attracted to the Windsor Free Festival; so anti-establishment in tone and yet with such a splendidly economical ring to it. I should have known better, really.

"*Arriving at Windsor Great Park, I was surprised at the lack of activity; that and the absence of signs, fences, food outlets and, in an ominous portent of things to come, anything remotely resembling lavatory facilities.*

"*A group of tents, teepees and polythene shelters were located in a clearing between the trees and I concluded that this must be the festival. Over the afternoon bits and bobs of equipment, a rudimentary stage and an assortment of flat-bed trucks coalesced nearby. I dimly recall huddling in a group around the chap who seemed to be the guiding light of the event as he discussed the goings-on with several policemen.*

"*I believe The Half Human Band – triumphant from their recent gig at Basingstoke Technical College – made an appearance, but the only group I definitely recall watching was an unnamed local band performing The Doobie Brothers' 'Long Train Running' in the warm sunshine, whilst perched on the back of one of the flat-bed trucks. It was to prove the only pleasant experience of my time there.*

"*Feeling the call of nature, I dived behind a handy hedge. My boy scout training to the fore, I had a digging tool ready to bury the consequences of my actions. I guess the people who preceded me had missed that bit of the scout handbook, and it was with much trepidation that I gingerly picked my way back to the festivities.*

"*After a day of not much in the way of bands playing or any kind of music really, evening fell and those in charge decided that a spot of recorded music was needed to brighten the proceedings. Unfortunately all they had to hand was a lone copy of* What A Bunch of Sweeties *by The Pink Fairies. Much as I love that album, by the time 'The Portobello Shuffle' rolled around at earth-shattering volume for what seemed the twentieth time in succession, any youthful enthusiasm I possessed for it had evaporated completely.*

"*Abandoning my attempts to sleep, at 6 a.m. I joined an enormous trail of fellow hippie types queuing to use the nearest public lavatory; a continuous torrent of use for which it was never designed, with the inevitable consequences.*

"*I squelched my way slowly back to the site in time to hear an urgently shouted appeal for a doctor over the PA: rumours were rapidly circulating that someone had contracted typhoid. This was the final straw for me. With a heavy heart I loaded up my rucksack and headed wearily home.*

"*I timed my exit well. Half an hour after I left, the massed ranks of the local constabulary arrived and brought the proceedings to a close with much cracking of truncheons across hippie heads.*

"*When I got home my parents asked me if I'd had a nice time.*"

CHAPTER 40

1974 – The Tipping Point

"There was a point in the mid-Seventies when the bands were overreaching themselves and I had to confess that they weren't all beyond criticism. I could see why people didn't like aspects of them. The musicians themselves had become so successful and to be honest a lot of [them] had run out of ideas, run out of steam as well." – Chris Welch, interview with the author, 2013

We left Robert Fripp back in Chapter 4, having just disbanded King Crimson in September 1974 at its artistic peak and when it seemed that the group were on the cusp of doing some pretty big business in the USA. He had already made *No Pussyfooting*, a tape-loop based album with Brian Eno, and was keen to pursue other avenues and escape from his role as the de facto leader of a big rock group that he felt was inevitably going to start repeating itself.

Shortly afterwards he said that it was the time when "all bands in the progressive genre should have ceased to exist. But since the rock'n'roll dinosaur likes anything which has gone before, most of them are still churning away, repeating what they did years ago without going off in any new direction."

Fripp also chose to break up the group before it got stuck on the US touring treadmill and became part of progressive and mainstream rock's expansion into stadia and spectacle.

King Crimson drummer Bill Bruford remembers Fripp using the "dinosaur" simile. He was, however, surprised when the guitarist broke up the group.

"From my point of view, I'm sitting at the drums, the crowds are going berserk, we're doing well in America and the fees are going up. Our manager, David Enthoven, had just come in from the box office at the Chicago auditorium where we were headlining, saying, 'We've just taken $9,000,' which we thought was a fortune and it meant that we were beginning to stop losing money on the road. But Robert called a halt and to this day I think people tend to see the golden period of progressive rock as being from *In The Court Of The Crimson King*, pretty much, to 1975-ish."

When King Crimson started out in 1969, Fripp described the group as a superb liberal education for a young man. Back then there was a connectedness between the group members, an engagement in collective musical exploration and a refusal to accept barriers or limitations.

But this kind of creative wave cannot last forever and by the mid-Seventies, although Fripp's assessment seems particularly harsh, many progressive rock groups had already done their best work. Fripp himself embarked upon an extraordinary alternative career of collaborator, producer and catalyst, as a "small, mobile, intelligent unit". Although it wasn't immediately apparent what that actually meant, it was a phrase that put him apart from his peers. Back then he could see that the prevailing "bigger is better" ethos was unsustainable and so he trusted his intuition, to "follow his feet when they go walking".

His actions resonated with some of the ideas put forward in one of the radical economics books of the day, *Small Is Beautiful: A Study Of Economics As If People Mattered*, by E. F. Schumacher. The diseconomies of scale of one of progressive rock's biggest bands, Emerson, Lake & Palmer, would be revealed in a couple of years.

Firstly Fripp's feet guided him into retreat at The International Academy For Continuous Education at Sherborne House in Gloucestershire, set up by J. G. Bennett. He participated in a programme designed to fulfil individual potential, based on the teachings of Armenian philosopher and mystic, George Gurdjieff. Then he relocated to New York City, where he first started doing solo guitar performances with Frippertronics, the same tape delay system with two tape recorders in tandem that he had used with Eno.

GENESIS

August 1975 brought even more of a shock, when Peter Gabriel announced that he was leaving Genesis. The bizarre, fantastical, satirical, surreal, allegorical world of which he had been chief architect was now crumbling. *The Lamb Lies Down On Broadway* tour had ended rather wearily in May 1975 and Gabriel, who had already decided to leave, held back his statement until the group got a replacement singer. Although besieged with applications, they decided on drummer Phil Collins who had sung backing vocals for the group and had a lighter voice than Gabriel's, but with a similar timbre.

Gabriel wrote and personally delivered a letter to the music papers, which he asked to be reproduced in full or not at all. In it he gave his reasons for leaving. This is an edited version (sorry Peter):

"OUT, ANGELS OUT – an investigation."

"The vehicle we had built as a co-op to serve our songwriting became our master and had cooped us up inside the success we had wanted. It affected the attitudes and the spirit of the whole band. The music had not dried up and I still respect the other musicians, but our roles had set in hard. To get an idea through 'Genesis the Big' meant shifting a lot more concrete than before. For any band, transferring the heart from idealistic enthusiasm to professionalism is a difficult operation.

"I believe the use of sound and visual images can be developed to do much more than we have done. But on a large scale it needs one clear and coherent direction, which our pseudo-democratic committee system could not provide.

"As an artist, I need to absorb a wide variety of experiences. It is difficult to respond to intuition and impulse within the long-term planning that the band needed. I felt I should look at/learn about/develop myself, my creative bits and pieces and pick up on a lot of work going on outside music. Even the hidden delights of vegetable growing and community living are beginning to reveal their secrets. I could not expect the band to tie in their schedules with my bondage to cabbages. The increase in money and power, if I had stayed, would have anchored me to the spotlights. It was important to me to give space to my family, which I wanted to hold together, and to liberate the daddy in me.

"Although I have seen and learnt a great deal in the last seven years, I found I had begun to look at things as the famous Gabriel, despite hiding my occupation whenever possible, hitching lifts, etc. I had begun to think in business terms; very useful for an often bitten once shy musician, but treating records and audiences as money was taking me away from them. When performing, there were less shivers up and down the spine.

"I believe the world has soon to go through a difficult period of changes. I'm excited by some of the areas coming through to the surface, which seem to have been hidden away in people's minds. I want to explore and be prepared to be open and flexible enough to respond, not tied in to the old hierarchy."

The above reads like the end of a certain kind of idealistic exercise, specifically the Genesis songwriting collective, which required that ideas were approved by committee. Gabriel wrote more and at the end he tries to make light of the situation, by saying that some thought he would "do a Ferry", others thought he should "do a Bowie" and others thought he should "do a furry boa and hang myself with it". The humour feels more than a little forced.

In the mid-Seventies this felt like the abdication of royalty. Firstly Fripp and now Gabriel, two icons of the progressive rock movement's creative scope and ambition, had now turned their back on the whole shebang.

They both felt that their creativity was becoming compromised by their role within an ever-expanding and increasingly corporate music business, with its constant demands for more, in which the glory days of just a few years before, when unfettered creativity was the driving force, now seemed like distant memories. The fact that both had drastically cut their long hair might seem trivial now, but at the time even those acts appeared symbolic.

Things were beginning to change and although few could say what they were changing into exactly, both Gabriel and Fripp had held up wetted fingers and decided that the prevailing winds had shifted enough for them to have a major rethink. And pity poor old Genesis. What the hell were they going to do now?

Their next step was already being written, an album that was released in January 1976, *A Trick Of The Tail*. "The whole thing was very buoyant in many ways," says Tony Banks. "I missed Peter a lot but from every other point of view it was great.

"When we got to *A Trick Of The Tail* I thought, let's credit it as who wrote the bloody thing rather than trying to pretend everybody wrote anything. Also Steve had just done a solo album and so he was dry of ideas and he wasn't even around when we were writing some of the early things, and so that was one of the reasons. But later on we went back to crediting everything by everybody."

Steve Hackett's solo venture, *Voyage Of The Acolyte*, came out first, in October 1975, a conceptual journey through the Tarot pack with Collins on drums and vocals, Genesis bass guitarist Michael Rutherford on bass and Hackett's brother John on flute and keyboards. It's very much like a Genesis album in feel and some of the music had reached the rehearsal stage when the group were putting *Foxtrot* together back in 1972.

It's on a par with *A Trick Of The Tail*, which starts in high drama with 'Dance On A Volcano' with majestic verse sections, underpinned by huge bass pedal notes, which demonstrated that in terms of production, this was their best sounding effort so far, and Collins' vocals fit in perfectly. *A Trick Of The Tail* contains some of the group's most haunting moments, particularly the twelve-string guitar mesh of 'Entangled', which is gently whisked away at the end by Banks's ghostly Mellotron. The album closes with the instrumental 'Los Endos', which demonstrated Collins' fascination with American jazz fusion groups like Weather Report, although it is a composed piece. This fed into his project Brand X, an idiosyncratic, more British sounding jazz-rock group with whom he drummed from 1975–78.

With Gabriel's departure, some of the lyrics, particularly those on 'Squonk', come across as a little too twee, as a scene is set of a hunter trying to capture the titular creature, who when caught dissolves into a pool of tears. In fact, the group got the story from an American cryptozoological publication from the 19th century.

The real clunker, though, is 'Robbery, Assault And Battery', which finds Collins revisiting the best-left-alone territory of 'The Battle Of Epping Forest' and running through a number of characters à la Gabriel, including a plod-ish policeman and a geezer-ish criminal. At the end section of 'Los Endos' there is an instrumental reprise of 'Squonk' and Collins salutes his departed bandmate with a reference to the angel standing in the sun from 'Supper's Ready'.

But it worked. Genesis then toured America in 1976 and found that audiences there were clearly beginning to warm to the group. "I think one of the advantages for us when we came to the next tour after Peter leaving was we could pick from the whole repertoire," says Banks. "For the last three songs we had 'Supper's Ready', that built to a real big high, then 'I Know What I Like' because it's easy and everyone can sing along and then 'Los Endos' which is very exciting. That made a lot of difference to us, made us realise that *The Lamb…* for all its good intentions, was perhaps not the best show to do."

The first drummer helping out with live work in the new Genesis line-up was Bill Bruford, who was ostensibly still in National Health, but as little was happening at that juncture he took up their offer.

"They thought I was a star, I think, and that they were lucky to get me. I thought I was lucky to get them!" says Bruford. "But it was the first time that I'd been in a major band where I didn't have any input into the music, so I didn't feel emotionally connected. Yet somehow I seemed to know all the answers. I don't think I was very well-behaved."

Recordings of concerts with Bruford suggest a certain amount of mischief in his application to the Genesis repertoire as he introduces some of the more outré breaks and patterns he might have played in King Crimson.

"It probably wasn't mischievous so much as that I was trying to remember the music, because it was assumed that I knew Genesis's repertoire from A to Z. I hadn't really heard Genesis at all,"

Bruford explains. "I remain grateful to them for putting up with me, to be honest."

PINK FLOYD

Pink Floyd have admitted that after *The Dark Side Of The Moon* they had felt trapped creatively. What to do now? The album cast such a long shadow over its creators that they retreated away from commercial expectation and back into the avant-garde, having started work on *Household Objects* in 1974, using hammers, cutlery, saws and rubber bands as their basic sound sources. One can only imagine the record company's horror had the project not been abandoned.

Gilmour said many years later that he had been wishing for something a bit more musical – in a group sense – than the mainly Waters vision that was *The Dark Side Of The Moon*.

But in the intervening period of general ennui and lack of group confidence, Waters grabbed the reins once more with *Wish You Were Here*, this time an album on themes of absence. The title track is a sad, simple acoustic song, whereas 'Welcome To The Machine' – a rather unoriginal metaphor for work or a situation that takes a person over – finds Wright coaxing some spectacular synthesizer effects over a mechanistic pulse. 'Have A Cigar', a looser, funkier number, features guest vocalist Roy Harper – drafted in as Waters felt that he couldn't deliver the right vocal performance – singing an appropriately intense tirade against the crassness and greed of the music business.

The centrepiece is the longest of Waters' new songs, 'Shine On You Crazy Diamond', which was premiered during the 1974 tour. He had plaintively whispered, "Syd…" at the end of the 1968 B-side 'Julia Dream', but this exhortation to Syd Barrett to shine once more – creatively or in any other way – takes up twenty-six minutes of the album. Communicating with him directly was unlikely to yield any results and so getting the message out there in song was rather like tying a message to him on a balloon and hoping it might eventually land somewhere nearby. But no one could have predicted what happened next.

The album was recorded at Abbey Road studios from January 1975 and by weird coincidence, Barrett, as he had done with *Atom Heart Mother*, turned up at the sessions, although now with a shaven head, *sans* eyebrows and considerably heavier than before. He stood silently in the control room for a while without anyone recognising him, until Rick

Wright asked who he was. It was an excruciating meeting, and one that apparently left Waters and other onlookers close to tears.

The group kept scrutinising a short recorded passage and Barrett, whose own recording sessions were infamously chaotic, was genuinely confused as to why they kept listening to a take over and over. What was the point? But Pink Floyd were in the habit of going over sections time and time again in their pursuit of sonic perfection.

Pink Floyd's default setting now was the slow 4/4, which here suited the music's drift and grandeur. And from the beautiful drone of synths and rubbed wine glasses – an idea explored during the *Household Objects* sessions – that opens the album, along with Gilmour's meditative guitar figures, it's a more open record than the dark inner landscapes of *The Dark Side Of The Moon*. But in the mixed bag of reviews it prompted, many pointed out the fact that excitement levels were low.

It was an early example of technological imperatives impinging on the music, with careful isolation of sounds to give maximum separation of channels, and therefore maximum control over mixing. Mason, who was essentially a straightforward player anyway, was urged to favour accuracy over expression. This careful layering of instruments might have sounded good, but, as Mason wrote in 2004, "It did nothing to help the sense that we were not a band playing together".

The great architectural span of 'Shine On You Crazy Diamond' that opens and closes the album is a mix of anthemic vocal sections and atmospheric instrumental sections. It returns as Parts VI–IX halfway through side two with Waters flanged one note bass pulsing across open space as on 'One Of These Days', accompanied by Wright's synth skywriting. It lurches into a quicker, if decidedly stiff rhythm and Gilmour tries to kick some life into proceedings with some incisive, choppy rhythm guitar and a stinging slide solo. At this point the listener is also just waiting for it to take off, to push the beat slightly beyond that foursquare plod, for someone to add some flourishes. Come on!

Mason begins to throw in some tom-tom accents and the listener by now is cheering them on from the sidelines to reach some dynamic peak. *Come on!* But then it settles back down to a straight rhythm, Gilmour reintroduces the melodic verse motif and it all just decelerates back into the slow 4/4. All sense of dynamics had been bled out of the group by their obsessive tidiness; it's the only song this writer has heard that actually sags from one section to another.

After the final verse comes a breezier section with Wright playing clavinet and it slowly drifts off, with the keyboard player again coming to the fore in an achingly sad coda of synth and piano, the album's most affecting moment.

Pink Floyd headlined Knebworth Festival on July 5, 1975, on a bill that included The Steve Miller Band, Captain Beefheart & His Magic Band and Roy Harper & Trigger.

Pink Floyd's love of special effects, which Mason recognises was "excessive" – and which involved explosives – had recently caused more than the usual stir at a North American sports stadium, where one of the crew blew up the scoreboard in an explosion that also damaged surrounding houses.

At Knebworth when Pink Floyd came onstage, two Spitfires made a fly-past. Mick Brown from *Sounds* was impressed: "Floyd have long since transcended the boundaries of musical definition, and their performance has been refined to the point where it is a spectacle which bombards all the senses, leaving one gasping for both air and the suitable adjectives to describe it all.

"Floyd have the ingenuity and skill to spring from a deceptively simple melodic base into the most esoteric of electronic realms, using the quadraphonic speaker system as a series of walls off which notes are bounced and skimmed around the arena, at one moment with a ruthless metallic compulsion, at another with the mystic, transcendental intensity of North African holy music."

Pink Floyd's live extravaganzas attracted such fervent write-ups. They were impressive affairs, with their lights and films and special effects, and their obsession with sound quality. Maybe it was a symptom of progressive rock excess, but a lot of people loved it. But sometimes it was apparent that technology had outgrown the means by which it could be electrically powered in the middle of a field. During Pink Floyd's headlining set, Rick Wright particularly was experiencing major problems.

"As darkness fell and the stage lights were operated, Rick's keyboards were changing pitch in unison with lights," Mason recalled. "It sounded awful. It transpired that every time the master volume was turned up, the keyboards went out of tune.

"...Somehow or other we staggered through the show using only one piano and one less sensitive keyboard, and a more modest light show."

RICK WAKEMAN

Since leaving Yes in 1974 Rick Wakeman's life had been eventful to say the least. He had premiered his orchestral rock extravaganza *Journey To The Centre Of The Earth* at the Royal Festival Hall in January.

But he could have taken permanent early retirement when he performed *Journey...* on stage at the Crystal Palace Bowl in July. He collapsed at the end of the show, and the next day was admitted to Wexham Park Hospital following a heart attack at the age of 25. He remained in hospital for some weeks and whilst convalescing wrote *The Myths And Legends Of King Arthur And The Knights Of The Round Table*, and once he had recovered he pushed ahead with the project.

Wakeman recalls having conversations with David Bowie about the hard and simple fact that if you have money you are less likely to compromise and the only reason that *Journey...* was made, as mentioned in Chapter 5, is that Wakeman was able to plough his own money into it. "The record company didn't want me to do *King Arthur* but David Bowie's words kept ringing in my ears – you must do what you believe in," he says. And the album was another mix of historical sources and storytelling, but this time without the narration.

The initial idea had been to perform the album live at Tintagel Castle in Cornwall, one of the sites that has connections with the Arthurian legends, but Wakeman ran up against practical problems. The castle itself is stuck out on an outcrop of rock and joined to the land by a narrow causeway, making it a health and safety nightmare. If he were to play in an adjoining field he was still going to have problems clearing the venture with the Duchy Of Cornwall, which owned the land.

"Believe you me, it's still going to happen if I have to buy Cornwall to do it," Wakeman told Welch. "I'm convinced it can work very well without upsetting any of the people down there."

But instead Wakeman looked at the more practical option of London venues and was keen on Empire Pool, Wembley. At the time he wanted to book, it was being prepared for an ice skating event and the surface that would normally have seats was frozen. So, pragmatically, he turned his proposed live show into an ice pageant.

Journey To The Centre Of The Earth had struck a chord with the public in a cinematic kind of way and *King Arthur* went to number two in the UK album charts, but one cannot escape the fact that it's very kitsch. Wakeman was borrowing from "high" art, with an operatic narrative, and as with opera, it demanded a huge suspension of disbelief.

The best way was just to view it simply as light entertainment, but it wasn't presented as such. And ultimately it was another example of an orchestra sounding like it had been tacked on to a rock performance, with clear pretension of grandeur and the story reduced to workaday rock lyrics.

Looking at footage of it now, while the group, choir and orchestra take up a lot of space, it was not really much of a spectacle for the punter, with a few knights brandishing replica broadswords skating around and having the occasional fight, and Guinevere going through some solo ice dance routines. All of which produced a feeing of bathos. But whereas Wakeman was obliged to put a significant chunk of his own money into realising *Journey To The Centre Of Earth*, the cost of the *King Arthur* extravagance put him in quite serious debt.

It was a world away from the concise and charming instrumental vignettes of *The Six Wives Of Henry VIII*. In composing that album, Wakeman had read a lot about the wives and he had let the music bubble up from his unconscious as an impressionistic reaction to the stories of their characters, life and times, not as a straightforward musical allegory where each musical episode represented something specific, like a rock version of programme music. But with *King Arthur*, it had all got too literal.

In promotional photo shoots Wakeman seemed to be having a hoot, appearing alongside chain mail-clad minstrels from the English Rock Ensemble, pewter tankard in hand, and sporting a conical hat like some latterday Merlin, the embodiment of the Seventies keyboard wizard.

The album received mixed reviews. Ian MacDonald of *New Musical Express* was one journalist who was not impressed: "If your idea of a good time is listening to a big bass choir solemnly intoning that they are the Lady of the Lake... then, young man, you're in."

MacDonald continued: "If Rick Wakeman has a saving grace, it's that he doesn't take this crap too seriously – which is just as well with taste as beerily crazed as his. Faced with the incongruities of pitching the "legit" voices of The Very Serious English Chamber Choir against the hoarse inadequacies of rockers Ashley Holt and Gary Pickford Hopkins, young Rick just orders another round, gets his head down, and charges up, down, over, and under every keyboard in the vicinity. (Cheers.)

"He doesn't so much 'solo' as fill in vacant spaces in the score with as many different notes in the relevant key as he can locate in the given time."

Wakeman had recently played Thor in Ken Russell's film *Lisztomania,* with The Who's Roger Daltrey as Franz Liszt. Perhaps inspired by the director's stylistic car crash of high and low art, Wakeman had thought of making *King Arthur* as a comedy film, with Tommy Cooper as Merlin and Harry Secombe as Sir Galahad, but then *Monty Python And The Holy Grail* came out a matter of days after he mentioned the idea to Welch, so that approach was no longer an option.

Although MacDonald claimed that Wakeman didn't take *King Arthur* seriously, there was no obvious humour in it either, so there wasn't much chance of laughing with it.

Wakeman told Chris Welch of his proposed next move: "Hopefully it'll be something on the gods of mythology – a Suite Of Gods. That idea came from a piece of music I was going to use for *Arthur*. I don't know how many gods I'll use, there are thousands of the buggers. They do tend to get around a bit. It'll be nice to get Thor in and Zeus."

YES

Wakeman's old group Yes were supposedly contributing to the "sillinesses" that Robert Fripp had identified as being prevalent at the time (see Chapter 4), but apart from appearing onstage with what drummer Alan White calls "a general surreal setting" – a set of illuminated perspex blobs and semi-animated sculptures of fantastical crab-like or arachnoid creatures looming up behind the keyboards and drum kit, all designed by Roger Dean and his brother Martyn – there wasn't a great deal of silliness about the group. In fact they were about to record their most aggressive and exploratory album.

After Wakeman had left in 1974, there were rumours that Vangelis Papathanassiou might be the new Yes man. He had come to fame with Greek progressive rock band Aphrodite's Child, who had delivered the – literally – apocalyptic album *666* in 1972. But Yes chose Swiss keyboardist Patrick Moraz. He had been in Refugee, with the former Nice rhythm section of Brian Davison on drums, and Lee Jackson on bass and vocals, and together they had released a critically acclaimed self-titled debut album in 1973. For a while they looked in line to be the next big thing. Moraz realised that he was leaving them high and dry as Keith Emerson had done in 1970 and requested that they should receive some money from his deal with Yes.

Moraz went to see Yes in rehearsal and was "blown away" by hearing 'Sound Chaser'. This is hardly surprising as the convoluted, complex track lurches from part to part, shifting metre like it was going out of fashion, with one particular riff appearing at three different speeds at various points in the song.

Relayer was the last Yes album to be produced by Eddy Offord, on a mobile twenty-four-track machine in bass guitarist Chris Squire's home studio. The album went Top 10 in the UK and US, but has a far more aggressive edge to it than any of their previous music.

Side one is a single track 'The Gates Of Delirium', which portrays a kind of rallying of the clans followed by an instrumental battle section. And after all the sound and fury, it concludes with the sweet and lustrous ballad, 'Soon', demonstrating the redemptive power of peace. It was apparently loosely based on Tolstoy's novel *War And Peace*, but when you condense a 1,000-page novel into a twenty-minute rock suite, that is basically what you get: war and peace.

"It certainly was a more tangled up record, more brittle. I was playing a Fender [Telecaster] guitar for the first time," Howe informs. The model of guitar is renowned for its trebly attack.

Although it's all rather preposterous, as the Yes heavy cavalry gallop into the battle section – the charge led by Moraz's synth bugle calls – the effect is nonetheless thrilling, with Howe allying his considerable speed and technique to an appropriately manic intensity.

White recalls how he sourced some of the percussion used on the track: "I remember doing some sessions and Jon Anderson and myself were driving together and we'd stop at a scrap yard and pick up pieces of cars and were banging them in the studio.

"For 'The Gates Of Delirium', we had a whole rack of car parts in the studio and Jon and I we were banging on that for certain overdubs. At the end of 'Gates Of Delirium', I pushed the whole thing over in the studio."

Anderson joins in with the clattering car part percussion, as the group veer through a zig-zagging jazz funk groove and an into a triumphal theme played by Howe on Telecaster and pedal steel, before the track's blissful resolution. Howe basically pieced together a template of the track from rehearsal sessions.

"There was a demo of us playing 'The Gates Of Delirium' in a very loose sort of way," says Howe. "I edited it together, stuck it together on quarter-inch tape and then we went in and I played it on the speakers and said, 'Now we've got to play this again and make it sound good.'"

The line-up never recorded again, although Moraz initially fitted in seamlessly and played live with Yes for three years. In 1975, Yes took a collective breather and concentrated on making solo albums. They were to emerge with the rejuvenated prodigal Wakeman on board once more at the height of punk.

JETHRO TULL

After the musical convolutions of 1972's *A Passion Play* and all the hoo-ha and fake news that surrounded Jethro Tull's supposed retirement as a result of negative criticism of that album, the group came back to critical favour with 1974's *War Child*, with Charles Shaar Murray giving it a guardedly positive review in *New Musical Express*.

It was complex for sure, with Barrie Barlow's tight, dense drumming pressing hard at every time change, and the concept was anything but obvious, although it clearly referenced World War Two, but it felt like the songs had been formed as individual entities rather than panels in some conceptual rock tapestry.

The dazzling 'Skating Away On The Thin Ice Of A New Day' stands as one of the band's most inspired song arrangements. Initially just acoustic guitar and voice, it becomes layered with the gradual addition of parts by drums, bass, guitar, tuned percussion, accordion and strings. It's another of Anderson's existential songs with the London Underground used as a metaphor for the cycles and journeys of life, as on 'Life's A Long Song'. Here the protagonist is appropriately riding the Circle Line and Anderson, as commentator, says that the story he is telling is *"too damn real"* and it's happening now.

On 'Only Solitaire', Anderson describes himself as perceived as *"court jesting"* and has a few more comments to aim at the music press, pre-empting any negative reactions with a line about critics queuing up to say that Anderson is *"boring"*, partly because he never caught VD from a public toilet seat.

"*War Child* was definitely a conscious move to keep things in a more finite song framework, with beginnings and ends and choruses and bridges, and short solos," says Anderson. "For the most part it's an easier, more accessible album, with songs that are not related in a strong way to the point that would ever be considered a concept album.

"But then with *Minstrel In The Gallery* [1975] it took on another tack with more emphasis on the acoustic side of things and more selfish singer-songwriting on my part where the band didn't have so big a role as they'd had on previous albums, in the sense that there were a lot of sections where they didn't play. Or their contribution was occasional and more decorative.

"*Too Old To Rock'N'Roll, Too Young To Die* [1976] is a more theatrical set of songs, loosely outlining a storyline, because it was conceived of as being something for musical theatre. It was a naïvely optimistic approach on my part because long before I had finished recording the album, I knew this was never going to happen – just as with *A Passion Play*, I knew that was never going to become a movie – but that didn't stop me finishing the album."

VAN DER GRAAF GENERATOR

Van Der Graaf Generator had imploded in 1972, shortly after making *Pawn Hearts*, although the group members contributed to Hammill's subsequent solo albums. But in October 1975 the reformed, rejuvenated group released a new album, *Godbluff*.

A number of record companies had shown an interest in them, but after some difficulties they negotiated a three-album deal with their former label, Charisma.

"It was only a few years but there was also a shift in attitude, a shift in possibilities within the industry," says drummer Guy Evans. "For a record company we were tantalisingly slightly successful. We would sell 20,000 albums and also Peter [Hammill] did write some things that, given the right lighting and the right hair-do, could be sold as hit material, like 'Refugees'. And so I think that Charisma thought that maybe just around the corner there was that major hit.

"When we crashed and burnt [in 1972], we were in debt and I was particularly concerned with the notion that this debt would be recoupable from advances in a new deal. This would have made it impossible for us to operate. It took a long time for us to reach a workable compromise and a one-year wait in getting going.

"I'd been pretty dissatisfied with our previous situation, in which management and record company were the same organisation, especially when presented with a debt that seemed to be arbitrarily compiled, with no distinction between management and record company expenses. There had no doubt been naivety on both sides, with everyone caught up in the heady pursuit of the now, without properly defining who was liable for what and when."

With this delay the group had amassed, rehearsed and recorded well over an album's worth of new material. Although long songs were still the order of the day, they were played in a more concentrated, less excessive way. "We didn't go through quite as many corniche turns," says Hammill.

"There might be a case to be made for, yes, we were a progressive group from *The Least We Can Do Is Wave To Each Other* to *Pawn Hearts*, but were we a progressive group from *Godbluff* onwards? Did we get reversed into being an underground soul band in an odd sort of way?" Hammill muses. "I'm not positioning this as a major statement, but it does seem to me that there is something in that."

Those soul riffs were still there hiding in plain sight, but no one else was writing songs like this at the time. *Godbluff* is hard to unravel lyrically, but it was followed up by *Still Life*, released six months later.

To answer Hammill's question, these two albums contain some of progressive rock's most striking moments. And the subject matter was typically at odds with prevailing songwriting trends.

On *Still Life*'s 'La Rossa', rock's cocksure mating calls are internalised. Here the protagonist is agonising over whether or not to make a move on his female friend. They stay up late talking about philosophy and then he sleeps on the floor, but will they ever do the act that will irrevocably change everything between them? It's a brilliantly written soliloquy on platonic and sexual relationships between men and women, although, while he is agonising, he realises that she can read him as if he is *"glass"*. They finally break through their carefully managed psychological barrier as the group (pun definitely not intended) reach an exultant instrumental climax.

The title track takes sex into uncharted territory. It comes over as a kind of unholy hybrid of the H. P. Lovecraft short story, 'The Survivor', and Joris-Karl Huysmans' novel *Against Nature*, depicting a world of decadent meaninglessness, where death is forever kept at bay. At the song's denouement – surely the absolute antithesis of rock music's narcissistic phallocentricity – Hammill looks on numbly before climbing into bed to pleasure his withered, centuries-old wife.

Then there is 'Childlike Faith In Childhood's End', based on the Arthur C. Clarke novel, which describes the metamorphosis of the human race and where Hammill, searching for a sign of the hereafter, rails at the entire cosmos in the colossal finale. This is the sort of ambition that got him labelled as pretentious. But then he was at least reaching for something.

"And at times not quite getting there," he says. "But that would be better than repeating myself. Yeah, obviously pretension is in the eye of the beholder. For what it's worth, I think I wrote some lyrics that made a degree of sense at a time when there were an awful lot of nonsensical lyrics going around."

Van Der Graaf Generator produced the marginally less successful *World Record* later in 1976, although the group's collective playing was looser and more expansive.

But another significant album featuring the group members had been recorded in 1974 and released in 1975, a Peter Hammill solo album, *Nadir's Big Chance*. It was intended as a clearing of ground before the full group reunion, with Hammill keen that it should be quite different from what the group were soon to record. Featuring a number of his previously unrecorded early songs it was, according to Hammill's tongue-in-cheek sleeve notes, supposedly written by his 16-year-old alter-ego, Rikki Nadir, and comprised "beefy punk songs, ballads and soul struts", which were played with a brash, brassy immediacy that at times brought to mind early Roxy Music. The concept might sound a little arch, but was, in Hammill's opinion, "both fun and serious".

"But the interesting thing is that it got absolutely slagged when it came out, because, supposedly, it revealed that my creativity had run out and it spelt doom not only for me, but also for the upcoming Van Der Graaf Generator Mark II."

But as we shall find out, the album would have more of an impact than anyone could have predicted. For change was afoot.

CHAPTER 41

There's Gonna Be a Storm: UK Punk

"At one time NME *called us The People's Band. That was in 1973, but three years later we were rock dinosaurs."* – Steve Howe, interview with the author, *MOJO* 294 May 2018

One of the stories that most sticks in my mind from researching this book concerns Fruupp, a progressive rock group originally from the Belfast area, told to me by novelist and writer Paul Charles.

"I was one of the lyricists, I did the sound sometimes, I humped the gear, I got the gigs, and I was always the last person to be paid," Charles explains.

As with many groups from both Northern Ireland and Eire who came to prominence in the early Seventies, finding places to play this type of music was not easy. A bigger draw like Rory Gallagher might be able to play on the college circuit, but if a bunch of emergent hairies like Fruupp had delivered their lengthy and complex rock excursions to a showband crowd on the Irish ballroom circuit, they would have been booed off at the very least.

It was also a bit of a haul for A&R men to go over to Ireland, and Belfast especially was rarely a destination of choice. Outbreaks of sectarian violence, rather euphemistically named The Troubles, was all that British TV viewers ever saw of the city, and it seemed impossibly grim, with endless terrorist bombings and kneecappings. Bands were afraid to tour there on the college circuit, but Charles recalls it quite differently.

"People went about their day and the no-man's land was music – it was the only place that I could see where both sides were happily mixing and happily socialising and there wasn't really a border in the music or in the venue."

Fruupp made the inevitable move to London and developed a style not dissimilar to Genesis, who they supported on a number of occasions. They released four albums: *Future Legends* (1973); *Seven Secrets* (1974); *The Prince Of Heaven's Eyes* (1974); and *Modern Masquerades* (1975).

Fruupp had headlined the Drury Lane Theatre in London in the autumn of 1974 and when, in January 1975, Seymour Stein, the head of Sire Records, came over to the UK to see them live, it seemed possible that, as Charles says, "they would go off to fame and fortune, and we'd all live happily ever after".

But keyboardist Steve Houston suddenly quit the band, leaving them to play to Stein at a gig at Farnborough Technical College as a three piece. He declined to sign them up. The group then recruited a keyboard player, John Mason, for *Modern Masquerades*. When Mason also left, their label, Pye Records, still stuck behind the group. Then 1976 brought their demise.

Fruupp were camped out in Dublin at that point rehearsing what was to be the next album, *Doctor Wilde's Twilight Adventure*. It was going to be a concept album based on a story by Charles called *The Flight Of The Dove*.

One night Charles went to Moran's Hotel in Dublin, which hosted gigs in the basement and was a venue that Fruupp themselves had recently sold out. He had been aware that something new was happening musically at an underground level, but this was his first experience of what was soon labeled "punk".

"The Boomtown Rats were playing there and it was packed to the rafters," Charles recalls. "At the time they were really a poor man's Dr Feelgood, but there was such an energy from the audience and the band and a connection between both that hadn't been around before. With the prog rock bands, you are there and the audience is there beyond the line of the stage. With the punk thing it was combination of the energy that was going on both on and off stage.

"At the time punk came along, you either had to have made the grade like Genesis, or you weren't going to, as all the media attention was on this new wave which was starting to come through. And it was very, very clear that as we hadn't made the grade and were losing our momentum, the writing was on the wall."

Even the fact that the group were his friends and had a budget for a new album couldn't tempt Charles to stay.

"Fruupp really needed new energy to take it on to the next level in what, I felt for progressive music, was going to be troubled times," he explains. "I really felt I should leave before the new album project started rather than halfway through it, so I resigned. They tried a couple of managers but didn't find the correct person to continue with. And they ground to a halt about three or four months later."

While Fruupp were grinding to a halt in Dublin, over in Deptford in south east London, a teenage employee of Williams & Glyn's Bank, Mark Perry, was going through his own musical metamorphosis. Back then Deptford was not the most glamorous of places.

"I've never been partisan in my interest in bands, and when you're growing up in Deptford, it's almost all the same to you: it's exciting stuff that's not made in Deptford," says Perry. "So in the mid-Seventies, my favourite bands were The Who, ELP, Little Feat, Roxy, Bowie. When you are growing up in a working-class area you want to escape somehow, and before punk came there were other ways to escape, like going to a local gig on a Saturday night, buying the records and having your dad saying, 'Turn that bloody racket down!'

"I was open to things and a few weeks after buying ELP's *Pictures At An Exhibition* I had Ravel's orchestration of it, as it was originally just a [Mussorgsky] piano piece. So to me they were a way of getting into music. People forget what progressive rock means, but it was a progression from that basic rock format."

But something major had been brewing up for a while. In June 1975, *New Musical Express* New York correspondent Lisa Robinson wrote: "There's no denying that during the last few months an actual *New Band Scene* has begun to re-activate itself... Something is Definitely Going On." [sic]

Robinson mentioned Blondie, The Stilettos, Wayne County, The Dictators and Television amongst others as typifying a new attitude that was manifesting in New York City. Soon the words "punk rock" were being bandied around. This new music was urban, unashamedly a bit arty and decidedly confrontational. A spiky haired Richard Hell, bass guitarist of Television, sported shades, a ripped t-shirt and oozed attitude. He quit the group that year and joined guitarist Johnny Thunders of notorious glam-rockers New York Dolls in The Heartbreakers. Right at the end of 1975, Patti Smith recorded an album, *Horses*, a mixture of poetry and direct, very modern rock'n'roll that no one had quite figured out how to categorise. Blondie were influenced by Sixties garage bands and girl groups, and their striking peroxide blonde singer, Debbie Harry, was the focus of attention.

In the UK something roughly similar was slowly developing out of the indigenous pub rock scene. Groups like Ducks Deluxe, Brinsley Schwarz and Bees Make Honey all played variants on back-to-basics, good-time rock'n'roll, which was both undemanding and unexciting. Then in 1975, Dr Feelgood, who had been playing on that circuit for a few years already, released their debut *Down By The Jetty* – in mono. They were different, edgier, with Wilko Johnson's guitar style an amalgam of lead and rhythm, which felt both ancient in rock'n'roll terms, and strangely modern in its terseness and angularity. Into 1976, Eddie & The Hot Rods came to prominence, playing what could have passed as pub rock, but it was harder and faster.

That year saw a seismic moment in rock culture, the release of the self-titled debut album by the Ramones. The music they presented was a mix of the familiar and the alien, stripping rock'n'roll down to its bare bones of unremittingly basic drumming, a few chords of buzzsaw guitar – with no solos – and the bass rarely straying from the root notes. Over this, Joey Ramone, stick thin and well over six feet tall, sang songs like 'Now I Wanna Sniff Some Glue' and 'Judy Is A Punk'.

It was as if the Ramones had stumbled upon the dimensions of rock's golden section. All their songs sounded similar, but all had strong, simple tunes that harked back to Sixties pop. The four group members all purported to be brothers, and all wore leather biker jackets, t-shirts, ripped jeans and sneakers. And if you liked them in small doses, then that was OK as that was all you were going to get. Their fourteen-track debut clocked in at just over twenty-nine minutes, which was about five minutes longer than 'Supper's Ready' by Genesis.

The Ramones' cartoon gang image was crucial, for one of the most important things about this new wave of music was that its newness called for a certain amount of reinvention. And what was so delicious about the Ramones is that no one quite knew whether da Brudders, as they were affectionately known in the press, were either a rather dim bunch of gum-chewing New York mooks or a particularly intelligent quartet, in order to be able to put over all that rock'n'roll numbskull stuff so convincingly. The *New Musical Express* even referred to them as The Morones. Later on it turned out that the whole concept had been the brainchild of drummer Tommy Erdelyi aka Tommy Ramone.

This was the point in time when a certain branch of rock music would be re-calibrated forever. The Ramones were effectively saying: here's what you can do with a few chords; you don't need twenty to make a good song; and you don't have to stretch it out to twenty minutes when one minute forty seconds will do. It was inclusive in that never since Black Sabbath had young guitarists been able to play along to a record so easily, and catalytic in that it served as springboard for others to write their own songs. And as such they helped kick-start the UK punk scene.

Mark Perry saw the Ramones' first UK gig supporting the Flamin' Groovies at the Roundhouse in London on July 5, 1976. The epiphanic experience inspired him to immediately set about writing and editing his own fanzine *Sniffin' Glue*, which he initially photocopied, after hours, at his girlfriend's place of work.

"I got so enthused with this new music that I wanted my own magazine," Perry recalls. "I used to shop at the Rock On stall in Newport Court in Soho. I saw *Punk*, the New York magazine, but there was nothing in the UK.

"Initially, we had included groups like Blue Öyster Cult and the Flamin' Groovies as we saw a kinship with their attitudes, and also The Mothers Of Invention's *Freak Out* album. Things were moving forward so fast, so we needed to start defining it, and by the time we got to *Sniffin' Glue* issues three and four it was a case of 'This is punk; the rest of it can fuck off'.

"There was a year-zero attitude and even I jumped on that bandwagon. But if you are going to build something up you kind of need to criticise what went before – it's a way of empowering yourself. It would have diluted the message somewhat if we'd said, 'Yes, The Clash is the thing; we like Pink Floyd as well.' It just wouldn't have worked."

The idea of reinvention and revolution were key, as to mean anything, punk had to make a break with the past. The Clash's '1977' proclaimed that in that year there was no longer any place for Elvis Presley, The Beatles or The Rolling Stones and they also divorced themselves – initially at least – from the rock'n'roll motherlode with 'I'm So Bored With The USA'.

Out with the old, in with the new. There was no option but to appear to be killing the ancient kings. The dance of choice while watching these groups was the pogo, which was basically just jumping up and down rather than the expansive moves or "idiot dancing" of the hippies. Then there was the "gobbing", with hails of spit and phlegm directed stagewards from the audience. In lieu of an academic psychological study of the phenomenon, it was a display of anti-adulation towards the crowd's new heroes.

The word was out that none of these new groups could play. But that idea was blown apart by the first UK punk single, released in October 1976, 'New Rose' by The Damned. It sounded a bit like Eddie Cochran's 'Summertime Blues' played at double speed or the guitar figures of David Bowie's 'Hang On To Yourself' injected with high-octane fuel, and with a touch of early Who, including a thrilling drumming performance, complete with cymbal white-outs, by Chris 'Rat Scabies' Miller.

The Sex Pistols were also a tough, punchy rock group, but without Malcolm McLaren's management and his ability to sniff out controversy, they would have probably remained on the pub rock circuit doing Small Faces covers, which is how they started out when guitarist Steve Jones was their vocalist. McLaren found them a singer, John Lydon, who reinvented himself as Johnny Rotten. He was soon kitted out in distressed-looking arty duds that McLaren's partner Vivienne Westwood designed for their King's Road boutique, Sex. With Rotten on board *New Musical Express* journalist Nick Kent – who had played guitar in an early incarnation of the group – described the Pistols as "like The Stooges fronted by Albert Steptoe".

The Sex Pistols' early gigs were notorious for punch-ups. At the Screen On The Green, Islington, in late 1976, there was a fracas in the crowd that had been at least partly provoked by McLaren and Westwood, with the band themselves soon weighing in. It was captured by an *NME* photographer and gave them priceless publicity. The group initially signed to EMI outside Buckingham Palace in 1977 and another of McLaren's ideas was that the group should play on a boat on the Thames in that summer as a way of embarrassing the establishment during Queen Elizabeth II's Silver Jubilee year celebrations, particularly as it came on the back of their single 'God Save The Queen'. These incidents have been described as Situationist pranks, but that feels like dressing up what were good old-fashioned publicity stunts in rather oversized intellectual and theoretical garb.

After more contractual shenanigans with A&M, the group eventually signed with Virgin, which most definitely marked the end of one era and the beginning of another for the label.

While the bigger progressive rock – and other more mainstream rock groups and artistes – were engaged in an arms race for more and more equipment, bigger staging and more special effects, the emergence of punk showed that all that was essentially showbiz, and not actually necessary. In January 1977, Manchester band the Buzzcocks even did without a record company, rustling up £500 to record, press and distribute their debut EP *Spiral Scratch* on their own New Hormones label.

Never before in rock history had there been such a backlash at what had gone before. For a few brief months in early 1977 all seemed in turmoil. Johnny Rotten was one of the main focal points of UK punk. A prickly, misanthropic character who was set against everything – including sex – it was as if he had just appeared, fully formed, out of the void like some exterminating angel. At least that was the impression he and McLaren wanted to give.

Even though a massive suspension of disbelief was needed to countenance such a thing, fans have always loved their larger-than-life characters. Many really wanted to believe, for example, that Captain Beefheart hadn't slept for a year, and David Bowie's assertion, when he "outed" himself in 1972, that he was gay and always had been – even though he was then married with a son.

The Clash were viewed as purveyors of a particularly earnest brand of punk politique, their political ideas conveyed through music as broad brushstrokes. But their constant need to be seen to hate – and be divorced from – what had gone before in order to maintain their credibility, stretched credulity to breaking point.

Paul Simonon, the group's bass player, apparently hated Led Zeppelin so much that just looking at their album covers made him want to throw up. But then, on the quiet, The Clash guitarist Mick Jones was a big fan of their guitarist, Jimmy Page.

Guitarist and vocalist Joe Strummer, who Nick Kent first met while watching King Crimson at Plumpton Festival in 1969, was a diplomat's son who had been to public school. This fact soon got out, but then he claimed he wasn't like those *other* diplomat's sons who had been to public school. Keith Levene, the guitarist in their first line-up and who later went on to play with Lydon in Public Image Ltd, kept quiet about the fact that he had been a roadie for Yes guitarist Steve Howe while in his mid-teens.

Simonon's keenness to reject everything, to be seen to be more punk than anyone else, to come across as some yobbo savant, was found out by Barry Miles. A countercultural mover and shaker in London in the psychedelic Sixties, Miles could see threads that joined The Clash with the counterculture of a decade before, and he was keen to manage them. He later wrote: "They were all from a rather more middle-class background than they admitted to… There was a certain amount of myth making going on even at this early stage in their career.

"Paul Simonon said he used to get drunk every night and go around kicking people and smashing up phone boxes, but now he had the band as a means of expression and he hoped the audience would find their own bands, or find some creative outlet for their energy. I found this astonishing, as I knew Paul had studied at the private Byam Shaw art school in Chelsea. 'I used to draw blocks of flats and car dumps.'"

It was a clear case of the punk doth protest too much, but Simonon was trying to stick to a stereotype of punk that was also perpetuated in the media, as being working class, anti-intellectual and ageist in the extreme – everyone over about 23 had to lie about their date of birth. But was it really as based on class as some neo-Marxist commentators would have it? Phillip Sanderson of early Eighties post-punk electronic duo Storm Bugs, who lived in a suburban area of Kent and perceived himself as basically white middle class, offers these thoughts.

"After O-levels I dropped out of the grammar school and went to Erith Technical College to do A-levels. Most of the people there were doing engineering, far more working class, without any positives and negatives.

"Initially, we were playing these [punk] records in the common room and they'd be sticking their heads around the door saying, 'What's this crap that you are playing in there?' In six months they started listening to it. So although there was a perception of it being a very working-class thing, out in the suburbs, it was all the middle-class boys who were picking up on it first."

Come 1977 it was good to maintain that your band had only been going for a year. The supposedly newly formed Stranglers had, in fact, supported Fruupp at their ill-fated gig at Farnborough Tech in January 1975. And in order to separate themselves from the enemy, some punk musicians chose to almost reject music itself – at least all the fancy stuff. Guitarist and vocalist Jakko Jakszyk, now in King Crimson, recalls being confronted with this attitude when he played with his group 64 Spoons in 1977.

"[I had made] the time, the effort and the denial of social activity in order to be able to play at a level at which I could compete. And God's joke is preparing you for a world that won't exist by the time you get there. I remember we got a gig headlining the University College Union in London and the support band was one of these new-fangled punk groups we had heard of but hadn't really seen.

"We're onstage sound checking and messing with the amps, and I suddenly become aware of someone getting too close, getting in my space. I turned round and there he was, this guy, blond spiky hair, staring straight at me. And he started talking to his mate the drummer, who was dragging his drums in, while still looking at me, to be as intimidating as possible, chewing gum.

"He says, 'Kev, get this geezer.' And the drummer goes, 'What about him?' He says, 'He can play the guitar... really well... What a *wanker*.' That was the moment when I thought that everything I'd known as currency had turned to dust."

Some kids were genuinely frightened of, or at least disturbed by, punk. To Pink Floyd fans, that group represented something enlightening, the good old Floyd who had reached for the stars and set the controls for the heart of the sun. Then you had, in Johnny Rotten, some bug-eyed, sneering wretch wearing a Pink Floyd t-shirt defaced by the addition of 'I HATE' scrawled across it in marker pen, who was out to rip down all that you held dear.

The Sex Pistols provoked a near hysterical reaction from just about everybody, with gig after gig cancelled in late 1977 by promoters fearful of the trouble that booking them might cause, and with demonstrations taking place outside the ones that went ahead.

But then hold on… what had Rotten, born in 1956, been listening to for the last few years? Reports began to leak out that John Lydon from Finsbury Park was the Hawkwind fan who used to have green, shoulder-length hair. "The main people in punk were 19 or 20 years old and we had obviously been listening to Pink Floyd and ELP, and Johnny Rotten was a big Van Der Graaf Generator fan," says Mark Perry.

Steve Hillage recalls: "When I first met Johnny Rotten he looked me in the eye and said [adopts Rotten sneer], 'Flying Teapot', with a cheeky grin and I thought, 'Yeah mate, right.'"

This level of punk fundamentalism couldn't be sustained for long and many punk groups and fans admitted to liking David Bowie, T. Rex, and The New York Dolls, while the Sex Pistols covered 'No Fun' by Iggy & The Stooges. No one admitted to liking any progressive rock groups.

On 1977's 'Your Generation', Generation X sang that the previous generation meant nothing to them. Two singles later they released 'Ready Steady Go', and were singing about how great it had been in the Sixties.

For many teenagers at the time, one of the most significant cultural moments of 1977 was when Lydon was invited into Capitol Radio to bring in and talk about some of his favourite records. Rather than bringing in nothing and telling the listening public to fuck off, he created another shock, this time by playing and chatting – albeit warily – to host Tommy Vance about tracks by Tim Buckley, John Cale, Peter Hammill, Neil Young, Can, Captain Beefheart and the Third Ear Band as well as some choice reggae cuts. The *Third Ear Band*?

With that, the curtains of artifice were gently pulled aside to present a portrait of a young man with a wide-ranging taste in music. Malcolm McLaren was apparently furious at how Lydon had burst the Rotten bubble.

Lydon picked two tracks from Hammill's 1975 solo album, *Nadir's Big Chance*, even going so far as to say that Hammill was "a true original. I love all his stuff", and that David Bowie had "copied" him. In a time when statues were routinely kicked over, Hammill's was left standing, although it might have been gobbed on, or its base pissed against, from time to time.

Listening to 'Nobody's Business' from *Nadir's Big Chance*, a put-down song delivered by Hammill in a thrilling, slightly hysterical manner, with exclamatory upward turns at the end of the lines, it surely could have fed as an influence into Lydon's vocal delivery, which had become more mannered after the Pistols' early demos. Maybe so, but Hammill has been consistent in his denial of directly influencing punk, even going so far as to say that the album, whose title track finds him sneering at the fag-ends of glam rock still smouldering around him, wasn't even prescient of a sea change in rock music. "I kind of still go with that – that it didn't go *Nadir* to punk," he concurs. "But I'd say there was a parallel, because it was three chords on a loud electric guitar with a basic pulse and go 'Arrgh!'"

Mark Perry explains why he pulled the plug on *Sniffin' Glue* in 1977, after just a year, even though by the time it had reached issue 12, he had stepped up production and sold a massive 20,000 copies.

"What put me off was that [punk] narrows the rules," he says. "Suddenly you had three or four chords and that was it. And that's why in my own band I had a lot of influences from the pre-punk era. A lot of people got bored with it. I mean, Johnny Lydon got bored with it: Public Image Ltd was much more sophisticated than the Pistols.

"Something like Jethro Tull, *Dark Side Of The Moon*, it's serious music, complex music. If you just go back to three chords it doesn't work."

Perry was involved in setting up the Deptford Fun City and Step Forward Records labels, the latter with former Curved Air manager, Miles Copeland. He also fronted a band, Alternative TV, who were tough, minimal and uncompromising. Perry notes that some of their 1978 debut album, *The Image Is Cracked*, was influenced by King Crimson's *Red*, while his own primitive guitar style nodded back to some of Neil Young's ruminations on single notes.

At the time, slight gradations in age were crucial, and while he was willing to move on and experiment further with ATV and towards the end of the decade in the improvisational The Good Missionaries, some bands and fans resolutely stuck to the 1977 model.

"We used to be called 'hippie', because the punks that were younger, who were 16 when they got into The Clash, thought we were the sort of hippies they were supposed to slag off," Perry explains. "They thought, 'Hold on, this is the editor of *Sniffin' Glue*, the premier punk magazine that set all the ground rules, now he's fucking about with recorders and clarinets.' You could get away with that in London, but the provinces was where punk really meant something."

Steve Hillage still can't understand why journalists were so antipathetic towards hippies: "It wasn't the same, but we weren't exactly pillars of the establishment," he says. "They were having some sort of rebellion but I don't know why they were rebelling against me.

"I got a call from a magazine who wanted to do [an article on] punks vs hippies. I was chosen to be the hippie and [Sham 69 singer] Jimmy Pursey was chosen to be the punk. I went to where Sham 69 were rehearsing and started talking. The journalist was trying to provoke conflict and I found myself and Jimmy largely agreeing about many things politically, and he said that his grandmother was psychic and really into spirituality. It was not what you would expect at all; we actually found quite a good level of harmony. So the journalist was getting really disappointed. Finally he wanted us to do photos of us staring each other down aggressively. I said, 'I can't do that, were getting on OK and having a good chat.'"

Pursey suggested that the photographer took some pictures of them playing together, and after a jam he asked Hillage if he would play a gig with Sham 69. That gig was an appearance at the Reading Festival in August 1978, where Hillage guested on 'When The Kids Are United' before proceedings came to a halt with a stage invasion by skinheads, including a number wearing National Front t-shirts.

"It was quite a hardcore event," Hillage recalls. "There was a lot of aggro going on and fighting, and a guy came onstage and tried to attack Jimmy Pursey with a bottle, which he dealt with very well, actually."

In 1977 Daevid Allen and Gilli Smyth, now recording as Planet Gong, made the *Live Floating Anarchy* album, which included a punk-inspired track 'Opium For The People'. On it they were backed by Here & Now, who came across rather like a cross between The Pink Fairies and Gong.

Allen also noted that there was a youth culture overlap and that punks and hippies actually embodied "two different ways of saying no to the same people".

"At the time I was really inspired by John Lydon and all that new movement, and was very fed up with the clean hair and white clothes brigade that Yes and Genesis represented, and all the nice sweetish sounds. It was the beginning of a period when I detested prog and all the jazz aspects that were not really gutsy jazz, but were combed out and made rather middle class and nice. I went back to the gutsy.

"I did a gig in America with Bob Geldof upstairs and Gong downstairs. He saw us in the audience and said, 'I think there are some hippies in the audience. Kill a hippie.' The whole audience turned round and stared at us and we felt really shit scared, I can tell you. It was a good illustration of the power of the microphone against individuals. We fled downstairs. I've never really forgiven him for that, because that was a really bad thing to do to fellow musicians."

Just to emphasise that the kids could indeed be united, Perry's ATV were soon approached by Here & Now. "[They said] we really like your stuff, would you like to come and play some free gigs? We take a bucket around and you can sell your records. I just thought that was marvellous. Punk was good with all its rhetoric, but I thought that this is a way of giving something back, giving something to the people. It was a bit of a revelation to me.

"We played in unis, polytechnics – if the weather was nice we'd play outside in a field. To me it was more punk than punk. We were actually living it. We played at Stonehenge. You'd have a generator running the PA, and people were making veggie burgers. Sometimes there weren't any lights, so you'd get cars to shine their lights at the stage.

"I remember arguing with Miles Copeland. I said, 'Look, if we do this free tour we are actually building a new audience,' so that's why he let us do it."

It came to the notice of many that, in signing Wire, EMI's progressive subsidiary Harvest Records was once again ahead of the game in a very different milieu. The group's singer and guitarist Colin Newman had been an art student doing a foundation year at Winchester Art College, before going on to Watford. He recalls that Brian Eno occasionally used to come into the college because Peter Schmidt, with whom he had devised *Oblique Strategies*, tutored there.

"[Bass guitarist] Graham Lewis handed me a set of lyrics that turned into 'Lowdown' and at that point I knew that I had to do something that wasn't like I'd written before," Newman recalls. "I didn't want it to be traditional. I wanted it to be open. I wanted it to be progressive, actually. I probably came down more on the side of prog than against it, although I hated as much as anyone else its overblown moments."

Wire's 1977 Harvest debut *Pink Flag* was quite shocking in its starkness. The Ramones had managed fourteen songs in twenty-nine minutes but Wire managed twenty-one in thirty-five, with 'Field Day For The Sundays' weighing in at twenty-eight seconds. Wire were inspired in part by The Damned and the Ramones, and like the latter's debut, *Pink Flag* had some good pop tunes, as well as – despite the idea of some reviewers that it mirrored the grimness of Seventies life — a lot of humour, which could be discerned once the listener had recovered from its short, sharp shock.

The lyrics to 'It's So Obvious' find them already restless for more change, to leave 1977 behind, and although Wire did punk brilliantly, they had largely discarded its musical vocabulary by the time of 1978's *Chairs Missing*. It still sounded modern, but with its long songs, use of synthesizers and its psychedelic leanings, some reviewers pointed the dreaded "p" word at it.

"Why is *Chairs Missing* the first real Wire album? Because it's the first progressive record," Newman says. "That was definitely where I wanted to go. It was a little bit monochrome, some of *Pink Flag*, and that was part of the aim of it because we sort of cleared the decks. But we weren't attached to that material."

Newman notes that just as many of the original Harvest signings would have been birthed in psychedelia, this was also a major influence on Wire.

"What I liked about the new stuff was the experimental attitude with the tightness of the playing," he says. "'Practice Makes Perfect' is prog meets Steely Dan in a weird kind of way. It's rhythmic, it's got a sharpness to it. It speaks more to the psychedelic and unhinged things about Syd Barrett, but at the same time it has got more of a prog attitude than anything else that was going on around it at the time. And that's where Wire really established themselves."

A year and a bit had gone by since punk had emerged and things were changing fast. In 1977, Magazine, a group that vocalist Howard Devoto had formed after he left the Buzzcocks, had come out with the fast, aggressive single 'Shot By Both Sides'. In 1978 on their album *Real Life*, the opening track 'Definitive Gaze' starts off with a funky syncopated groove but soon blossoms into an instrumental chorus with a synthesizer melody line against a lush string synth backdrop that sounded more than a little like Genesis. It felt like after a brief, spasmodic convulsion, progressive rock had come back already, but rather that clean haired, white clad musicians singing escapist, fantasy lyrics about Squonks, these were edgier, younger, short-haired guys whose inspiration came from darker stuff, like the short stories of Dostoevsky and Kafka.

David Bedford had scored *The Orchestral Tubular Bells* and his modernist orchestral album *Star's End* had been released on Virgin in 1974. He then recorded a trio of solo concept albums for the label, which crossed into progressive rock, *The Rime Of The Ancient Mariner* (1975), *The Odyssey* (1976), and *Instructions For Angels* (1977). He sums up his career on the label: "It was clear that I wasn't selling the number of albums that they had hoped. If they were counted as classical albums, they would have been among the best sellers of the year, but for a rock label like Virgin they weren't selling huge amounts. So I did feel a bit under pressure.

"When punk came, so I went. My [Virgin] contract was just terminated. 'We feel that now you have had three albums, the time has come to part company.' It was due to lack of sales, plus the fact that they had signed the Pistols around this time."

And while received wisdom would have it that the music business was full of progressive rock leviathans bloated by their wealth, contracts were rarely generous so that financially, the majority of groups were just ticking by. Tony Banks of Genesis, who at this point were still in debt to Charisma, notes that "it wasn't until the mid-Seventies that the progressives started to be financially viable".

Pete Brown was just coming to the end of his time in a group, Party In The Rain, and is less than impressed by any claims that punk purveyed a genuine anti-authoritarian stance.

"It was phoney," Brown says. "They invented the clothes first and most of the people were invented. It was the first time that the record business had decided to create something that would sell rather than recording something that was there. And they did it in a very, very cynical way. And there was a demographic attached to it that working-class people didn't have any money and so they wanted to create these phoney working-class artists that middle-class people with money would have sympathy for.

"It didn't work. Commercially it was a total disaster. The punk thing destroyed the album market for ten years. They were putting an emptiness back onto the scene that fucked up anything."

Steve Hillage regards punk as a genuine movement, initially coming out of art school.

"Record companies are always looking for the new thing; I don't see anything unusual there at all," he says. "The one thing to stress is that record companies were launching into the new stuff and the new independent companies who were coming up, weren't necessarily dissing the old stuff, but the music papers were being partisan in a way that they were dissing the stuff that two years ago they had been overtly praising. It all gets a bit Soviet propaganda."

The main players in the music press – *Sounds* and *NME*, with *Melody Maker* lagging behind just a bit – all got behind punk, although all had their dissenting voices. *NME* had perhaps the greatest credibility in this respect as it had published Mick Farren's epochal article "The Titanic Sails At Dawn" in June 1976.

Farren's aesthetic, having been a member of The Deviants and part of the Ladbroke Grove freak scene, was at odds with the mainstream in 1976 as he perceived it, with its progressive rock indulgence, overblown stadium rock, and a new kind of rock star arrogance that was ever more divorced from reality. The writer felt that he had discerned, from reading letters of dissent posted in to the paper, the tip of a metaphorical iceberg. "The iceberg in this case seems to be one of a particularly threatening nature. In fact it is an iceberg that is drifting uncomfortably close to the dazzlingly lit, wonderfully appointed Titanic that is big-time, rock-pop, tax-exile, jet-set showbusiness," Farren wrote.

"Unless someone aboard is prepared to leave the party and go up on the bridge and do something about it, at least a slight change of course, the whole chromium, metal-flake Leviathan could go down with all hands."

He concludes: "Putting The Beatles back together isn't going to be the salvation of rock'n'roll. Four kids playing to their contemporaries in a dirty cellar club might.

"And that, gentle reader, is where you come in."

Most people were still unprepared for what followed, but Farren captured in words a staleness that many had begun to recognise. It was hard to get enthused, for example, over photographs of Rod Stewart in whatever tax haven he was living in with his latest squeeze, model Britt Ekland. He had graduated from the bog brush-haired jack-the-lad in the Faces, to someone who seemed now to be sporting an expensively sculpted coiffure and wearing a permanent smirk. And he wasn't going to be playing at your local venue any time soon.

On *Melody Maker* the staff were ambivalent. Chris Welch remembers going to see the Sex Pistols at Brunel University in Uxbridge. "That was quite an event, it was quite exciting to see them," he says. He also remembers on another occasion having a drink with bassist Glen Matlock and drummer Paul Cook and being heartened by the fact that they were both Thin Lizzy fans. But he was also concerned that all that he held dear was on the brink of being destroyed.

Chris Charlesworth recalls the mood in the camp: "*MM* was slow to react to punk, which was critical, because *NME* jumping onto punk put them ahead in the circulation race. But we'd been almost conditioned by editor Ray Coleman [and everyone else] on downwards to appreciate good musicianship and write about that, so it was difficult for us to appreciate the three-chord slam-bang thing, which took two months of guitar practice, rather than twenty years like Robert Fripp. We did eventually – I certainly did – but it took me a while. When I first saw the Ramones I couldn't tell if it was a joke or not."

Caroline Coon, like Barry Miles, was another seasoned countercultural figure who embraced this new music. In fact, they both managed The Clash at different times early on. She was an important figure in Release, the charitable organisation that gave advice on drug use and drug laws.

Looking back in 2016, Coon wrote: "You'd go into editorial meetings and say it was the next thing, and you'd be laughed at. I think journalists and editors were horrified that the next generation was coming along and they would become redundant. And they certainly didn't want to be told this by 'a girl'. There was a lot of misogyny around.

"By the summer of 1976, the *MM* couldn't ignore it any longer. So when I gave it the name 'punk rock' – the term had been used to describe the American rock bands of the Sixties and was more glamorous than 'rebel', I joined together the new groups on the British scene into a critical mass. I knew from the hippie era that there would be more security for youth if they belonged to a movement. It was about safety in numbers and also creating an identity."

New Musical Express went furthest out on a limb when they advertised for two "hip young gunslingers" to join the staff. Barry Miles described what was happening at the paper. "[Nick Logan] was a good editor, but he never went to a single gig the whole time I was there. He was into the publishing game and did well at it. A good example of his skill was in hiring Tony Parsons and Julie Burchill.

"Nick saw what was happening with punk so he wanted some young kids. At the time Julie had not written anything longer than a 600-word school essay but she was stroppy and looked the part. Parsons lied about his age."

Although *New Musical Express* journalist Nick Kent had played with the Sex Pistols, his association with the group was also marked, rather too literally, by an incident when Sid Vicious – who could only loosely be called the group's bassist, as he was more-or-less incapable of playing the instrument and was basically positioned like a gurning gargoyle during live shows – attacked him with a bike chain. That McLaren used this to gain the group notoriety was a sign of the dismal lows of publicity at any cost into which he was about to guide the group. Perhaps this is why Kent now comes out with this surprising assertion.

"Forty years later, I'm a lot more sympathetic towards the prog rock phenomenon than I was. I actually feel more sympathy for prog than I do for punk. Most of the punk people, they talk about their music as art, and frankly it's not – nor was prog rock, but at least the prog guys have a sense of humour about what they were doing, and there was a sense of musical exploration and experimentation. Even if it went down the wrong by-roads, at least they were trying to stretch themselves."

After a mid-Seventies period when he seemed to have lost direction, along with a lot of modern rock at the time, John Peel embraced punk as well as the reggae that had so incensed some of his listeners to the extent that he had received death threats and (human) turds through the post.

Peel's head was turned by the Ramones' debut album. "The initial reaction was one of, not hostility exactly, but people, rather as they had done when we first played reggae almost a decade previously, had written in and said, 'Come on, old fellow, pull yourself together.'"

Peel followed his instincts, which he admitted involved doing the opposite of what listeners, en masse, had asked him to do.

Alan "Fluff" Freeman, fifty years young in 1977, who had been a champion of progressive rock on his Saturday afternoon show, embraced punk, playing The Damned's 'New Rose' on its week of release. This made for some interesting playlists, with The Slits and Henry Cow on the same programme; and Siouxsie & The Banshees' then unreleased 'Metal Postcard' alongside something by Camel.

On TV *The Old Grey Whistle Test* seemed to be seriously lagging behind public tastes, with nothing resembling British punk or new wave groups on show. It was assumed that Bob Harris and his producers were simply being reactionary, but the real reason was both simple and unexpected. "It just got ridiculously overblown and over-produced, a lot of that stuff at that time, which is why it was very important that punk came along when it did as it took us back to rock'n'roll," says Bob Harris. "The energy they brought in was needed at that point.

"I'm not rewriting history here either, because all the new wave bands exploded on indie labels through singles, so we weren't able to feature them until they started putting out those albums, which was a year down the line."

But the programme's album-tracks-only remit was not common knowledge and its apparent indifference to most of what was going on around it provoked "an aggressive backlash" and to some Harris became, in his own words, "a hate figure".

If you were a progressive rock musician in 1977, punk or new wave most definitely wasn't made for you. It was all well and good to say that you had been a bit of a hooligan in your youth, but it was better to keep your counsel and just keep on doing your own stuff.

In a publicity masterstroke, one artist remained aloof of all this. In 1977 *"Heroes"* was released with the advertising strapline: "There's Old Wave. There's New Wave. And Then There Is David Bowie."

At the Knebworth Festival in 1978, Peter Gabriel, then a positively geriatric 28 years old, declared he was going to play the anthem of the BOF Brotherhood – that being an acronym for "boring old fart", an insult that sneering teenage punks would direct at anyone senior in years. He then played a comedy punk version of 'A Whiter Shade Of Pale'.

Steve Hillage made '1988 Aktivator', his own punk song, complete with sneering vocal inflections, but although Hillage had guested with Sham 69 and liked punk because "it was a short energy burst rather than a long, multi-levelled epic", it sounded all wrong.

As mentioned in Chapter 30, Gentle Giant were playing a similarly dangerous game when they recorded their "punk" song 'Betcha Thought We Couldn't Do It' on 1977's *The Missing Piece*. And the less said about Mike Oldfield's 'Punkadiddle' the better. It was best to leave well alone. Unless you were prepared to play with them live, as Robert Fripp did with The Stranglers and The Damned in the UK and Blondie in New York.

Sonja Kristina, who had been the singer with Curved Air, took to this new music with an enthusiasm that was not shared by all of her peers. "About the time that the band broke [in 1976] Stewart [Copeland] and I were going down to the Roxy club [in Covent Garden], which was where punk in England was born, and really enjoying what we were seeing. It wasn't a massive scene at the time but just good little bands with an agenda: play very fast, very short songs, very simple chords and proclaim passionately."

Like Mark Perry, most of the teenagers I knew at the time found that after the initial shock to the system, they assimilated all that they heard without too much bother about barriers or labels, and embraced both punk and progressive rock.

Video footage of one early gig by The Clash shows a front row of greatcoated hippie types pressed against the stage and all looking like they had got lost on their way to a Jethro Tull concert. With hindsight – and in common with many of my peers – punk had become the stroppy, scruffy, nay-saying single-finger-saluting yin to my clean-haired, white-clothed yang. To my mind they were, oddly enough, made for each other and I felt more complete as a result.

CHAPTER 42

The End of the Century

For upcoming progressive rock groups, the late Seventies was not the best period in which to embark upon a musical career. The band England recorded the album *Garden Shed* for Arista in 1977, having signed to the label the previous year. Their influences are clear with arrangements that bring to mind Yes and there's a dash of Supertramp in the melodic shape of their songs, which have a pop immediacy. And it's no surprise to find out that keyboard player Robert Webb had a few Genesis albums in his collection.

But *Garden Shed* is full of invention, with a subtle deftness to the drumming. There's also an English pastoralism about it, particularly on 'Three Piece Suite', with Webb's sweeping Mellotron to the fore. Being good at what you do has never been a guarantee of commercial success, but if this album had been released two years before or even after that year, it would surely have attracted favourable press and greater sales, but Arista failed to get behind the band – they actually considered not releasing the album – and by the following year England had folded.

But while some of the serious progressive rock groups were having a difficult time of it, the groups who were taking over the market were just a bit more fun. Actually, "fun" wasn't necessarily a way that one would have addressed Supertramp, but they had come out of progressive rock, then honed down their songwriting and released a sequence of big-selling albums and singles from *Crime Of The Century* (1974) – with its Top 20 single 'Dreamer' – through to the worldwide hit *Breakfast In America* in 1979.

Another group who had explored their pop side were Electric Light Orchestra, originally a spin-off from The Move. They had gone from the cello-heavy chamber pop of their self-titled 1971 debut album on the Harvest label to *ELO 2* (1973), which was right in the progressive rock field, including a version of Grieg's *In The Hall Of The Mountain King*, a favourite of instrumental groups since Nero & The Gladiators recorded it in 1961. Drummer Bev Bevan recalls the group's development: "[*ELO 2*] was totally experimental. We didn't quite know which direction we were going in to begin with. I like *ELO 2*, but the tracks go on and on. 'Kuiama' is about eleven minutes long.

"The turning point was probably *Eldorado* in '74, which was a concept album and I think it really worked. That's when Jeff [Lynne] really began to blossom as a songwriter, and he became a lot more confident in his singing ability and his production ability."

By 1977's *Out Of The Blue* their music still retained some of that progressive spirit but they had essentially become a pop phenomenon, selling out stadia in the US and playing onstage in a giant perspex spacecraft.

If you were looking for even more fun there was always Queen, who had mixed hard rock and progressive bombast on *Queen* (1973) and *Queen II* (1974), scored an enormous hit with the camp operatics of their 1975 single 'Bohemian Rhapsody', and thereafter seemed to be able to release anything in any style and it would sell bucketloads.

And 10cc were still making their erudite and witty pop confections, despite Lol Creme and Kevin Godley quitting in 1976. That duo went on to chart success but started in an unorthodox way that year with a triple concept album, *Consequences*.

One group who bucked all mid-Seventies progressive rock trends – and who were also fun – were The Enid. They were formed in 1974 by keyboard player and Royal College Of Music graduate Robert John Godfrey, together with guitarists Francis Lickerish and Steve Stewart, and Dave Williams on bass, who had all lived at Finchden Manor in Kent, a residential experimental educational facility which was known as a "therapeutic community" – a safe haven rather than a correctional centre. Musician and broadcaster Tom Robinson, who was in his own words "a suicidal sixteen-year-old" spent time in that establishment where the founder George Lyward had high success rates with rehabilitating young offenders.

After Lyward's death, the place closed in 1974 so these now displaced musical youths rented a house in Cranbrook. It is no wonder, then, that The Enid has always been based on a sense of community and communal living.

"The only way The Enid works is as part of a musical family," says Godfrey. "You think of all the sacrifices one has to make sharing one's domestic world with others – actually there are a great deal of pluses as well and you don't really miss the things you have to give up."

The group's name, which conjures up images of quaint and straight-laced maiden aunts, is about as un-rock'n'roll as it comes, although what it actually means is hard to define. "Somehow, Enid or The Enid, dependent on context, became a brief but potent byword within the

Finchden community," Godfrey explains. "Its meaning was non-specific – a joker in the pack – a "lost for words" word... which was either used as a substitute noun or to exemplify any adjective or verb which needed spicing up – a silly piece of fraternal amusement.

"I managed to interest my mother's cousin who was the same age as me, from the wealthy side of the family, and he spent a great deal of money on helping The Enid to get going – about thirty grand. My cousin paid for the recording of *In The Region Of The Summer Stars*, which was recorded at Sarm Studios in Whitechapel."

On The Enid's 1976 debut album, Glen Tollet replaced Williams on bass and drummer Dave Storey was recruited, and the music is based on material from Godfrey's 1974 solo album *The Fall Of Hyperion*, but with less showy pianistics and more intricately woven ensemble playing. The album was originally meant to have vocals, but the singer Peter Roberts committed suicide and so the group recorded it as an instrumental album. The album was released on BUK in 1976 and distributed by EMI, but was soon deleted.

Their second album *Aerie Fairie Nonsense* is another example of music written by rock musicians who, like Godfrey, "understand the language" of classical music. He explains the side-long 'Fand' as "an attempt to try to do something on a larger scale, like a little symphony. It's structured rather like that; it's born out of motifs so that all the musical themes are interconnected and related to one another." But *Aerie Faerie Nonsense* had been funded by one of The Enid's backers "with money he didn't have". He was supposed to be forming an EMI subsidiary called Honeybee, but went bankrupt and so *Aerie Faerie Nonsense* came out on EMI but was also soon deleted.

But The Enid came into their element in concert and were one of the most singular of all progressive rock groups. Newly recruited bass guitarist Terry "Thunderbags" Pack and Storey formed a tough, imaginative rhythm section and live, pieces like 'Fand' were thrillingly powerful. But there was something absurd and camp about them too.

Lickerish and fellow guitarist Steve Stewart flounced around the stage front, hair flowing. By contrast, the balding Godfrey, wearing a velvet jacket and bow tie, and clearly not much of a singer, would occasionally come and take the microphone, like a groovy music teacher trying to get down with the kids, delivering spirited cover versions of 'Wild Thing' and 'Pretty Vacant'.

They would also play 'The Dam Busters March'. "We did [that], really, for Martin Wallis who was the grandson of Barnes Wallis, and who was one of our roadies," says Godfrey.

If you thought that they looked ridiculous, well, they knew that already and didn't care anyway. Faced with a provincial college audience of hippies, punks, pseudo-punks, don't-knows and shoulder-shruggers who had just turned up because there was nothing else to do, The Enid had the remarkable ability to win them over and make them into fans – for that evening at least.

"I think that The Enid were a repository for the largely middle-class kids who were at university or doing A-levels, something serious like physics, and they wanted somewhere to go, as they didn't feel comfortable wrapping themselves in a bin liner and putting a knitting needle through their nose," says Godfrey. "Very quickly I realised that was more based on a fashion statement than anything to do with music and that sooner or later, the clever musicians, well-educated musicians [would re-emerge].

"The band had radical views. We were hostile to the dinosaurs that Keith Emerson and Yes had become, because they had lost it, basically. This concept of the supergroup had driven away any possibility for a band to get off the ground, because you needed £100,000 [sic] to spend on an organ especially made for you by Yamaha, and so it became just so overblown and bloated. People weren't any longer experimenting or achieving anything new."

The Enid had another disastrous deal with Pye Records in 1979, but they have continued until the present day. Keyboard player and Enid fan Gordon Reid has these memories of the group's halcyon days:

"Reading Festival 1977 – the year of the big mud. It was a horrible weekend. The rain barely abated, no matter where you walked you sank into the ground up to your knees, the girl I had gone with ended up in a sleeping bag with one of my mates, and even the music was atrocious, with at least one band being mud-bombed off stage. So there I was, disconsolately walking around the stalls at the back of the arena when I heard something remarkable, and the first few bars of 'In The Region Of The Summer Stars' saw me pushing and jostling to reach the front of the crowd. Melodramatic as it sounds, it was the day that I discovered The Enid, and it was a day that helped shape my life.

"Released in 1976, In The Region Of The Summer Stars *remains perhaps the most successful marriage of classical music and rock music ever recorded. Neither a rock album with an orchestra plastered uncomfortably over the top, nor a classical album with guitars, bass and drums shoe-horned awkwardly into the mix, the marriage was at the cellular level, where the two art forms became inseparable from one another. The result was music on a grand scale, powerful, humorous, emotive, tongue-in-cheek and bombastic in equal measure.*

"*Following The Enid soon became a major part of my social life and, at a breakthrough concert at the Victoria Palace Theatre later in 1977, my new girlfriend and I met one of the band's two guitarists, Steve Stewart, for the first time. Innumerable further concerts followed,* Aerie Faerie Nonsense *was released, and we soon got to know the band well, attending parties at their communal house in Hertford, and occasionally helping to move equipment when extra hands were needed.*

"*But over it all towered Godfrey's dominating form. Publicly avuncular, often a bully behind the scenes, and sometimes remarkably generous to his friends and fans, his word was law, and he drove the band mercilessly.*

"*Supporting them throughout this era was The Enid Society, a loose collection of fans who provided accommodation for one another as the band travelled up and down the country.*

"*For me, nothing that followed The Enid of the* In The Region *and* Aerie Faerie *tours quite equaled the magic of those early years. It was tie-dyed t-shirts versus safety pins, Mahler's 9th versus* Never Mind The Bollocks, *us against the world. And the incredible thing was that we didn't get beaten to a pulp. In fact, the world joined in with us and sang along as The Enid pumped out 'The Dam Busters March' and 'Land Of Hope And Glory' alongside 'Wild Thing' and 'Pretty Vacant'. It will never happen again – things have changed far too much for that to be possible. I'm just glad that I was there to be a part of it when it did.*"

Fans and journalists have a view of musicians, their motivations, their place within a certain scene, which is often completely at odds with the view of the musicians. They try to make sense of what is going on, while musicians try to play their best within what is going on. Bill Bruford's incisive drumming, with its rock drive and jazz intricacy and exciting, risky fills effectively defined a certain style of questing progressive rock drumming in the Seventies.

He was one of the musicians who one most associates with that style of music, but as he has said, if he had been born ten years earlier he might have been a bebop specialist; if he had been born ten years later he might have been a new romantic.

For, like groups, individual musicians rarely have master plans. Instead they act on hunches, whims, play what's there to be played at the time and hopefully do all this while earning money. After leaving King Crimson in autumn 1974, Bruford played with National Health, Genesis, Roy Harper & Trigger, Phil Collins' jazz fusion group Brand X, Gong and American band Pavlov's Dog. He even tried to persuade Fripp to reform King Crimson. Many fans would have assumed that he would have walked into a high-profile band straightaway.

"Musicians don't say no; they never do," says Bruford. "Someone might have thought that I was famous because I was in Yes or something, but that didn't mean anything to me; that's three or four years earlier. I'd been around Crimson, which to all intents and purposes had gone flat on its back, so I was up for playing with anyone who'd have me.

"It's a bit like you are interviewing an actor. Actors are notoriously insecure and will jump at the first job they can get if they are resting – musicians also. So what came into my purview were people like Gong and Roy Harper. That should explain my behaviour. It's not that I've gone mad, it's just that somebody's asking me to play.

"Another misconception from the outsider's viewpoint is that all we players want to stay in one group forever: get wealthy, get silly, retire. A jazz background, like mine, suggests a different process: you join a group and contribute as best you can, and move on if you've not got anything more to offer."

Bruford decided to start preparing for a solo album. And rather than a typical drummer's solo vehicle where other musicians are recruited to basically write all the material, Bruford played piano, albeit as a "beginner". He had also written 'Five Per Cent For Nothing' on Yes's *Fragile* and contributed the odd melodic phrase to 'And You And I' and King Crimson's 'Starless'.

"Back in the Seventies I was watching how other people did it, thinking I could probably do it too, and that's why I formed a band around 1977," he says.

Bruford describes his particular way of composing: "I hear some rhythm and it's easy to put a bass line to a rhythm, even if it's only one note. The next thing you know is that you've got a different note and then a chord is implied and you are off and running. So I hear it that way, seldom from a vocal down."

One of the first pieces that he composed for his debut solo album, *Feels Good To Me*, released in January 1978, was 'Beelzebub', which had also been rehearsed by a short-lived and tentative trio of Bruford, Wakeman and John Wetton. Bruford describes it as being "from the same pot as 'Five Percent For Nothing' – very staccato from the short sounds of the drums, often with a legato bridge for contrast".

For his group, Bruford hired keyboard player Dave Stewart, who he had played with in National Health, guitarist Alan Holdsworth who had recently featured in Soft Machine and Gong, and American bass guitarist Jeff Berlin. Bruford had played sessions for American singer Annette Peacock and so was keen to have her involvement.

The drummer also demonstrated a genuine songwriter's ear for melody with the jazzy ballad 'It Seems Like A Lifetime Ago', which he sketched out on a Portastudio, then a state-of-the-art multi-track cassette recorder.

"I wanted and loved Annette's prototypical rap on 'Back To The Beginning' and 'Adios A La Pasada': that in-between-ness – is she going to sing this phrase or talk this phrase?" Bruford says. "She could half sing the phrase and drop it away in speech, all kinds of things like that, which were becoming really interesting. If we'd had more time we could have gone further, but she was only around for one album.

"I wasn't sure that we thought of ourselves as 'fusion'," he explains. "We wanted to be a rock group with electricity and guitars, powerful, but then we wanted some serious harmony in it, with the focus being primarily on the instrumentalists."

Bruford – as the group were now billed – were a popular live draw, playing at colleges and small theatres. "We played with brio, gusto, and fun, but with serious intent. The notes had to be played in the right order," he says. At this time the drummer was also involved with U.K., one of the last new high-profile progressive rock groups of the Seventies.

U.K. – U.K.
Original Label: EG
Producer: U.K.
Recorded: December 1977–January 1978
Released: March 1978

After their aborted trio with Wakeman, for their new group, Bruford and Wetton each invited a musician to join. Bruford had a huge admiration for Allan Holdsworth, who had played on *Feels Good To Me*, while Wetton brought along violin and keyboard player Eddie Jobson, who had first appeared in the spotlight as a teenage wunderkind with Curved Air and had gone on to play with Roxy Music and also Frank Zappa. Collectively they were inevitably described as a potential supergroup.

But this was going to be big, not least because of the America effect regarding King Crimson. Bruford notes that it can take a long time for some groups' music to spread through the States. King Crimson had been gaining popularity as a live band and although they had broken up before *Red* was released in late 1974, their posthumous reputation had continued to grow. Bruford's playing on the album was remarkable, and Wetton was the lead singer and had proved himself a technically adept and formidably heavy bass player. Add to that the perennial allure of early Yes and an enthusiastic record company, and an audience was guaranteed.

The group's self-titled debut opens in dramatic fashion on 'In The Dead Of Night', with a juddering bass drum and bass guitar figure that opens out with a keyboard countermelody and Bruford playing fills on rototoms – a newly developed type of shell-less drum that could be tuned by rotating, giving a well-defined, flat, punchy sound.

"Allan Holdsworth's guitar solo on 'In The Dead Of Night' is fantastic as a little work of art – I could do a musical analysis on that," says Bruford. "And of course that caught Eddie Van Halen's ear in the States because it was the lead track on the album. At the time of doing it I was probably so relieved that the track had been cut, that I went, 'Oh great, give me another cup of coffee' – just getting through it. Same with every King Crimson album: getting an album done without breaking up. None of it was a breeze and I wish I could say otherwise. But I don't blame my colleagues.

"It's never easy: if it were easy everyone would do it. I'm one of these people who never found music particularly easy anyway. Making an album is, for me, a hazardous process, full of various shades of anxiety."

U.K. is a mix of songs and instrumentals. Jobson's 'Alaska' starts with a frozen landscape of synths and shifts into a speedy accented group performance. His 'Presto Vivace And Reprise', the last section of 'In The Dead Of Night', is full of staccato keyboard figures that sound decidedly Zappa-esque. He composed a similar section on 'Mental Medication', although on that song, Bruford's lyrics aren't a patch on his efforts on *Feels Good To Me*, his musings on music itself coming across as rather trite. Wetton's evocations of Soho on 'Nevermore' as a place where people's *"spirits"* are raised and so the people who go there aren't *"so low"* are similarly rather clunky, although the tune is typically strong. Holdsworth's acoustic guitar introduction is a gorgeous showcase and he plays another evocative electric solo into the song.

The album was produced by the group, who had a celebratory playback gathering at Advision. "It would be the last time that you would hear it in such quality," says Bruford. Guests were invited and bottles of champagne were opened. One of the attendees was Zappa himself who was over playing in the UK, although his opinions on the music are unknown.

Bruford is complimentary about Jobson's compositional abilities, but ironically a split was already beginning to form within the group along a particular fault line.

"Eddie was very good, a very efficient musician, but one of the people whose mission in life is to produce what the audience wants, or what he thinks the audience wants," Bruford says. "A very dangerous game, as the chances are that you might fail.

"There's the camp that says, 'This is a product and I'm producing it, and I want all you guys to buy it and I'll make it as shiny, nice, and agreeable as possible.' And then there's the process camp who say, 'I'm a maturing musician. What you are paying me to do is to get better within myself and produce something neither of us has heard before. That's what I think my obligation and function is as a musician as opposed to selling a product.'

"So Eddie and I split on that, but Eddie was a fine craftsman, a great musician with a great set of skills who came up with good compositions. It's very strong, that first album, and sold like hotcakes and continues to sell."

Holdsworth thrived on spontaneity and U.K. was the most commercial context in which he was ever likely to play. And he didn't take too kindly to being asked by Jobson, on occasion, to replicate something that he had played previously. Going back to Bruford's comments about what musicians do and what commentators want, for the fan, that the initial U.K. line-up broke up within a year constitutes an "if only..." moment. To which Bruford says: "Musicians and artists are wise to avoid getting caught up in all that, otherwise next thing you know you're a parody of a heritage act, wasting away on the nostalgia circuit."

In this case it's not just that fans want more of the same, but in the case of this initial U.K. line-up, new ground was being broken and so business felt unfinished. Especially as the group's subsequent releases were markedly inferior. The fans and commentators, those who buy the musicians' records and go to their concerts, had a good reason to feel disappointed.

By the late Seventies, taste was slowly shifting more towards the product, whereas in the earlier part of the decade, in Bruford's words: "When the musicians took to the stage the expectation was that neither listener nor performer knew quite what was going to happen in advance." And sad to say, with U.K., Bruford fell on the wrong side of that dividing line.

"There was a conversation with John in the car going back to New York after a big show in Philadelphia and he said, 'Eddie and I want to do it this way, and if you don't want to, why don't you leave?' Or I said, 'I don't want it to go that way and so I'll leave.' I can't remember quite what was said. It wasn't unpleasant, but clearly John and Eddie had got the bit between their teeth and thought that they were the creative heart of U.K. and could [progress] with a simpler drummer and a simpler guitar player."

Bruford and Holdsworth went back to play in Bruford and both that group and U.K. folded in 1980.

The last group in this overview of who came to prominence towards the end of the Seventies are the most difficult to categorise. In November of 1977 this writer chanced upon, and recorded, a new song on a John Peel session. Over an ominous, nagging guitar riff, a singer with a harsh adenoidal whine, who out-sneered John Lydon, ended up singing the old marching tune 'Lillibulero' as the song slid into chaos.

Another ferocious piece changed tack at least every half minute, before ending up subsumed into an abstract coda of bells, percussion and organ chords. It was the second session by This Heat and the tracks were 'Makeshift Swahili' and 'Rimp Romp Ramp/Basement Boy'. Peel announced that: "I've had letters asking me to play more music like This Heat. But to my knowledge there is no other music like This Heat."

Drummer and vocalist Charles Hayward had fulfilled both roles in Quiet Sun. Looking further back he was initially influenced by another singing drummer, Tony Meehan from The Shadows. Later on, his interest was piqued by The Who, Jimi Hendrix, The Beatles, The Beach Boys, Spirit, Ornette Coleman, Miles Davis, East Of Eden and King Crimson.

Soft Machine were also important. Hayward didn't go to the group's house in Dalmore Road, Dulwich, south London, as his friends Bill and Ian MacCormick had done, but the way Soft Machine influenced him went beyond technicalities and could be summed up by their production of a feeling of visceral excitement, a noise that went almost beyond music.

"A lot of it was the rush rather more than the detail," Hayward explains. "Just the sheer fuzziness on *Third*, the opening of 'Facelift'. Even before the main theme there was the improvised section [an abstract group improvisation with Mike Ratledge's searing fuzz organ to the fore], that 'Eeargh!' The theme was only there to make the 'Eeargh!' happen more. The notes were only there to let the sound have a reason to be there. It was more about the sound than it was about anything else."

After Quiet Sun had recorded *Mainstream* in 1975, a new version of the group briefly formed, with Bill McCormick on bass, Hayward on drums and guitarist Charles Bullen, who had played with Hayward in two other groups, Dolphin Logic and latterly Radar Favourites. The new Quiet Sun had been set to play a major London showcase, but being reduced to just Hayward, Bullen and former Radar Favourites manager

Gareth Williams, by that time, the trio, who now were called This Heat, were instead offered their inaugural gig at a club in Hampstead in early 1976.

This Heat were quite unlike Quiet Sun. They were an example of what progressive rock could potentially become, but operated apart from their peers. They came to prominence in punk, but had nothing to do with that style of music either, so the trio ended up treading a somewhat lonely path, an avant-rock group before anyone had even thought of the term.

Both the Charleses were experienced musicians, who in Hayward's opinion, "knew too much, but in the wrong sort of way", while Williams was both the rogue element and a vital catalyst: in the parlance of the time he was, like Brian Eno, a "non-musician", completely unbounded by technique, but possessed of an innate musicality and full of new ideas.

One view about Seventies rock – and fusion – groups is that many of the more gifted players couldn't see far enough beyond the impressiveness of their own technique, so while they could produce grandstanding solos, this did not necessarily serve the music as a whole. "That's why I didn't like later Soft Machine," says Hayward. "There's something that I've always known and it's very hard to quantify, but some players only bring you to the surface of their playing, because they are so concerned with their relationship with the instruments that it's all they know, and that's all you hear. And other players take you behind the playing where you go into this other world where playing isn't really what they are thinking about."

There was an instinctual "start from scratch" mentality about their approach, which ran contrary to trends in the era. This proved more important to the music they produced than any list of influences. And although Hayward had heard the Music Improvisation Company – featuring percussionist Jamie Muir – before he'd heard King Crimson's *Larks' Tongues In Aspic*, rather than being influenced by free improvisers, This Heat went back to square one, seeing what they could produce with improvising as the most essential form of musical self-expression and explored their own fascination with tape, editing them for use in the studio and in concert.

As well as being adept at both compositions – some of which were complex – and improvisation, This Heat also explored pure sonics, utilising different recording media in different physical spaces and environments. Although musically very different from Bruford, they epitomised his idea of process as opposed to product, only releasing two albums and a 12-inch single in their six-year lifespan.

This Heat initially rehearsed daily in Hayward's parents' house in Camberwell, south London. Then in 1977, they moved operations into a derelict meat pie factory in Brixton that had been converted into artists' spaces. The trio put in regular eight-hour shifts at their rehearsal area and studio named Cold Storage, as it was originally built as a cooling facility.

The group came to the notice of David Cunningham from Flying Lizards, who was talent-scouting for Andrew King and Peter Jenner's Blackhill Enterprises. But commercial priorities meant that they never managed This Heat, although they kept hold of the publishing on their first album and got them some dead time sessions at an East End 24-track studio, The Workhouse, at which Cunningham was ostensibly the producer. He remembers studio co-owner Manfred Mann eavesdropping on some of the amazing sounds they were making. For their self-titled debut they also recorded on reel-to-reel at Cold Storage and on cassette, their most audacious piece being '24-Track Loop', which was made by dubbing a cassette recording of organs, viola and drums onto the two-inch master tape and running it around the studio. The sound was manipulated with an Eventide Harmonizer, which enabled pitch-shifting, delay and feedback generation.

On *This Heat*, 'Horizontal Hold' exemplifies Hayward's love of "Eaargh!" It features Can-like drum rhythms, brutal stop-starts, a baleful groaning sound and a single strummed guitar chord gradually distorted to oblivion, before a melodic interlude and Williams' chaotic keyboard solo.

"With 'Horizontal Hold' it would be more the overall textures and more of a soundworld rather than D sharp against whatever," Hayward explains. "There are whole hunks of what we call 'music' missing, because we've stripped away all this stuff that everybody talks about and worries about, but we've got this other thing. We've exposed the wiring. It was a three-day process refining the playing more and more to get to that final shape."

This Heat didn't fit anywhere, although their songs are unmistakably English with Hayward nodding towards Robert Wyatt and Syd Barrett on 'Not Waving But Drowning' with its sombre marine fogscape of viola, clarinet, tape loops and ship's bell.

Hayward recalls that as they came into prominence, they were then lumped in with punk and the post-punk scene, which wasn't a comfortable fit.

"There was this thing that Gareth couldn't really play and most of the punks couldn't really play, so there was a thing going on there that was giving us a parallel. And the DIYness. Partly it was, 'Hey you guys, you are settling down into this punk thing – it's too fucking easy. I mean as far as we understand it, this punk thing is perpetual revolution, so why are you all sounding the same and looking the same? You have these gods that you want to tear down. Fucking wake up because you're falling asleep as well.'"

This Heat released *Deceit* in 1981, after which Williams left. They carried on into 1982 with a revised line-up and then disbanded.

As we get to the end of this particular journey, it's time to catch up again with progressive rock's big hitters as they head for the Eighties.

EMERSON, LAKE & PALMER

Emerson, Lake & Palmer had taken a break in late 1974. And just as Keith Emerson had no idea how long the group's success would last at the outset, so by the time they had reached the apex of their popularity, no one would have known how easy it would be for them to lose both their momentum and their creative bearings. Lake describes his feelings about the group when it took its break in 1974:

"I think that we had begun to run out of steam. That was combined with the fact that we toured too much. We were playing about 200 shows a year, and we never had time off and we were burnt out. You do feel that there is a limit to what you can keep creating with three people and it would be different every time. What can we do next?"

ELP's albums had always been a mix of Lake's ballads and love songs, Emerson's classical adaptations and the group's original material. Their last album, 1973's *Brain Salad Surgery*, was hallmarked by group playing of a particular energy and intensity.

On *Works Volume 1*, released in 1977, each musician had their own side and only one featured the group. Emerson played his *Piano Concerto No. 1* with the London Philharmonic Orchestra, which with its combination of romantic and more modernist elements is a short, attractive piece. Leonard Bernstein was disparaging when asked to conduct it, but then the classical establishment has never taken kindly to outsiders encroaching on their territory.

Lake's side featured acoustic-based songs written with Pete Sinfield, and Palmer's side veered erratically from 'LA Nights' with Joe Walsh of The Eagles on lead guitar, to reworkings of Prokofiev. The highlight of the album is undoubtedly the trio's version of Aaron Copland's 'Fanfare For The Common Man' with its dramatic synth clarion calls, which unexpectedly went to number two in the UK singles charts in the summer. The sole group original, with lyrics by Sinfield, is the orchestrated 'Pirates', which is something of an over-egged pudding. The album charted at nine in the UK and twelve in the US.

"The concept of having a side each and a side for the group playing collectively wasn't really the thing to do after a three-year hiding away in the woods," says Palmer.

"Keith had this idea that he wanted more to follow this classical path. And I understood that," says Lake. "I could also see that we weren't really classical; we were rock. And I think that doing interpretations of classical was one thing but to actually become a classical form of music, I just didn't feel comfortable about it.

"It became the voice of ELP through an orchestra. But previously when we made records ourselves, I produced them, [and] it was the band itself that decided everything. With *Works Volume 1* there were all kinds of fucking people involved with it, orchestras in Switzerland and Paris, conductors coming out of the woodwork. It cost us over a million pounds to record.

"Although there are things I like about it, it's not something the public really liked. If you ask someone what's their favourite ELP album you'll get one of the first five records. Maybe one in ten, maybe one in fifty will say *Works Volume 1*. That was the beginning of the end."

Then came the 1977 tour of the USA, and some brief, infamous aerial film footage taken of a convoy of three articulated trucks with the diseconomies of scale literally writ large, with the words EMERSON, LAKE and PALMER painted on the roofs of the three containers. That said, if one thinks more carefully about how much space the band's gear, PA and lights would actually have taken up, claims that the whole thing was a publicity stunt have credibility – although if this was the case it clearly backfired.

Melody Maker journalist Chris Welch has noted that ELP were a bit like lottery winners in a way, as most musicians then were really broke and living in poverty. "I remember going to see Carl Palmer with Vincent Crane when he was in Atomic Rooster and they were living in this awful squalid flat in Stratford overrun by mice and they had very little money. Keith Emerson was living in a bedsit. Then all of a sudden there's all this money from album sales and touring and they are flying in jets and staying in posh hotels and it went to their heads as it would do."

Palmer thinks now that if the group had come out as a trio and then been joined by the orchestra at selected dates then it might have worked, but the overheads were so high that they had to sell out every concert.

"We had to cancel three weeks with the orchestra and still had to pay them," says Palmer. "It was not a case of being bankrupt. But then we toured for three weeks and then went out again as a trio for six weeks to put the books in order and everything was OK."

Later in 1977 came *Works Volume 2*, which reached the Top 20 in the UK charts and thirty-seven in the US, and which was basically a compilation of bits and pieces. It included 'Brain Salad Surgery' that had been given away as a flexi disc with *New Musical Express* in 1973 and Keith Emerson's solo single 'Honky Tonk Train Blues'. But if that seemed a bit desultory, what came next in 1978 was, to use a phrase, the dreaded end. It was part contractual obligation album, part misguided attempt to be commercial, with its cover photo portraying Messrs Emerson, Lake and Palmer as grinning, tanned holiday makers... Ladies and Gentlemen, *Love Beach*.

"Quite honestly I think if *Love Beach* had a different cover, we wouldn't have been referred to as some sort of new Bee Gees," says Emerson.

"I didn't produce ELP albums after [*Works Volume 1*]," says Lake. "It wasn't the ELP that I wanted. Like *Love Beach* was a version of ELP, but it didn't have the soul of ELP, it didn't have that handmade innovative spark that those albums had. What you are doing is diluting the very thing that made it popular."

The album went to forty-eight in the UK charts then made a quick disappearance and Emerson, Lake & Palmer split in 1979. They reformed at times over the years but never fully regained their creative impetus.

JETHRO TULL

In 1977 Jethro Tull's Ian Anderson demonstrated that as long as your fanbase is large enough you could do what the hell you liked and still have record company backing. On the cover of the overtly rural *Songs From The Wood* Anderson is photographed in a forest clearing cooking something in a pot – a squirrel, perhaps – coming across like some background character from Thomas Hardy's *The Woodlanders*. Onstage he dressed like a country squire and it had been noted in the music press that Anderson was indeed something of a laird as he owned and ran a salmon farm on the Strathaird Estate on the Isle Of Skye from 1978.

Then, pictured on the cover of *Heavy Horses* that year, he carried the humble air of a Victorian ostler in charge of some shire horses. These two albums and *Stormwatch* (1979) were also more overtly folk oriented than before and although still intricate, the music feels less dense, with greater use of space than on some of their earlier Seventies albums.

Anderson says: "There are those who become arch noodlers, those who become besotted with playing very, very quickly with a huge amount of detail. It's the spaces between the notes which give the notes their poignancy and relevance, and give shape to music."

He wasn't bothered, it seemed, by anything except making the music he wanted to. And if anyone really pointed the finger at him, he always had the response that he had bought the Sex Pistols' *Never Mind The Bollocks* and was quite happy to admit it, and whatever John Lydon said about Jethro Tull, he knew for a fact that he had been a fan – maybe was still – of the group's *Aqualung*.

"When you look at Johnny Rotten's stage persona in the early days he has that hunched, slightly one shoulder up thing that looks just like the guy on the *Aqualung* cover," Anderson observes.

"It would be a bit ridiculous to over-react to the punk thing; it was just the re-emergence of screaming youth and simplicity," says Anderson. "I was onstage in 1969 with the MC5 long before the era of punk as we knew it, and saw the absolute archetype of punk music. So everything that came after was a pale shadow of the MC5, who started off their most famous song, *"Kick out the jams, motherfuckers!"* – that's pretty brave stuff. Even Johnny Rotten never went that far."

YES

In 1977 Yes came up with *Going For The One*. Reviewing the album in *Sounds*, Phil Sutcliffe was delighted that the group were back on track: "It sounds to me as if 'Going For The One' was the track that got them excited about Yes all over again. The energy is colossal – and the words are fascinating. That track is exactly the one: exactly where Yes should be at in '77."

Patrick Moraz had gone and the prodigal Rick Wakeman was back in the fold.

"Rick came back to sort of assert his place again," says guitarist Steve Howe. "So *Going For The One* was kind of joyous. It was a lot of fun. It's got a lovely contrast. 'Going For The One' is an out-and-out stomping rock song, then you've got 'Turn Of The Century', which is nothing like a rock song. Then we did it again with 'Parallels' and 'Wonderous Stories', from heavy to light. And of course the thing that we had up our sleeve was the wonder of 'Awaken'. That's the last Seventies composition of Jon and I. We'd lost [producer] Eddy Offord but we'd got John Timperley who was another British guy who was working in Switzerland and we went the distance."

The follow-up *Tormato* was different again. From its irreverent tomato-spattered sleeve designed by Hipgnosis, which served to distance it further from Roger Dean's mythical landscapes, to its shorter songs, it seemed to be signposting a need for change without knowing how to achieve it. The group made the mistake of not going in to record with enough good quality material, and with arguments and uncertainty about the direction that it was all going to take. "It was intricate and it was kind of OK, but it wasn't the most satisfying or gratifying record to make," says Howe.

After touring there came the 1979 Paris sessions for which Yes thought they would just work up material in the studio. Howe reckons that was "a huge mistake" and "the whole bottom fell out of the band". They effectively spelled the end of that incarnation of Yes. Howe and Squire began writing new material together and Anderson had a bunch of songs. But the singer soon left, along with Wakeman.

"The band was fragmented by then," says Anderson on his decision. "[There was] no real direction, no harmony, a tired energy, too many tours." Yes would carry on without Anderson and Wakeman for *Drama* (1980) in a short-lived line-up featuring Trevor Horn and Geoff Downes aka The Buggles, a rather arch, avowedly modern pop duo, who came across as the antithesis of early Yes. It was bold move that some fans were unable to accept.

PETER GABRIEL, STEVE HACKETT & GENESIS

After we left Peter Gabriel in Chapter 41 having left Genesis, growing cabbages and threatening to commit suicide with a feather boa, he slipped comfortably into a solo career. As a marker he scored a hit single with 'Solsbury Hill' in 1977, one of the few pop hits in 7/4 time. But that little dink in the rhythm just adds a pinch of spice as the way the verses are sung feels like a regular 4/4. More importantly it was memorable, melodic and was metaphorical in many ways, with Gabriel playing a self-referential role as rock star.

Whereas Roger Waters wrote 'Welcome To The Machine' essentially as a grim parable about the music industry, Gabriel had decided to leave *"the machinery"* by quitting Genesis. He climbs the hill near Bath to look out over the city with a feeling of exhilaration and a guardian figure tells him that he's come to take him home, but home in this case is somewhere else, a spiritual home, somewhere he belonged but had never been before.

Gabriel remained on Charisma and must have delighted them by simply titling each of his first solo four albums, from 1977–82, *Peter Gabriel.*

Some of the songs on Gabriel's debut solo album, like 'Moribund The Burgermeister', would have been at home in a Genesis set, but overall it had a tougher, leaner sound. Produced by Bob Ezrin, it found Robert Fripp on guitar, joined by Steve Hunter and Dick Wagner, the guitar team who had played with Alice Cooper, and on Lou Reed's 1973 album *Berlin* and his 1974 *Rock'n'Roll Animal* tour. But the highlight is the deeply moving 'Here Comes The Flood'. Like a member of the band that was playing when the Titanic went down, Gabriel describes the unfolding details of the apocalypse, which are set against a dramatic orchestral backdrop.

On *Peter Gabriel 2* the sort of third-person characters that he so often adopted with Genesis appears here with Mozo, the furtive pirate radio operator in some dystopian future in a makeshift house in a junkyard by a river. There's the new army recruit of 'Animal Magic', while 'Have A Wonderful Day In A One Way World' is a deliciously witty observation of day-to-day banality. Robert Fripp produced the album and delivers a soaring guitar solo on 'White Shadow'.

Peter Gabriel 3 (1980), which features Phil Collins on drum kit *sans* cymbals and hi-hat, explores disassociated inner states on the sinister 'Intruder' and the tale of the failed assassin of 'Family Snapshot'. 'Biko', the story of ANC activist Steve Biko's death in police custody in Port Elizabeth, South Africa, remains one of the most elegantly phrased and emotionally resonant of all political rock songs.

Genesis had survived Gabriel's departure with scarcely a breaking of stride and, almost as surprisingly, they easily weathered the departure of guitarist Steve Hackett in 1978. Hackett realised that Genesis had managed well without him being fully engaged in the writing process on *A Trick Of The Tail*. He was also rocking the proverbial boat with a solo career that was gaining momentum.

"I know that Tony and Mike were very concerned to not create another Peter Gabriel, a star within the ranks, so they said, 'You can't stay within the band and have a separate solo career,' and they weren't prepared to give me a fair proportion of the songwriting. They said, 'If you don't like it, you know what you can do.'

"I stuck it out stoically for another album, *Wind And Wuthering* [1976]. I think it was a very good album, but I was anxious to get more ideas recorded, and ultimately my allegiance was to music itself."

Genesis seemed to have some kind of charmed life in that their fans loved everything they did. When Hackett left, there were more prophesies of doom and gloom for the band. But their momentum was unstoppable. The remaining trio released *And Then There Were Three* (1978), which, with its accurate, but slightly naff title, and Michael Rutherford having to cover for Hackett's lead guitar, did not augur well. It was less adventurous and expansive than *Wind And Wuthering*, but with a few rather mawkish exceptions, it was set of strong, concise songs.

"Steve wasn't even there for the first week when we wrote 'Dance On A Volcano' and 'Squonk' [for *A Trick Of The Tail*], so it was easier to write with four people and when we went down to three it was even easier in a way," says Tony Banks. "It meant that you could get more ideas through. There was less committee stuff and things seemed to work more easily, but the personnel obviously made a difference to the music."

Not only that, fans loved this new poppier direction as it dovetailed neatly with their melodic but more expansive early material. In 1977 Genesis released *Seconds Out*, a live album with Phil Collins singing some Gabriel-era material like 'Supper's Ready' and in effect reclaiming it for the new line-up.

And when Genesis headlined the Knebworth Festival in 1978, with live drummer Chester Thompson joined by lead guitarist Daryl Stuermer, they delivered a powerful set that found them dusting off the 1971 epic 'The Fountain Of Salmacis' together with the rather sappy new single 'Follow You Follow Me' and the crowd just lapped it all up. In 1980 they made *Duke*, which got to number one in the UK and number eleven in the US and so continued on an upward trajectory that made them one of the world's biggest bands.

VAN DER GRAAF

Van Der Graaf Generator seemed to have run aground in 1976 and carried on as Van Der Graaf as they were depleted by the departure of saxophonist David Jackson. But they also welcomed Graham Smith from String Driven Thing on violin and the return of bass guitarist Nic Potter. The four-piece created the exceptional *The Quiet Zone/The Pleasure Dome*, which had the sort of strong Hammill melodies that would prick up the ears of record company bods hoping beyond hope for a possible hit. The new line-up was lean and hungry, but with bursts of flamboyant playing.

But in concert they were spectacularly heavy and produced *Vital*, a live album recorded at The Marquee in early 1978, that could equally have been titled *Brutal*. By this time Charles Dickie had been added on cello and keyboards. So you had a rhythm section of drums, cello and fuzz bass, which was tight and also packed a hefty punch, with Hammill on keyboards and guitar – on which he made an alarming racket – and Smith on wah-wah violin. In essence *Vital* found the group looking over to the punks – as well as the proggers and the new wave of heavy metal bands – and saying, "Oh yeah? Well get a load of *this*."

Van Der Graaf had made a demo of 'Ship Of Fools' which was in Guy Evans's estimation "liquid metal". Here Hammill's rather uncertain and noisy guitar starts the riff, joined by Potter's monstrous fuzz bass, Guy Evans's drums and edgy swoops of violin and cello. As Hammill declaims this allegory of human folly, it starts off intense and peaks with him screaming himself hoarse. The band lurches along, Hammill plays a fabulously ham-fisted guitar solo and it all seems to be falling apart until the initial riff is restated. As Hammill has said, Van Der Graaf (Generator) never delivered a polished product. He's right: the performance sounds like a band careering to the end of a particularly fraught set. Amazingly, this was the opening song – they were just warming up. They split shortly after the concert recording was made.

Ryan Baptiste was in the audience at the Marquee gig at which *Vital* was recorded. He writes:

"The platform for becoming an angry young man began when Lord Beeching ruthlessly ended the glorious steam era of British Railways. Not too far down the line, my mum left 'for a holiday' from which she, voluntarily, never returned, by which time my beloved Manchester City's Football League Division 1 Championship seems but a distant memory.

"Thus, fleeing the nest and grasping the modest amount of independence afforded me by becoming a student, unleashed a torrent of pent-up frustration, the perfectly timed soundtrack to which was punk. But the musical foundations had been laid a couple of years earlier when Alan 'Fluff' Freeman introduced me to Van Der Graaf Generator/Peter Hammill on his Saturday afternoon show.

"Whilst there wasn't a remotely seamless transition from prog to punk, at least VdGG's music had hallmarks of what was to follow... Hammill's often angst-ridden lyrics mated with the energy of The Damned, the urgency and intensity of Wire and the discordant chaos of The Fall. The band was never a bunch of virtuosos by prog rock standards; whilst album tracks were lengthy, they were usually broken down into contrasting segments, and members never indulged in the extended and pompous drum or keyboard solos of, say, Emerson, Lake & Palmer.

"VdGG were the anti-establishment punks of prog, if you like. They didn't sound remotely like Yes, Genesis, Pink Floyd or ELP, and Hammill certainly sounded a lot darker and angrier than just about anyone else at the time.

"When the norm would have been to go to gigs headlined by the likes of Wire, Television or Gang of Four, seeing VdG – just Van der Graaf by then – live at the Marquee in 1978, neither seemed out of place nor time and certainly didn't lack the high-powered energy of bands ten years their junior. There was also a raw sound to this gig compared with VdG's studio albums, no doubt enhanced by the venue's modest size. It was an electric atmosphere and confirmed for me that VdG was still very relevant."

PINK FLOYD

Pink Floyd were such a press-resistant, hermetically sealed entity that it was hard to gauge what outside forces, if any, affected them after *Wish You Were Here*, but in 1977 they came up with their most aggressive album, *Animals*.

Although it was released at the height of punk, there's nothing to suggest that it had anything to do with all that, especially as the music for 'Dogs' and 'Sheep' was basically taken from the 1974-era tracks 'Gotta Be Crazy' and 'Raving And Drooling' respectively. But now Roger Waters was articulating his ever-souring vision of the human race by drawing on George Orwell's novels *1984* and *Animal Farm*.

Here 'Dogs' are the charming business-people, the successful sort, who are basically psychopathic, but will die of cancer anyway. 'Pigs' are dysfunctional oddities, but 'Sheep' are perhaps the most disturbing. In Orwell's *1984* the forlorn hope uttered by Winston Smith was that in a totalitarian state, "if there is hope it MUST lie in the proles", as there were so many of them – if only they could be assembled or even made aware of their own strengths. But they never were. At the end of 'Sheep', however, when the placid, bleating hordes are faced with the dogs, they turn angry, violent and out of control.

The song embodies the dynamics that were in short supply on *Wish You Were Here*. Rick Wright's poised, cool electric piano intro gradually makes way for Waters' 'One Of These Days'/'Careful With That Axe, Eugene' one-note bass line brought out of the cupboard once more. Gilmour plays some inspired angular rhythm guitar and even Wright's spuming synths have a toxic edge.

Barry Miles, who gave *Animals* a favourable review in *New Musical Express*, also saw the group play Madison Square Garden in New York City. The cover features the shot of a giant helium balloon in the shape of a pig restrained by wires so that it hovered above Battersea Power Station. Indoors it was not so well behaved.

Miles wrote: "Then the Floyd filled the place with smoke and brought out a huge inflatable pig – like the Goodyear blimp – which cruised about the vast space of the auditorium, the pencil beams of light from its eyes casting a malevolent gaze over the stalls. It came to rest and hovered, as if about to take a dump on the mixing console. For a while, several thousand people couldn't see the group because there was a huge pig in the way."

Now Pink Floyd purveyed a curious mix of jaundiced musings on the fame they had made for themselves, and corruption and greed in society, but all presented within Seventies' rock's grand showbiz spectacle. And it all got curiouser and curiouser with their concept album/live show/film, *The Wall*.

The album was released in November 1979 and was born from a moment when something in Waters' brain "snapped" during a stadium tour that he was not enjoying. Even now it feels a perplexing and thoroughly odd choice of concept. The fourth wall is a name for the invisible barrier that separates the actors in a play or film from their audience. So if an actor goes out of character and directly addresses the audience, by delivering a commentary on the play or their role within it, that is breaking the fourth wall.

So in that respect there was nothing new in *The Wall*'s exploration of the relationship between the audience and the performer. Roger Waters had once been an affable spokesperson onstage communicating with the audience, so this was basically his Big Problem swathed in dry ice, raked by spotlights, strobes and with the occasional inflatable pig hovering over it, as if to do its business.

In terms of rock music the fourth wall had never been an issue to start with, but was assuming greater importance. Now Waters was so taciturn that if he had started chatting with the audience it would have seemed wrong somehow. And now to underline all that he was going to have a wall built between the group and the audience during each show. As a metaphor it was (both visually and otherwise) so heavy-handed, and so literal. It formed a huge spectacle, yet paradoxically a wall is utterly unglamorous, the antithesis of spectacle. It was both fascinating and ridiculous. And it would surely have been more appropriate for a wall to have been gradually built around Waters onstage.

Again, Waters was in control of Pink Floyd, although if he had not been, one wonders if anything would have been achieved. But the browbeaten Wright had essentially been sacked and then invited back on a wage, and onstage each musician had a double. It was all about wall-like separations in institutions, against individuals, in the music business, in personal relationships. Gerald Scarfe's projected onstage animations referenced totalitarianism with a striking section of marching hammers, and there was the teacher, the one who was the one who was instructed to leave the kids alone in a faux working-class idiom on the surprise hit single 'Another Brick In The Wall', in which Waters rails against the British education system. But why? Was it really full of brainwashing agents of the state trying to indoctrinate *"them kids"*?

All this came with a stiff disco beat and some school children singing that they don't need *"no education"*. Its message is laboured and awkward, but then the Brits have always liked a novelty song, and, incredibly, it reached number one in the singles charts both in the UK, and in the US.

It's by far the worst track on *The Wall*, which overall comes on like a grand statement that is sketchy, banal and doesn't particularly make sense. But it gives Waters a stage on which to wring his hands with angst, although 'Comfortably Numb' transcends all that as one of the few really affecting moments on the album.

In the early Seventies Nick Mason warned against Pink Floyd's tendency to trudge in slow 4/4 time. But by *The Wall* it was all so four-square that he seems to have become de-skilled. On 'Mother', there is one odd section in seven time. He had played 7/4 on 'Money'. But for some reason he couldn't get it and so the job was handed over to Jeff Porcaro of Toto. Taken on face value, that incident in itself, that easy admission of defeat when some serious practice – even some drum lessons – would surely have rectified the problem, acts as a dismal end to Pink Floyd in the Seventies.

It was the total antithesis of the unwritten progressive ethic: that musicians did not know what they could not do, that they were finding new areas to explore. It was rather that he knew what was a bit difficult, but he couldn't be bothered to try to surmount that difficulty.

What *The Wall* particularly shows is that the writer who had set the controls for the heart of the sun in 1968 now had come up with the monolithic, ugly and practically useless structure of a huge wall, which was left to stand like an outlier, a kind of monument to the end of the Seventies, emblematic of the emotional blankness and dysfunction that had gripped Pink Floyd. Nick Kent reviewed a live show for *NME*. He hated it. Millions of fans loved it.

One of the things that Rick Wakeman expressly loved about the early Seventies was that the musicians were ahead of technology and by necessity spent time experimenting with their synthesizers in an attempt to manifest the sounds that were in their heads. The Seventies had essentially been their decade, but now tastes were changing, attitudes were changing, hairstyles were changing and recording technology was changing. For progressive musicians or those of any of the big rock groups, the Eighties were, in a sense, an even bigger challenge than punk.

Now technological imperatives started to make themselves known and many musicians were only too happy to conform. Keyboards like the Yamaha DX 7 were programmable, but the process was so complicated that musicians often just used the instantly recognisable pre-sets. Then there were the dreaded gated reverb snare drums, going off like depth charges throughout songs no matter how inappropriately, which mitigated against any intricate snare drum work – and so many musicians, who were scared of appearing old fashioned, consented to this horrible sound ruining their music.

And if you hadn't had one already, it was time for a haircut. If you couldn't bear to be shorn, the genius compromise was the mullet cut, which was left long at the back. Then maybe get yourself a tub of hair gel to spike up the front, put on some eye liner and hope that you looked OK under the scrutiny of the camera compared to the aspirant pop stars who were ten years your junior. Because now was the decade of MTV and the ubiquity of the pop video, and your past achievements were no guarantee of entry into this particular party.

At the end of the Seventies and start of the Eighties there cropped up some newer progressive rock groups like Twelfth Night, Marillion, Pallas and Pendragon. But the reason we stop before we get to them is simple.

There was nothing wrong with being influenced by Yes and Genesis per se, but it seemed rather like a backward step, harking back more than pushing on. It marked the time when progressive rock was "officially" recognised by that name and became a category rather than loosely describing musicians who could take what was around them and make something new and exciting.

Personally, the cut-off point was sitting with a group of friends watching Marillion play 'Forgotten Sons' on TV in the early Eighties. Lead vocalist Fish was plastered in make-up like an approximation of Rael-era Gabriel. He drew some groans and a few derisive titters from the assembled company as he mimed shooting himself in the mouth with the mike stand while the band galloped away in a sub-Genesis manner in the background. When musicians around them were changing, exploring, it seemed that Marillion were essentially a born-too-late parody of the recent past.

To these ears the spirit that fuelled progressive rock from the early Seventies was now infusing the radical approach to sonics of a one-off like This Heat and post-punk groups like Magazine who played direct rock music, but with greater texture and complexity than many of their young peers. Later on it cropped up in Kate Bush's idiosyncratic approach to song arrangement on *The Dreaming* and *Hounds Of Love*. It surfaced in the lengthy structures of Sonic Youth's *Daydream Nation*. It reared its head unashamedly in the expansive sounds of the so-called post-rock groups like Godspeed You! Black Emperor and Sigur Rós. It could even be discerned in the lavish complexity that could be constructed in a remix, particularly Ui's thirteen-minute extravaganza, 'The Grand Piano'; in Trans Am's mix of rock and electronics; in Jah Wobble's conceptual albums like *The Celtic Poets*; even the teeming soundscapes of The Future Sound Of London. Then there are Sonar, Mogwai and their ilk who explore complexity through nuance within what sounds repetitive. Those are just a handful of examples.

Some will violently disagree with the above and come up with counter arguments, but I will pre-empt all that by quoting a diplomatic former bandmate of mine who would say, "I kind of like your idea... but I kind of like mine better".

The Ramones sagely sang that the end of the Seventies was the end of the century. The decade had produced so much, so whatever could lie beyond? For the purposes of this exploration, we have reached our journey's end. What a long, strange trip it's been. And despite what I was led to believe, we have encountered so few wizards, witches, elves and hobbits en route, that I feel rather short-changed. So it only seems right to leave, as the last words, those that Frodo Baggins directed towards Sam Gamgee when they were in peril on the Stairs of Cirith Ungol.

"You and I, Sam, are still stuck in the worst places of the story, and it is all too likely that some will say at this point: 'Shut the book now, Dad; we don't want to read any more.'"

Acknowledgements

This book is dedicated to the memory of my godfather and staunch supporter, Kenneth McAndrew, who died on April 9, 2018.

When we spoke on the phone he would always enquire as to how it was taking shape. When I told him of my slow progress and moaned about the enormous amount of work involved, he would say: "Well, you've just got to get up earlier and work harder". He was right.

Thank you:

To all the interviewees who gave their time to help shape the story and to all the fans who vivified it through their personal testimonies.

To those who contributed through advice, discussions, arguments, information, text, audio and visual material, and general encouragement: Chris Bohn, Lesley Carver, Gill Cassidy, Declan Colgan, Dave Cousins, Ian Crockett, Chris Cutler, Jerry Ewing, Robert John Godfrey, John "Harpo" Harris, Annie Haslam, Tony Herrington, Emy Horsell, Mick Houghton, Billy James, Jo Kendall, Robert Lipson, Gary Lucas, Shelagh McDonald, Peter Muir, Colin Newman, David Parker, Dave Pegg, Edwin Pouncey, Andrew Reader, Andy Saunders, Sid Smith, Dave Stewart, Ian Sturgess, David Trevor-Jones, Derek Walmsley and Rob Young.

And to Chris Charlesworth and David Barraclough at Omnibus for commissioning the book, and for their saint-like patience.

I'd also like to give a respectful nod to the late David Cavanagh, my first reviews editor at *Select* back in 1990. In terms of music writing he set the bar high for the rest of us and kept it there. I had been meaning to drop him a line about this book, but left it too late.

And a tip of the hat to the late Mike King for the assiduously researched timeline in his book, *Wrong Movements: A Robert Wyatt History*.

Author's Source Notes

Introduction
Author's interviews with Ian Anderson (2015) and Mike Oldfield (2013); Keith Altham, *New Musical Express* (July 20, 1968) and Mark Williams, *International Times* (March 13, 1970).

Chapter 1
Author's interviews with Brian Eno, *MOJO* 184 (March 2009), Alan Barnes (2016), Pete Brown (2013), Keith Emerson, *Prog* 40 (2014), Jon Hiseman, *Prog* 52 (2015), Peter Daltrey, *MOJO* 258 (May 2015), Steve Howe (2015), Barry Miles (2014), Robert Wyatt (2013), Judy Dyble (2015) and Nik Turner (2016); Joe Boyd, *White Bicycles: Making Music In The 1960s* (Serpent's Tail, 2006); Mike King, *Wrong Movements: A Robert Wyatt History* (SAF, 1994).

Chapter 2
Author's interviews with Steve Howe (2015), Peter Daltrey, *MOJO* 258 (May 2015), Arthur Brown, *MOJO* 237 (August 2013), Keith Emerson, *Prog* 44 (2014), Nick Kent (2014), Toby Manning (2016) and Tony Banks (2016); Chris Welch, *Melody Maker* (February 24, 1968); writer unknown, *Melody Maker* (January 3, 1970); Ian MacDonald *Revolution In The Head: The Beatles' Records And The Sixties* (Fourth Estate, 1994).

Chapter 3
Author's interviews with Nick Kent (2014), Michael Giles (2013), Robert Fripp (*The Wire* 159, May 1997; *The Wire* 368, October 2014; *MOJO* 231, February 2013), Ian McDonald (1997), Judy Dyble (2015), Greg Lake (1997), Robert Lipson (2013), Alan Cowderoy (2013), Michael Giles (2013), Pete Sinfield (1997), Richard Williams (2013) and Keith Tippett (2014); *International Times* (March, 1969); *The Essential King Crimson: Frame By Frame* box set notes (1991); *International Times* (June 13-15, 1969); Alan Lewis, *Melody Maker* (October 25, 1969); Richard Williams, *Melody Maker* (September 20, 1969; May 9, 1970; December 19, 1970); writer unknown, *Melody Maker* (January 3, 1970); writer unknown, *Disc* (November 8, 1969).

Chapter 4

Author's interviews with Bill Bruford (1997 & 2017), Robert Fripp (*The Wire* 159, May 1997; *The Wire* 368, October 2014; *MOJO* 231, February 2013) and John Wetton (1997); Caroline Boucher, *Disc* (May 27, 1972); writer unknown, *Melody Maker* (August 5, 1972); *Ptolemaic Terrascope* (c.1991–92); *The Essential King Crimson: Frame By Frame* box set notes (1991); *New Musical Express* (September 1, 1973).

Chapter 5

Author's interviews with Steve Reich, *The Wire* 153 (Nov 1996), David Bedford, *The Wire* 325 (March 2011), Chris Cutler (2014), Rick Wakeman, *Prog* 37 (2013), Mont Campbell (2016), Graeme Downes (2016) and Robert John Godfrey (2015); film documentary, *The Best Of Both Worlds*, 1969; Vincent Budd, Malcolm Arnold and Jon Lord, Classical Music On The Web, 1997, musicweb-international.com/arnold/lord.htm; *Beat Instrumental* (November 1970); The Nice – *Five Bridges* sleeve notes; Official Keith Emerson website; Chris Roberts, *Prog* 45 (2014); Chris Welch, *Melody Maker* (April 13, 1974); Keith Altham, *Fusion* (March 6, 1970).

Chapter 6

Author's interviews with Ron Geesin (2002; *The Wire* 235, (September 2003) and Nick Kent (2013); Nick Jones, *Melody Maker* (October 20, 1966); Chris Welch, *Melody Maker* (August 5, 1967); Barry Miles, *New Musical Express* (May 15, 1976); BBC, *Look Of The Week* (May 15, 1967); Nick Mason, *Inside Out: A Personal History Of Pink Floyd* (Phoenix, 2004); Tony Stewart, *New Musical Express* (February 19, 1972); Chris Welch, *Melody Maker* (April 10, 1969); writer unknown, *Record Mirror* (November 1969); John Peel, reprinted in *Private Eye* (1969); Ron Geesin, *The Flaming Cow* (The History Press, 2013); Tony Stewart, *New Musical Express* (February 12, 1972); Chris Charlesworth, *Melody Maker* (November 16, 1974); Lester Bangs, *Creem* (November/December, 1970); Nick Kent, *New Musical Express* (November 23, 1974); Pete Erskine, *New Musical Express* (January 1975).

Chapter 7

Author's interviews with Carl Palmer, *Prog* 44 (2014); Keith Emerson, *Prog* 44, (2014); Greg Lake (1997; *Prog* 44 2014), and Robert Fripp, *MOJO* 231 (February 2013); Chris Welch, *Melody Maker* (5 September, 1970); Charles Shaar Murray, *Creem* (July 1972); Penny Valentine, *Sounds* (October 13, 1970); Caroline Boucher, *Disc* (May 13, 1972); *Mainlines,*

Blood Feasts And Bad Taste: A Lester Bangs Reader, edited by John Morthland (Serpent's Tail, 2003).

Chapter 8
Author's interviews with Peter Gabriel (2002), Michael Rutherford, *MOJO* 209 (April 2011), Tony Banks (2016), Steve Hackett (2015), Paul Whitehead (2016), David Hitchcock (2013) and Ron Geesin, *The Wire* 235 (September 2003); unknown writer, *ZigZag* (1971); Jerry Gilbert, *Sounds* (September 30, 1972); *Genesis: Chapter And Verse*, by Phil Collins, Peter Gabriel, Tony Banks, Anthony Phillips, Bill Bruford, Mike Rutherford, Steve Hackett (St Martin's Griffin, 2007); Barbara Charone, *New Musical Express* (October 13, 1973); Chris Welch, *Melody Maker* (August 23, 1975).

Chapter 9
Author's interviews with Chris Welch (2013), Steve Howe, (2014; *MOJO* 294, May 2018), Jon Anderson (2017; *MOJO* 294, May 2018), Bill Bruford (2017), Rick Wakeman *Prog* 37 (2013), *Planet Rock* (September 2017) and Nick Kent (2014); Chris Welch *Close To The Edge: The Story Of Yes* (Omnibus, 2007); sleeve notes to *Yes* by Yes (Atlantic 1969); Mark Williams, *International Times* (July 18, 1969); Mark Williams, *International Times* (April 9, 1970); Eddy Offord interview with Joe Bosso *Music Radar* 3 (February 3, 2013); Steve Howe interviewed in *Prog Rock Britannia: An Observation In Three Movements* (BBC Four, 2009); Richard Cromelin, *Rolling Stone* (March 1972); Bill Bruford, *The Autobiography* (Foruli, 2009); Andrew Tyler, *Disc* (May 27, 1972); Andrew Tyler, *Disc* (June 2, 1973); Chris Welch, *Melody Maker* (December 1, 1973).

Chapter 10
Author's interviews with Ian Anderson (2015), Martin Barre (2015), Chris Welch (2013) and Nick Kent (2014); Derek Boltwood, *Record Mirror* (August 17, 1968); interview with Jethro Tull, *Thick As A Brick* 25th anniversary edition bonus track; John Swenson, *Crawdaddy!* (August 1972); Dave Marsh, *Creem* (August 1972); Chris Welch, *Melody Maker* (March 11, 1972); Charles Shaar Murray, *New Musical Express* (date unknown, 1972); Steven Rosen, *Circus* (December 9, 1975); Rob Partridge, *Melody Maker* (September 1, 1973).

Chapter 11
Author's interviews with Peter Hammill (*The Wire* 138, August 1995; *The Wire* 277, March 2007; *MOJO* 222, May 2012; 2016) and Guy Evans

(2015); Van Der Graaf Generator, *The Box* sleeve notes, (2000); interview with Mick Gillingham (1990) vandergraafgenerator.co.uk; unknown writer, *Melody Maker* (November 6, 1971); unknown writer, *Disc & Music Echo* (January 1, 1972).

Chapter 12
Author's interviews with Mike Oldfield (2013), Steve Hillage (*Prog* 37, 2013; 2014) and Chris Cutler (2014); BBC Four, *Tubular Bells: The Mike Oldfield Story* (2013); Paul Gambaccini, *Rolling Stone* (November 1973).

Chapter 13
Author's interviews with Chris Cutler (*The Wire* 158, April 1997; 2014), Fred Frith, *The Wire* 168 (February 1998), Jakko Jakszyk (2017), Dagmar Krause, *The Wire* 394 (December 2016) and Robert Wyatt (2013); transcript of public discussion at the British Academy in January 2011, published in *Red Strains: Music And Communism Outside The Communist Bloc*, edited by Robert Arlington (Oxford University Press, 2013); Fred Frith and Chris Cutler, sleeve notes to Henry Cow, *The Road: Volume One* box set (2009); Ian MacDonald, *New Musical Express* (April 7, 1973); Charles Shaar Murray, *New Musical Express* (August 31, 1974); Steve Lake, *Melody Maker* (April 5, 1975); Tim Hodgkinson, sleeve notes to Henry Cow, *The Road: Volume Two* box set (2009).

Chapter 14
Keith Altham, *Record Mirror* (January 1971); Bud Scoppa, *Circus* (August 1970); Malcolm Dome, *Prog* 34 (March 2013); Sylvie Simmons, *Creem* (December 1986); John Mendelsohn, *Rolling Stone* (December 1970); Simon Frith, *Let It Rock* (March 1973).

Chapter 15
Author's interviews with John Lees, *Prog* 69 (2016), Robert John Godfrey (2015) and Annie Haslam (2016); Richard Green, *New Musical Express* (March 21, 1970); Jerry Gilbert, *Sounds* (March 1974).

Chapter 16
Author's interviews with Guy Evans (2015), Keith Emerson, *Prog* 44 (2014) and Mont Campbell (2016).

Chapter 17
Author's interview with Arthur Brown, *MOJO* 237 (August 2013).

Chapter 18
Author's interviews with Andrew Poppy (2013), Kevin Ayers, *MOJO* 184 (March 2009), Pye Hastings (2013), Daevid Allen, *The Wire* 233 (July 2003), Bill McCormick (2015), Robert Wyatt (live interview on *Scratching the Surface*, Resonance 104.4 FM, September 30, 2003; *The Guardian*, April 25, 2008; 2013), Mont Campbell (2016) and Phil Miller (2013); Mike King, *Movements: A Robert Wyatt History* (SAF, 1994); Daevid Allen, *Gong Dreaming 1*, originally published in 1994 on GAS (SAF, 2007); Graham Bennett, *Soft Machine: Out-Bloody-Rageous* (SAF 2005); unknown writer, *Melody Maker* (September 4, 1971).

Chapter 19
Author's interview with Robert Wyatt (2013); Mike King, *Movements: A Robert Wyatt History* (SAF, 1994); Ian MacDonald, *New Musical Express* (July 27, 1974).

Chapter 20
Author's interviews with Pye Hastings (2013), Robert Wyatt, *The Wire* 142 (December 1995), David Hitchcock (2013) and Geoffrey Richardson (2016); sleeve notes, Hatfield And The North, *Hatwise Choice* (2005); Andrew Tyler, *Disc* (June 24, 1972).

Chapter 21
Author's interviews with Mont Campbell (2016) and correspondence with Dave Stewart (2013); Dave Stewart, *Copious Notes: The Inside Story Of Egg, Uriel, Arzachel & The Ottawa Company* (2007).

Chapter 22
Author's interviews with Phil Miller (2013), Nick Kent (2014), Bill Bruford (2017) and Mont Campbell (2016); sleeve notes, Hatfield And The North, *Hatwise Choice* (2005); Jonathan Coe, *The Rotters' Club* (Viking, 2001).

Chapter 23
Author's interviews with David Bedford, *The Wire* 325 (March 2011), Kevin Ayers, *The Wire* 226 (December 2002) and Geoffrey Richardson (2014); Karl Dallas, *Melody Maker* (April 5, 1975); Barry Miles, *New Musical Express* (July 3, 1976).

Chapter 24
Author's interviews with Rick Wakeman, *Prog* 37 (2013), and David Trevor-Jones (2014).

Chapter 25
Author's interviews with Allan Cowderoy, Robert Lipson and Tim Wheatley (2013).

Chapter 26
Author's interviews with Andy Latimer, *Prog* 55 (2015) and David Hitchcock (2013); Chris Welch, *Melody Maker* (April 3, 1976); Paul Morley, *New Musical Express* (May 27, 1978).

Chapter 27
Author's interviews with Chris Welch (2013), Richard Williams (2014), Nick Kent (2014), Chris Charlesworth (2013), Barry Miles (2014), Bob Harris (2015) and Dave Pegg (2016); John Tobler, *ZigZag* 30 (April 1973); *Peeling Back The Years* Part 3 BBC Radio 1 (1987).

Chapter 28
Author's interviews with Michael Rother, *The Wire* 290 (2008); Lester Bangs, *Creem* (1975).

Chapter 29
Author's interviews with Jon Hiseman, *Prog* 52 (2014), Dave Greenslade (2014), Pete Brown (2008), Robert Wyatt (1995) and Keith Tippett (2014); Mike King, *Wrong Movements: A Robert Wyatt History* (SAF, 1994).

Chapter 30
Author's interviews with Derek Shulman (2013) and Graeme Downes (2016); Arlo West, Blazemonger.com/GG (1995); *Contemporary Keyboard Magazine* (May/June 1976); writer unknown, *MOJO* 75 (February 2000) reproduced on Blazemonger.com/GG; Thomas Wictor, *Bass Player* (July 1997).

Chapter 31
Author's interviews with Gary Brooker, *Prog* 86 (2018), Chris Wright, *Prog* 46 (2013), John "Poli" Palmer (2013) and Chris Welch (2013); Chris Wright, *One Way Or Another: My Life In Music, Sport & Entertainment* (Omnibus Press, 2013); unknown writer, *MOJO* (Summer 1994) reproduced on winwoodfans.com/articles/traffic-spirit.htm; Chris

Welch, *Melody Maker* (December 16, 1967); David Dalton, *Rolling Stone* (May 3, 1969); Tony Stewart, *New Musical Express* (January 13, 1973 & January 27, 1973); Gary Sperrazza, *Shakin' Street Gazette* (October 10, 1974); Connor McKnight with help from Al Clark, *ZigZag* 34 (September 1973).

Chapter 32
Author's interviews with Shirley Collins, *The Wire* 219 (May 2002), Dave Pegg (2016), David Oberlé (2016) and Dave Cousins (2014); strawbsweb.co.uk/hist/hist2.asp; Ken Barnes, *Rolling Stone* (September 12, 1974).

Chapter 33
Author's interviews with Gail Colson (2015) and John "Poli" Palmer (2013); *Kermode And Mayo's Film Review* (February 2, 2018); Germaine Greer, *The Female Eunuch* (Harper Collins, 1970); Graham Masterton, *Penthouse* (1973), Ian MacDonald, *New Musical Express* (September 1, 1973).

Chapter 34
Author's interviews with Sonja Kristina (2014, 2018) and Darryl Way, loudersound.com/features/fiddling-about-the-violin-in-prog (2014).

Chapter 35
Author's interviews with Ron Geesin, *The Wire* 235 (September 2003), Phil Shiva Jones (2014), Nik Turner (2013) and Nick Kent (2014); unknown writer, *ZigZag* 4 (August 1969); Steve Lacy, *Beat Instrumental* 132 (October 1971); Paul Moody, *Uncut* (September 2007); James Johnson, *New Musical Express* (February 5, 1972); hawkwindmuseum.co.uk; Ira Robbins, *Zoo World* (December 19, 1974).

Chapter 36
Author's interviews with Robert Wyatt live on *Scratching the Surface*, Resonance 104.4 FM (September 30, 2003), Guy Evans (2015), Steve Hillage (2014), Chris Cutler (2014), Dagmar Krause, *The Wire* (December 2016), John Lees, *Prog* 69 (2016), Nik Turner (2016), Bill MacCormick (2015), Robert John Godfrey (2015) and Dave Cousins (2014).

Chapter 37
Author's interviews with Daevid Allen, *The Wire* 233 (July 2003), Kevin Ayers, *The Wire* 226 (December 2002), Steve Hillage (*Prog* 37, 2013; 2014) and Charles Hayward (2017); Peter Funnell, *Hiawatha Fanzine* (7 July, 1991); Ian MacDonald, *New Musical Express* (September 6, 1975); Jon Young, *Trouser Press* (January 1978).

Chapter 38
Author's interviews with Geoffrey Richardson (2016), Brian Eno, *MOJO* 184 (March 2009), Charles Hayward (2017), Robert Fripp, *MOJO* 231 (February 2013), Bill MacCormick (2015) and Simon Phillips (2015).

Chapter 39
Author's interviews with Nik Turner (2013) and John "Poli" Palmer (2013); John Peel, Reading Festival 2: Here Come The Beers Again, *Sounds* (September 10, 1977).

Chapter 40
Author's interviews with Robert Fripp, *MOJO* 231 (February 2013), Bill Bruford (2017), Tony Banks (2016), Rick Wakeman, *Prog* 37 (2013), Alan White, *MOJO* 294 (May 2018), Steve Howe (2014), Ian Anderson (2015), Guy Evans (2015) and Peter Hammill (2016; *The Wire* 277, March 2007); Irwin Stambler, *The Encyclopedia Of Pop, Rock And Soul* (St Martin's Press, 1989); Peter Gabriel, letter to the music press (1975); Nick Mason, *Inside Out: A Personal History Of Pink Floyd* (Phoenix, 2004); Mick Brown, *Sounds* (July 12, 1975); Chris Welch, *Melody Maker* (April 5, 1975); Ian MacDonald, *New Musical Express* (April 5, 1975).

Chapter 41
Author's interviews with Paul Charles (2017), Mark Perry (2014; *The Wire* 378, August 2015), Nick Kent (2014), Philip Sanderson, *The Wire* 412 (June 2018), Jakko Jakszyk (2015), Steve Hillage (2014), Peter Hammill, *The Wire* 277 (March 2007), Daevid Allen, *The Wire* 233 (July 2003), Colin Newman (2013), David Bedford, *The Wire* 325 (March 2011), Tony Banks (2016), Pete Brown (2013), Barry Miles (2014), Bob Harris (2015) and Sonja Kristina (2014); Lisa Robinson, *New Musical Express* (June 1975), Barry Miles, *In The Seventies: Adventures In The Counter-Culture* (Serpent's Tail, 2011); Mick Farren, *New Musical Express* (June 19, 1976); *MOJO* 267 (February 2016).

Chapter 42

Author's interviews with Bev Bevan, *Prog* 89 (2018), Robert John Godfrey (2015), Bill Bruford (2017), Charles Hayward (*The Wire* 363, May 2014; 2017), Greg Lake, *Prog* 44 (2014), Carl Palmer, *Prog* 44 (2014), Chris Welch (2013), Keith Emerson, *Prog* 44 (2014), Ian Anderson (2015), Steve Howe, *MOJO* 208 (March 2018), Jon Anderson, *MOJO* 208 (March 2018), and Steve Hackett (2015); Tom Robinson, *The Guardian* (September 1, 2005), robertjohngodfrey.org/my-life/autobiography/2-uncategorised; Phil Sutcliffe, *Sounds* (July 9, 1977); Barry Miles, *New Musical Express* (July 23, 1977); Mark Blake, *Pigs Might Fly: The Inside Story Of Pink Floyd* (Aurum, 2007); J. R. R. Tolkien, *The Two Towers* (George Allen & Unwin, 1954).

Bibliography

Allen, Daevid, *Gong Dreaming 1: From Soft Machine To The Birth Of Gong* (SAF, 2007)

Alther, Lisa, *Kin Flicks* (Knopf, 1976)

Bangs, Lester (Greil Marcus ed.), *Psychotic Reactions And Carburetor Dung: The Work Of A Legendary Critic* (Anchor Press, 1987)

Bangs, Lester (John Morthland ed.), *Main Lines, Blood Feasts And Bad Taste: A Lester Bangs Reader* (Anchor Press, 2003)

Beckett, Andy, *When The Lights Went Out: Britain In The Seventies* (Faber and Faber, 2009)

Bennett, Graham, *Soft Machine: Out-Bloody-Rageous* (SAF, 2005)

Blake, Mark, *Pigs Might Fly: The Inside Story Of Pink Floyd* (Aurum, 2007)

Boyd, Joe, *White Bicycles: Making Music In The 1960s* (Serpent's Tail, 2006)

Bruford, Bill, *The Autobiography* (Foruli, 2009)

Cousins, Dave, *Exorcising Ghosts: Strawbs And Other Lives* (Witchwood Media, 2014)

Cutler, Chris, *File Under Popular: Theoretical And Critical Writings On Music* (November, 1984)

Fabian, Jenny and Byrne, Johnny, *Groupie*, 3rd edition (Omnibus, 2005)

Frame, Pete (ed.) *The Road To Rock: A ZigZag Book Of Interviews* (Charisma, 1974)

Greer, Germaine, *The Female Eunuch*, revised edition (Harper Collins, 2012)

Hammill, Peter, *Killers, Angels, Refugees* (Charisma, 1974)

Harris, Bob, *Still Whispering After All These Years: My Autobiography* (Michael O'Mara, 2015)

Herrington, Tony (ed.), *Invisible Jukebox* (Quartet, 1999)

Irvin, Jim (ed.), *The MOJO Collection: The Albums That Define Popular Music* (MOJO Books, 2000)

Jack, Richard Morton (ed.), *Flashback* 2 (Winter 2012)

Kent, Nick, *The Dark Stuff* (Penguin, 1994, Faber and Faber, 2007)

Kent, Nick, *Apathy For The Devil: A 1970s Memoir* (Faber and Faber, 2010)

King, Mike, *Wrong Movements: A Robert Wyatt History* (SAF, 1994)

Knee, Sam, *Memory Of A Free Festival: The Golden Age Of The British Underground Festival Scene* (Cicada Press, 2017)

Laing, R. D., *Knots* (Vintage, 1970)

MacDonald, Ian, *Revolution In The Head: The Beatles' Records And The Sixties* (Fourth Estate, 1994)

Mason, Nick, *Inside Out: A Personal History Of Pink Floyd* (Phoenix, 2004)

Miles, Barry, *In The Seventies: Adventures In The Counter-Culture* (Serpent's Tail, 2011)

O'Dair, Marcus, *Different Every Time: An Authorised Biography Of Robert Wyatt* (Serpent's Tail, 2014)

Peel, John and Ravenscroft, Sheila, *Margrave Of The Marshes: His Autobiography* (Bantam, 2005)

Peel, John, *The Olivetti Chronicles* (Bantam, 2008)

Pegg, Dave and Schofield, Nigel, *Off The Pegg: Bespoke Memories Of A Bass Player* (Pegglets, 2018)

Sandford, Jeremy and Reid, Ron, *Tomorrow's People* (Jerome Publishing Co. Ltd, 1974)

Savage, Jon, *England's Dreaming: Sex Pistols And Punk Rock* (Faber and Faber, 1991)

Sheppard, David, *On Some Faraway Beach: The Life And Times Of Brian Eno* (Orion, 2008)

Stump, Paul, *The Music's All That Matters: A History Of Progressive Rock*, 2nd edition (Harbour, 2008)

Sounes, Howard, *The Seventies: The Sights, Sounds And Ideas Of A Brilliant Decade* (Pocket Books, 2007)

Welch, Chris, *Close To The Edge: The Story Of Yes* (Omnibus, 1999)

Young, Rob, *Electric Eden: Unearthing Britain's Visionary Music* (Faber and Faber, 2010)

INDEX

Suggested Listening

'Itchycoo Park', Small Faces

'Legend Of A Mind', The Moody Blues

'21st Century Schizoid Man – Including "Mirrors"', King Crimson

'It Happened Today', Curved Air

'The Barbarian', Emerson, Lake & Palmer

'Introduction', Gracious

'Golf Girl', Richard Sinclair, David Sinclaire, Pye Hastings, Richard Coughlan, Caravan

'Killer', Van Der Graaf Generator

'One Of These Days', Pink Floyd

'Roundabout', Yes

'Can-Utility and the Coastliners', Genesis

'Kemp's Jig', Gryphon

'Mother Goose', Jethro Tull

'Son Of 'There's No Place Like Homerton'', Hatfield & The North

'The Advent of Panurge', Gentle Giant

'A Last Straw', Robert Wyatt

'Nirvana for Mice', Henry Cow

'Master Builder', Gong

'In The Dead Of Night', U.K.

'Northern Lights', Renaissance

'Absorbing, revealing and immersive' Kathryn Williams

The definitive biography of Kate Bush, revised and updated for 2024.

Detailing everything from Bush's upbringing through her evolution into a fascinating visual and musical artist and featuring over 70 revealing interviews from old school friends, early bandmates, collaborators, former managers, musicians and many more, this is the story of one woman's life in music.

Focusing on her unique working methods, studio techniques and albums from the beginning of her career, Under The Ivy has been updated to include coverage of Bush's return to the top of the charts in 2022. An eye-opening journey of discovery for anyone unfamiliar with the breadth of Bush's work, this Remastered edition also rewards the long-term fan with new insights and fresh analysis.

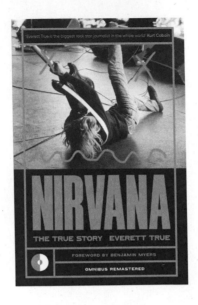

'Everett True is the man who runs England' Courtney Love

Everett True is responsible for bringing Nirvana, Hole, Pavement, Soundgarden and a host of other bands to public attention. He introduced Kurt to Courtney, performed on stage with Nirvana on numerous occasions and famously pushed Kurt onto the stage of the Reading Festival in 1992 in a wheelchair.

This is the true story written by the only journalist allowed into the Cobain house immediately after Kurt's death. True reveals the details of what the legendary band was really like from start to finish, what happened to Cobain in Olympia and Seattle, how Kurt first met Courtney and gives the lowdown on the scenes, the seminars, the live dates, the friends and the drug dealers surrounding the grunge explosion.

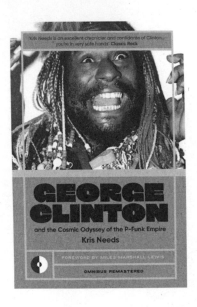

GEORGE CLINTON

and the Cosmic Odyssey of the P-Funk Empire

Kris Needs

FOREWORD BY MILES MARSHALL LEWIS

OMNIBUS REMASTERED

The first comprehensive biography of one of funk music's most fascinating and innovative black pioneers.

A member of Parliament and Funkadelic, Clinton stands alongside James Brown, Jimi Hendrix and Sly Stone as one of the most influential black artists of all time who, along with his vast P-Funk army, took funk into the mainstream, dominated the US charts and sold out stadiums.

Containing first-hand interview material with Clinton, Bootsy Collins, Jerome Bigfoot Brailey, Junie Morrison, Bobby Gillespie, Afrika Bambaataa, Jalal Nuriddin (Last Poets), Juan Atkins, John Sinclair, Rob Tyner (MC5), Ed Sanders (The Fugs), Chip Monck (The Voice of Woodstock) as well as other P-Funk associates and friends, this Remastered edition presents an insider's view. It covers the rise of Parliament and Funkadelic from the doowop era and LSD-crazed early shows through to P-Funk's huge rise, the era of the Mothership and beyond.